BUDDHAS
BOUDDHAS
BUDDAS
BOEDDHA'S

Godefriduskaai 22
2000 Antwerp
Belgium
Tel: + 32 3 226 66 73
Fax: + 32 3 226 53 65
www.booqs.be
info@booqs.be

ISBN: 978-94-60650-376
WD: D/2010/11978/038
(Q056)

Editor & texts: Paz Diman
Art direction: Mireia Casanovas Soley
Layout: Maira Purman
Translation: Cillero & de Motta

Editorial project:

maomao publications
Via Laietana, 32, 4.º, of. 104
08003 Barcelona, Spain
Tel.: +34 932 688 088
Fax: +34 933 174 208
maomao@maomaopublications.com
www.maomaopublications.com

Printed in China

BUDDHAS
BOUDDHAS
BUDDAS
BOEDDHA'S

booQs

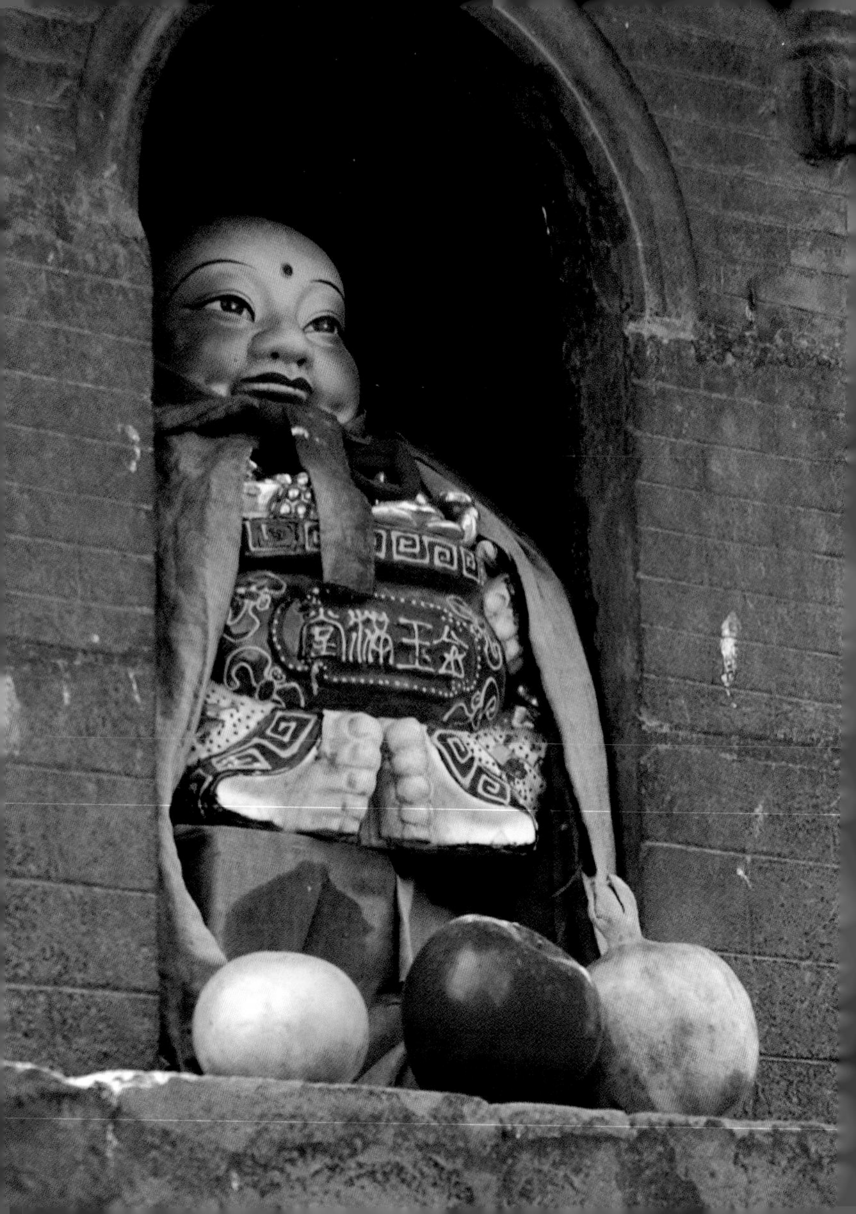
金玉滿堂

CONTENTS

Introduction

Contrary to popular belief, the word "Buddha" is not a name, but an honorific title bestowed upon those who have achieved spiritual awakening. A Buddha is someone who has achieved a state of complete mental peace, liberating themselves from any mundane obstacle and being completely free.

However, even though any human being can achieve this state of transcendence from the material world, the term is generally associated with one of the historical figures of Buddhism- Siddharta Gautama.

Gautama is considered the founder of the Buddhist tradition. The story goes that he was born around 600BC in the north of India. On the day of his birth, the Brahman Asita, invited to foresee what was to come in his life, saw an inspiring future: the child would not only become a completely enlightened being, but that his words would influence the world for hundreds of years.

Siddharta decided to leave the opulence of his noble life to follow the path of spiritual awakening, moved by human suffering.

The errant path of the monk led him to fasting and to intense asceticism through what he knew of pain and sacrifice. He listened to other masters and practiced extreme famine, which drove him almost to the point of death.

Gautama finally achieved illumination the day he decided to sit beneath the Tree of Wisdom, determined not to get up until he found liberation from suffering. Through meditation he achieved nirvana and discovered the Four Noble Truths:

1. Suffering exists.
2. The origin of this dissatisfaction is desire.
3. Suffering can be extinguished.
4. To extinguish suffering we have to follow the path of wisdom, of ethics, and of meditation.

As the years went by, the Buddhist tradition spread among the different Asian cultures and towns until it arrived in the West. As such, not only did it grow with new perspectives to its philosophy, it also created hundreds of possible representations throughout the world of this inspired being.
It is from precisely these images that this book comes from, which takes photos of the five most usual poses of Buddha: standing, resting, sitting, fasting and smiling.
Temples, natural countryside and urban corners in remote regions of the globe show us the incredible beauty with that of the living heritage of a philosophy that has influenced the vast majority of the world.

Introduction

En dépit des confusions populaires, le mot “ bouddha ” n’est pas un nom, mais un titre honorifique utilisé pour nommer celui qui a réalisé un éveil spirituel complet. Un bouddha est une personne qui est parvenue à un véritable état de tranquillité mentale, s’affranchissant de tout type d’obstacle mondain, et qui est totalement libre.
Bien que n’importe quel être humain puisse atteindre cet état de transcendance du monde matériel, ce terme est généralement associé à l’une des figures historiques du bouddhisme: Siddharta Gautama.
Gautama est considéré comme le fondateur de la tradition bouddhiste.
Selon la légende, ce prince serait né au VIe siècle avant J.C., dans le nord de l’Inde. Le jour de sa naissance, le brahmane Asita, invité à lui prédire l’avenir, présagea qu’il aurait une vie qui inspirera de nombreuses personnes : non seulement l’enfant deviendrait un être complètement illuminé mais en plus il aurait une influence sur le monde pendant des siècles.
Siddharta, touché par la souffrance humaine, décida d’abandonner la vie noble et opulente afin de poursuivre le chemin de l’éveil spirituel.
Le chemin errant de moine le mena au jeûne et l’ascétisme intense, au cours desquels il connut la douleur et le sacrifice. Écoutant les autres maîtres, il pratiqua un jeûne très strict, frôlant de près la mort.
Gautama atteignit la vérité le jour où il décida de s’asseoir sous l’Arbre

de la Sagesse, déterminé à ne pas se lever jusqu'à ce qu'il fut parvenu à la libération de la souffrance. Par le biais de la méditation, il atteignit le nirvana et découvrit les Quatre Nobles Vérités :

1 – La souffrance existe.
2 – L'origine de cette insatisfaction est la " soif ".
3 – La souffrance peut être éradiquée.
4 – Pour éradiquer la souffrance nous devons suivre le chemin de la vérité, de l'éthique et de la méditation.

Avec le temps, la tradition bouddhiste s'est frayé un chemin parmi les différentes cultures et les peuples asiatiques, arrivant jusqu'en Occident. Ainsi, de nouvelles perspectives de sa philosophie ont vu le jour et des centaines de représentations possibles de cet être inspirateur ont été créées.
Et c'est précisément de ces images qu'est né ce livre qui rassemble des photos des cinq positions les plus fréquentes de bouddha : debout, allongé, assis, jeûnant et souriant.[1] Les temples, les paysages naturels et les recoins les plus éloignés du globe nous montrent une beauté incroyable, reflet de l'héritage vivant d'une philosophie qui a influencé une grande partie du monde.

Einleitung

Im Gegensatz zu dem allgemein verbreiteten Irrtum ist das Wort “Buddha” kein Name, sondern ein Ehrentitel, mit dem derjenige bezeichnet wird, der die vollständige geistige Erweckung erlangt hat. Ein Buddha ist eine Person, die einen vollkommenen Zustand der inneren Ruhe erreicht hat, sich von allen weltlichen Banden befreit hat und absolut frei ist.

Aber auch wenn jeder Mensch diesen Zustand der Transzendenz der materiellen Welt erreichen kann, so wird doch dieser Begriff im Allgemeinen mit einer der historischen Gestalten des Buddhismus verbunden: Siddharta Gautama.

Gautama wird als Gründer der buddhistischen Tradition betrachtet. Nach der Überlieferung wurde er als Prinz um 600 vor Christus in Nordindien geboren. Am Tag seiner Geburt sagte ihm der Brahmane Asita, der eingeladen war, um die Weissagungen über seine Zukunft zu machen, eine begeisternde Zukunft voraus: Das Kind würde sich nicht nur in ein vollkommen erleuchtetes Wesen verwandeln, sondern sein Worte würden die Welt jahrhundertelang beeinflussen.

Siddharta beschließt, den Überfluss seines adligen Lebens zu verlassen, um, bewegt durch das menschliche Leid, den Weg des geistigen Erwachens zu folgen.

Sein zielloser Weg als Mönches führte ihn zum Fasten und zu starker Askese, wodurch er Schmerz und Aufopferung erfuhr. Gautama erlangt schließlich die Erleuchtung an dem Tag, als er beschließt, sich unter dem Baum der Weisheit niederzulassen, entschlossen, nicht wieder aufzustehen, bis er die Befreiung vom Leid gefunden hätte. Während der Meditation erreicht er das Nirwana und entdeckt die Vier Edlen Wahrheiten:

1.- Das Leid existiert.
2.- Die Ursache dieses Leidens ist die Begierde
3.- Das Leiden kann ausgelöscht werden.
4.- Um das Leiden auszulöschen, müssen wir dem Weg der Weisheit, der Ethik und der Meditation folgen.

Im Lauf der Jahre verbreitete sich die buddhistische Überlieferung in den verschiedenen asiatischen Kulturen und Völkern, bis sie in den Westen gelangte. Auf diese Weise wurde ihre Philosophie nicht nur durch neue Sichtweisen ergänzt, sondern es wurden hunderte Darstellungsweisen dieses erleuchteten Wesens auf der ganzen Welt geschaffen.
Und dieses Buch, das Fotographien der gängigsten Gestaltungen des Buddhas versammelt, geht von genau diesen Darstellungen aus: stehend, liegend, sitzend, fastend und lächelnd. Tempel, Naturlandschaften und Orte an den entlegensten Teilen der Welt zeigen uns die unglaubliche Schönheit, mit der das lebendige Erbe einer Philosophie, die einen großen Teil der Welt beeinflusst hat, aufgenommen wird.

Inleiding

Ondanks de algemene begripsverwarringen is het woord "boeddha" geen naam, maar een eretitel die wordt gebruikt om degene die het volledige spirituele ontwaken heeft bereikt te benoemen. Een boeddha is een persoon die een toestand van volledige mentale rust heeft bereikt en zich heeft bevrijd van elk aards obstakel. Het is een geheel vrij mens. Maar hoewel ieder mens deze transcendente toestand van de materiële wereld kan bereiken, wordt de term over het algemeen geassocieerd met een van de historische figuren van het boeddhisme: Siddharta Gautama. Guatama wordt beschouwd als de oprichter van de boeddhistische traditie. Er wordt verteld dat hij als prins rond 600 jaar voor Christus in het noorden van India werd geboren. De dag van zijn geboorte voorzei de brahmaan Asita, die was uitgenodigd om zijn leven te voorspellen, hem een inspirerende toekomst: het kind zou niet alleen veranderen in een geheel verlicht wezen, maar zijn woorden zouden eeuwenlang van invloed zijn op de wereld.

Siddharta besloot, aangedaan door het menselijk lijden, om zijn weelderige leven te verlaten en de weg van de spirituele ontwikkeling te volgen.

Het nomadisch bestaan van de monnik bracht hem tot het vasten en het intensieve ascetisme, door middel waarvan hij pijn en opoffering leerde kennen. Hij luisterde naar andere meesters en deed aan extreem vasten, wat hem bijna de dood in joeg.

Guatama bereikte uiteindelijk de verlichting op de dag dat hij besloot om onder de Boom van de Wijsheid te gaan zitten en pas weer op te staan als hij de bevrijding van het lijden had gevonden. Door te mediteren bereikte hij de nirwana en ontdekte hij de Vier Nobele Waarheden:

1- Het lijden bestaat.
2- De oorzaak van deze ontevredenheid is het verlangen.
3- Het lijden kan worden opgeheven.
4- Om het lijden op te heffen moeten we het pad van de wijsheid, de ethiek en de meditatie volgen.

In de loop van de jaren vond de boeddhistische traditie zijn weg in de verschillende Aziatische culturen en volkeren en bereikte tevens het Westen. Zo werden niet alleen nieuwe perspectieven aan de filosofie toegevoegd, maar werden er ook honderden mogelijke voorstellingen in de hele wereld van dit bezielde wezen gemaakt.
En juist vanuit deze beelden is dit boek ontstaan. Er zijn foto's van de vijf meest gebruikelijke boeddhavoorstellingen in opgenomen: staand, liggend, zittend, vastend en lachend.
Tempels, natuurlandschappen en plekjes in de stad uit alle uithoeken van de wereld laten ons de ongelooflijke schoonheid zien waarmee de levende erfenis van een filosofie die een groot deel van de wereld heeft beïnvloed wordt bijeengebracht.

Standing Buddha
Bouddha debout
Stehender Buddha
Staande Boeddha

The representations of Buddha are normally closely linked to the artistic traditions of each of the cultures that produce them. However, it is believed that there are 32 major physical signals and 80 minor ones that show that were look upon a being that has achieved illumination, and that they can indeed be seen.
While some traditions have observed them and others have not, there are two characteristics that are generally repeated throughout Buddha art: a protruding forehead, (showing his mental sharpness), and large ear lobes, (which symbolise his great ability to listen).
In the following images of Buddha standing up, we can mainly see another two: his hair growing upwards and his finger and toenails, which are exceptionally long. Also, holding both palms of his hands upwards, or at least one of them, and out in front of him (an action recognised as a mudrâ or sacred gesture), is a symbol of friendship towards strangers and of good intentions.

Les représentations de Bouddha sont, généralement, étroitement liées aux traditions artistiques propres de chaque culture qui les produits. Cependant, on considère qu'il existe 32 marques physiques majeures et 80 mineures sur le corps d'un Bouddha qui démontrent qu'il s'agit d'un être qui a atteint l'illumination et l'on peut, par ailleurs, voir ces marques.
Bien que certaines traditions les aient repris et d'autres non, il existe deux marques qui se répètent dans l'art bouddhiste : une protubérance sur le front (démontre l'acuité de son intelligence) et de grands lobes au niveau des oreilles (symboles de la grande capacité d'écoute).
Sur les représentations de Bouddha debout, il est possible de remarquer deux autres signes récurrents: ses cheveux poussent vers le haut et les ongles de ses mains et de ses pieds sont extrêmement longs. De plus, le fait d'avoir la paume des deux mains tournée vers l'extérieur ou uniquement l'une d'elles, inclinée vers l'avant (action reconnue comme un mudra ou un geste sacré), est un symbole d'amitié envers les étrangers et des bonnes intentions.

Die Buddha-Darstellungen sind normalerweise eng mit den besonderen künstlerischen Traditionen jeder einzelnen Kultur, die sie hervorbringen, verbunden. Man geht jedoch davon aus, dass es 32 größere und 80 kleinere physische Merkmale gibt, die darauf hinweisen, dass wir uns vor einem Wesen befinden, das die Erleuchtung erlangt hat. Und diese Anzeichen sind tatsächlich feststellbar.
Auch wenn einige Traditionen sie aufgenommen haben und andere nicht, gibt es zwei Merkmale, die sich in der buddhistischen Kunst wiederholen: Ein Höcker auf der Stirn (der geistige Schärfe bedeutet) und große Ohrläppchen (die seine große Fähigkeit zum Zuhören symblisiert).
Bei den meisten der folgenden Figuren des stehenden Buddhas kann man zwei weitere Merkmale feststellen: Sein Haar wächst nach oben, und seine Finger- und Fußnägel sind extrem lang.Außerdem ist die Haltung der Hände, beide Handflächen, oder nur eine, erhoben und nach vorne gerichtet (Geste, die als ein Mudra oder heilige Geste gilt) ein Symbol der Freundschaft und der guten Absichten gegenüber Fremden.

De voorstellingen van Boeddha zijn vaak nauw verbonden met specifieke artistieke tradities van de culturen die ze produceren. Er wordt echter vanuit gegaan dat er 32 primaire en 80 secundaire fysieke kenmerken bestaan die aangeven dat wij ons voor een wezen bevinden dat de verlichting heeft bereikt, en die feitelijk waargenomen kunnen worden.
Er zijn twee kenmerken die steeds in de boeddhistische kunst terugkeren, hoewel niet in alle tradities: een bult op zijn voorhoofd (die op zijn mentale scherpzinnigheid wijst) en grote oorlellen (die zijn grote luistervermogen symboliseert).
In de volgende figuren van de staande Boeddha kunnen meestal ook twee andere karakteristieken worden waargenomen: zijn haar groeit omhoog en de nagelwortels van zijn handen en voeten zijn extreem lang. Bovendien is het feit dat hij zijn opgeheven handpalmen, of een daarvan, naar voren houdt (wat wordt gezien als een moedra of heilig gebaar) een symbool van vriendschap ten aanzien van vreemden en van goede bedoelingen.

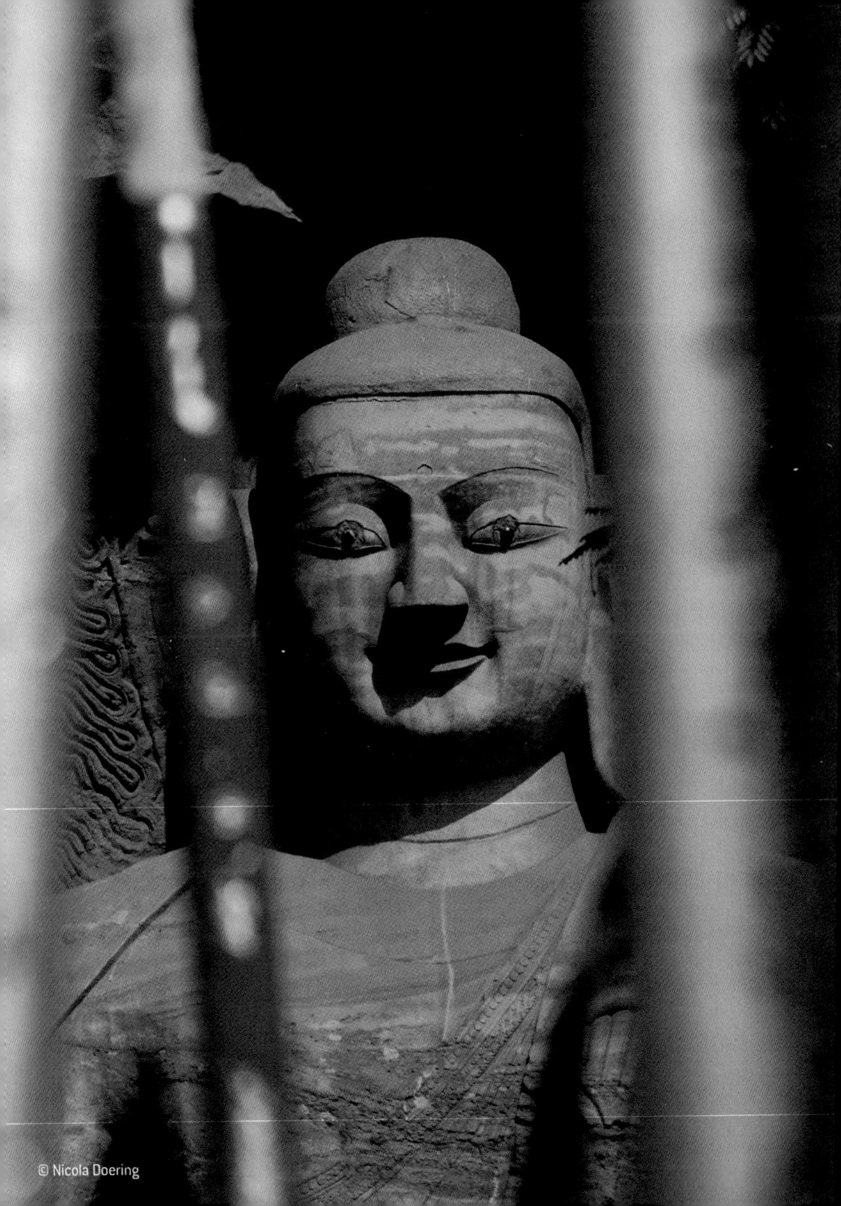

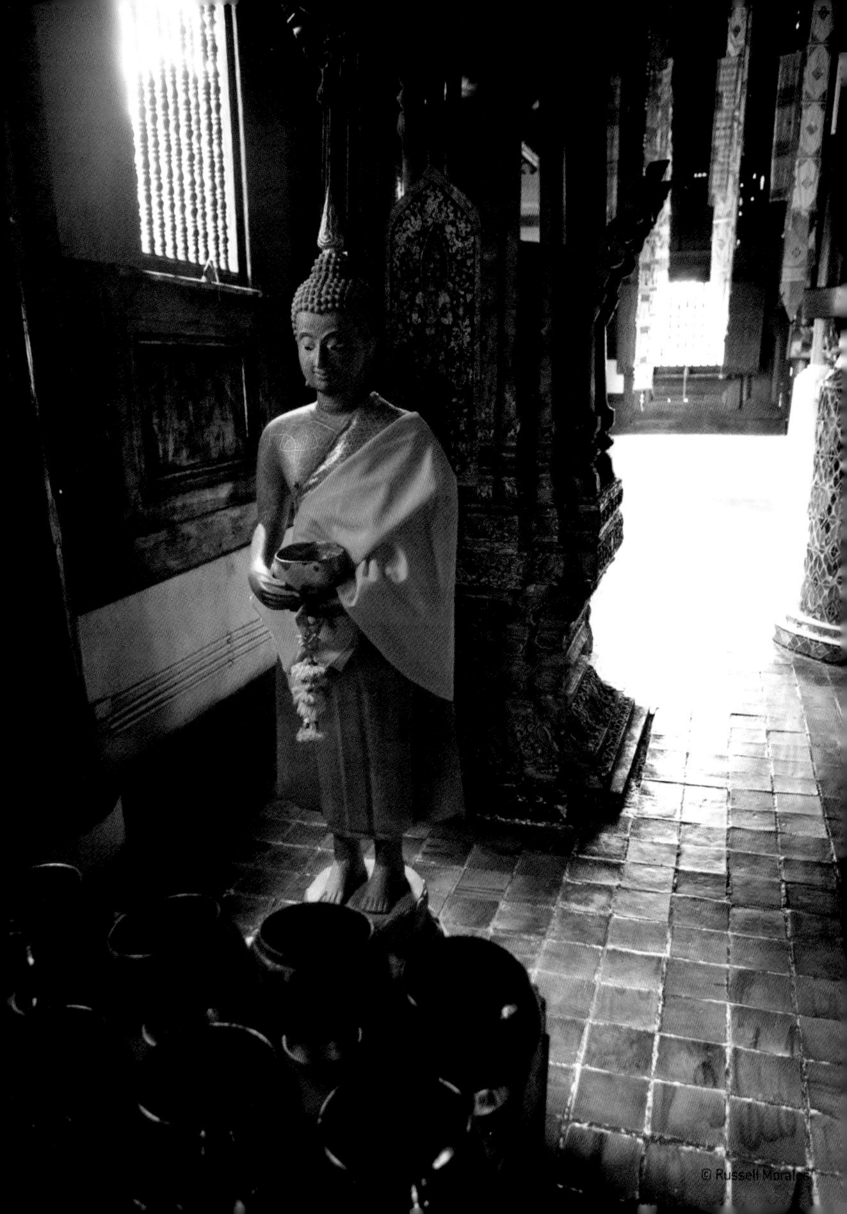

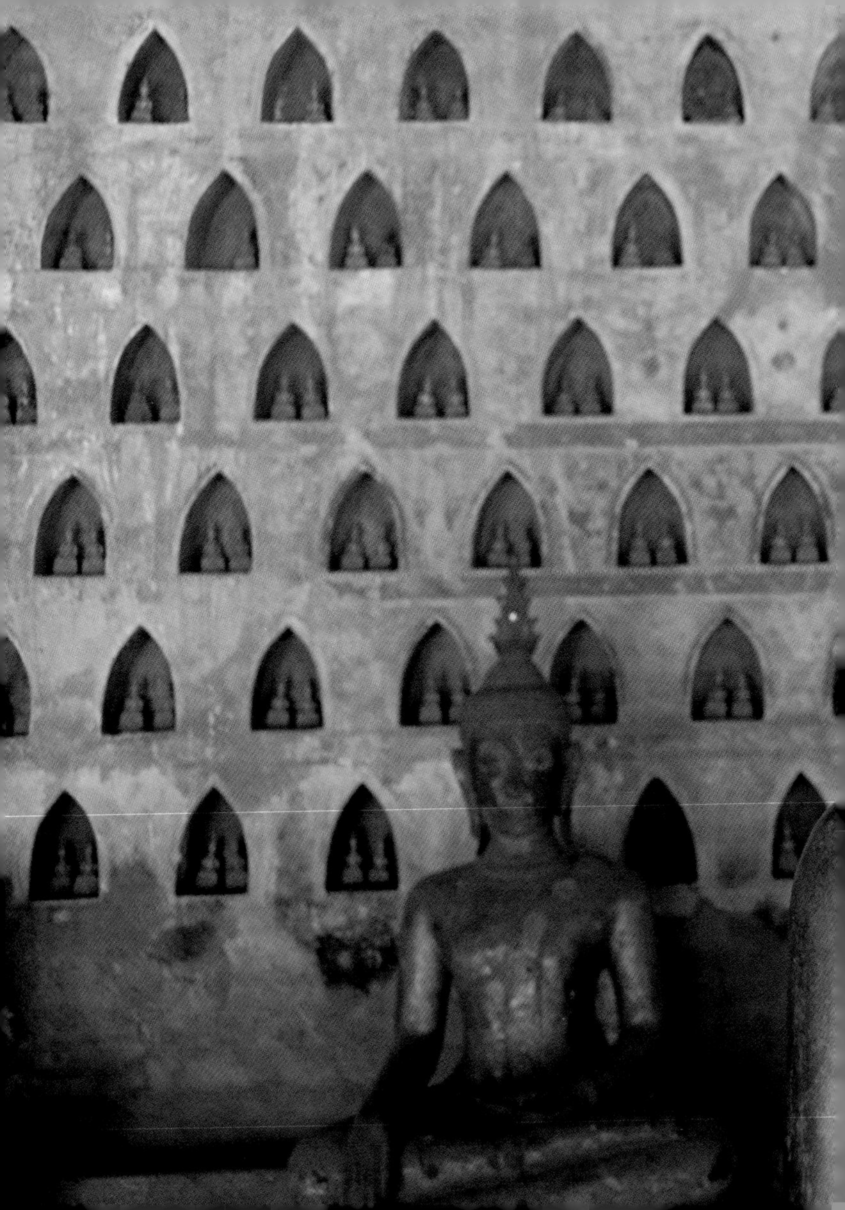

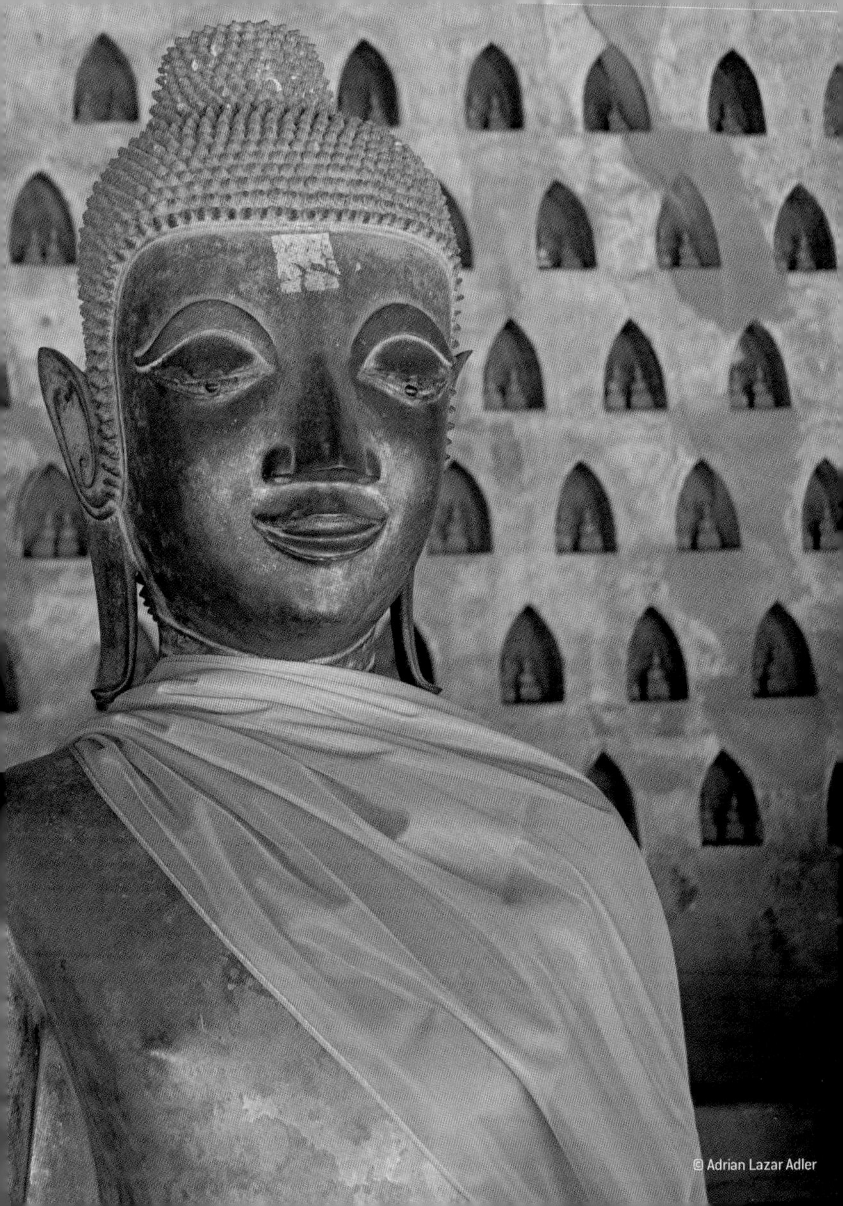

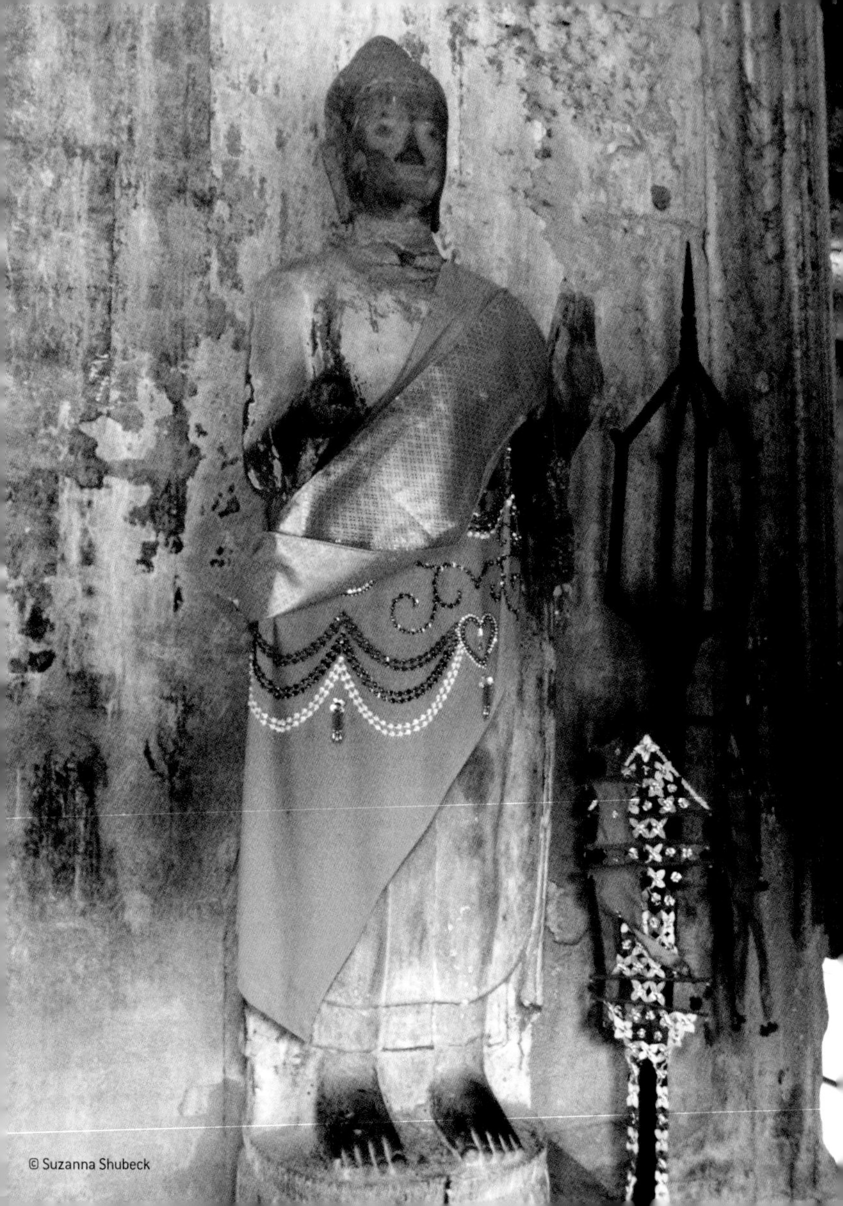

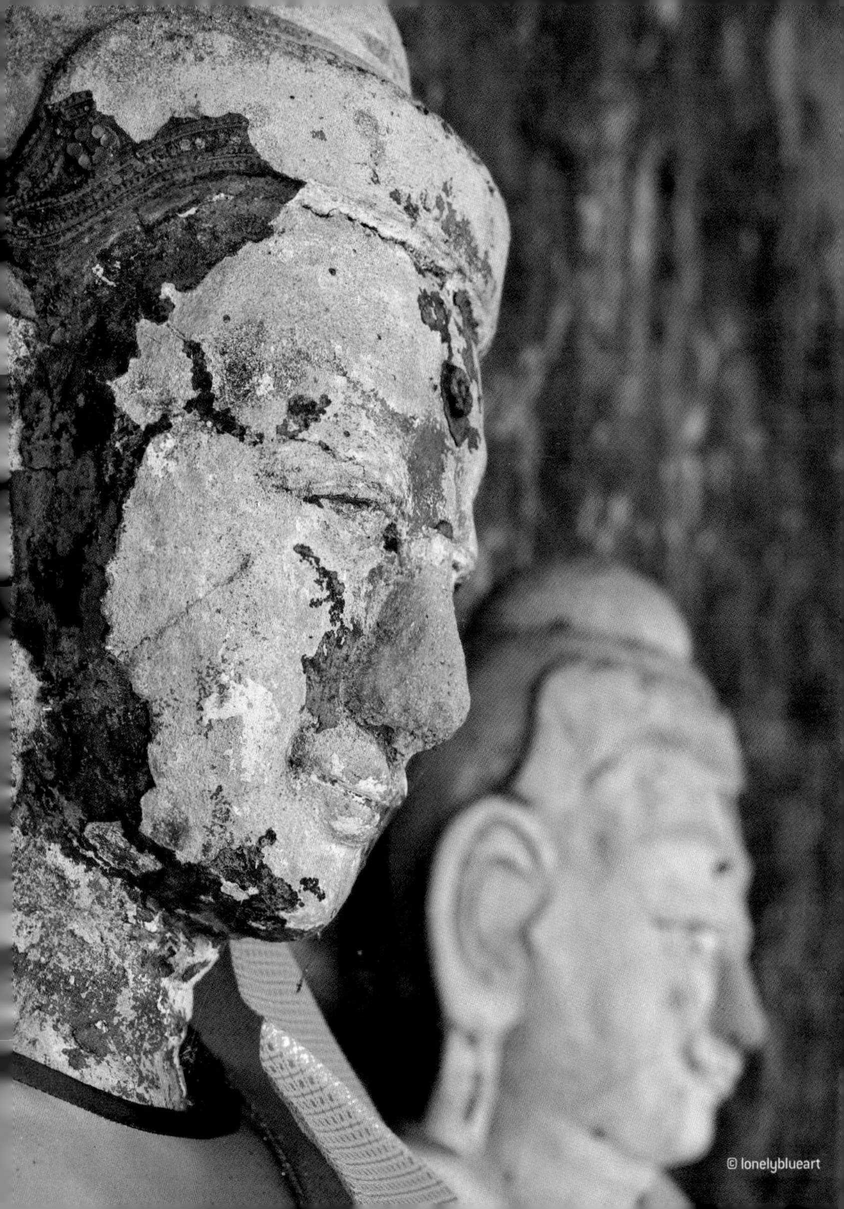

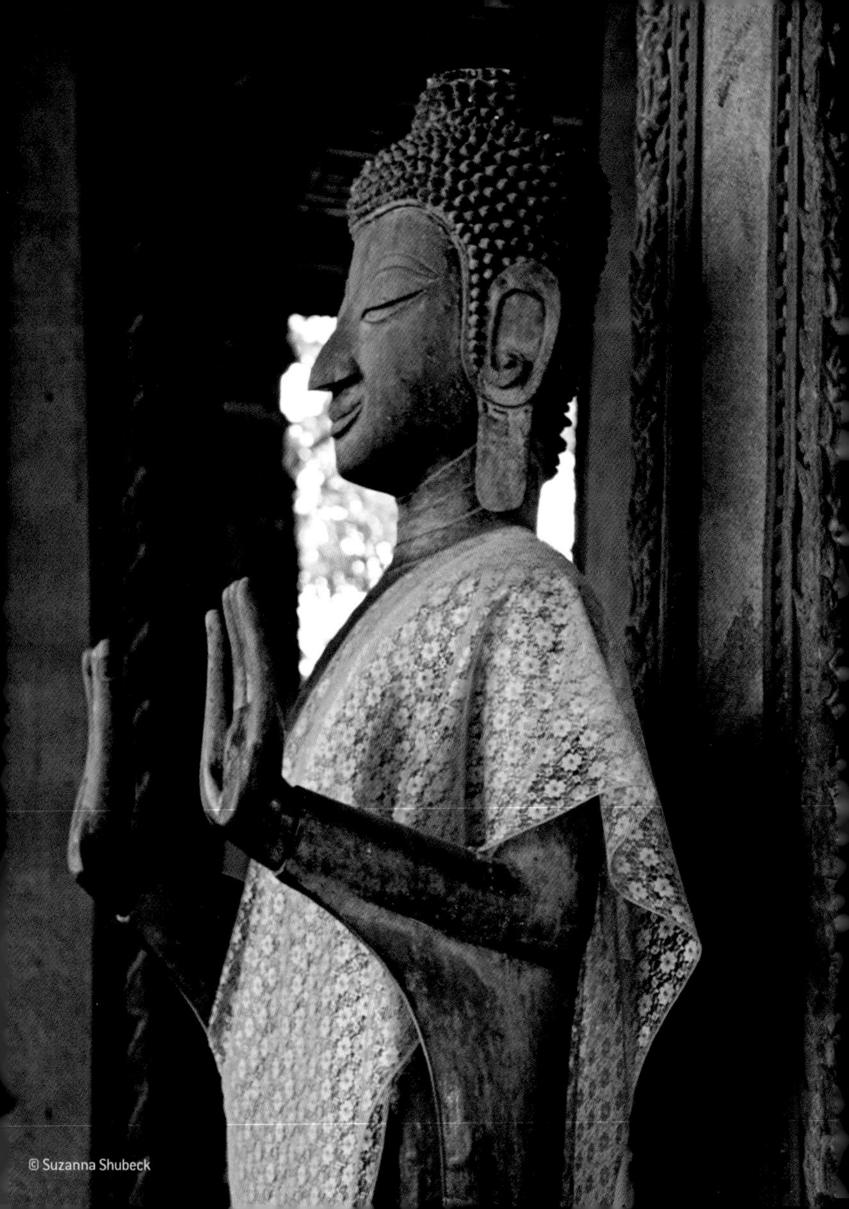

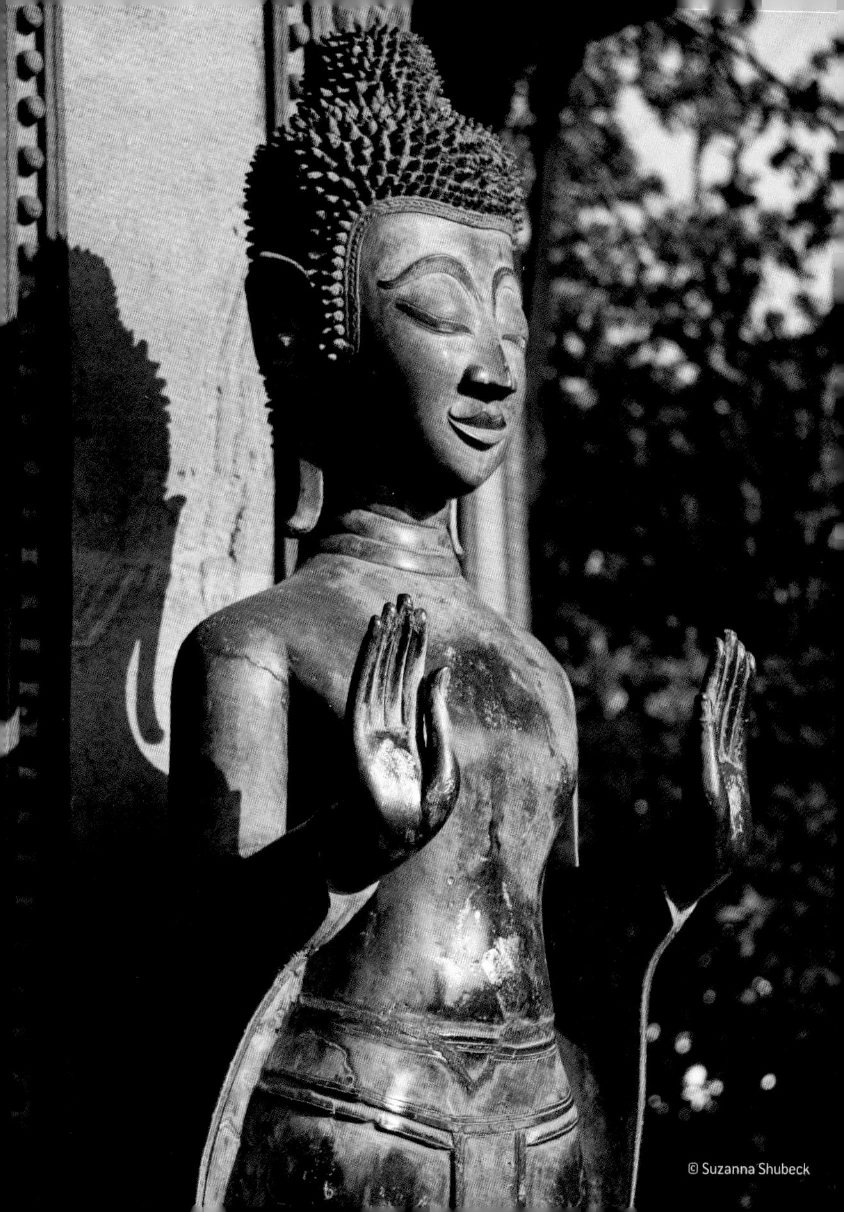

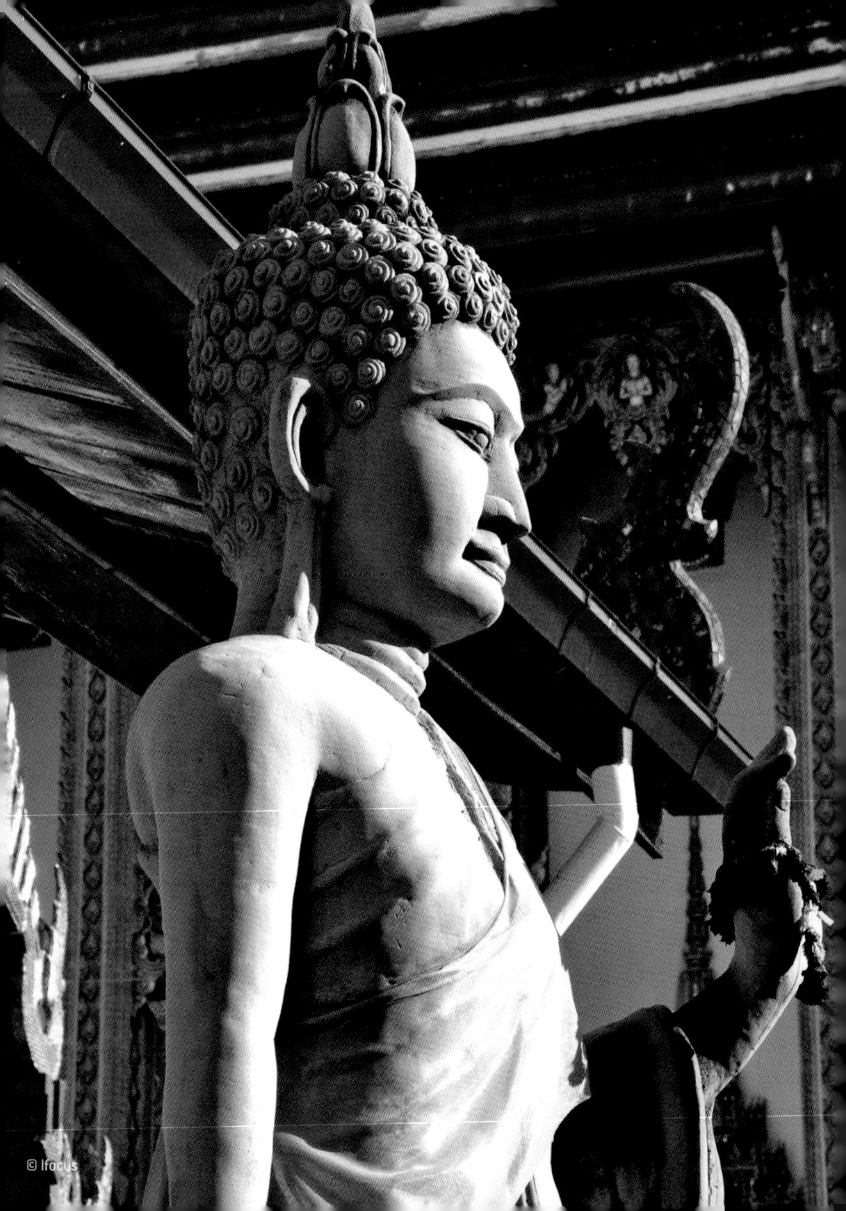

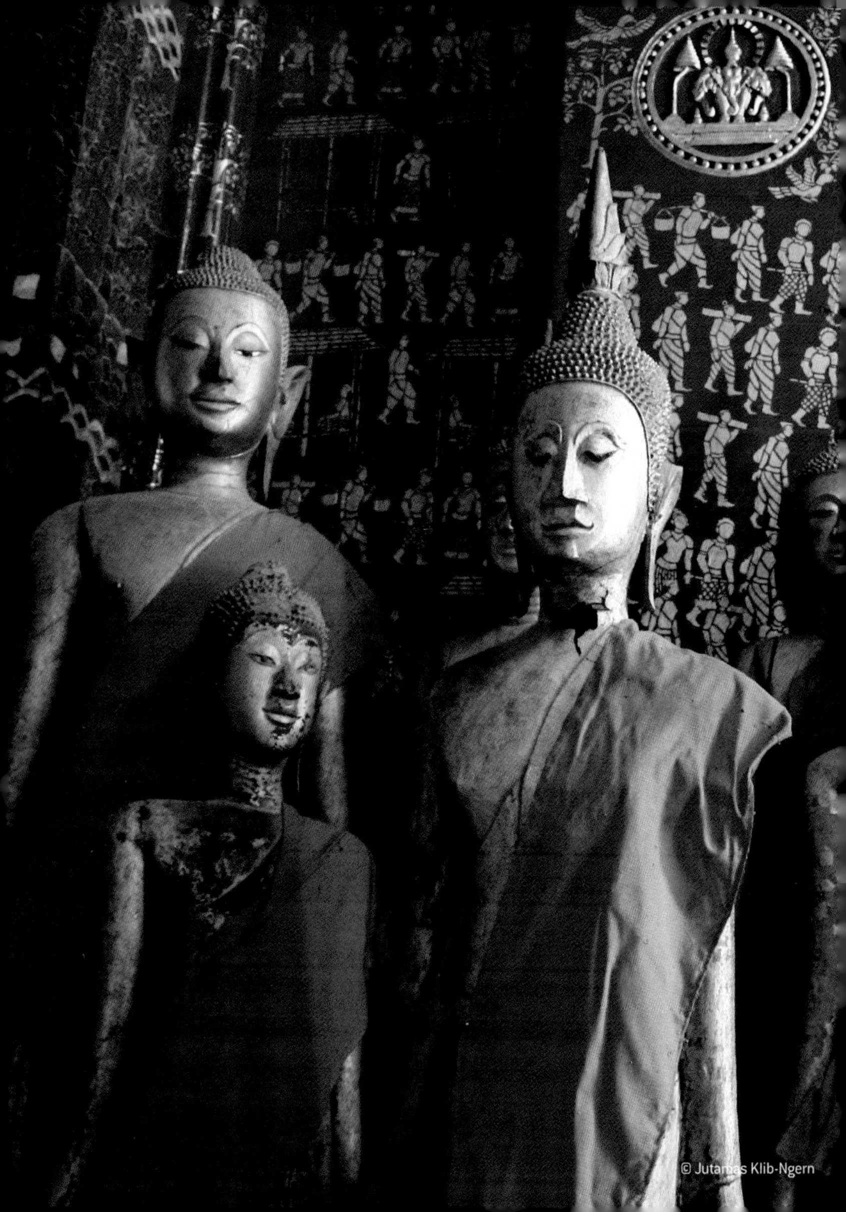

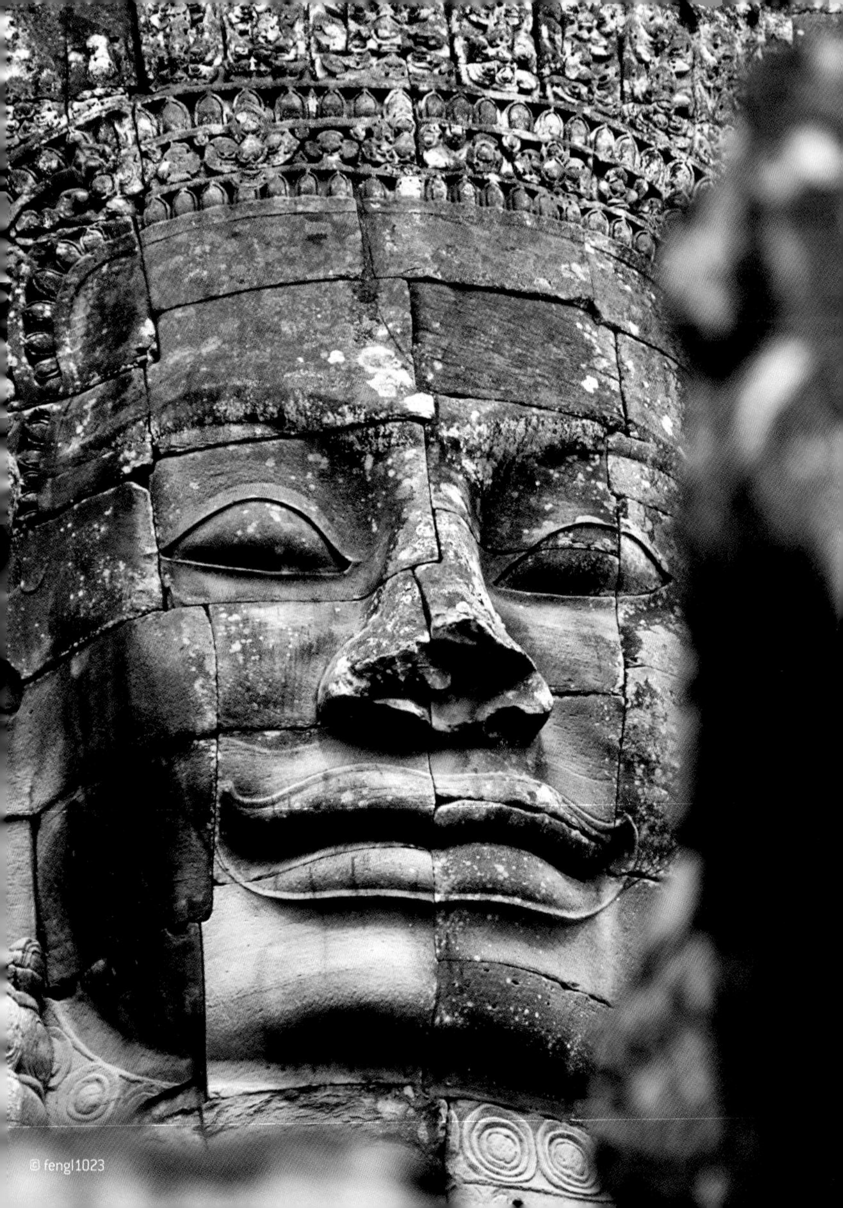

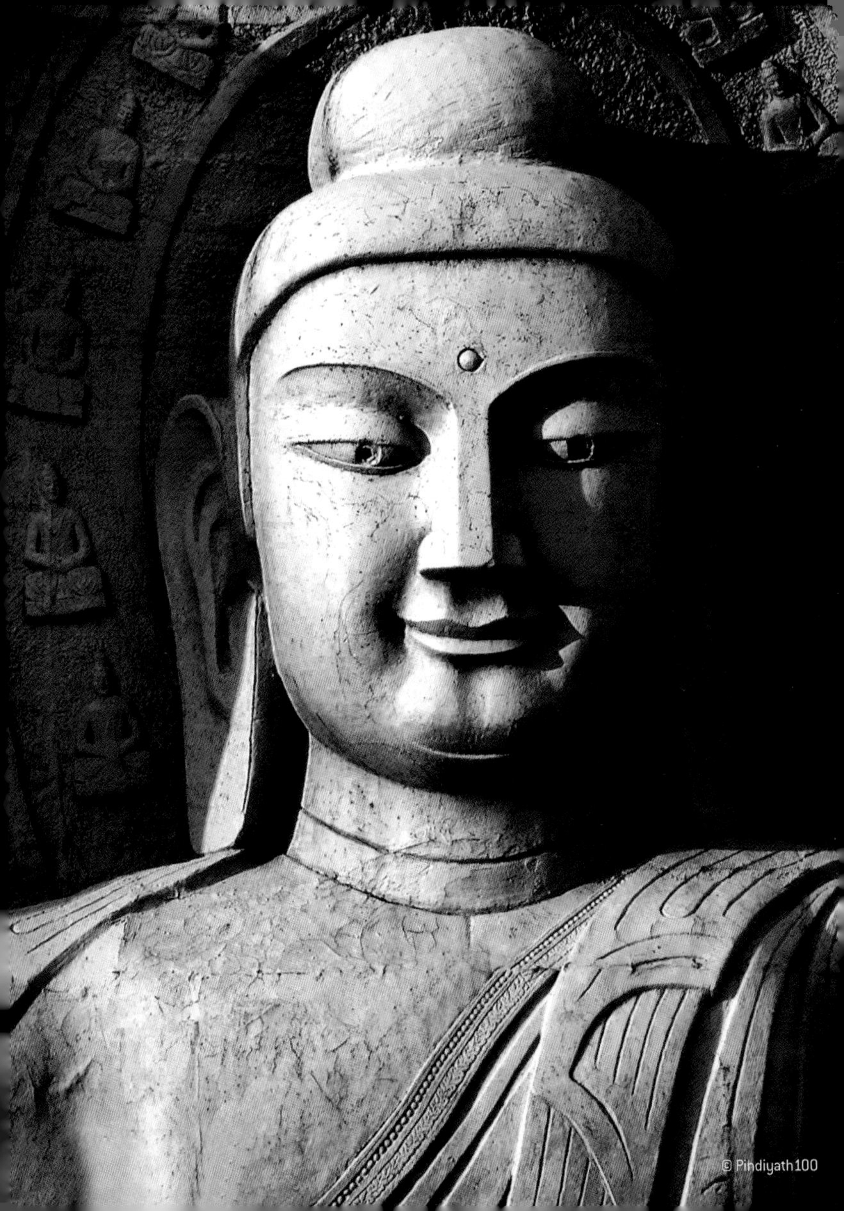

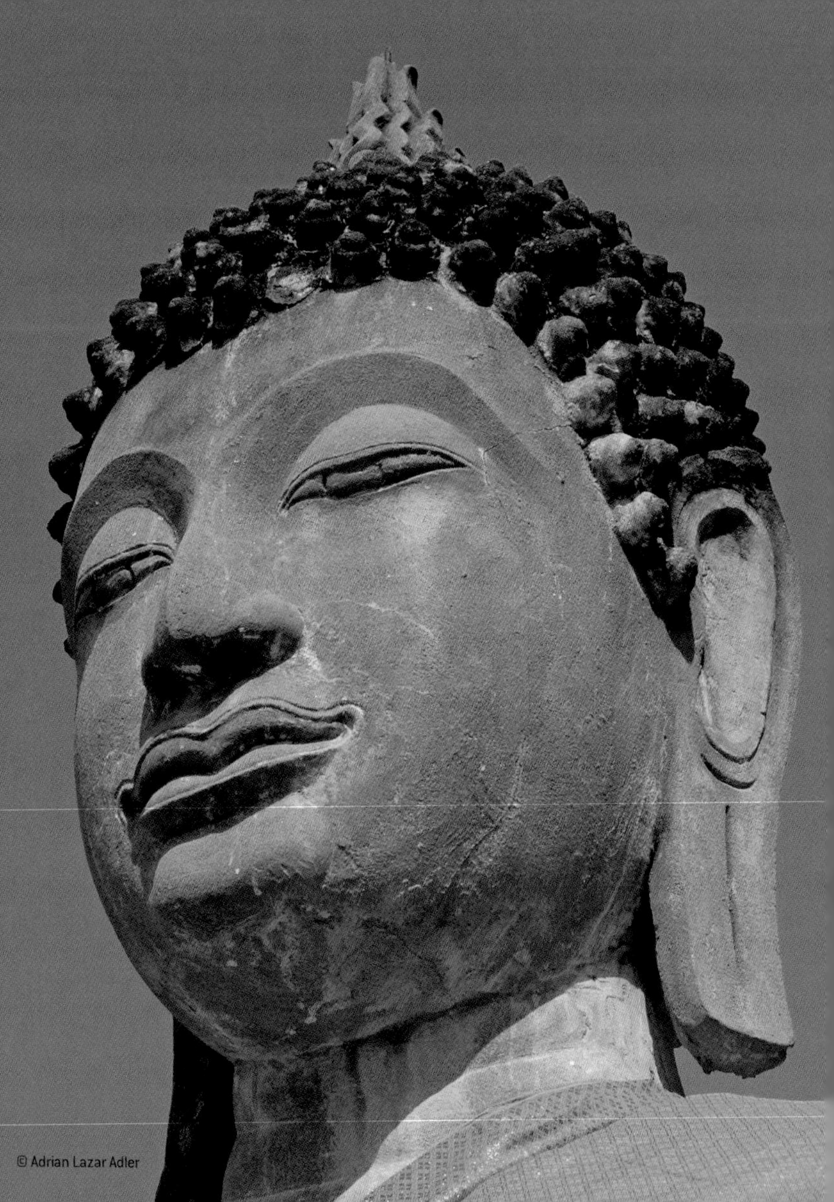

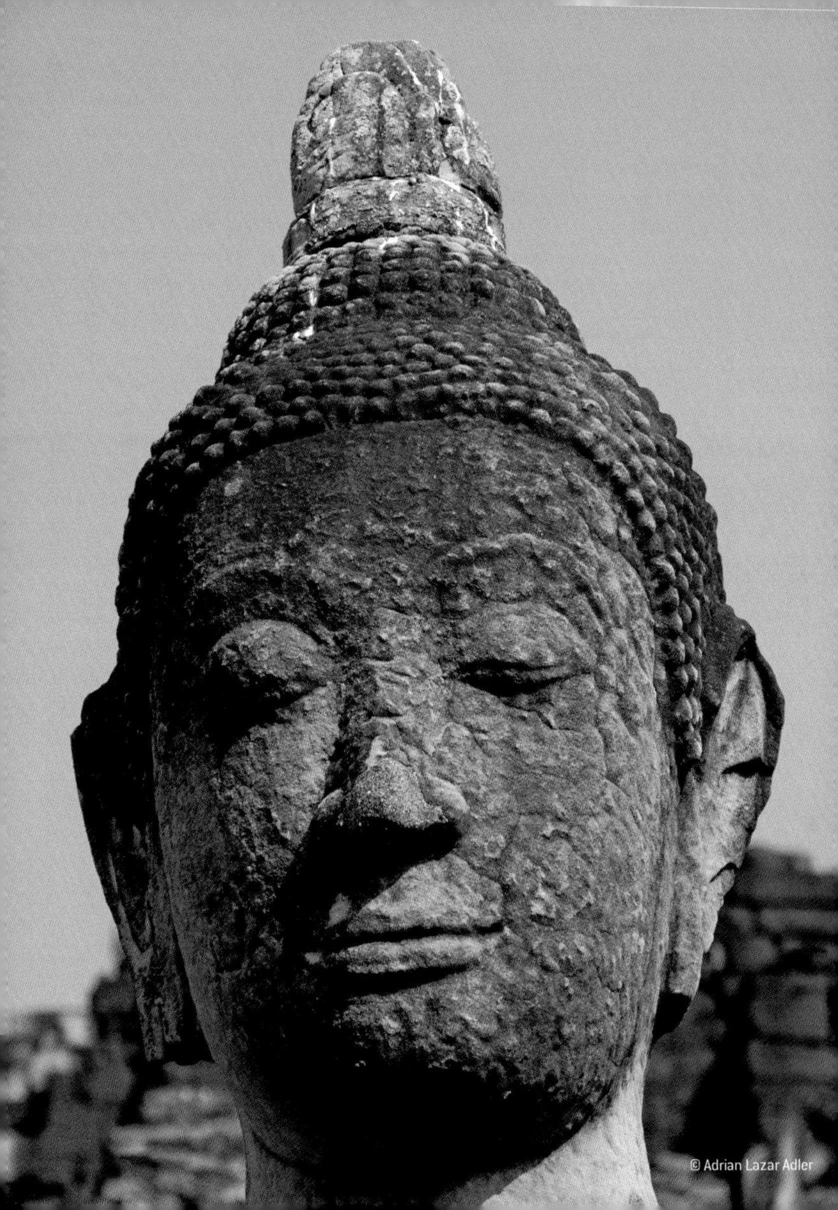

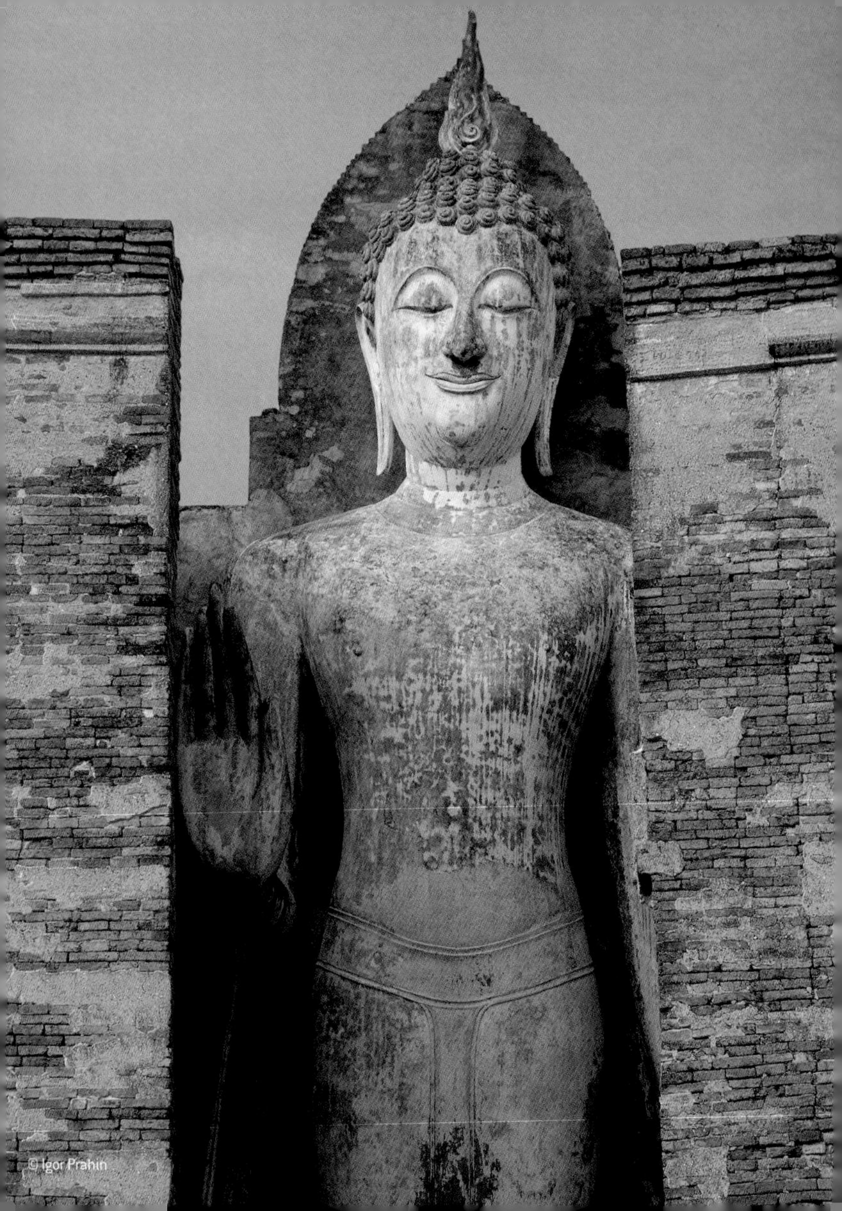

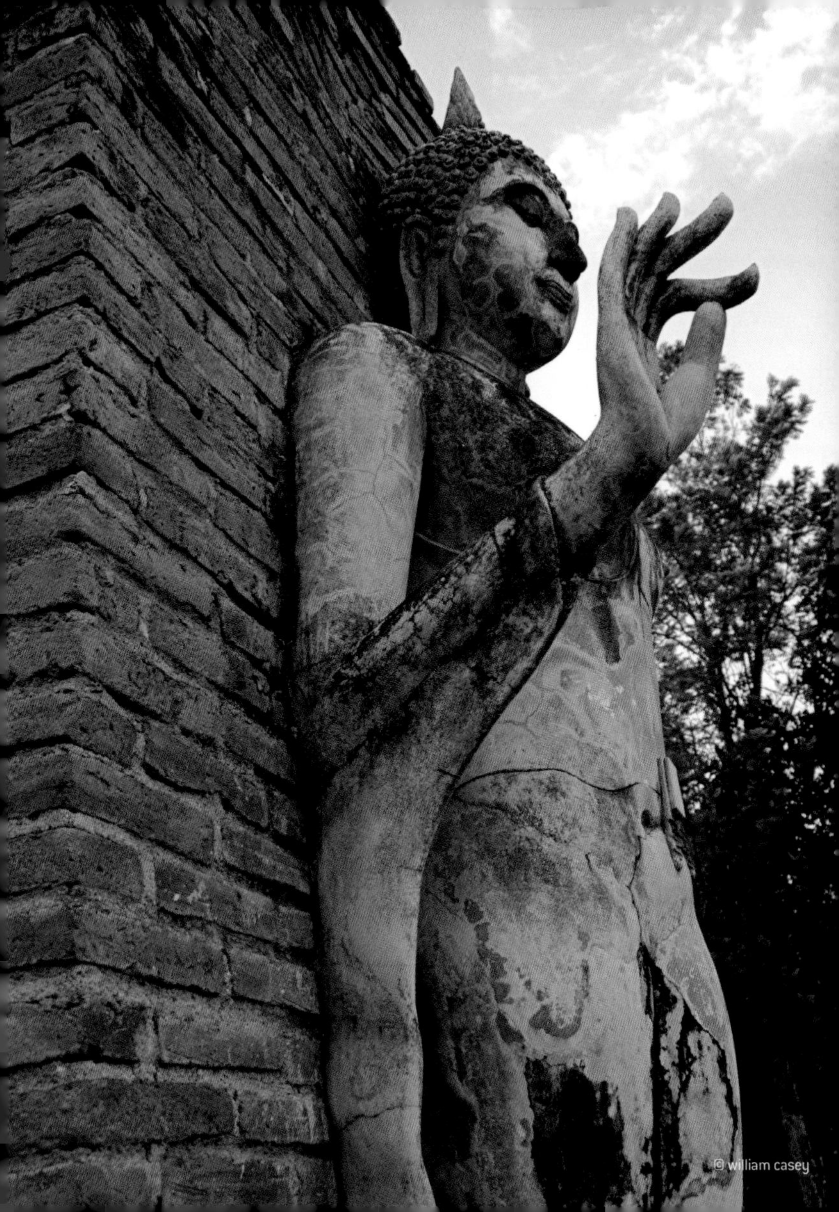
© william casey

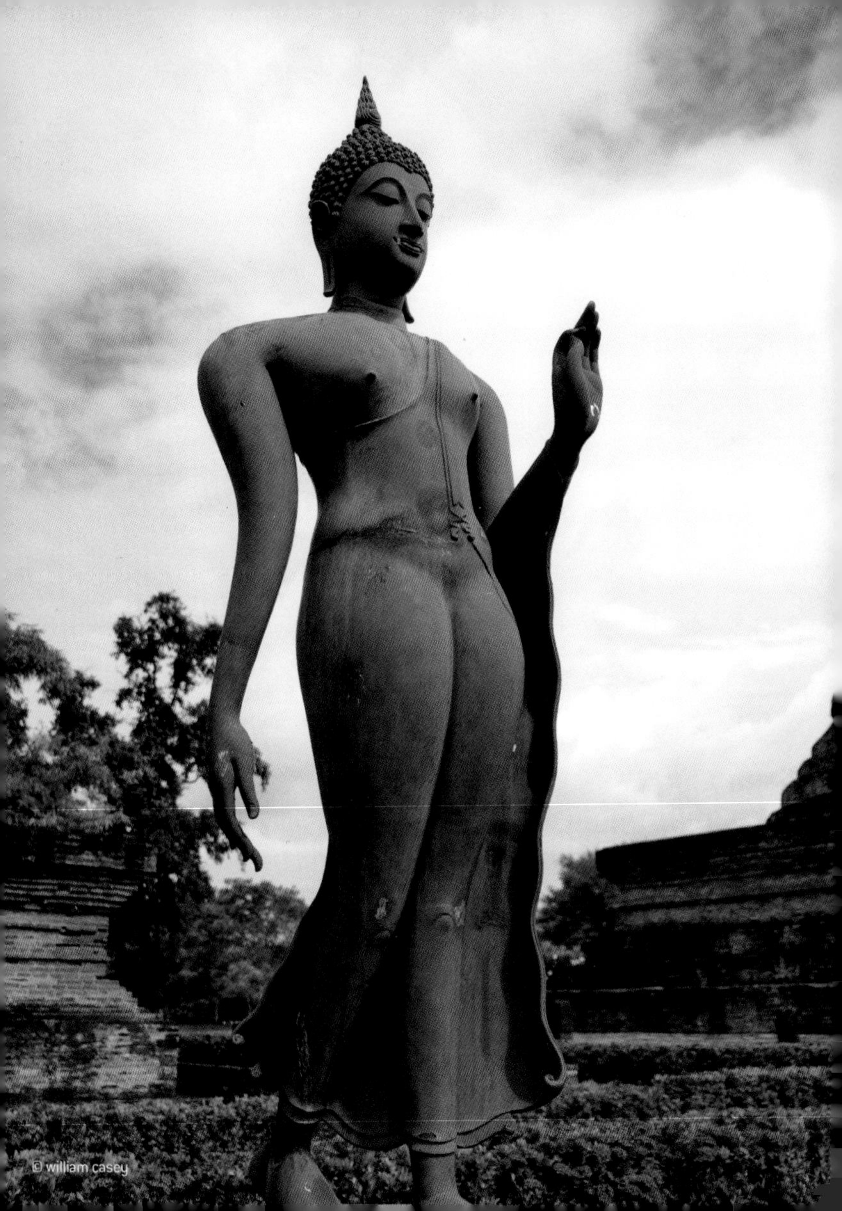

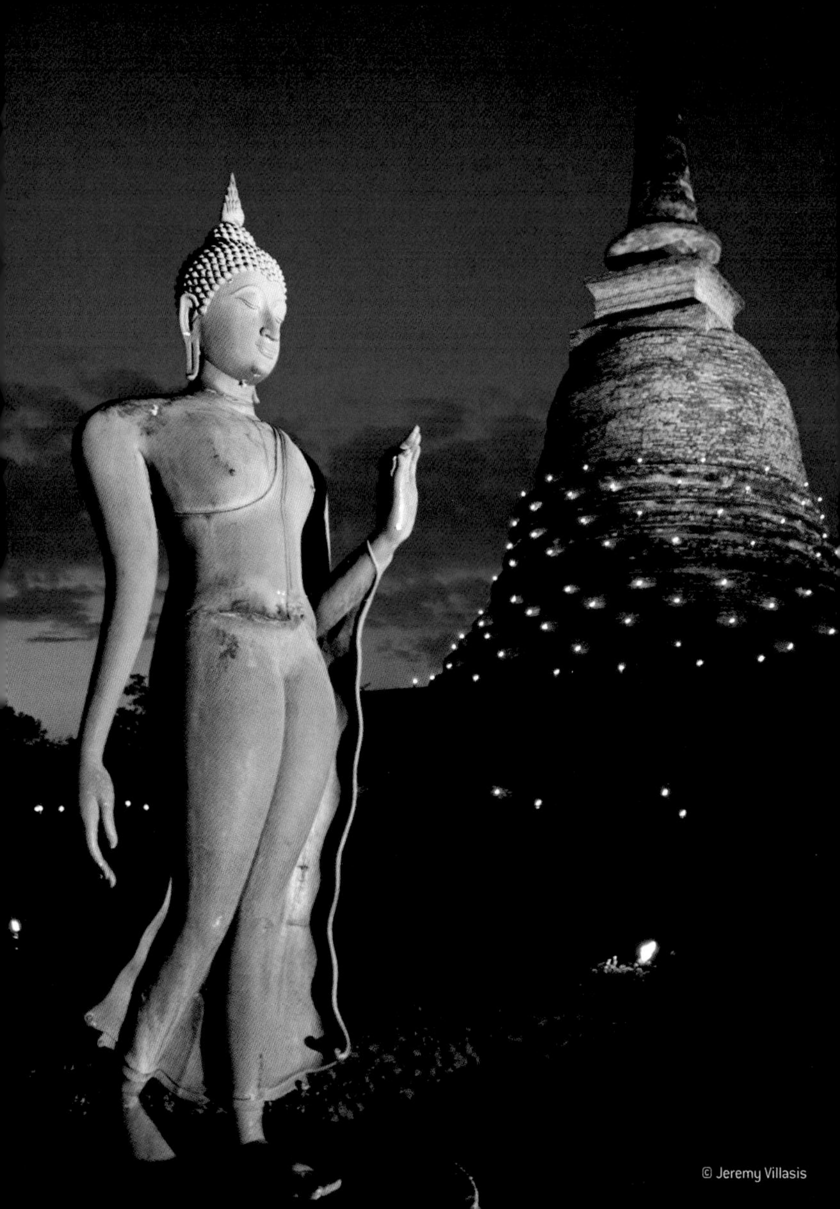

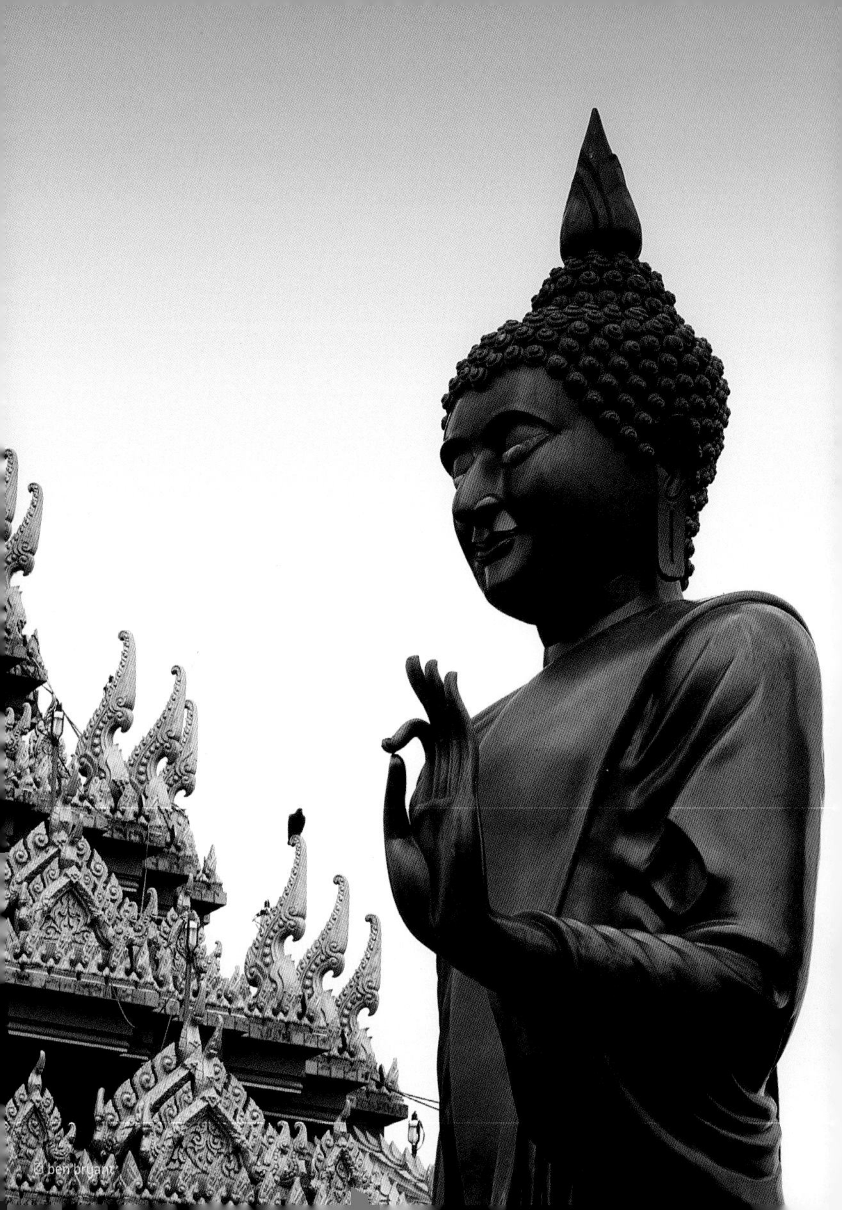

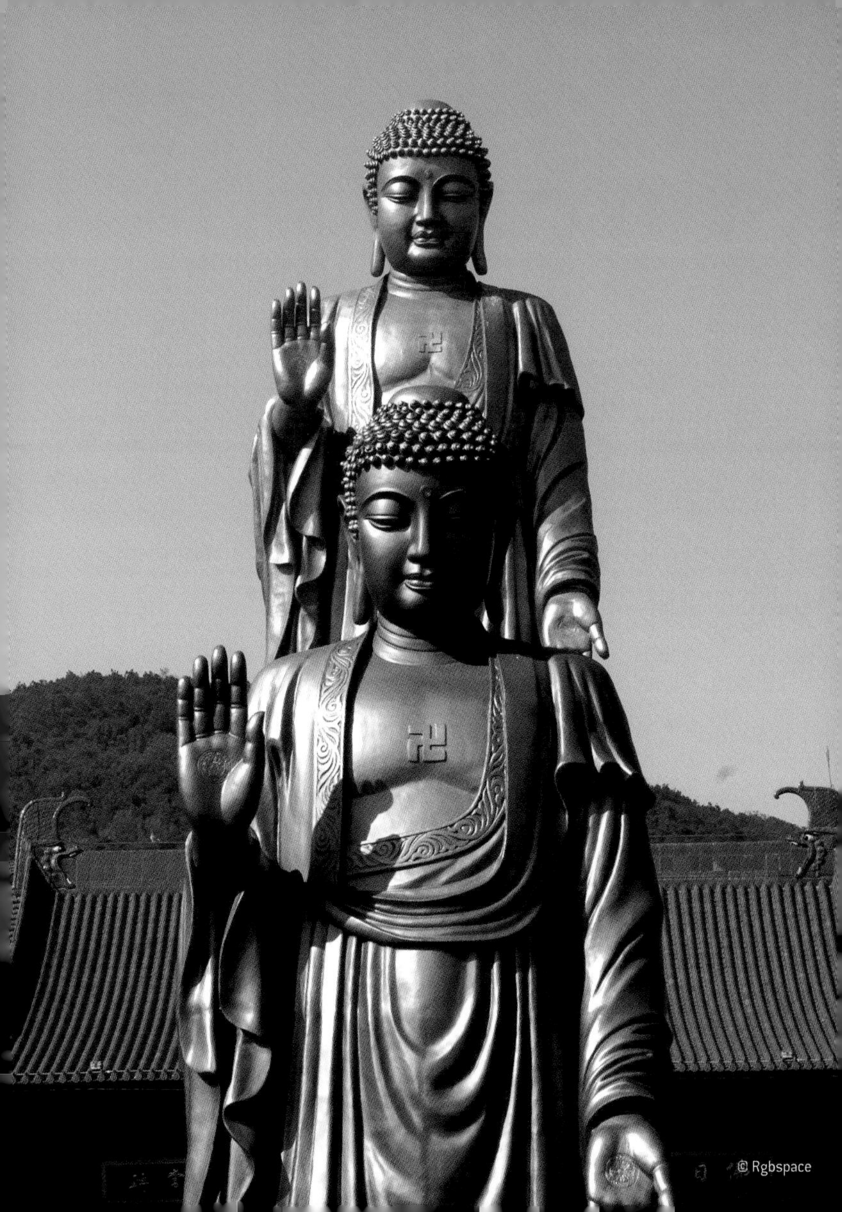

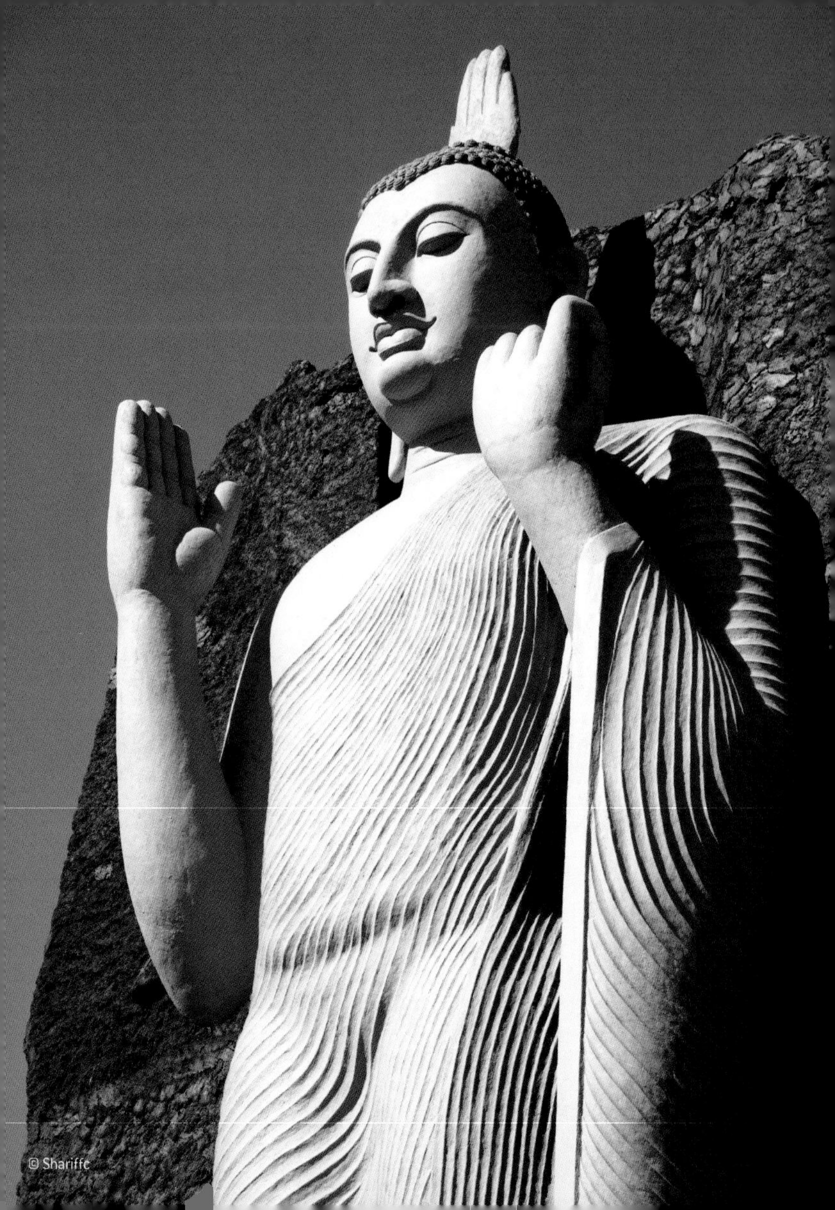

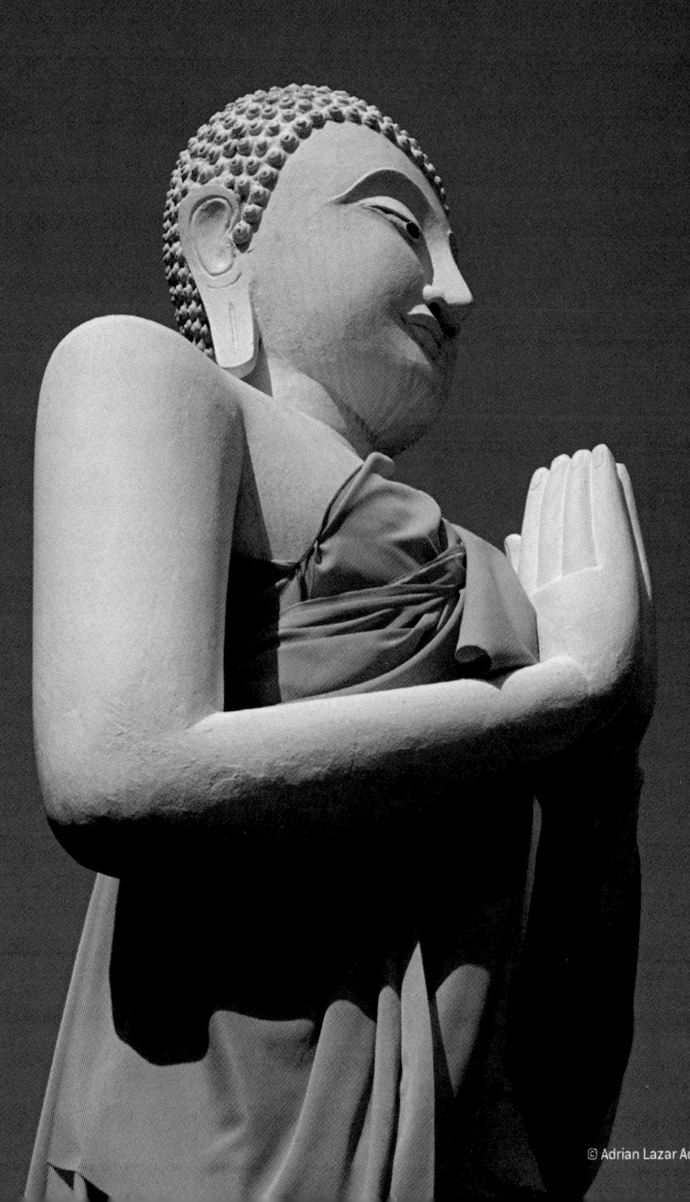

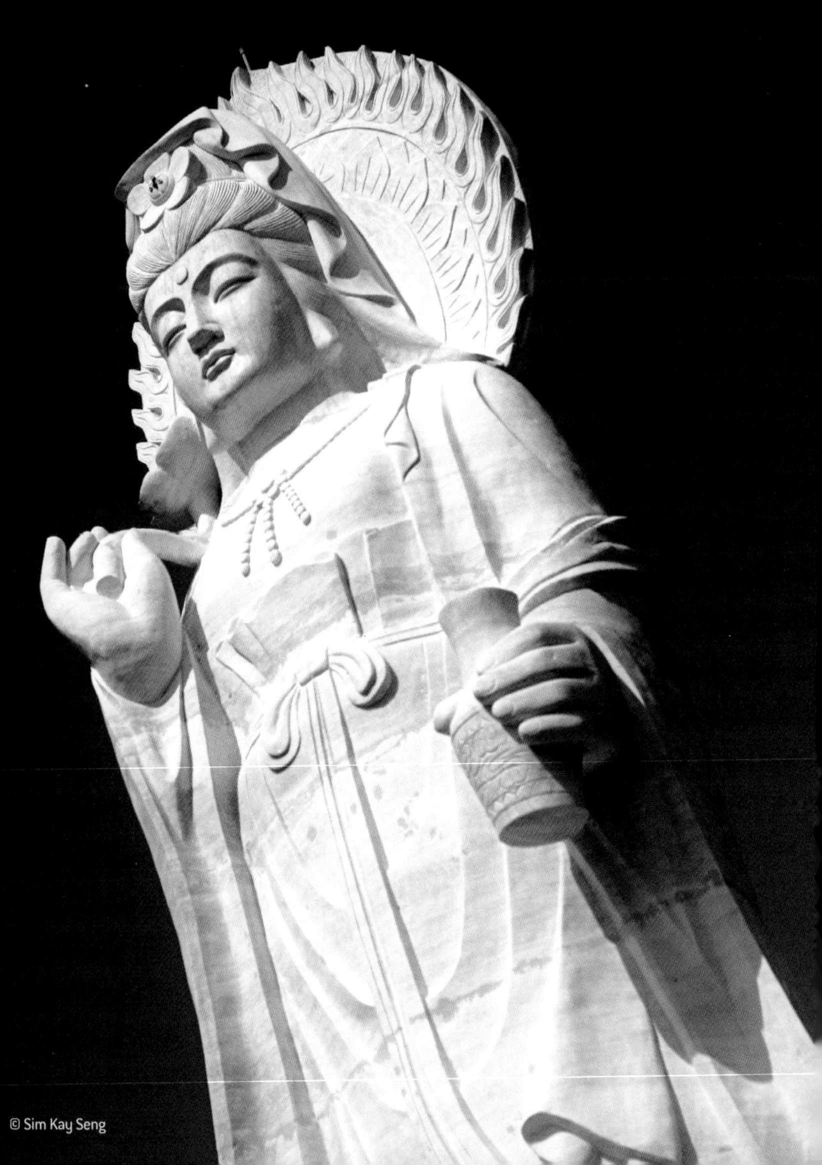

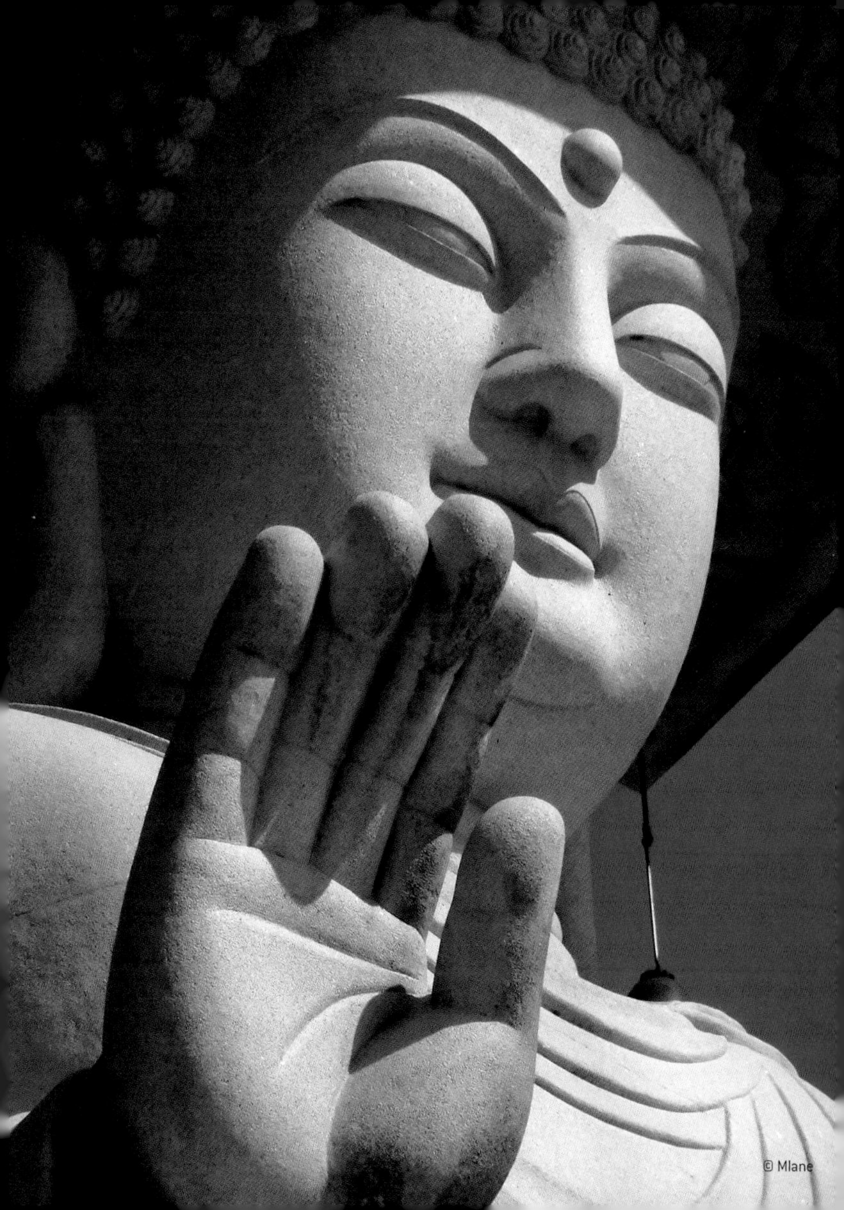

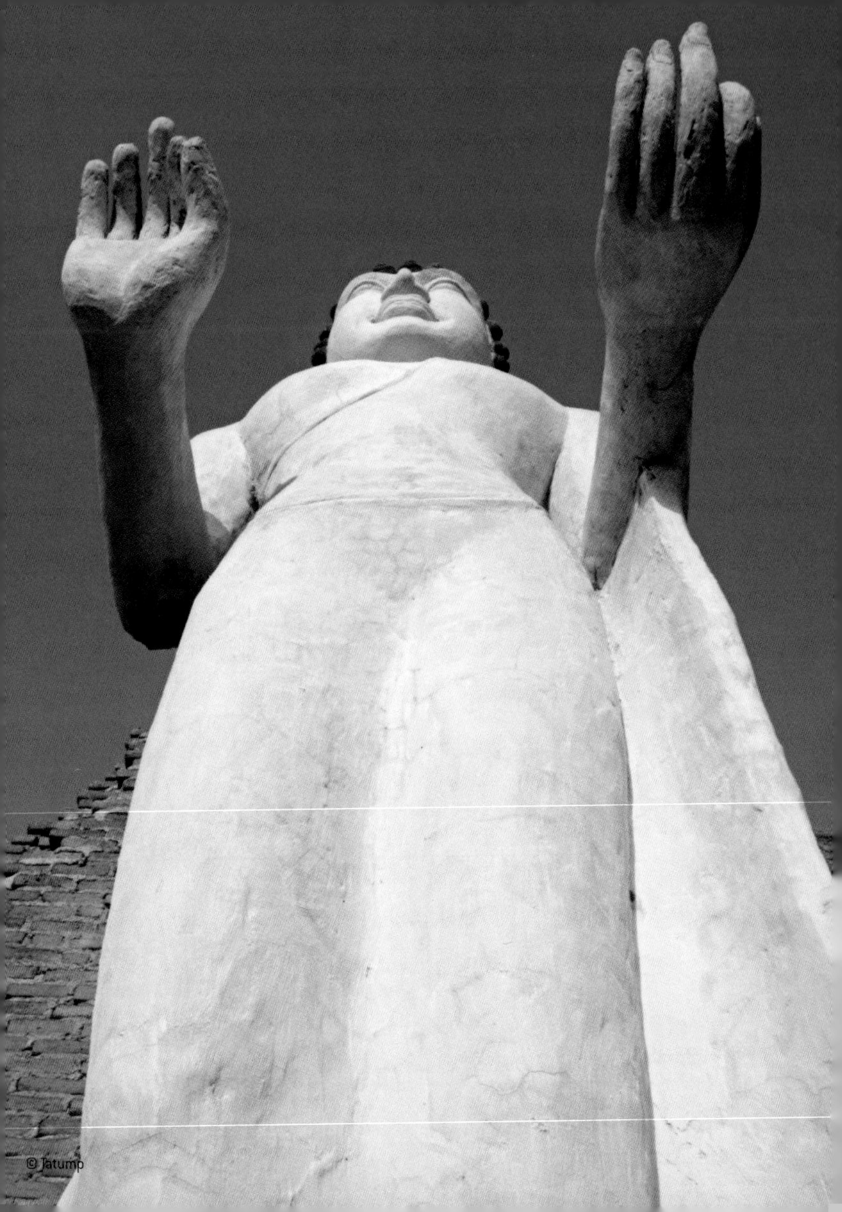

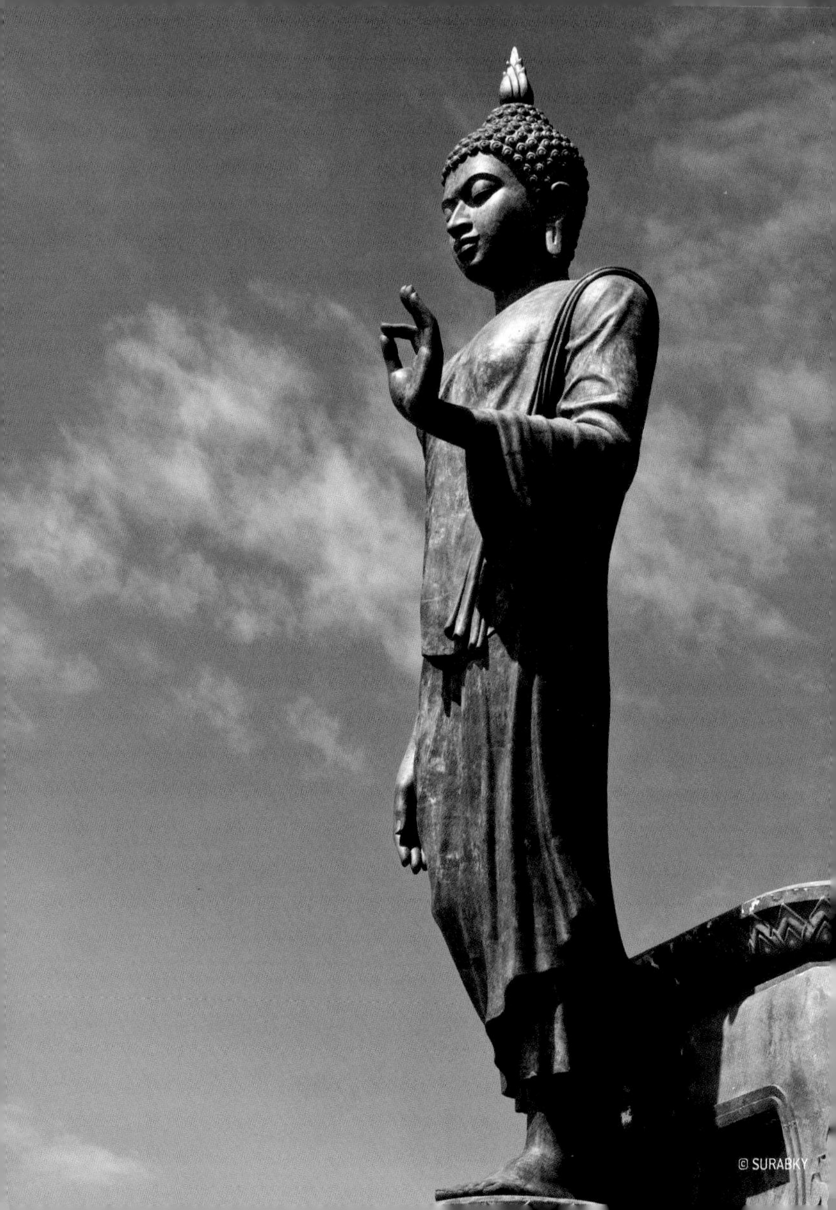
© SURABKY

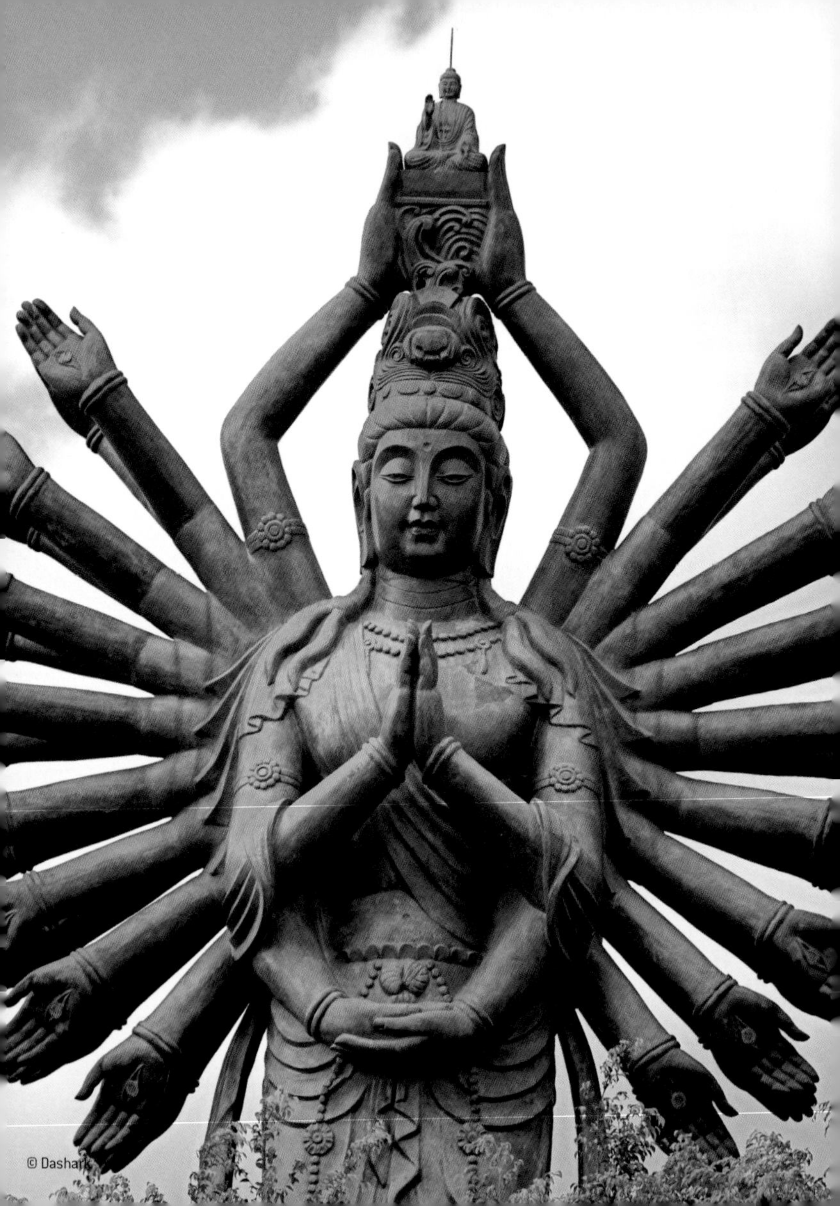

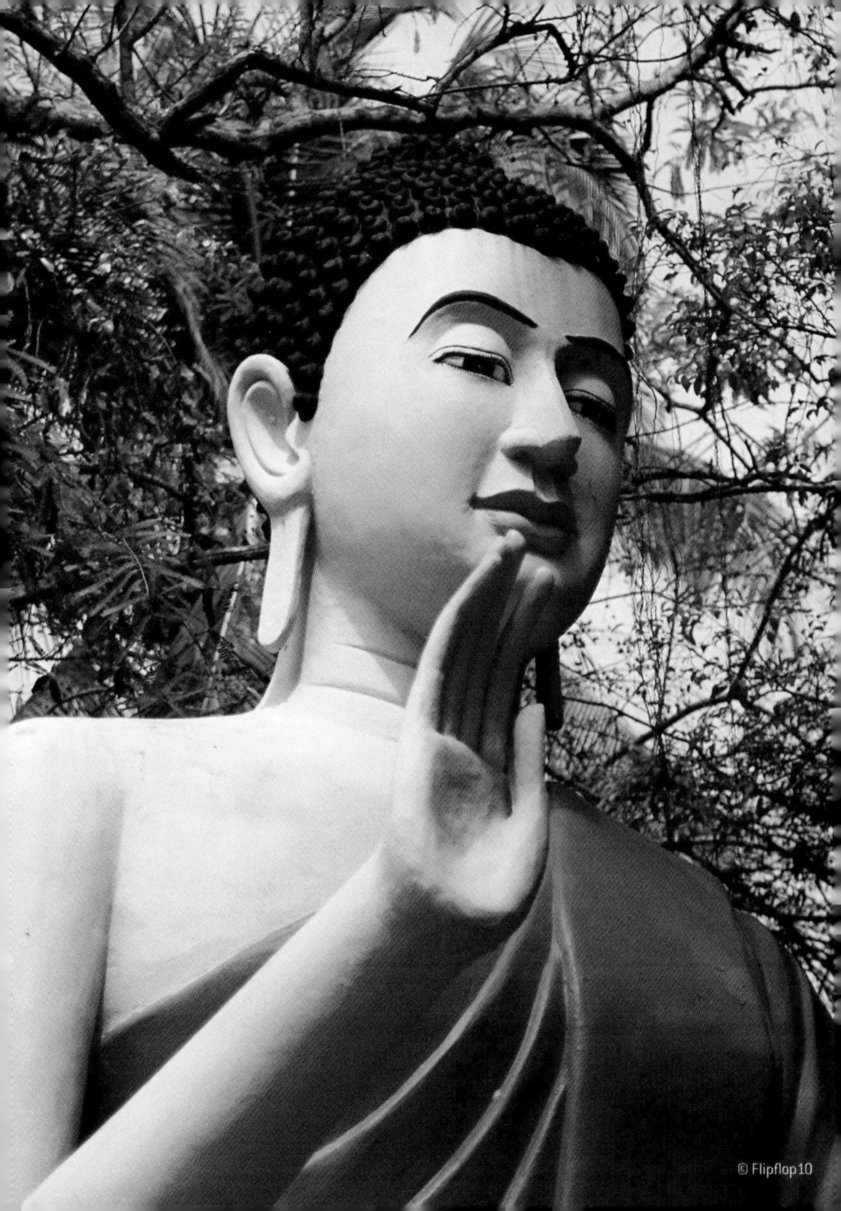

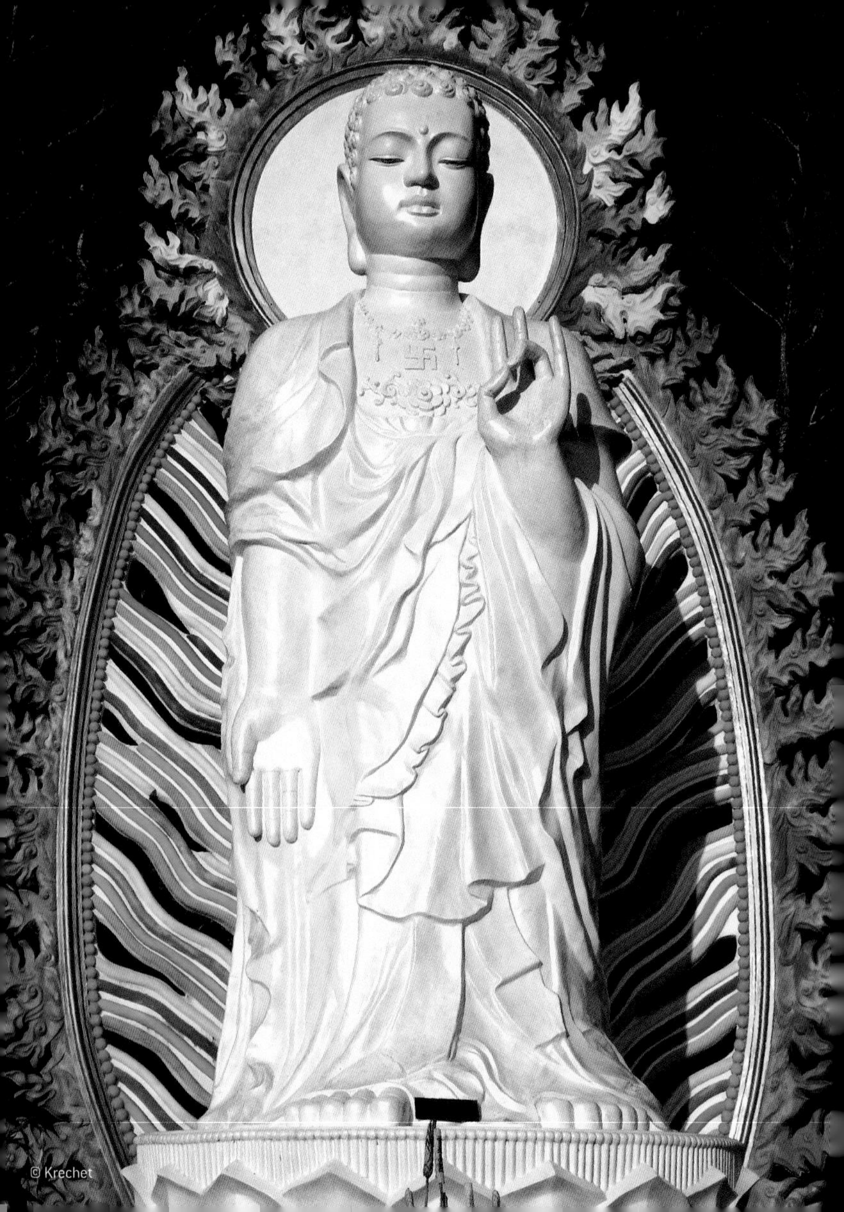

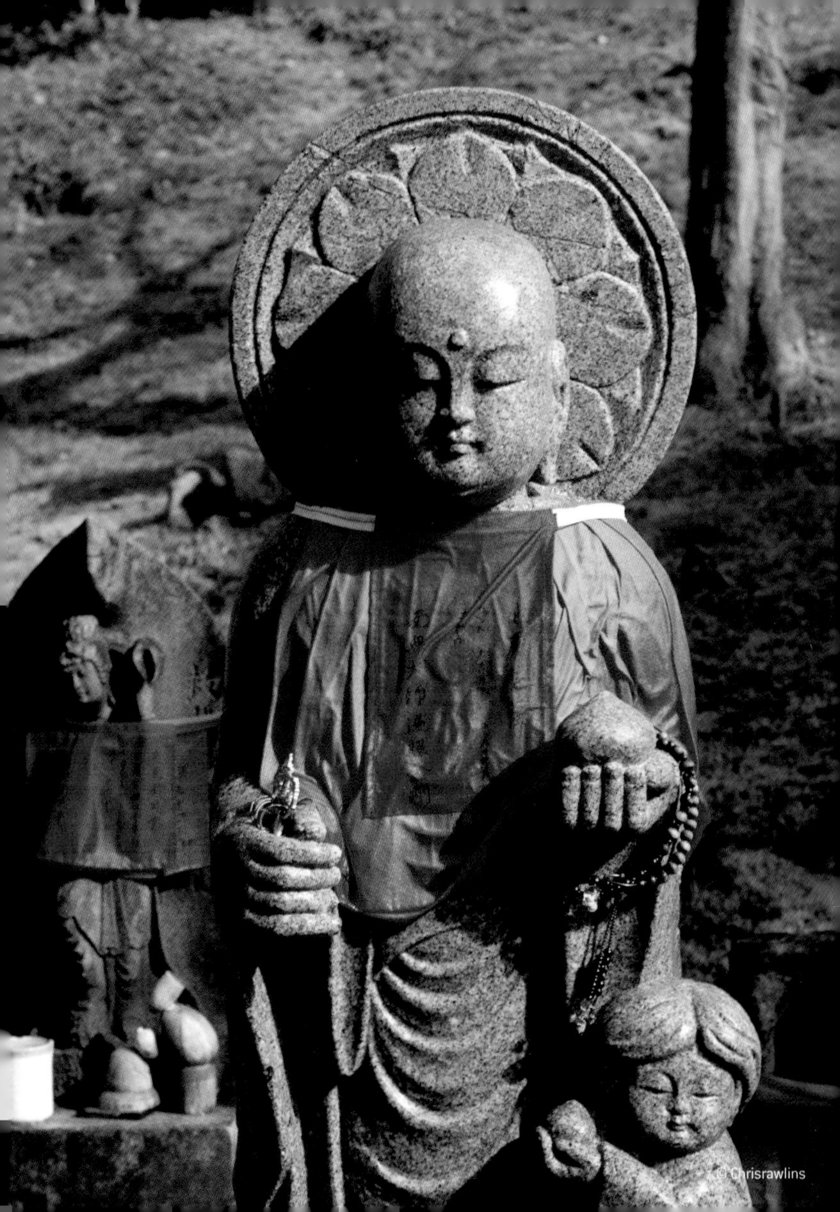

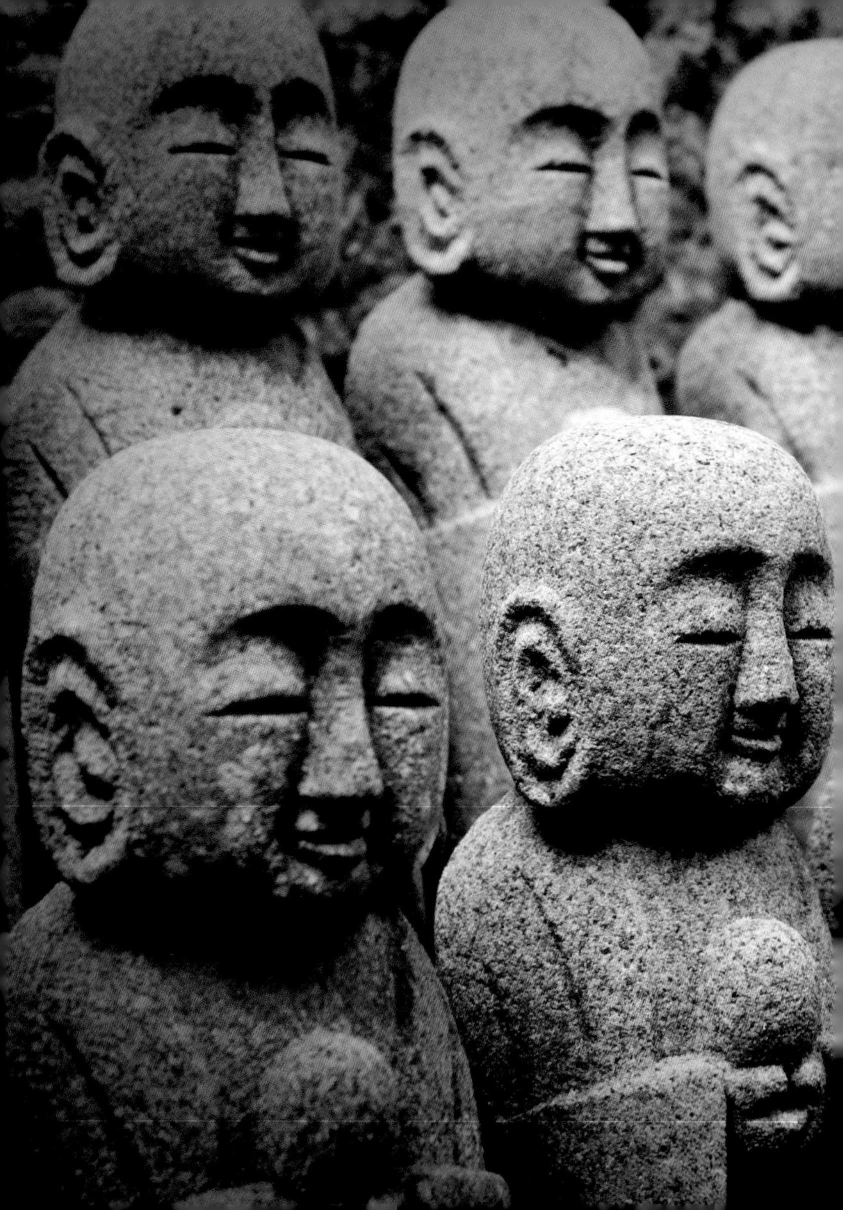

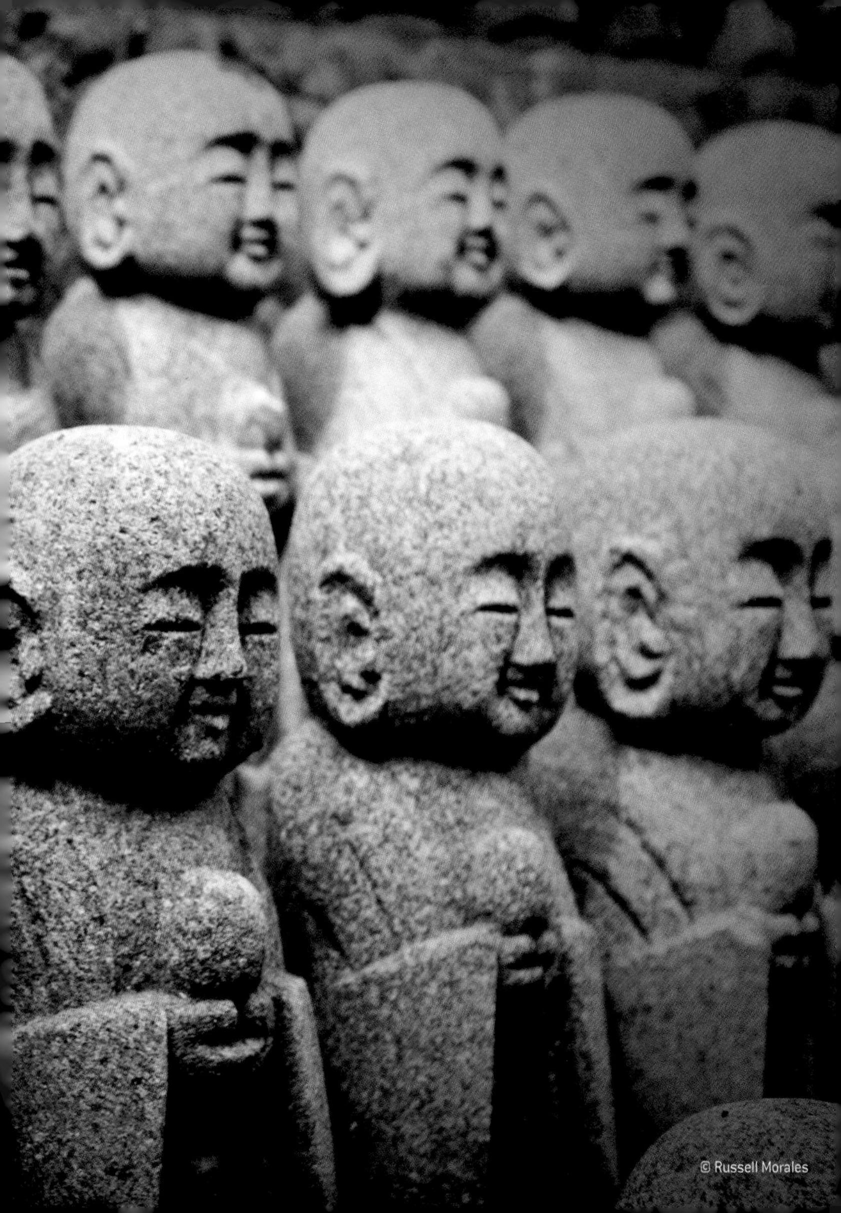

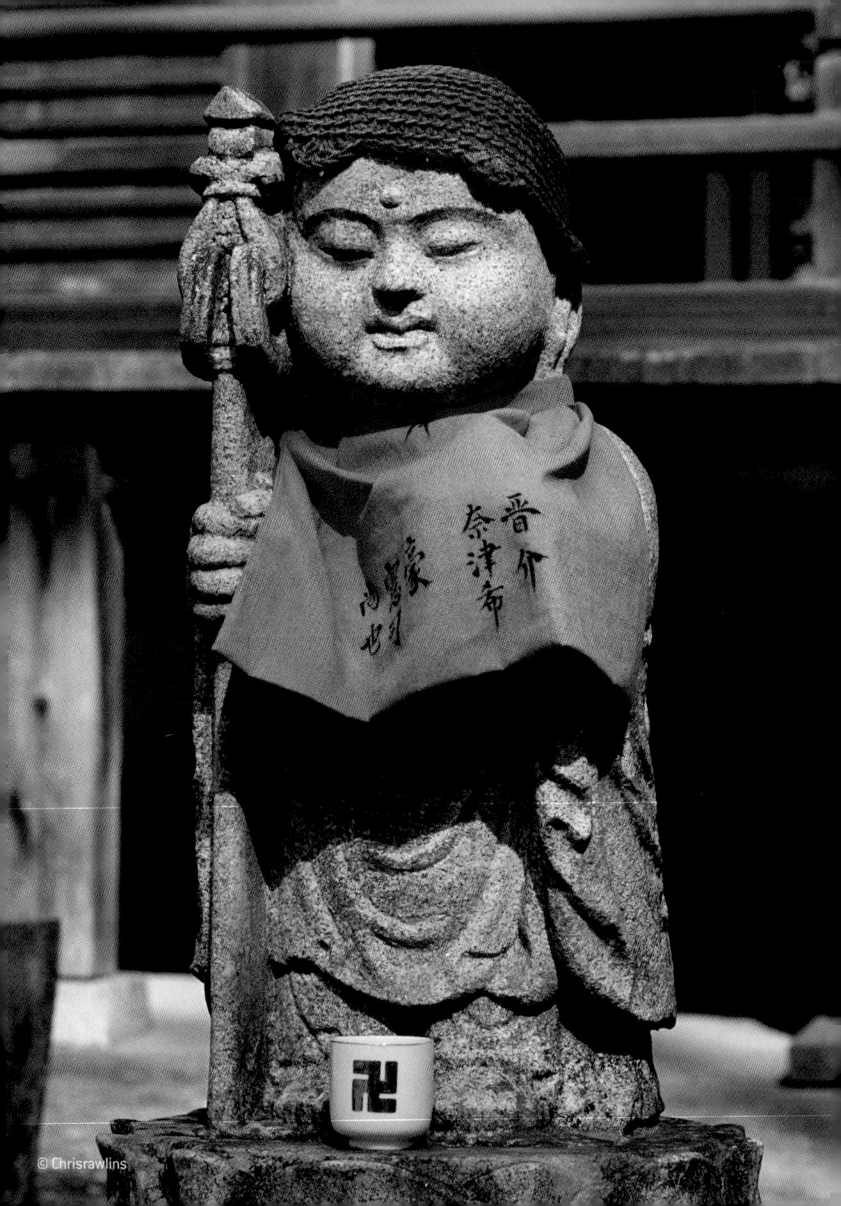

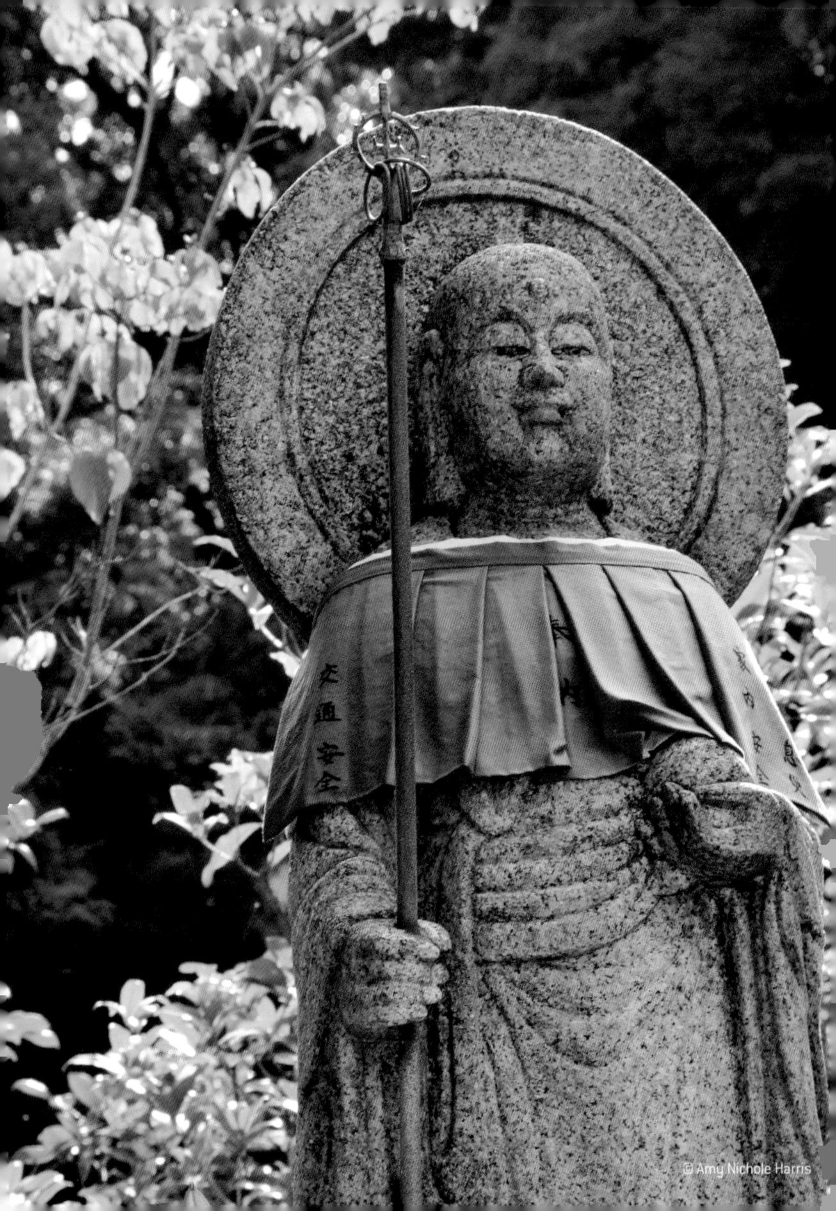
交通安全
© Amy Nichole Harris

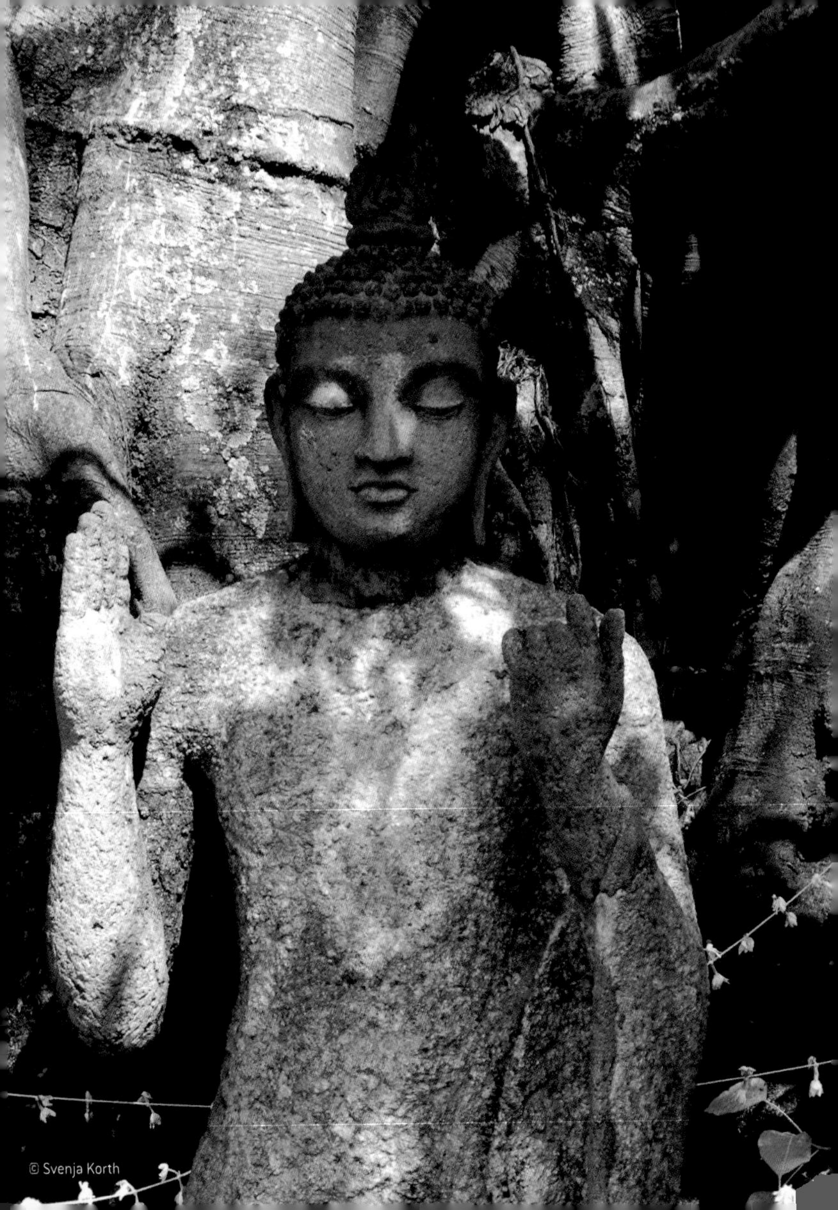

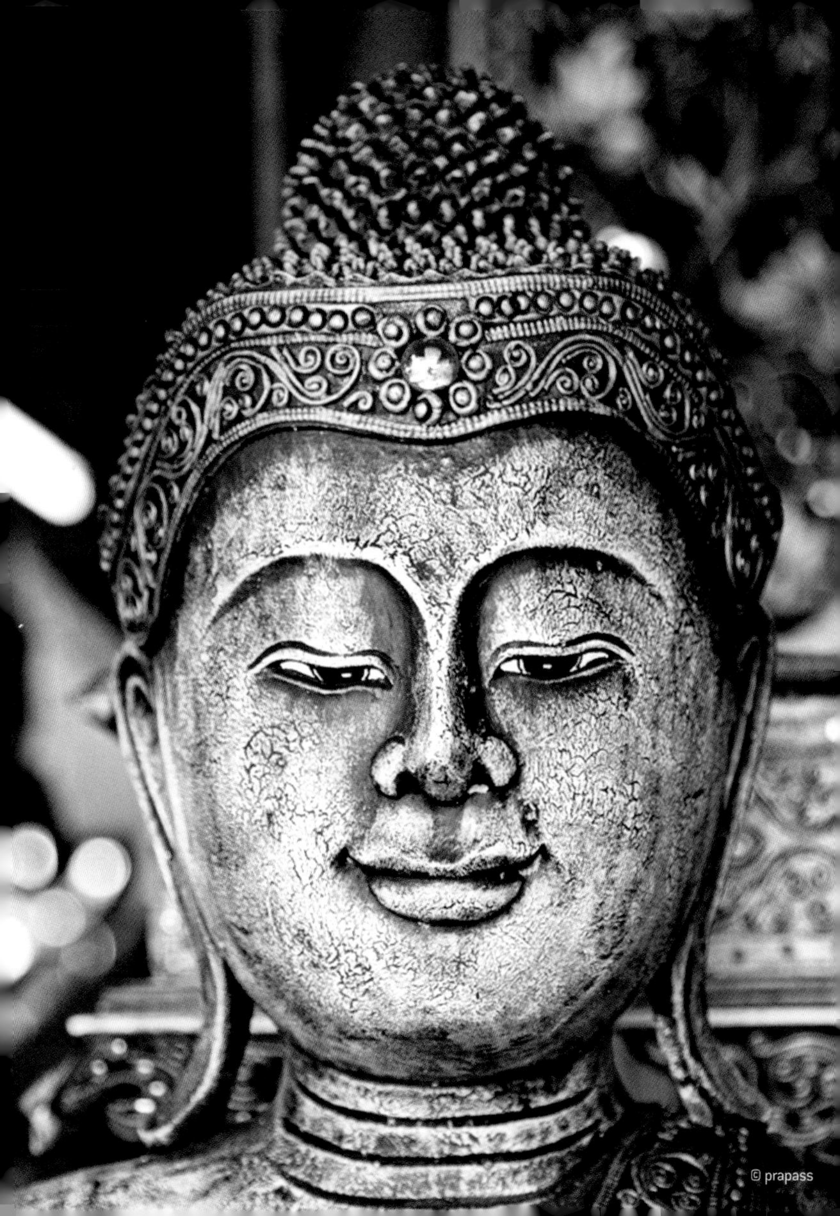

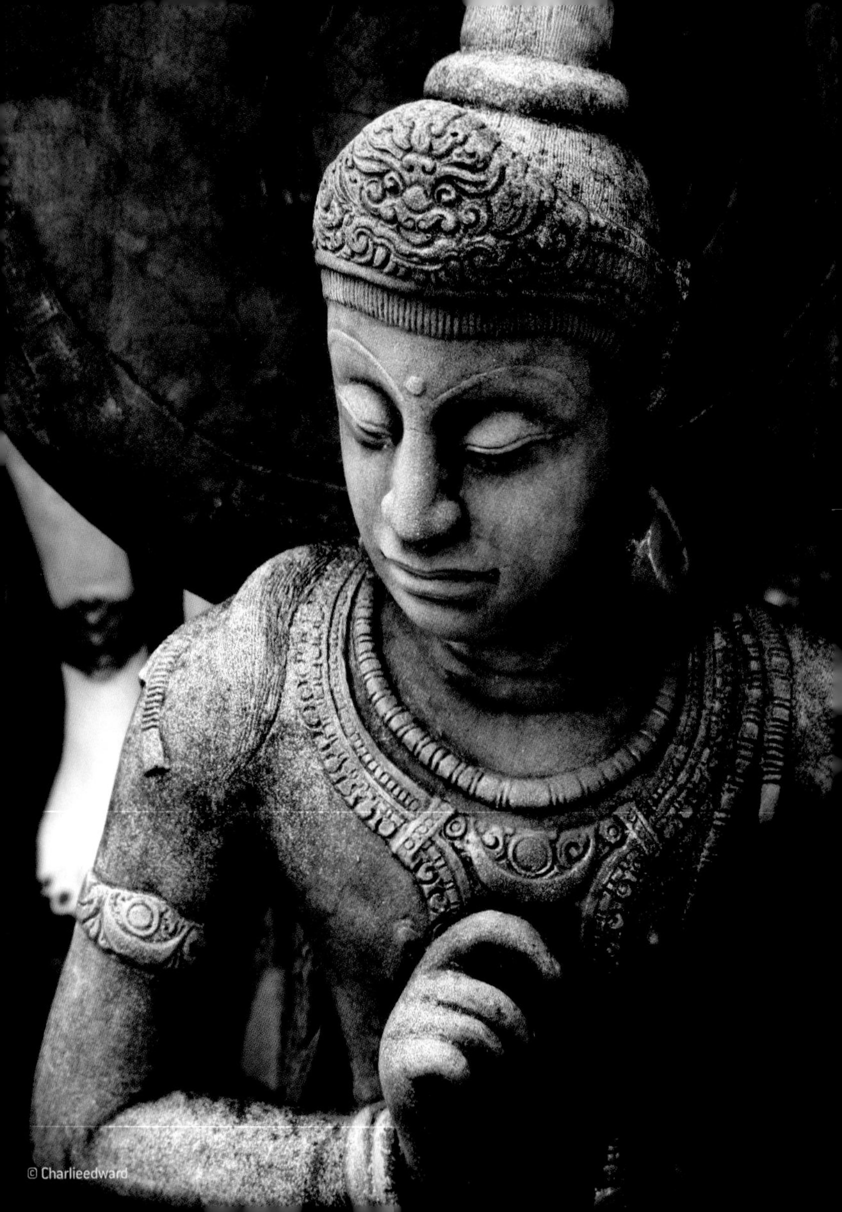

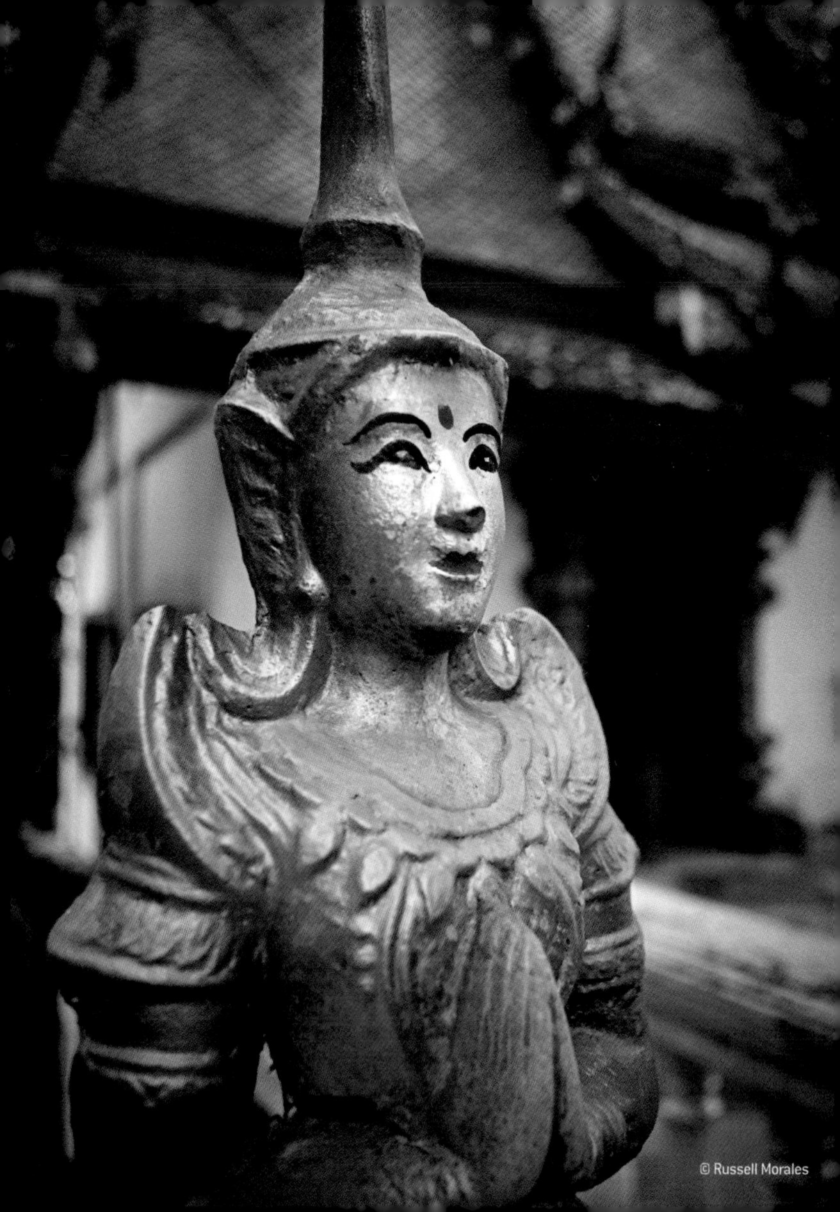

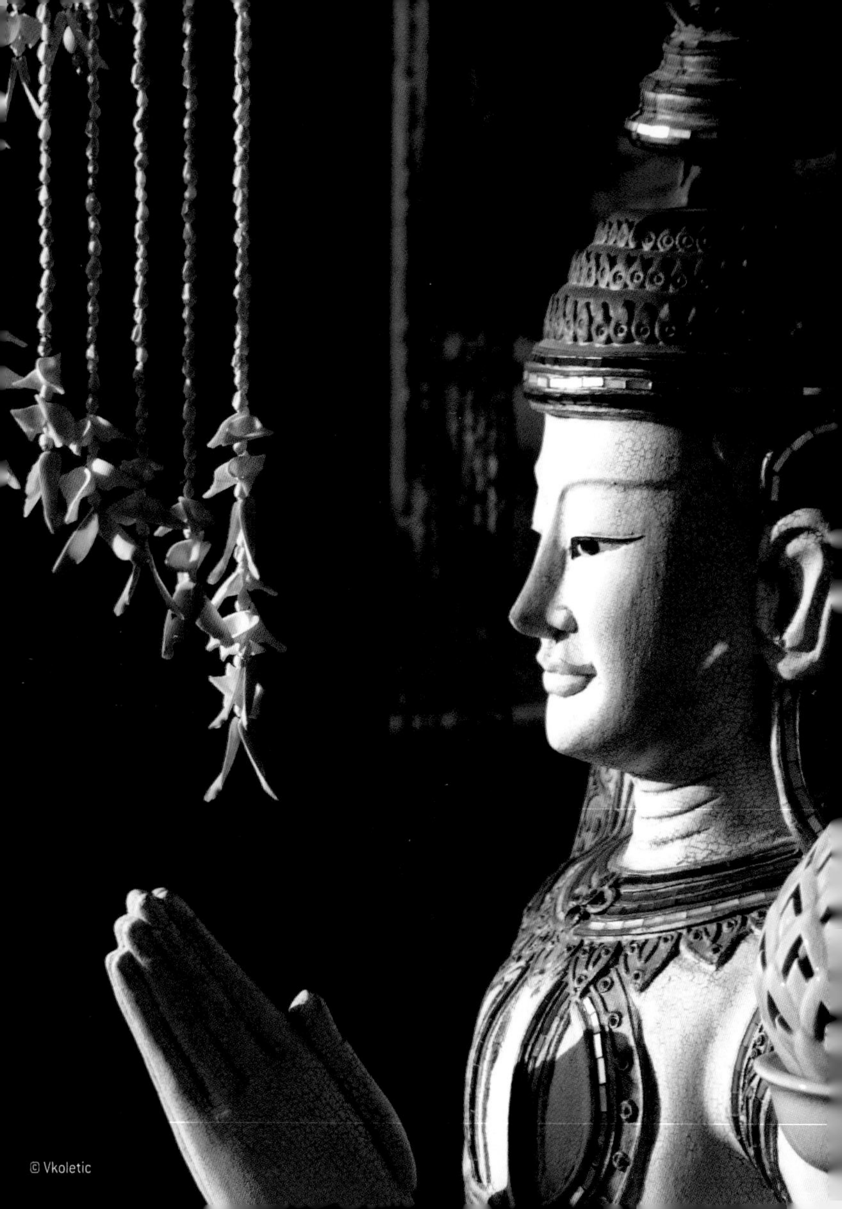

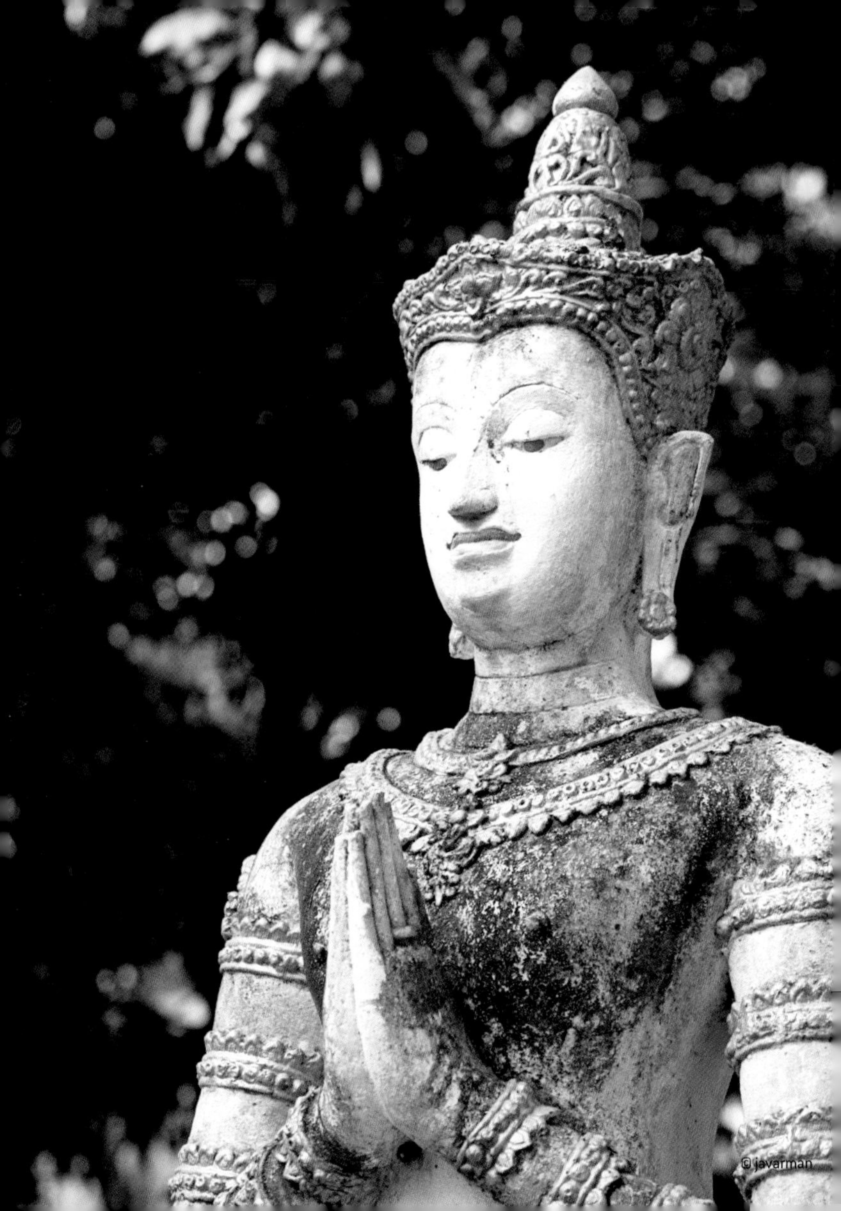
© javarman

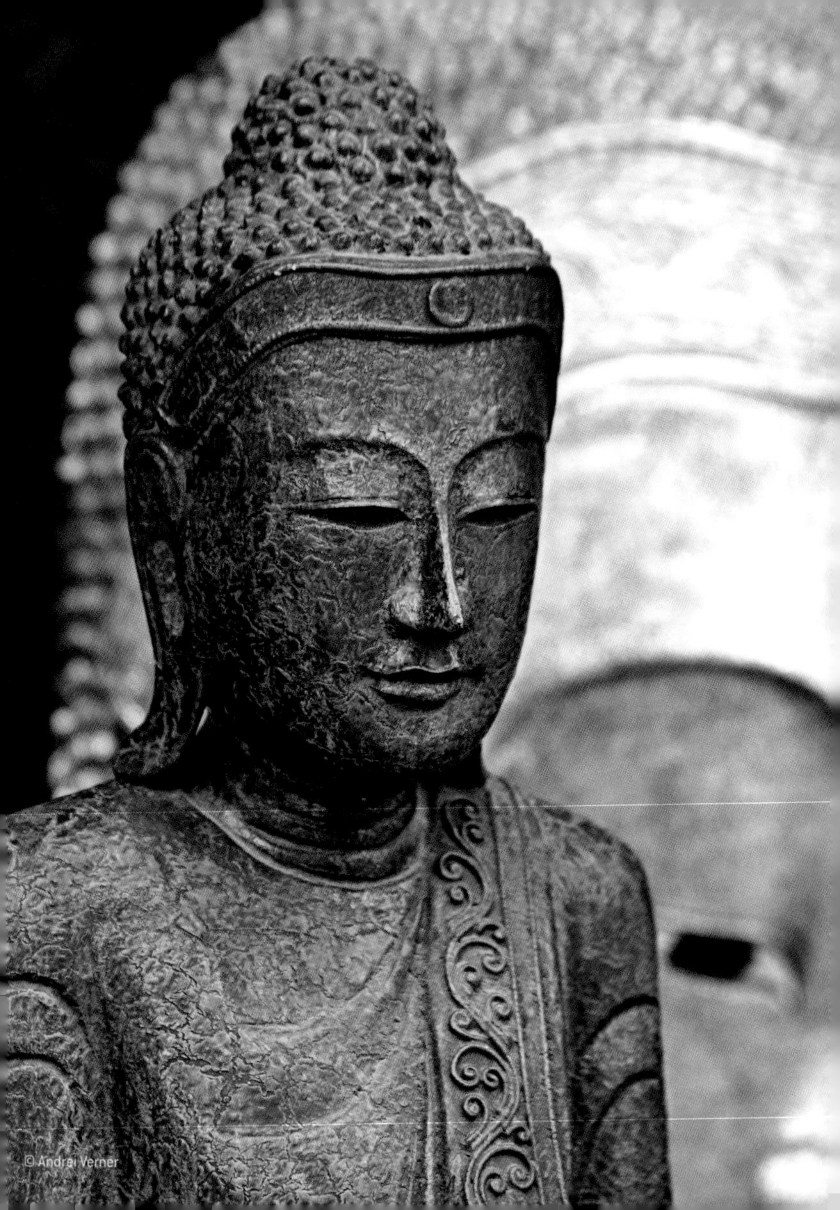

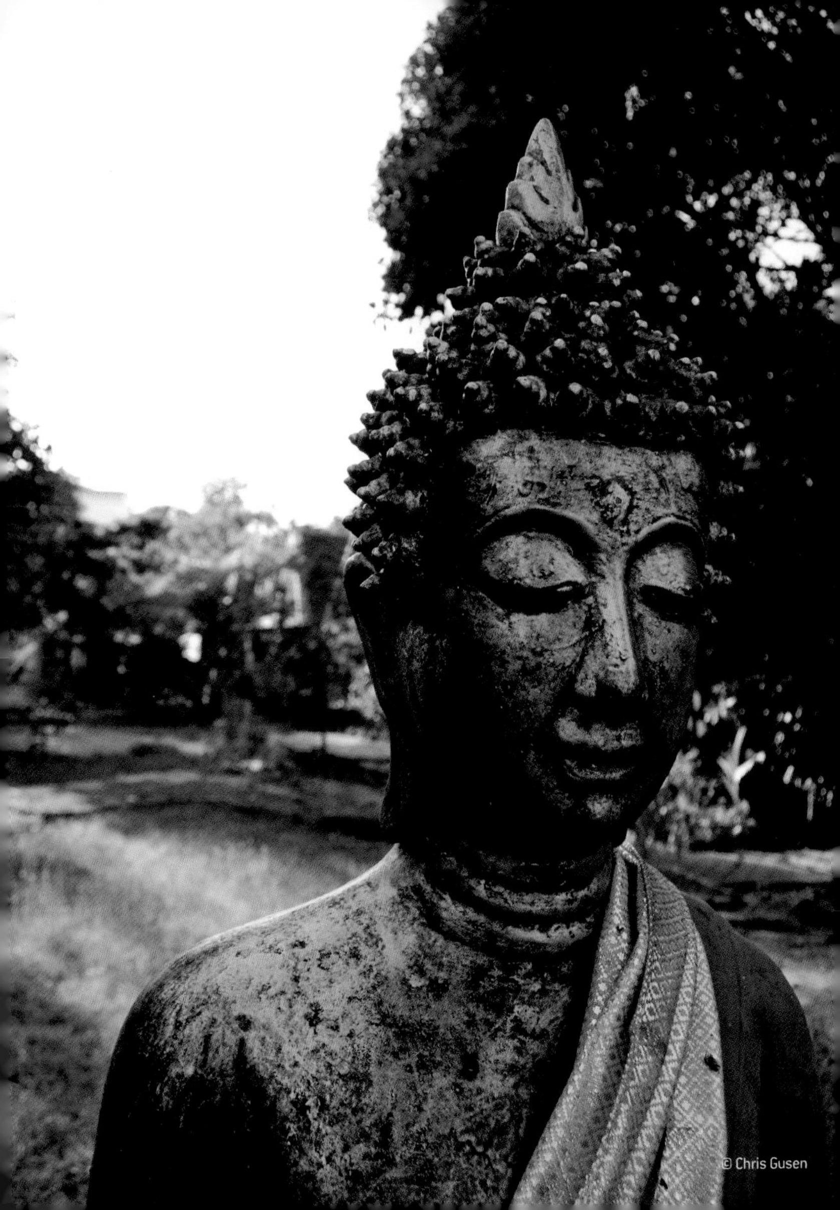

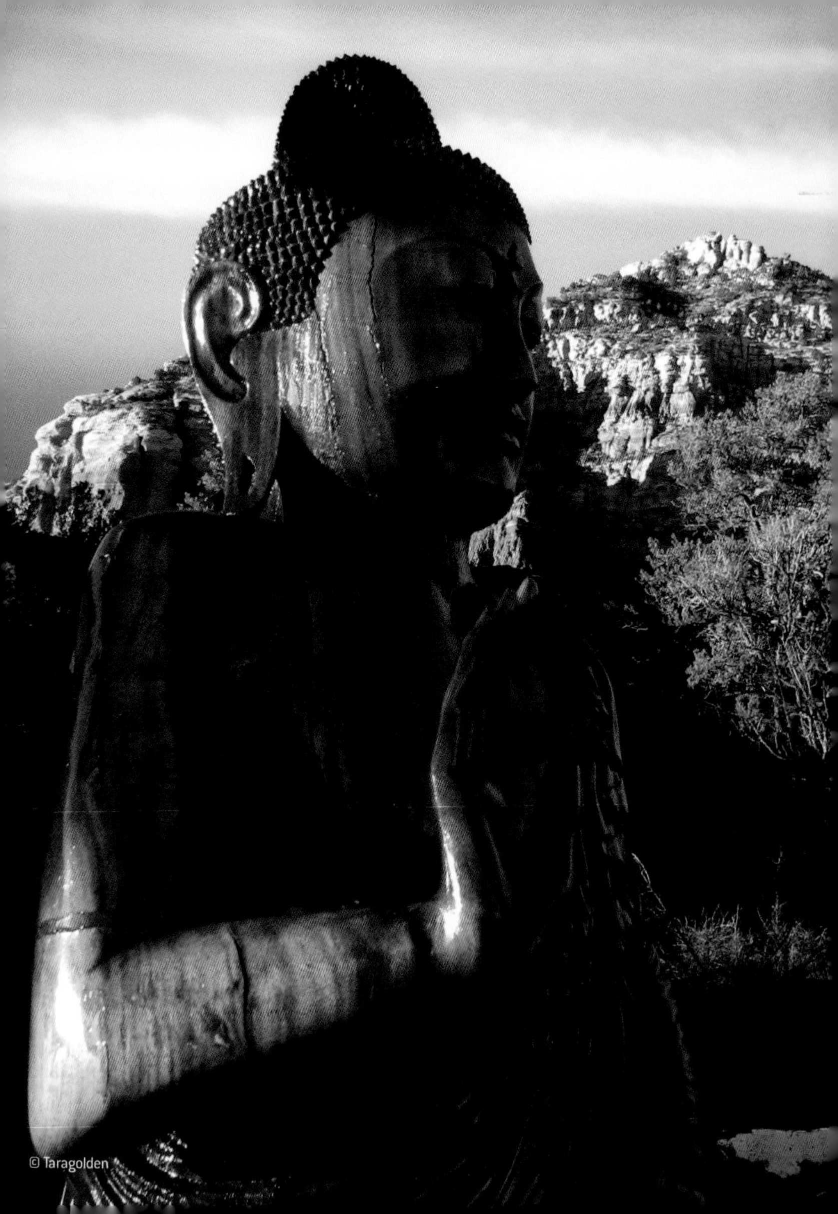

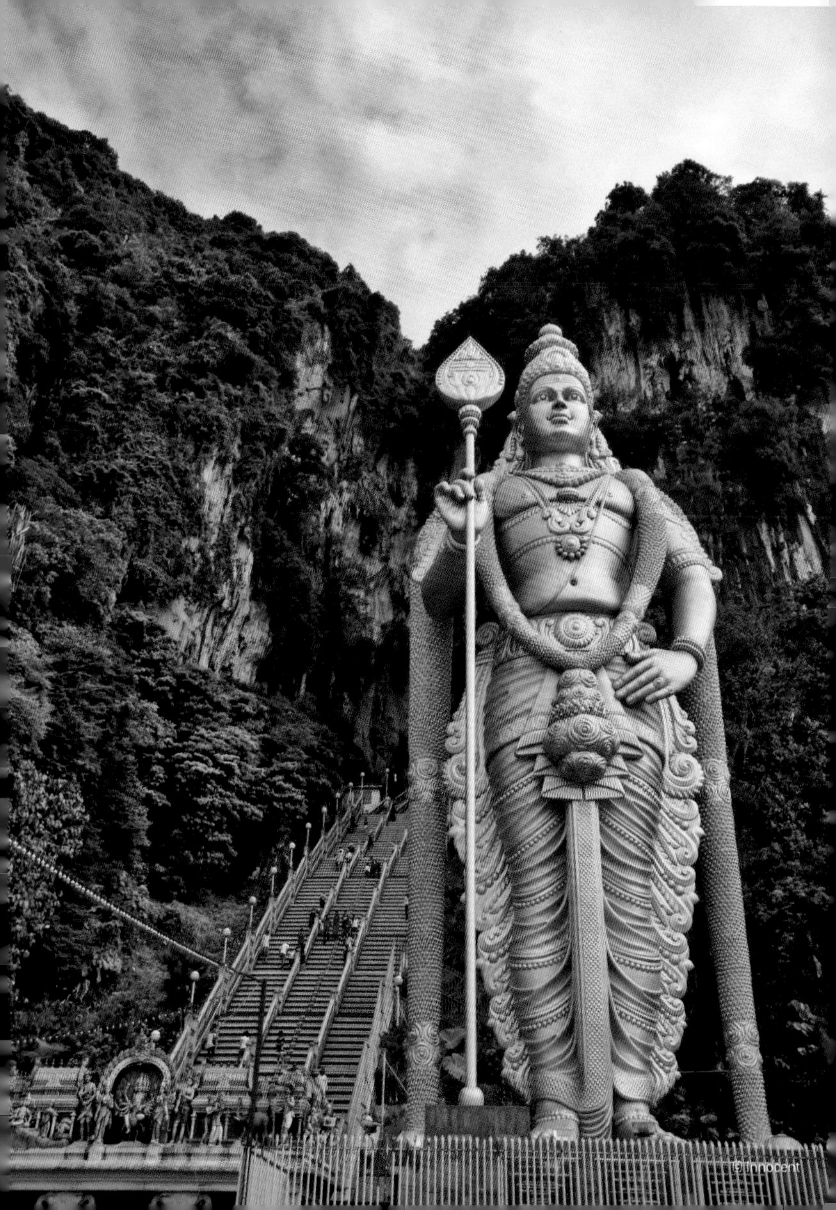

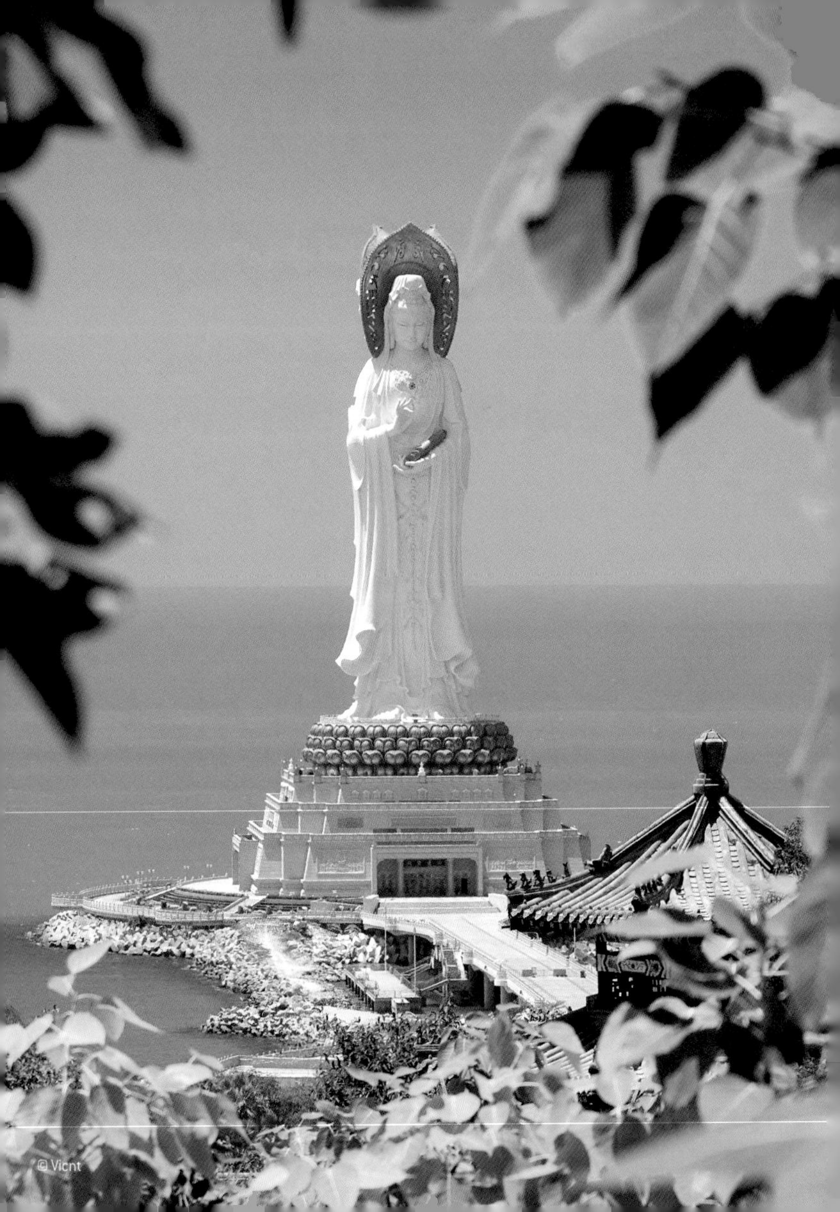

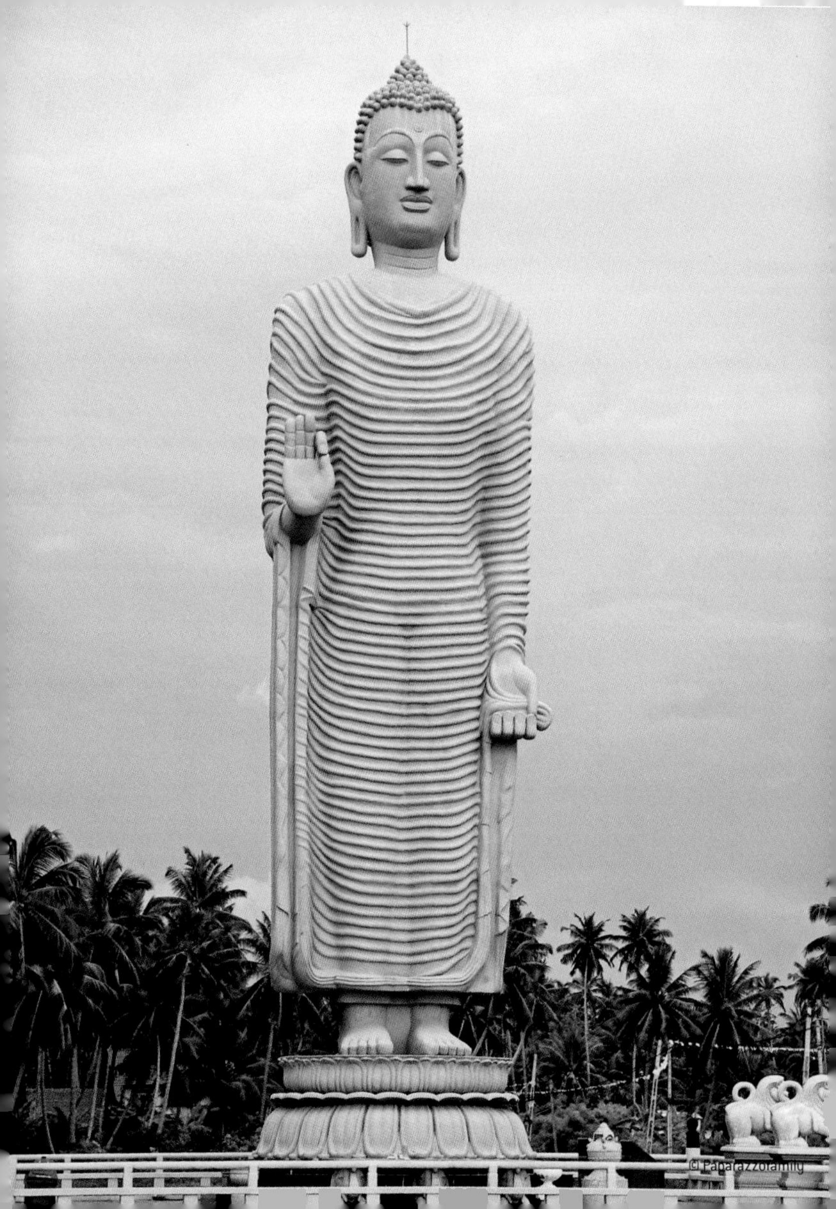

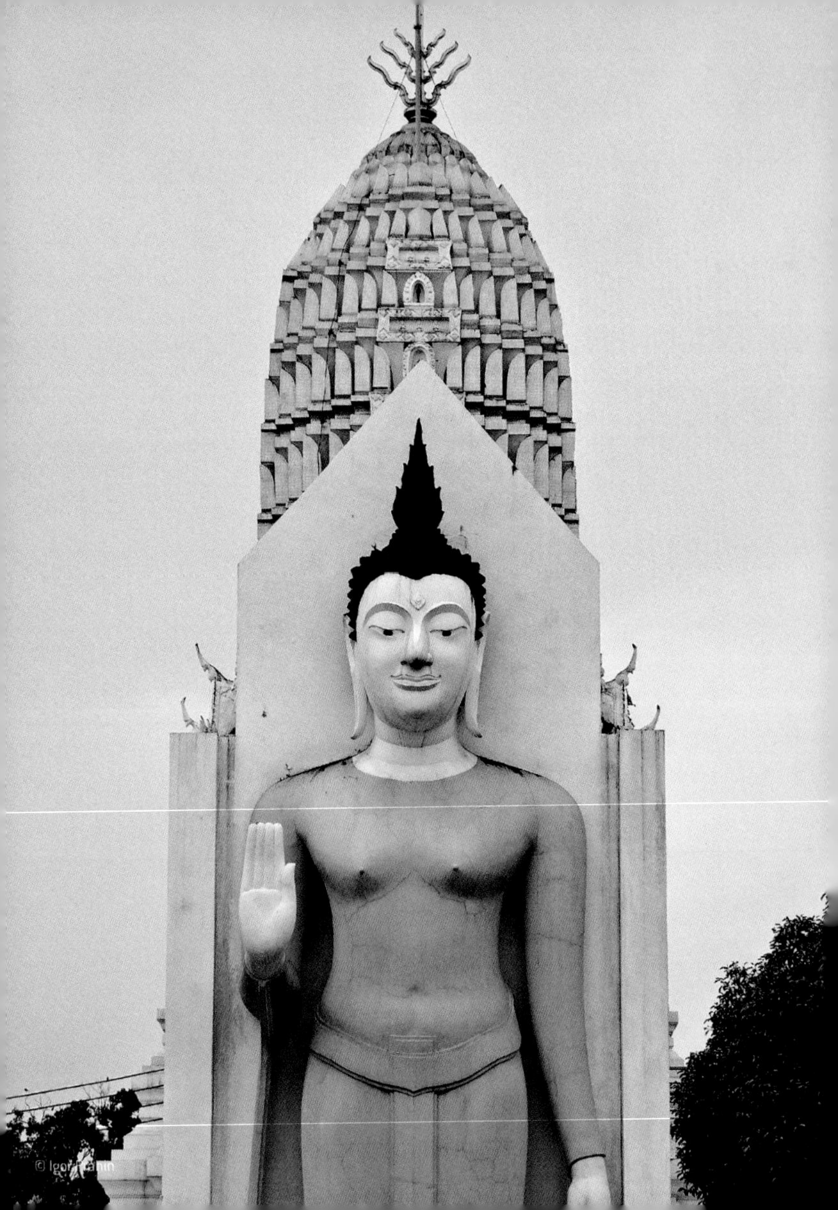

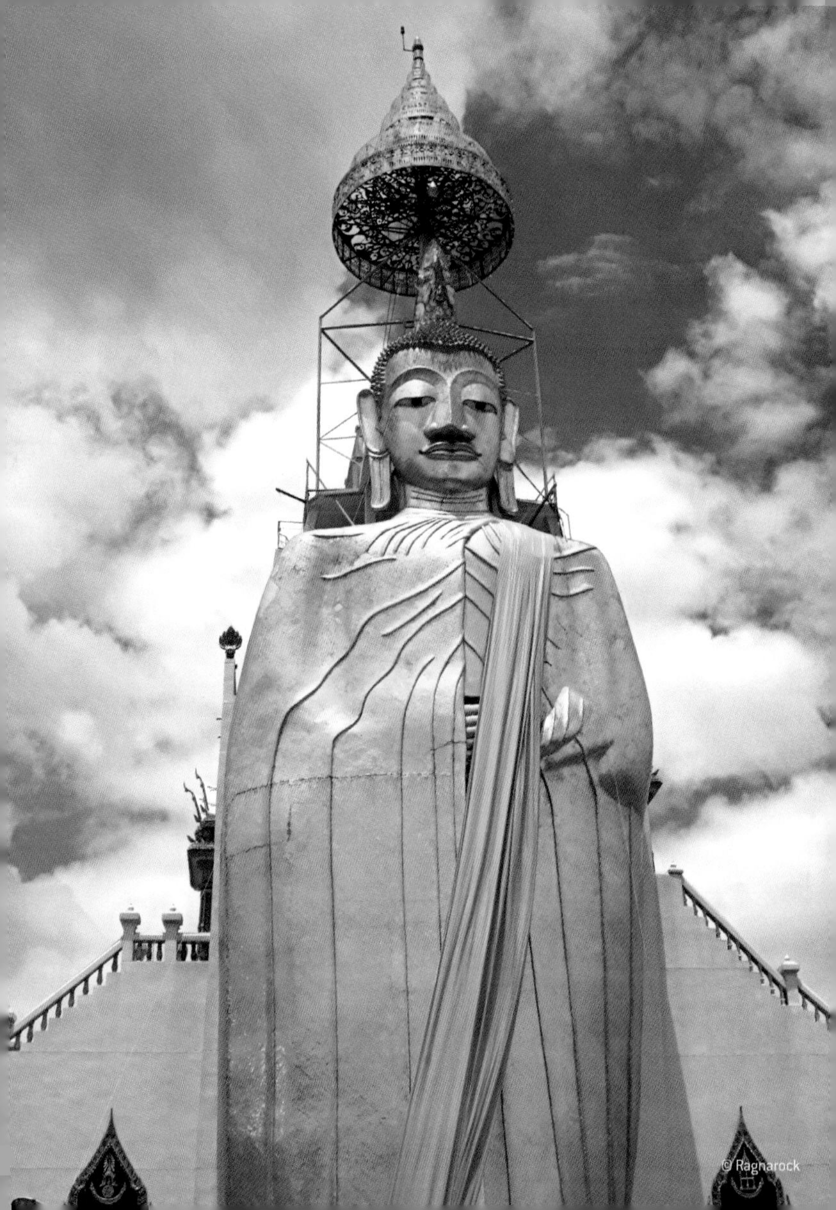

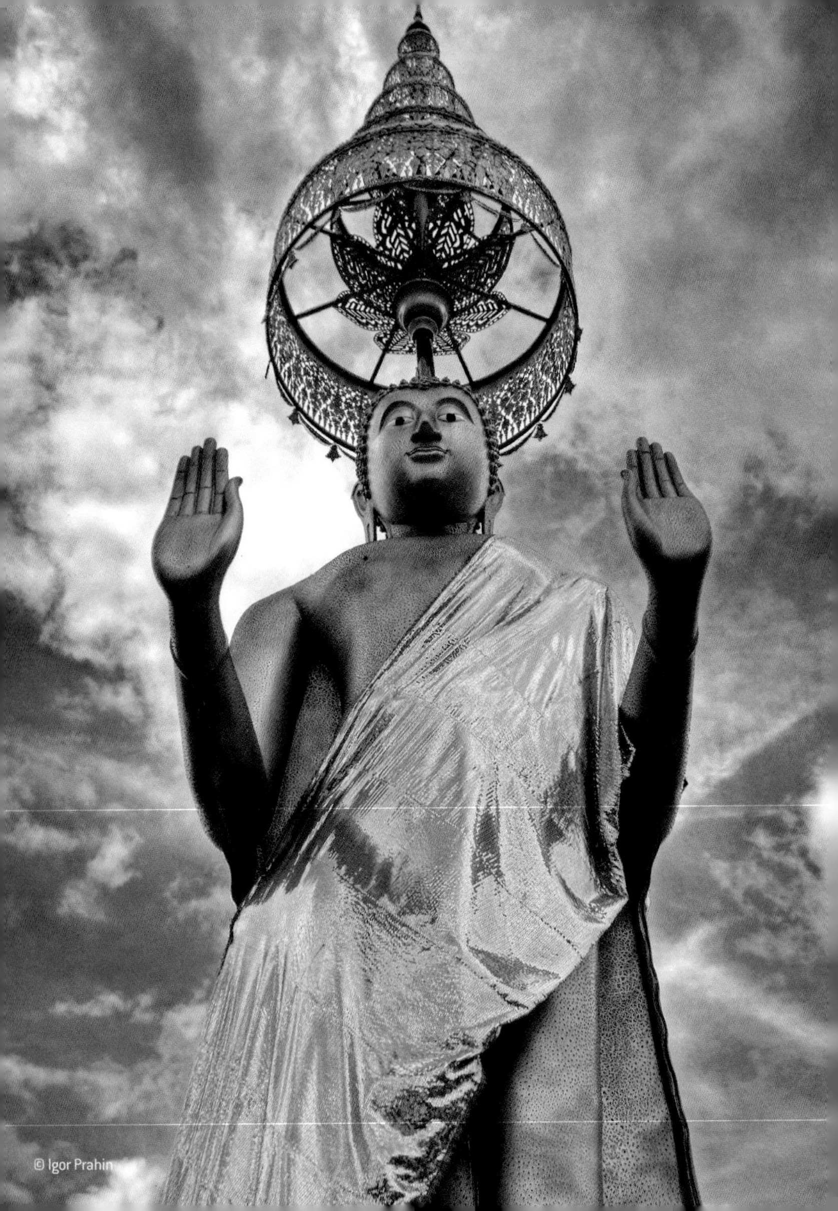

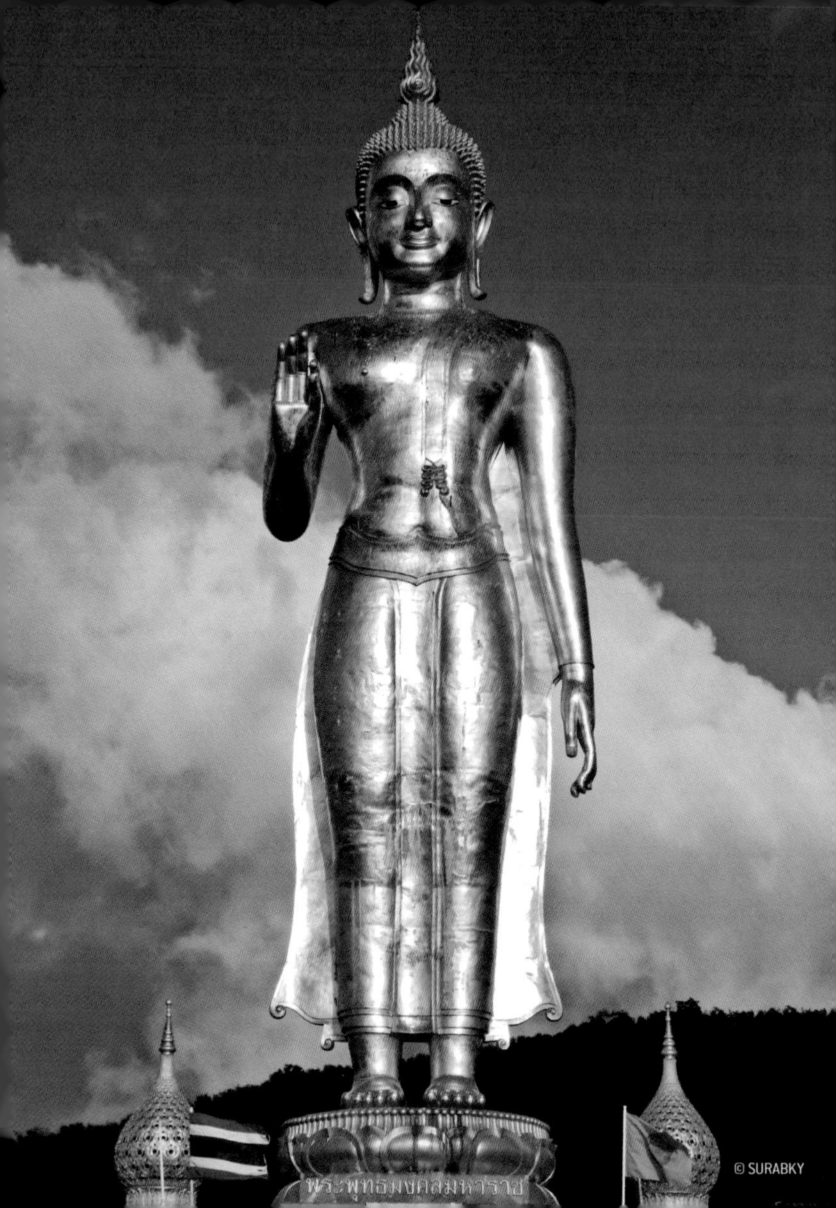
พระพุทธมงคลมหาราช

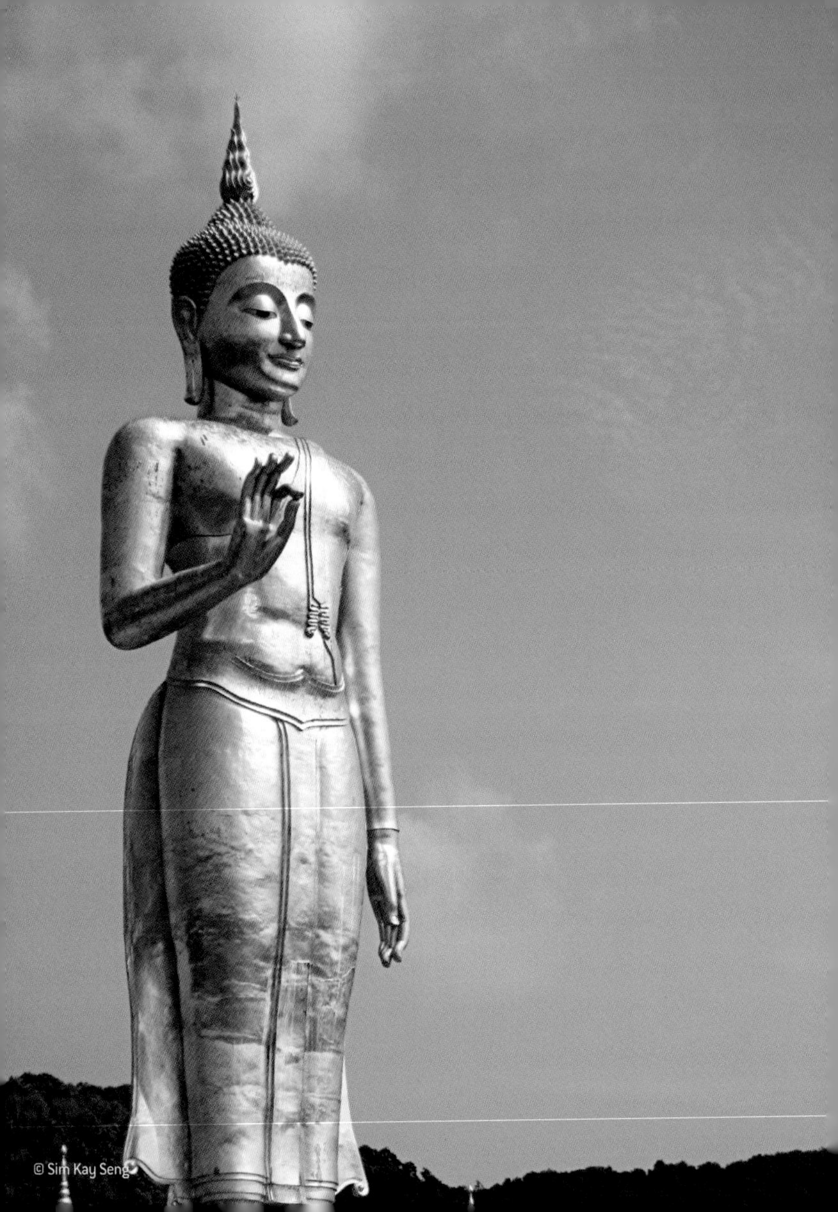

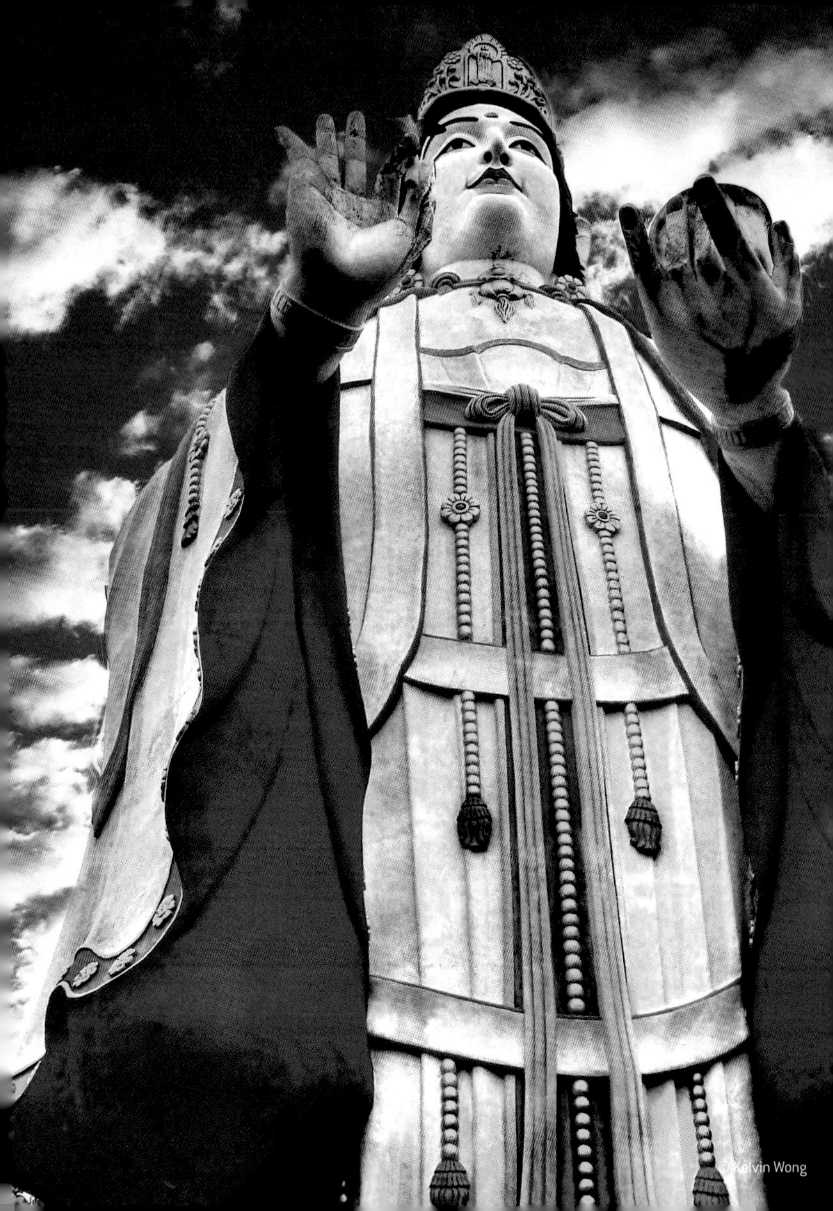

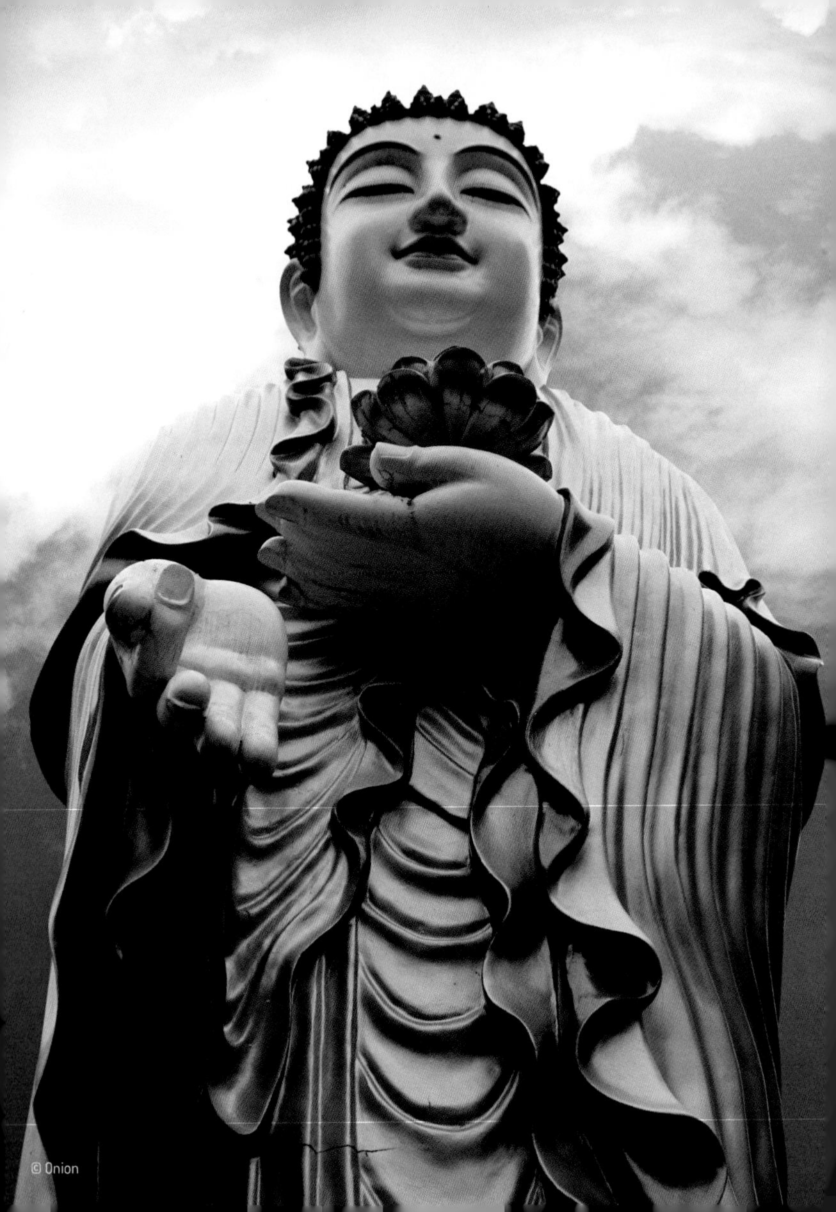

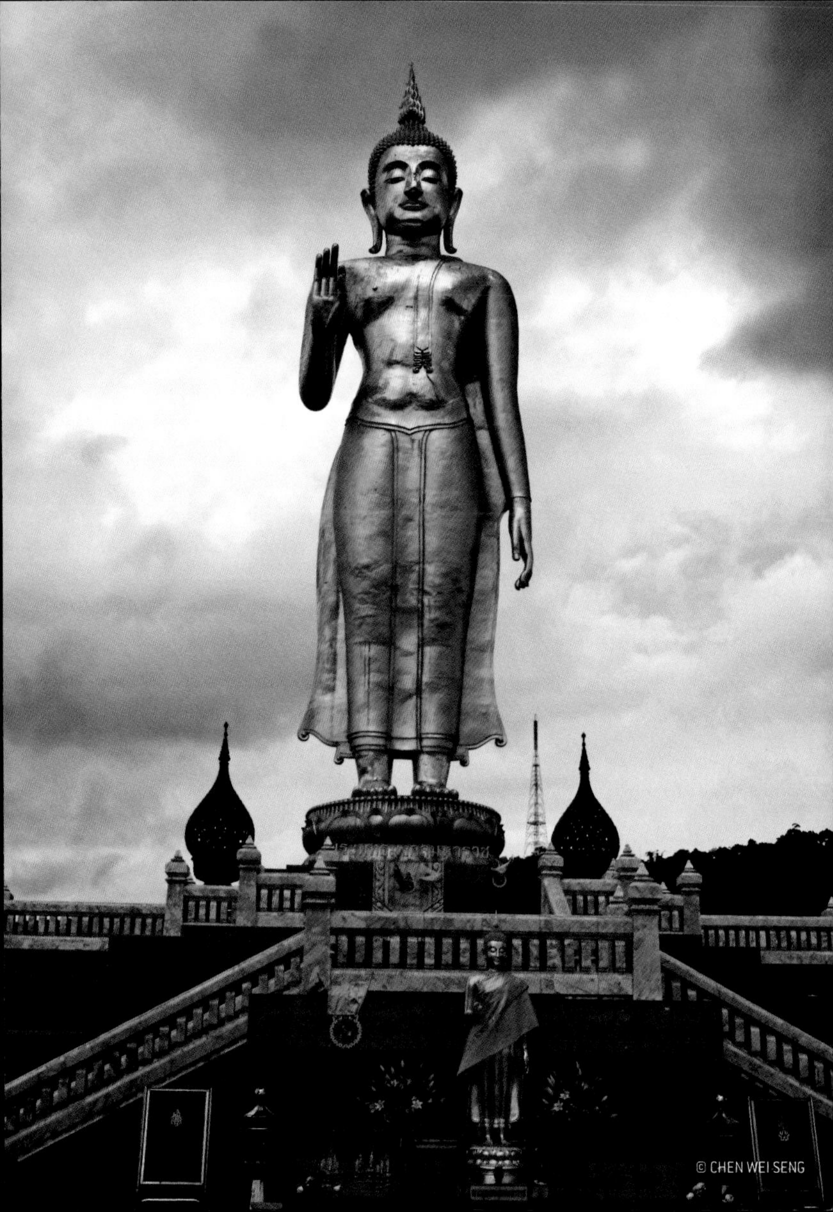

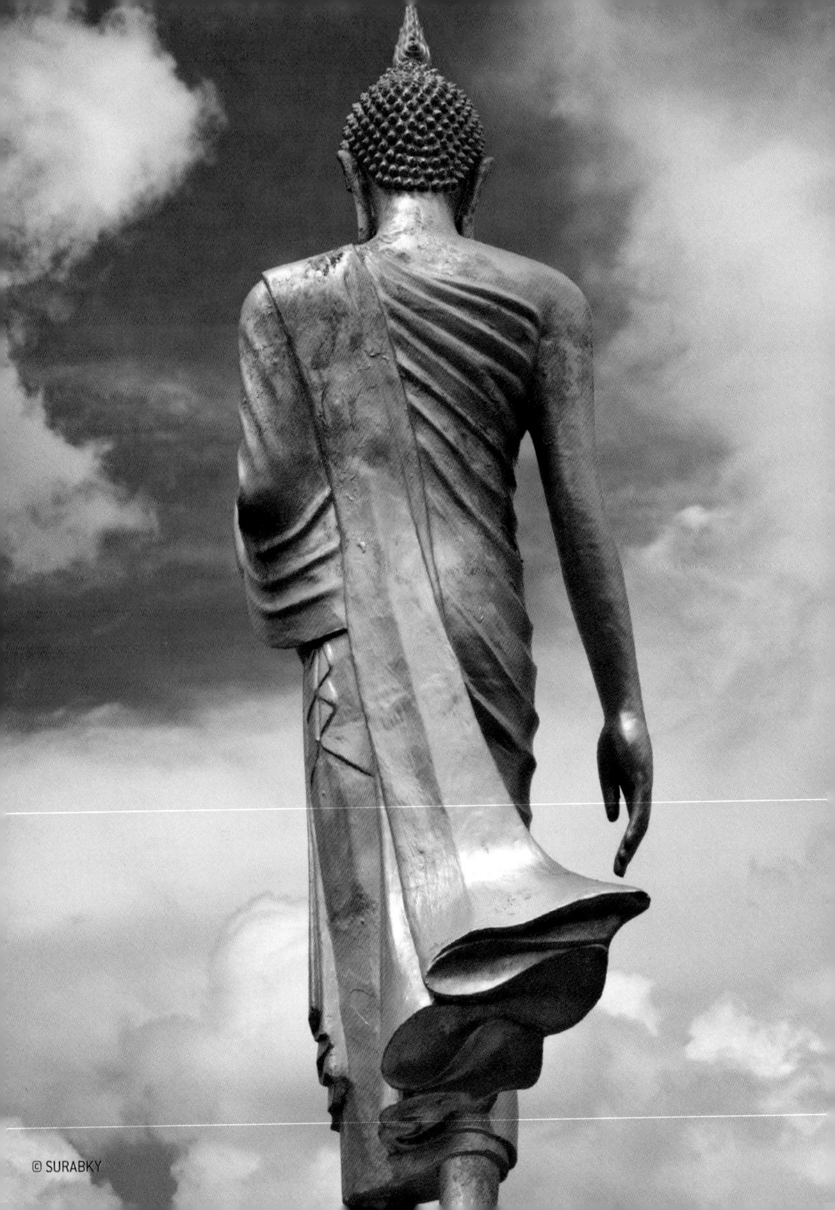

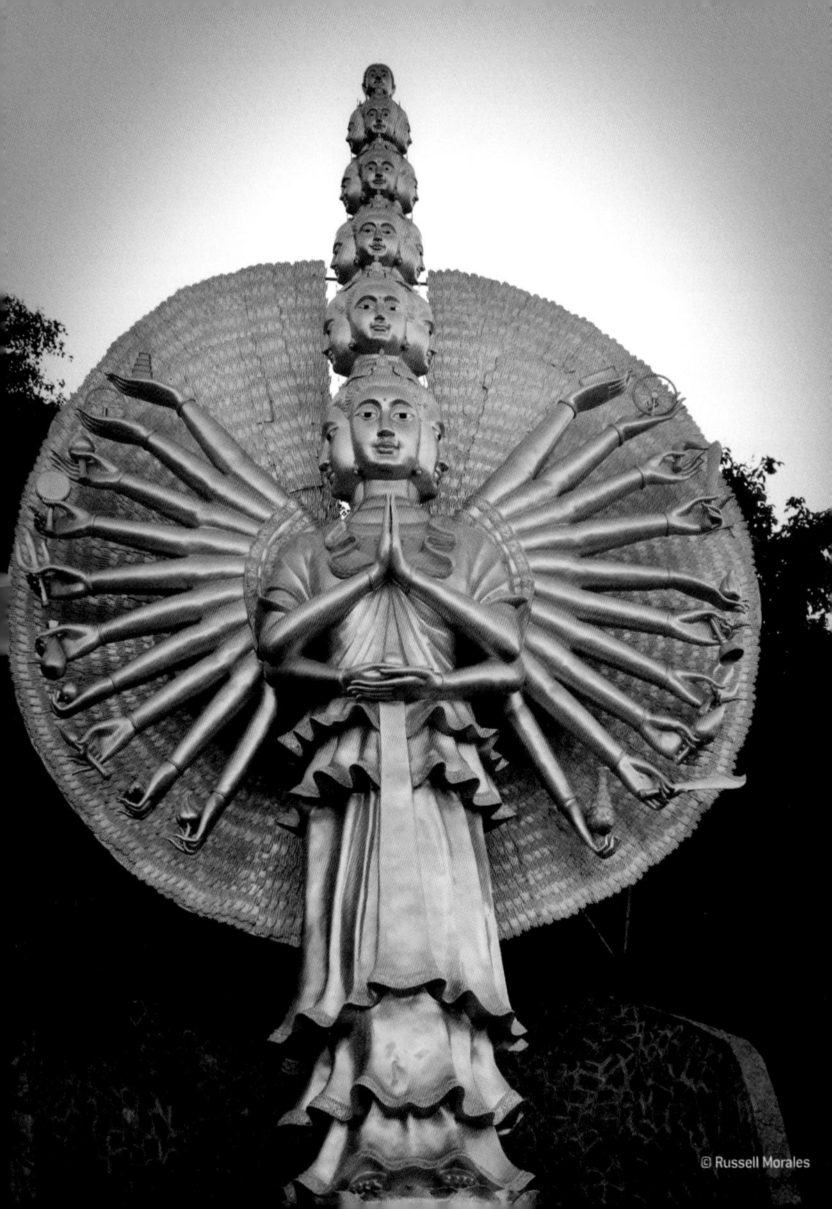
© Russell Morales

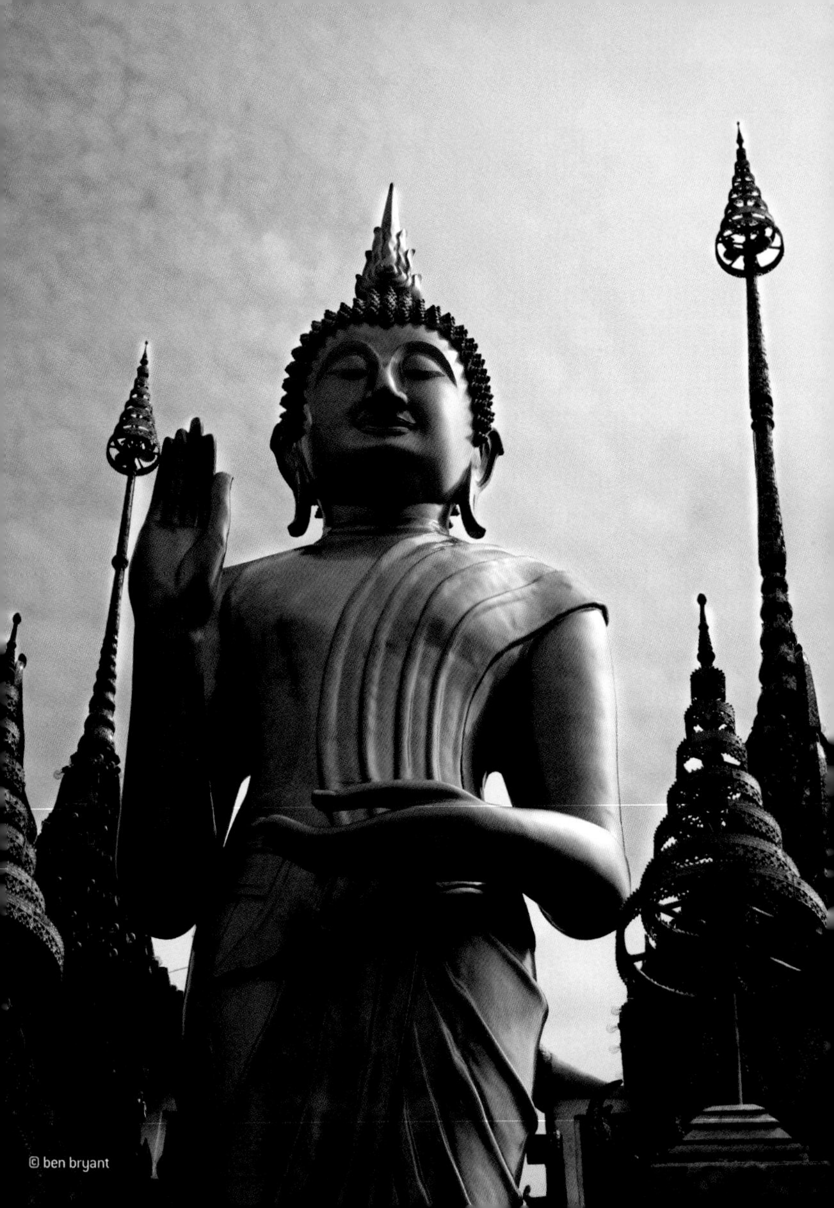

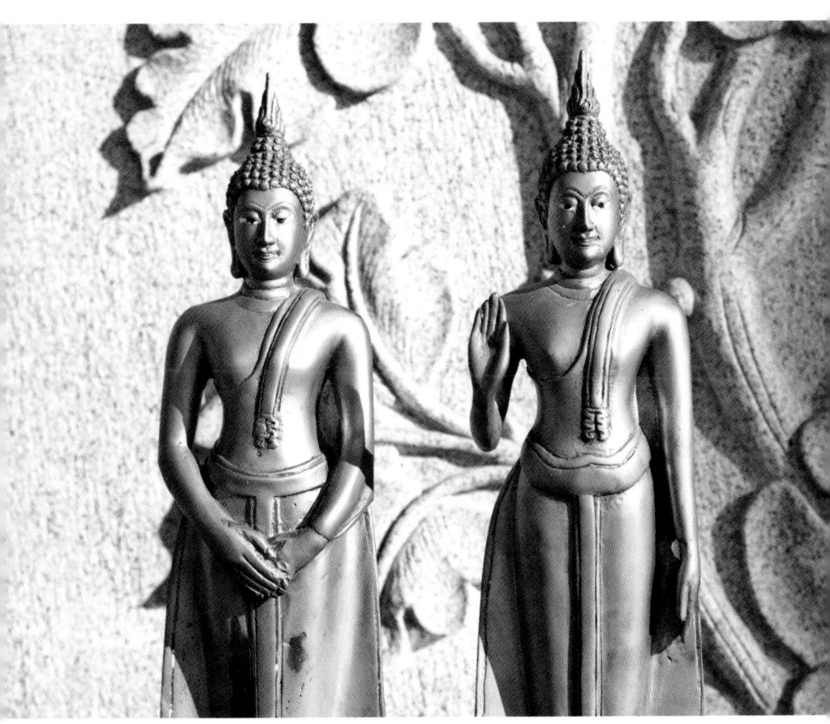

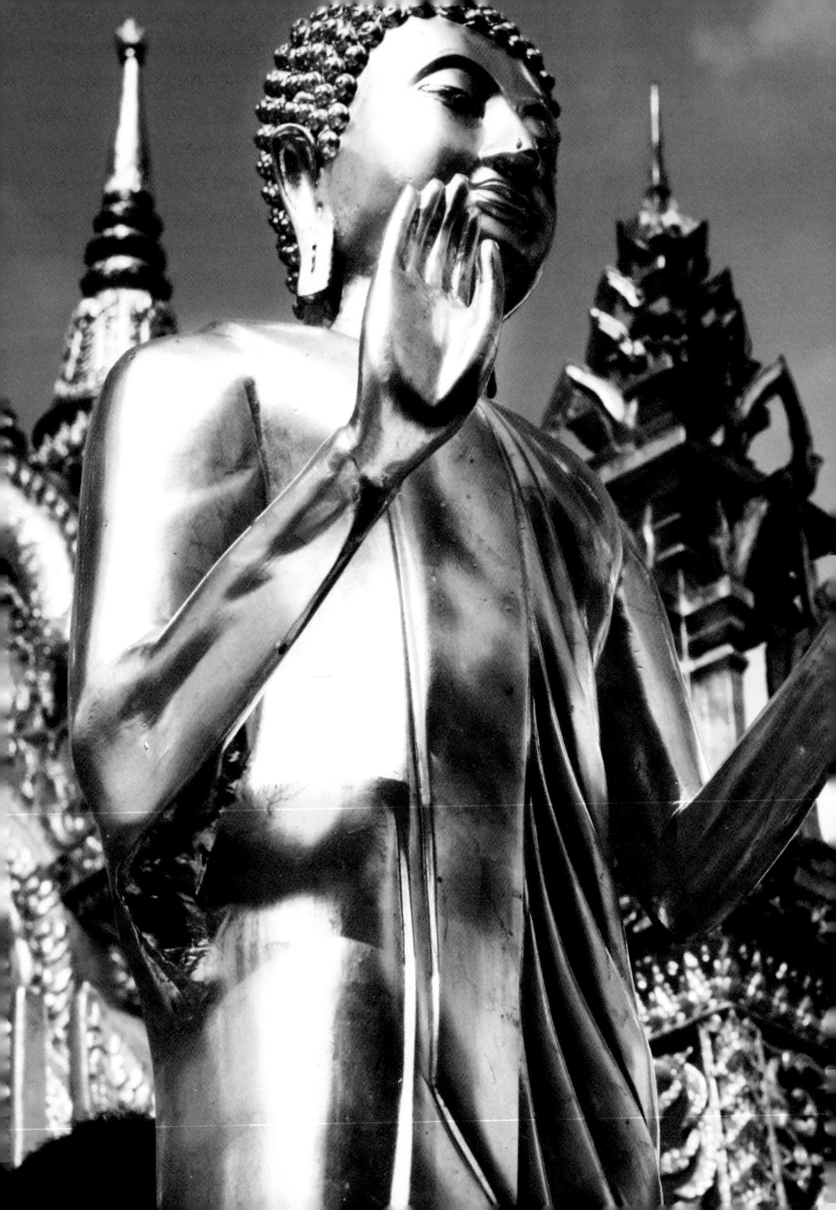

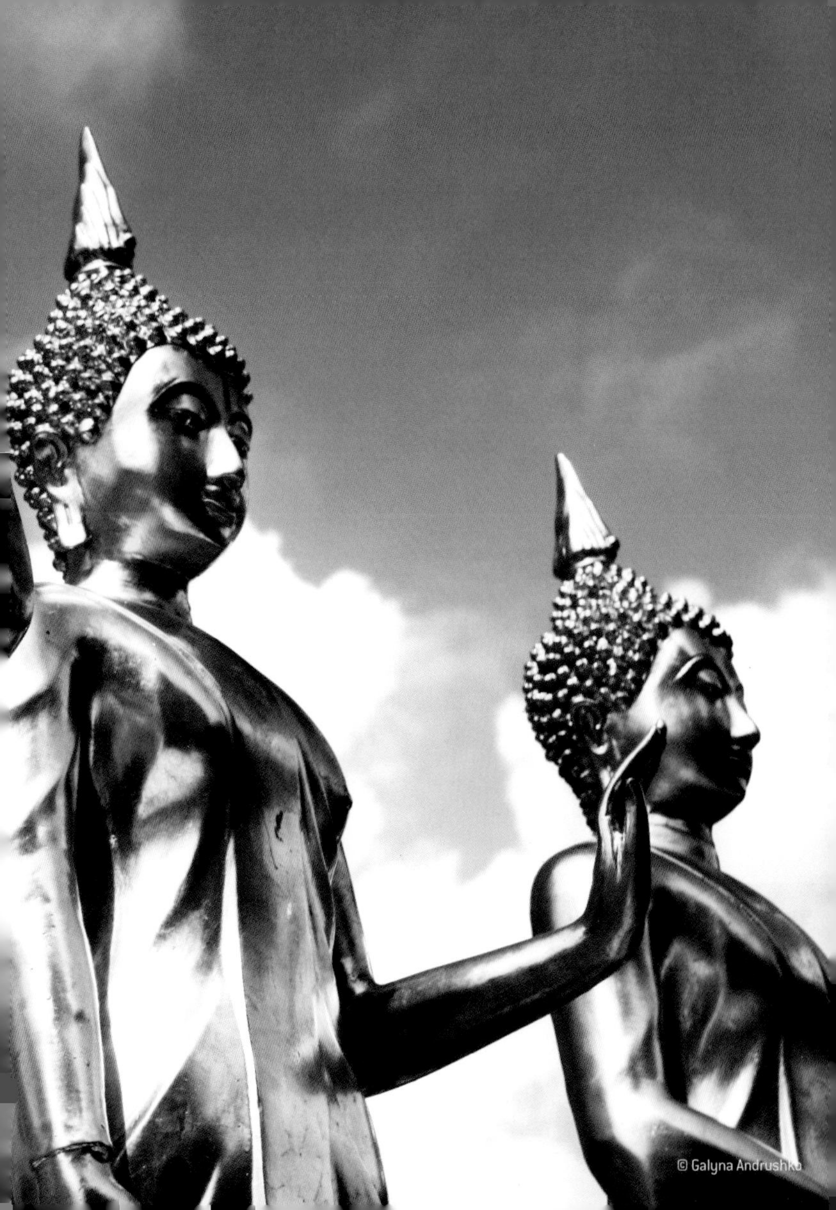

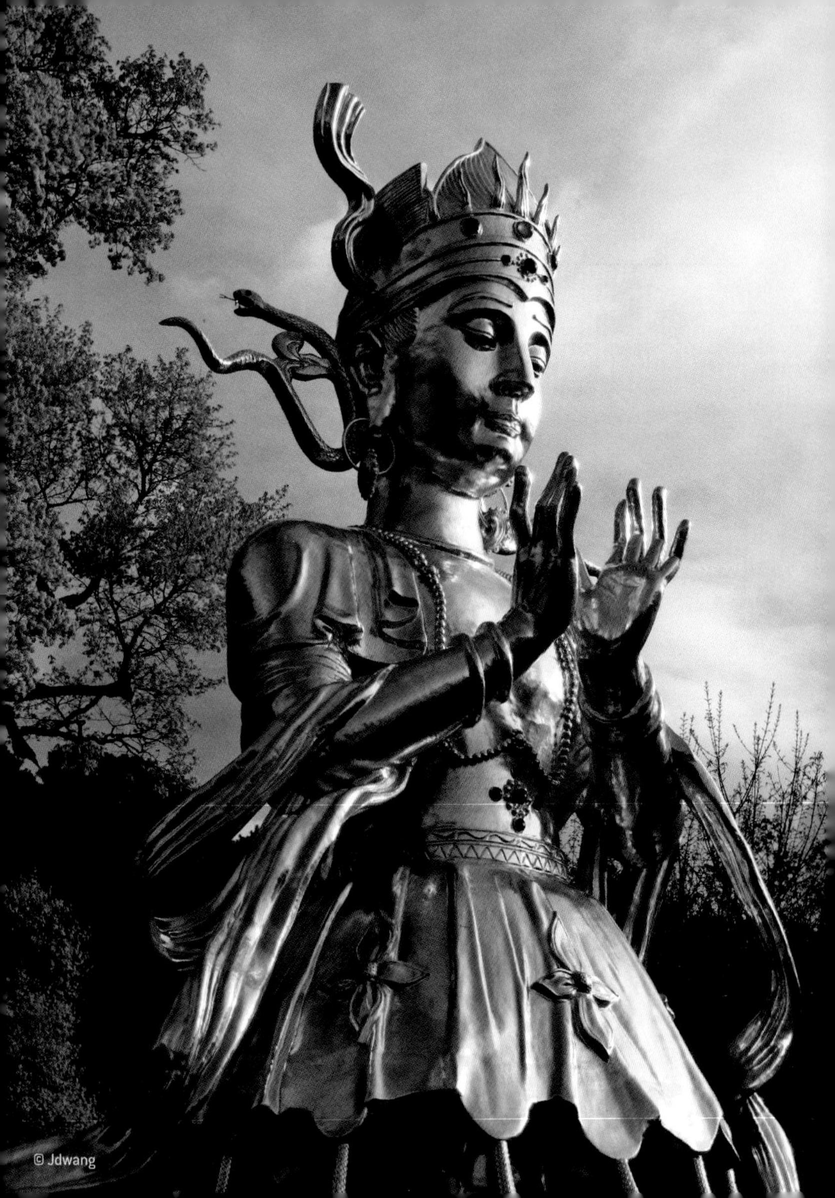

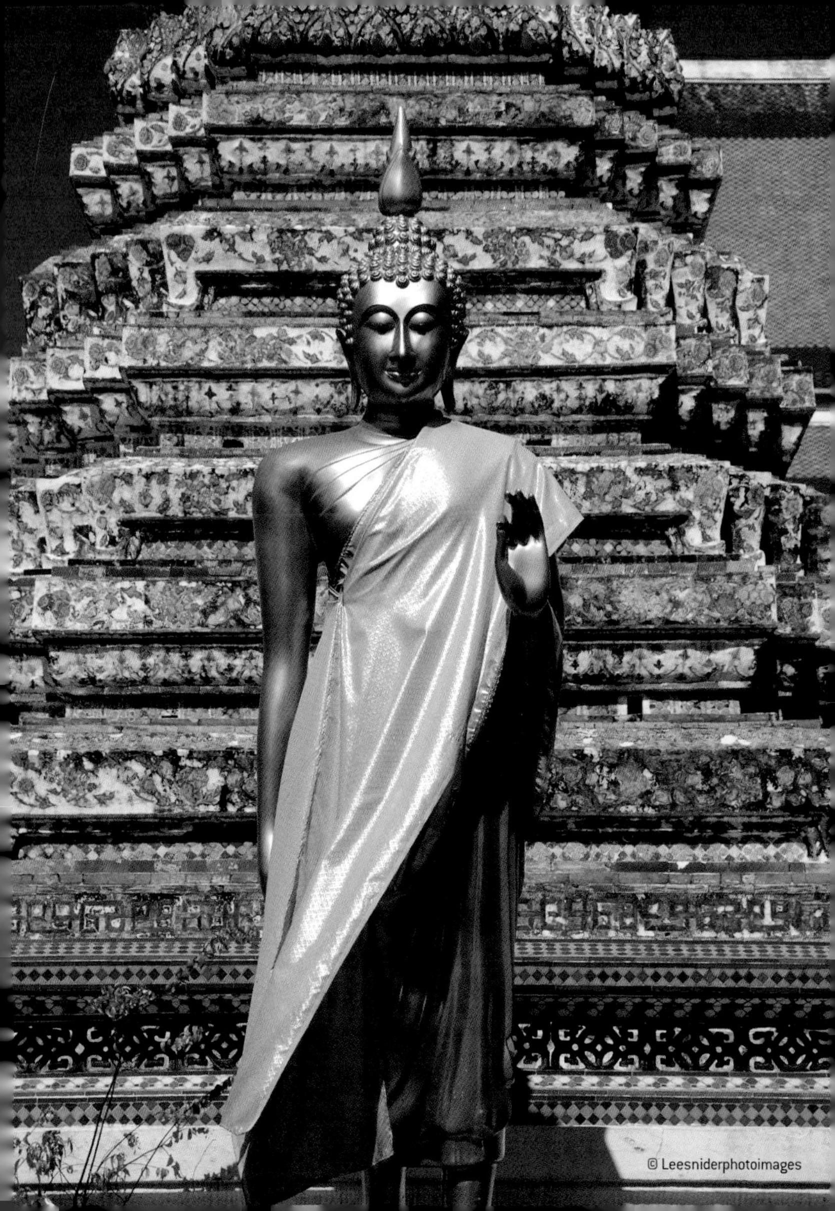

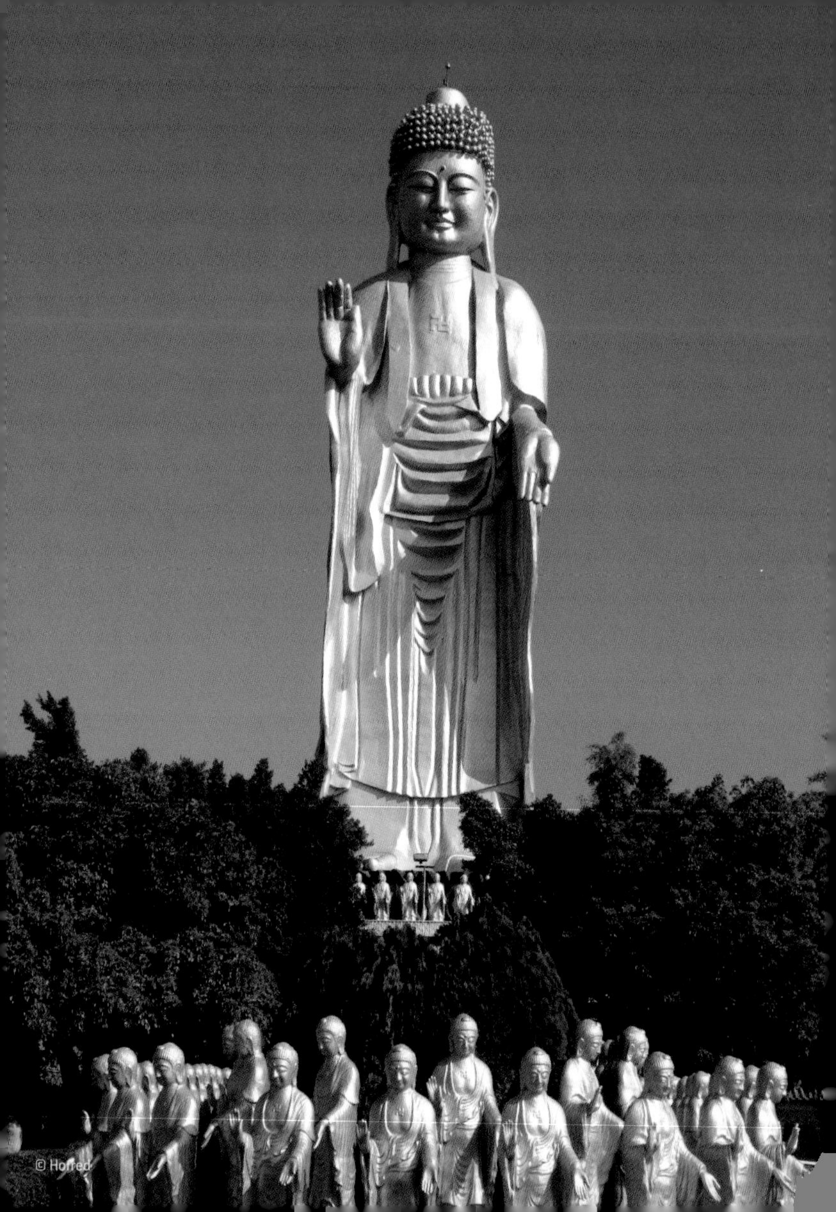

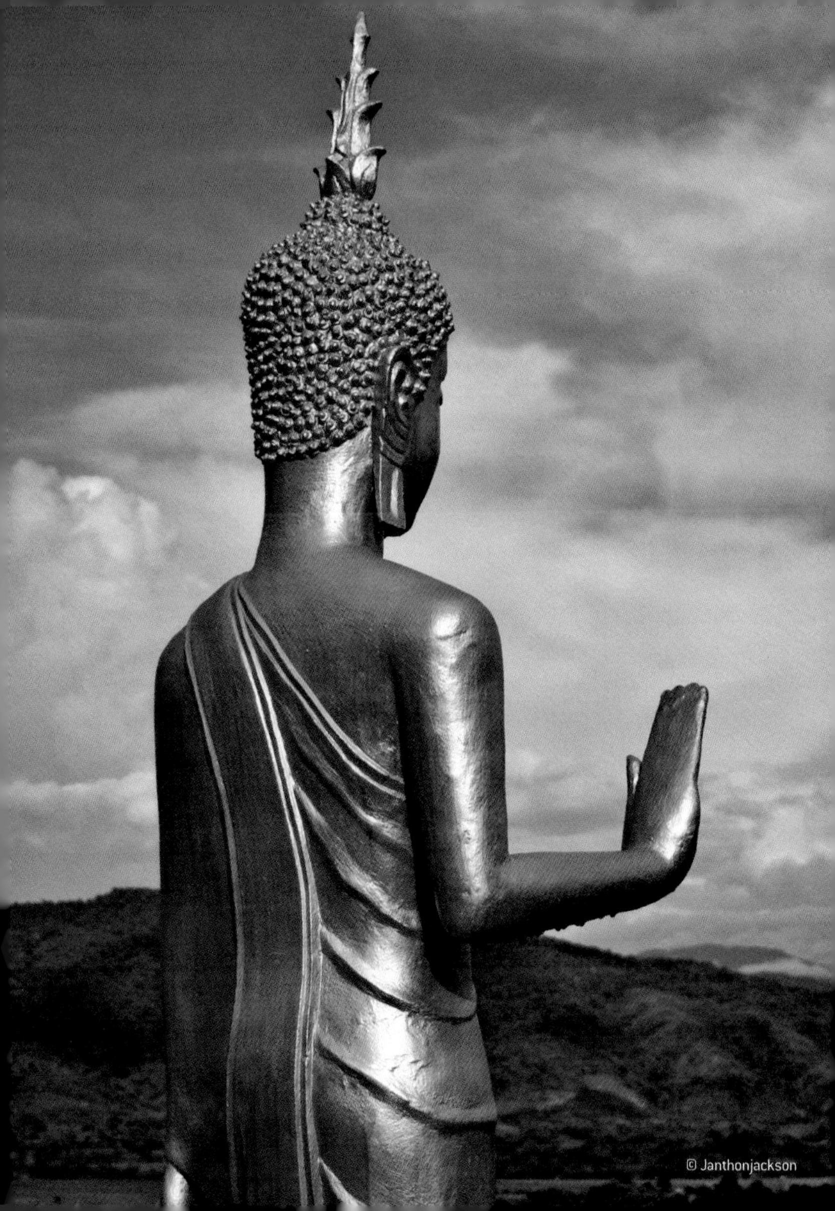

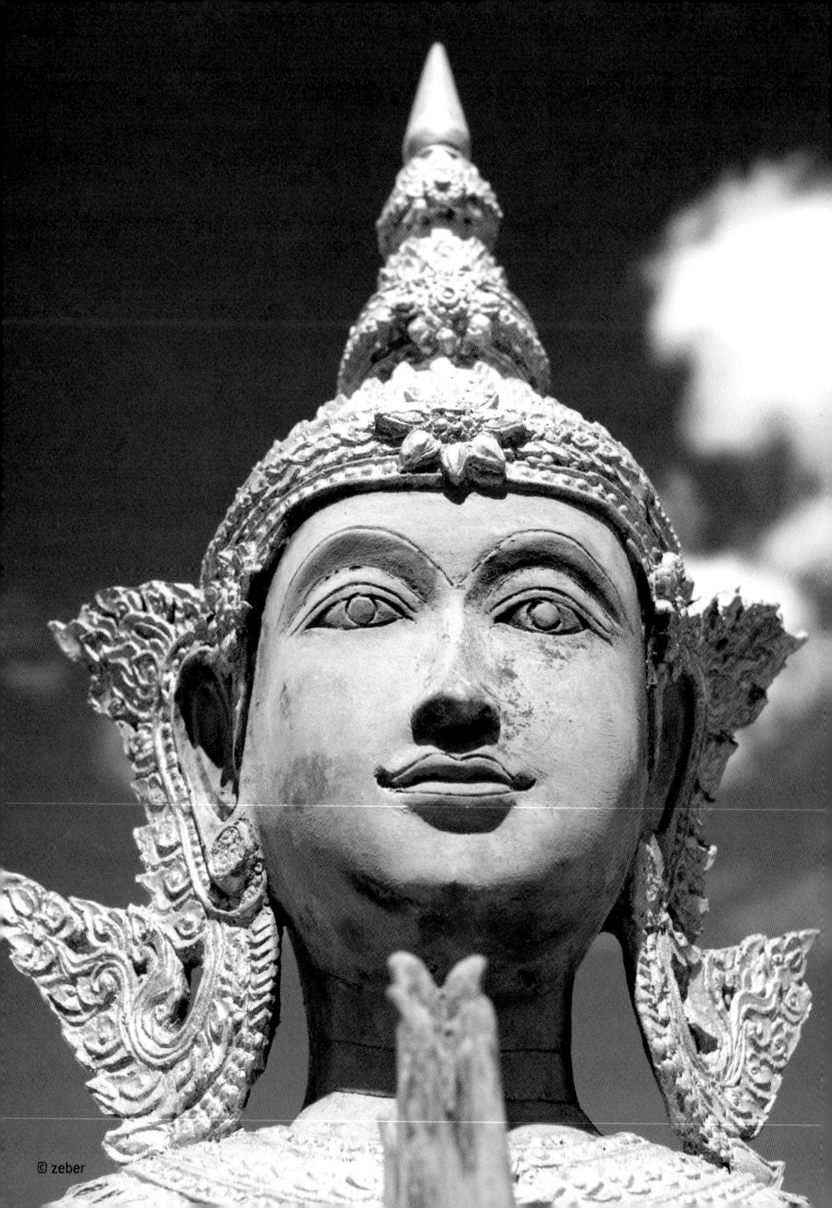

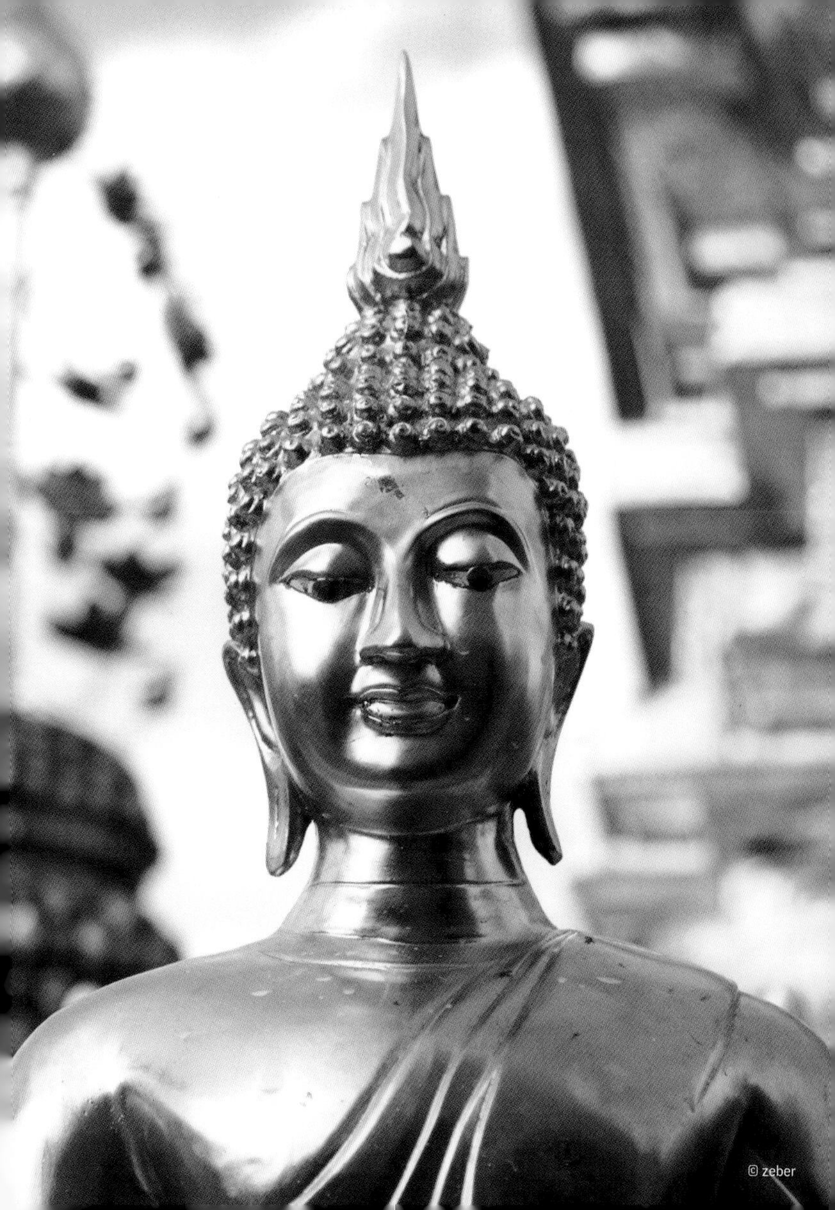

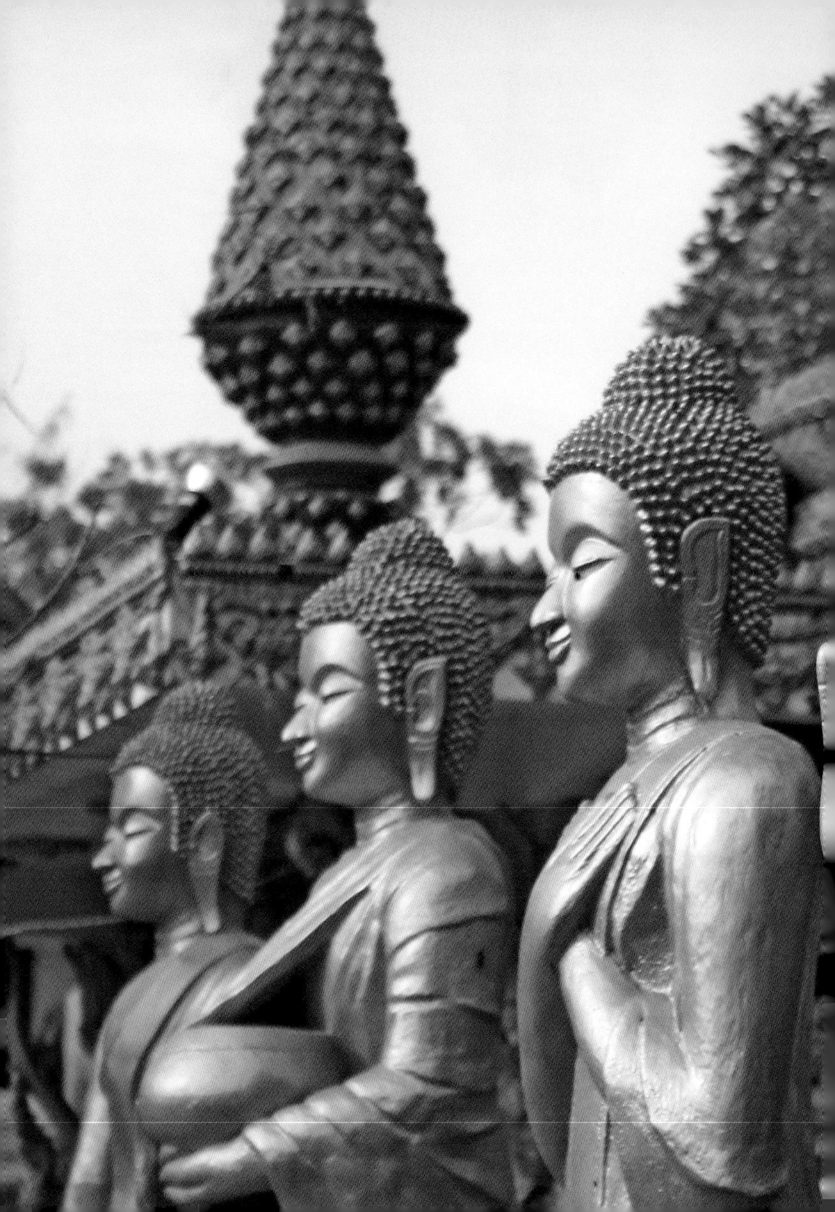

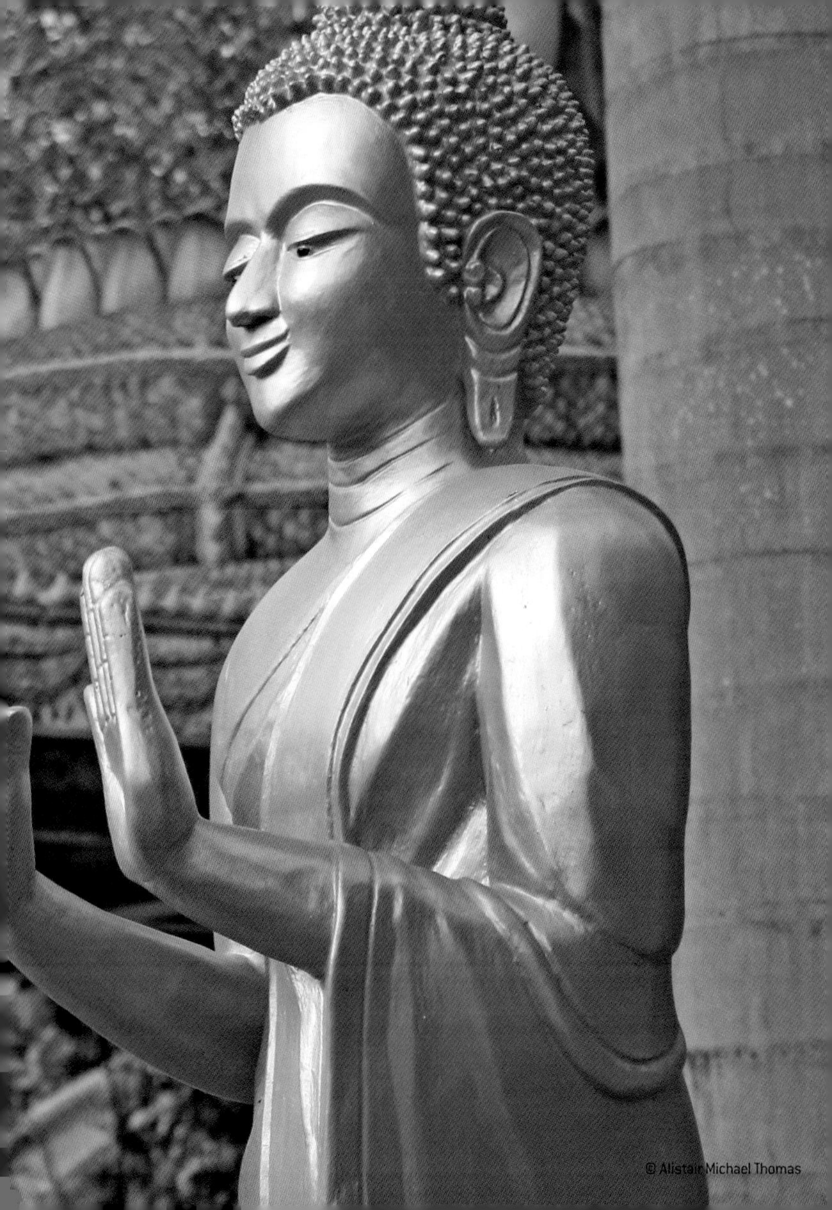

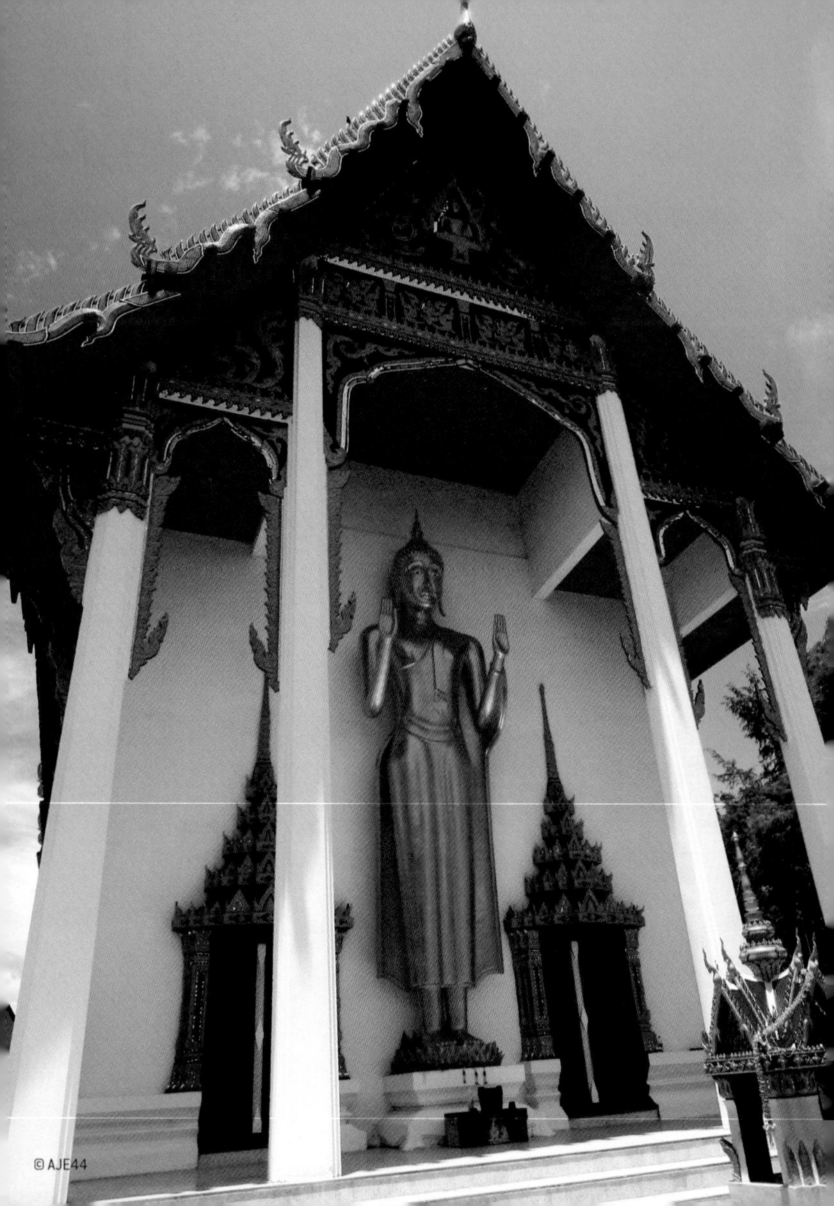

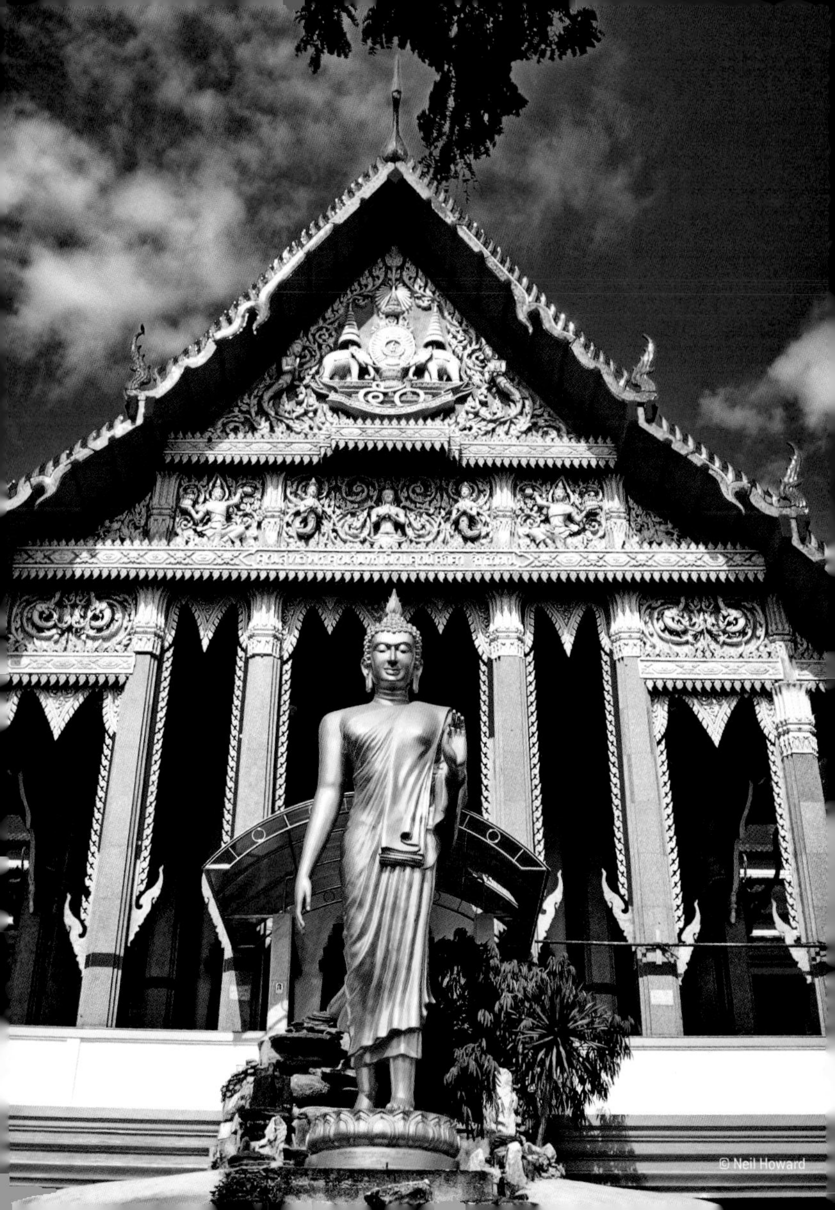

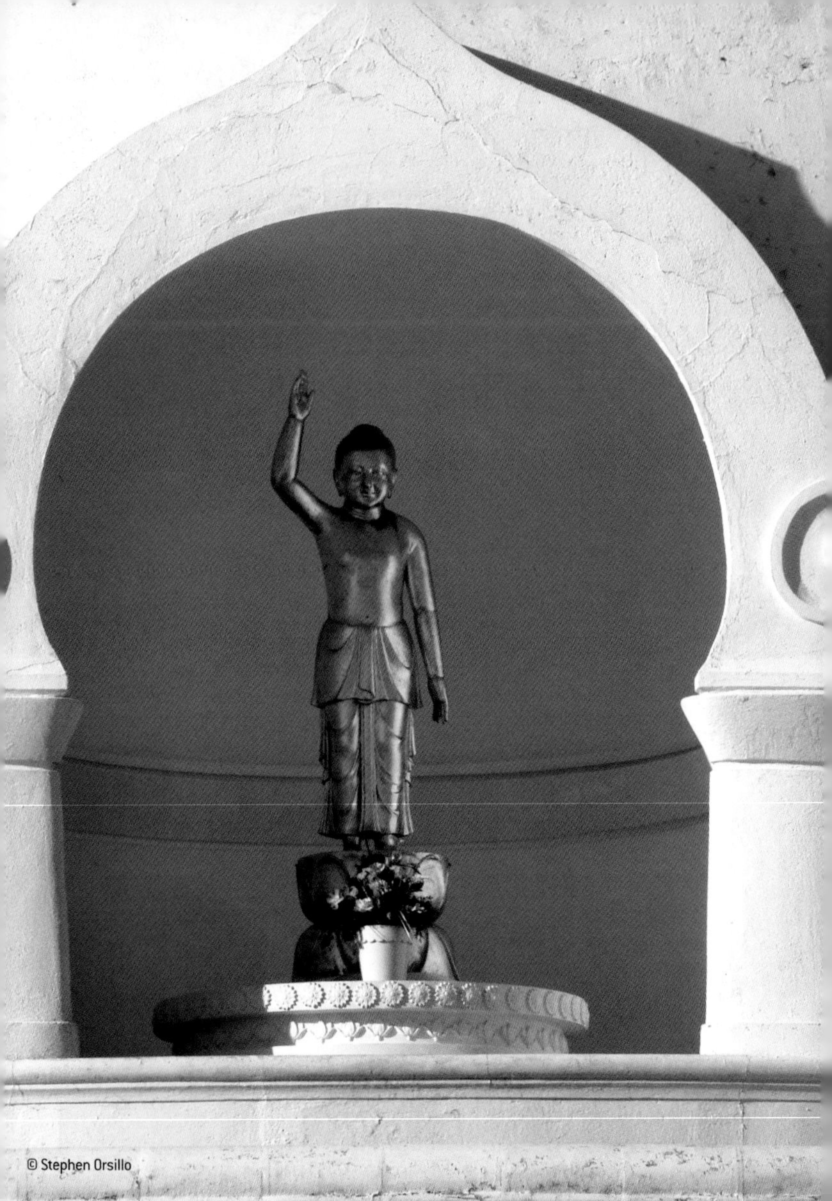

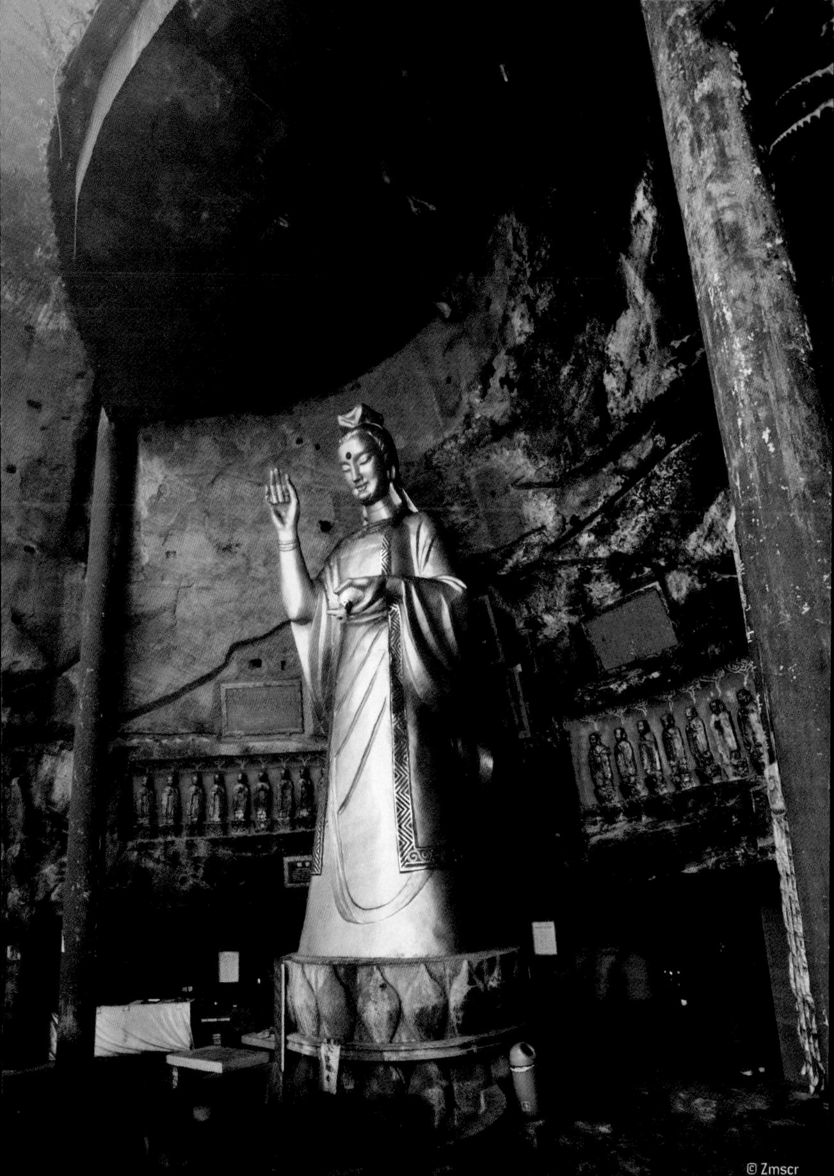

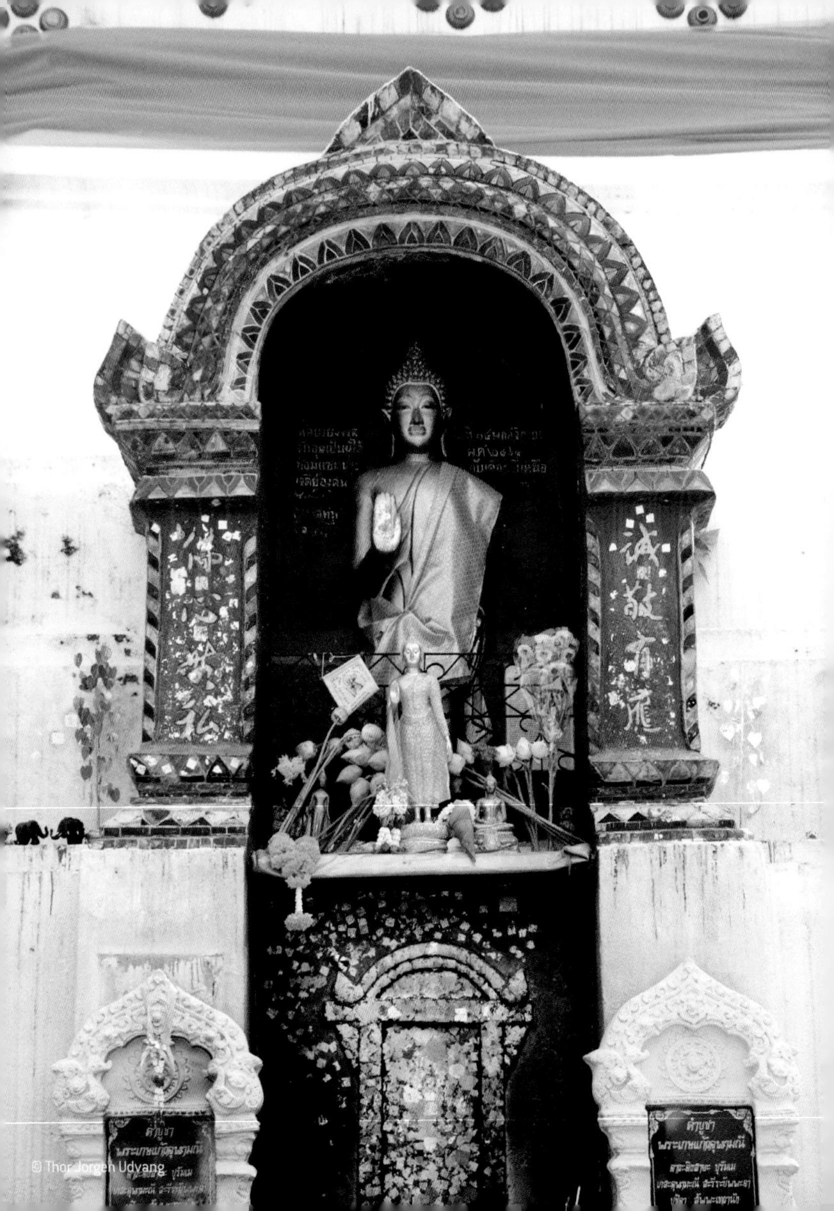

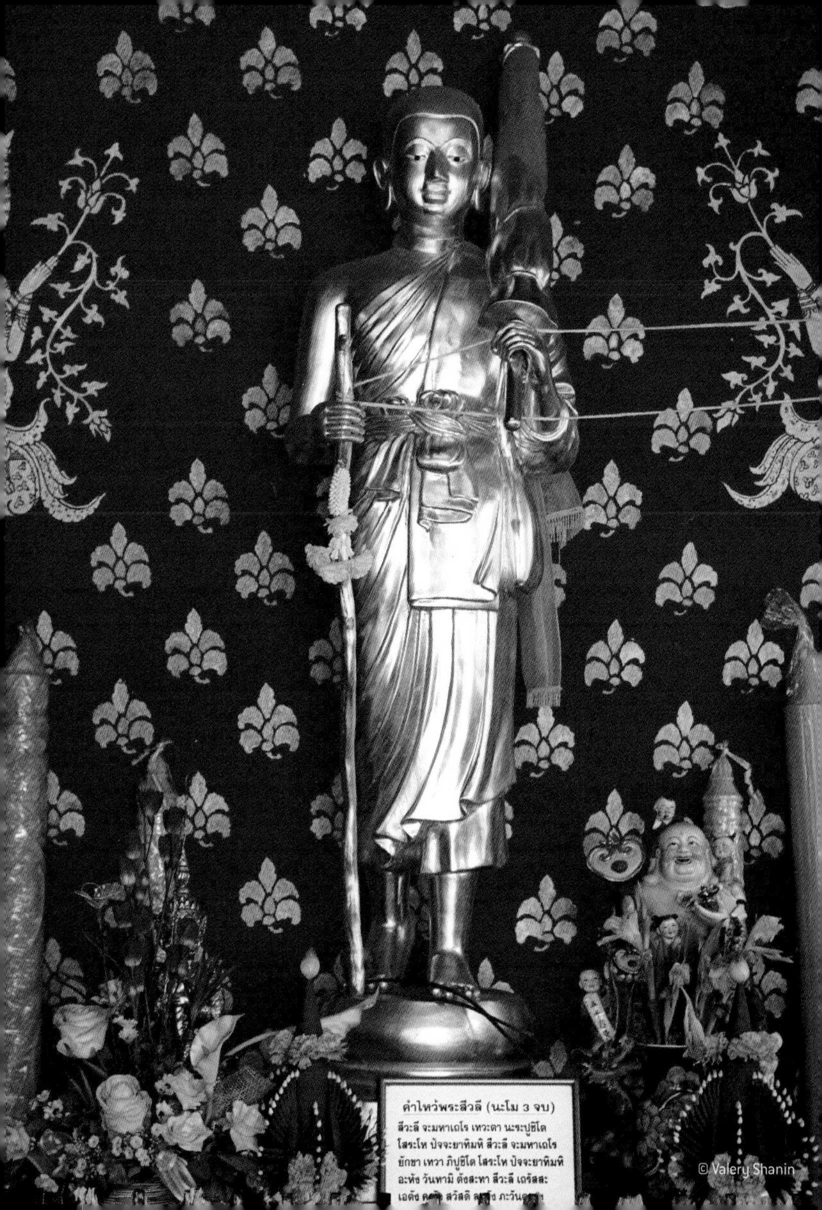
คำไหว้พระสีวลี (นะโม 3 จบ)
สีวะลี จะมหาเถโร เทวะตา นะระปูชิโต
โสระโห ปัจจะยาทิมหิ สีวะลี จะมหาเถโร
ยักขา เทวา ภิปูชิโต โสระโห ปัจจะยาทิมหิ
อะหัง วันทามิ ตังสะหา สีวะลี เถรัสสะ
เอตัง สวัสดิ

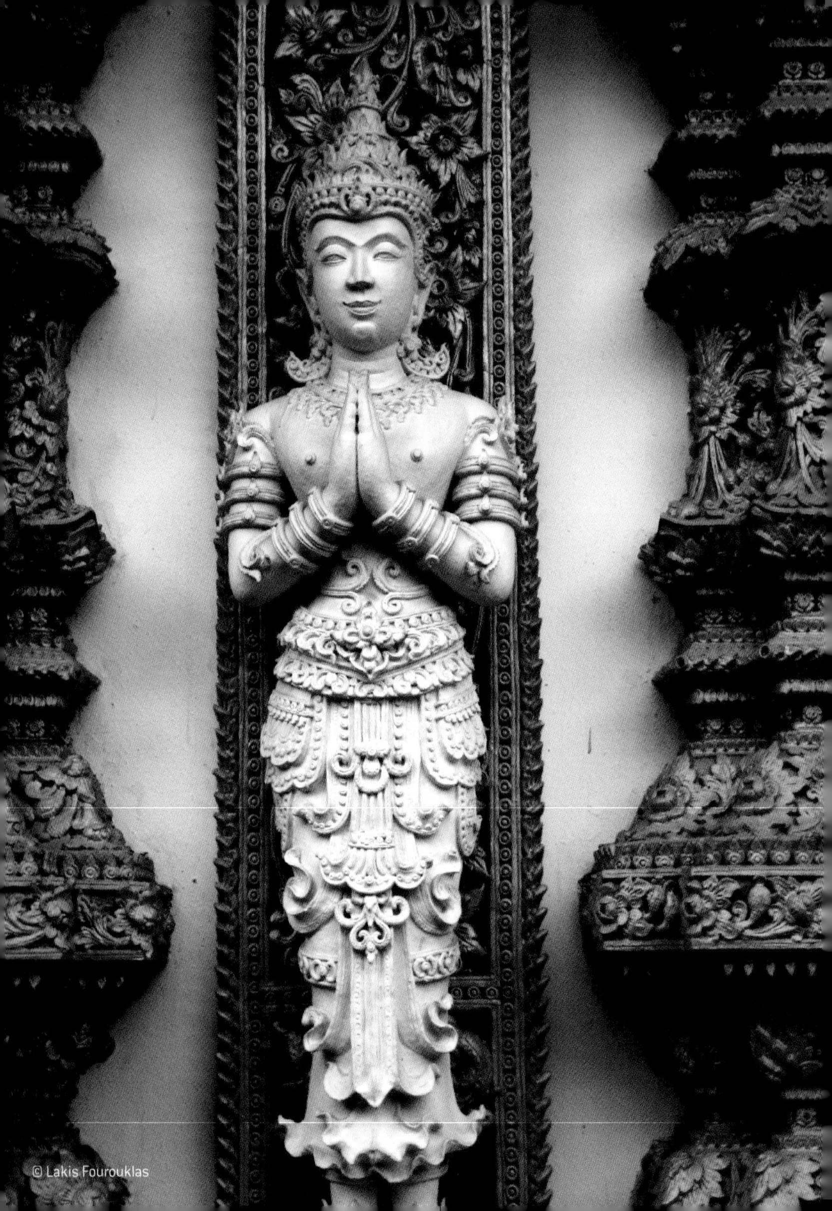

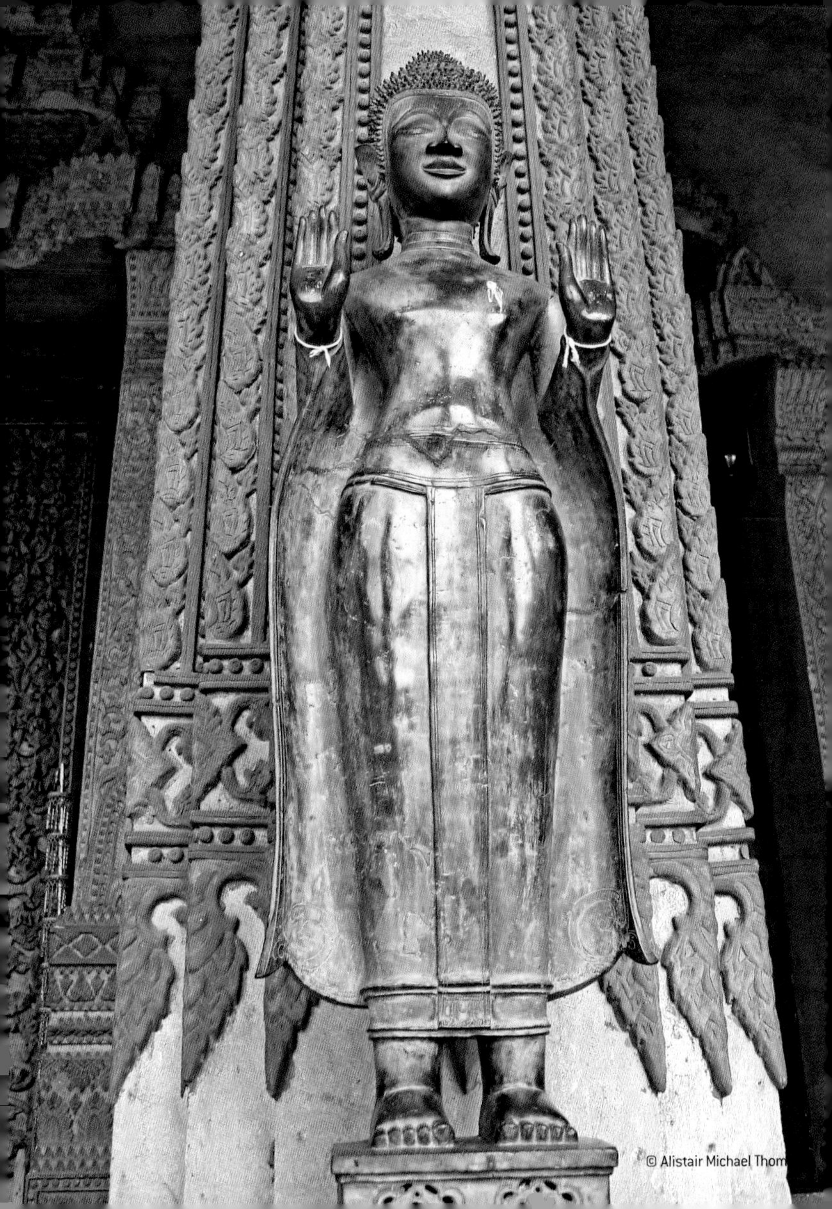

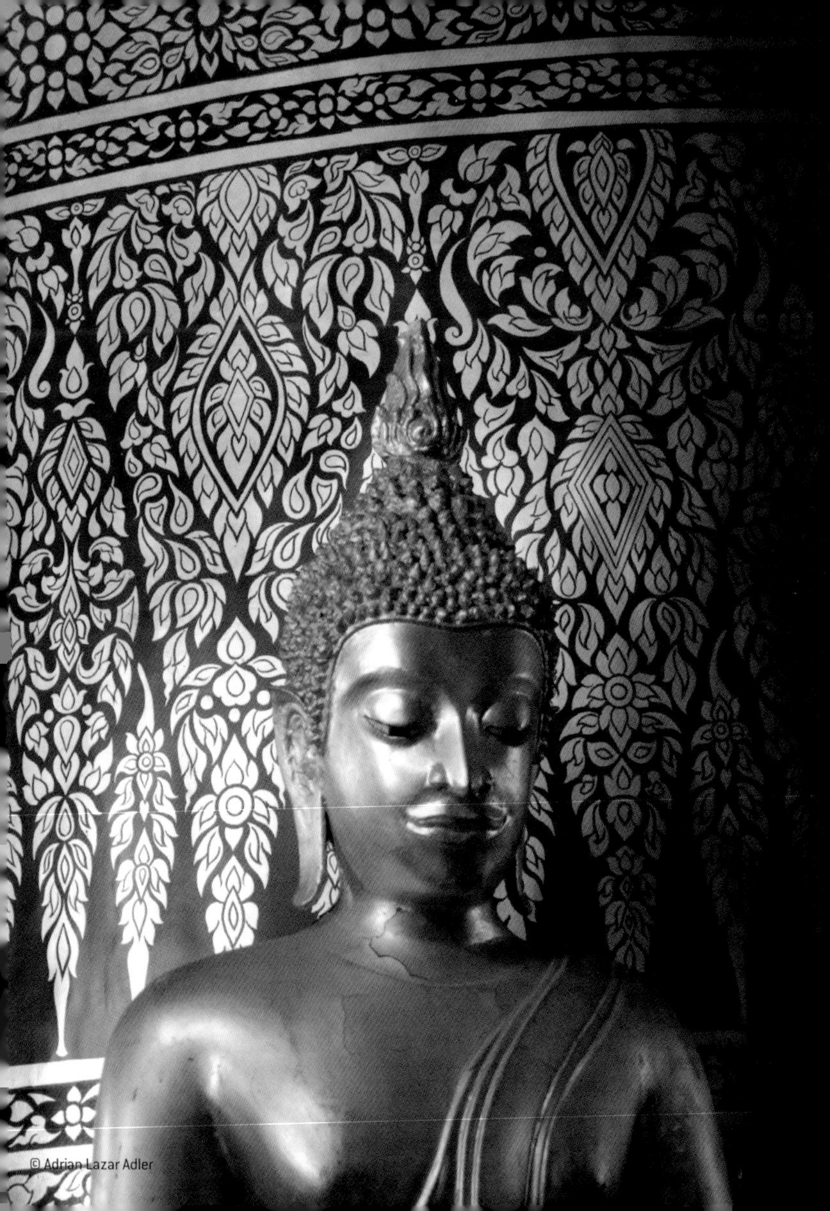

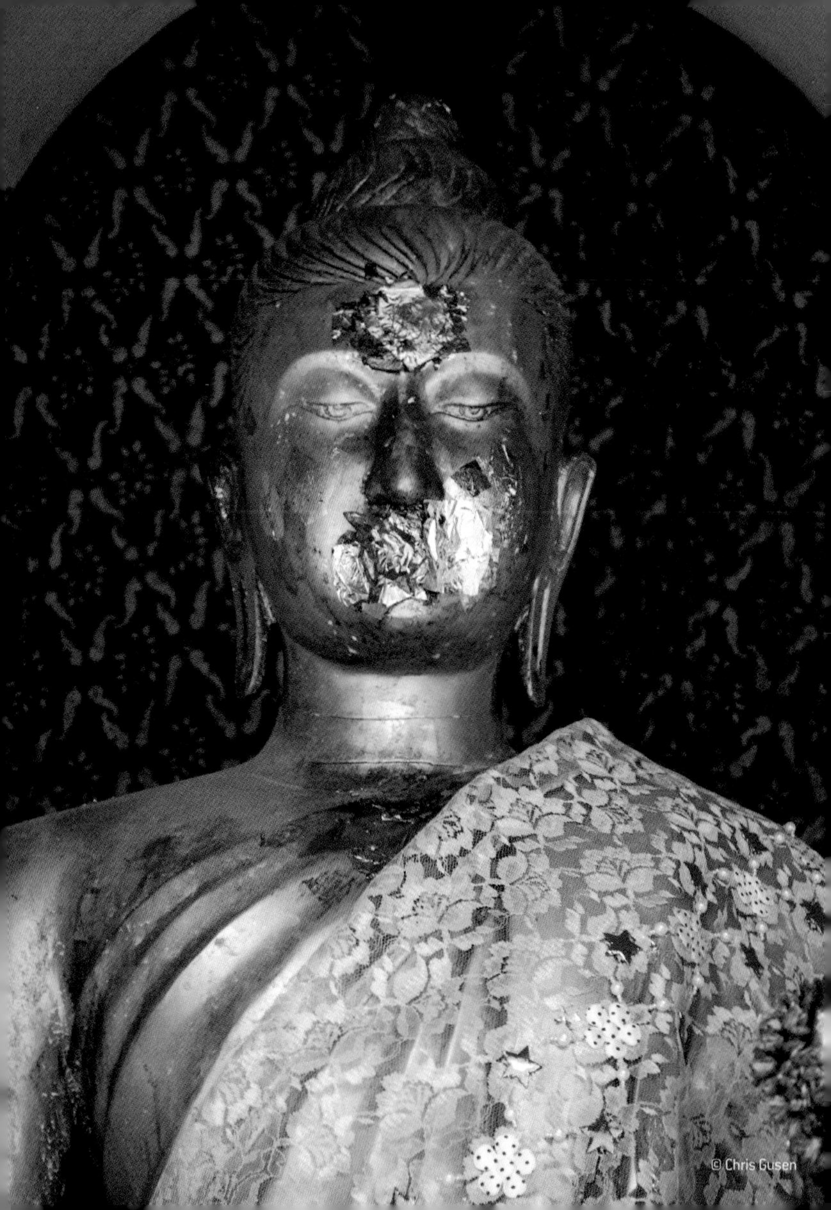

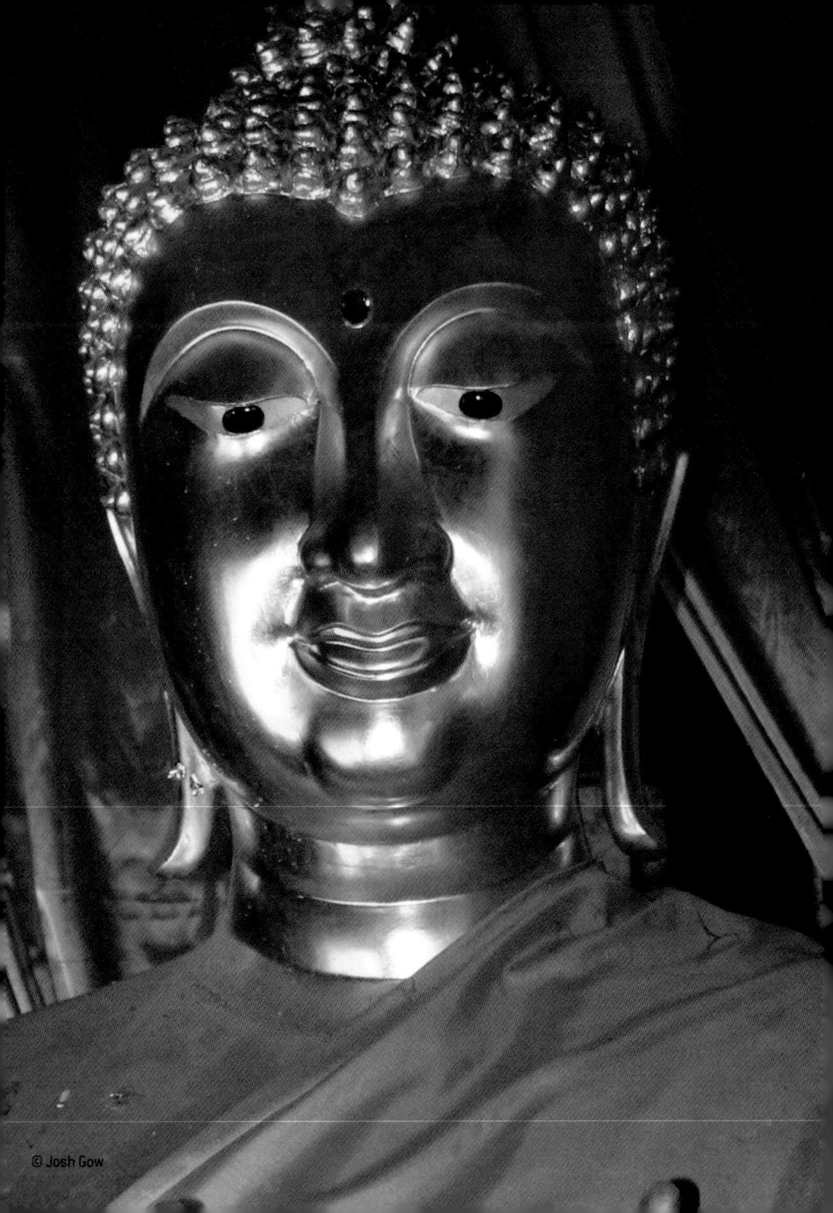

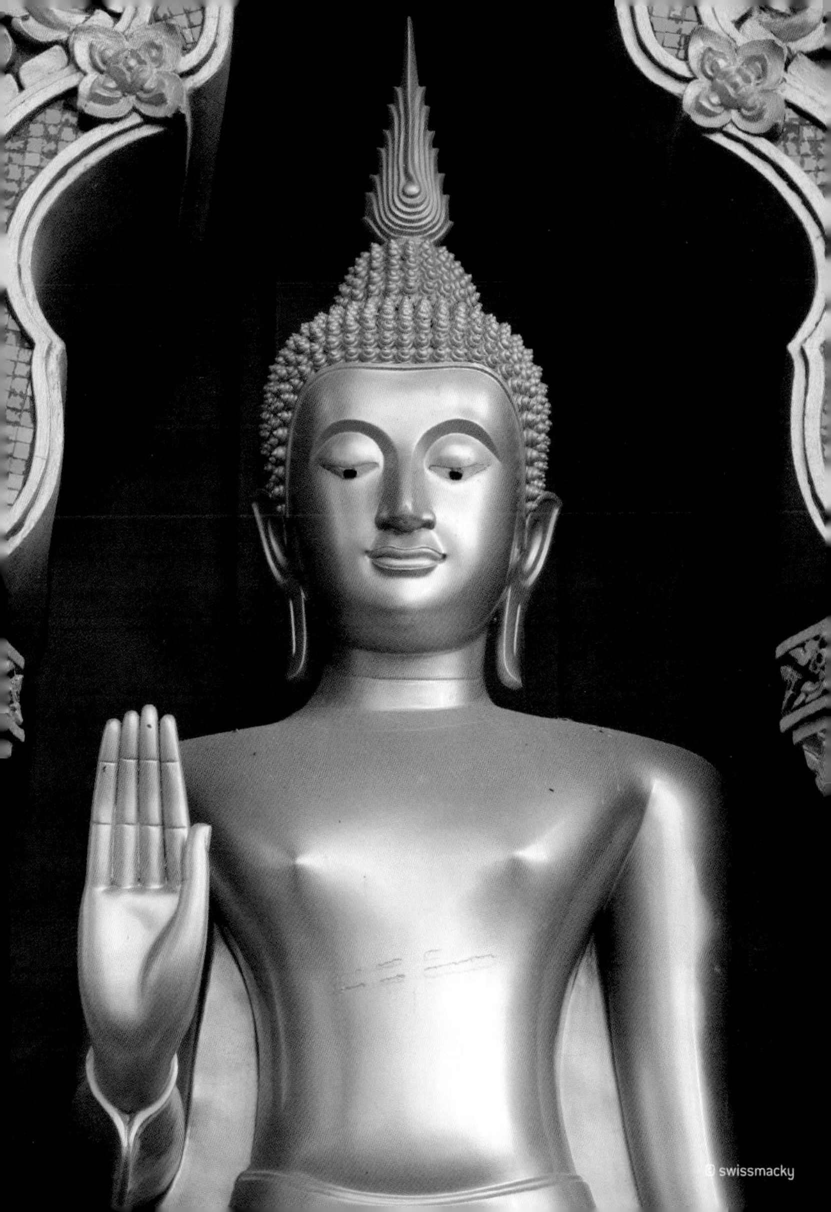
© swissmacky

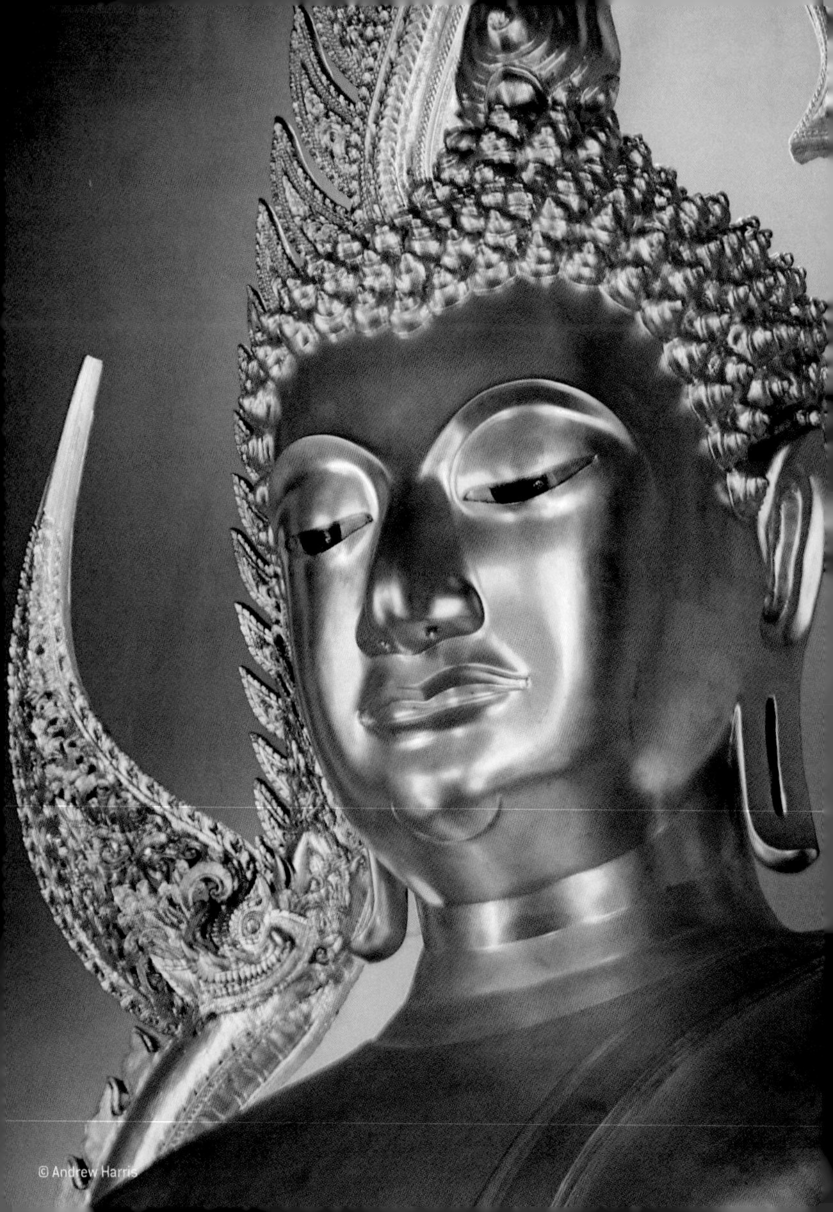

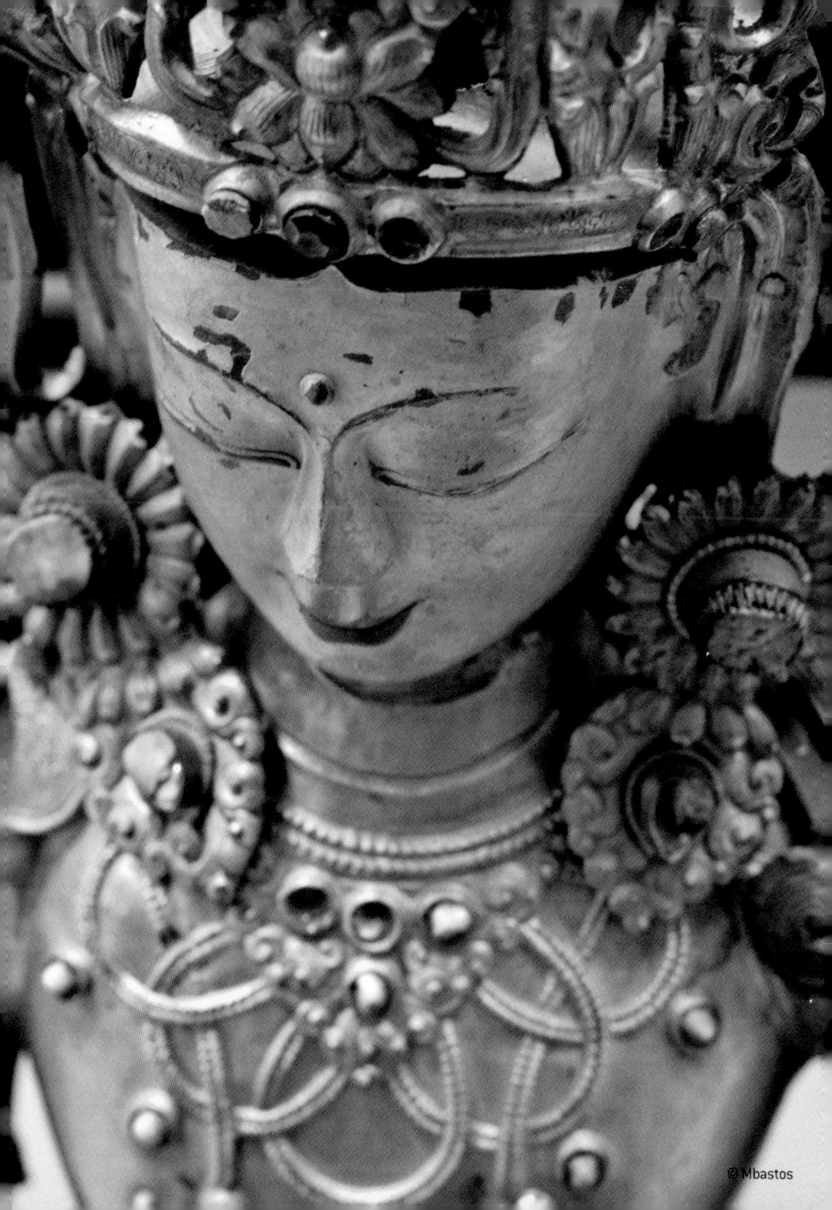

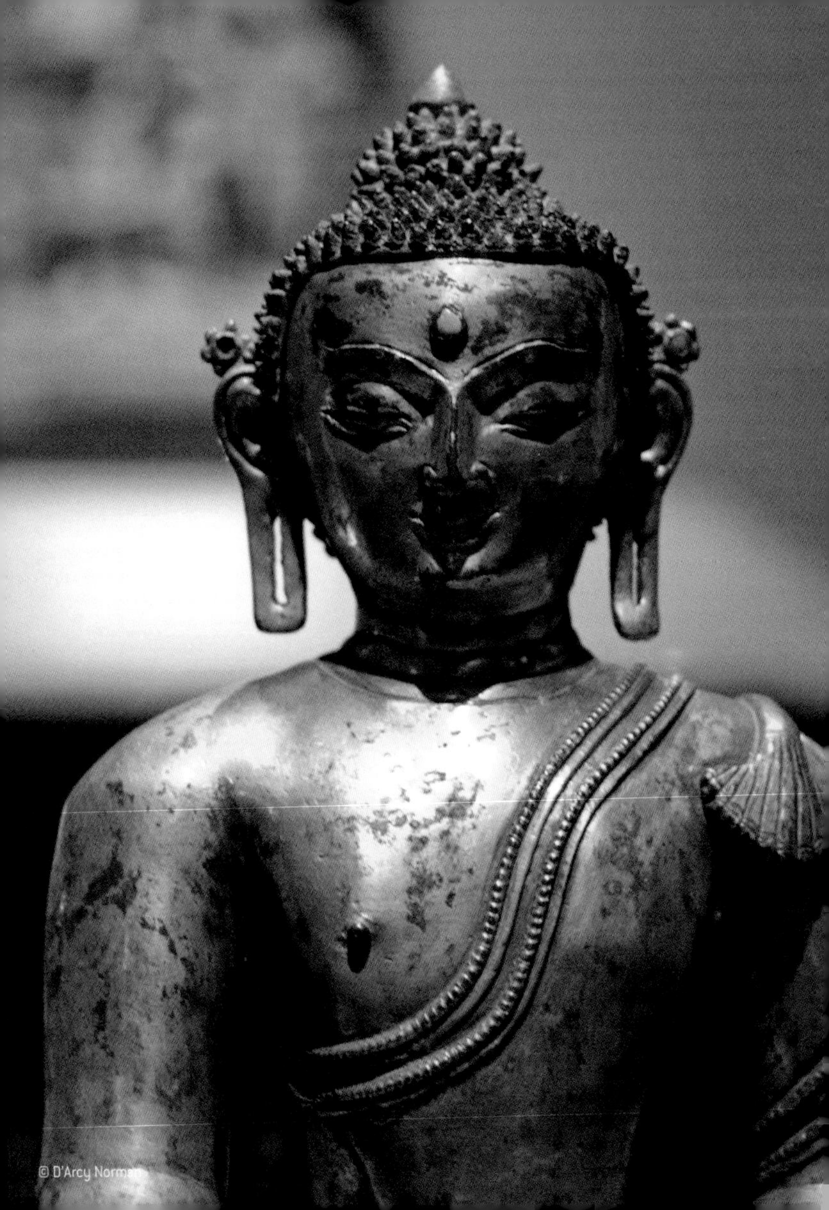

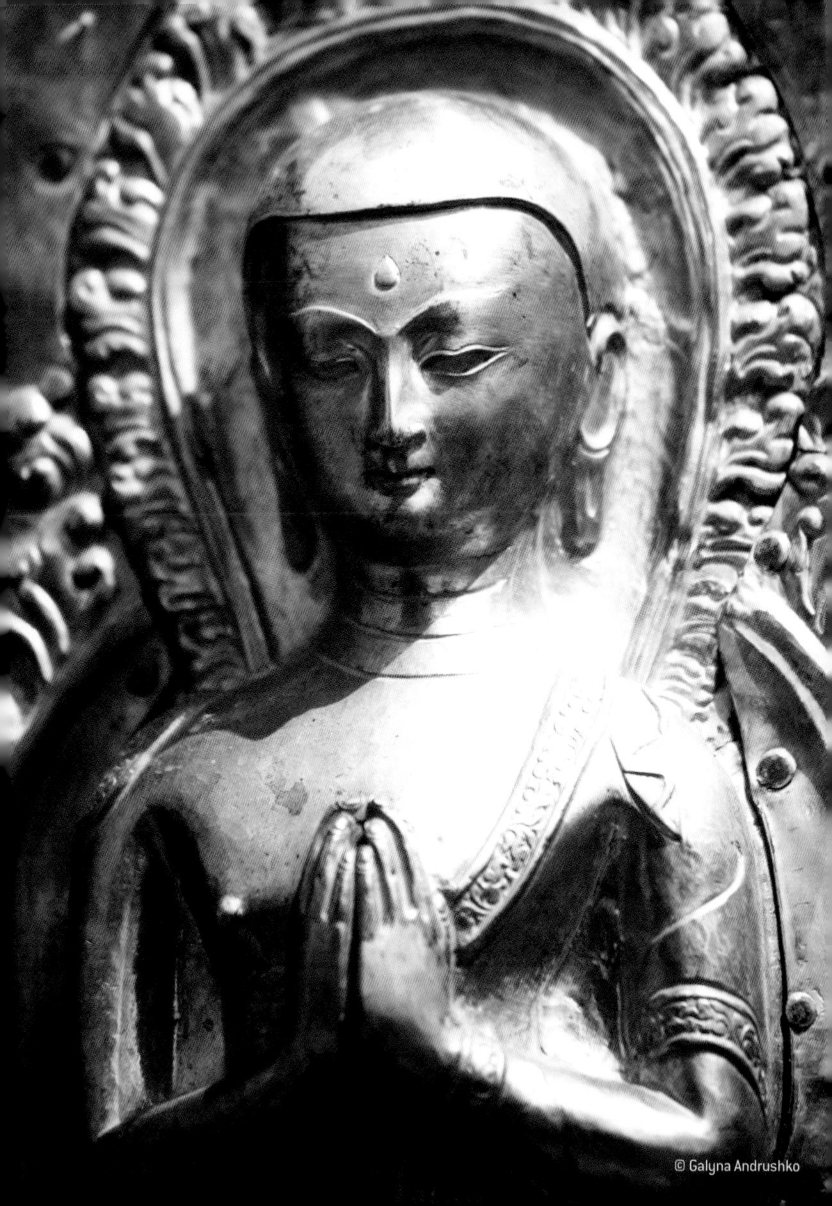

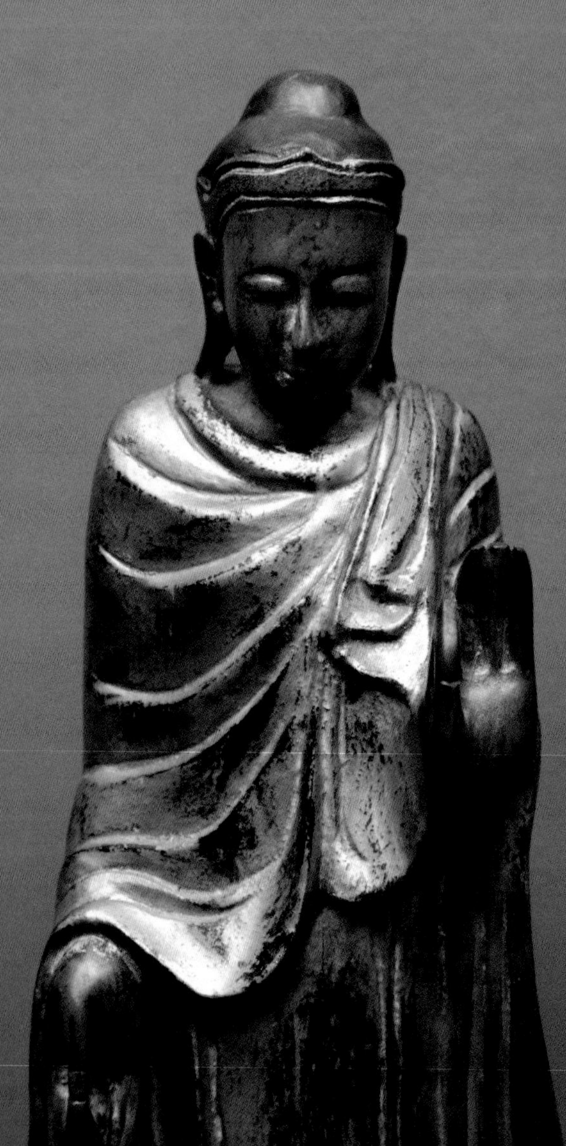

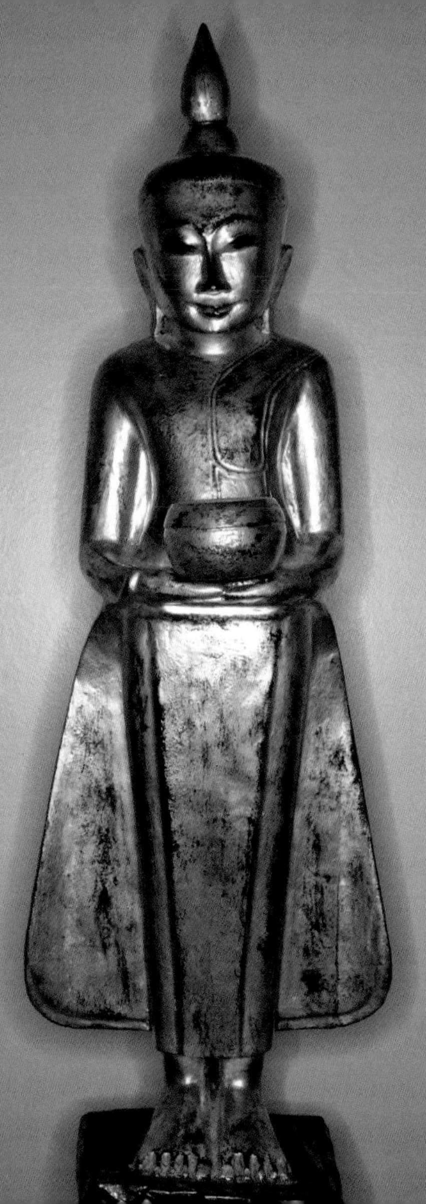

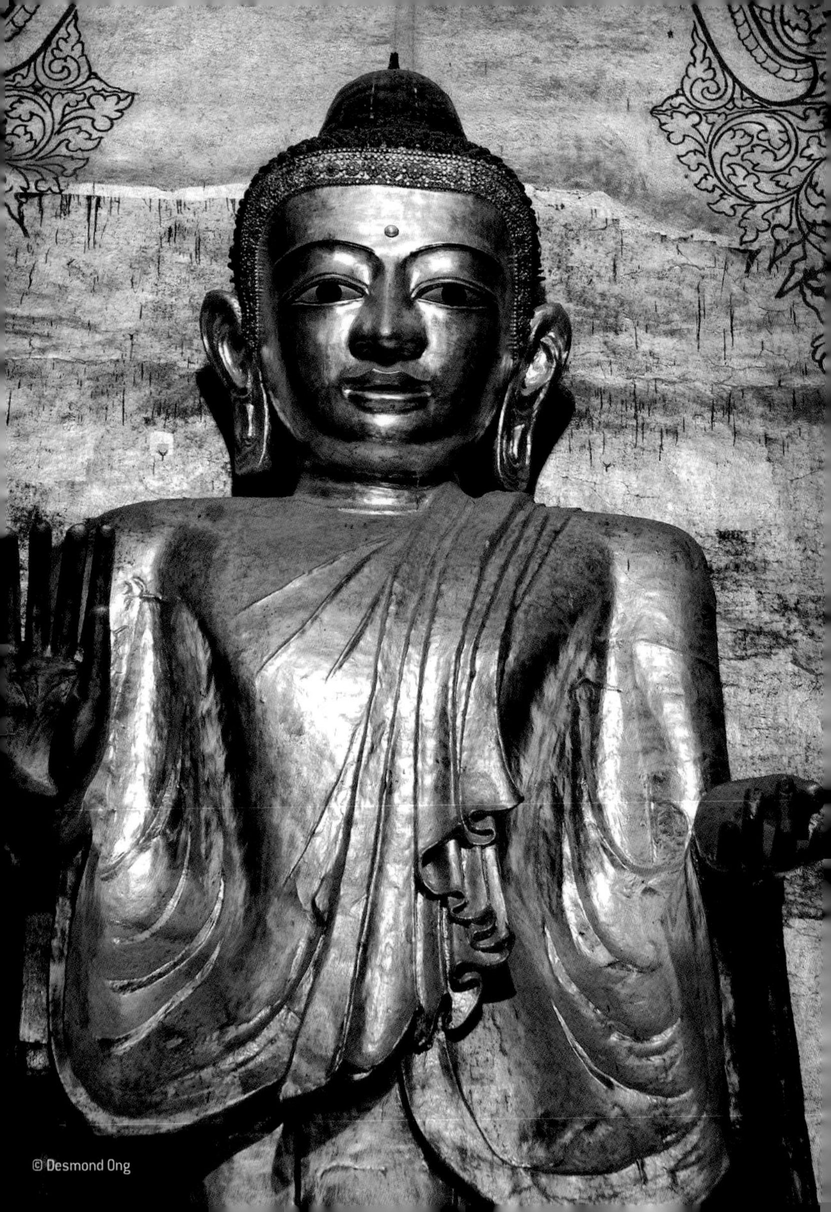

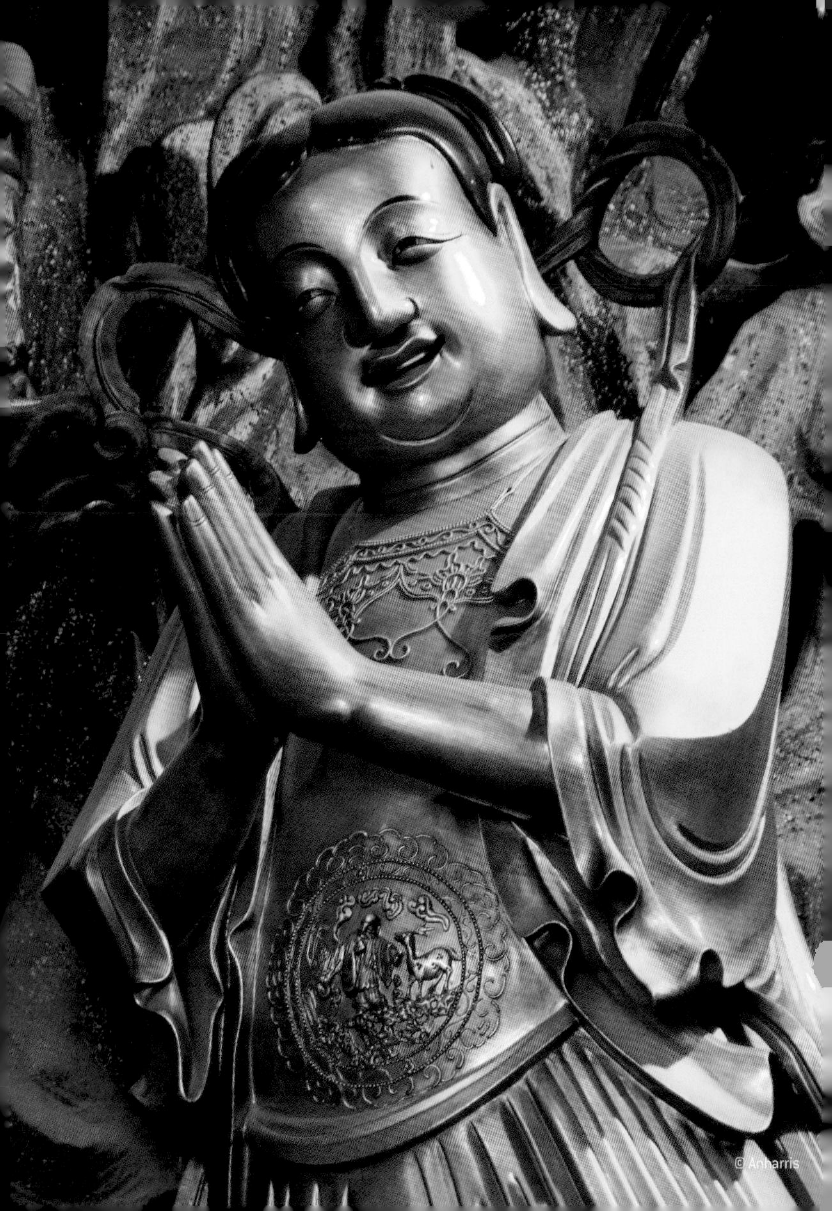

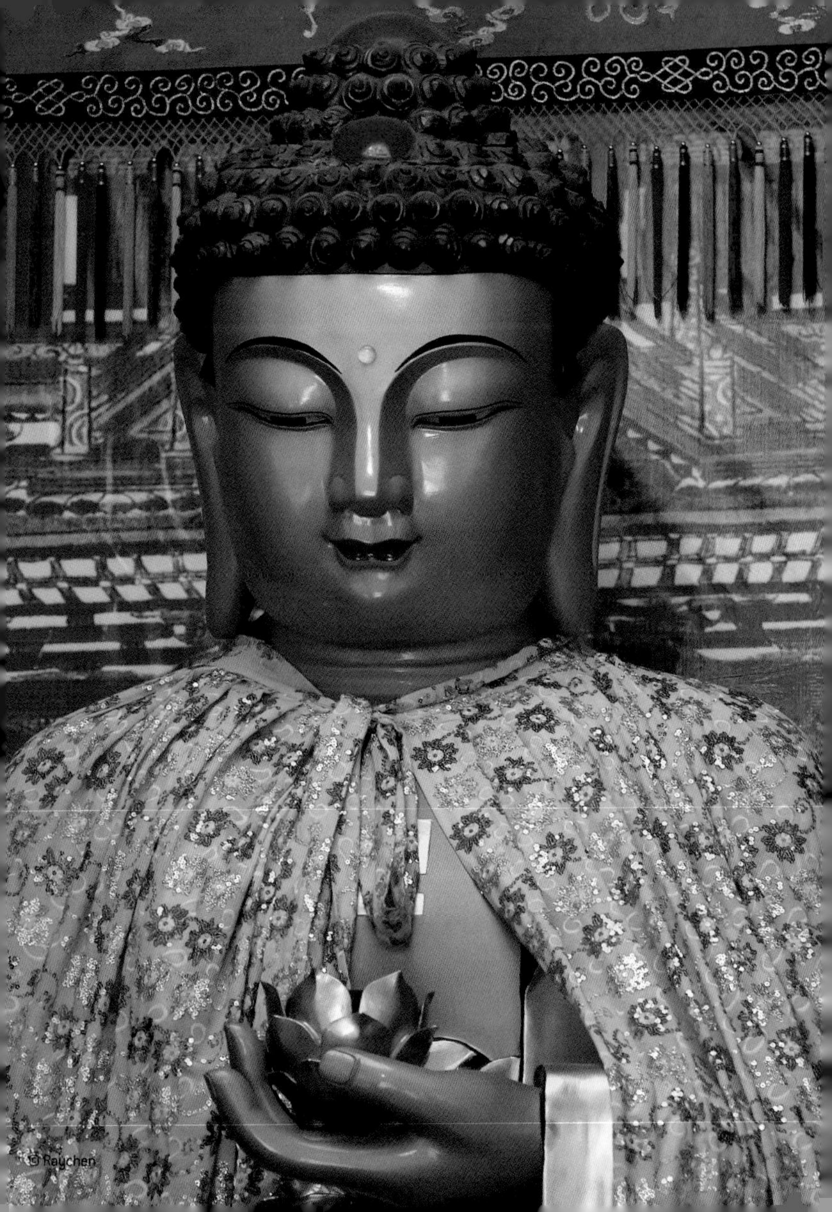
© Raychen

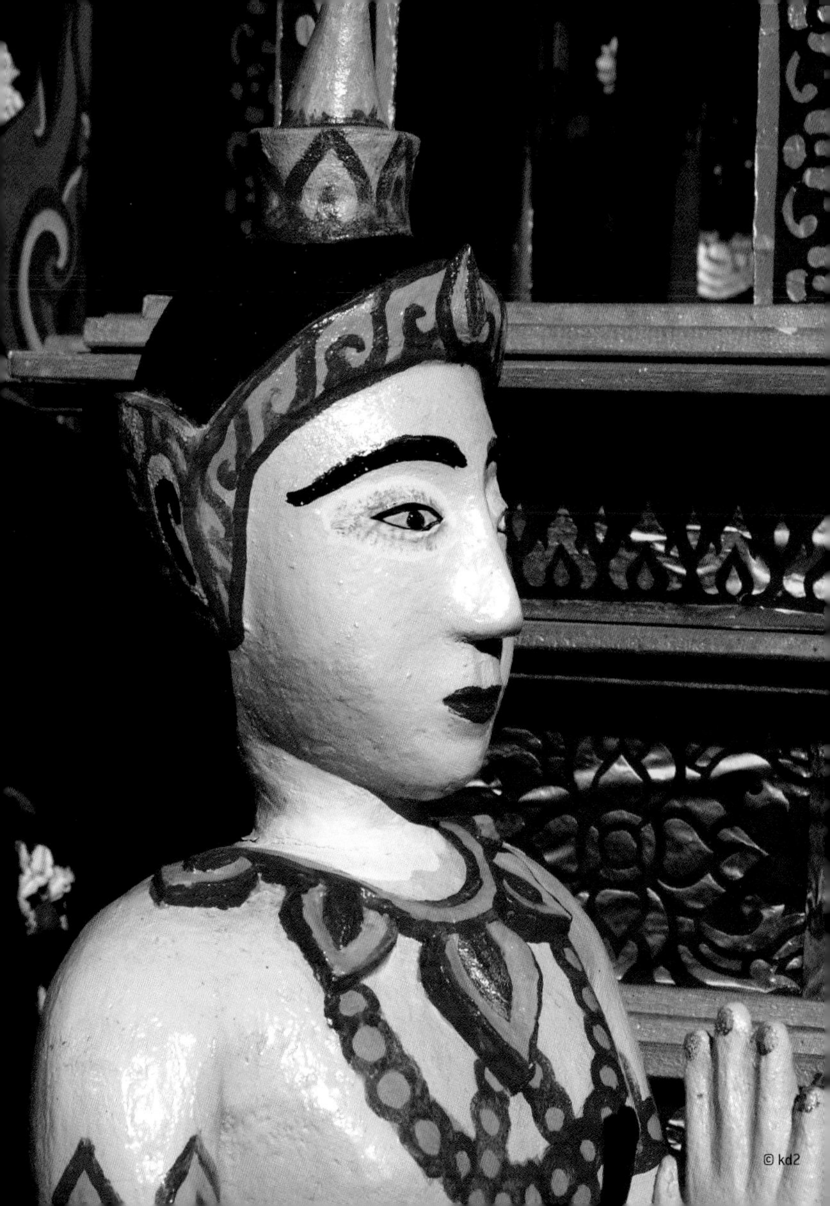
© kd2

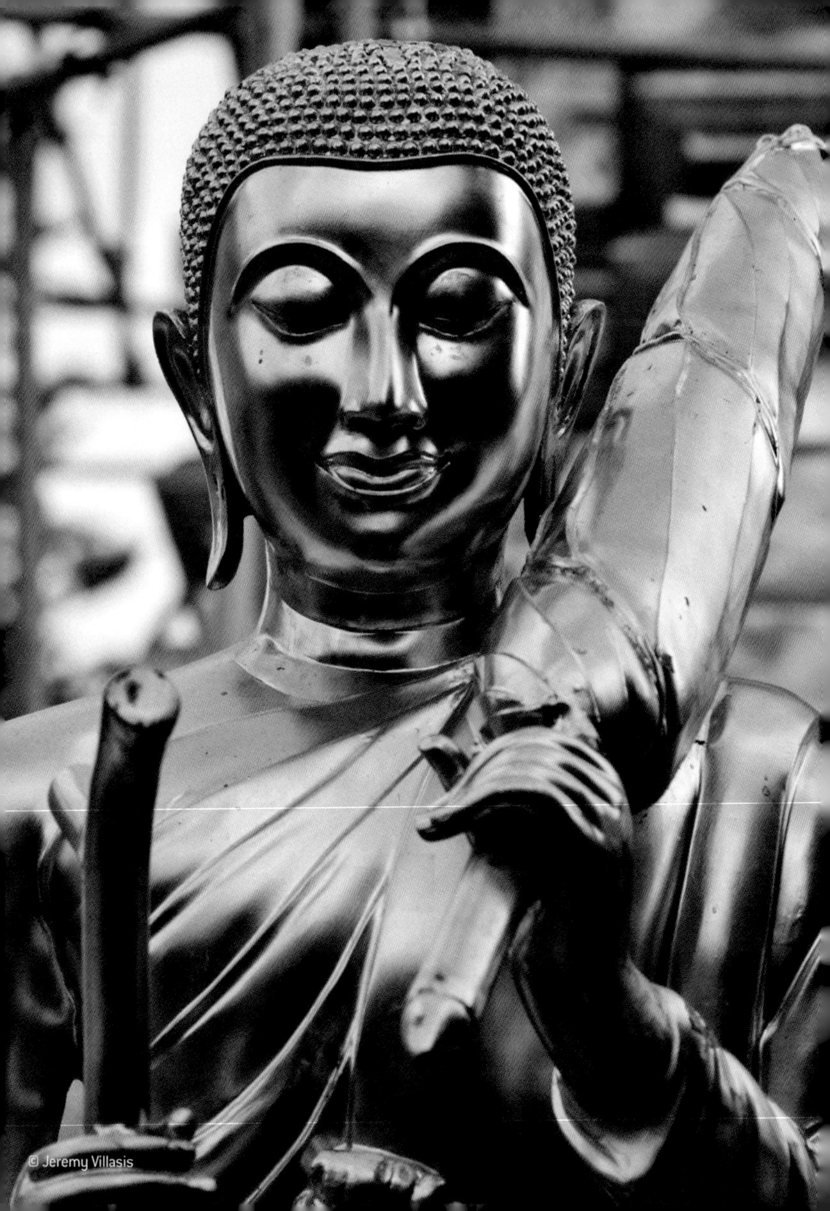

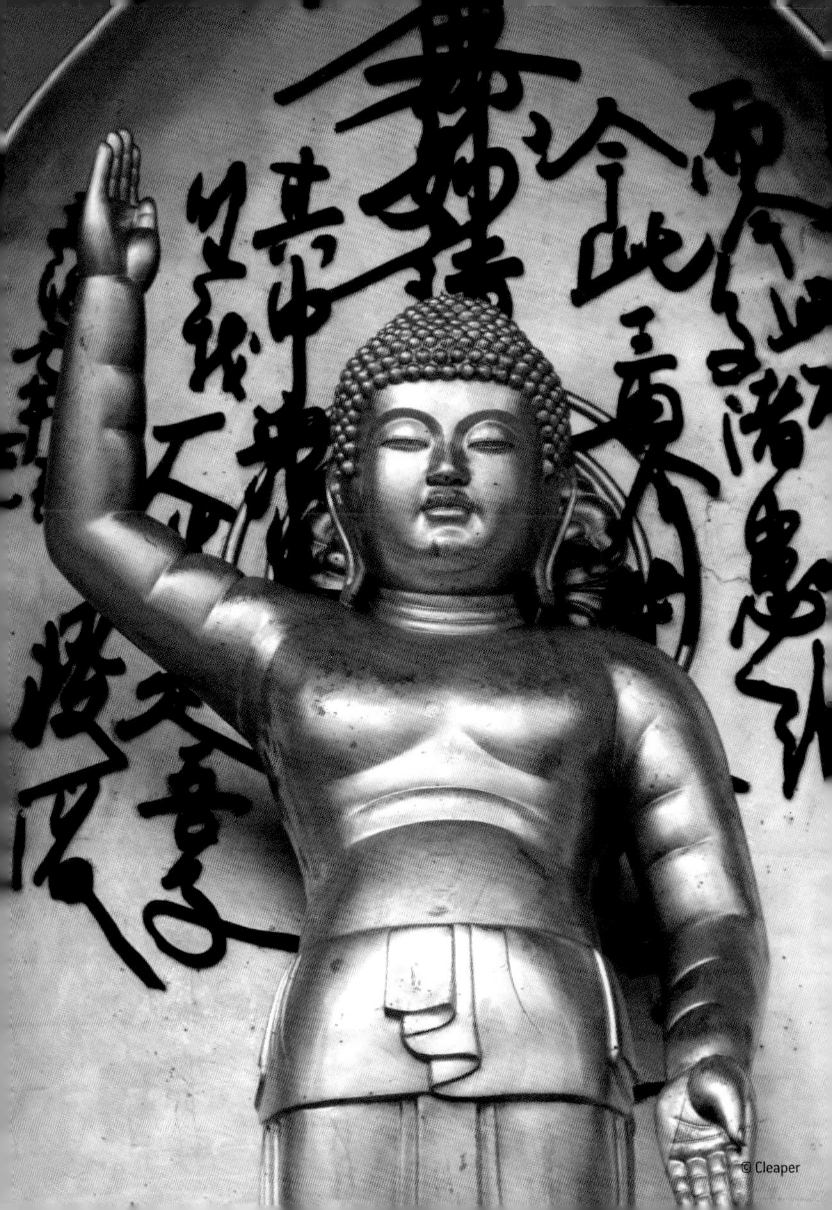

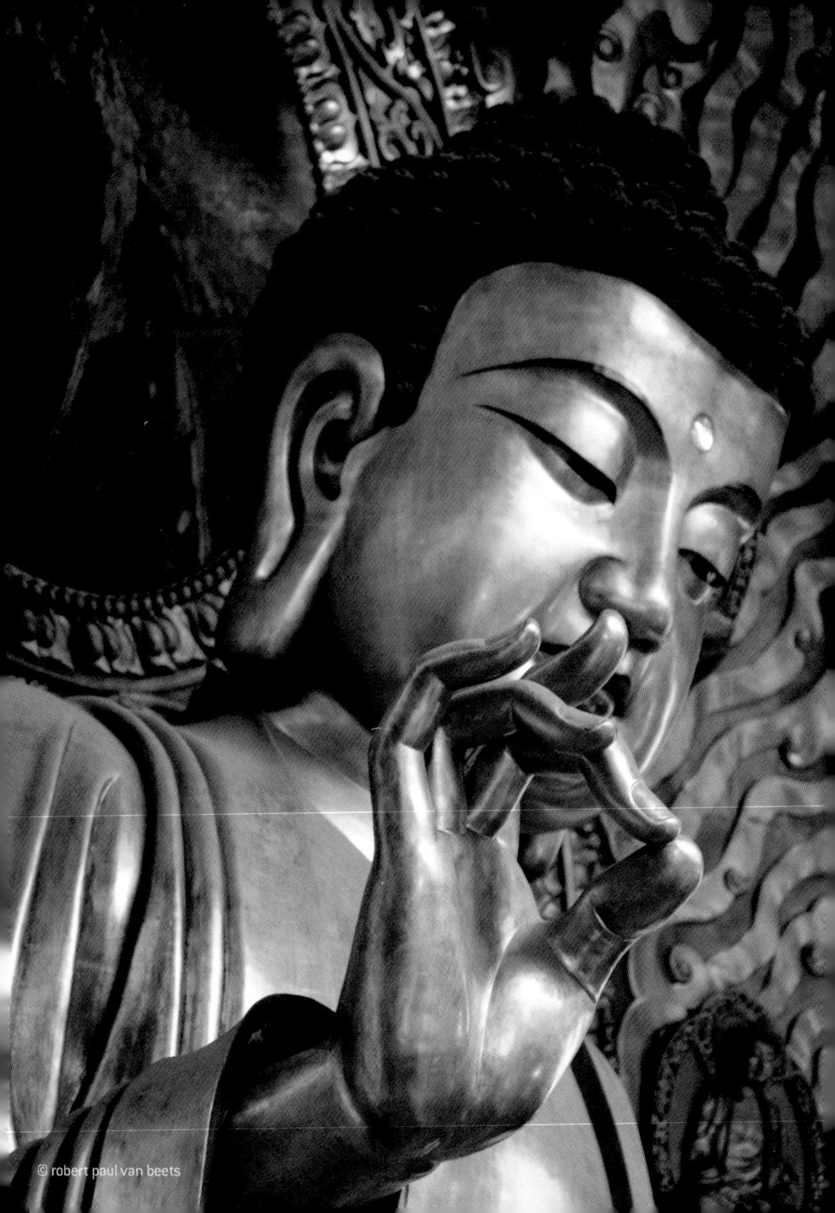

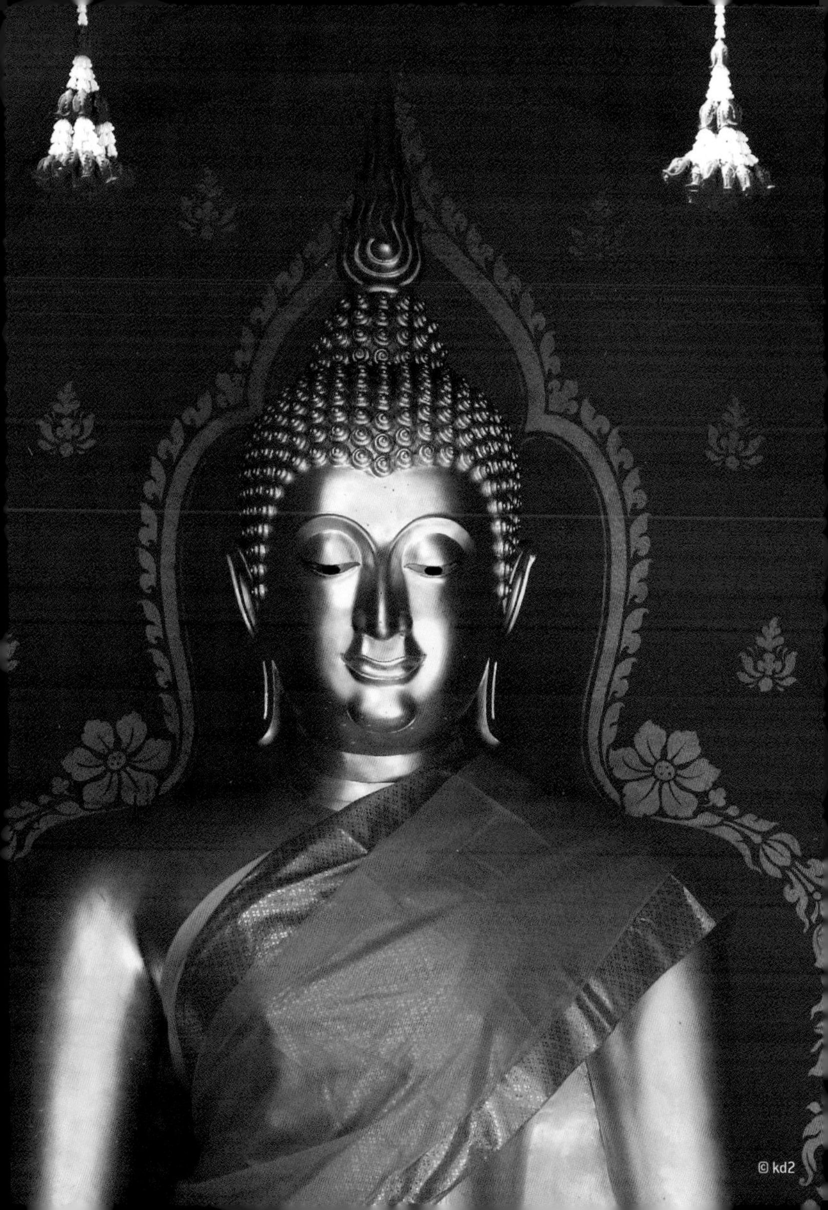

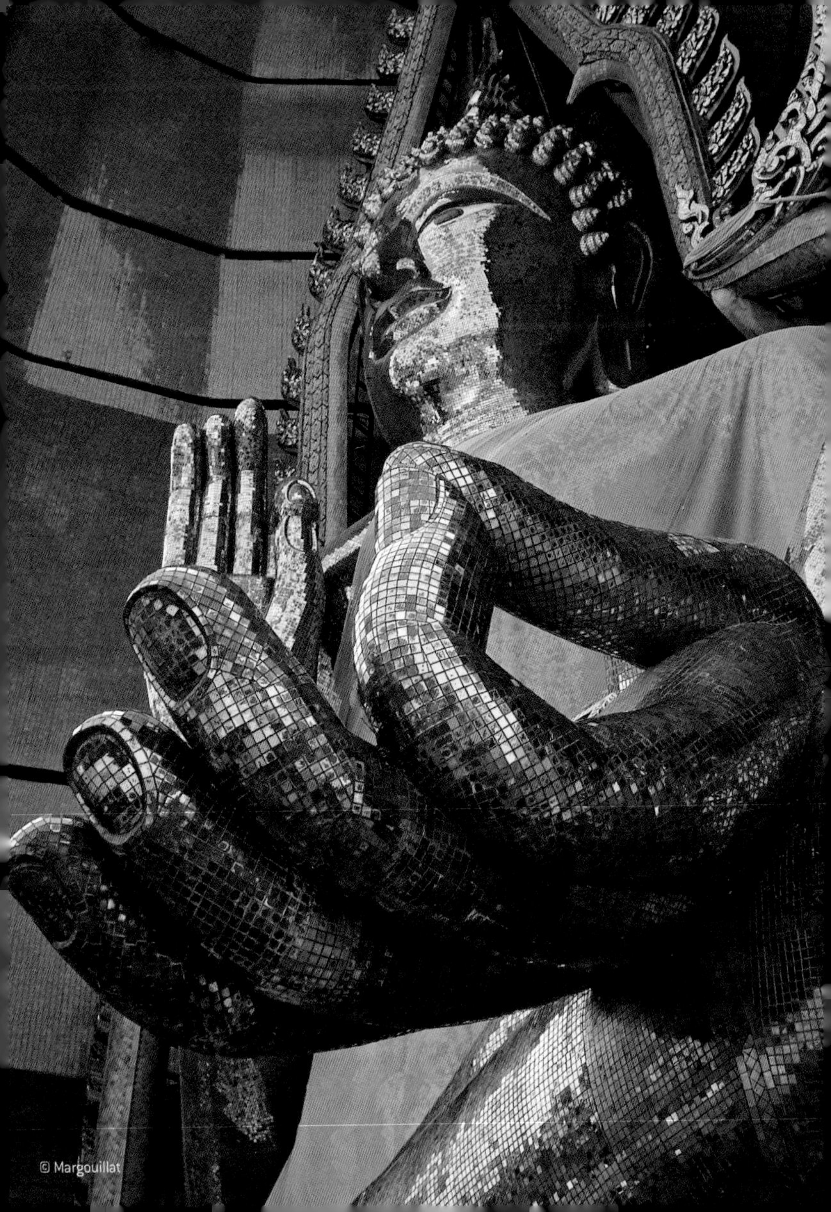

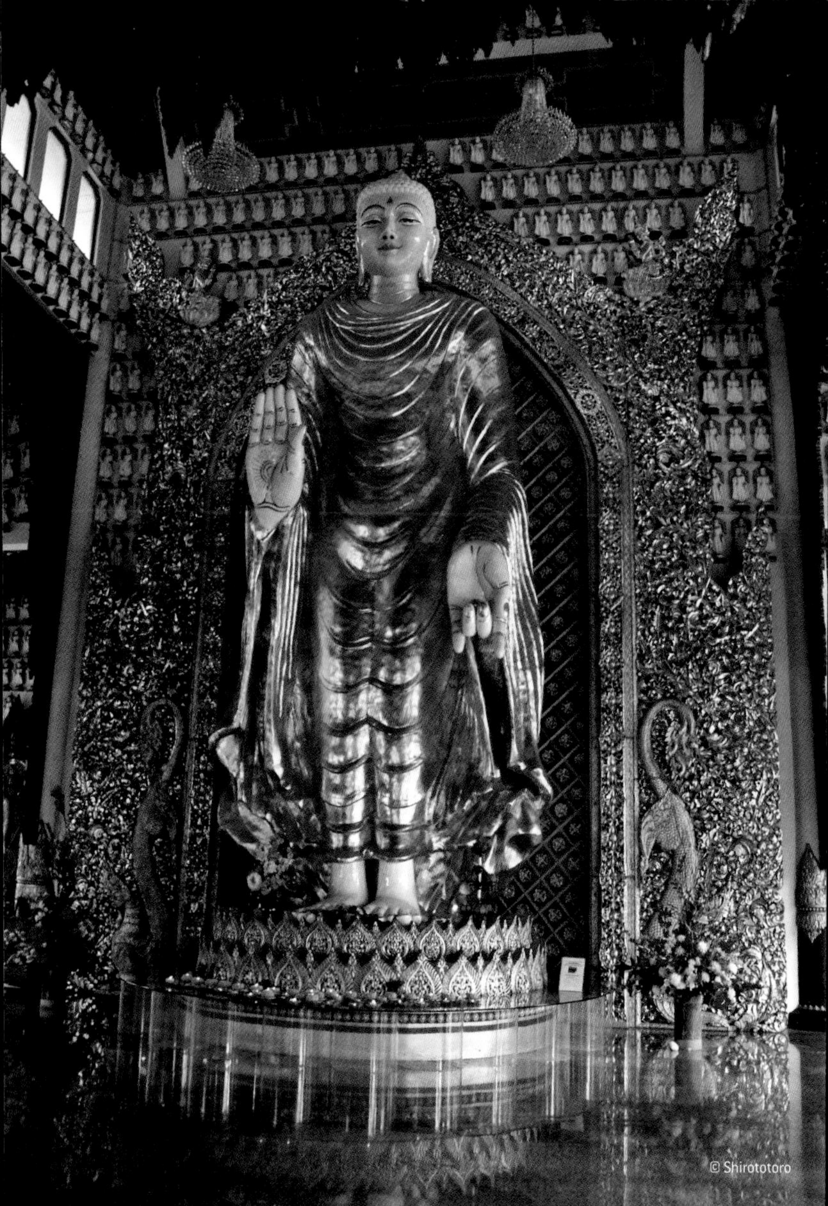

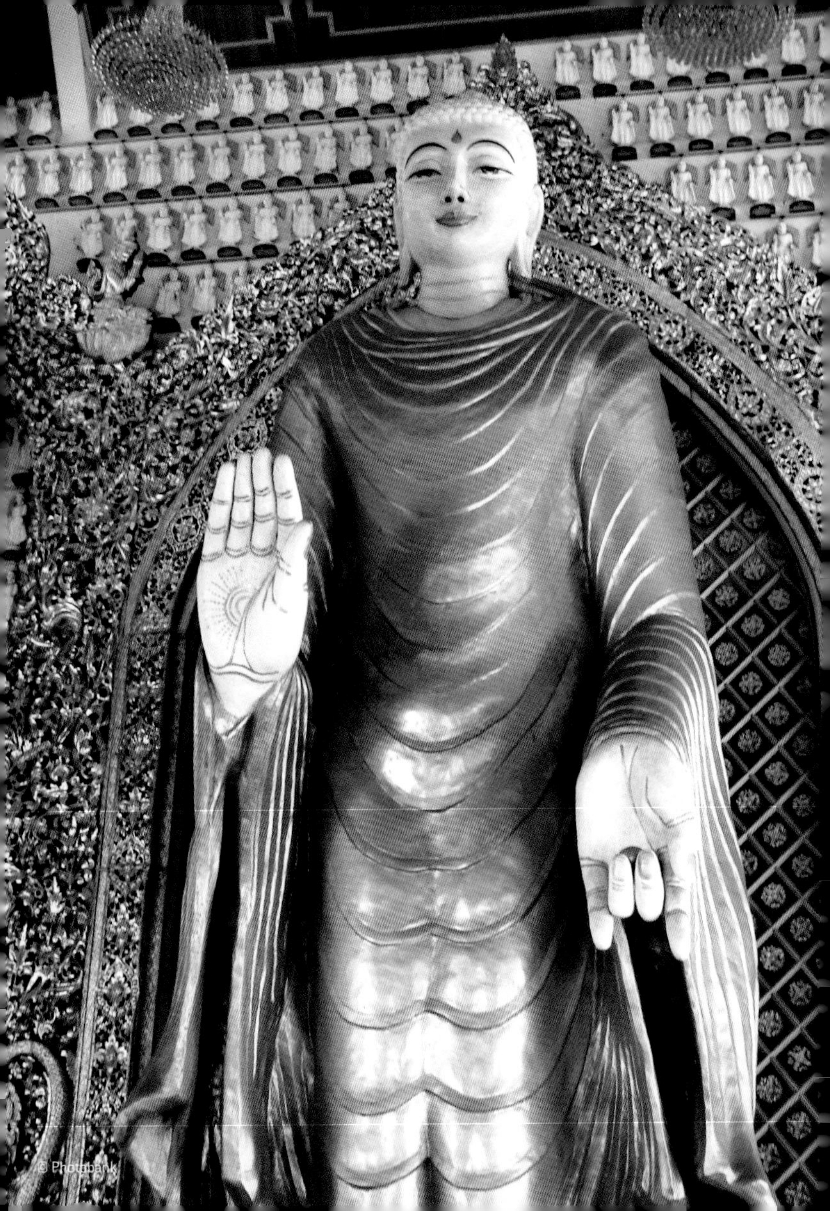
© Photobank

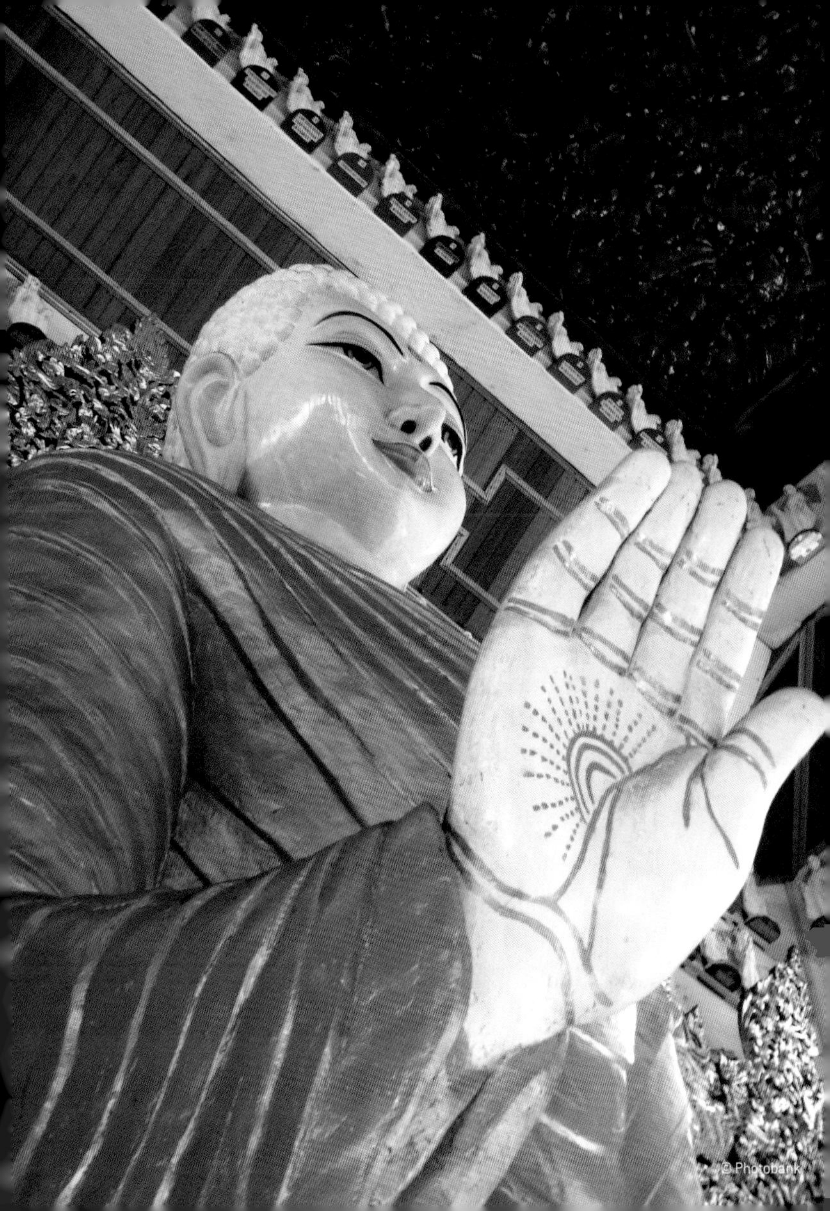

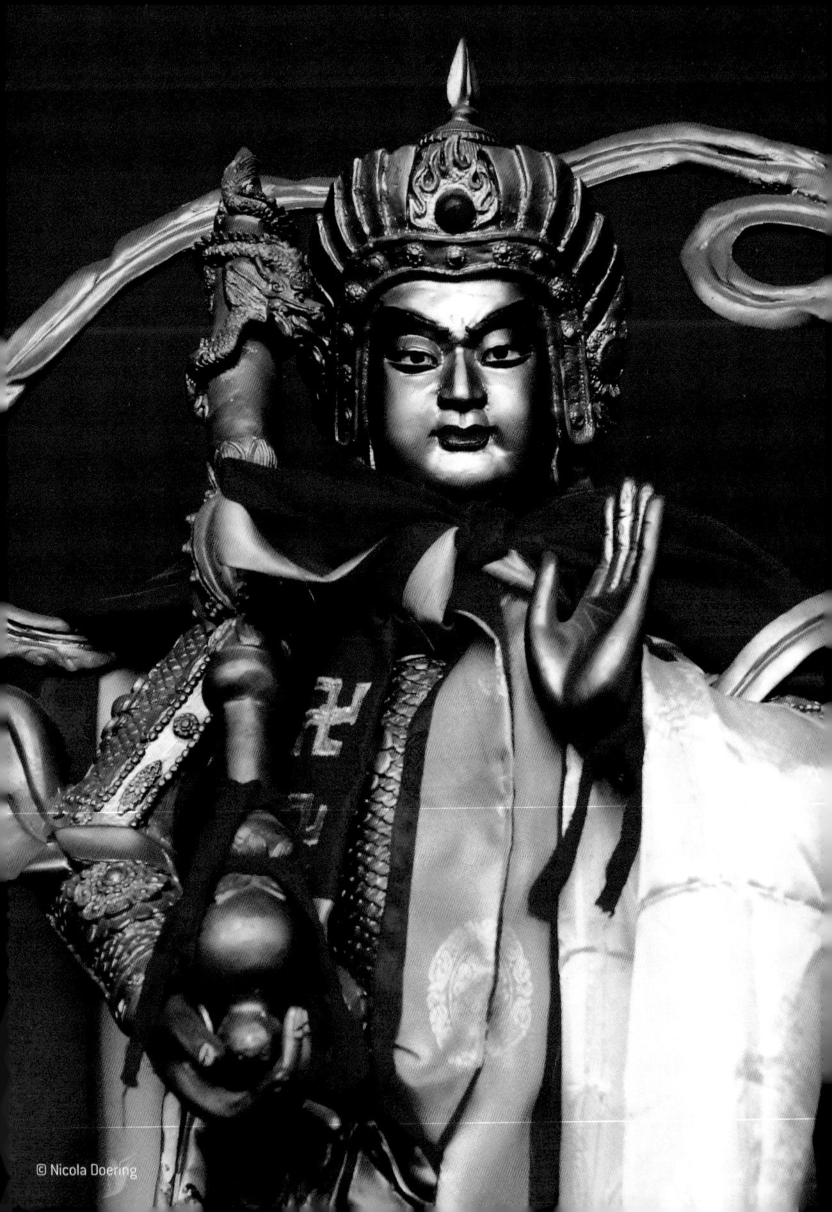

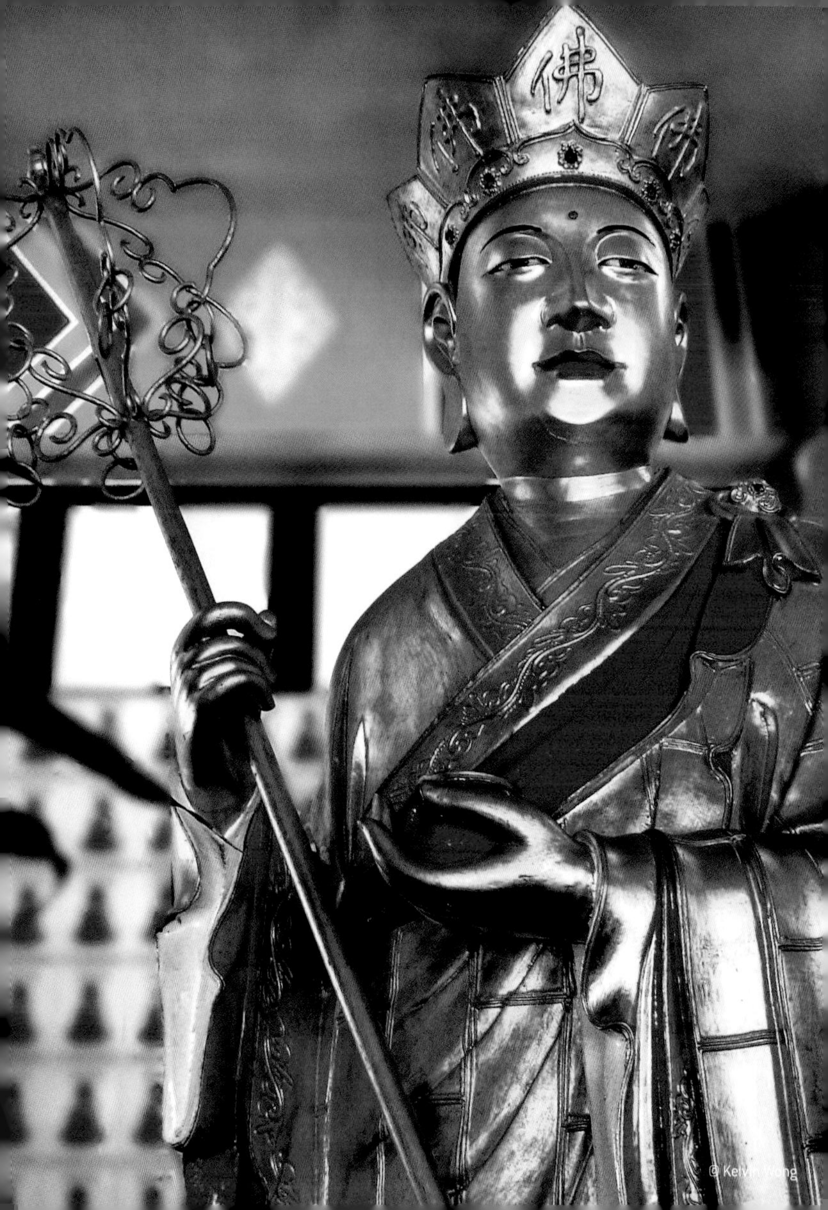
佛

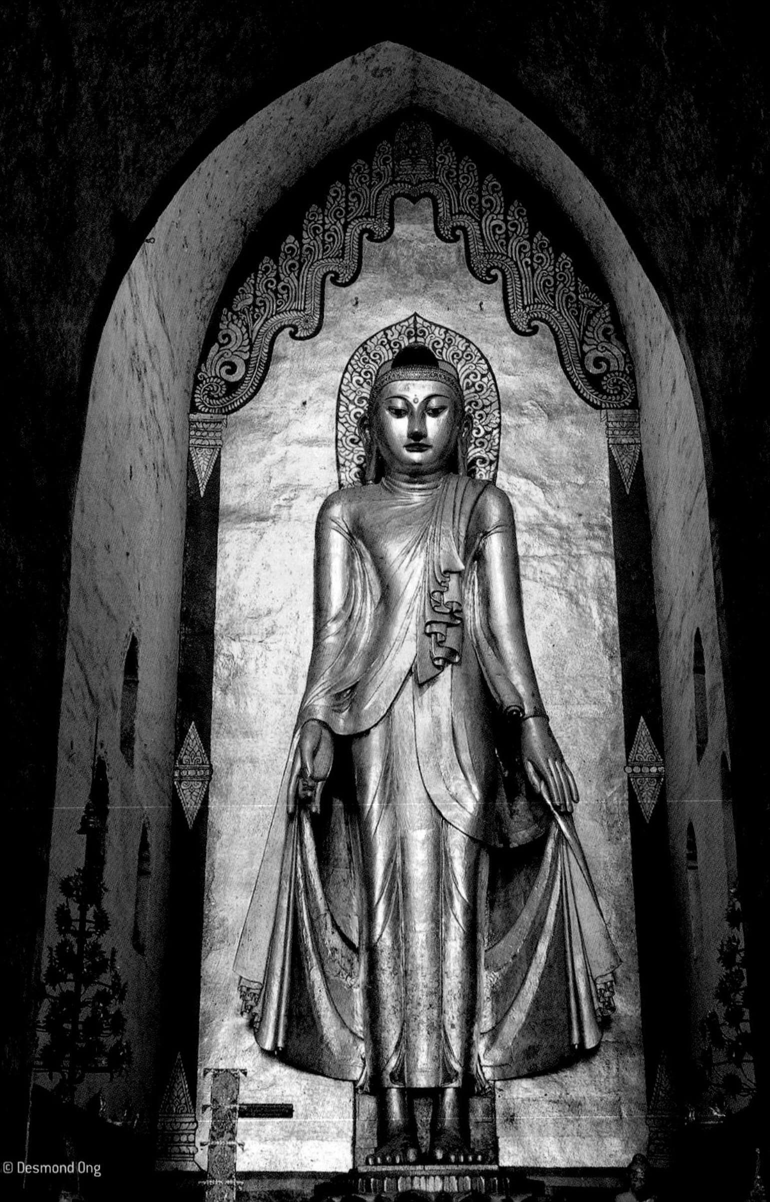

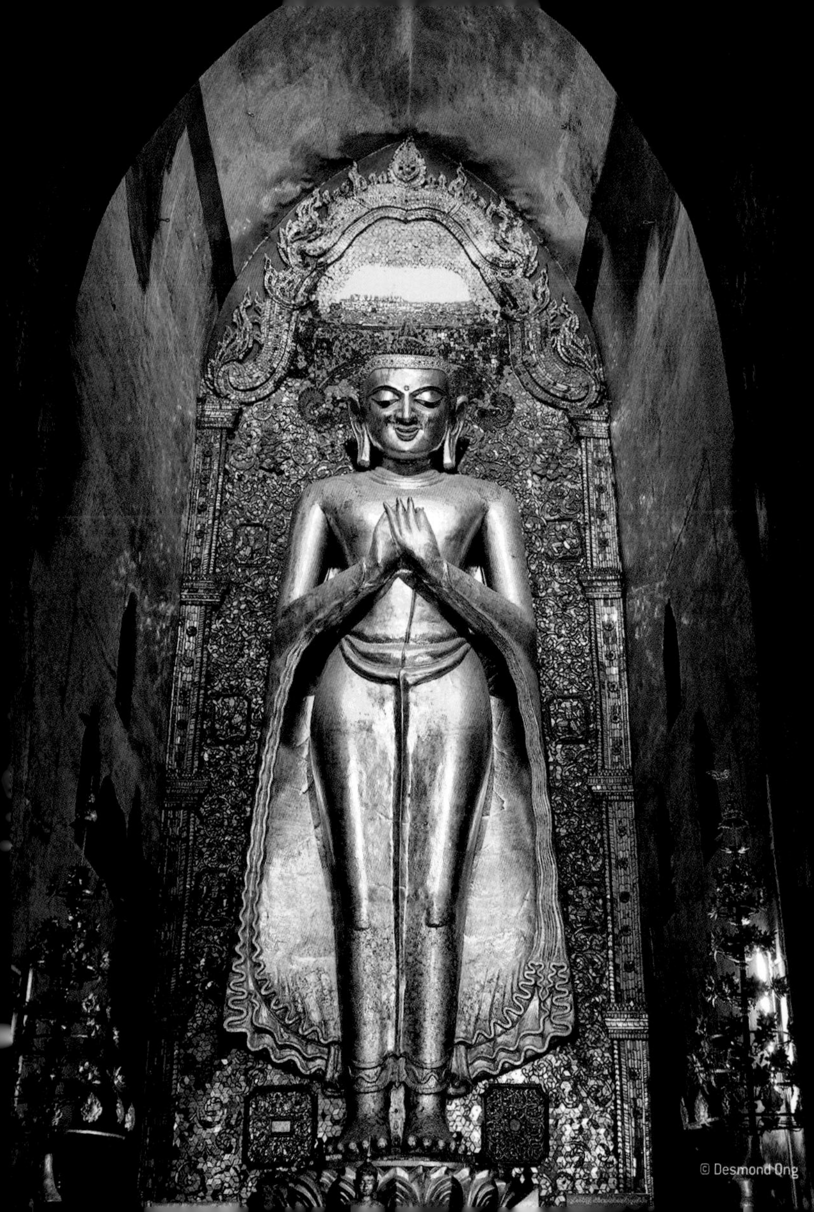
© Desmond Ong

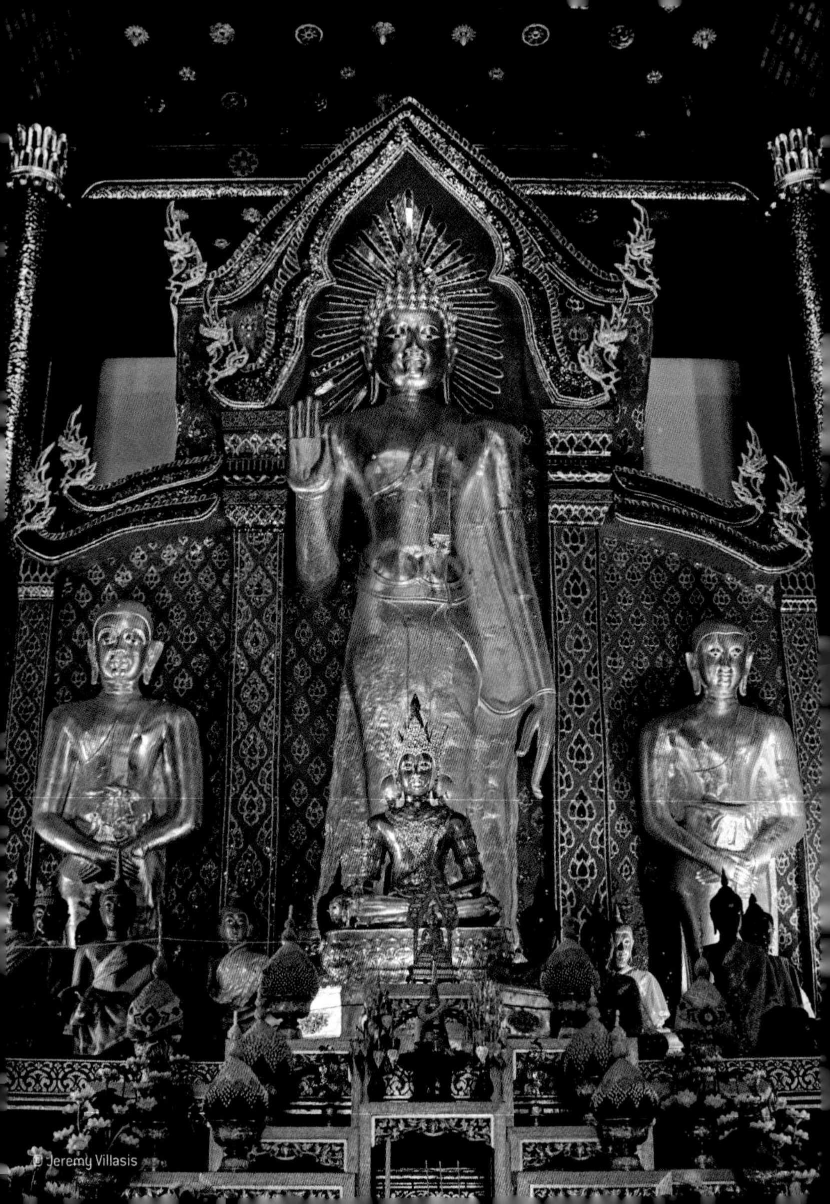

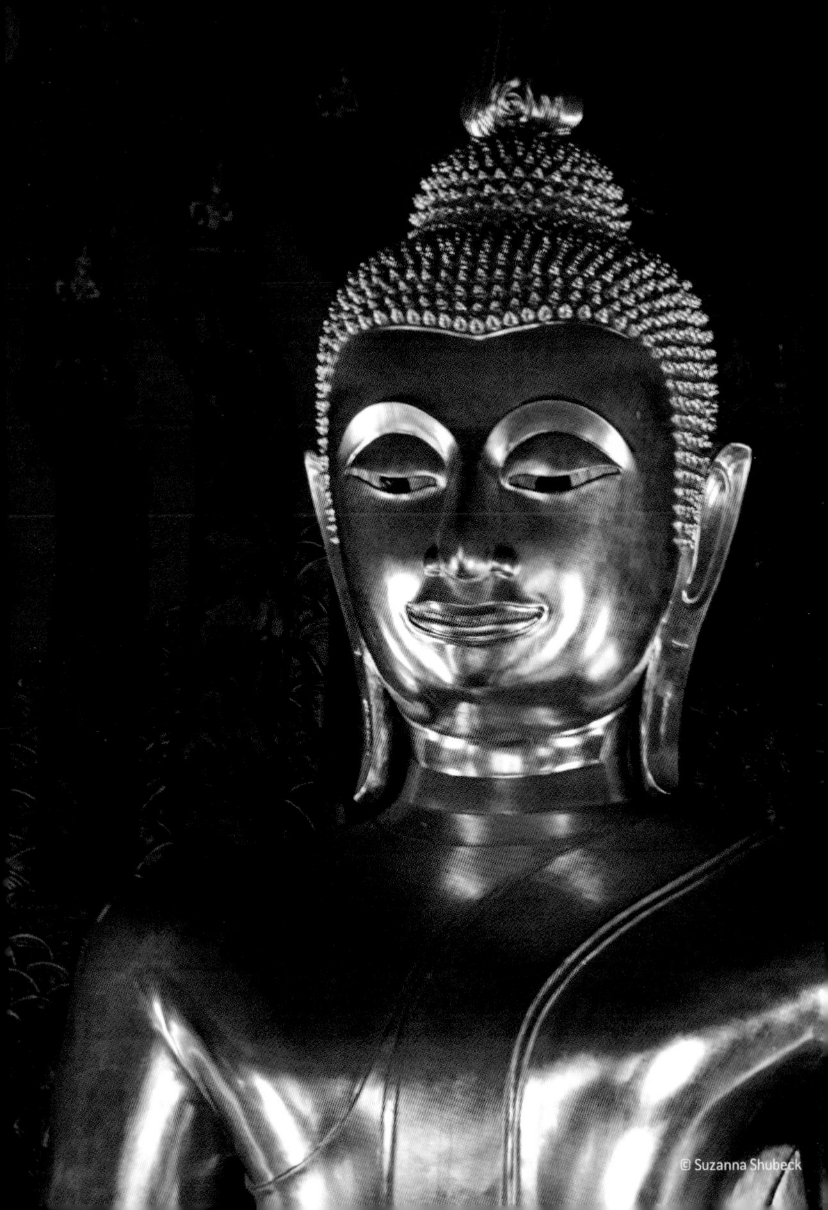

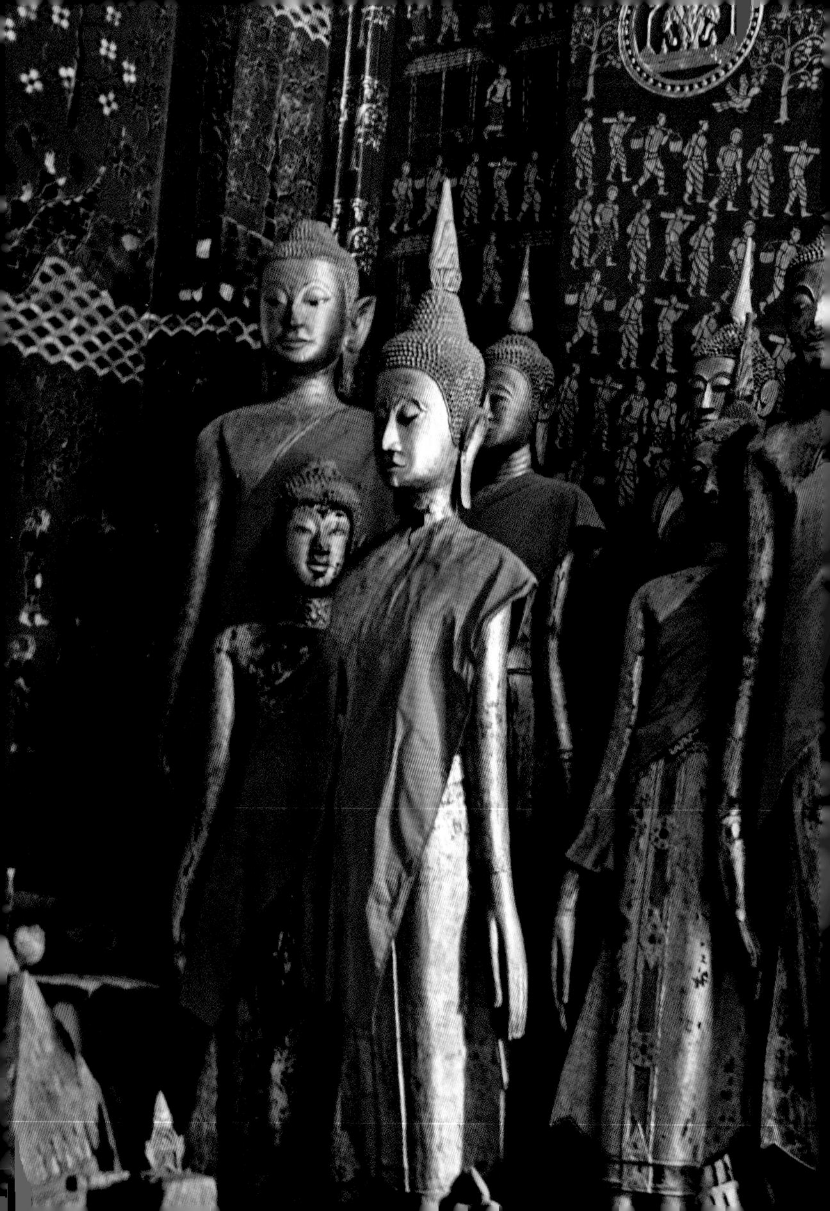

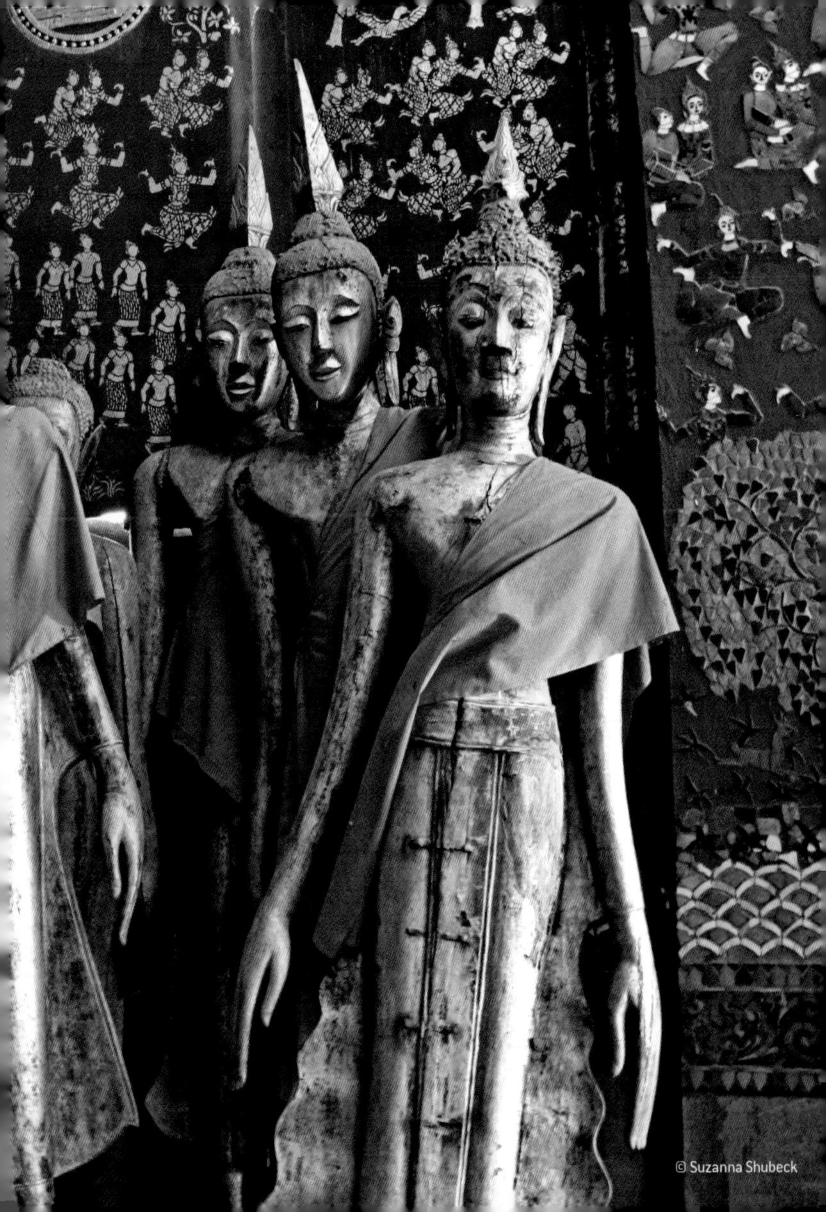

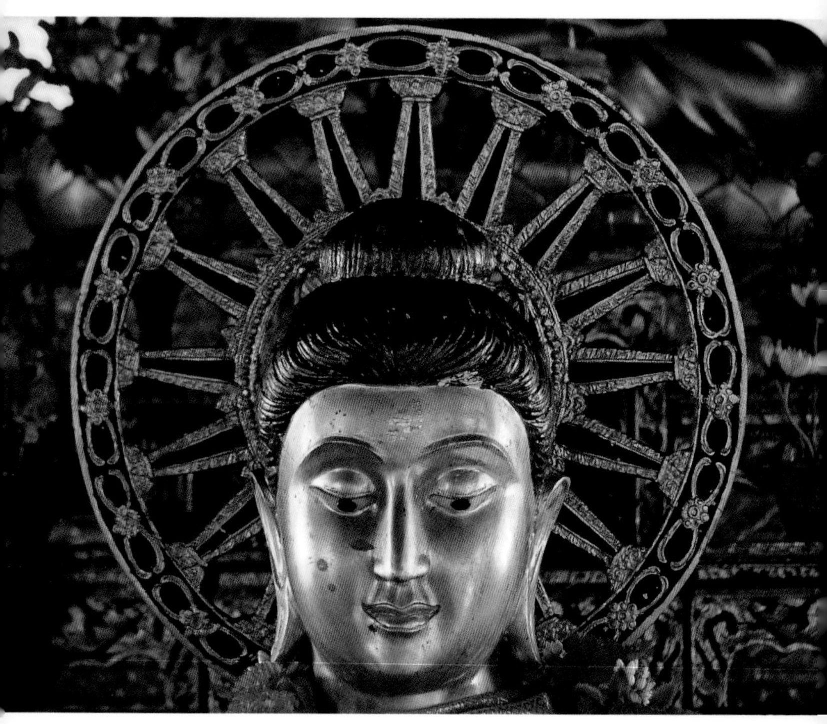

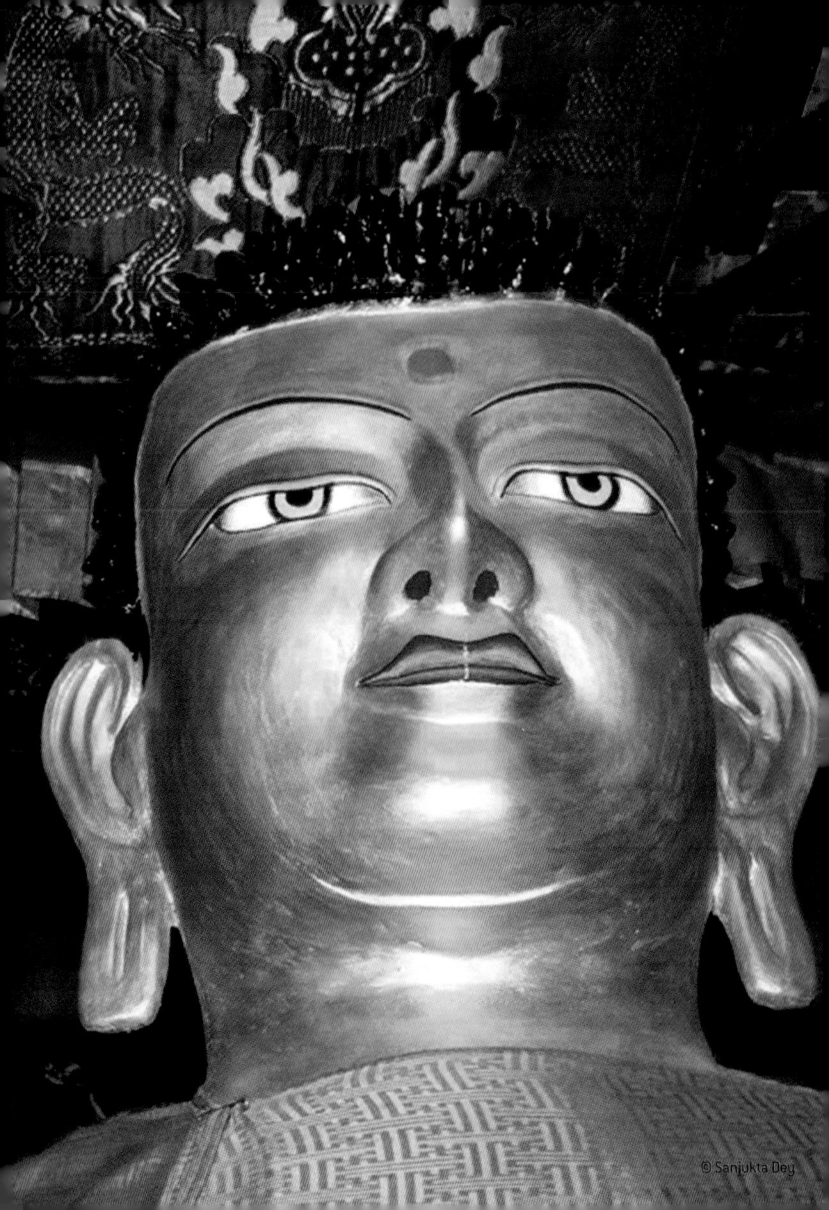
© Sanjukta Dey

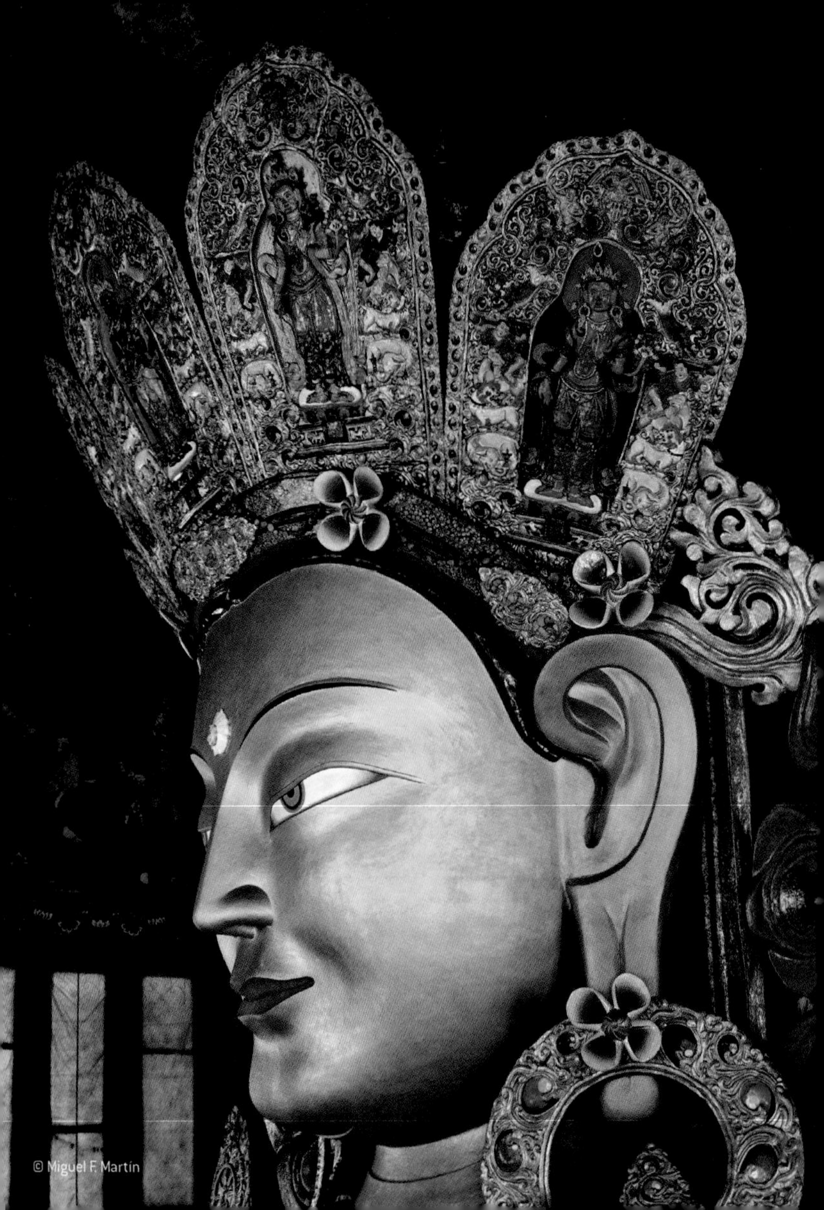

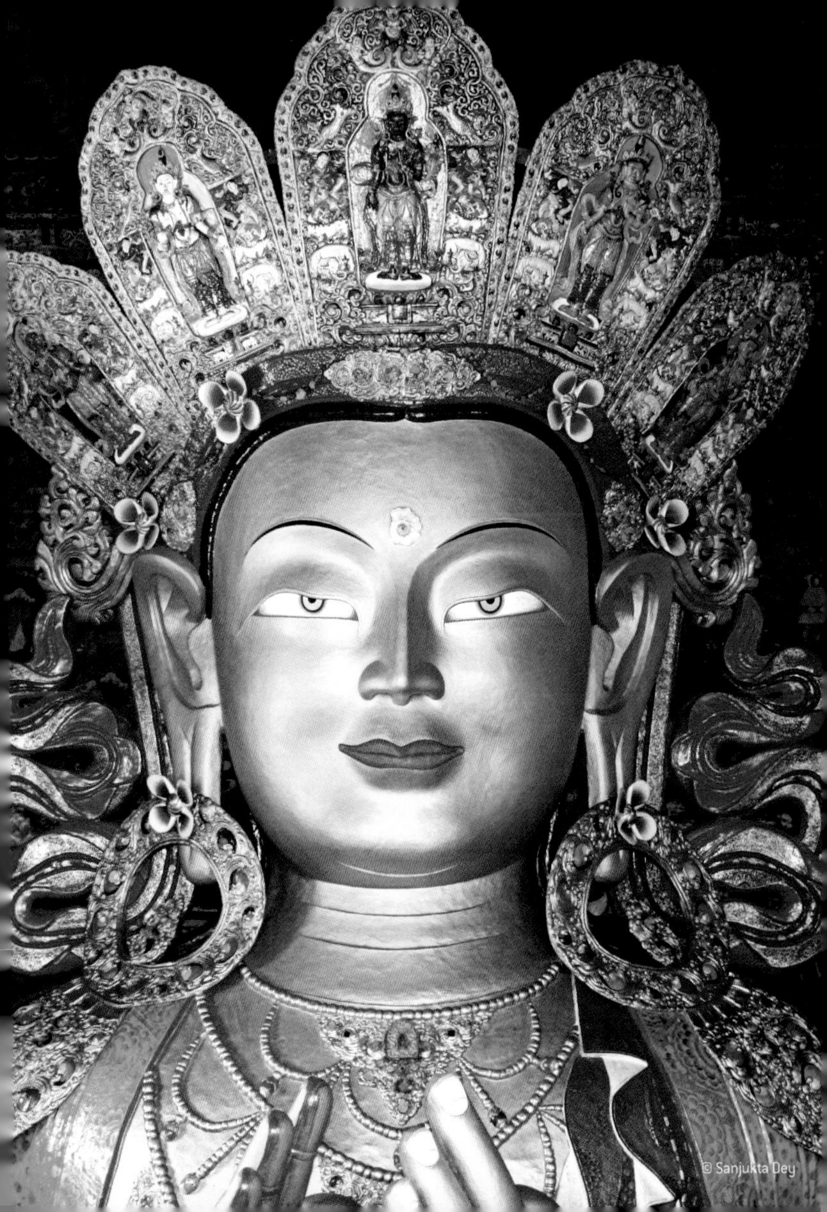
© Sanjukta Dey

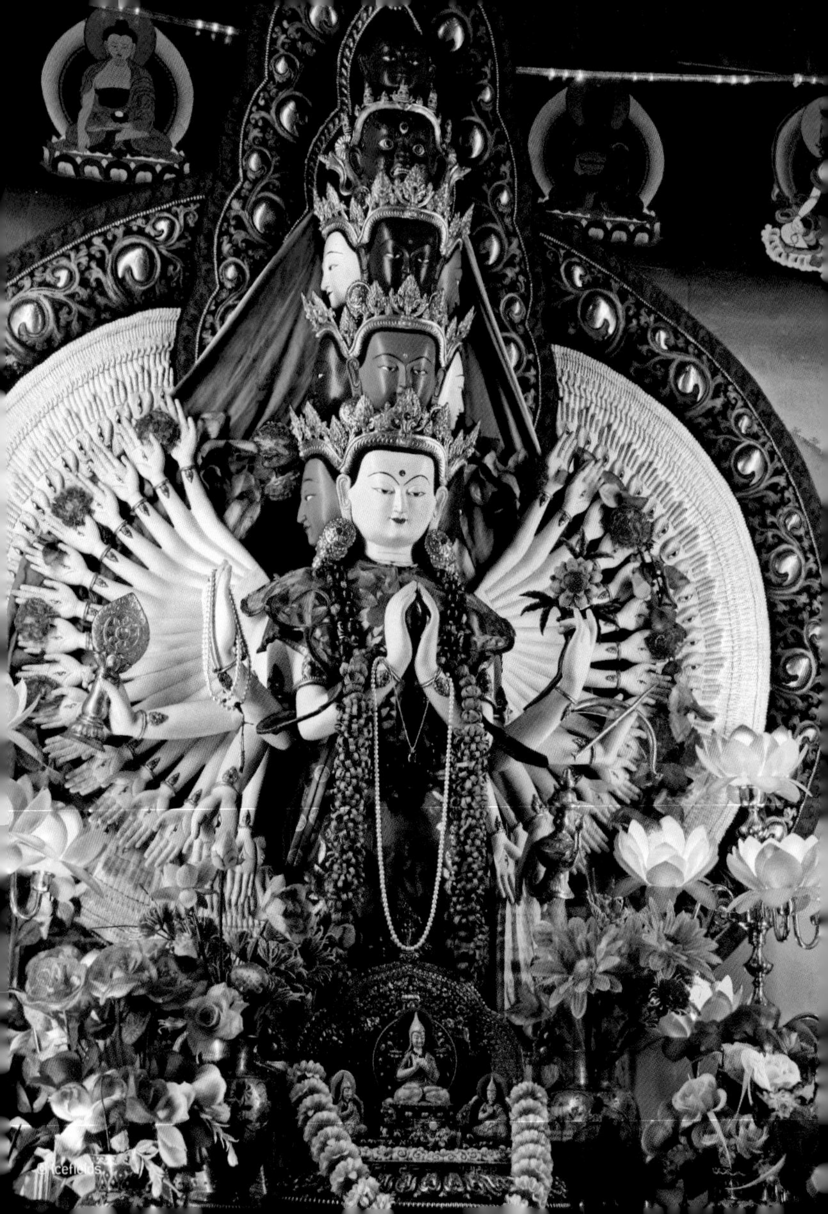

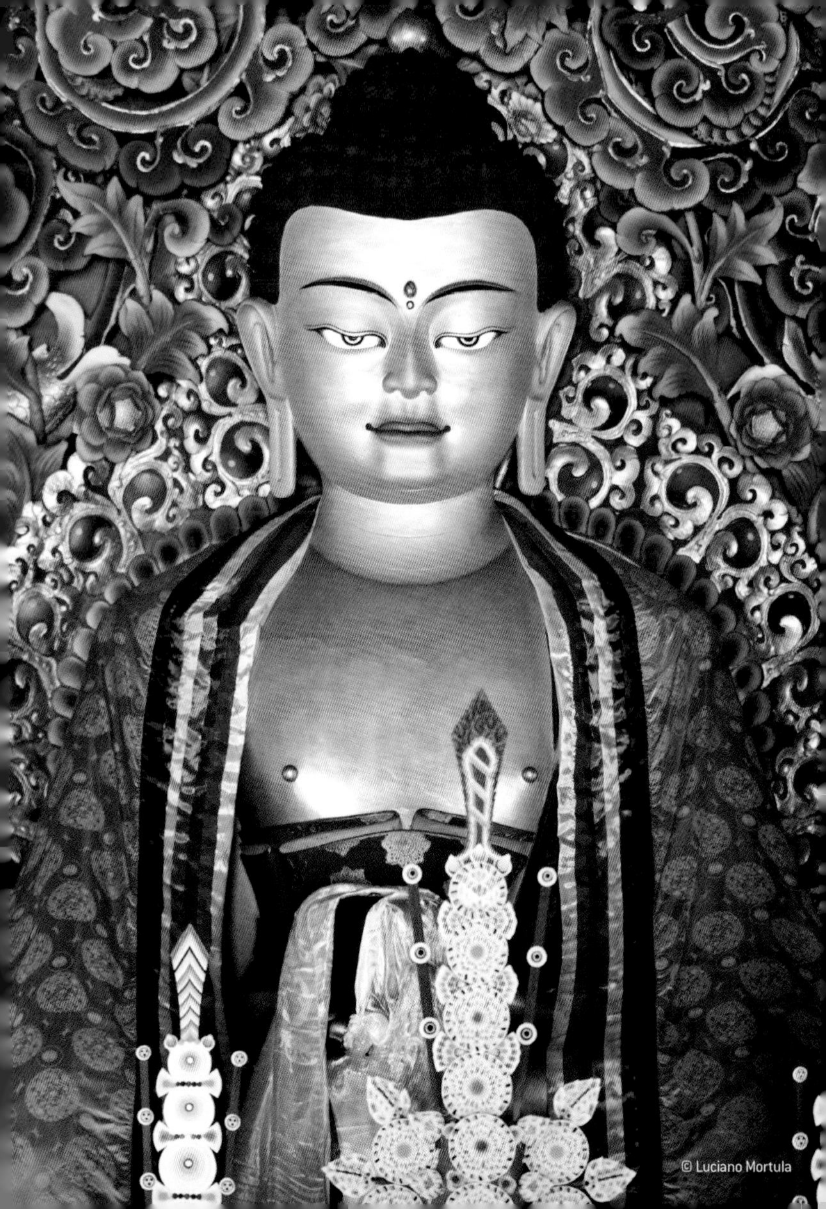

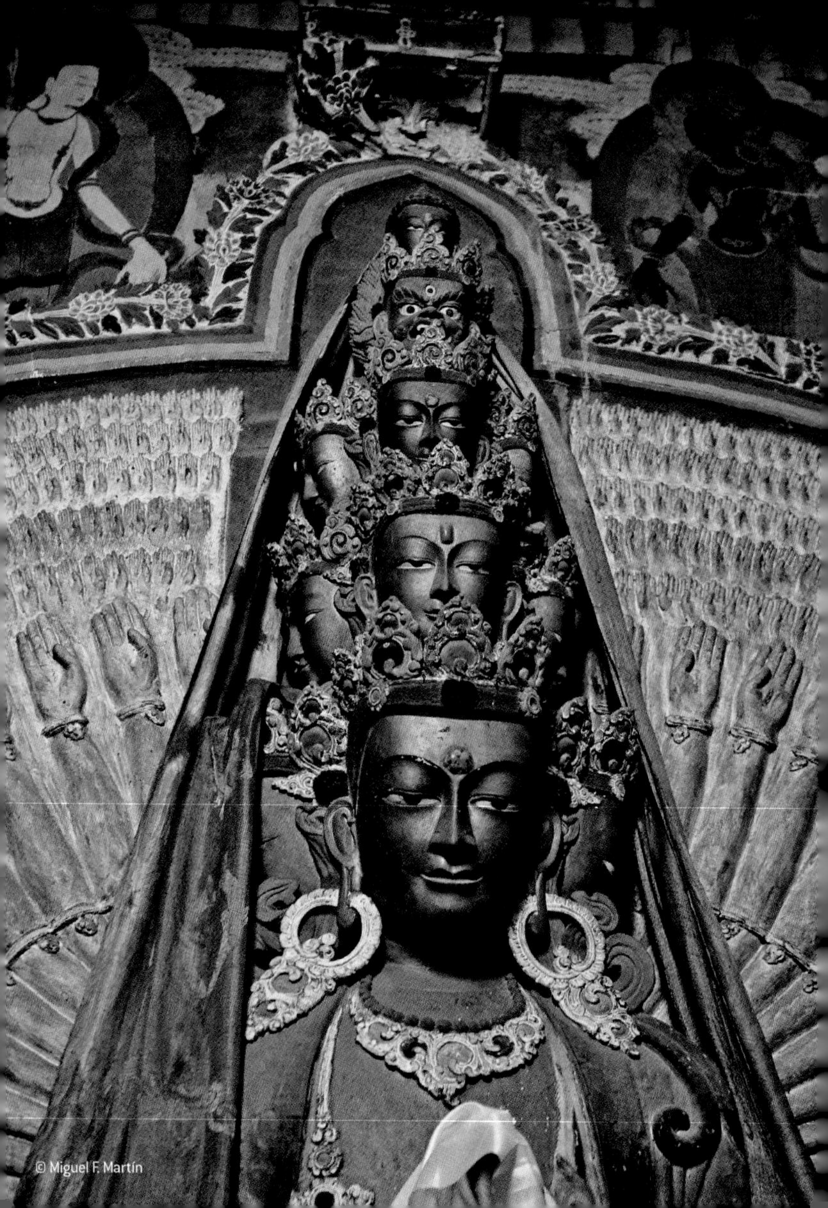

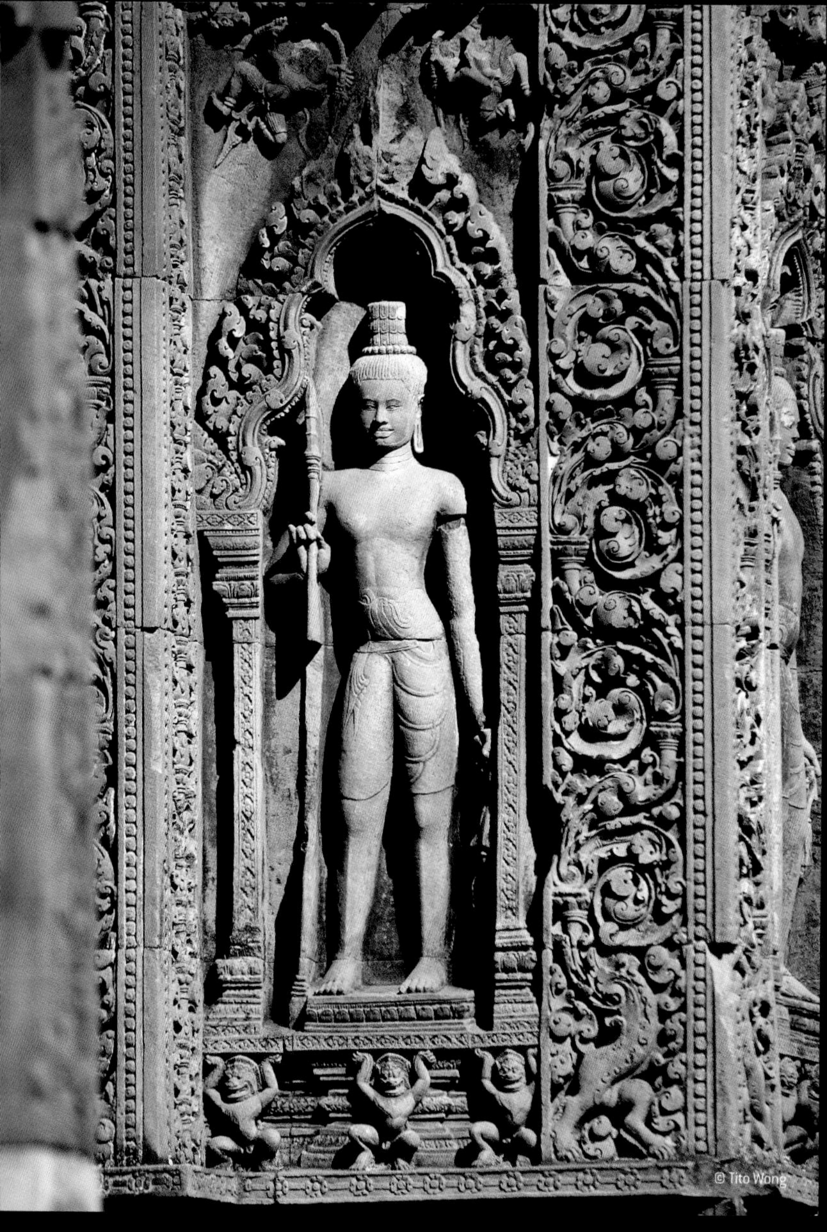

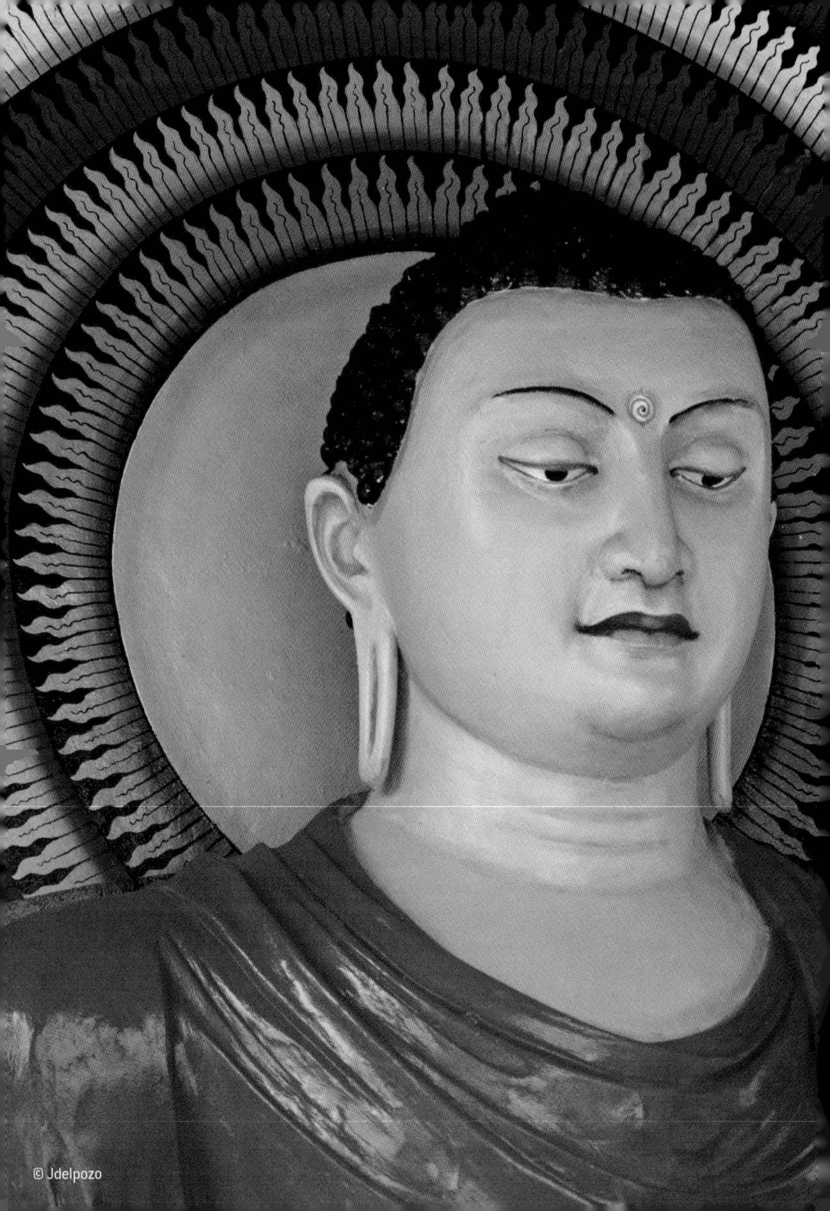

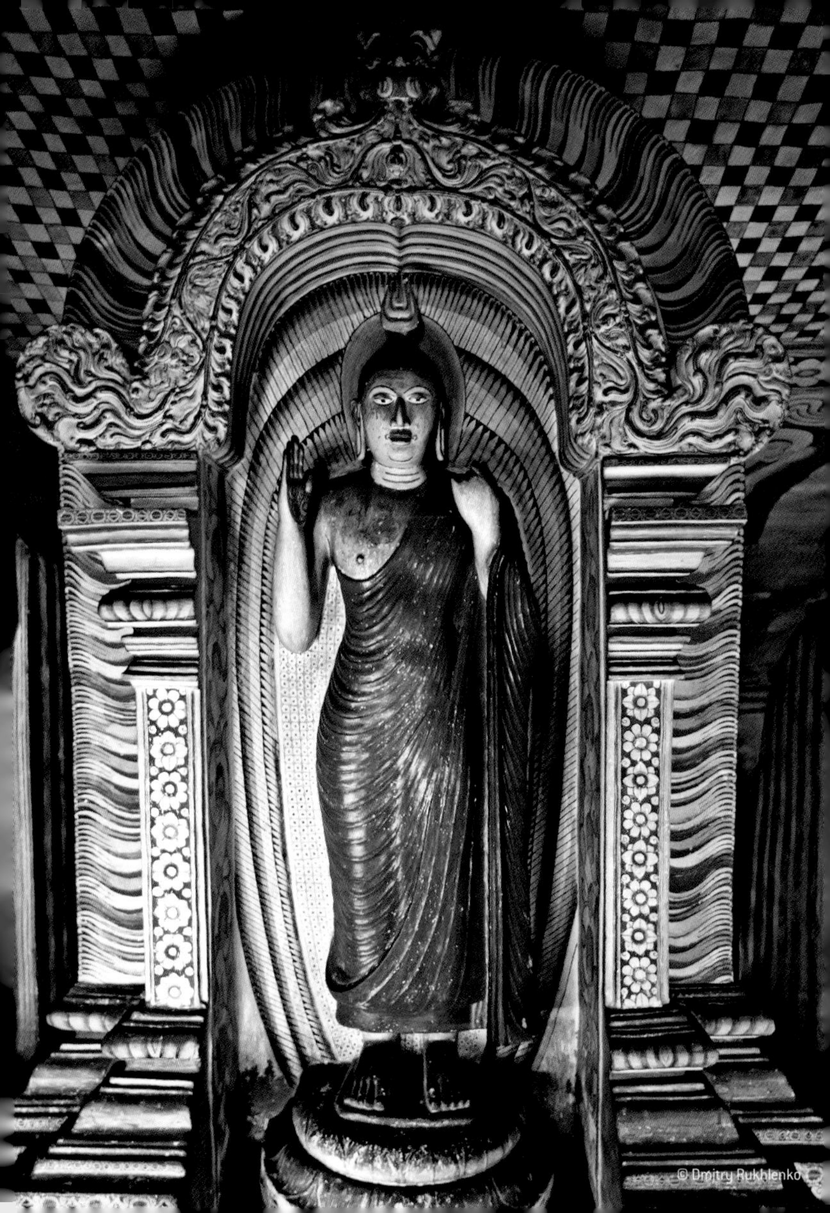
© Dmitry Rukhlenko

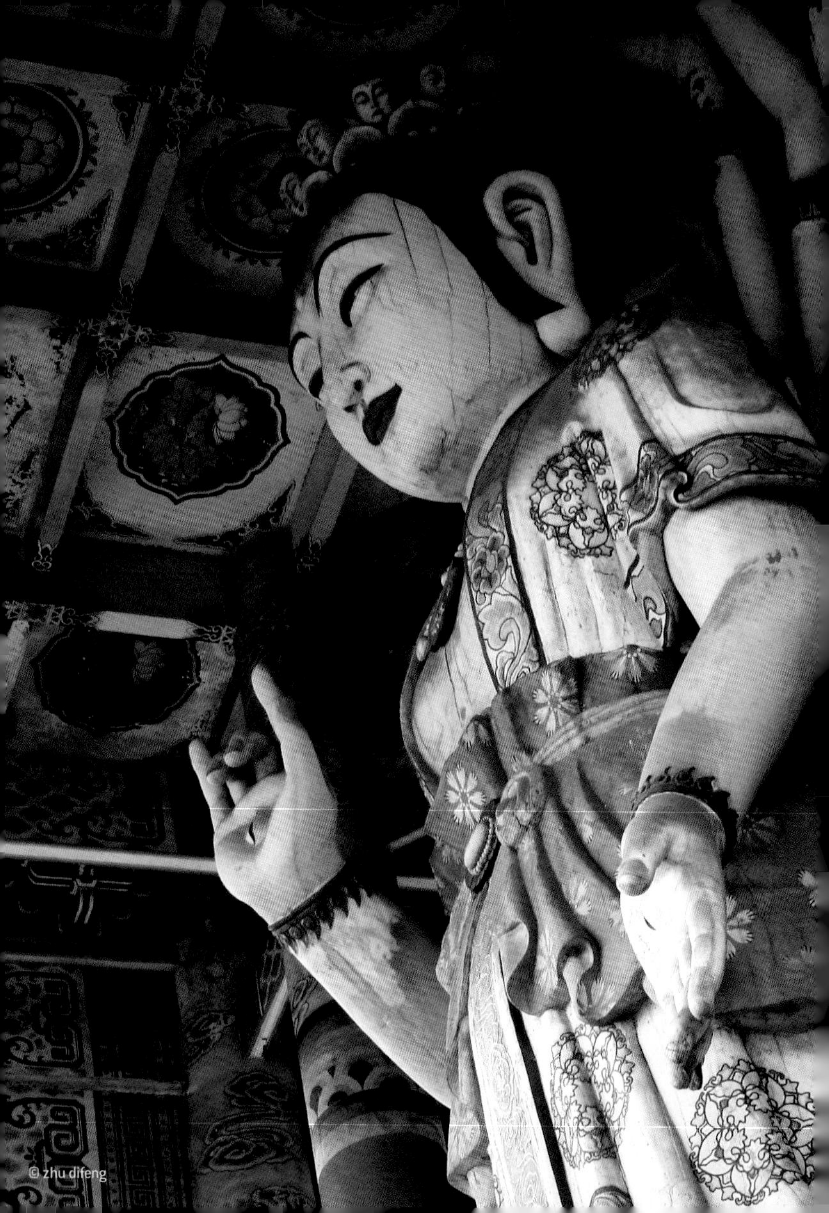

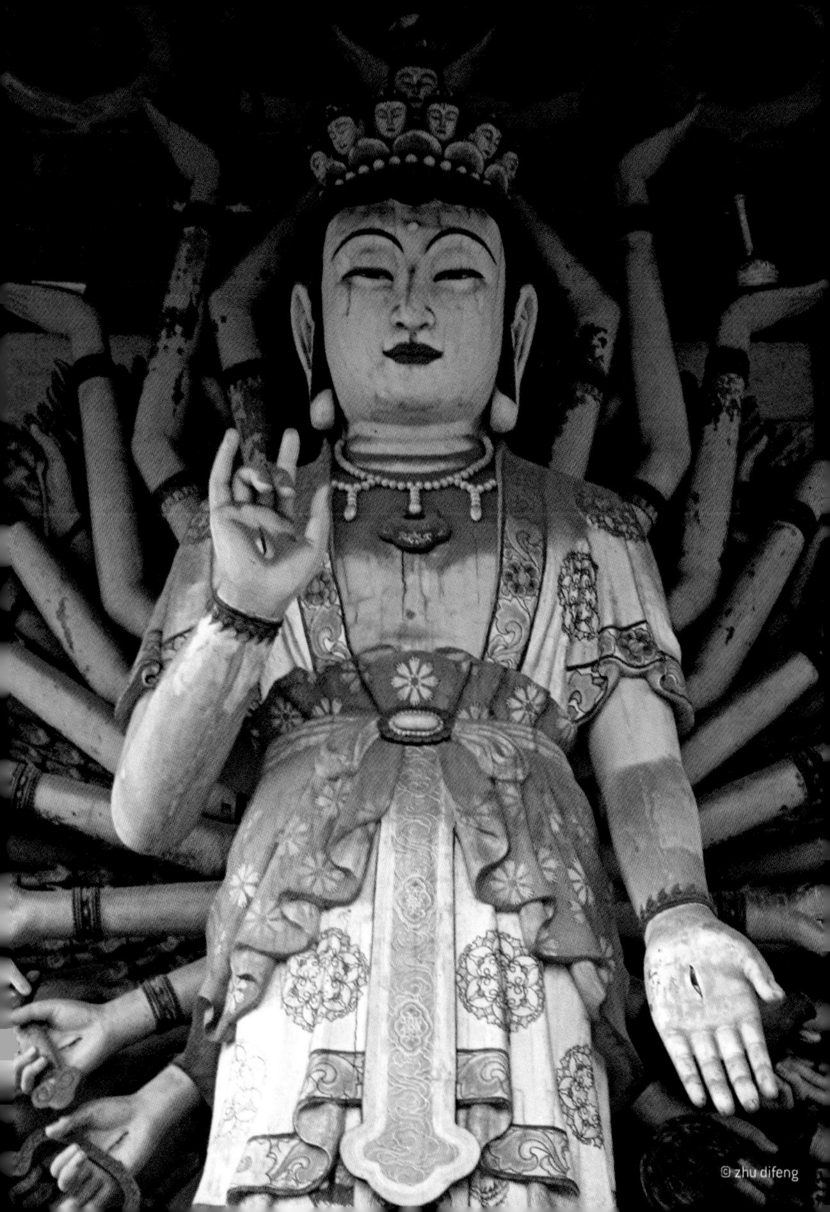

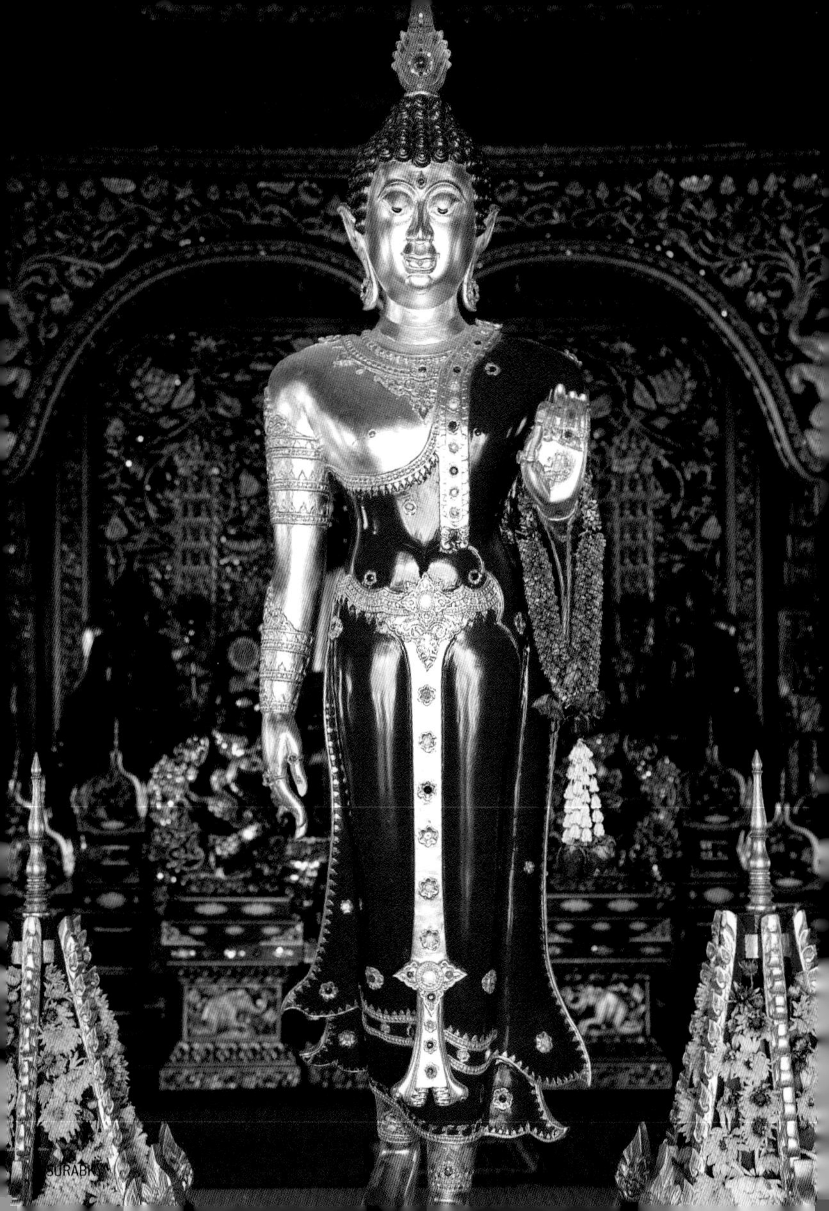

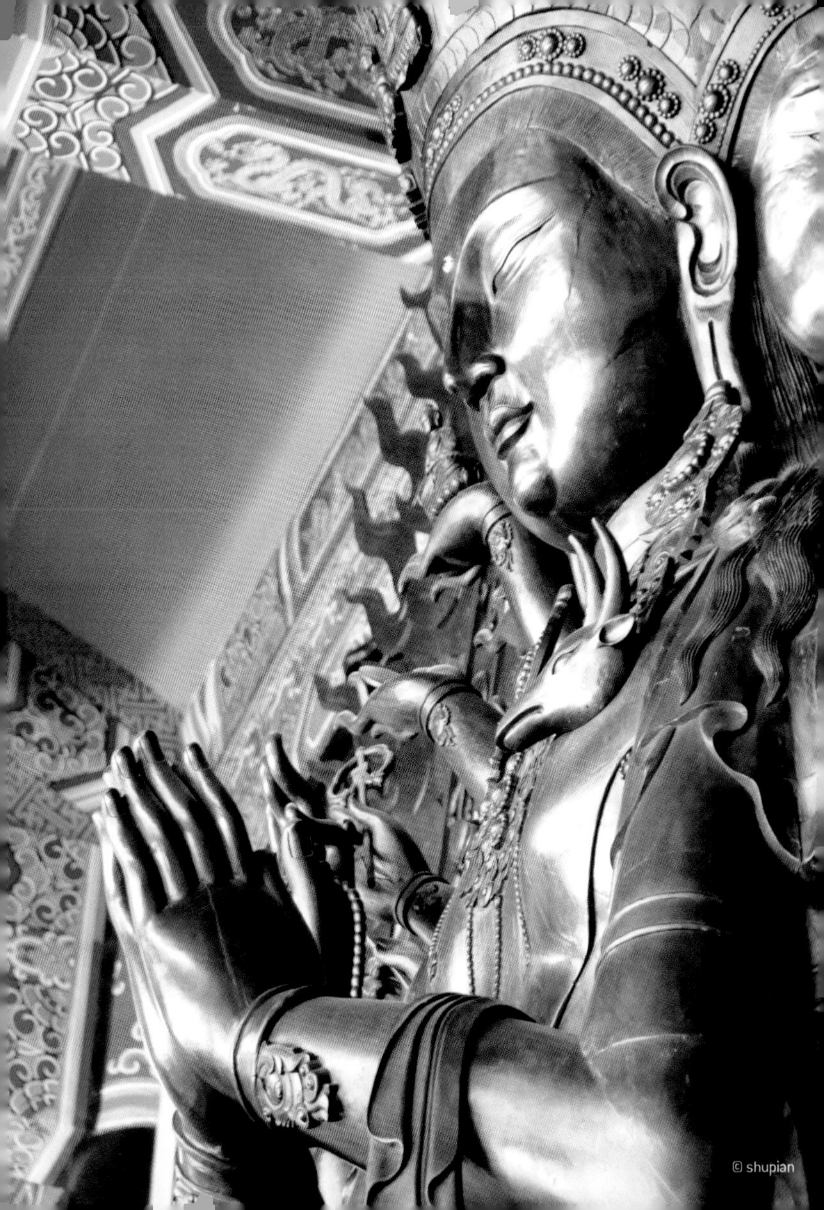
© shupian

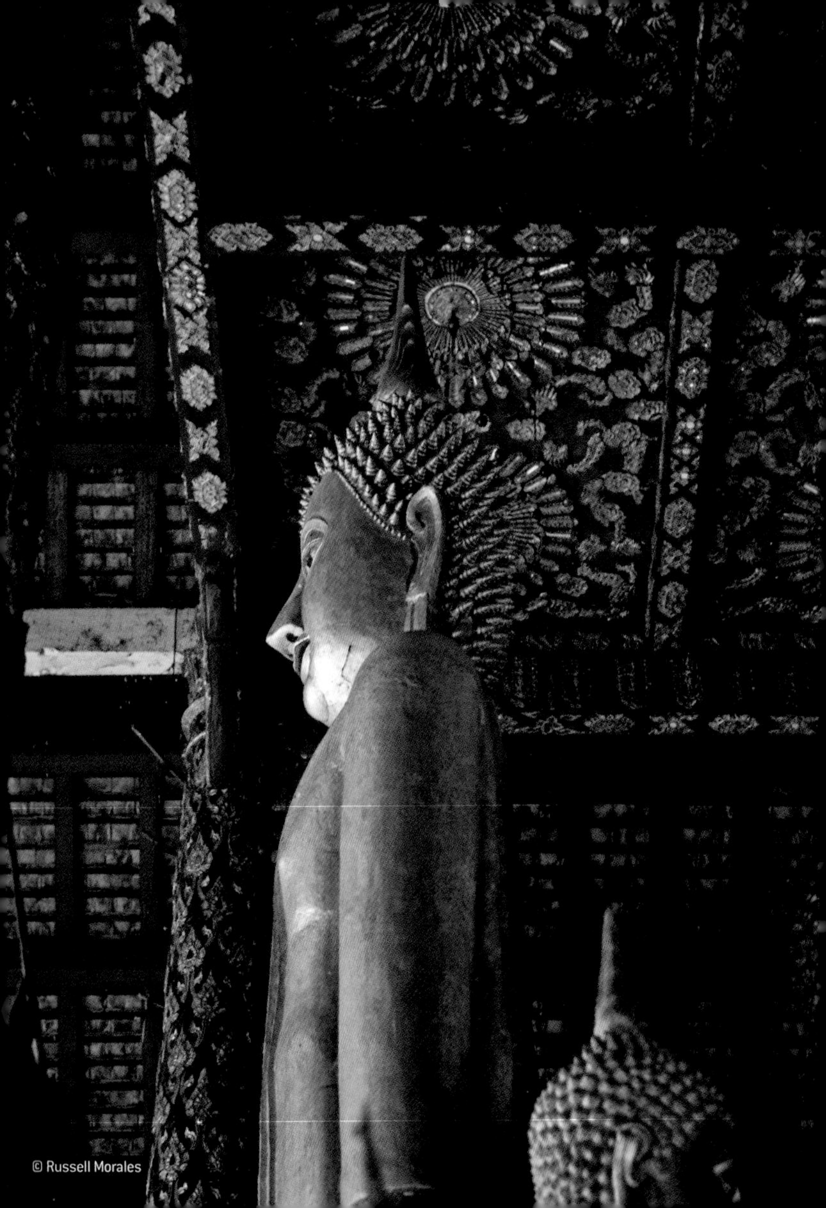

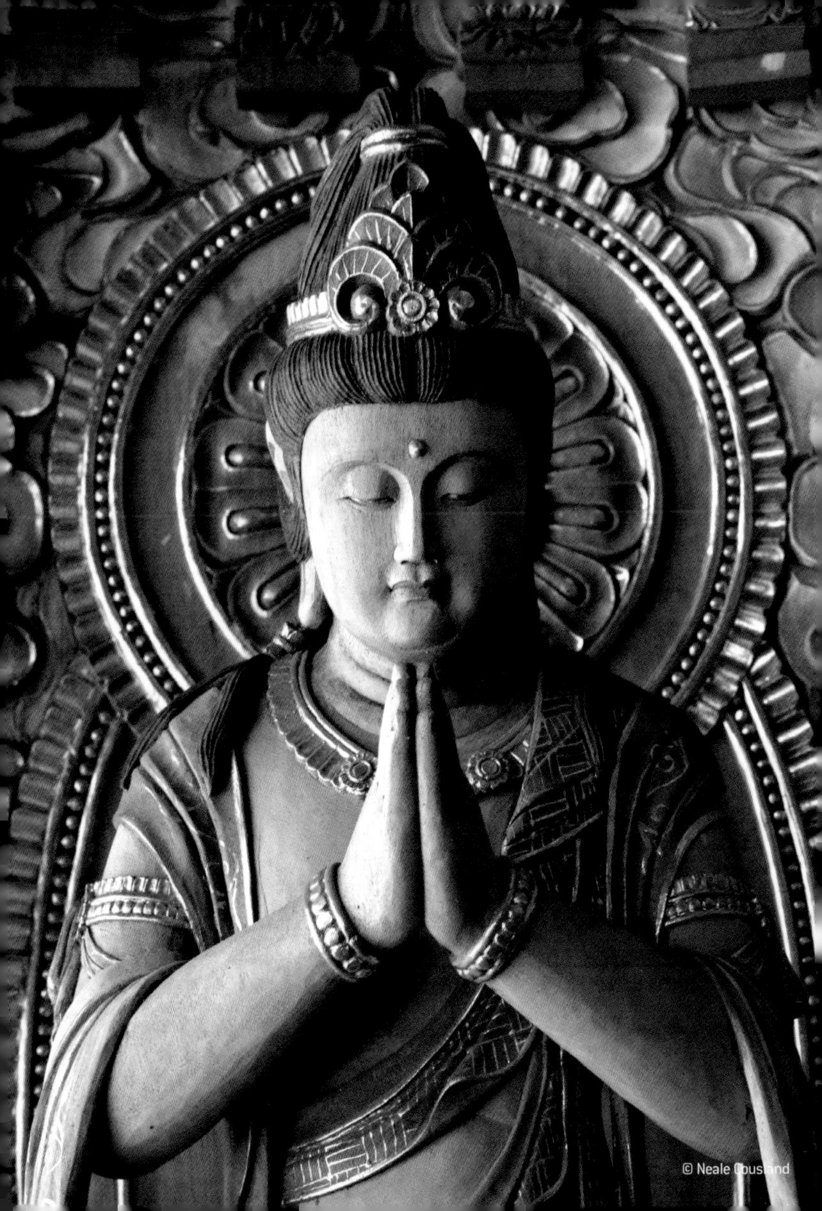

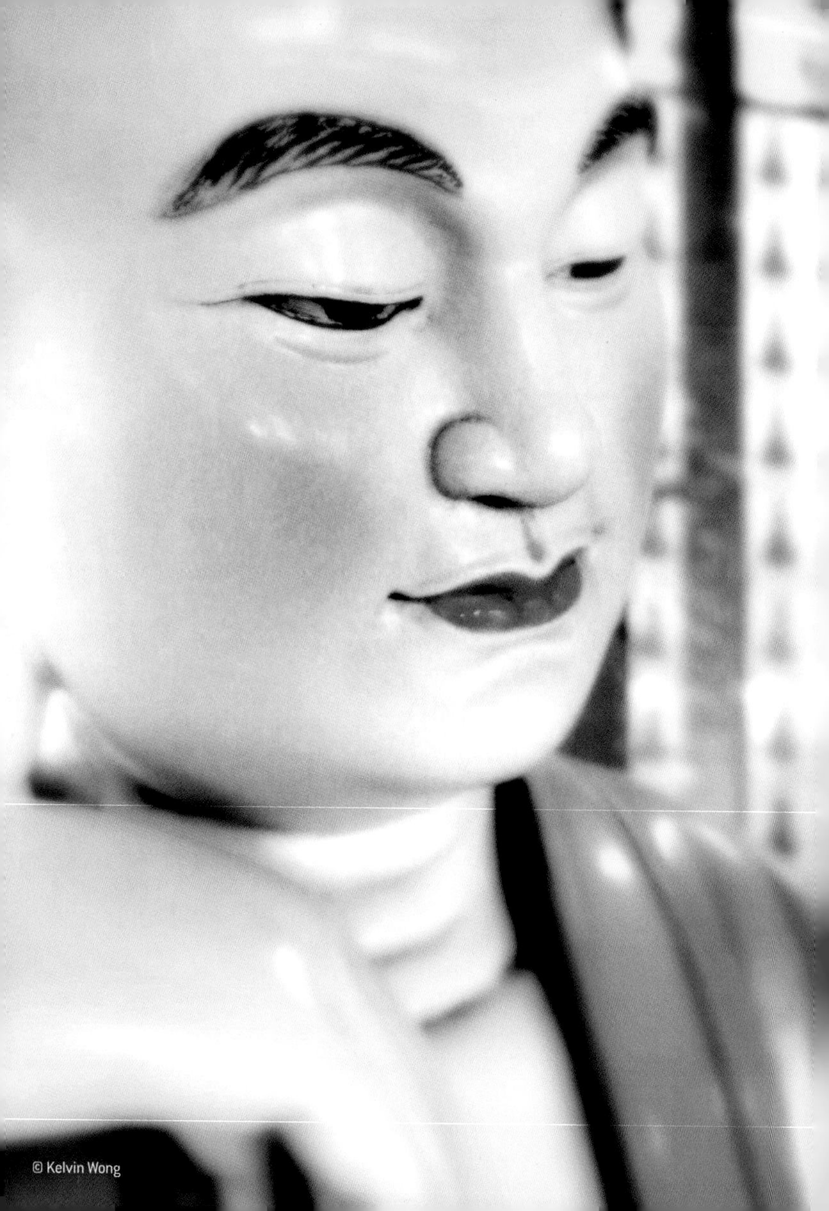

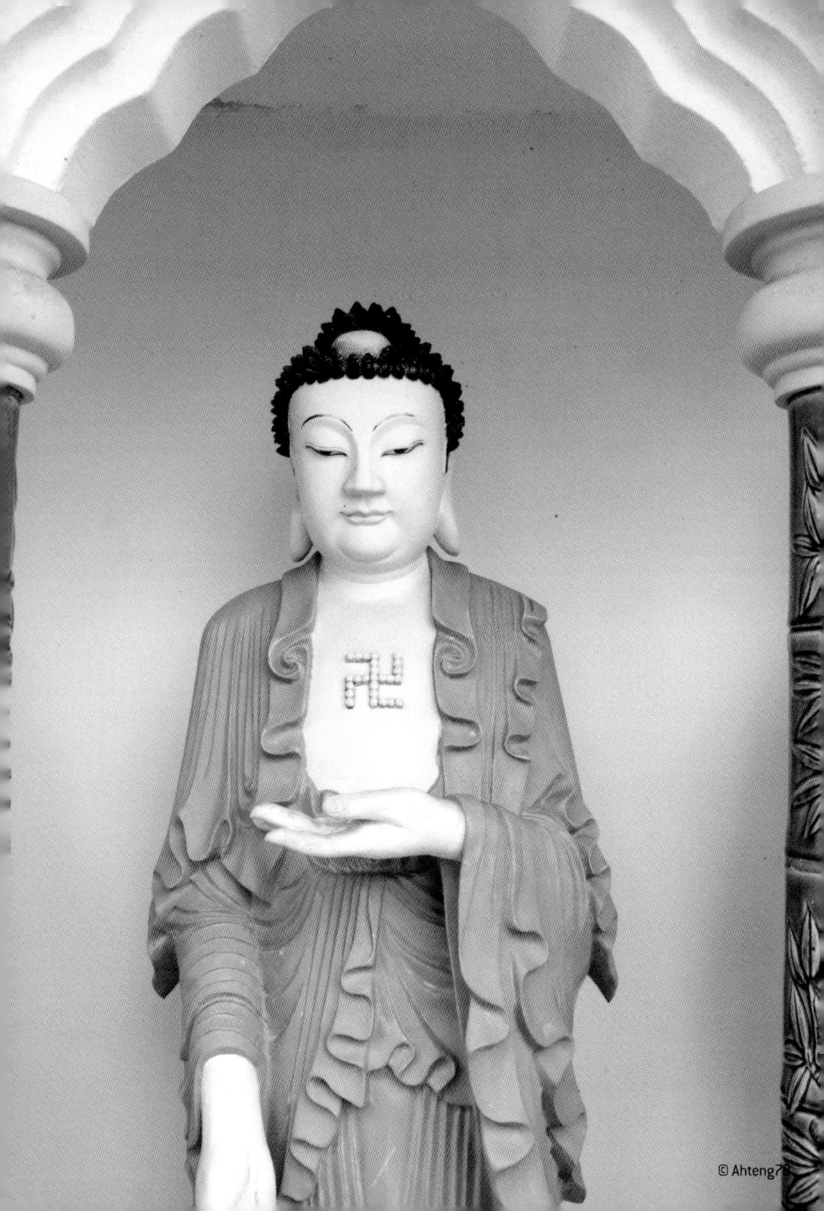

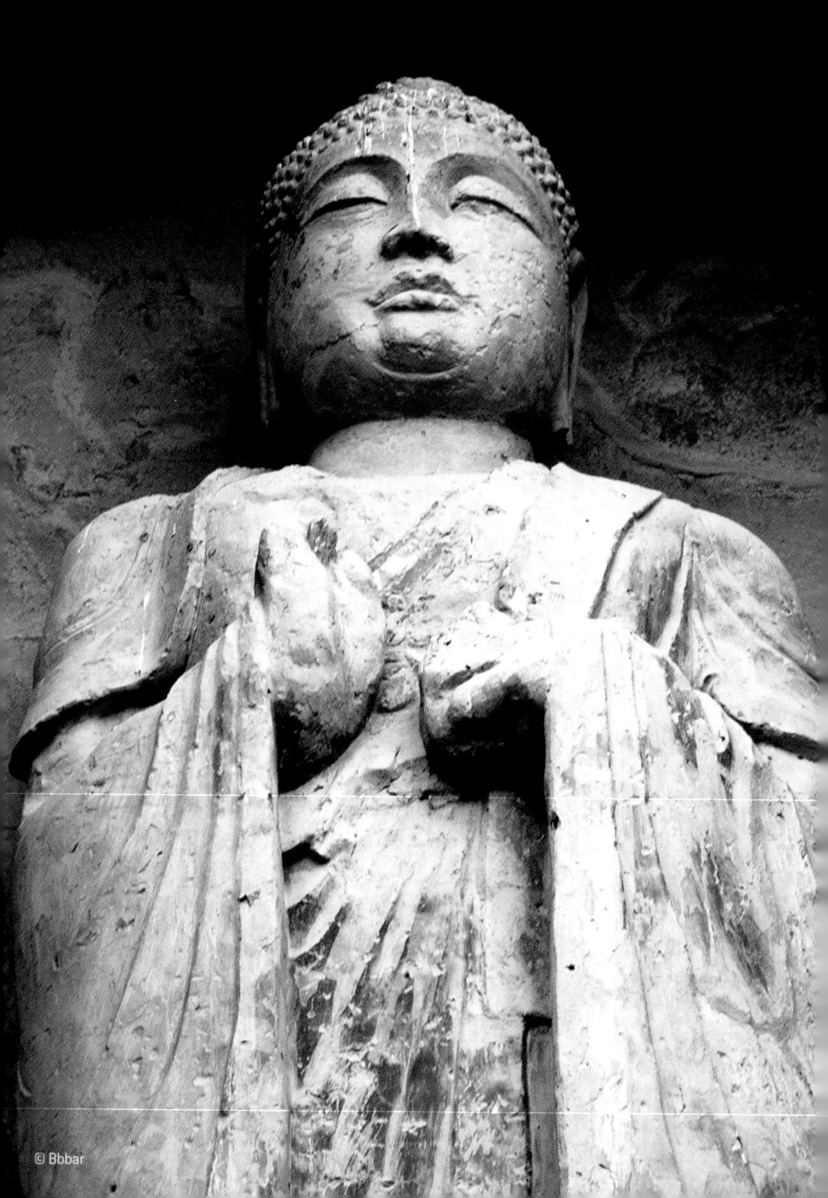

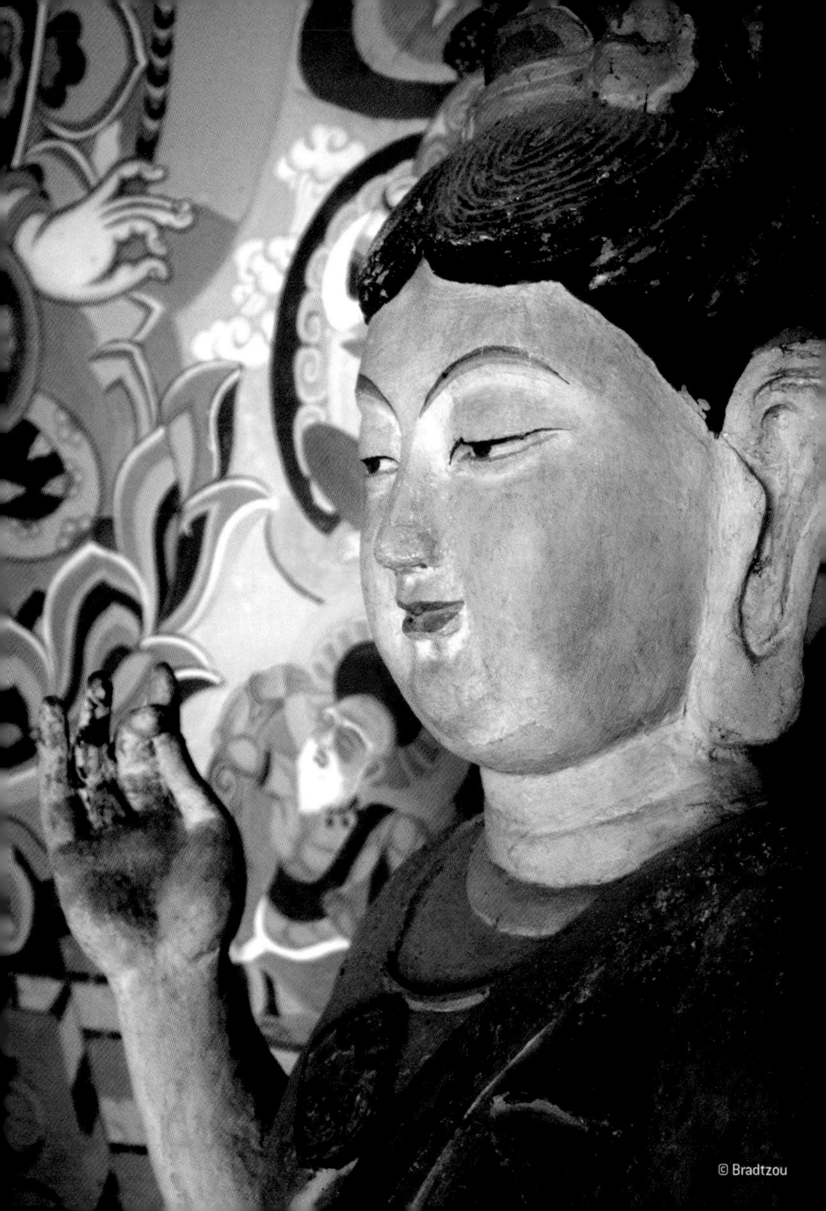

Resting Buddha
Bouddha allongé
Liegender Buddha
Liggende Boeddha

In the images where Buddha is resting one can see some of his other sacred marks: the print of the Dharma wheel with one thousand rays. The word “Dharma” is of sand script origin and can be translated as “social order”, “virtue” or good conduct”.
The Dharma wheel is the oldest Buddhist symbol found in Indian art and its clear marking on the soles of Buddha’s feet are a reminder of the many twists and turns that the Buddhist path can take. Also, they say that a true Buddha walks as though he were floating in the air, but despite the fact that his feet do not touch the ground, (so as not to disturb the creatures that live in it), his footprint leaves the mark of the Dharma.
It is not a coincidence that many of the statues of the resting Buddha are gold in color: it is said that his skin is light and smooth for having offered help to all beings.

Sur les représentations de Bouddha allongé, on peut voir d’autres marques sacrées : la roue de Dharma aux mille rayons. Le terme dharma provient du sanskrit et peut se traduire par “ ordre social ”, “ vertu ” ou “ bonne conduite ”.
La roue de Dharma est le symbolc bouddhiste le plus ancien rencontré dans l’art indien. Les marques nettes sur la plante des pieds de Bouddha rappèlent les diverses tournures que peut prendre la voie bouddhiste. De plus, on raconte qu’un vrai Bouddha marche comme s’il flottait dans l’air, cependant, bien que ses pieds ne touchent pas la terre afin de ne pas perturber les créatures qui y vivent, il laisse sur son passage la marque du Dharma.
Ce n’est pas non plus une coïncidence qu’une grande partie des statues de Bouddha allongé soit dorée : il semblerait que sa peau est lumineuse et douce en raison de l’aide qu’il a apporté à tous les êtres.

Bei den Figuren, die den Buddhaliegend darstellen, kann man weitere heilige Merkmale feststellen: Den Abdruck des Dharma-Rads der tausend Speichen. Das Wort Dharma kommt aus dem Sanskrit und kann als „gesellschaftliche Ordnung", „Tugend" oder „richtiges Verhalten" übersetzt werden.
Das Dharma-Rad ist das älteste buddhistische Symbol, das in der indischen Kunst gefunden wurde, und seine deutlichen Abdrücke auf den Fußsohlen des Buddha erinnern an die vielen Wendungen, die der buddhistische Weg nehmen kann. Außerdem wird gesagt, dass ein echter Buddha läuft, als ob er in der Luft schweben würde, aber obwohl seine Füße die Erde nicht berühren, um die Geschöpfe, die sie bewohnen nicht zu stören, hinterlässt er die Spur des Dharma.
Die große Zahl von goldfarbenen, liegenden Buddha- Statuen ist ebenfalls kein Zufall: Es wird vermutet, dass seine Haut leuchtend und weich ist, weil er allen Lebewesen Hilfe zuteil werden liess.

In de beelden waar Boeddha ligt kunnen andere van zijn heilige kenmerken worden opgemerkt: de afdruk van het Dharma-wiel met duizend strepen. Het woord dharma komt oorspronkelijk uit het Sanskriet en kan worden vertaald als "sociale orde", "deugd" of "juist gedrag". Het dharma-wiel is het oudste boeddhistische symbool dat in de Indische kunst is gevonden en de duidelijke afdrukken op de voetzolen van Boeddha herinneren aan de vele wendingen die het boeddhistische pad kan nemen. Bovendien wordt gezegd dat een ware Boeddha loopt alsof hij in de lucht zweeft, maar ondanks het feit dat zijn voeten de aarde niet aanraken om de schepsels die daar wonen niet te storen, laat hij de sporen van de Dharma achter.
Ook is de grote hoeveelheid goudkleurige liggende boeddhabeelden geen toeval: aangenomen wordt dat zijn huid lumineus en zacht is omdat hij alle wezens zijn hulp heeft geboden.

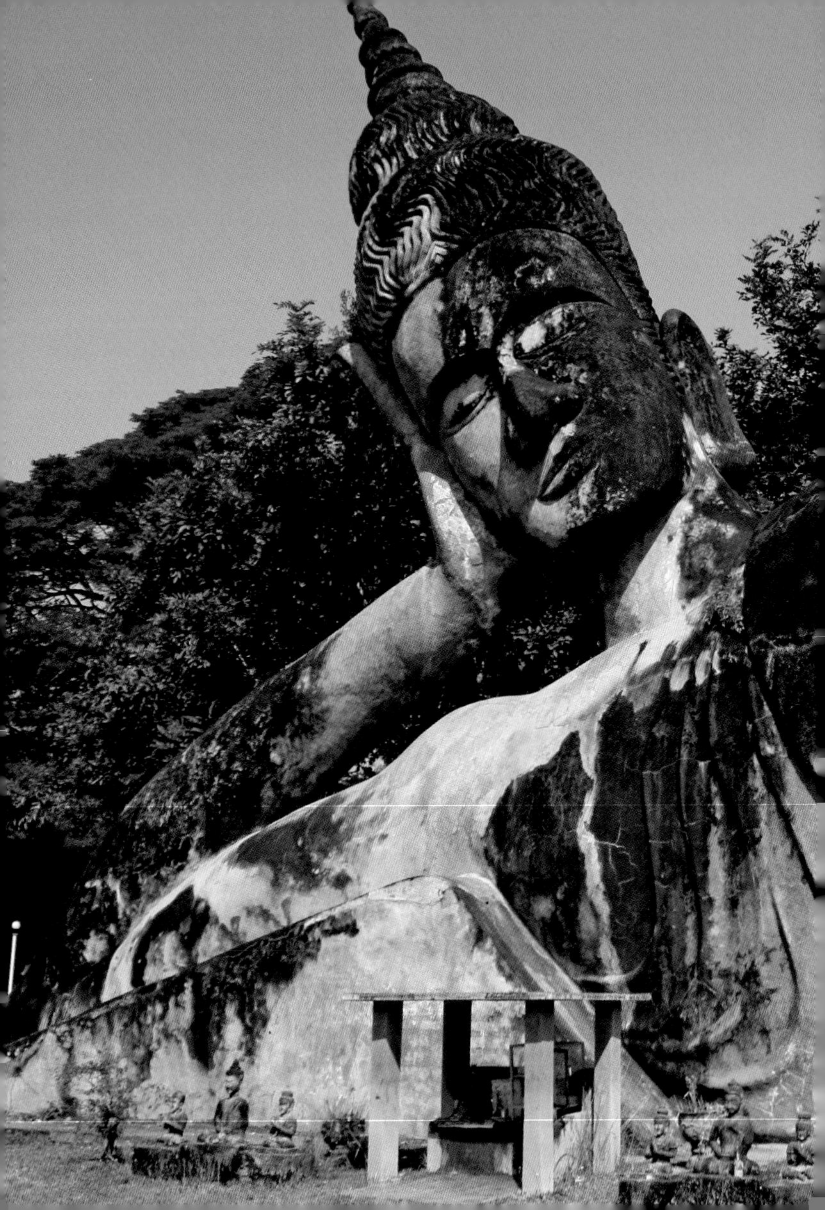

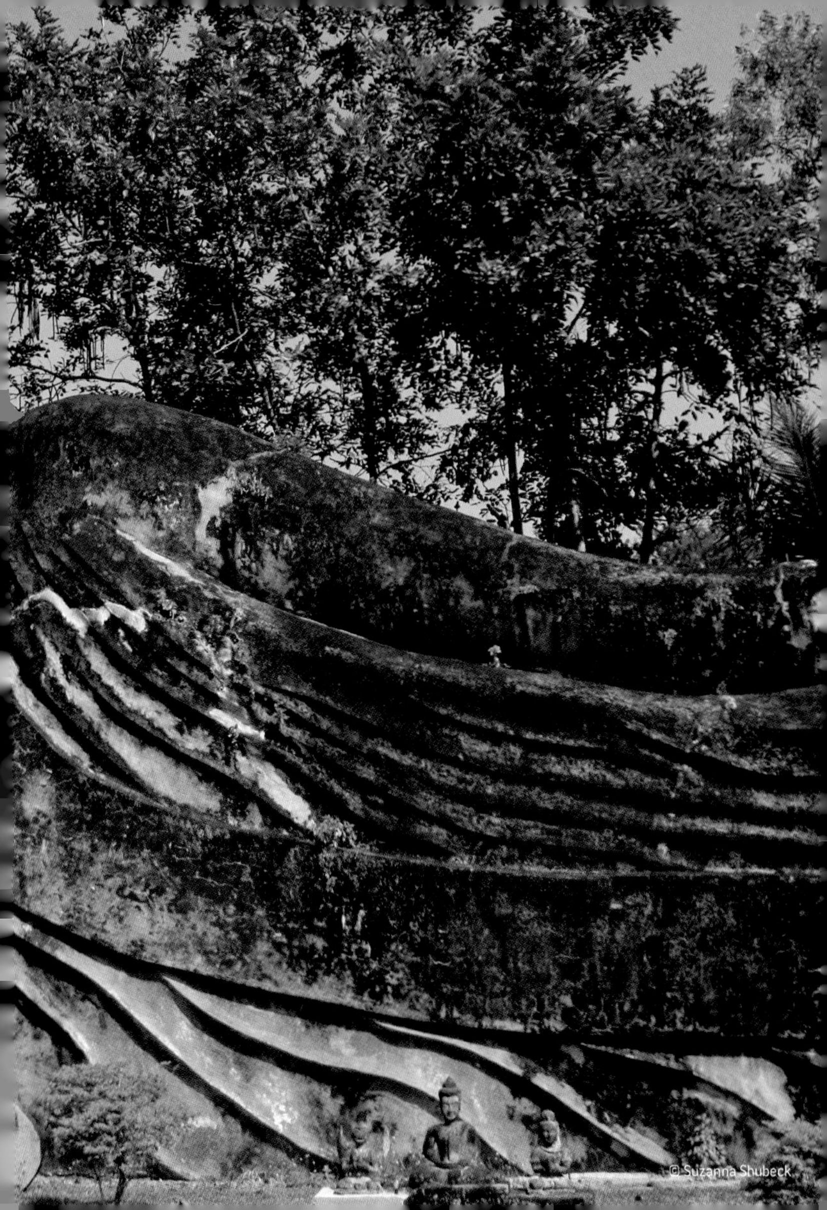
© Suzanna Shubeck

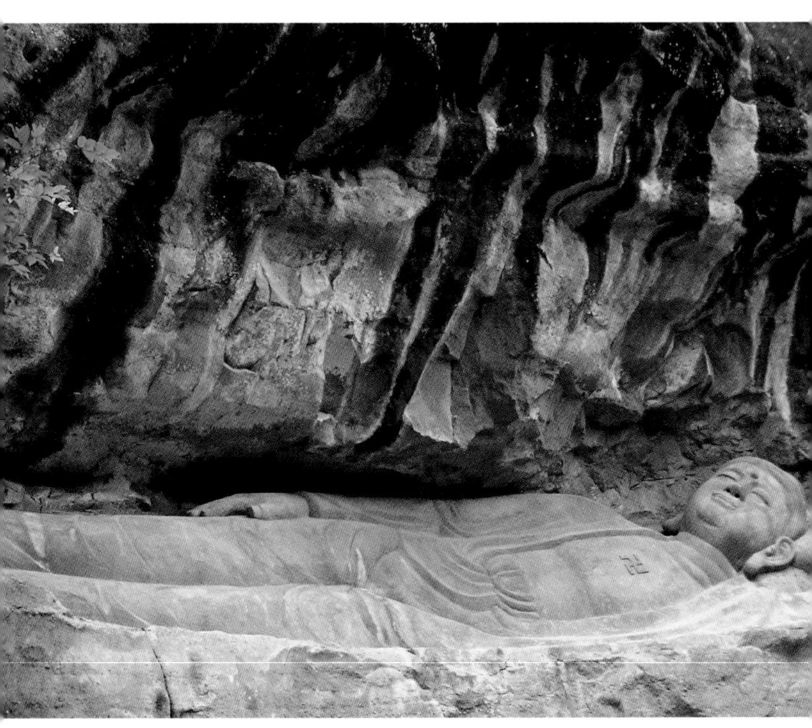

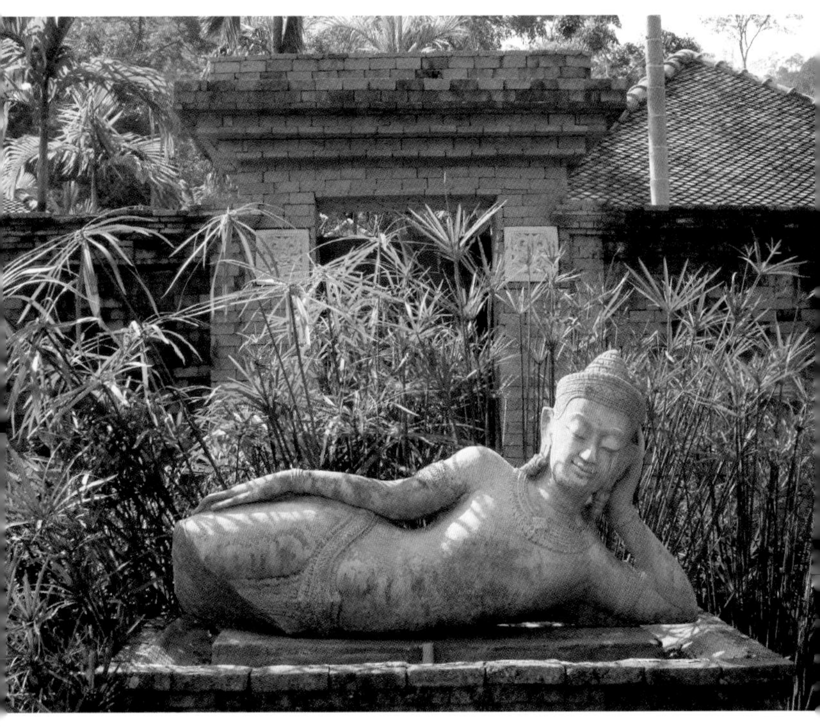

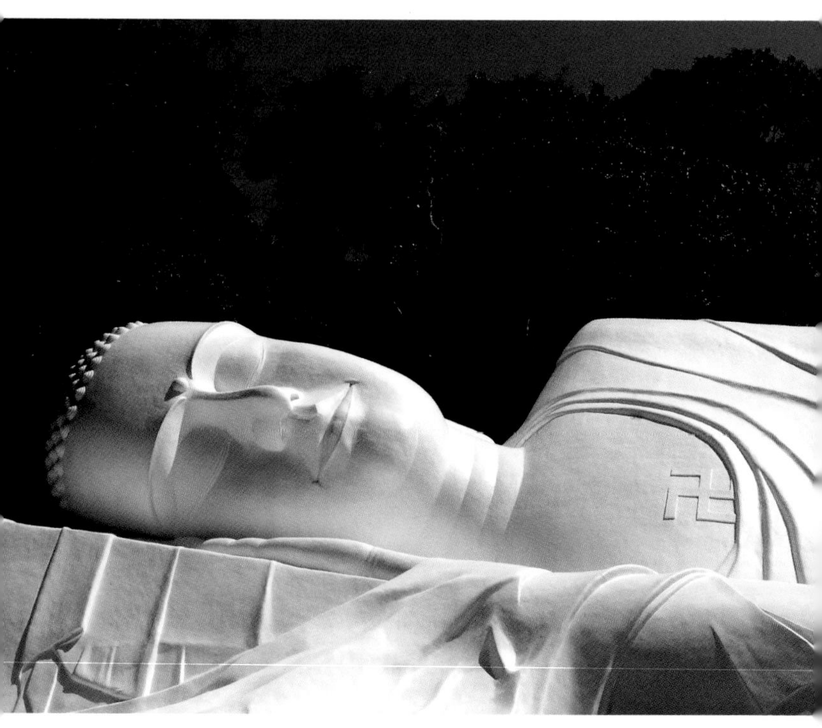

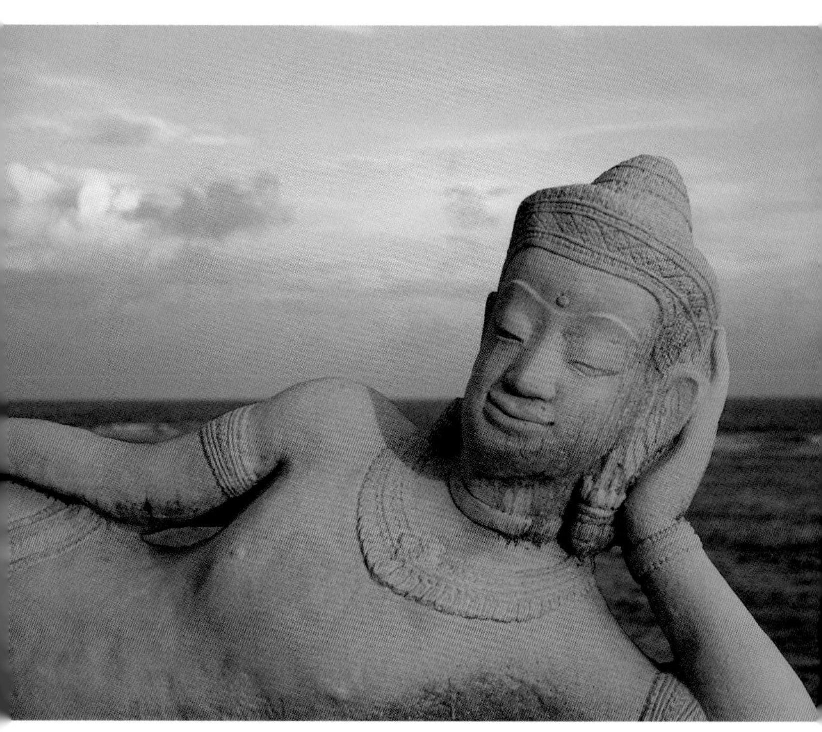

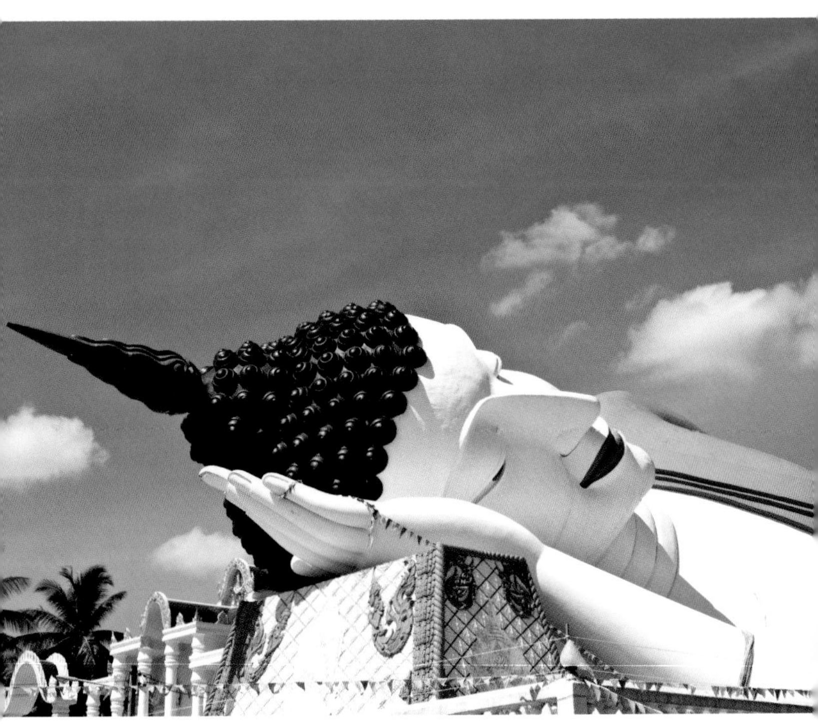

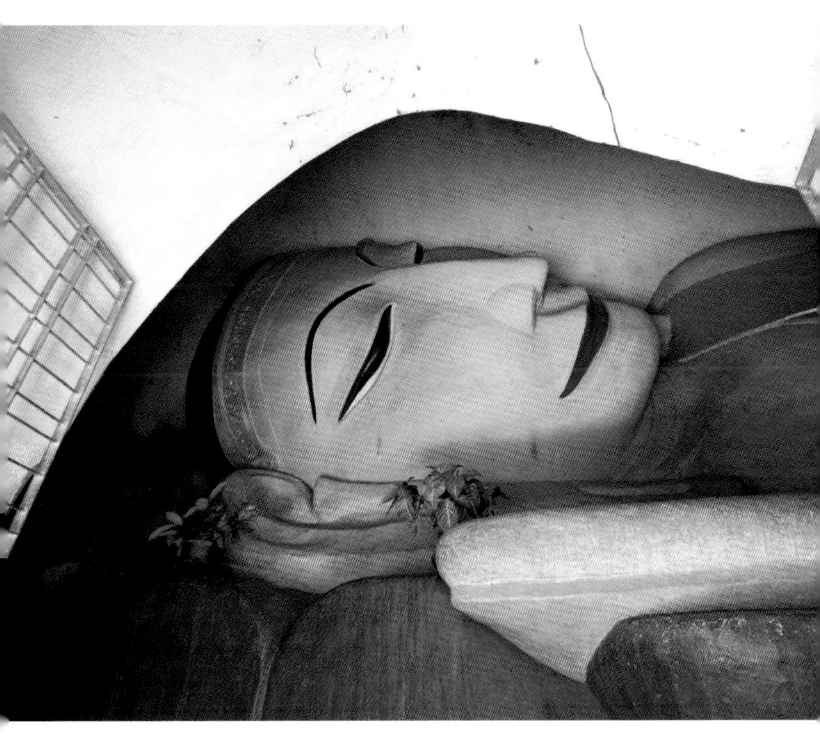

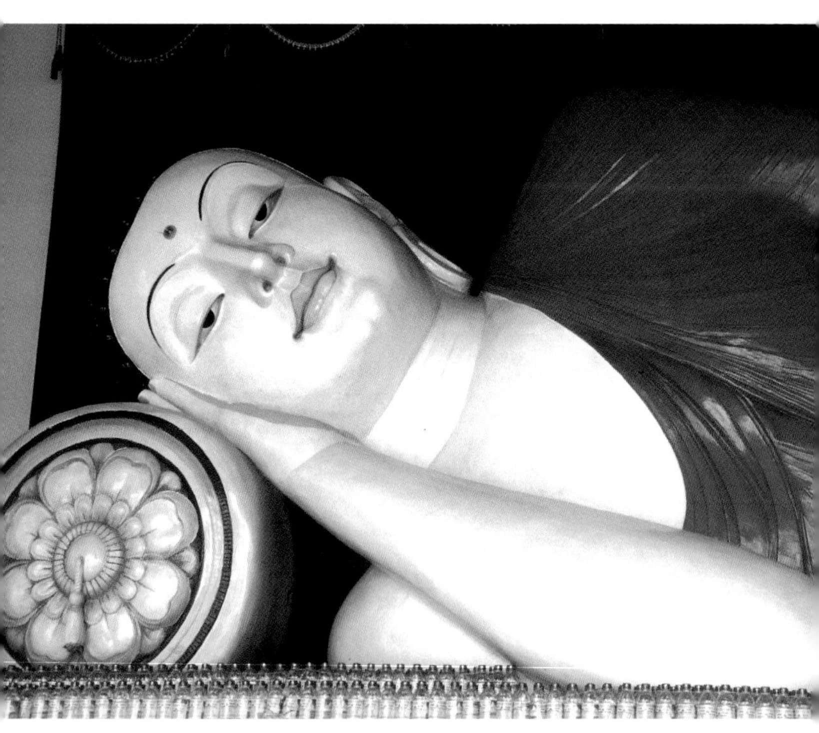

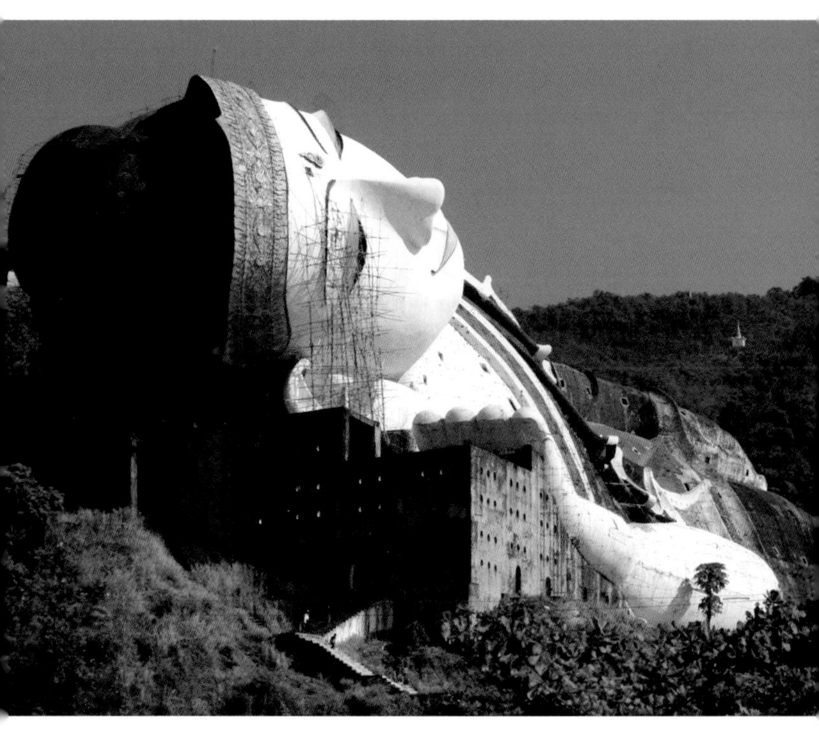

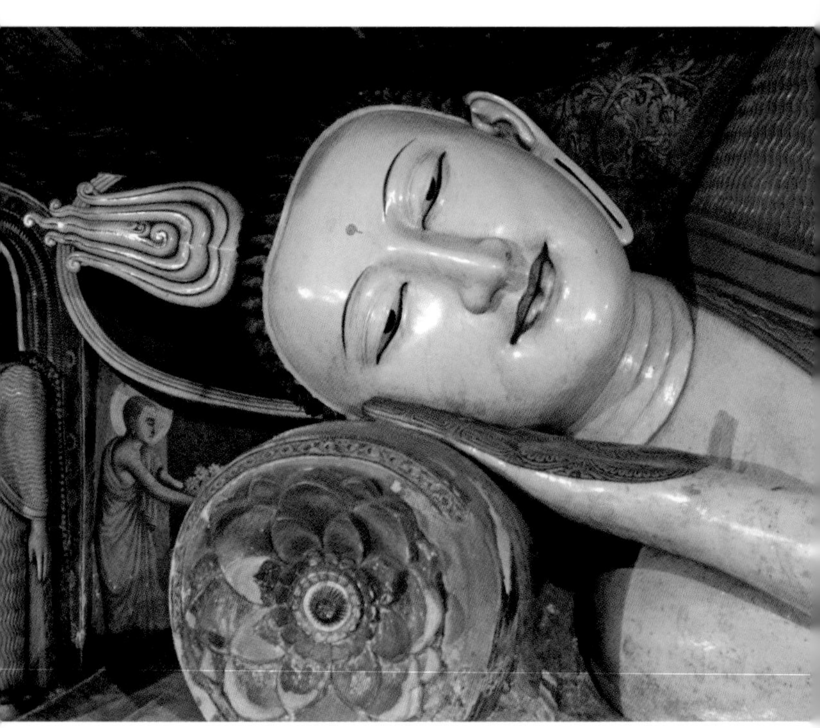

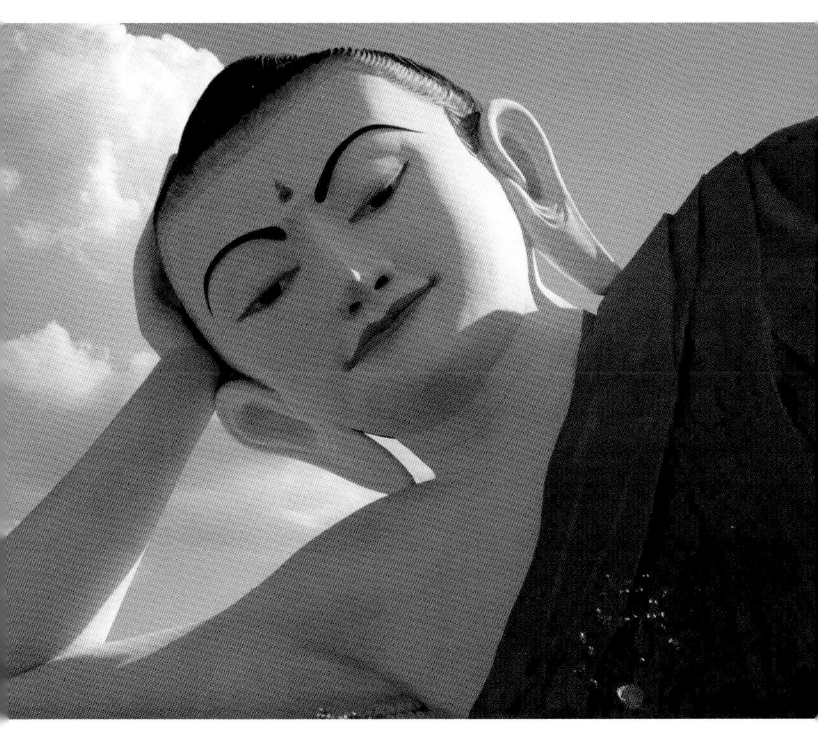

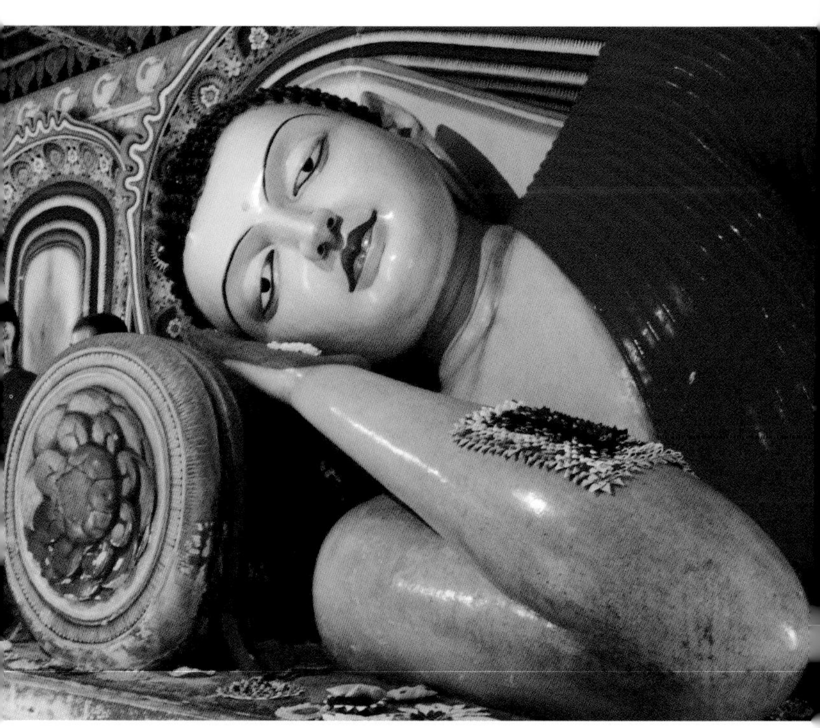

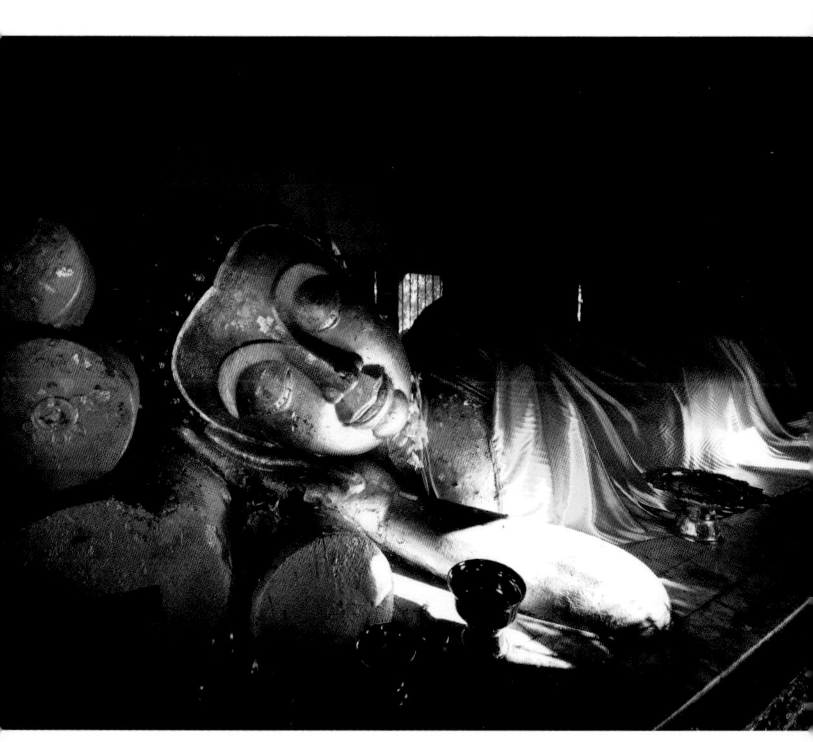

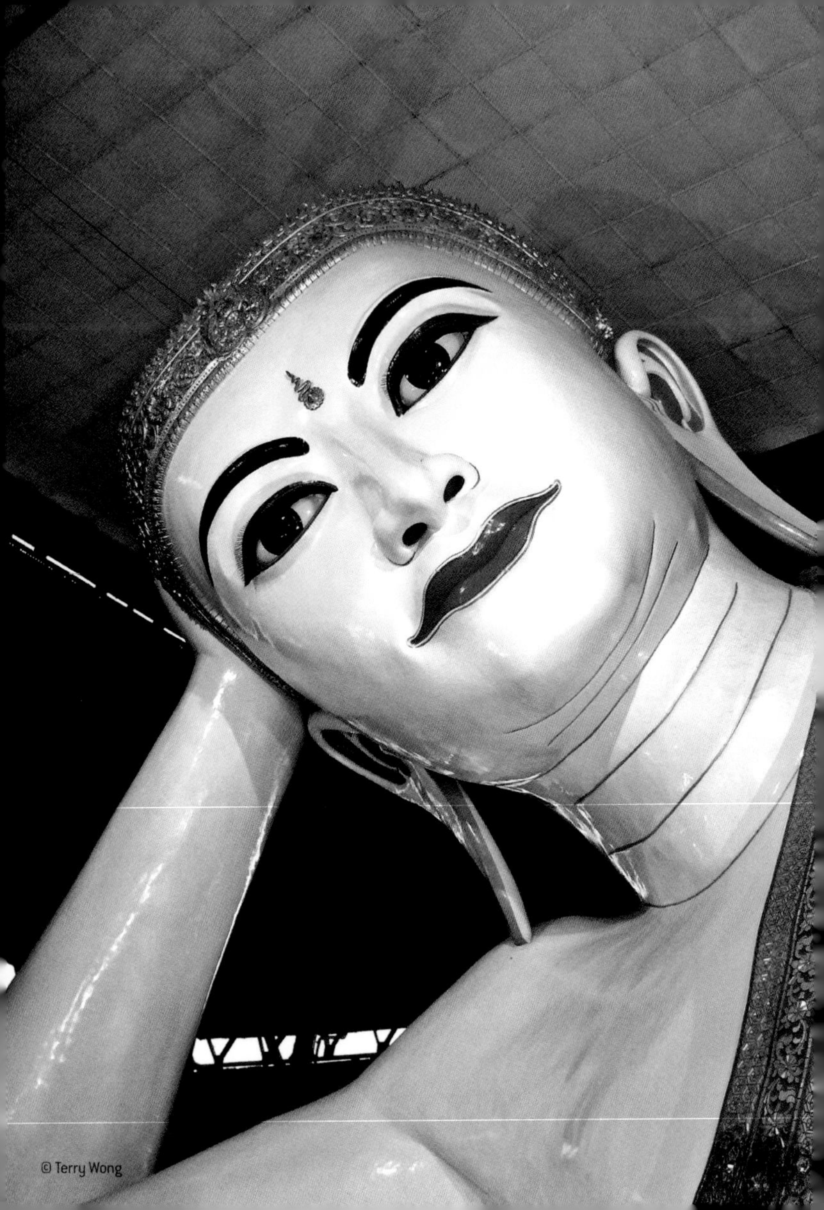

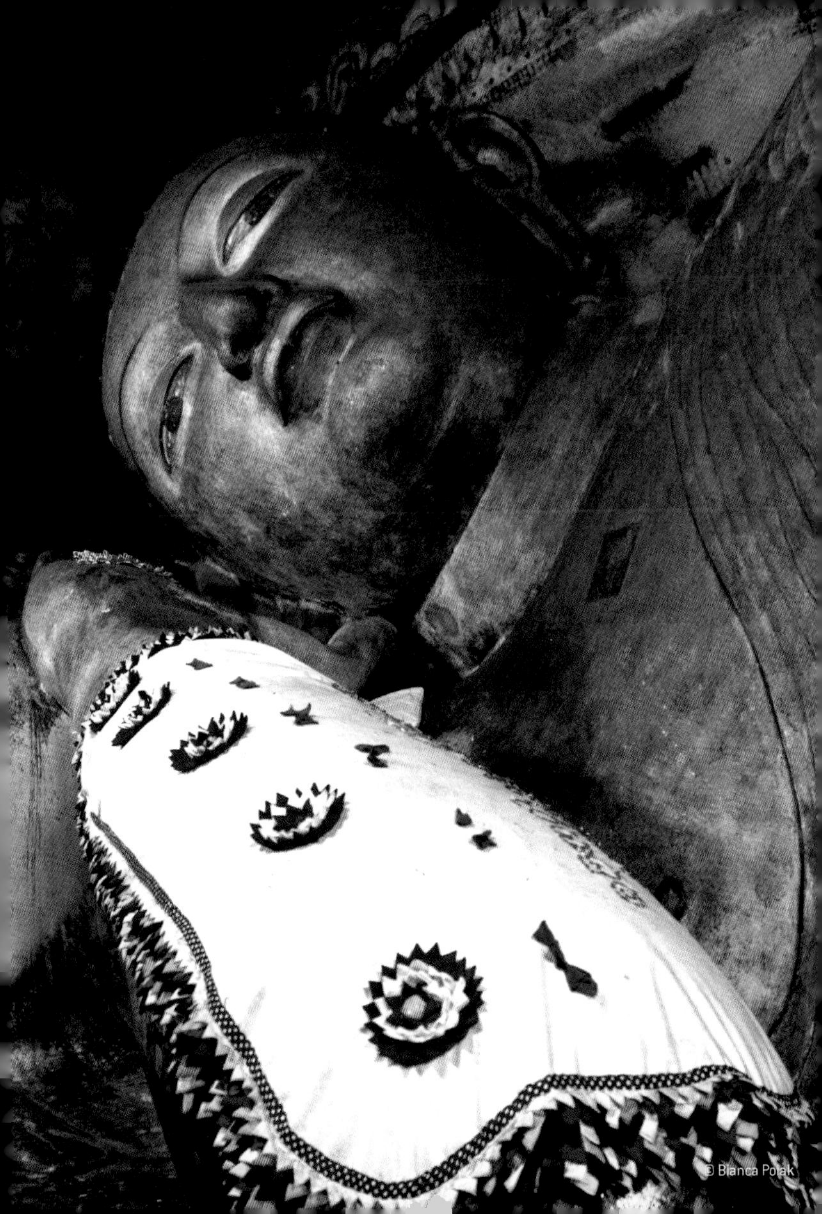

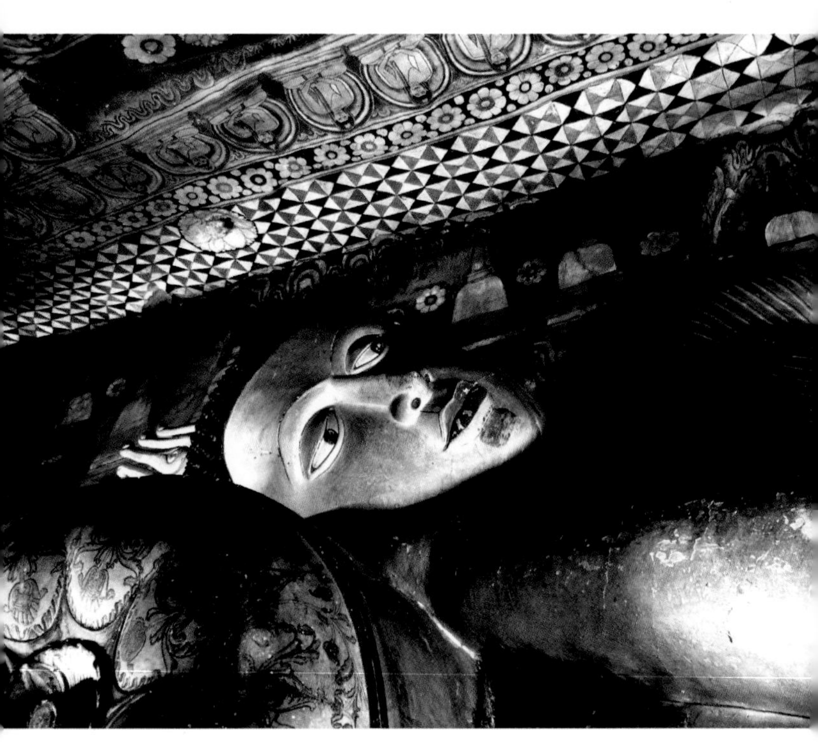

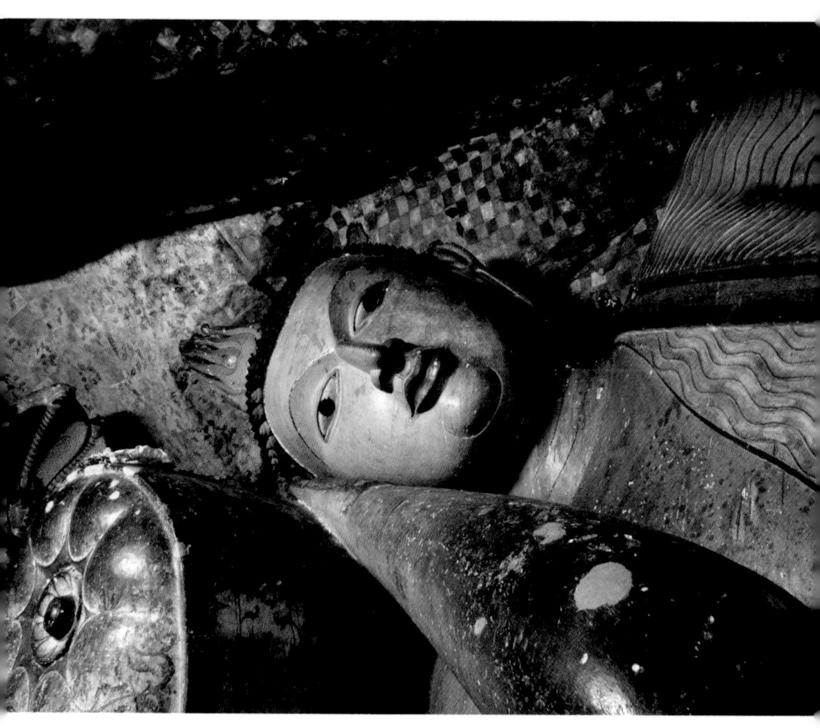

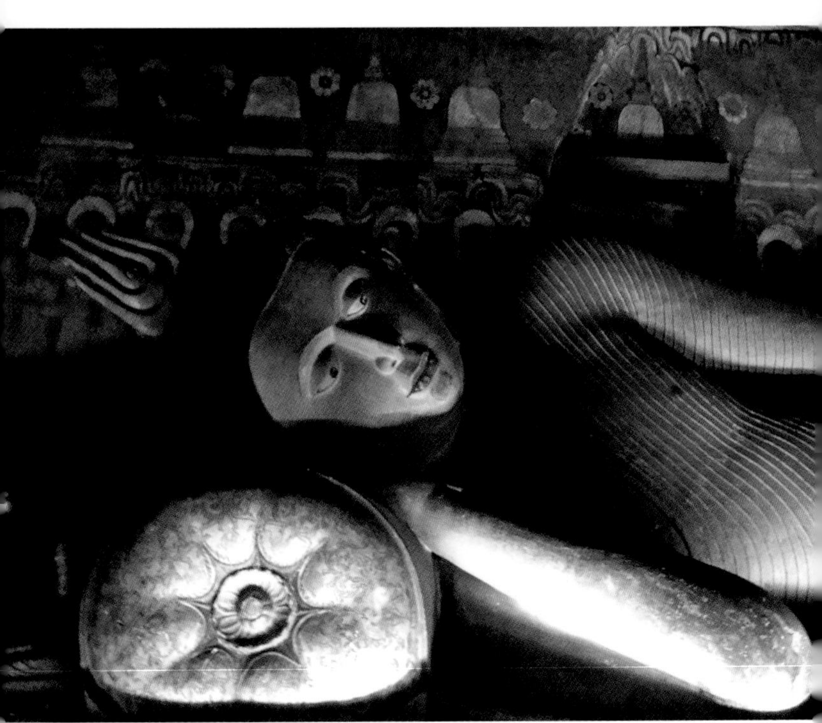

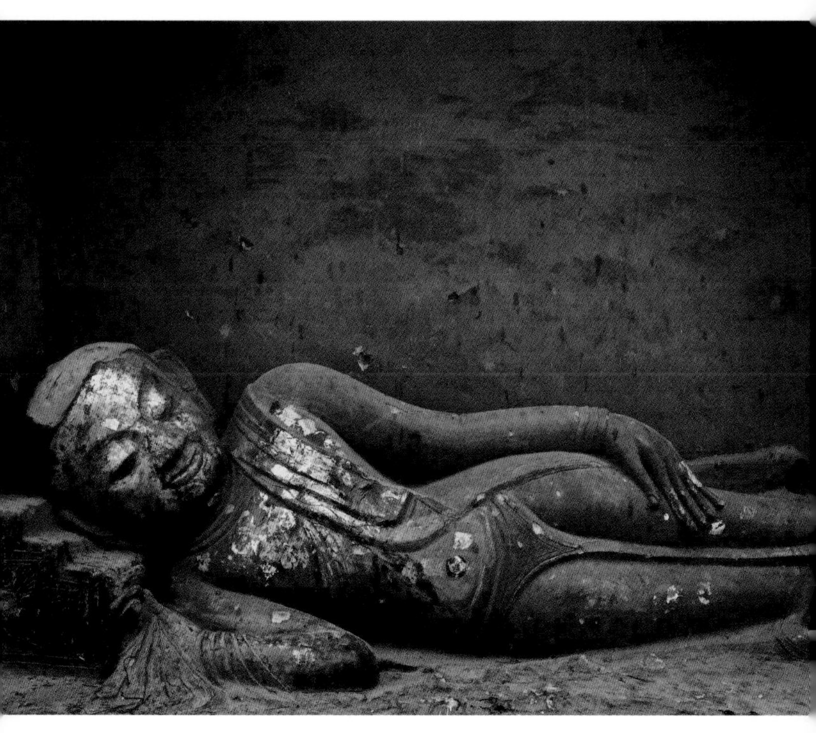

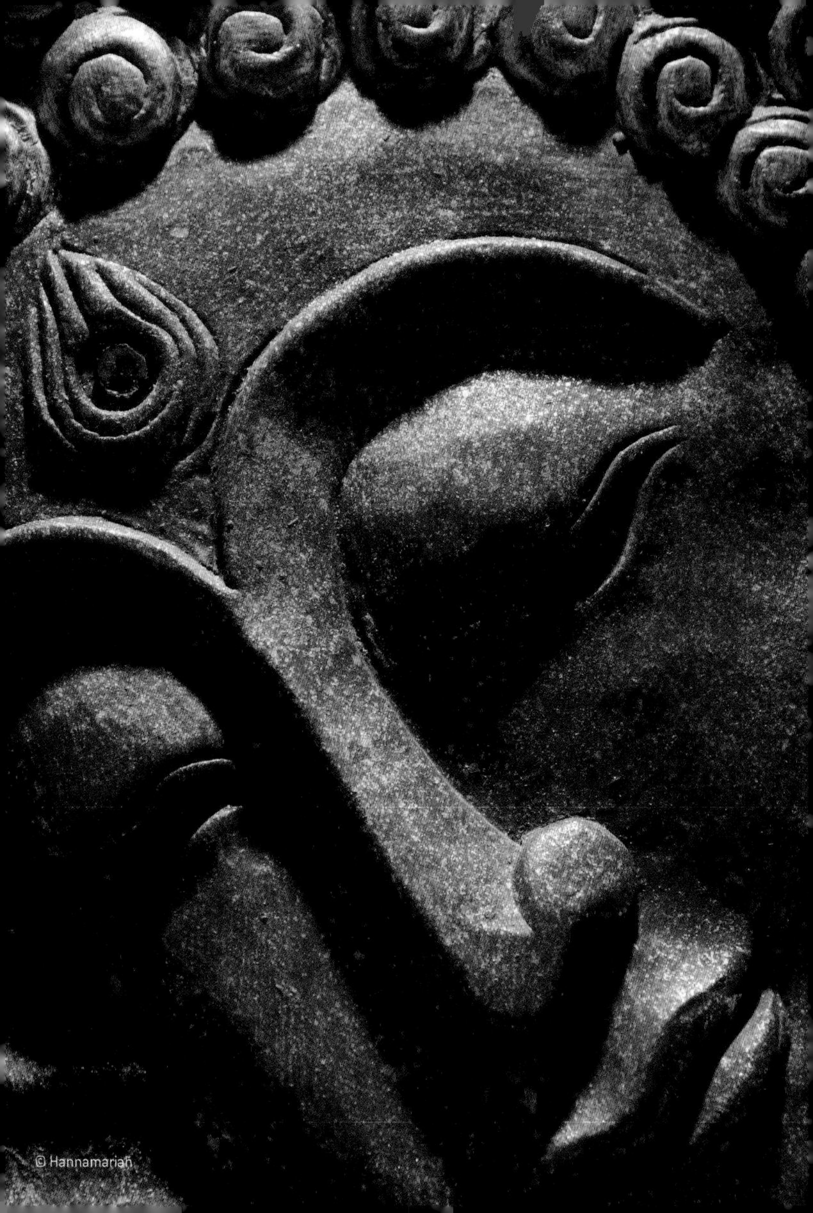

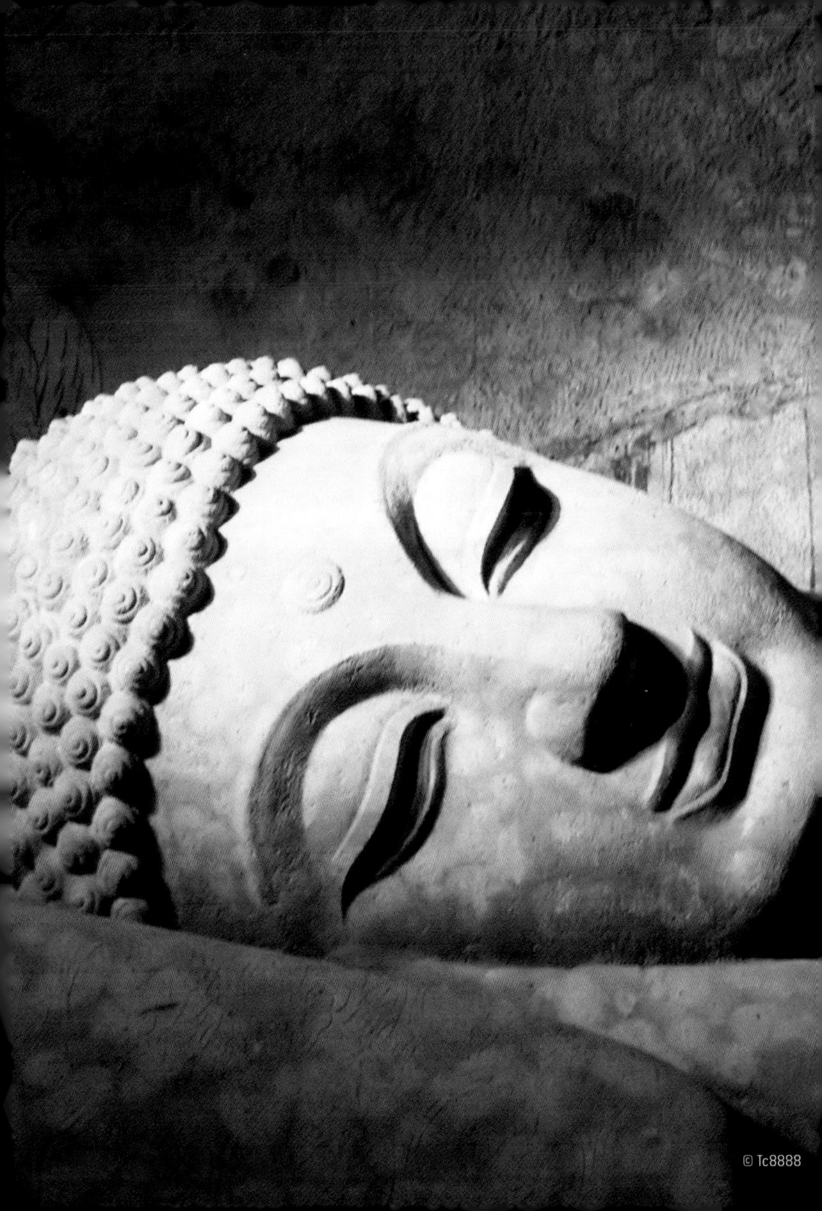

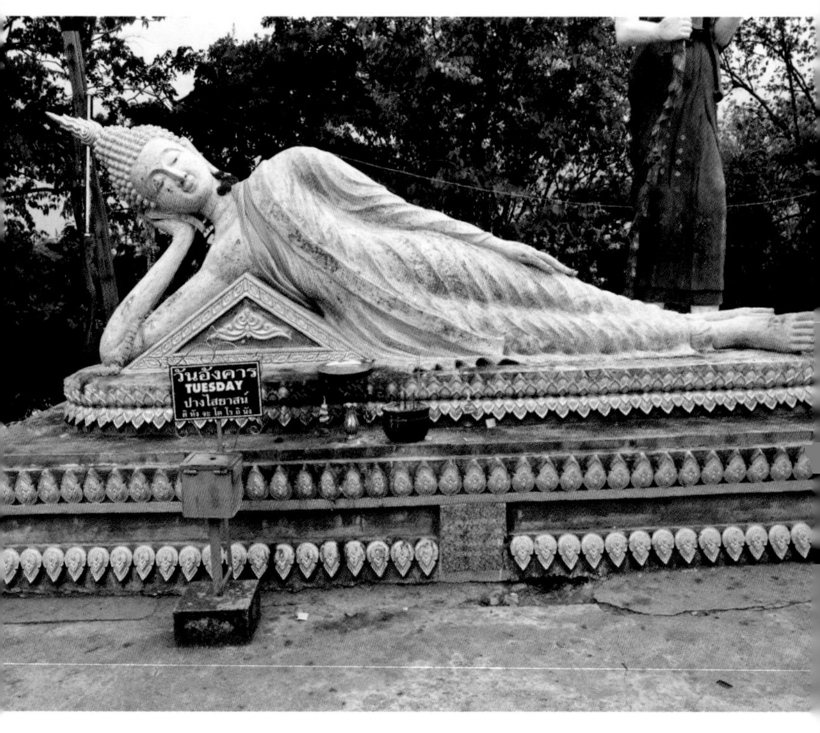
วันอังคาร
TUESDAY
ปางไสยาสน์

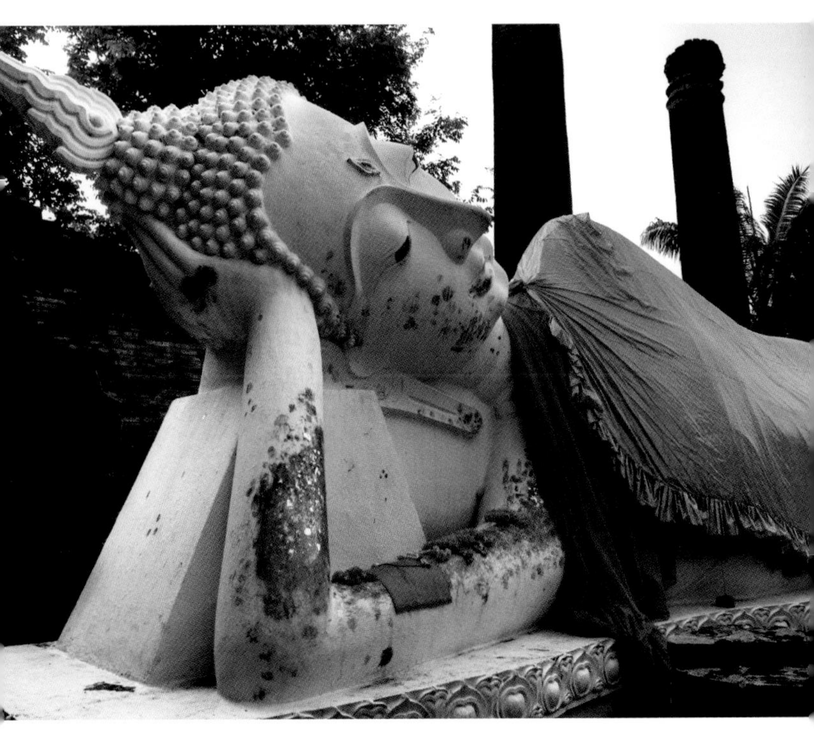

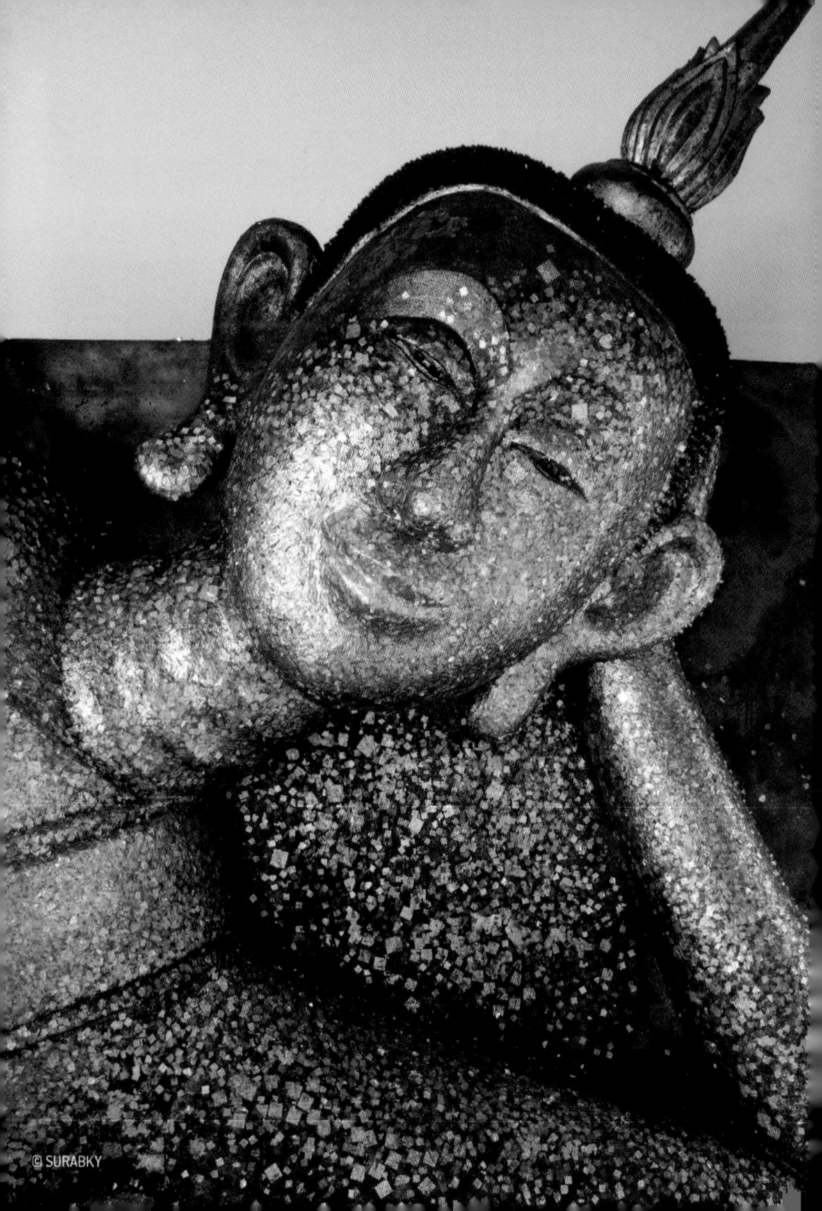

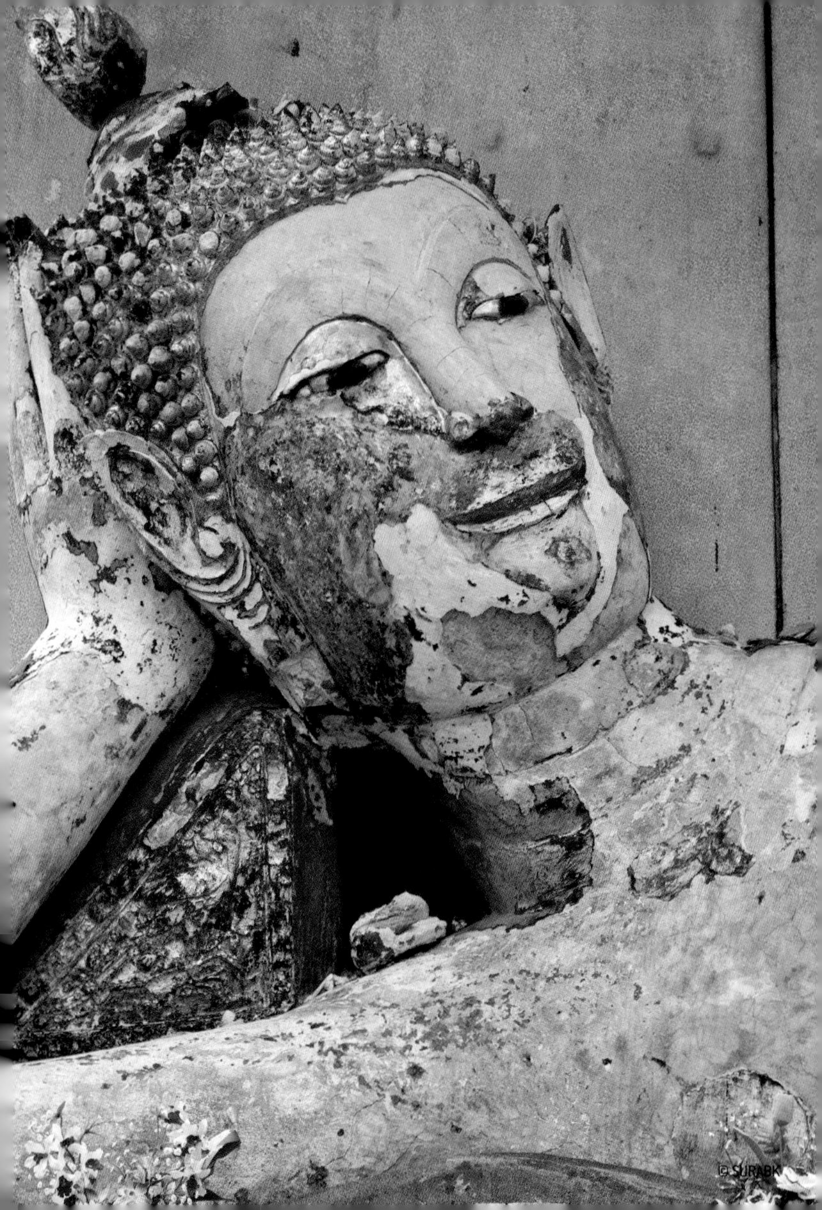
© SURABK

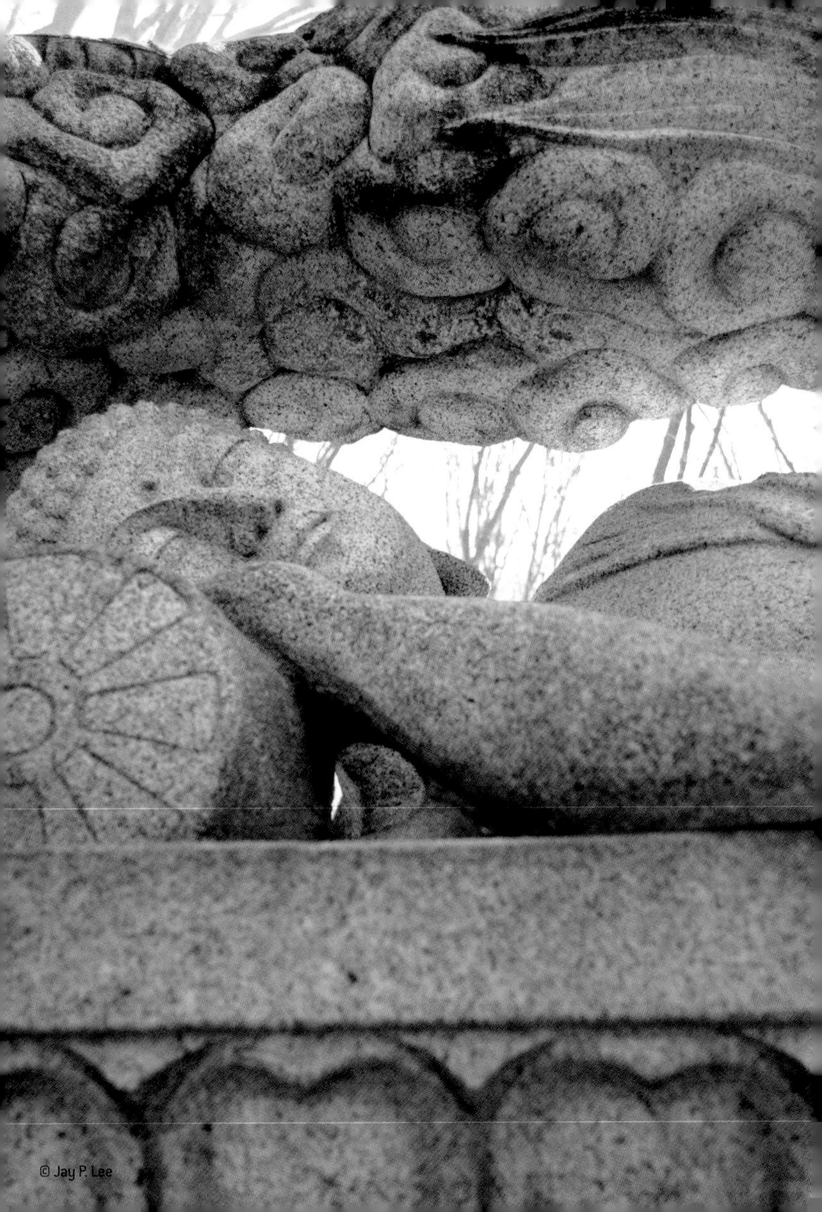

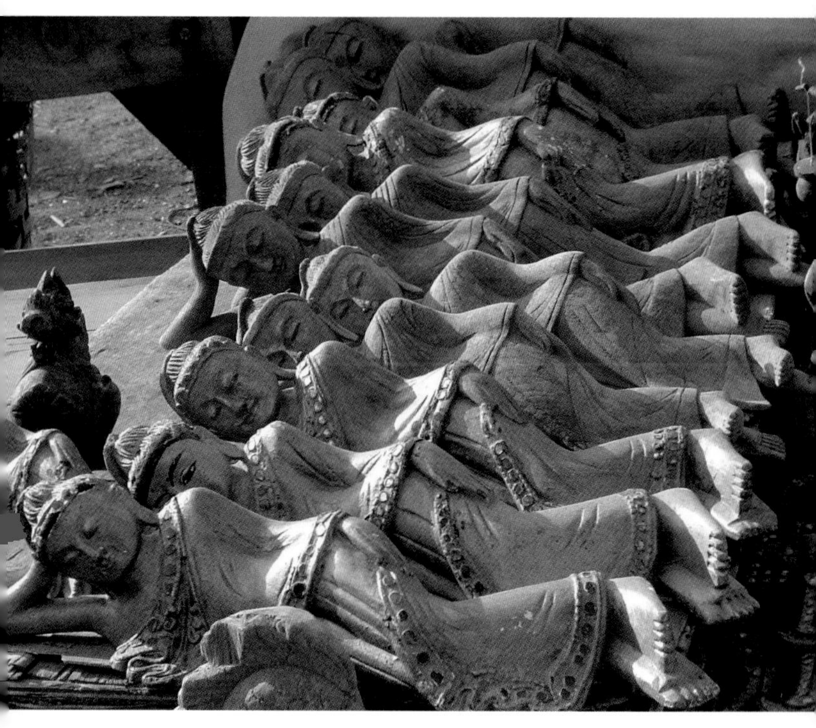

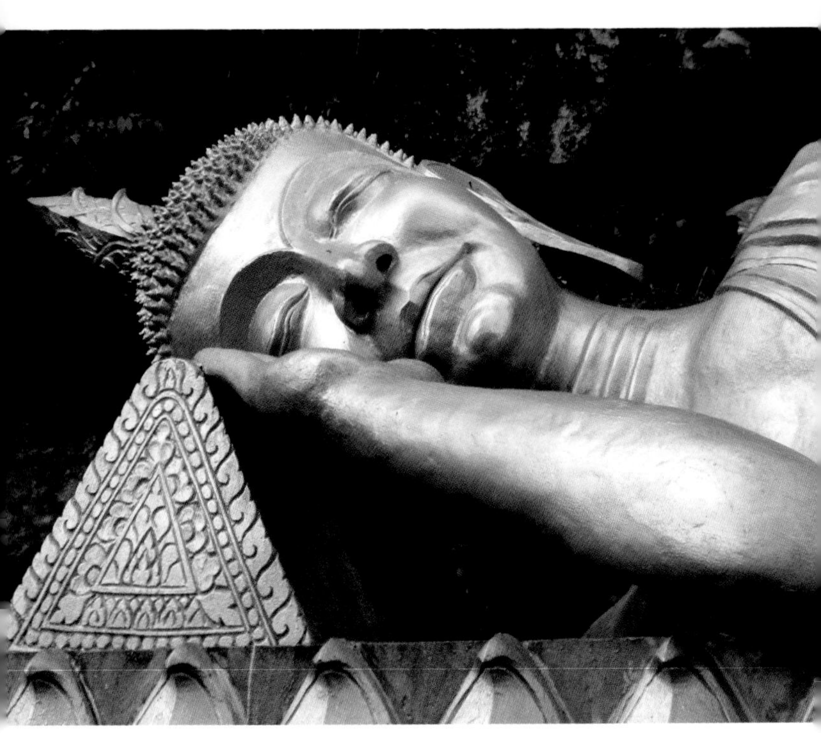

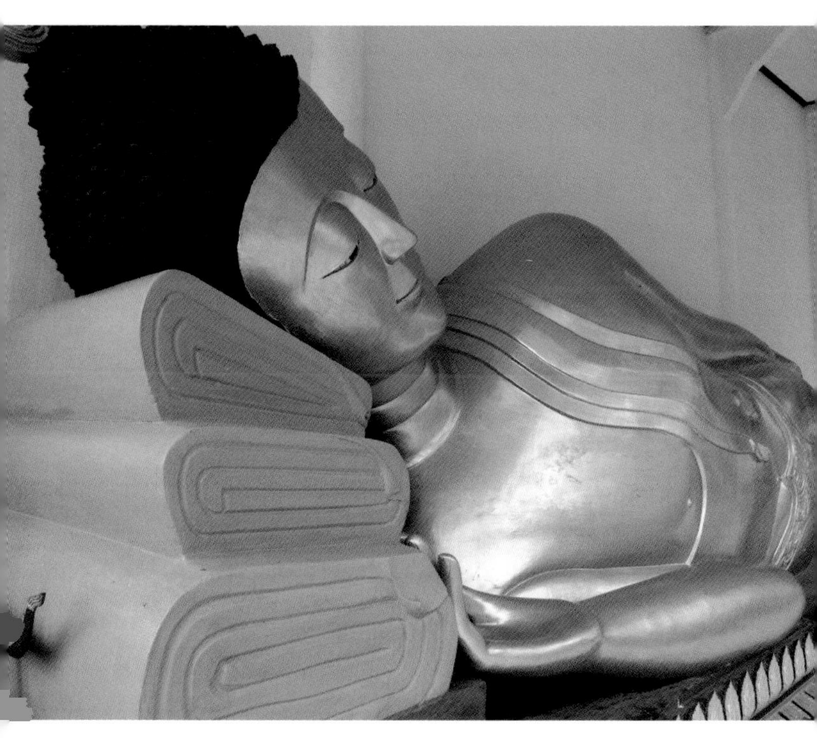

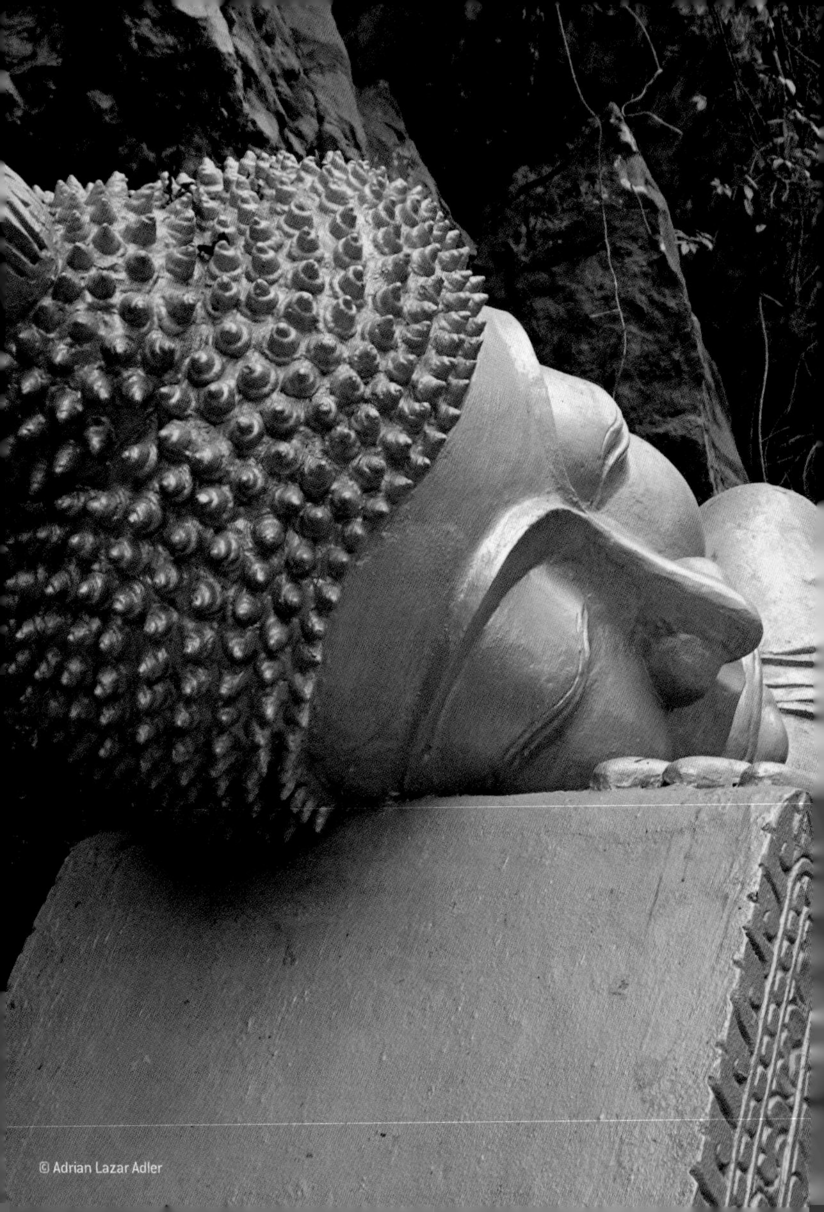

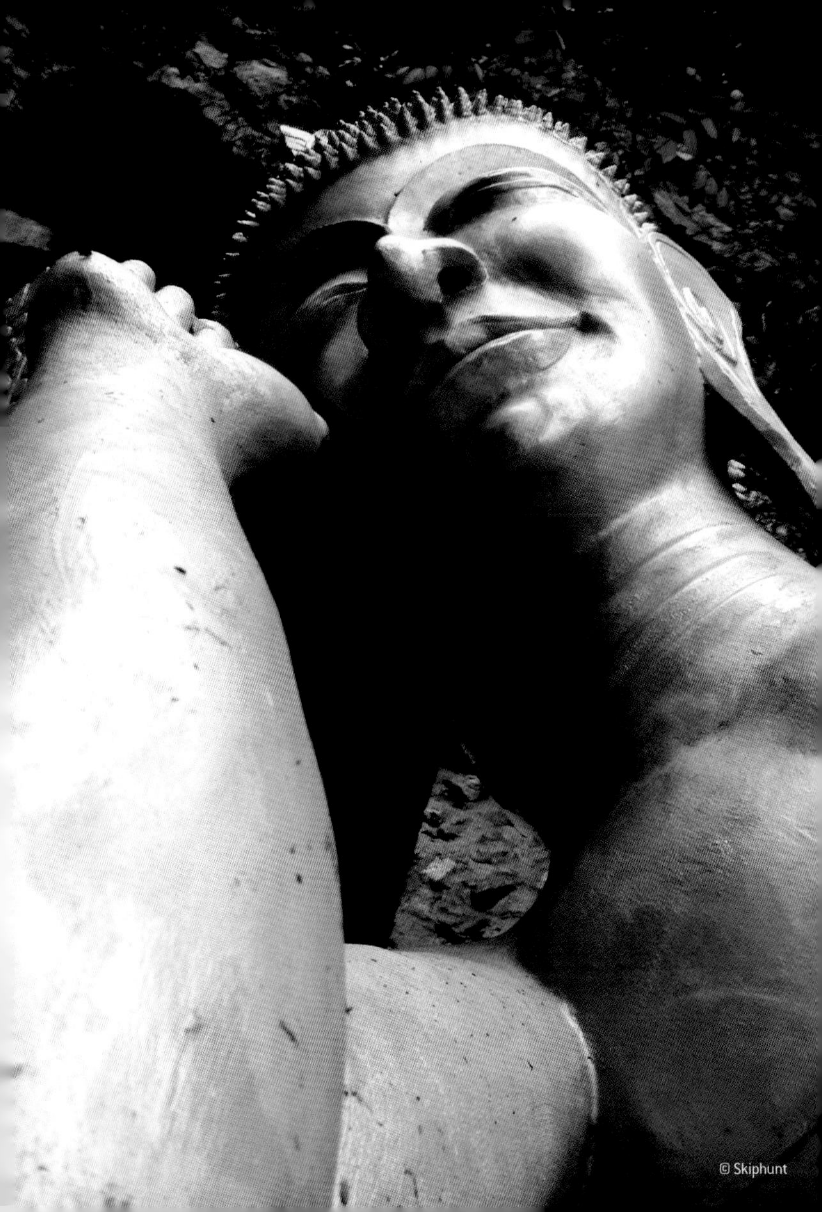

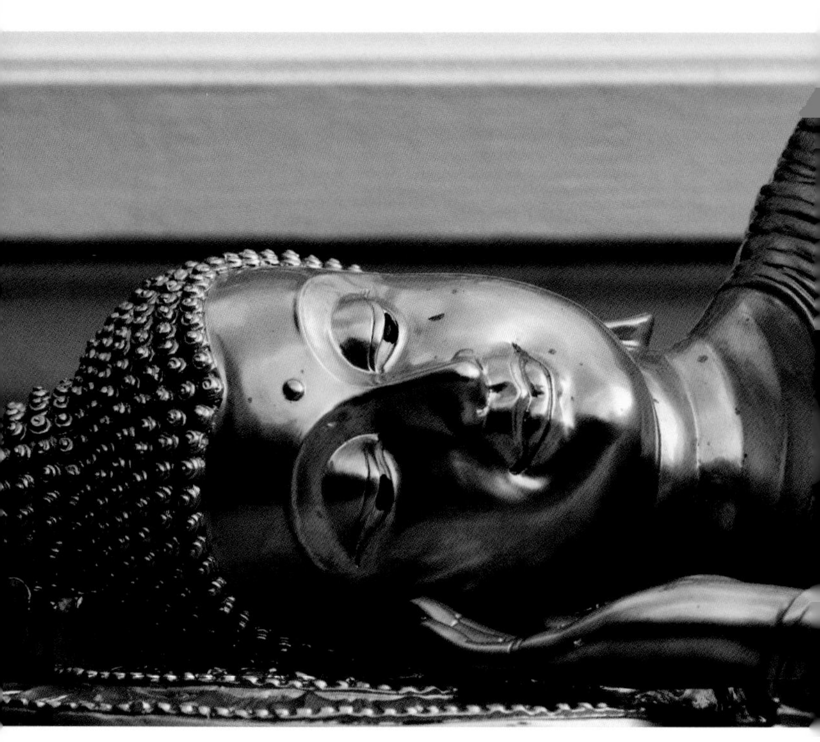

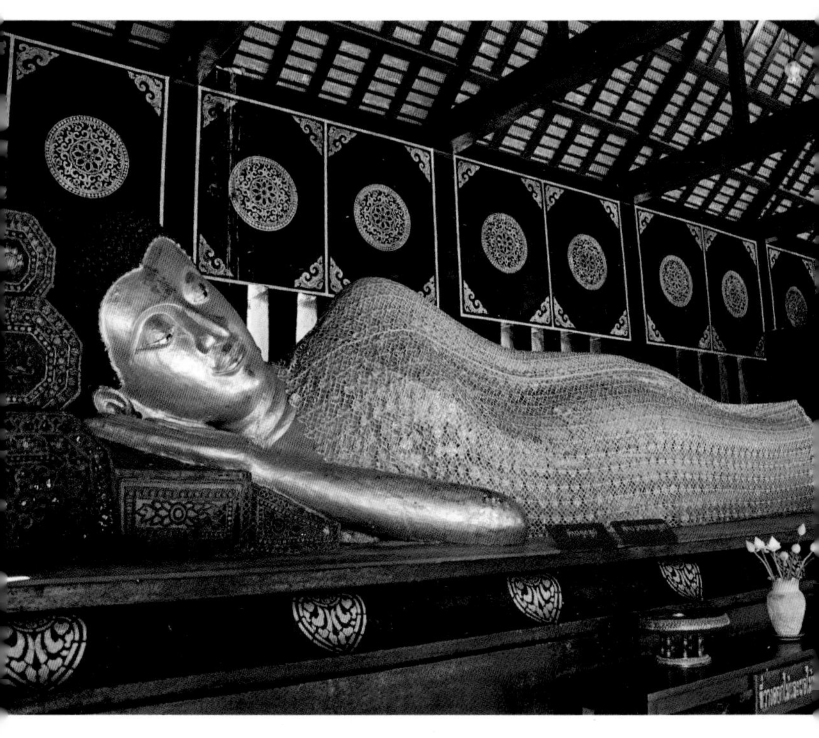

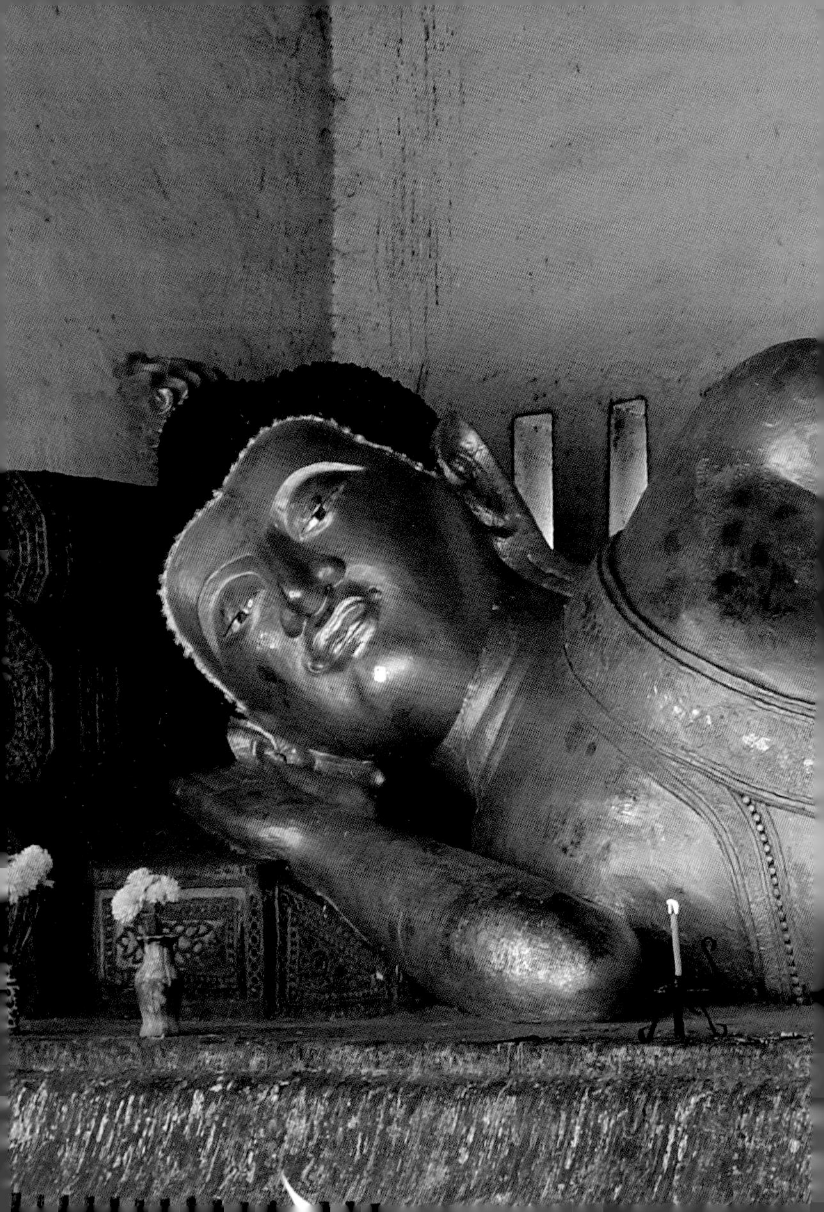

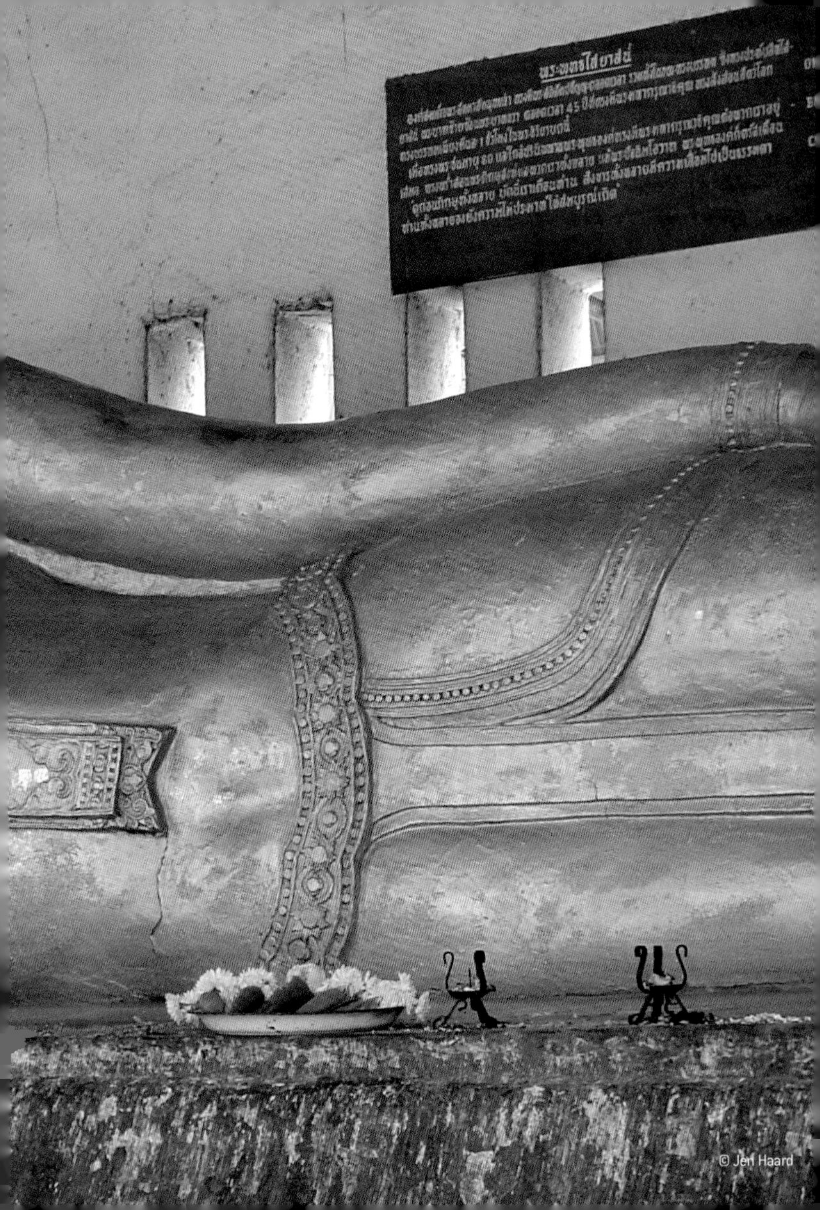

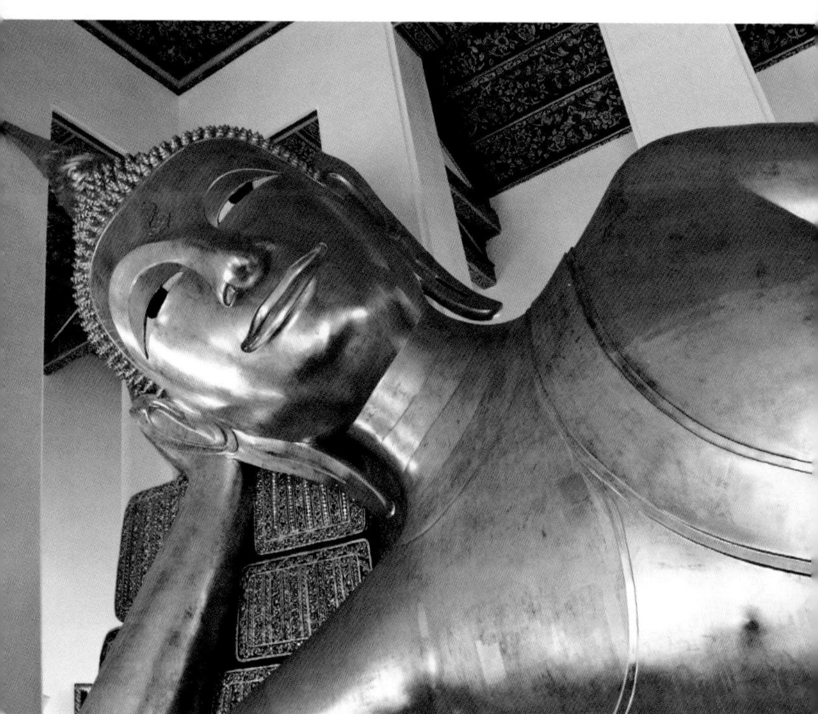

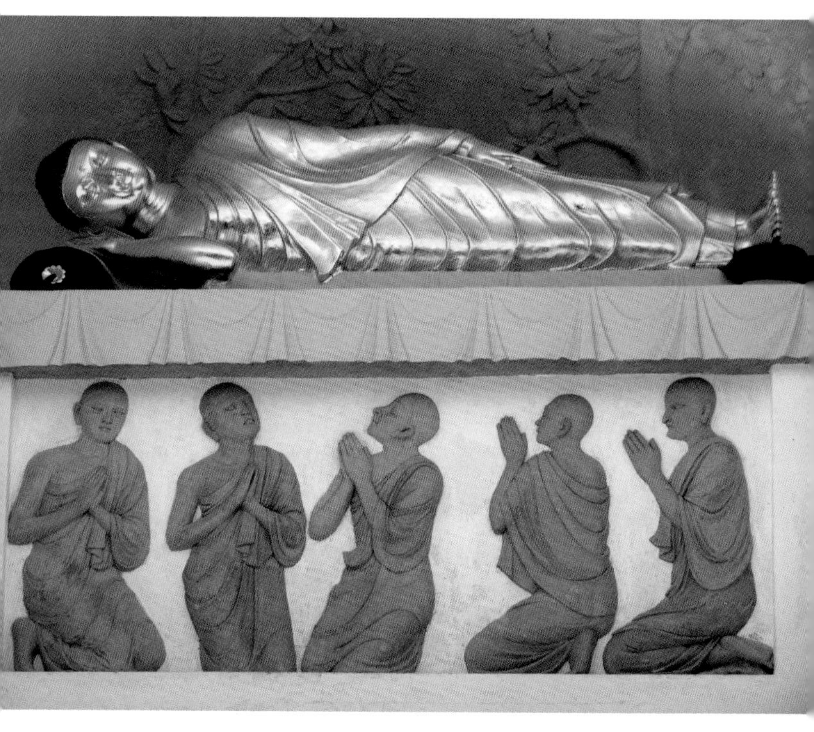

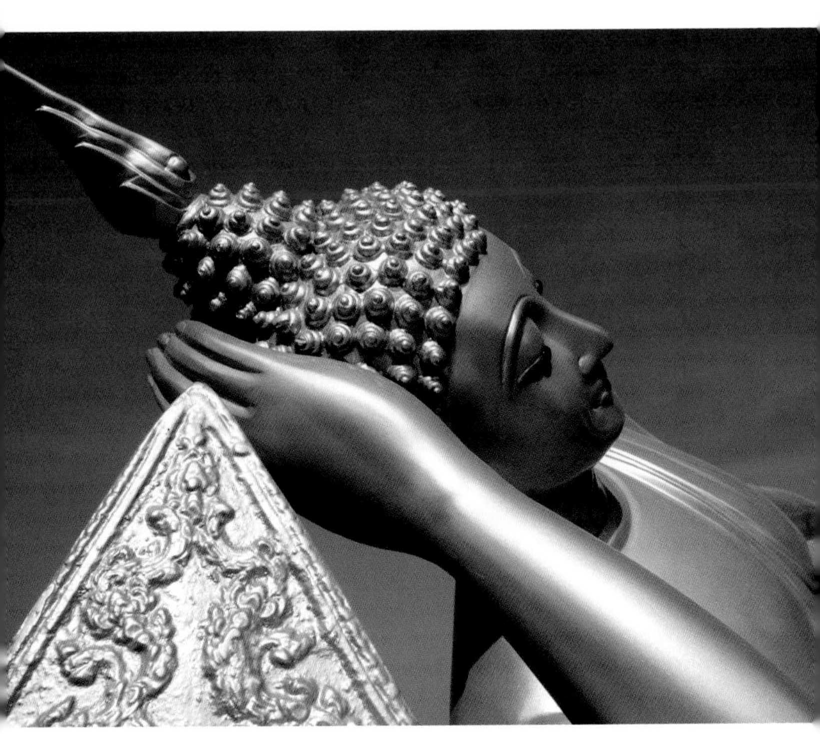

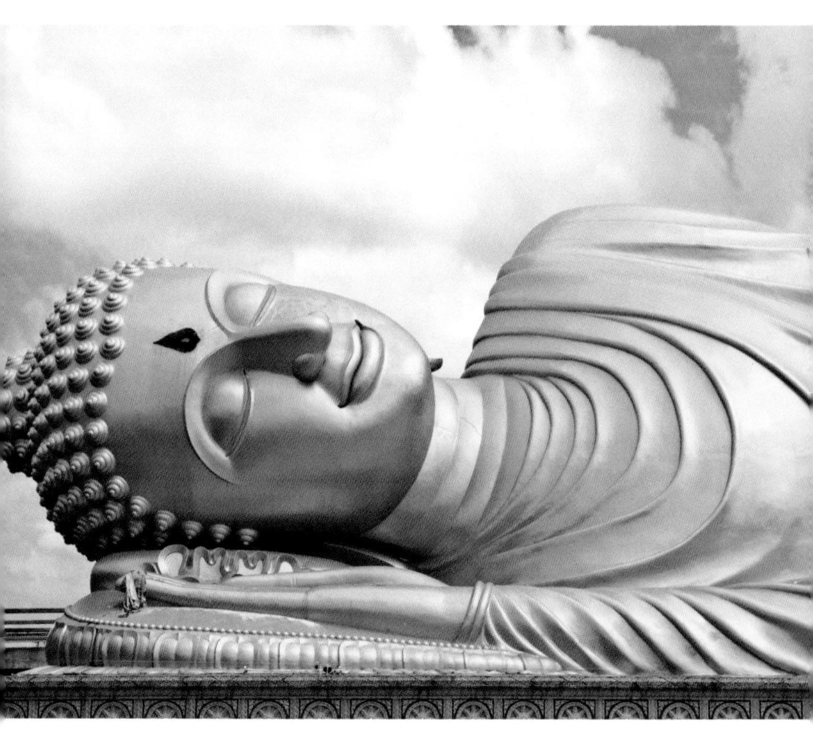

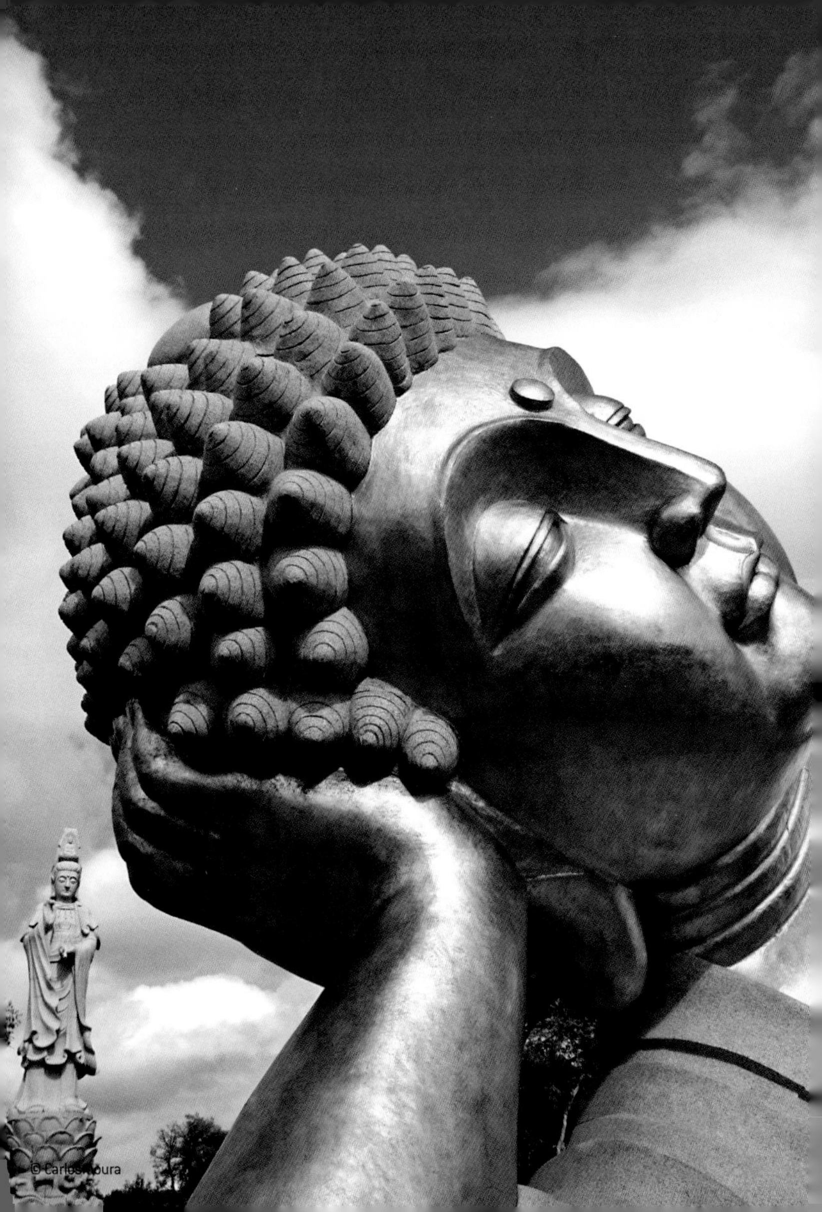

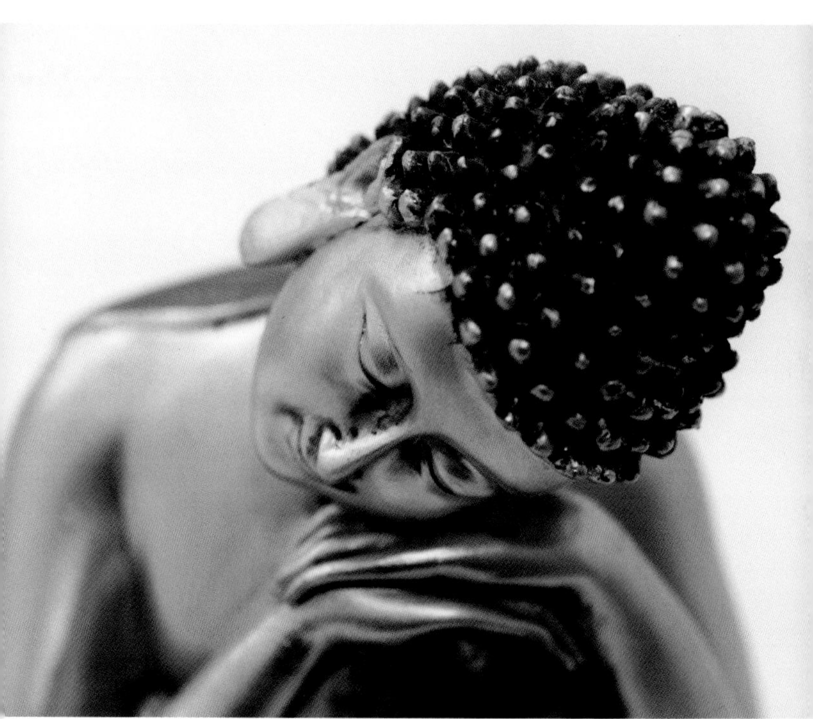

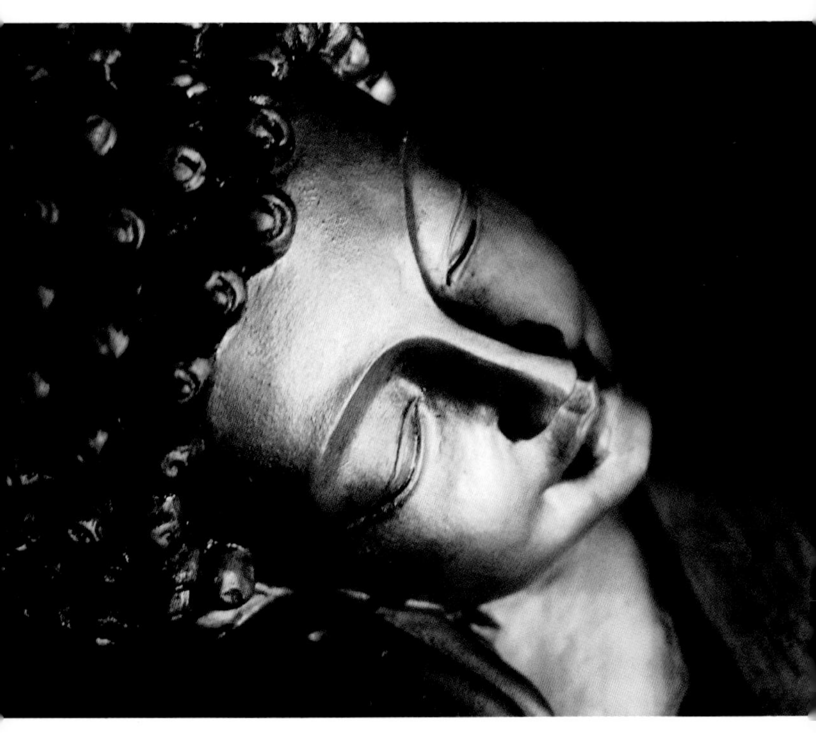

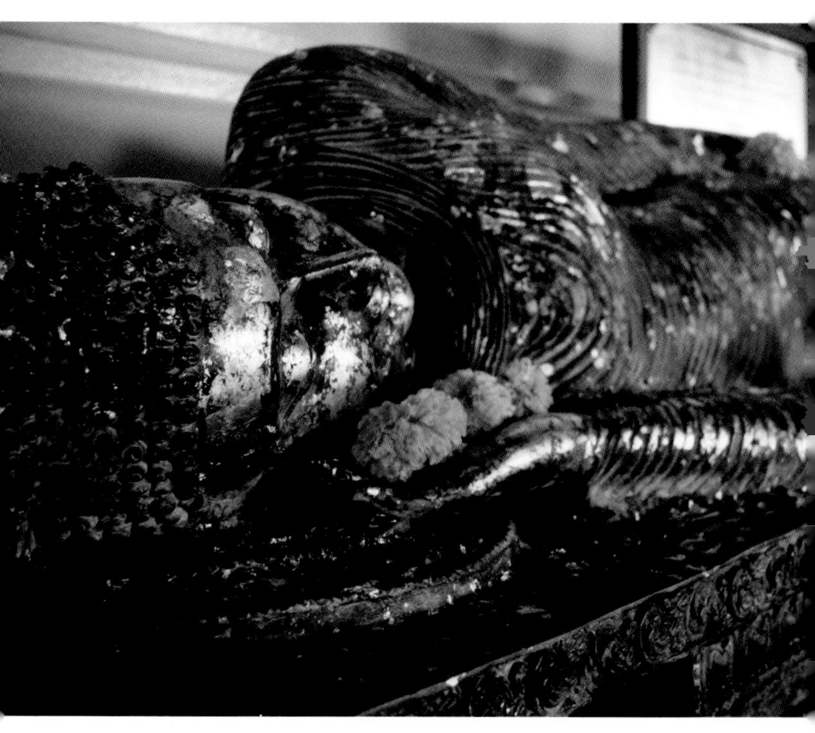

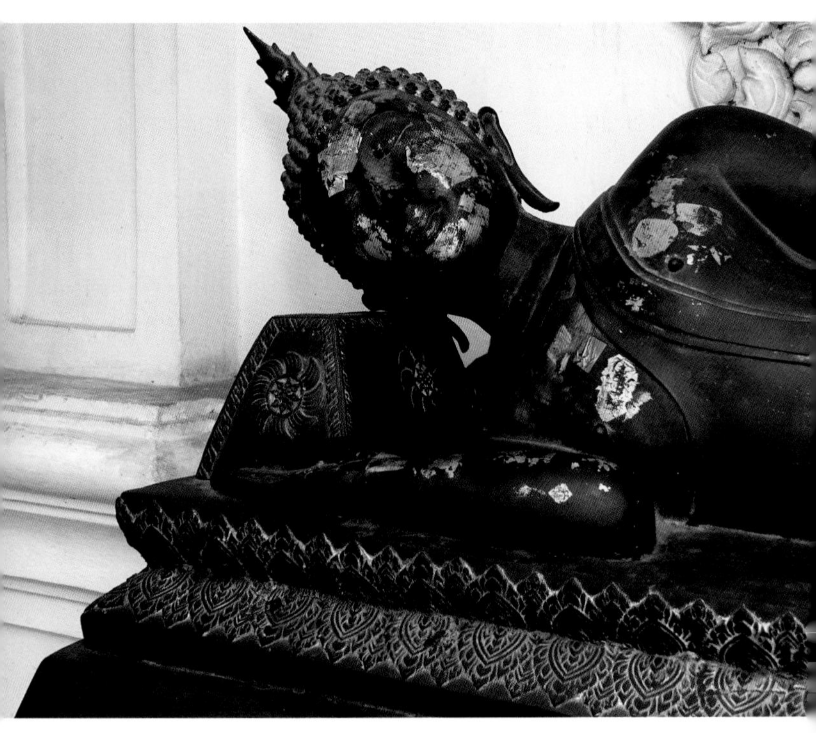

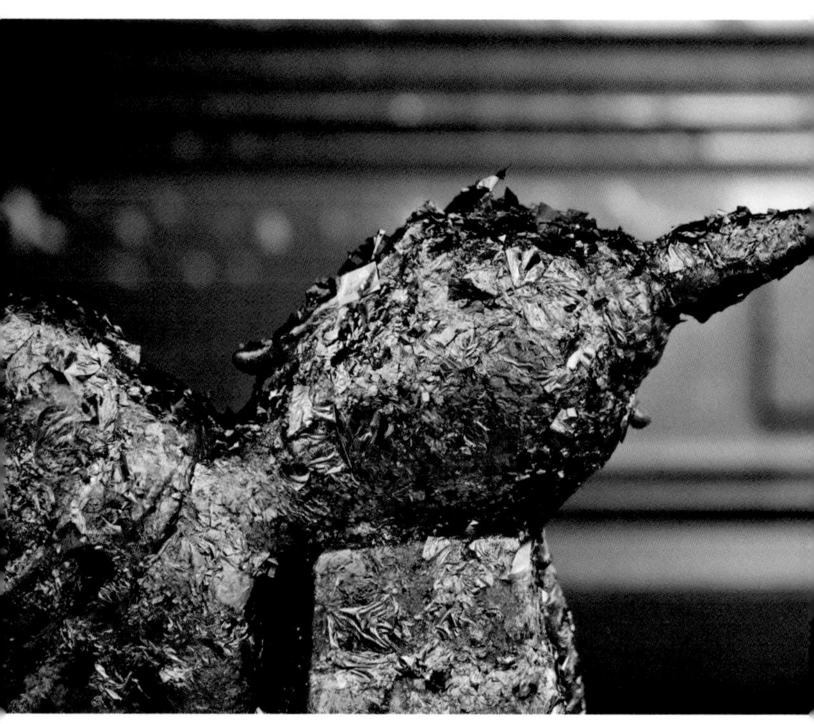

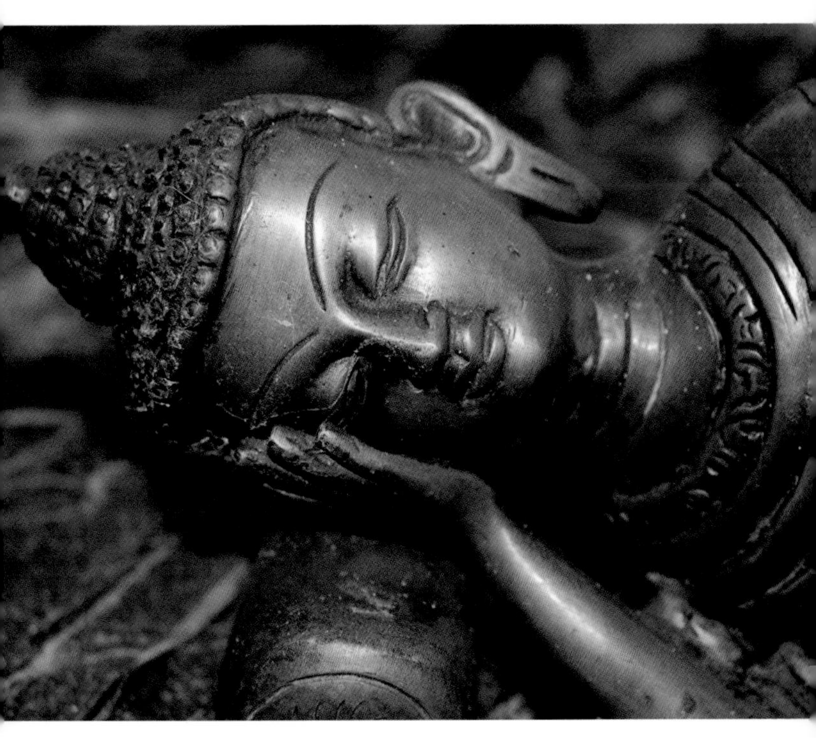

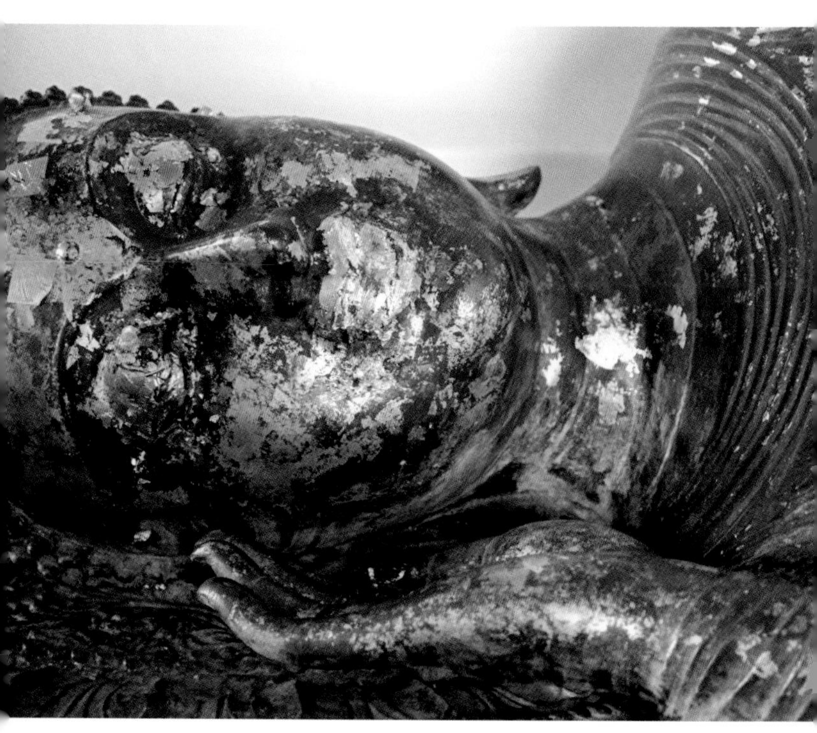

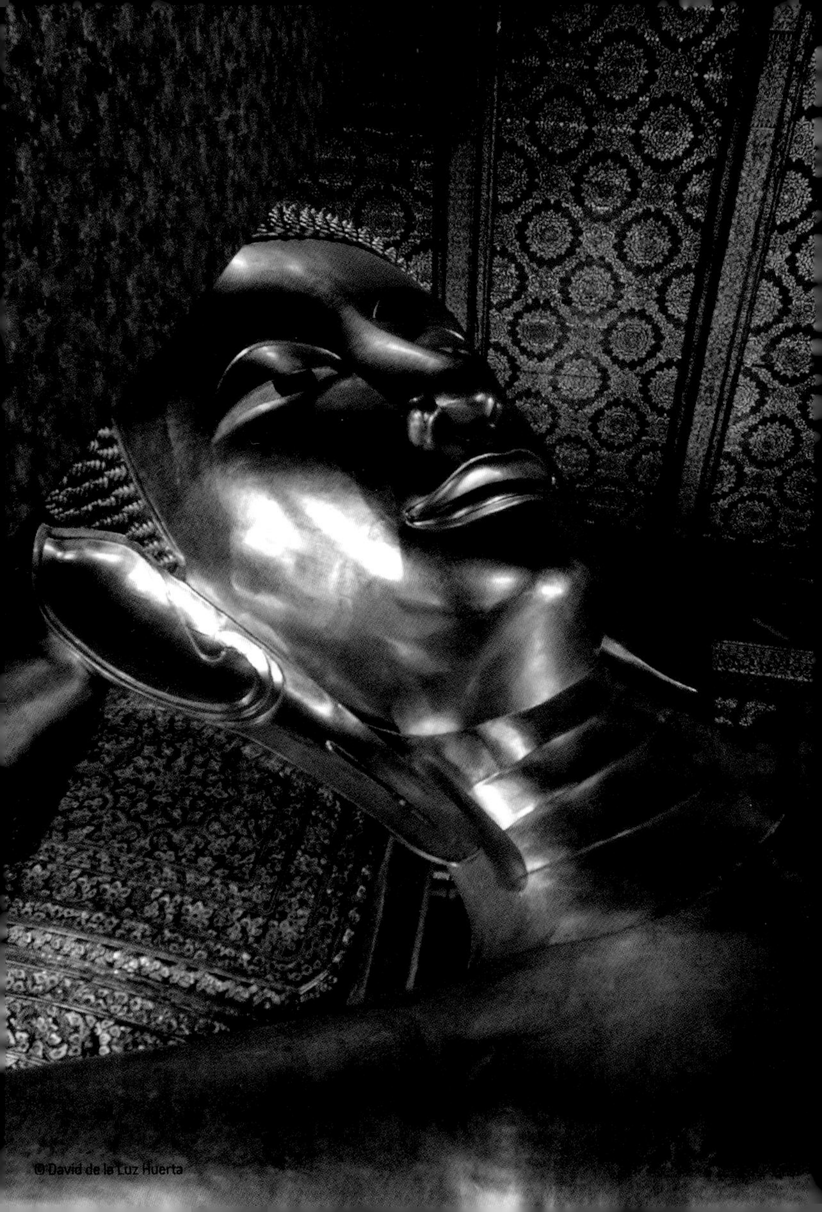

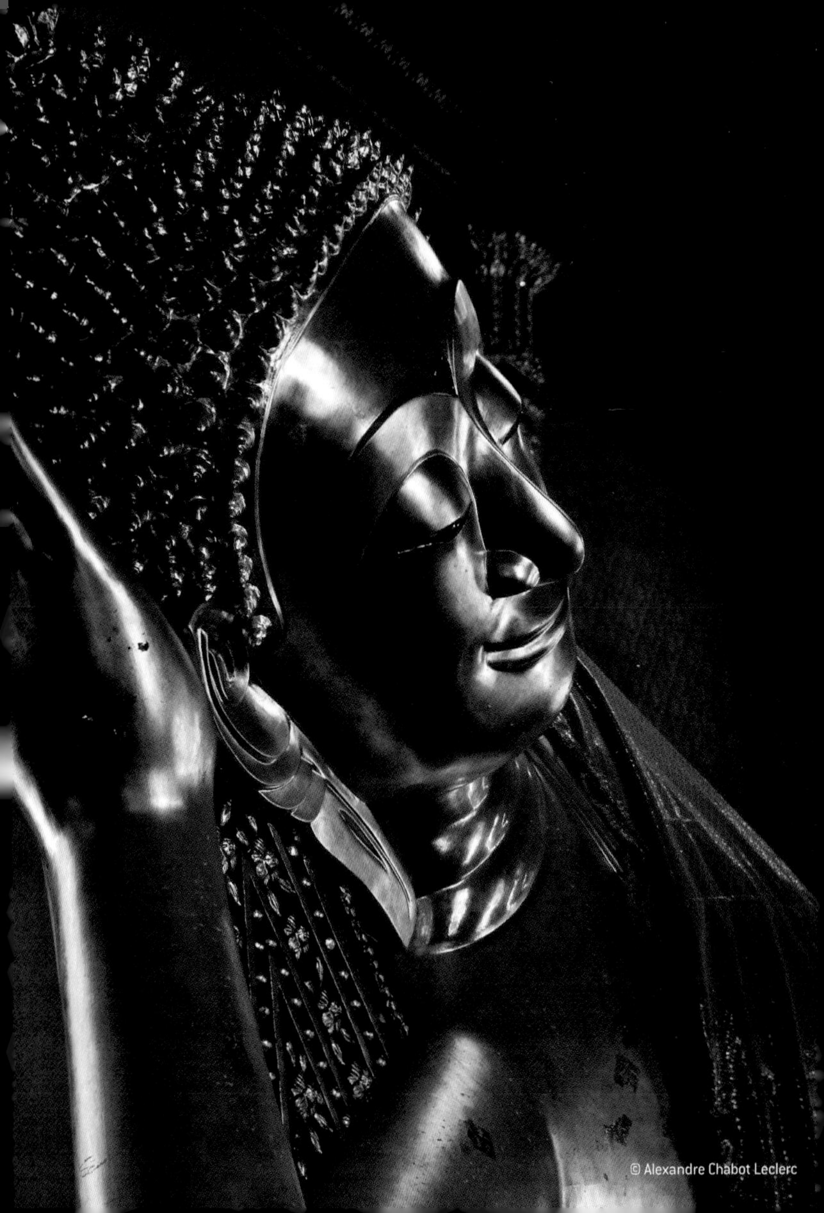

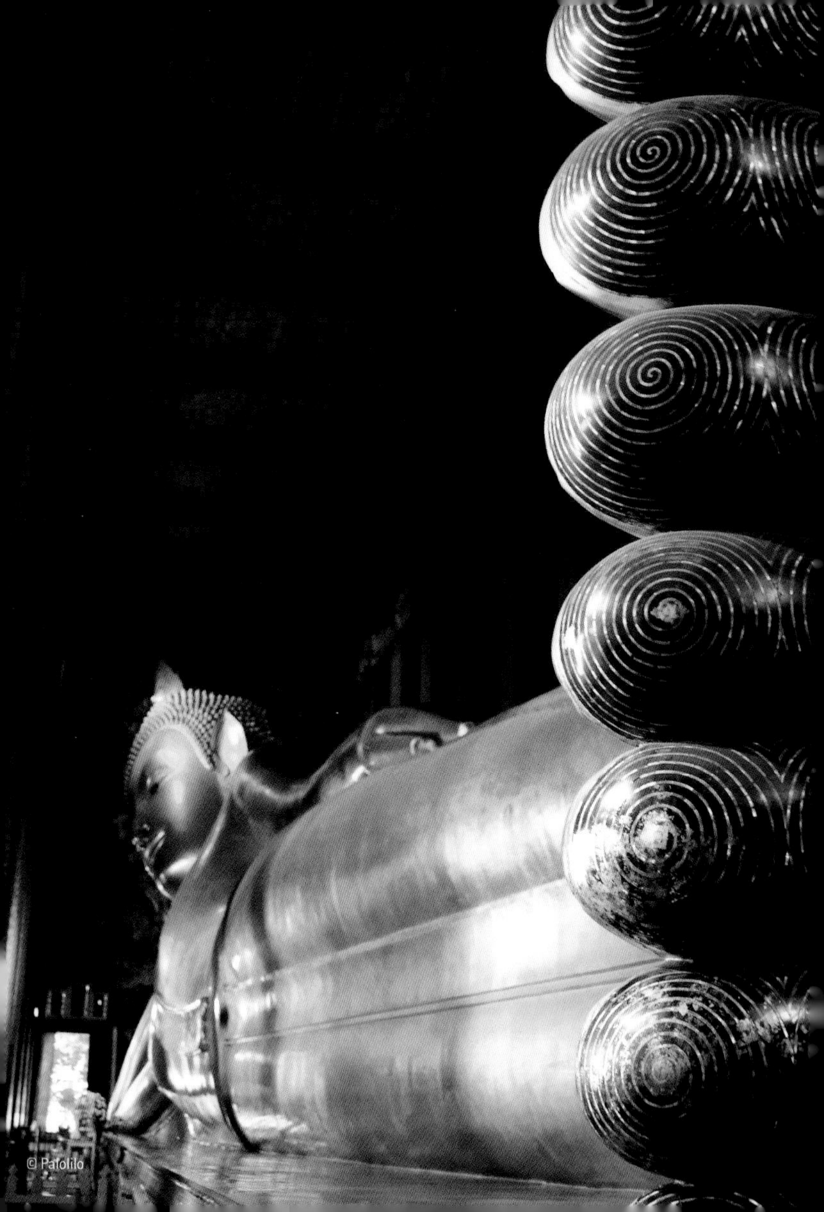

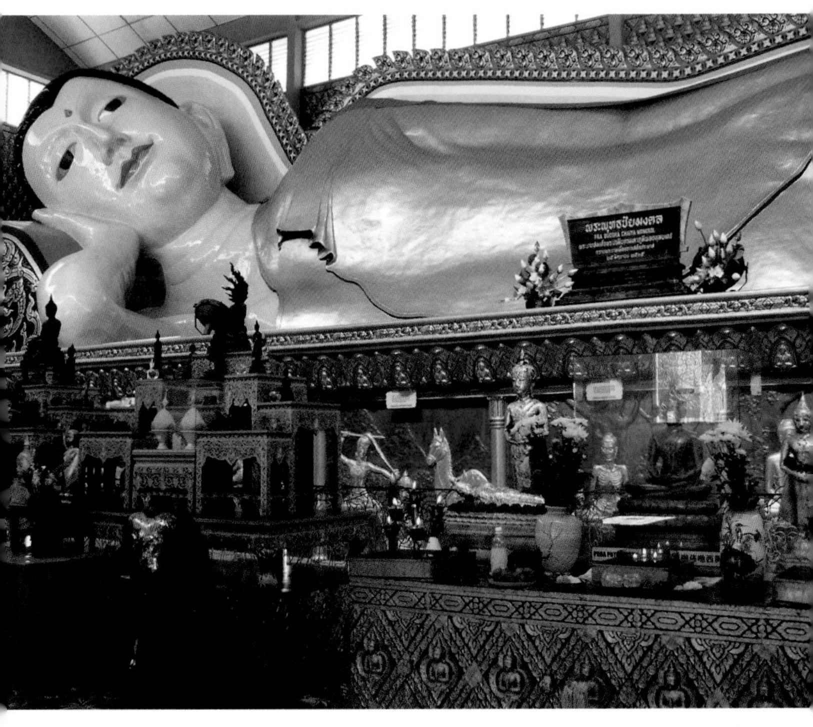

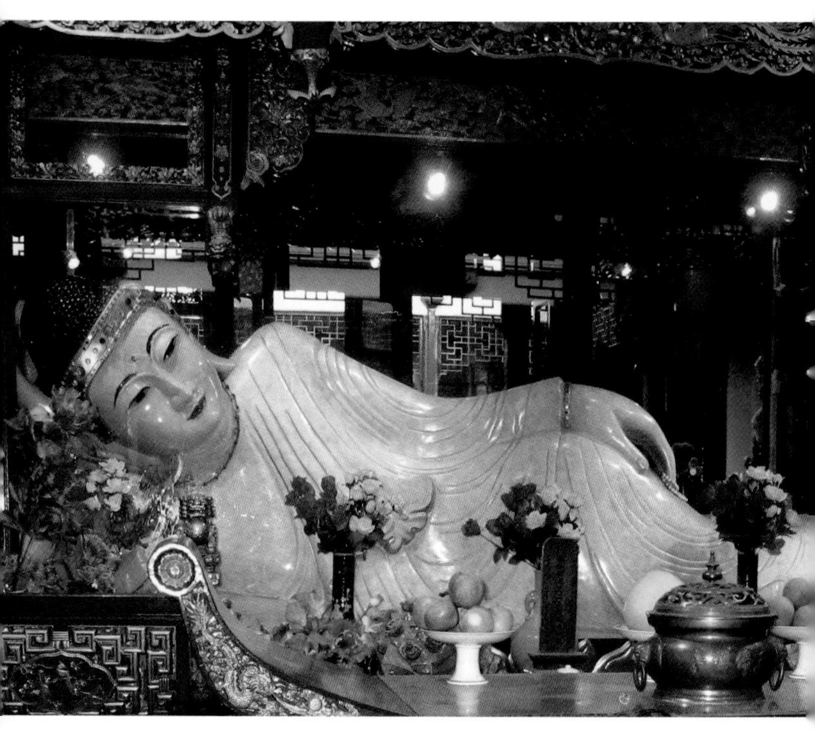

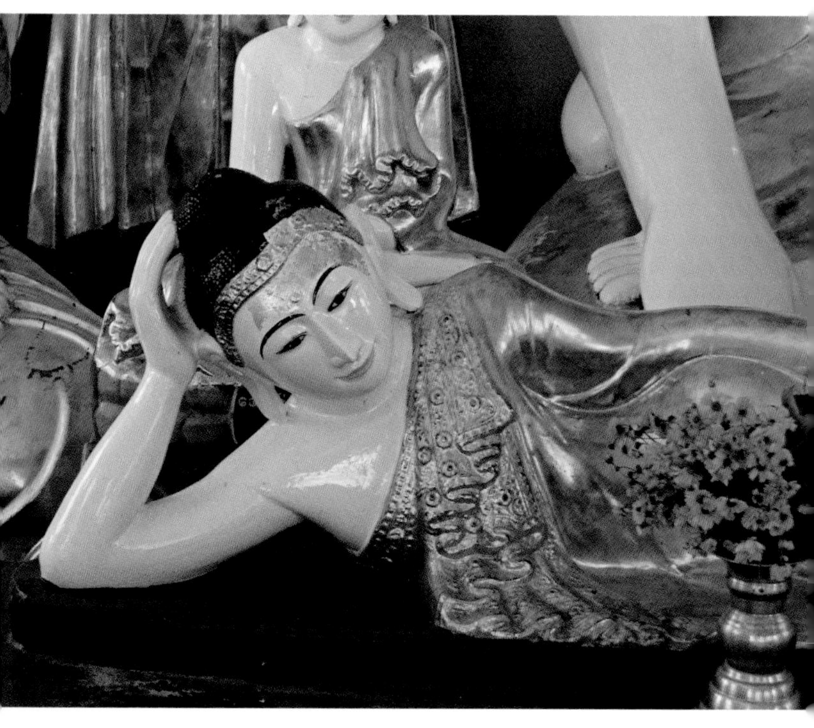

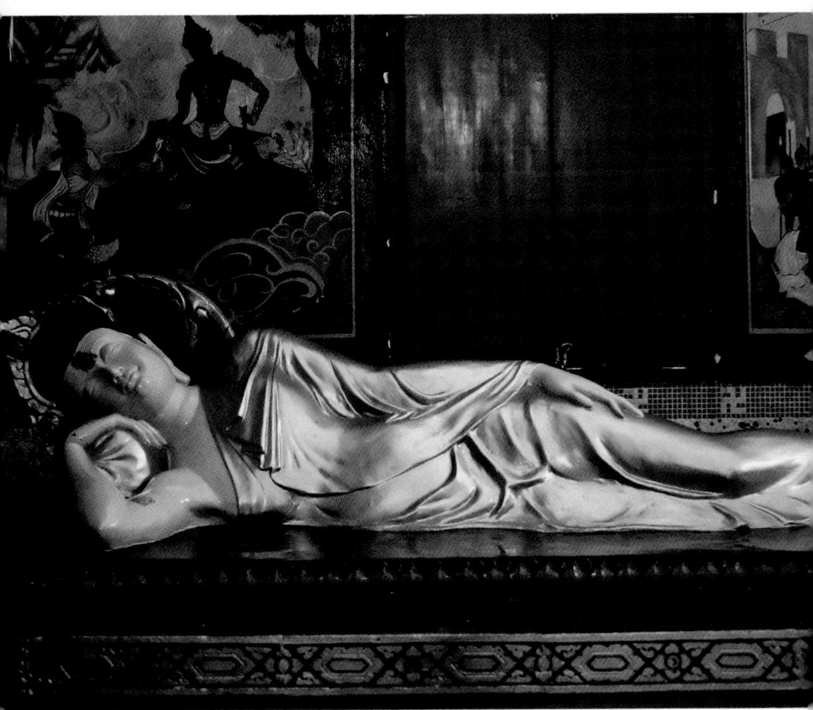

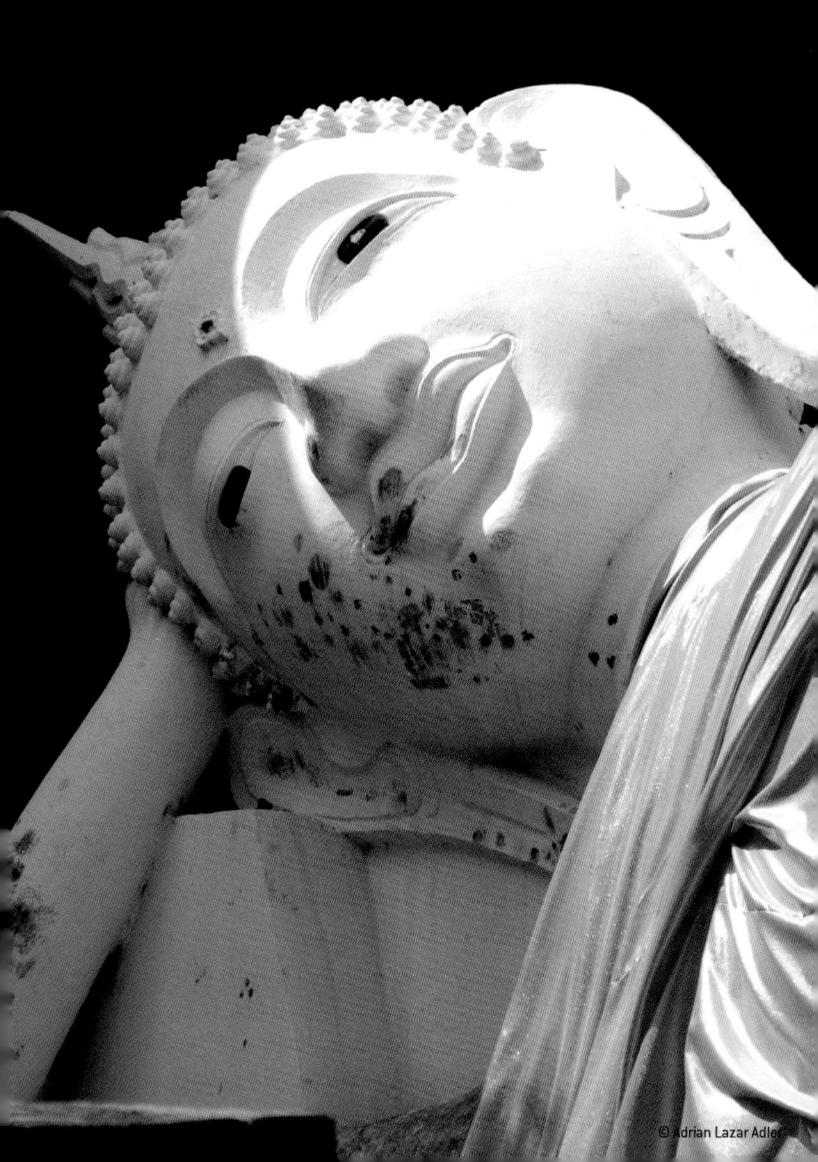

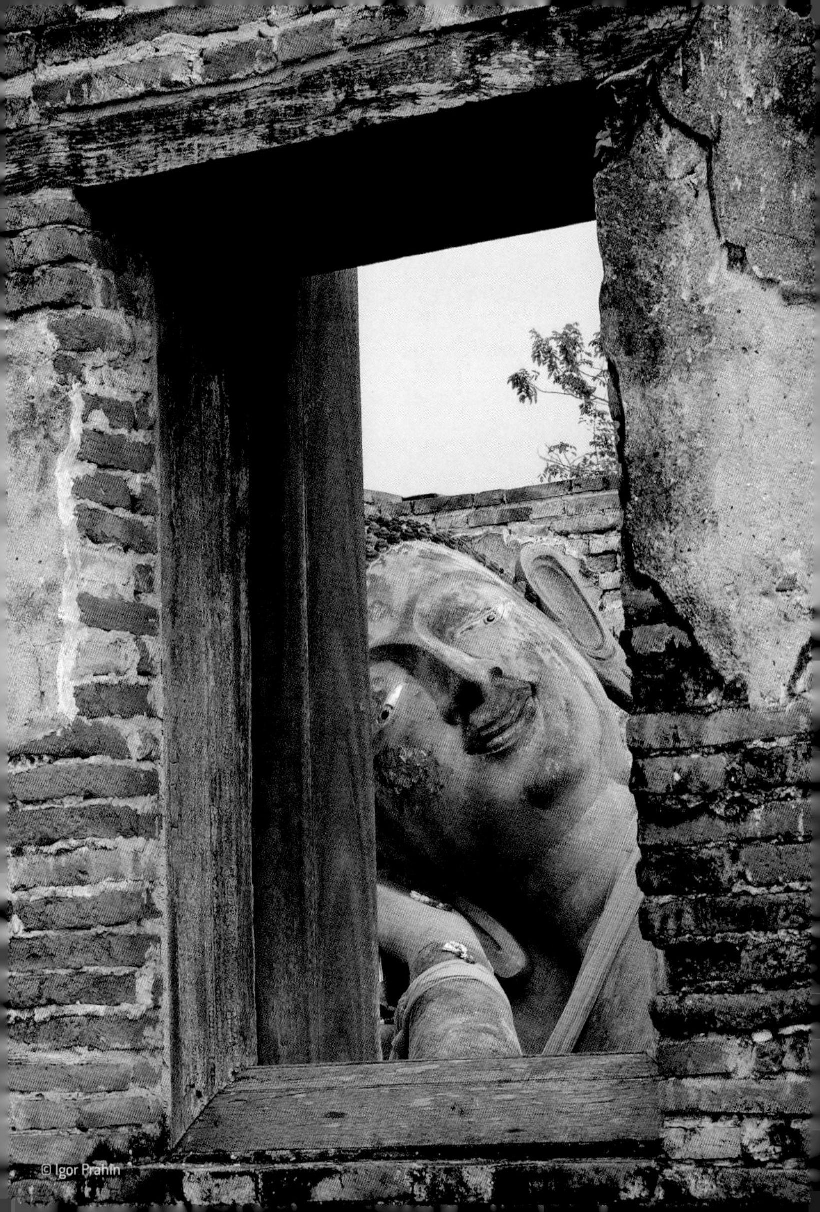

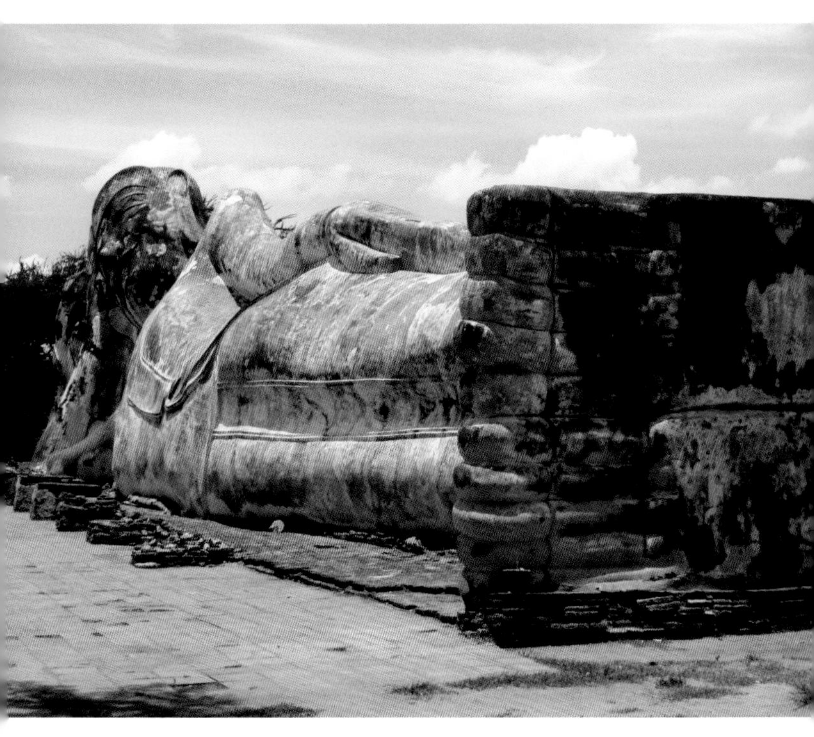

© Dhaneesha Senaratne

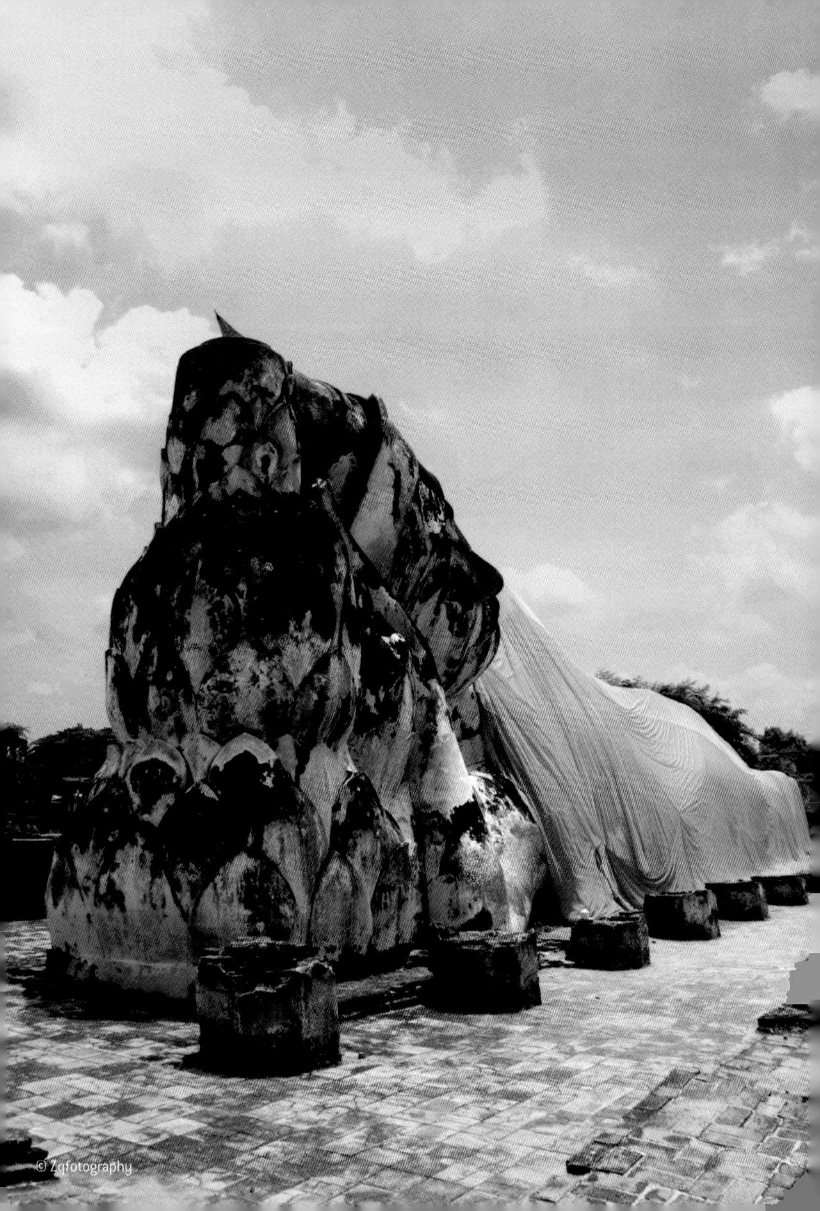

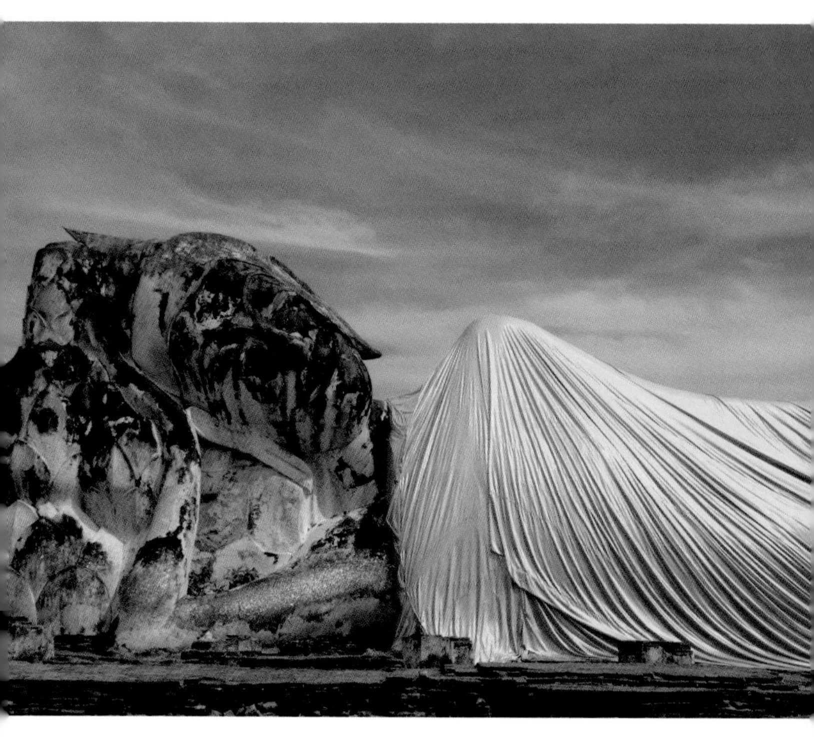

© javarman

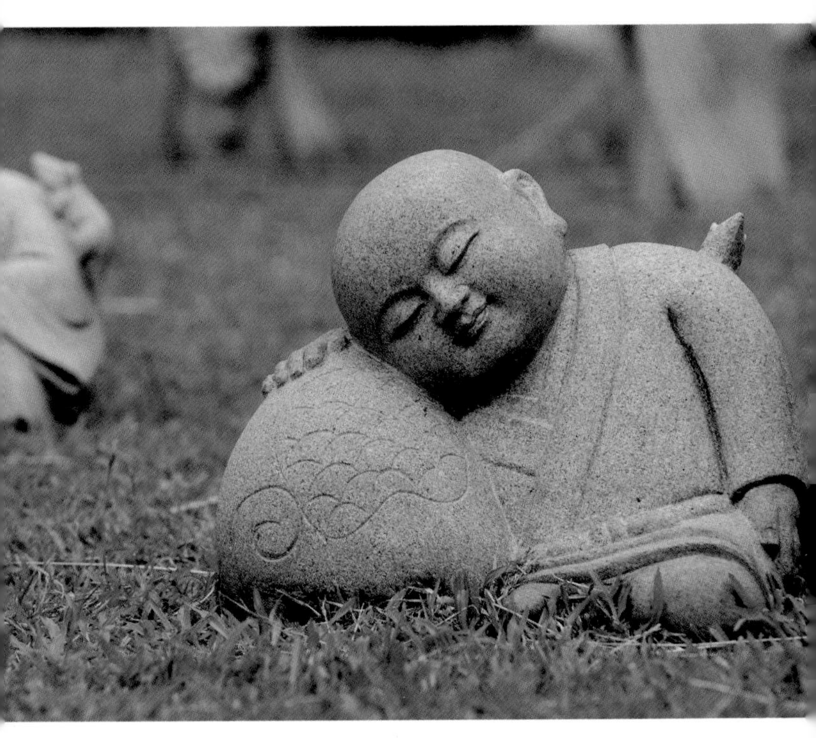

© sunsetman

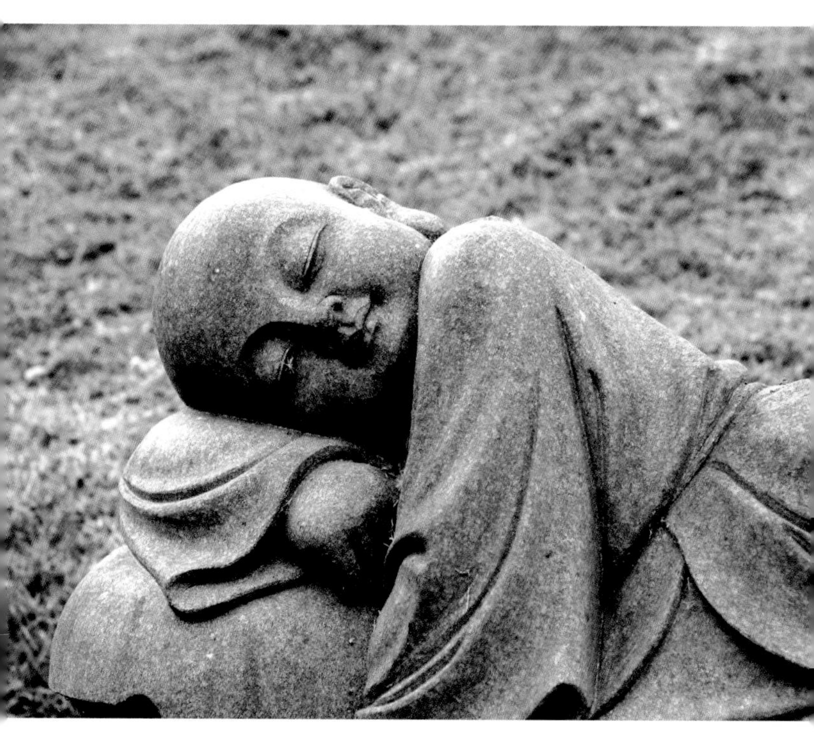

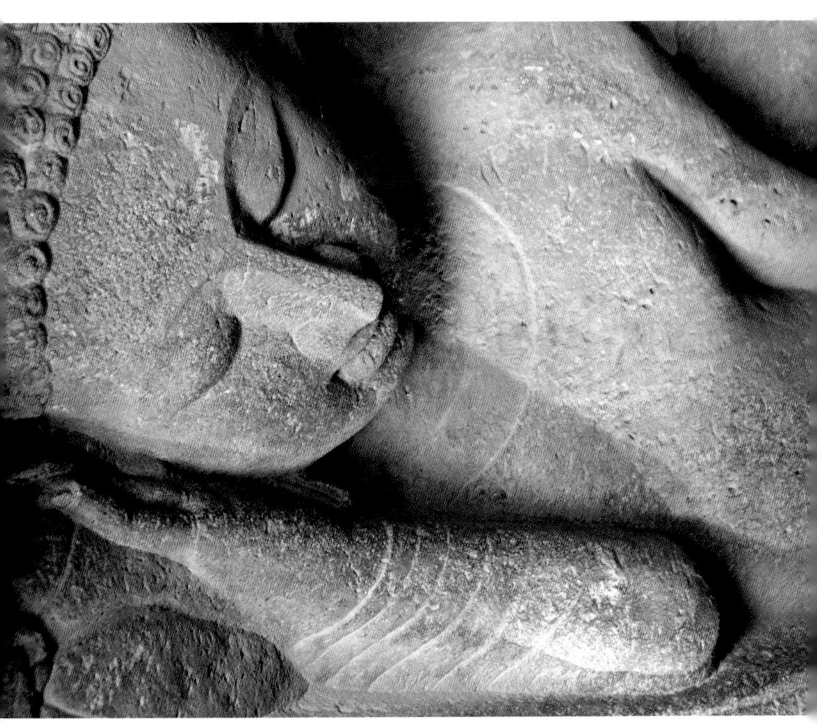

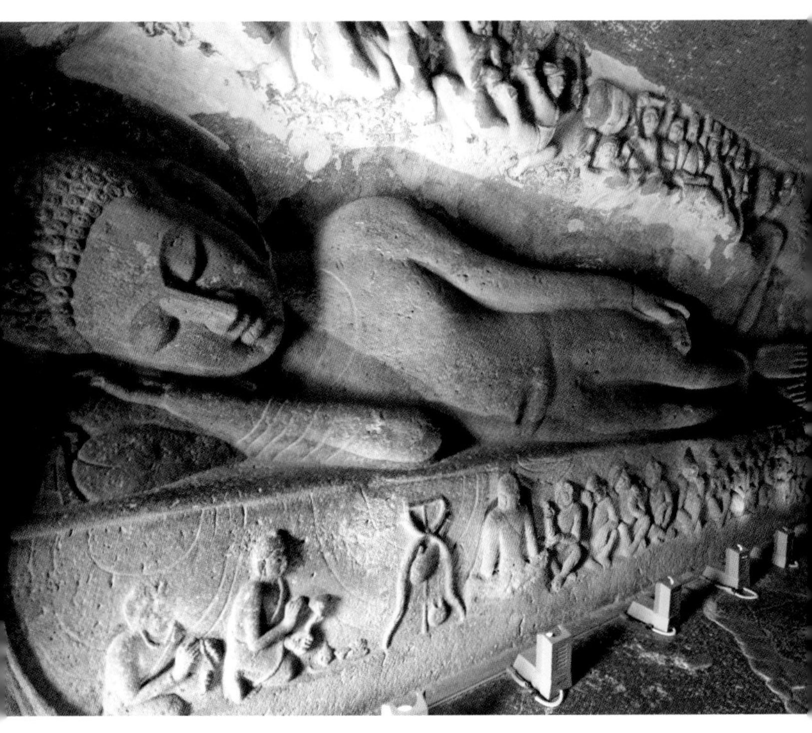

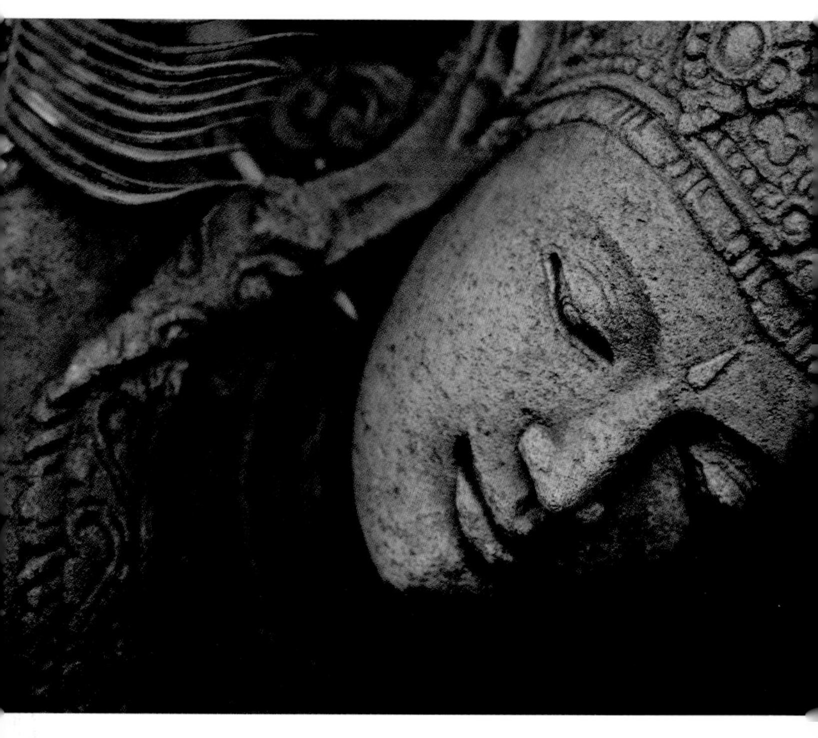

© zhu difeng

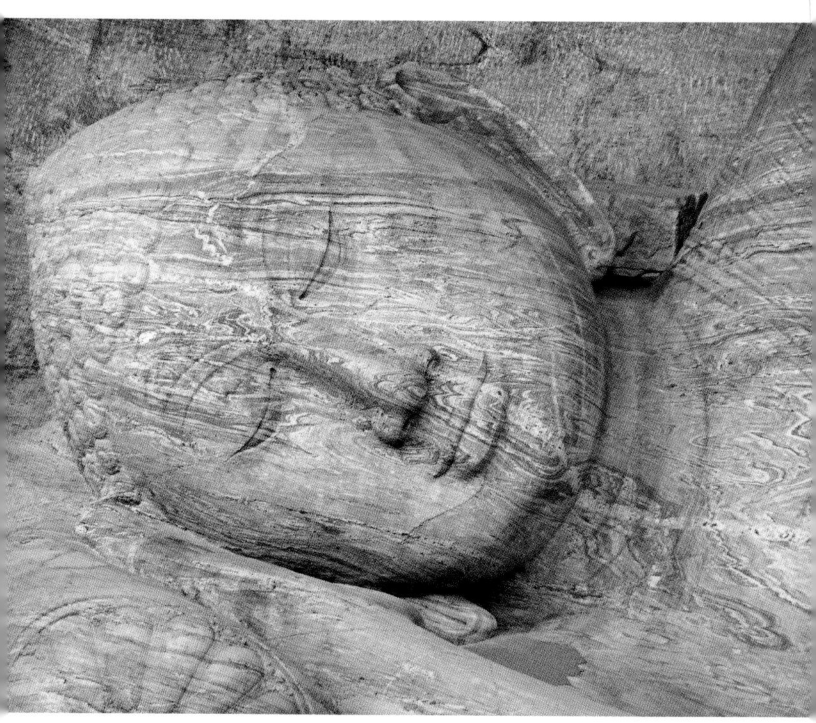

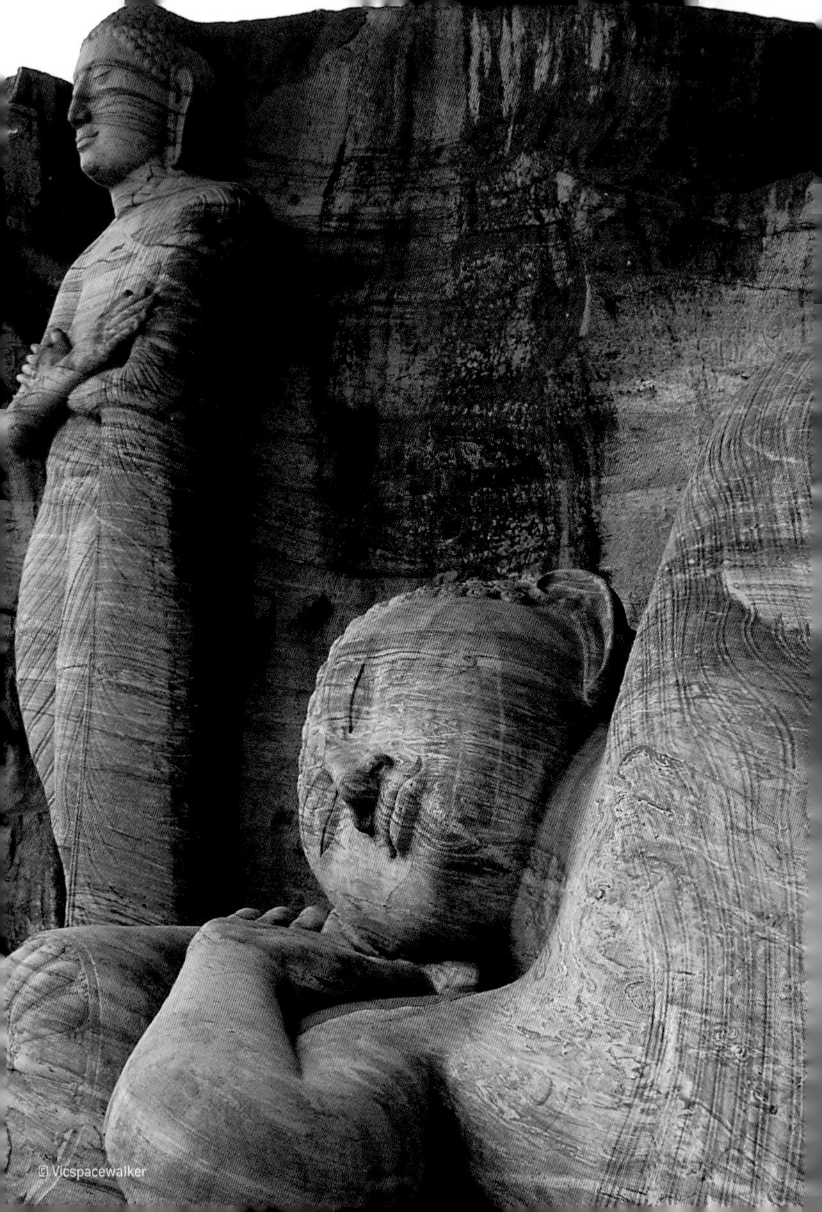
© Vicspacewalker

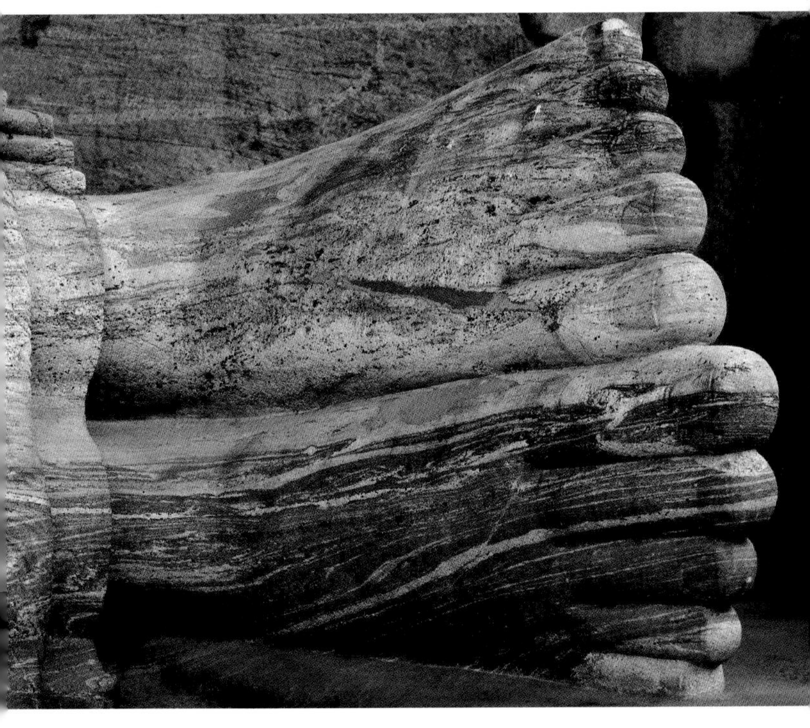

Smiling Buddha
Bouddha souriant
Lächelnder Buddha
Lachende Boeddha

It is believed that the figure of smiling Buddha takes its origins from the Liang Dynasty, China, and that really, he is a monk known as Hotei. The idea that it represents Maitreya, the next Buddha, is linked to the political context in which he lived, since the figure of the Buddha, the sign of what is to come, was the object of intense political conflict. As such, Hotei is used as the allegory that personal salvation must be achieved in the present, and by vain hope.

He is generally seen with a cloth bundle, in which he carries rice plants, (which represent happiness), sweets for children, and food. That he is normally surrounded by children is no coincidence, as children are considered to be beautiful beings.

His prominent belly gives alludes to the Chinese tradition: the stomach is considered to represent his good heart and a symbol of happiness, good fortune, and fullness. It is for this reason that his body is seen as a luck charm.

Il semblerait que la figure du Bouddha souriant tire son origine de la Dynastie Liang, en Chine, et qu'il s'agisse en réalité d'un moine connu sous le nom d'Hotei. L'idée qu'il représente Maitreya, le prochain Bouddha, est liée au contexte politique de l'époque à laquelle il a vécu, étant donné que la figure du prochain bouddha faisait l'objet de luttes politiques intenses. Ainsi, Hotei est utilisé comme une allégorie selon laquelle le salut personnel doit se faire au moment présent et non par une attente vaine.

Il est généralement représenté portant un sac en tissu qui contient des plantes de riz (symbole du bonheur), des sucreries pour les enfants et de la nourriture. Ce n'est pas un hasard qu'il soit souvent entouré d'enfants : les enfants sont considérés comme des êtres précieux.

Son ventre proéminent provient de la tradition chinoise qui considère l'estomac comme une allégorie de la bonté et un symbole du bonheur, de la chance et de la plénitude. C'est pour cette raison qu'il est considéré comme un porte-bonheur.

Man glaubt, dass die Figur des lächelnden Buddhas ihren Ursprung in der chinesischen Liang Dynastie hat, und es sich in Wirklichkeit um einen als Hotei bekannten Mönch handelt. Die Vorstellung, dass er Maitreya darstellt, den nächsten Buddha, ist mit dem politischen Kontext verbunden, in dem er lebte, da die Figur des künftigen Buddhas Gegenstand heftiger politischer Kämpfe war. So wird Hotei als Alegorie dafür benutzt, dass die persönliche Erlösung in der Gegenwart geschehen muss und nicht durch eine vergebliche Erwartung.

Normalerweise sieht man ihn mit einem Stoffbündel, in dem er Reispflanzen, die das Glück darstellen, Süßigkeiten für die Kinder und Speisen trägt. Die Tatsache, dass er oft von Kindern umgeben erscheint, ist kein Zufall, da die Kleinen als kostbare Wesen betrachtet werden.

Sein hervorstehender Bauch geht aus der chinesischen Tradition hervor, die den Magen als Sinnbild seines guten Herzens und als Symbol für Glück, und Erfüllung ansieht. Daher dient seine Figur auch als Amulett.

Men denkt dat de lachende Boeddhafiguur zijn oorsprong vindt in de Chinese Liang-dynastie. In werkelijkheid gaat het om een als Hotei bekende monnik. Het idee dat dit beeld Maitreya, de volgende Boeddha, voorstelt wordt in verband gebracht met het politieke kader waarin hij leefde. De nog te komen boeddha was namelijk het voorwerp van intense politieke strijd. Zo werd Hotei gebruikt als een zinnebeeld van het feit dat de persoonlijke redding zich in het heden moet voordoen, en niet aan de hand van een zinloos wachten.

Over het algemeen draagt deze boeddha een bundel stof, waarin hij rijstplanten draagt die voor geluk, zoetigheid voor de kinderen en eten staan. Het feit dat hij vaak wordt omgeven door kinderen is geen toeval, want de kleintjes worden beschouwd als mooie wezens.

Zijn uitspringende buik is afkomstig van de Chinese traditie, die de maag beschouwd als een zinnebeeld van een goed hart en een symbool van gelukzaligheid, geluk en volkomenheid. Daarom fungeert zijn beeld ook als amulet.

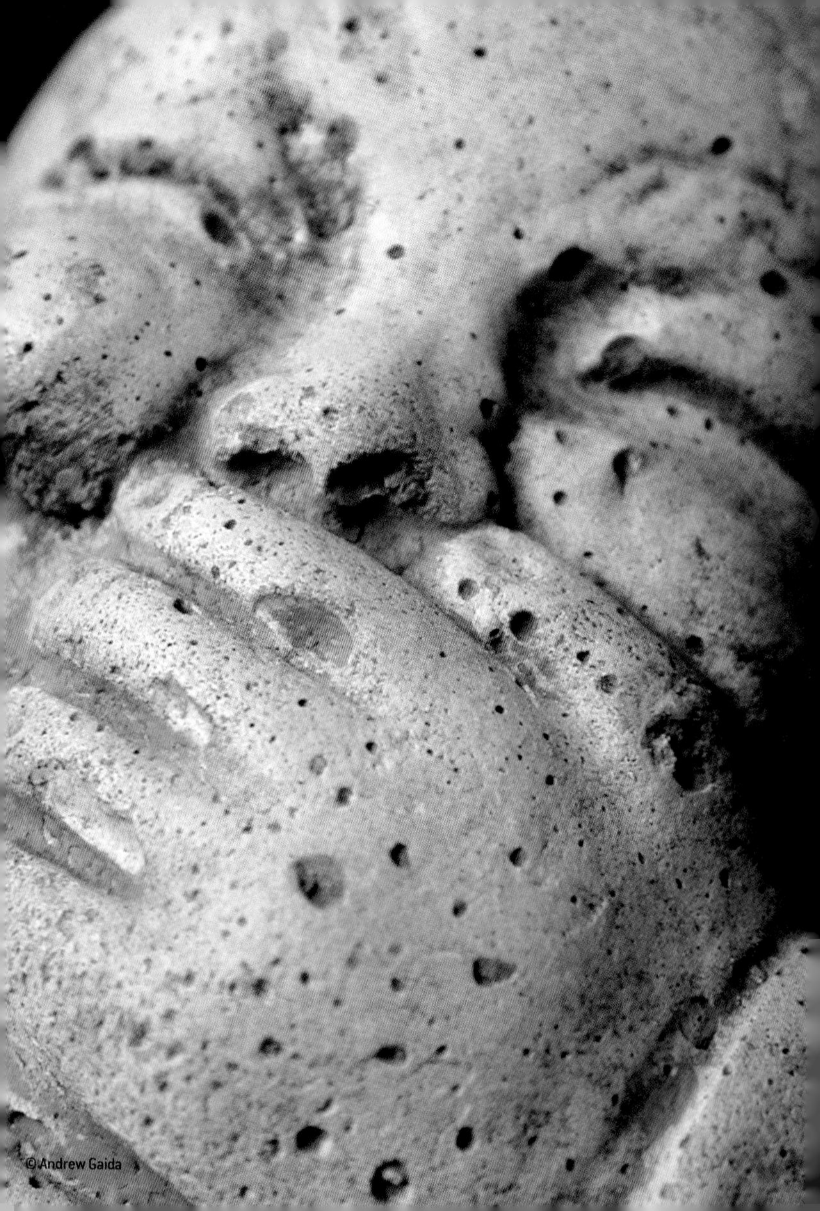

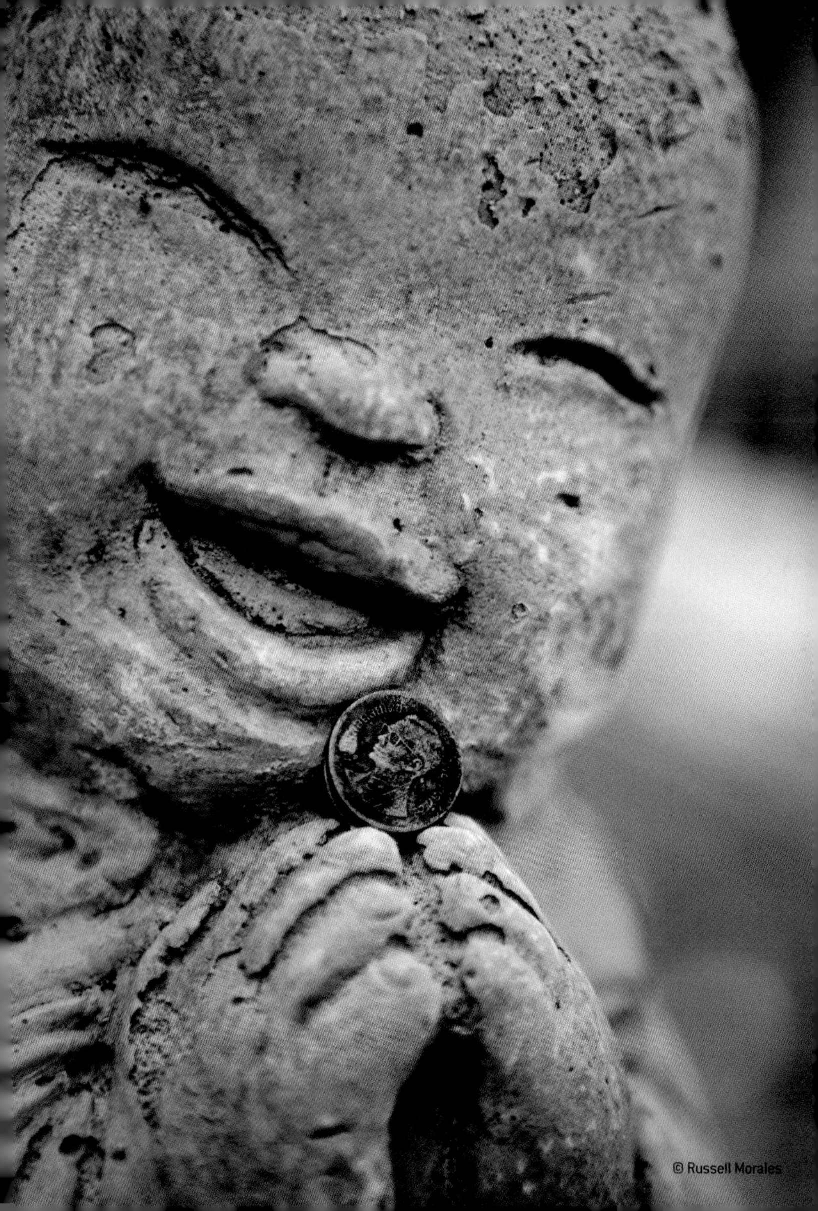

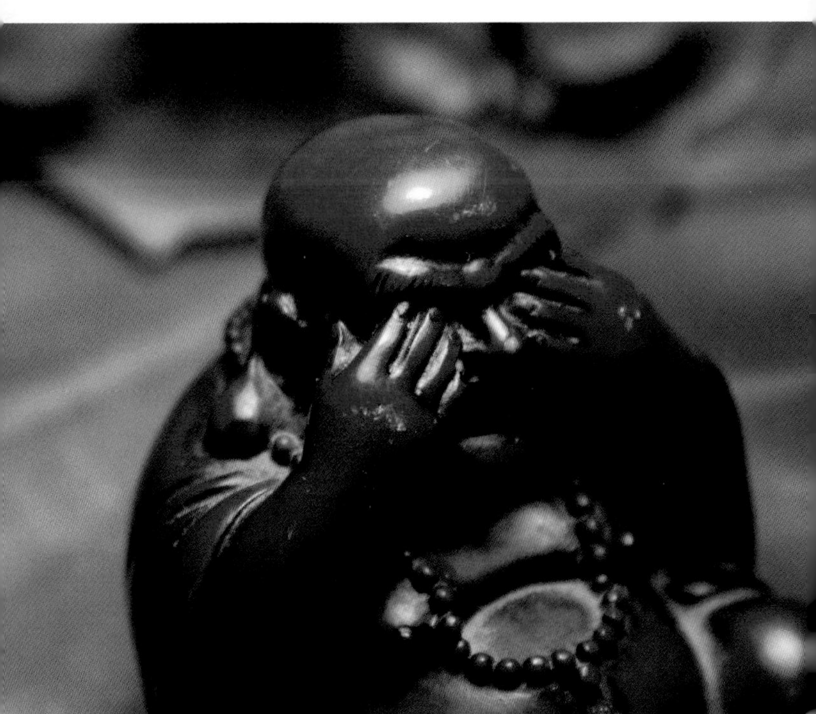

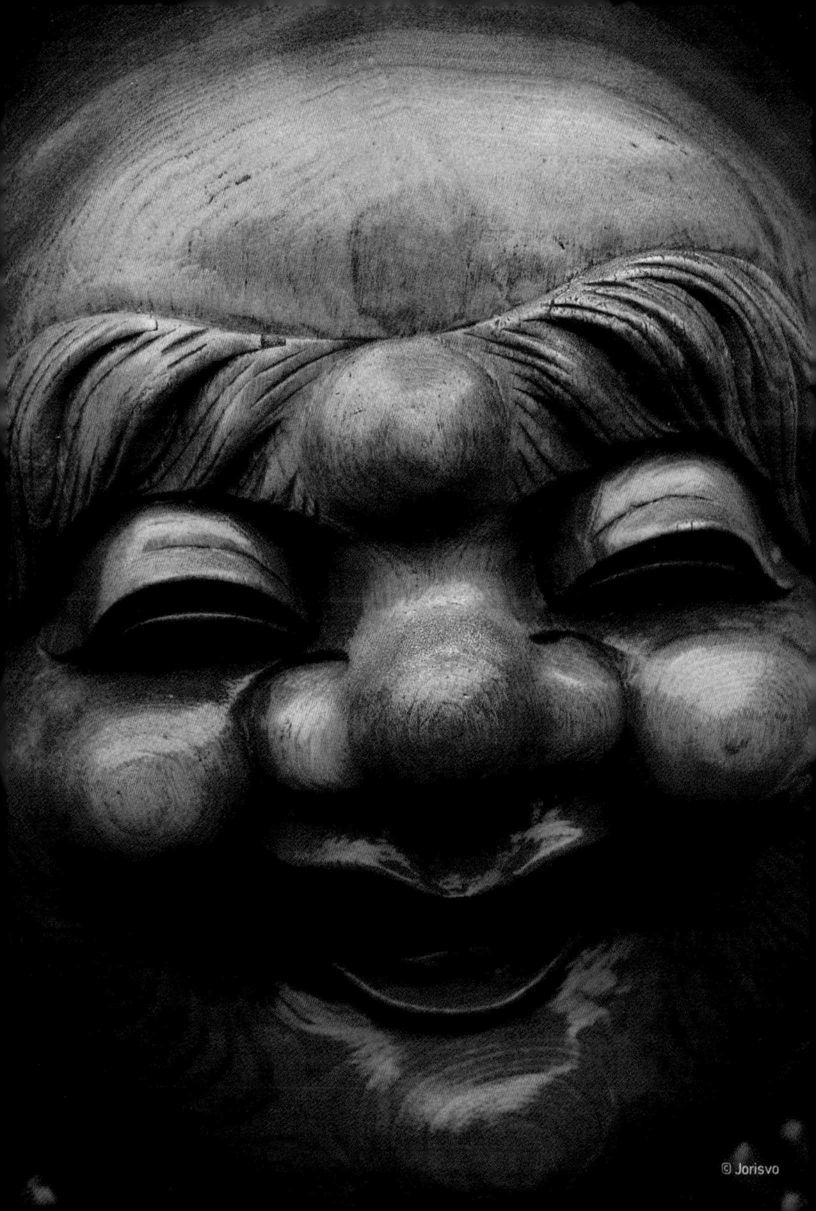

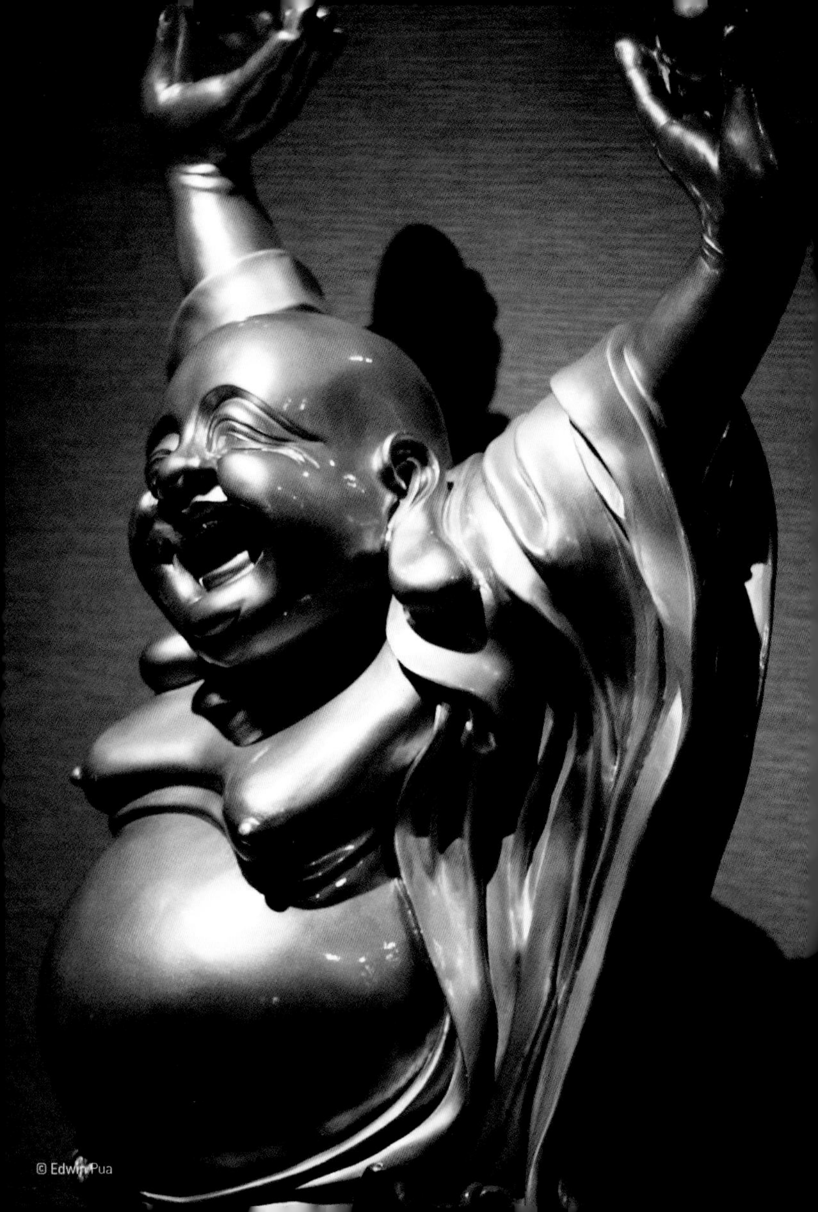

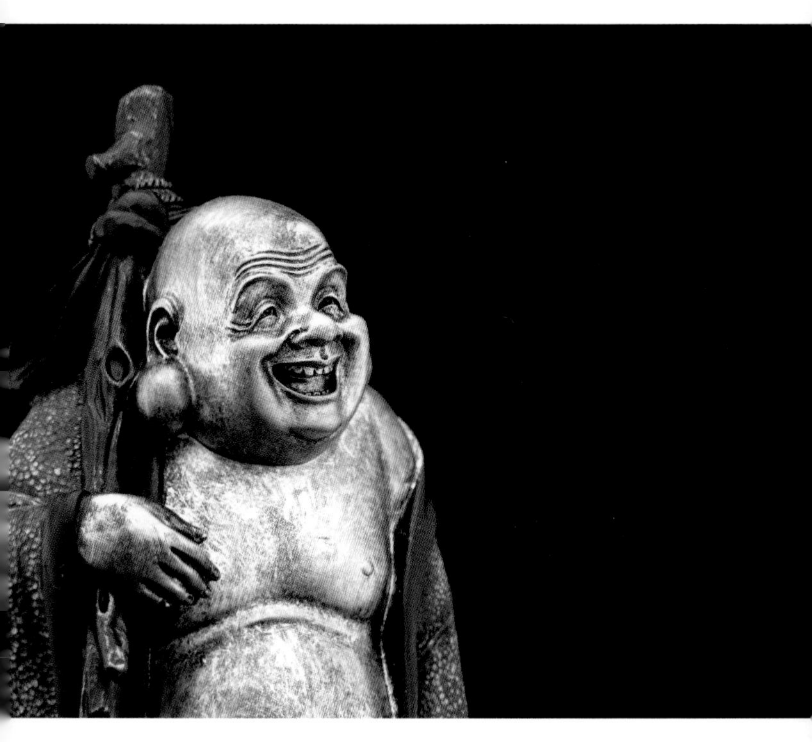

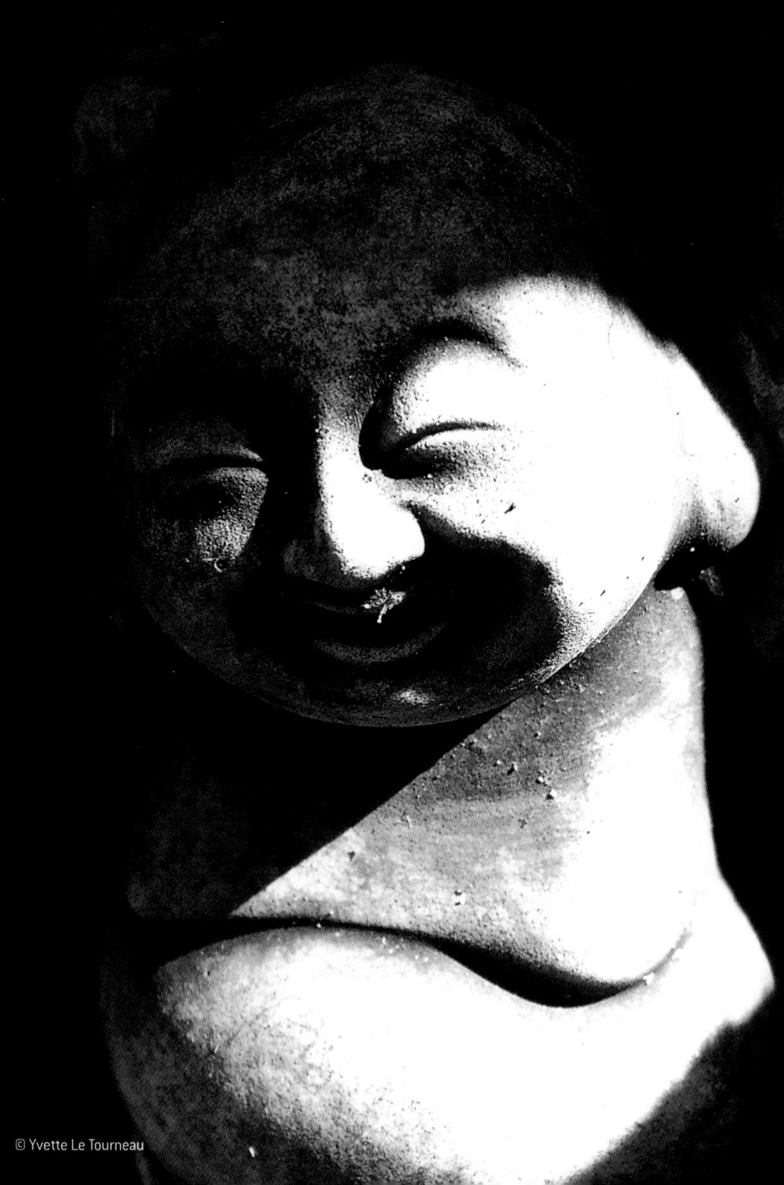

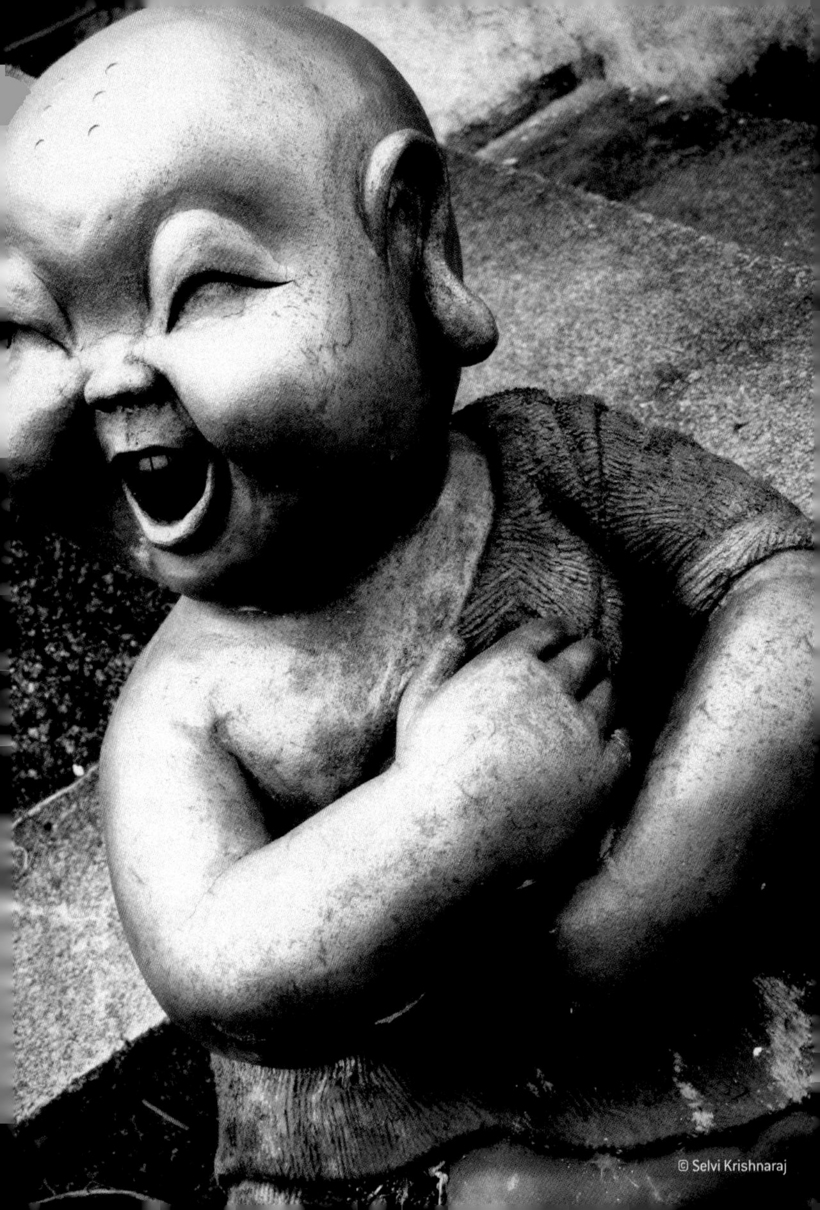

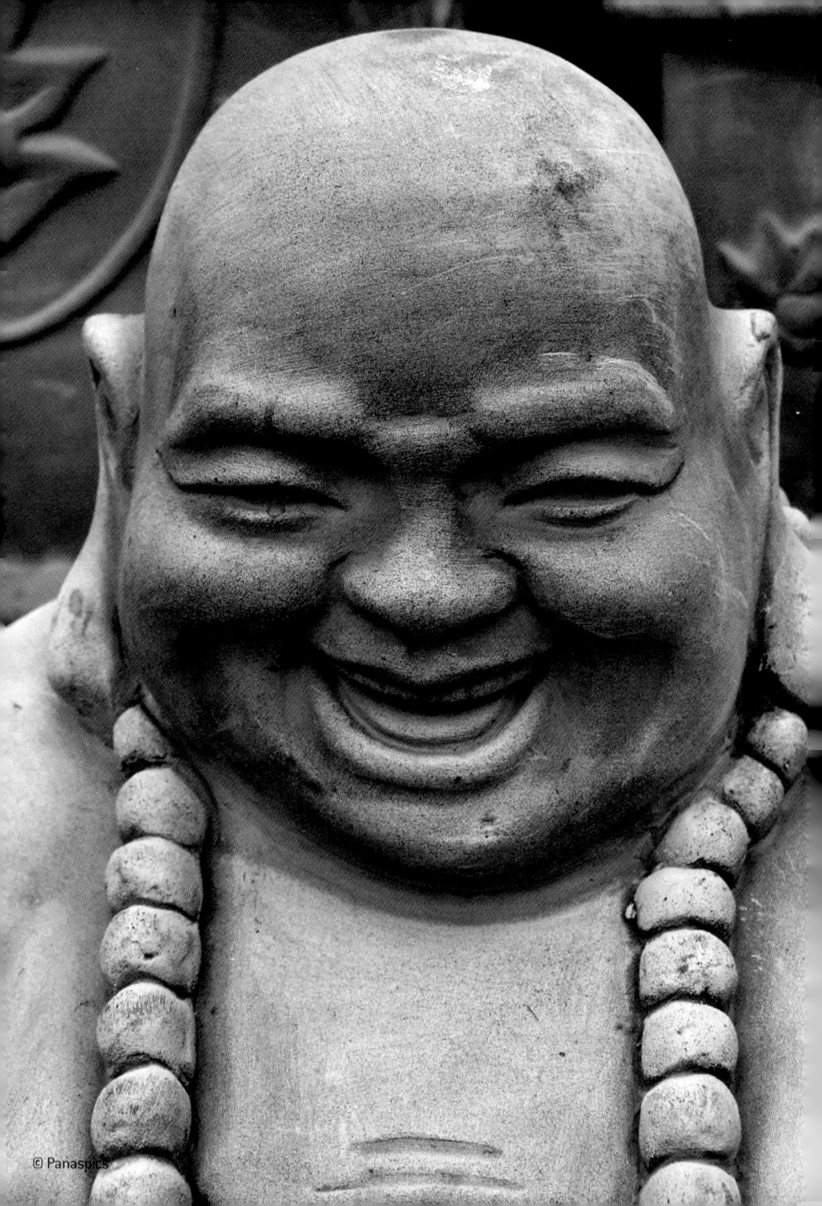

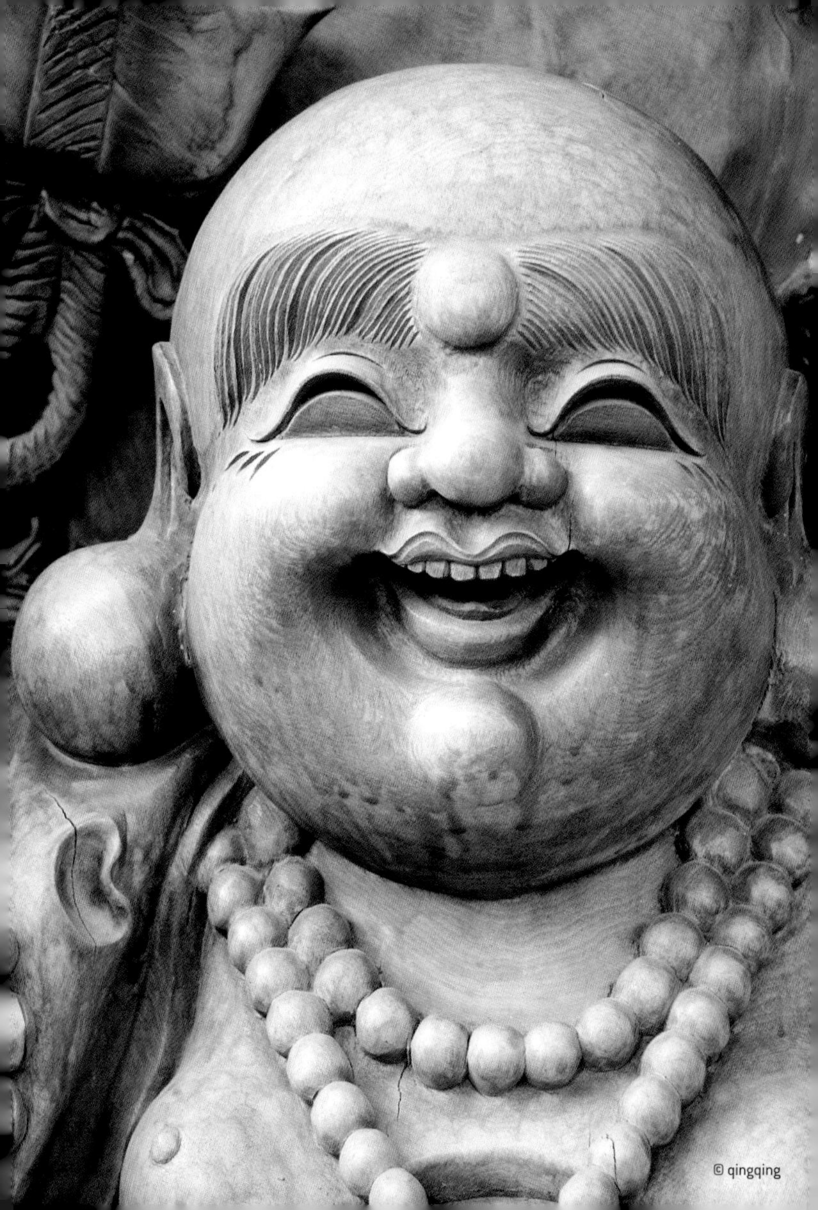
© qingqing

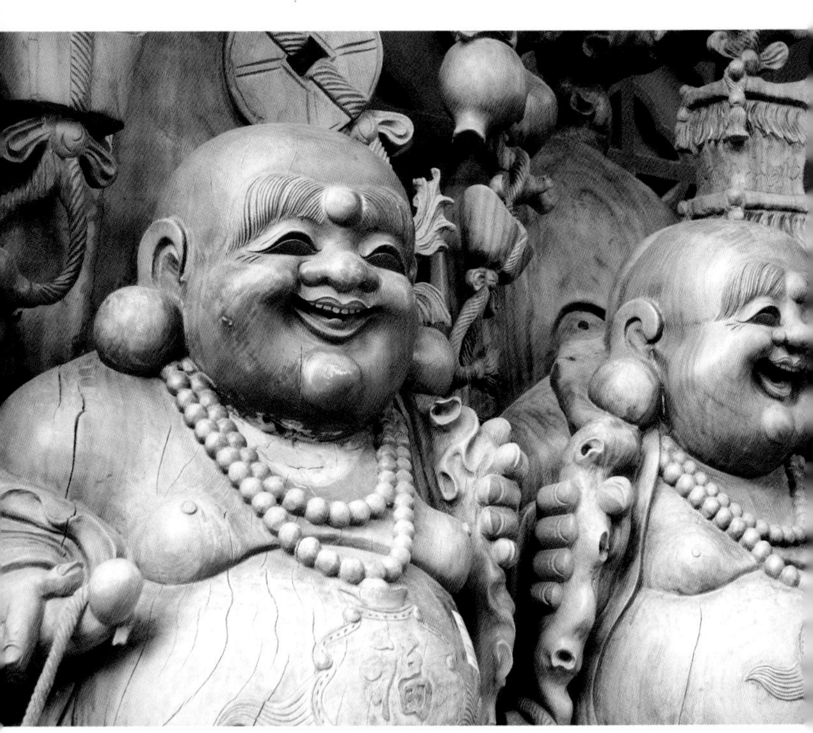
福

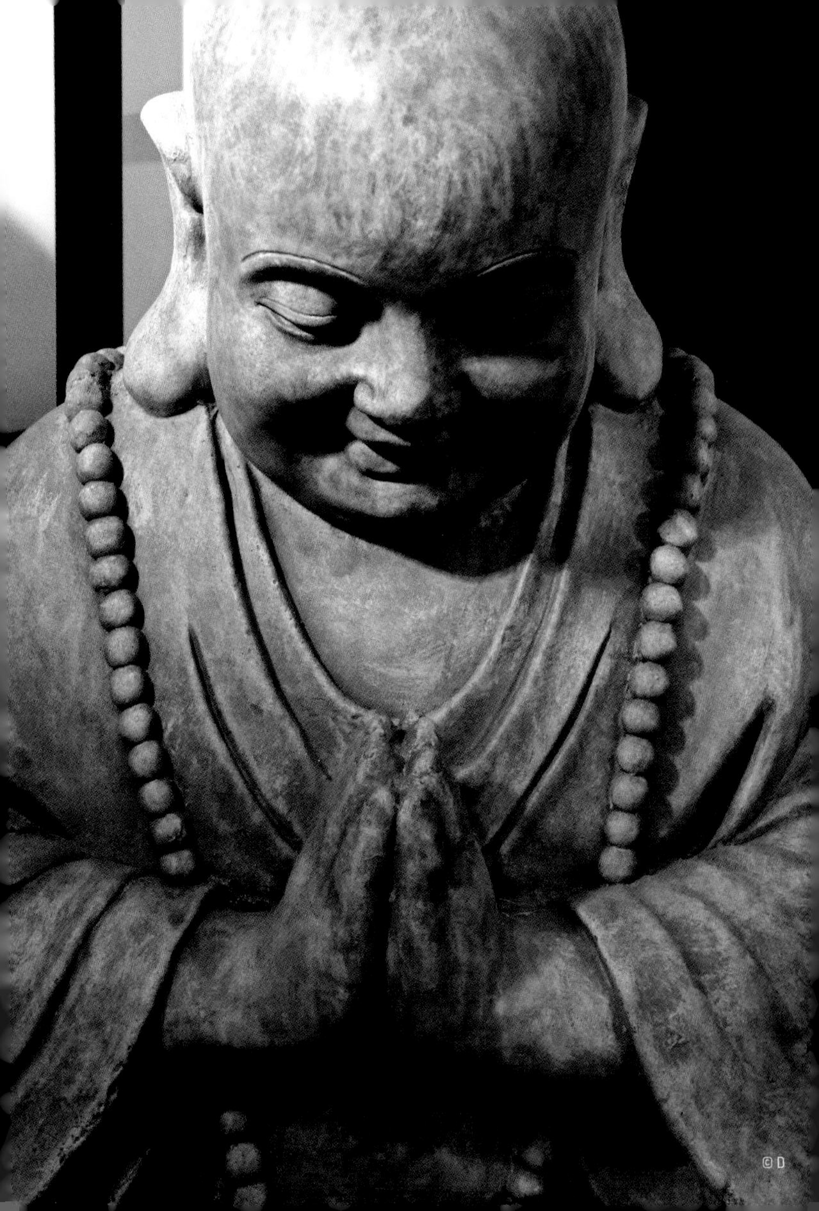

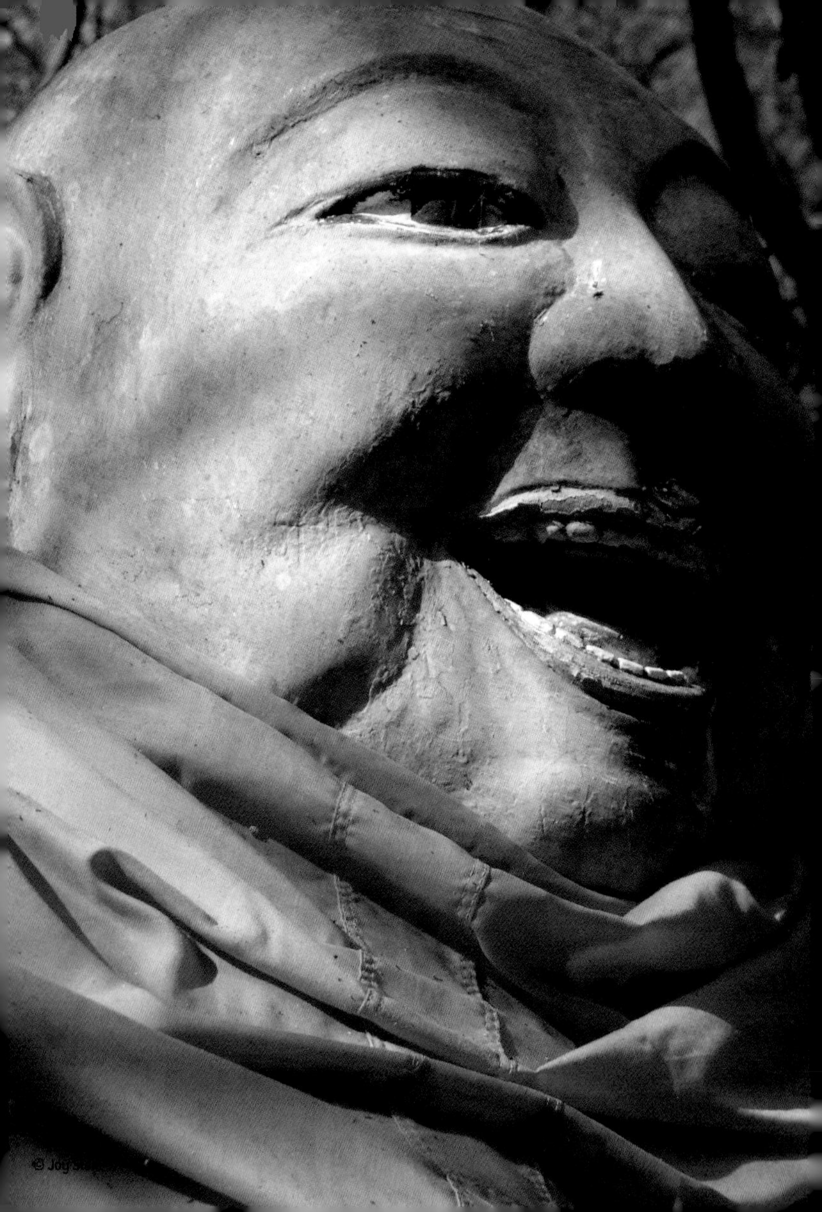

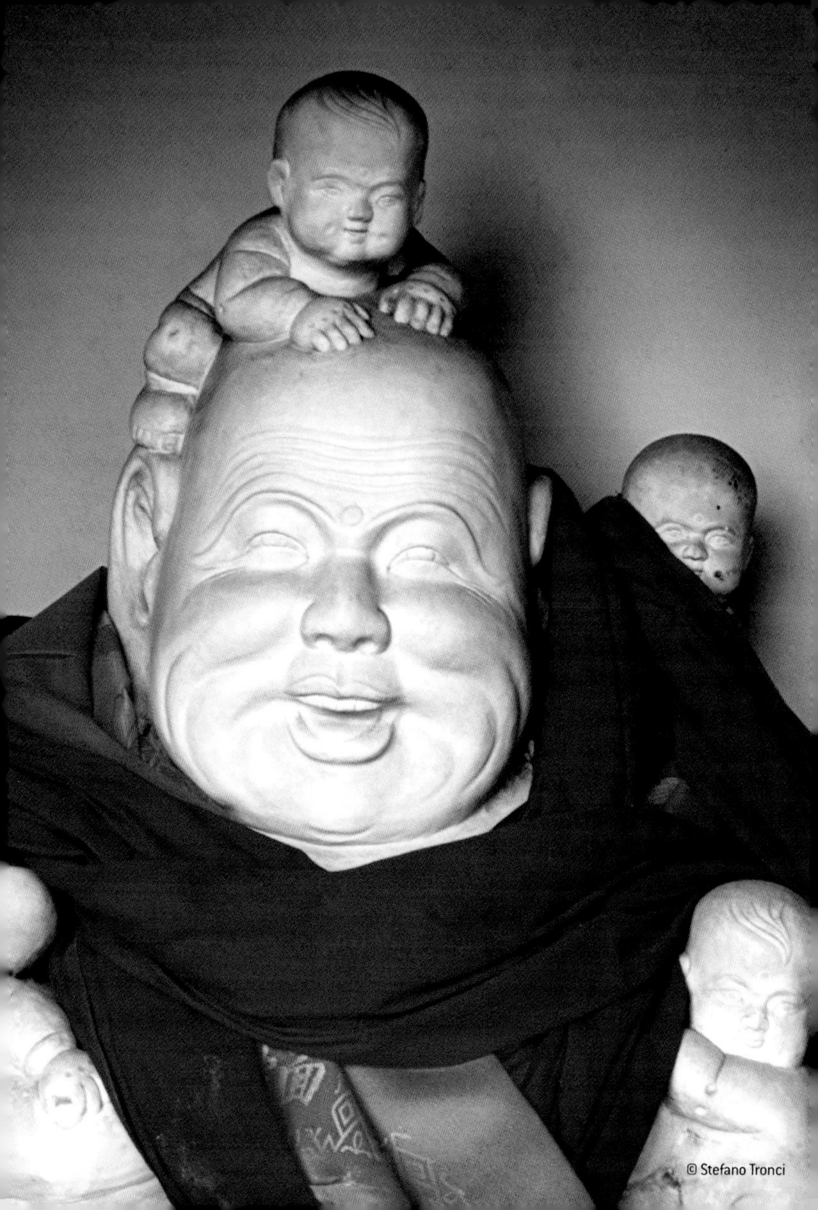

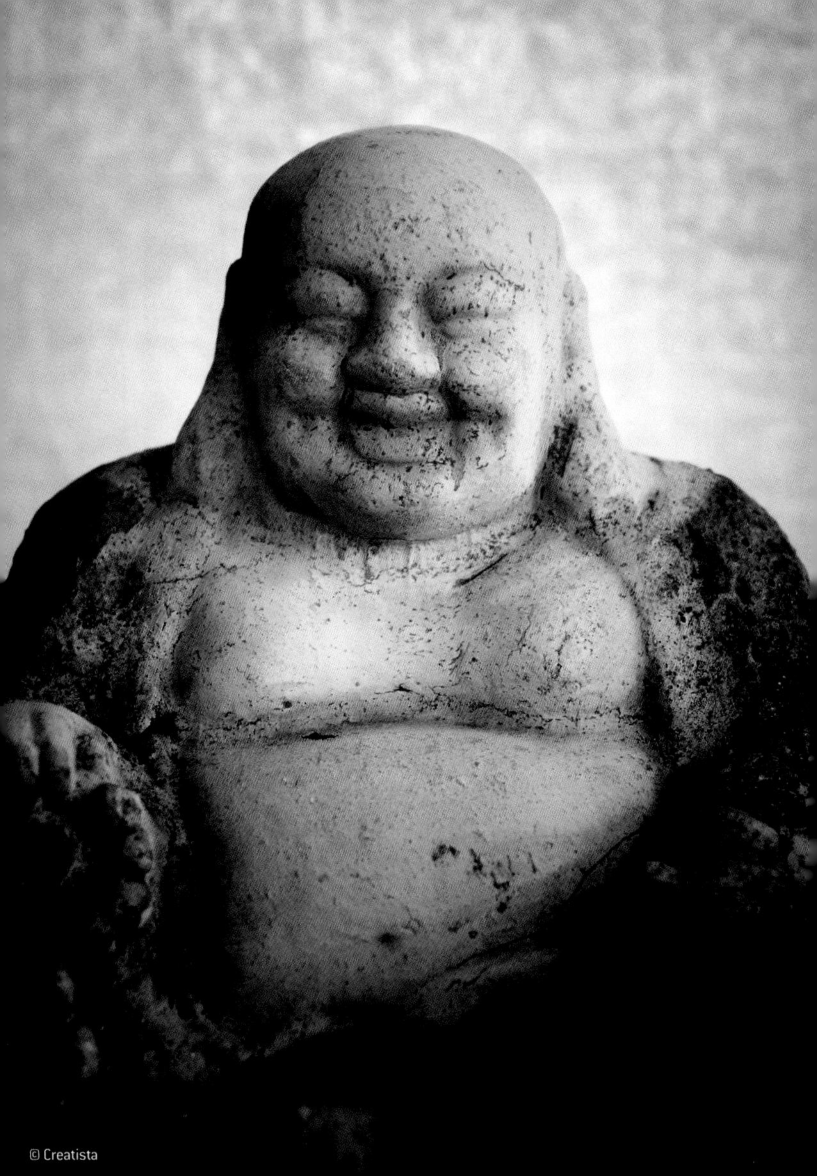

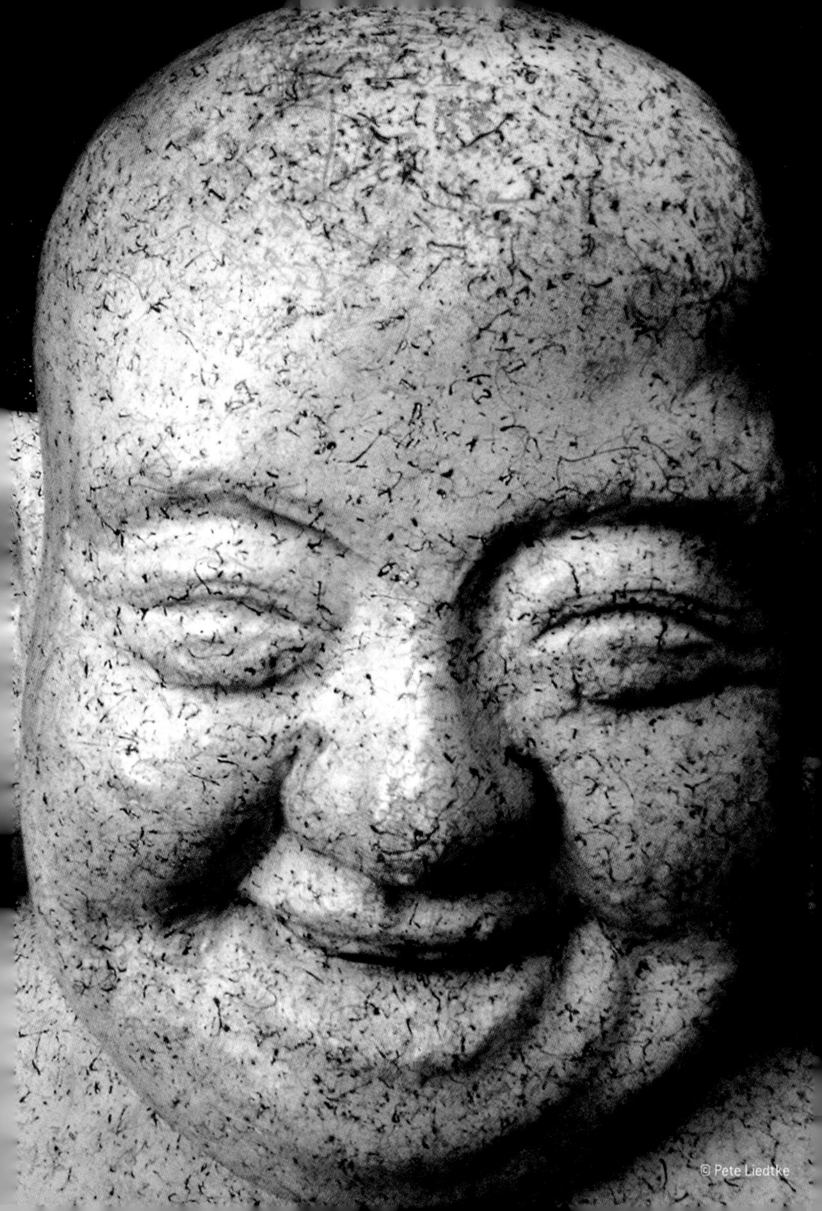

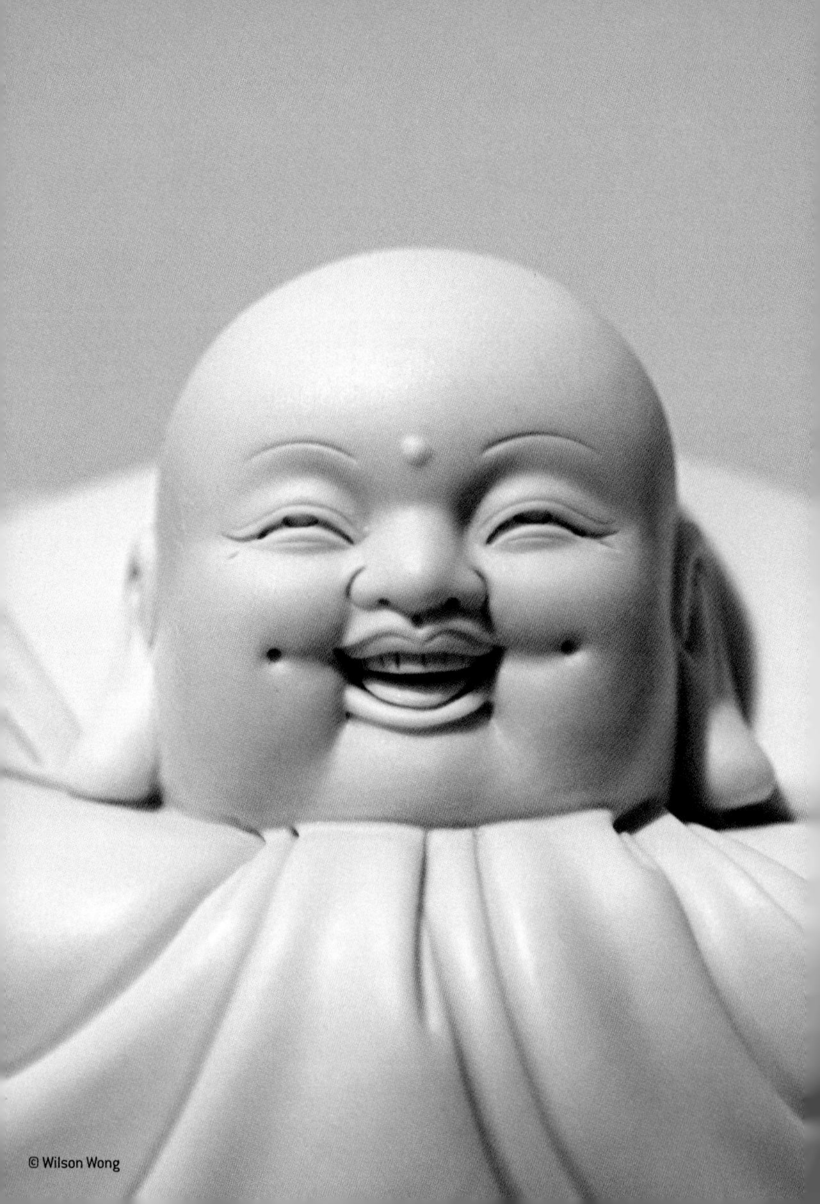

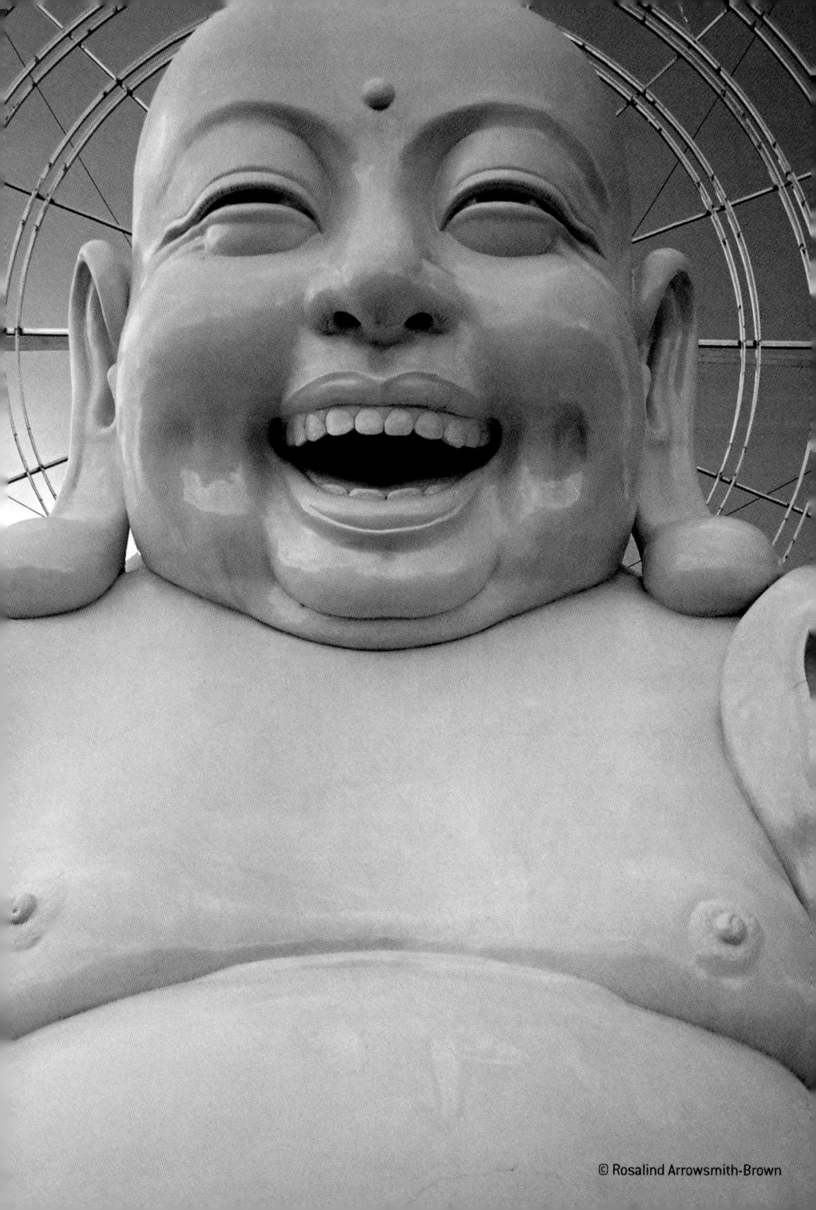

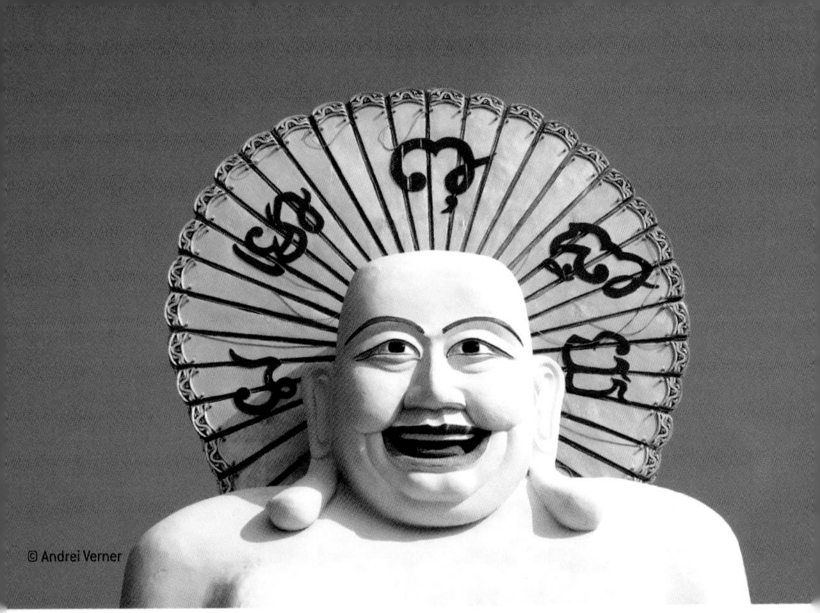

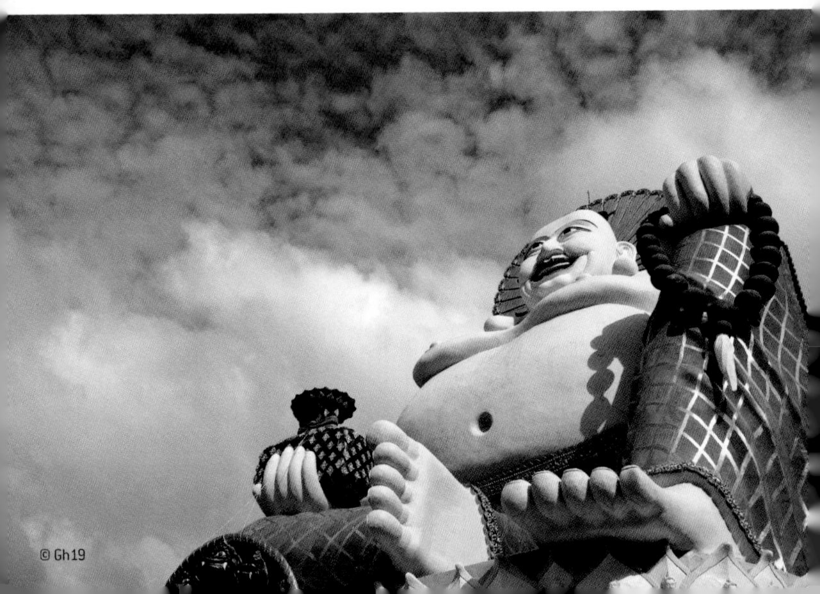

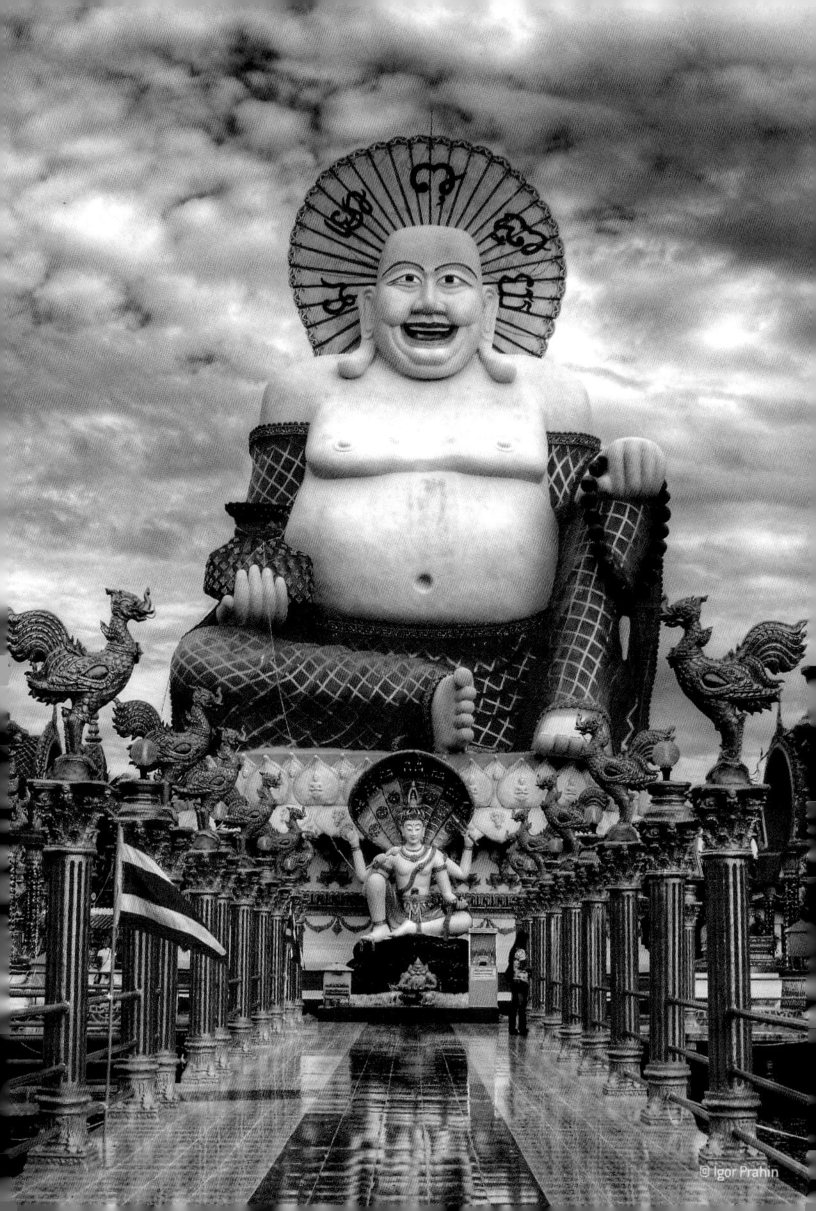

© Igor Prahin

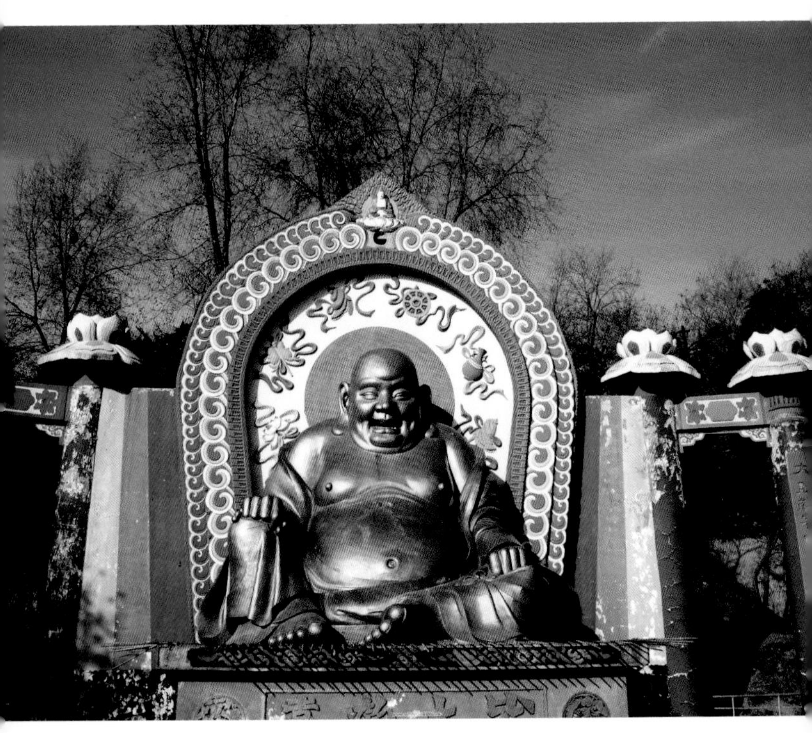

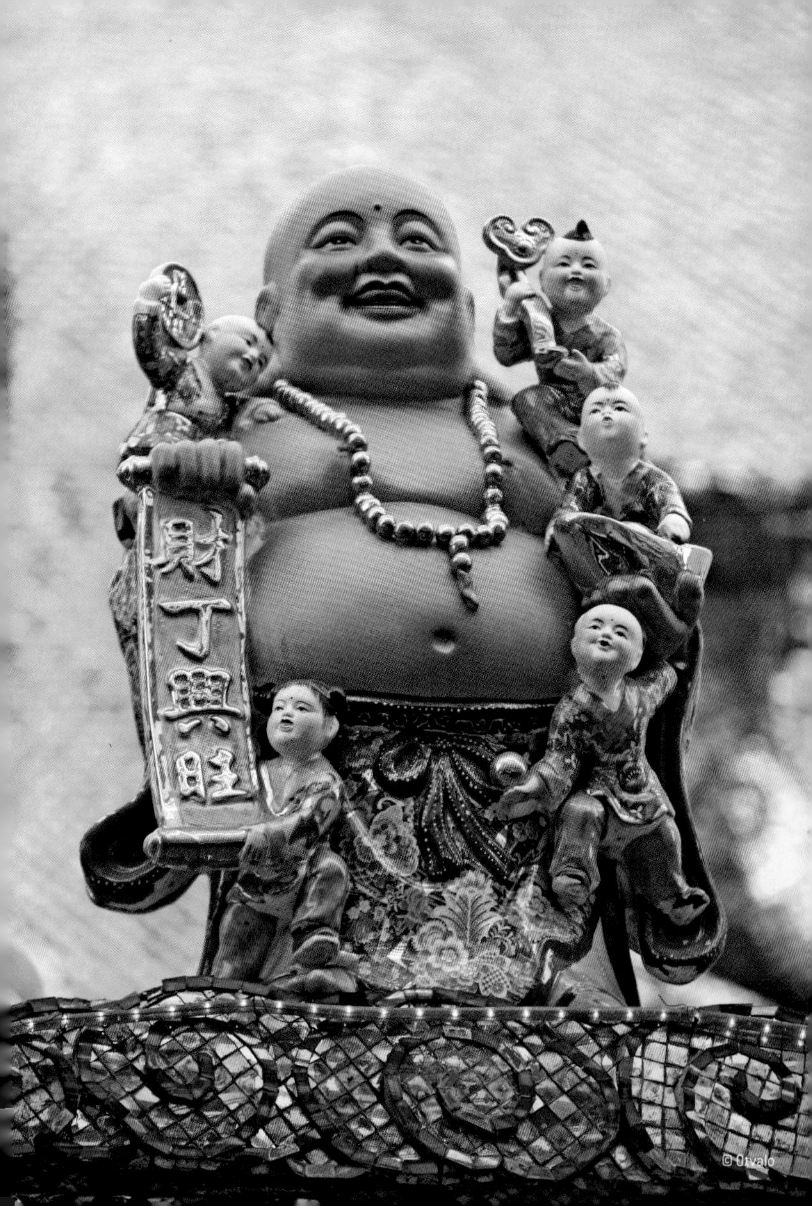
財
丁
興
旺

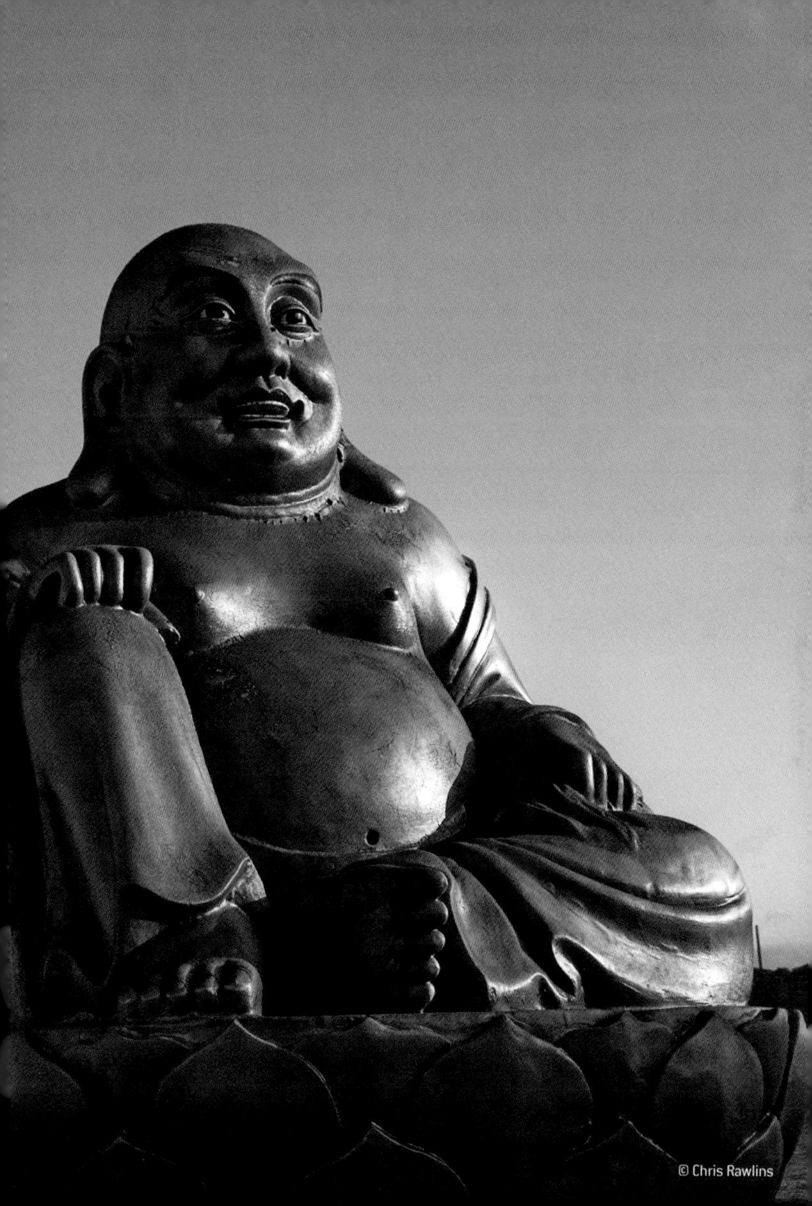

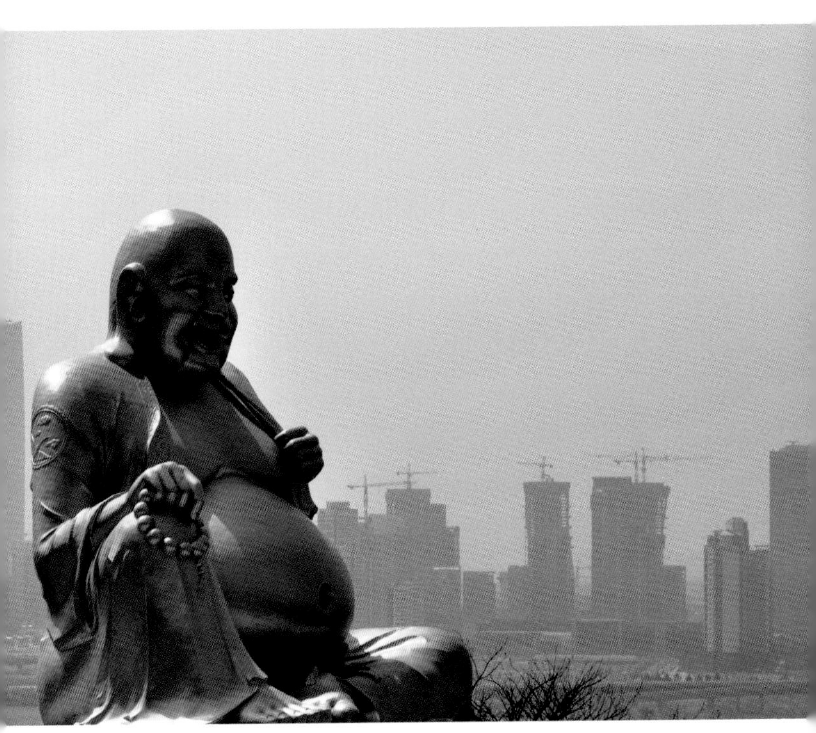

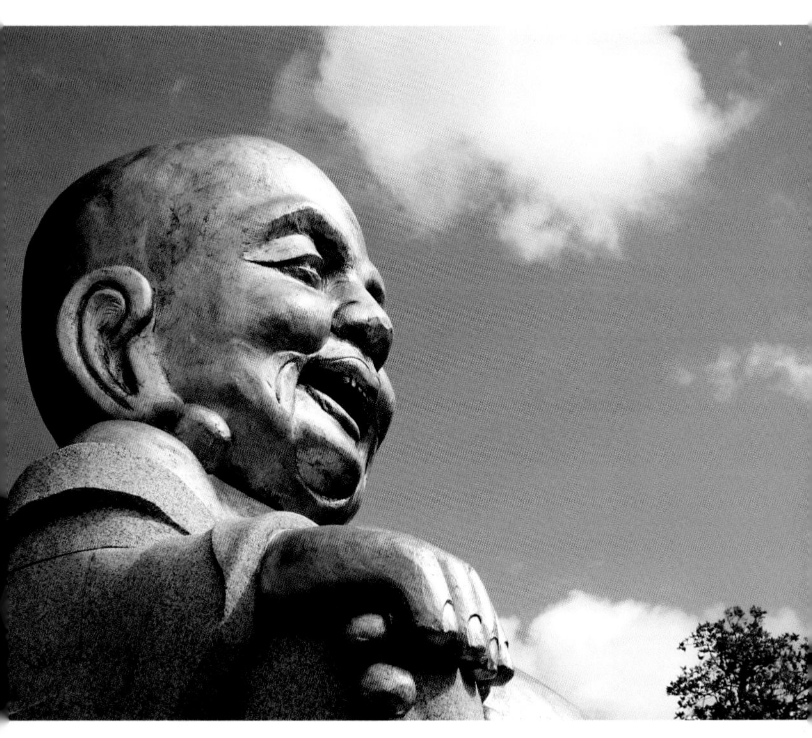

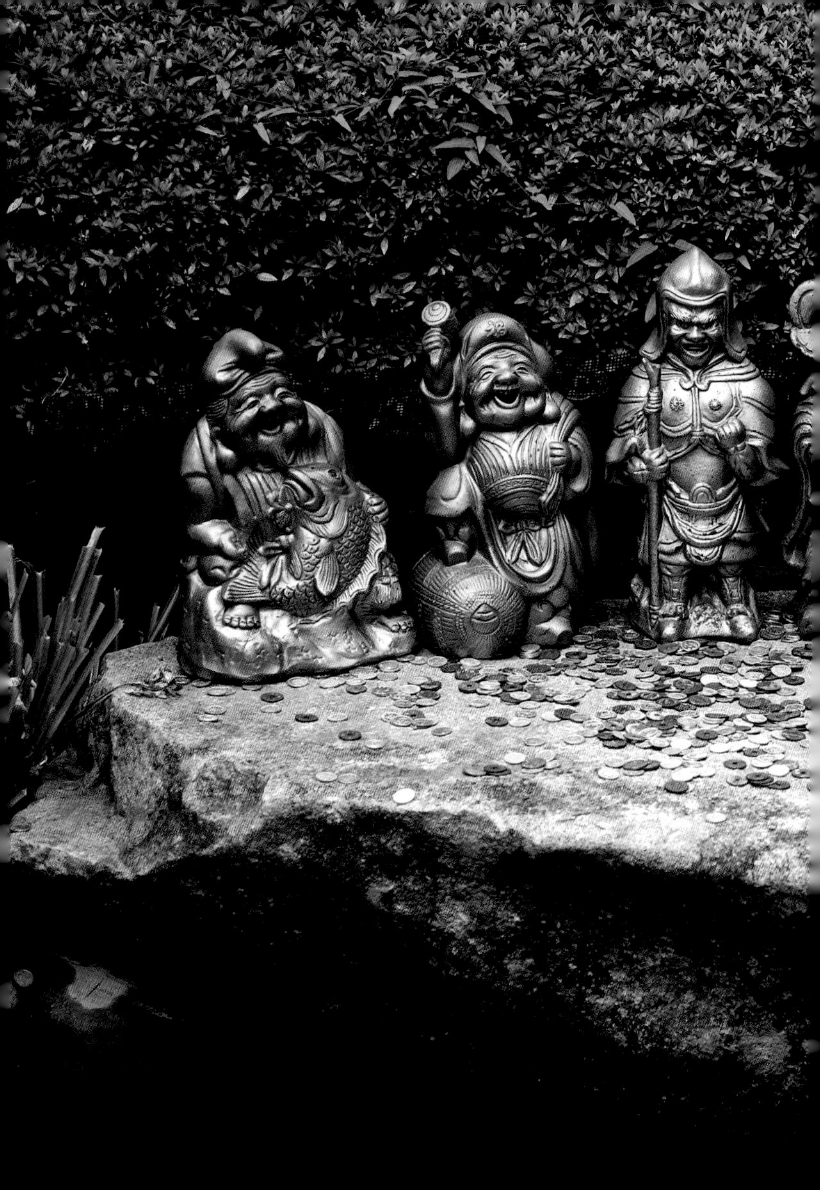

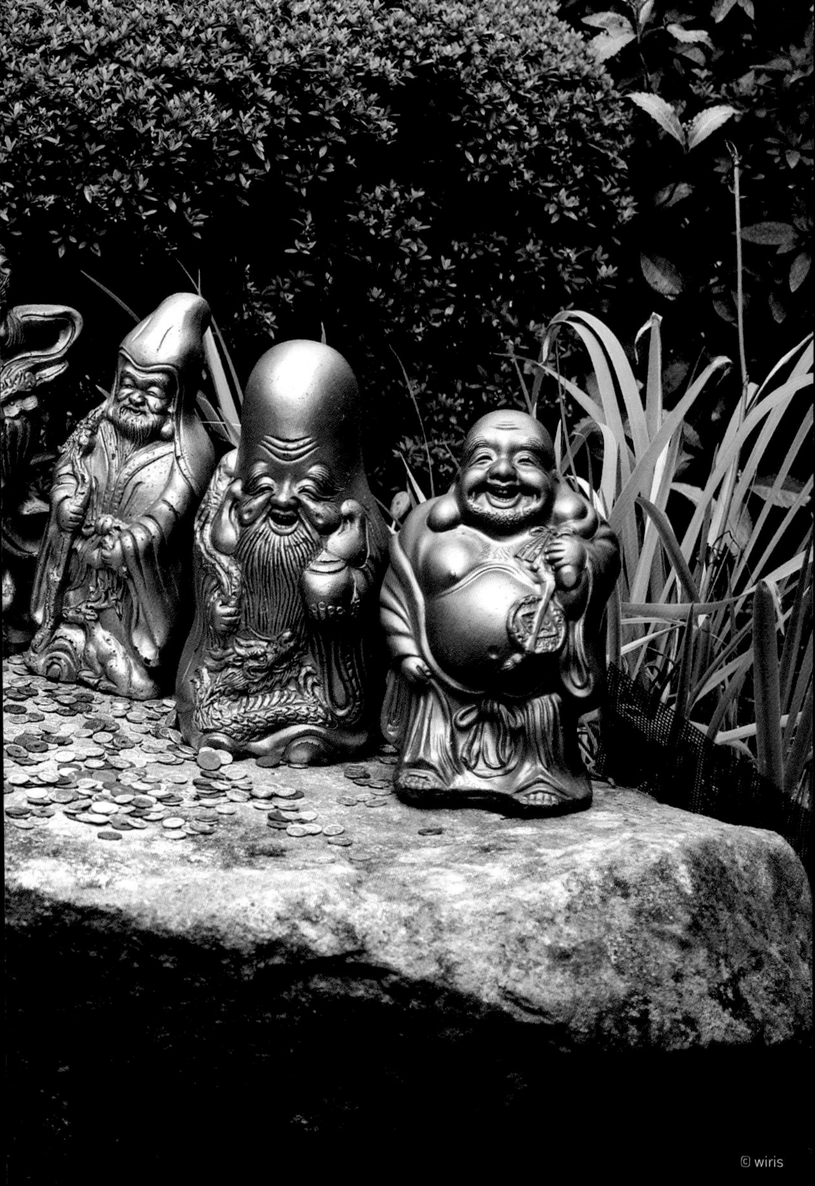

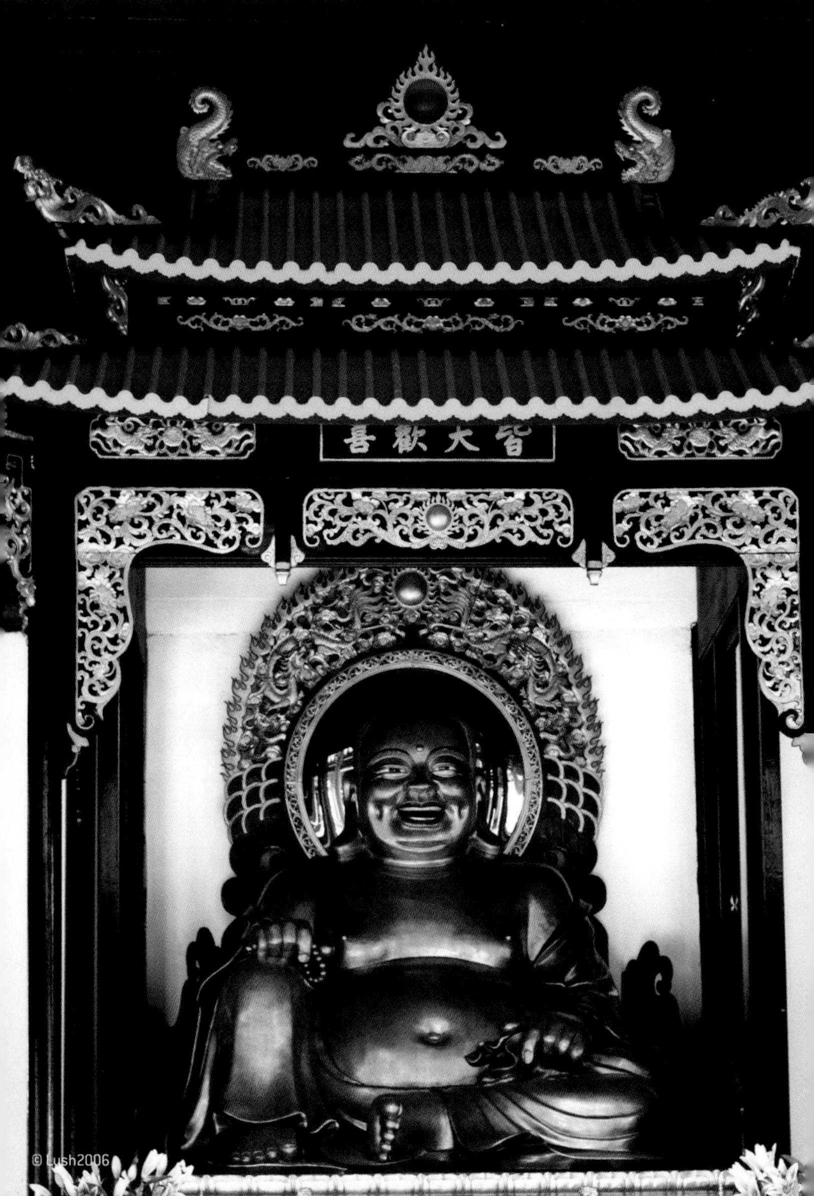
皆大歡喜

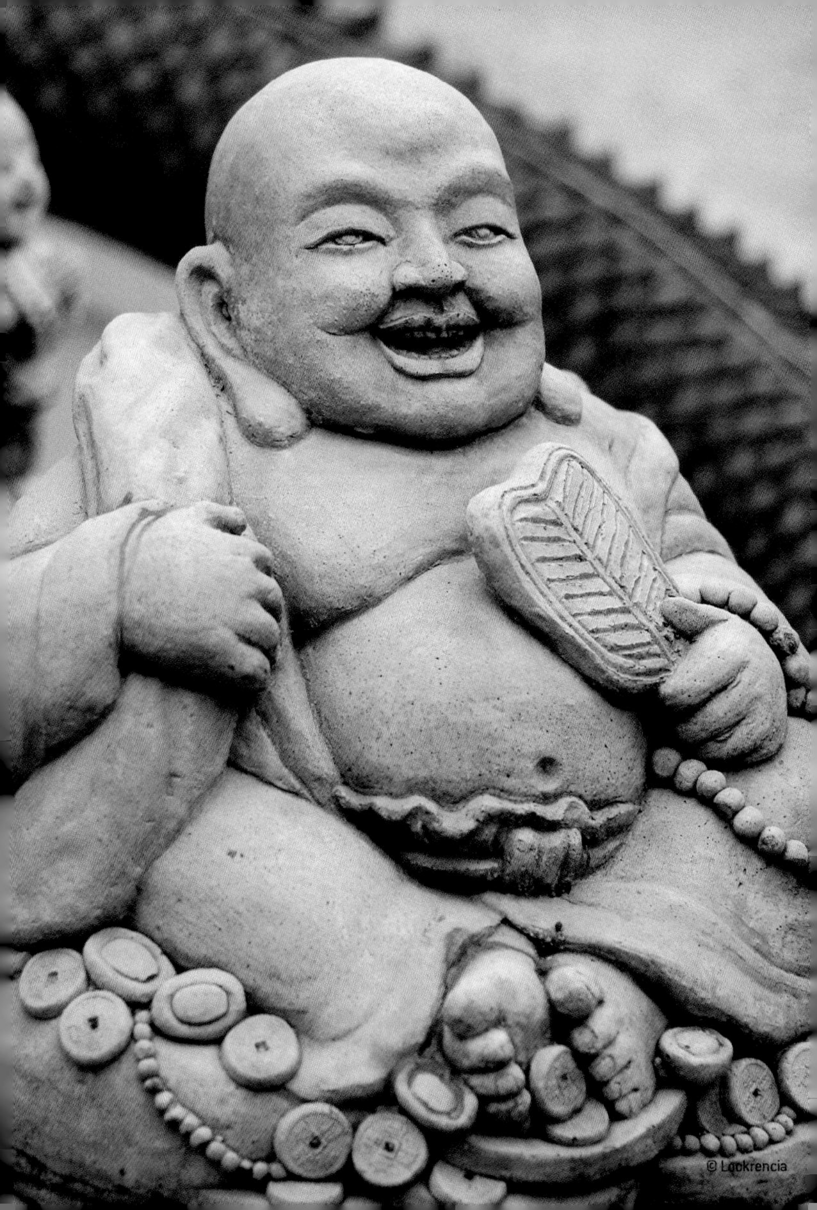

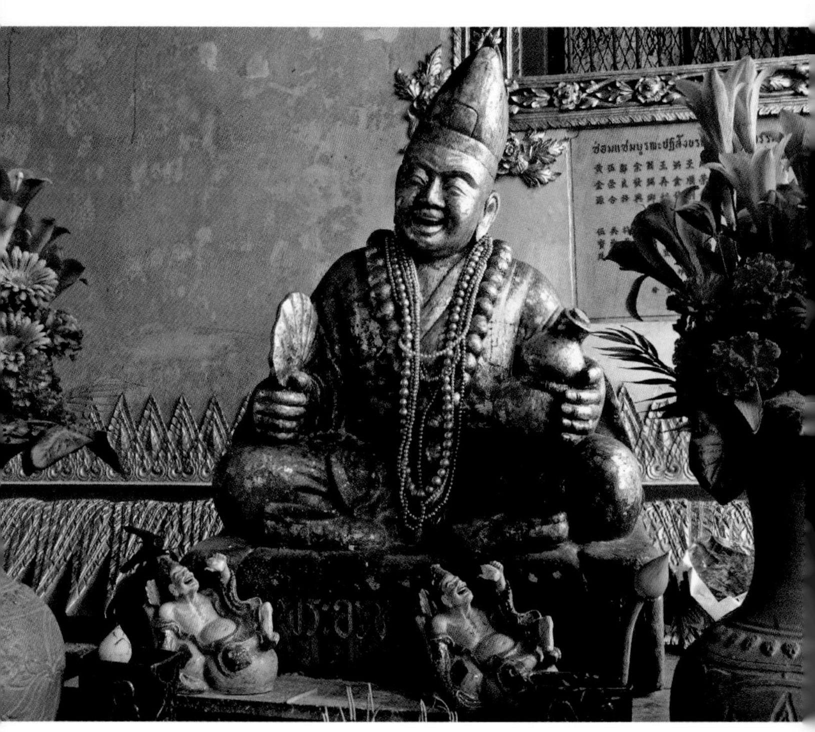

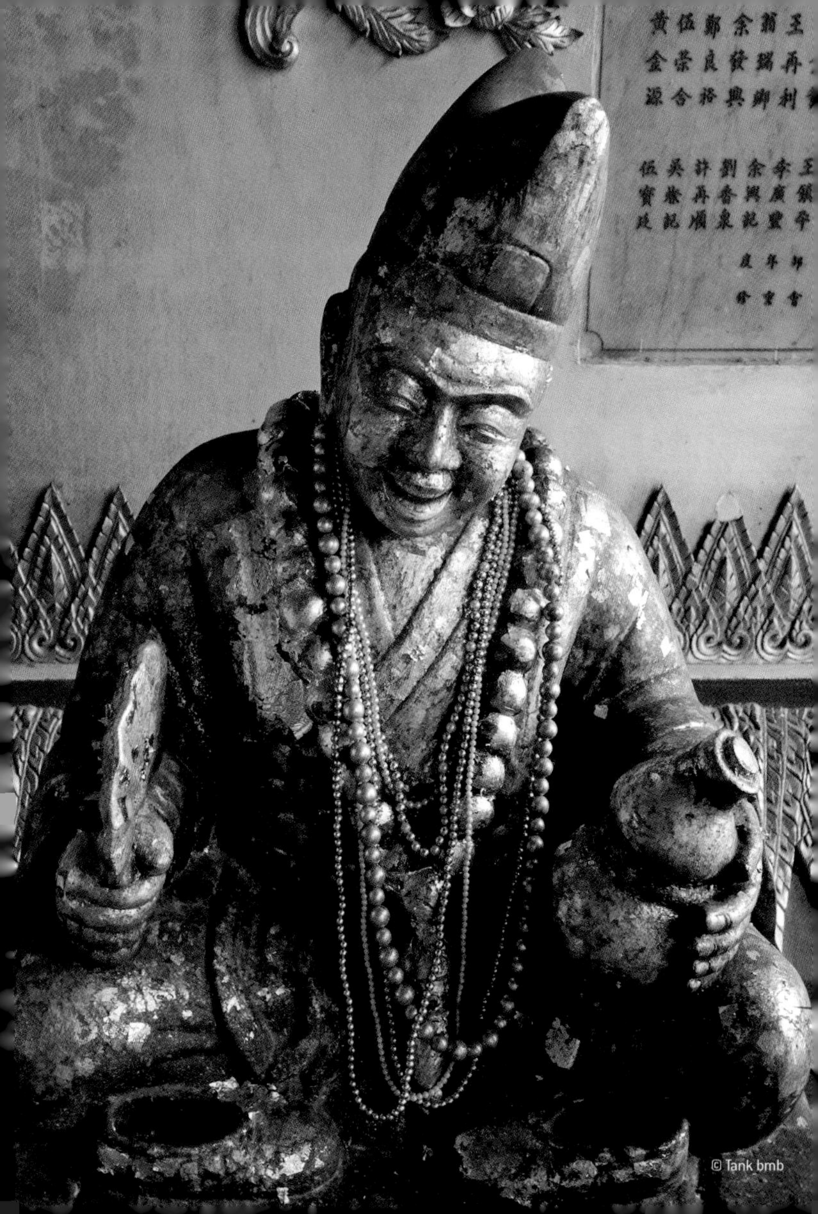

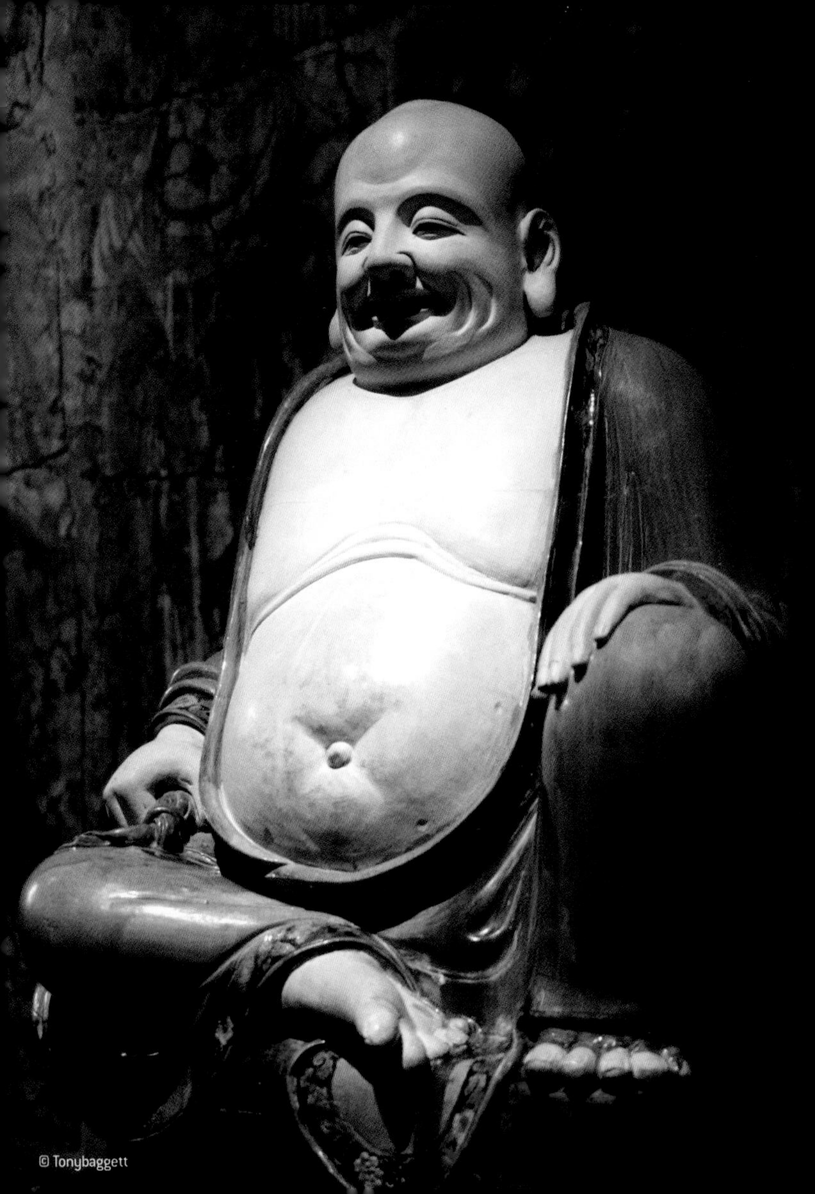

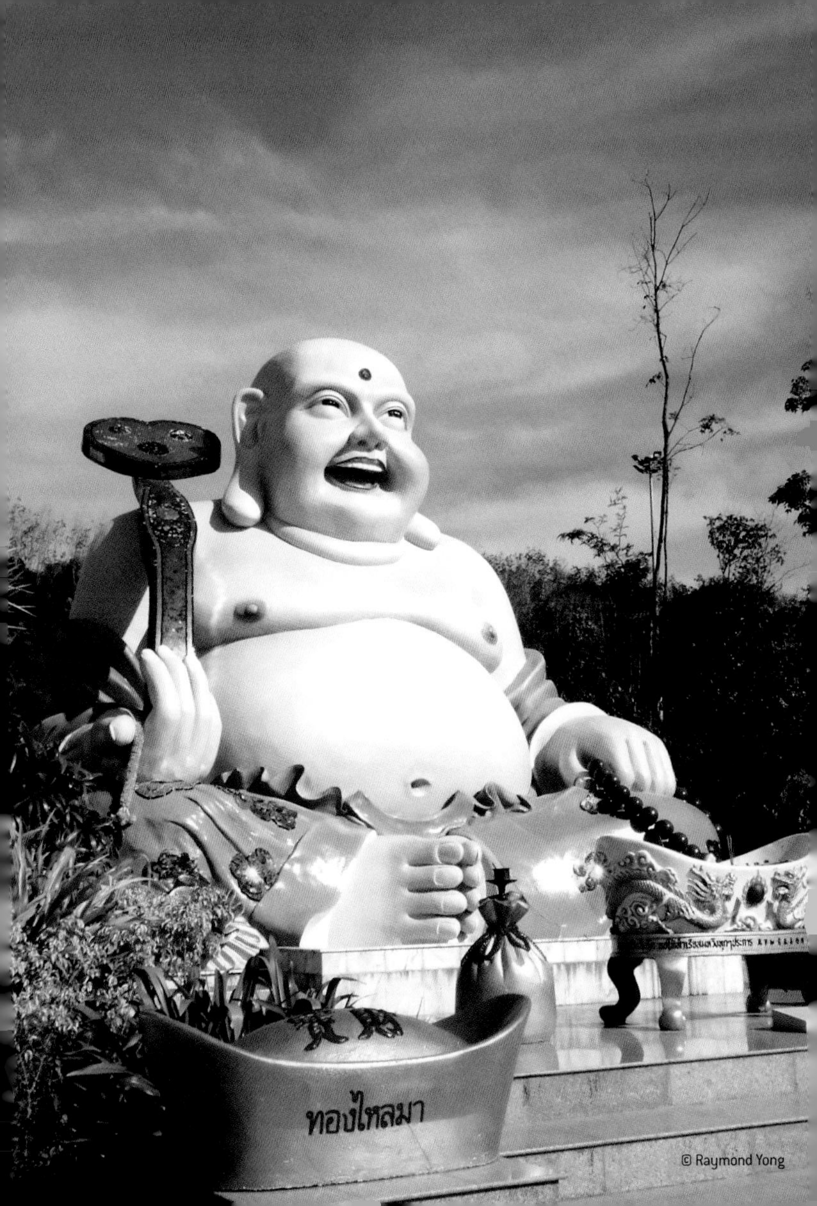
ทองไหลมา

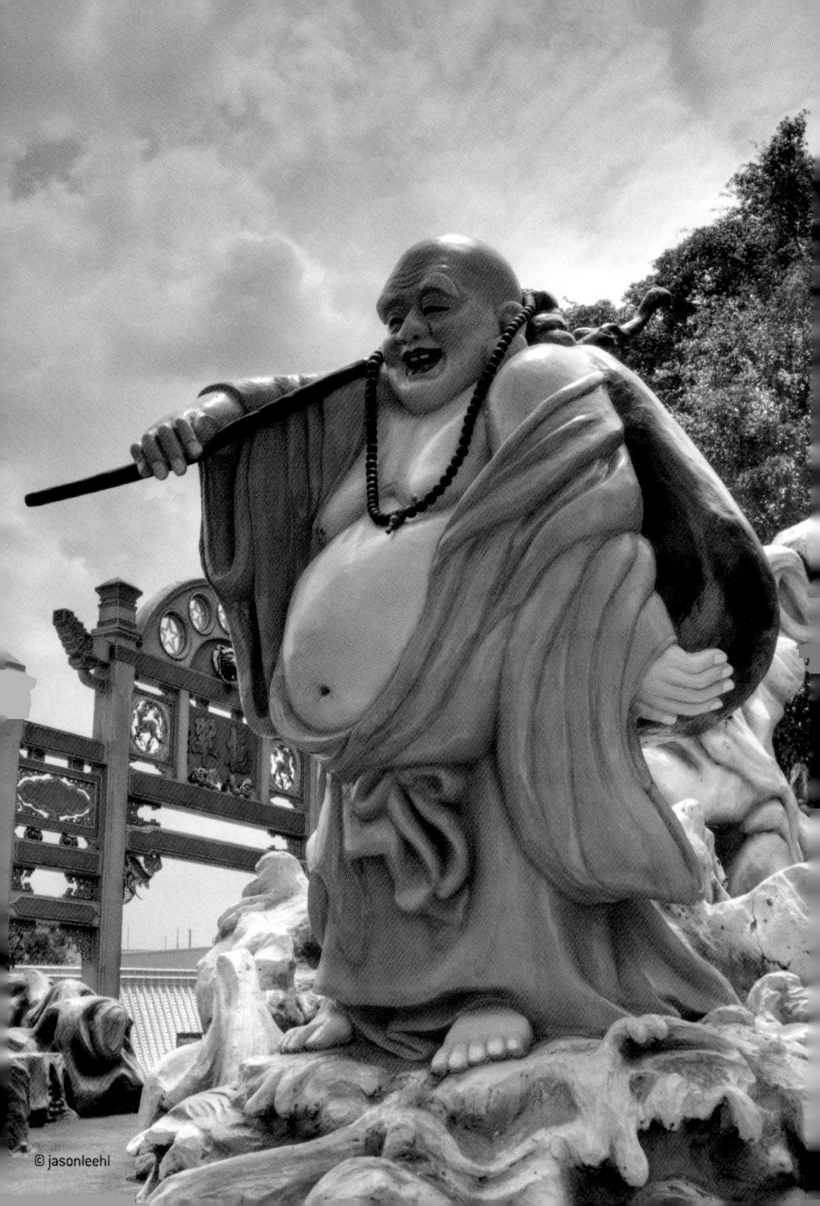

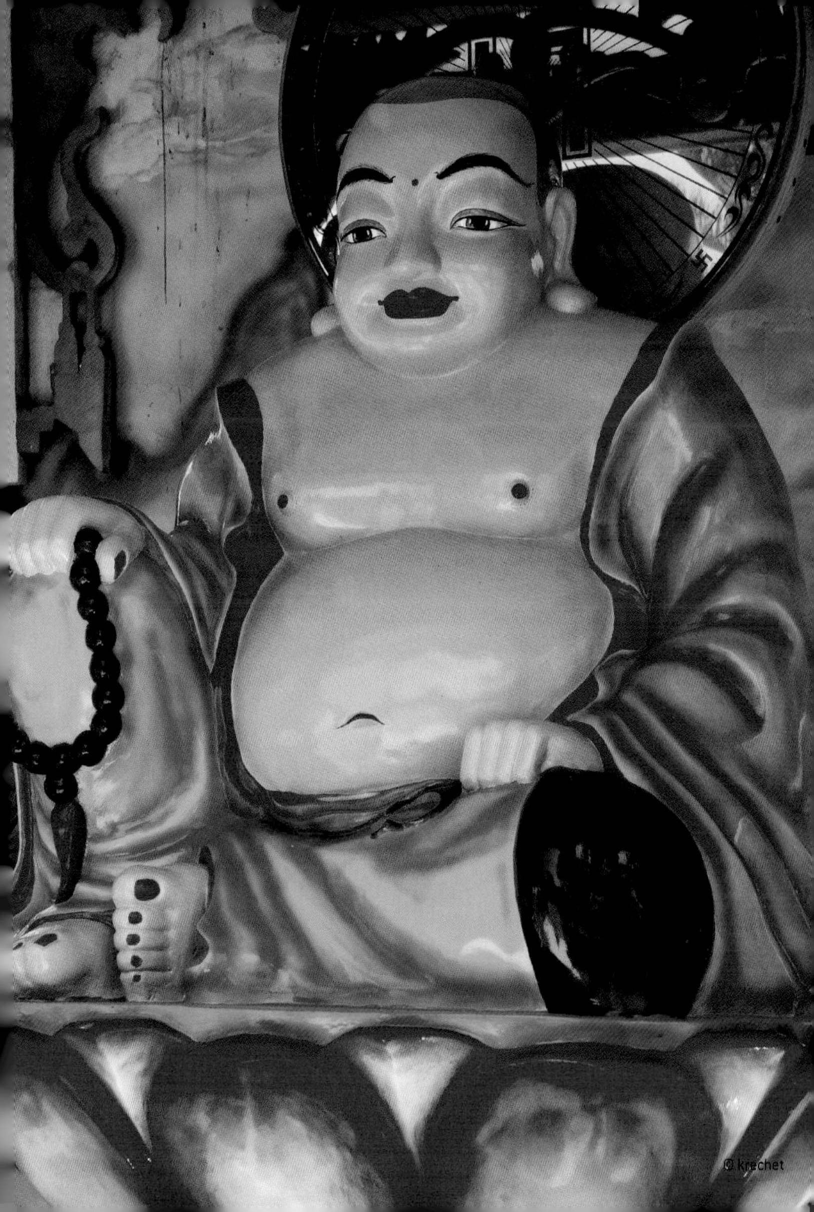
© krechet

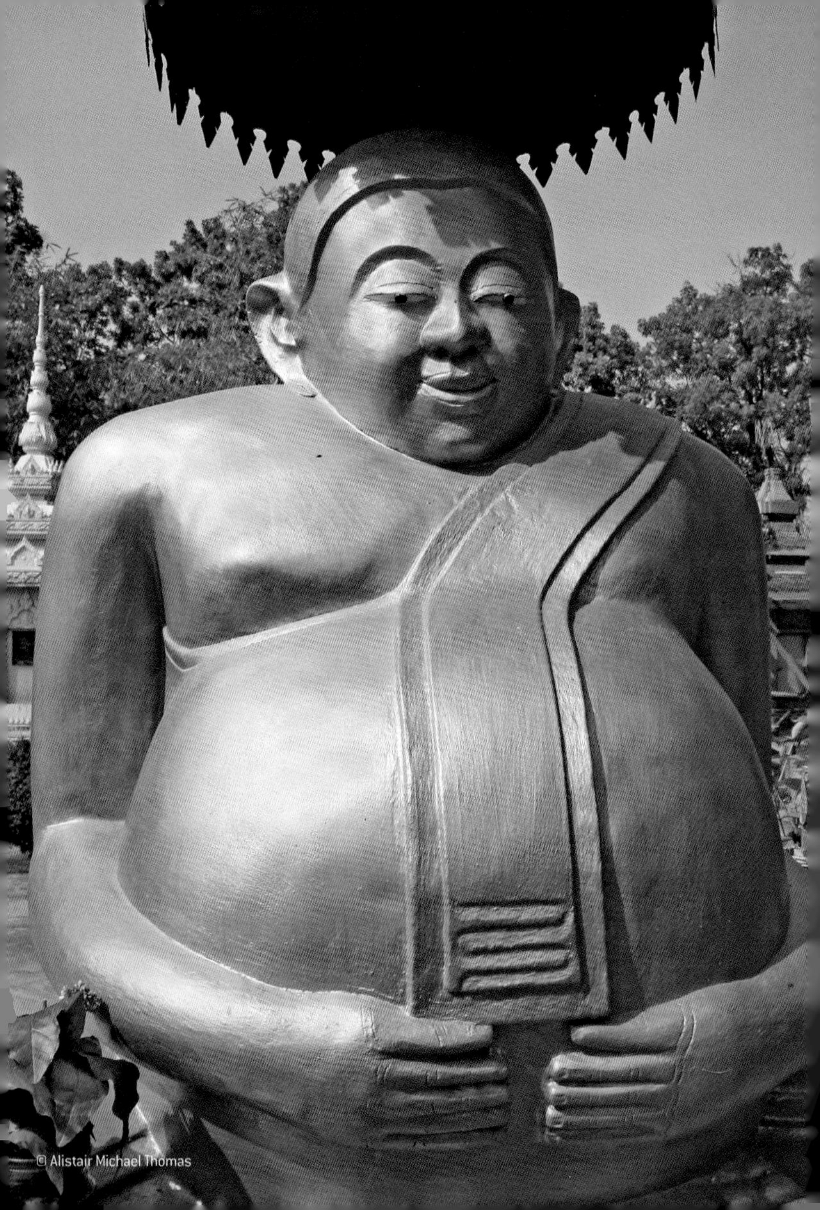
© Alistair Michael Thomas

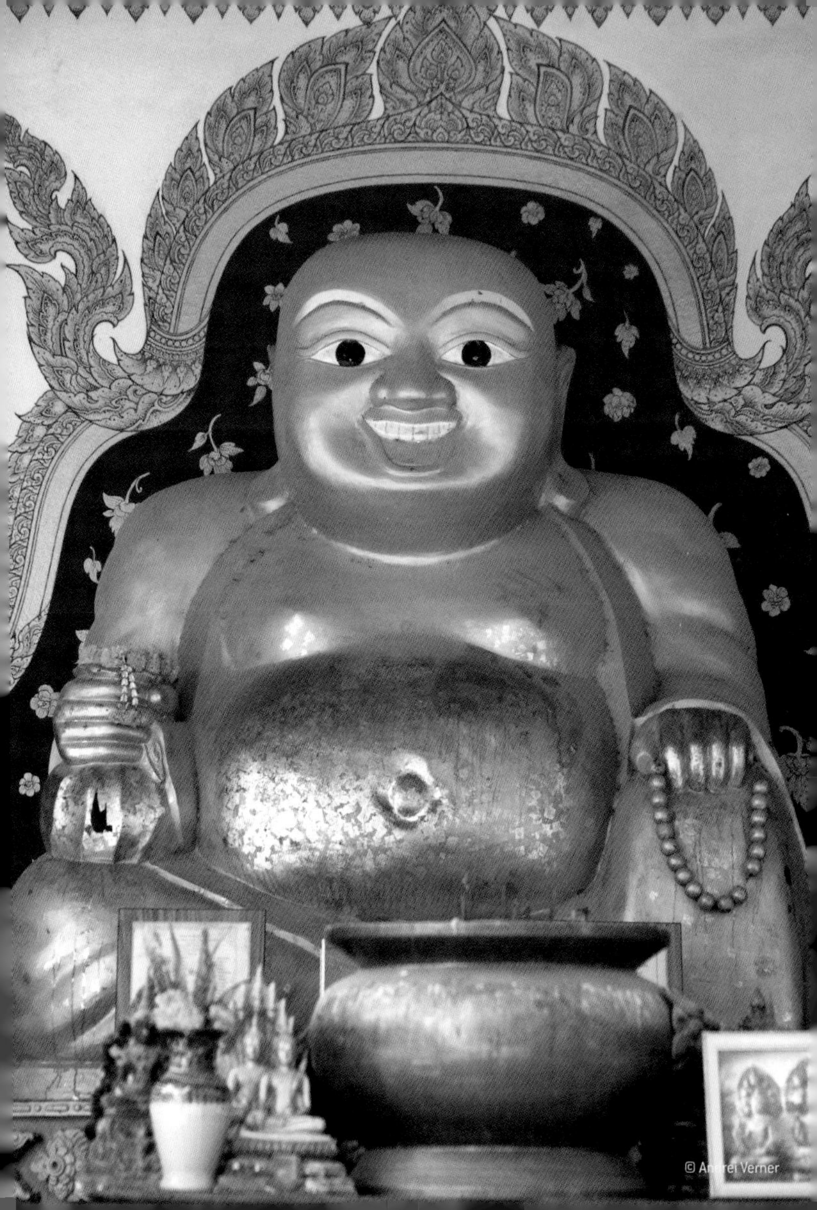

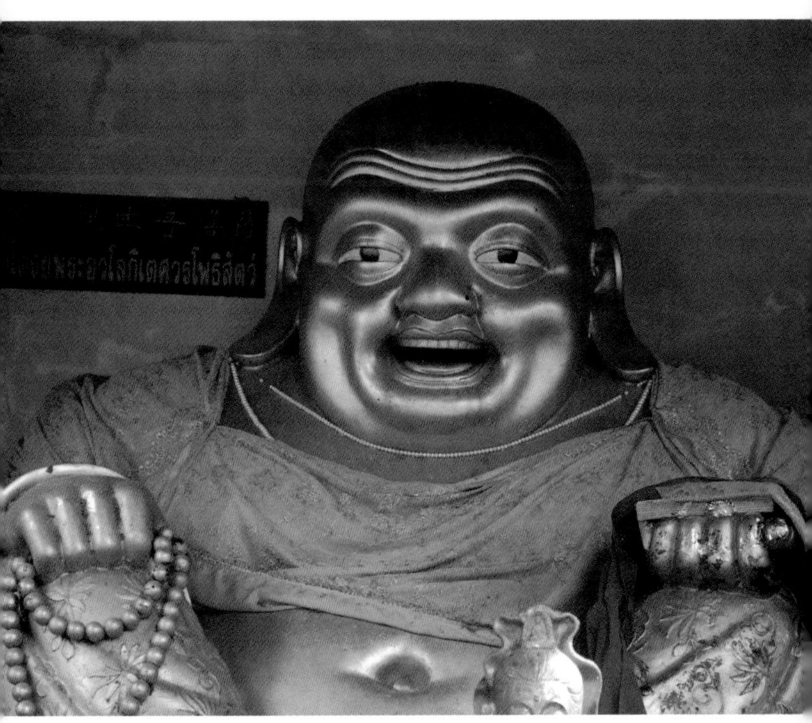

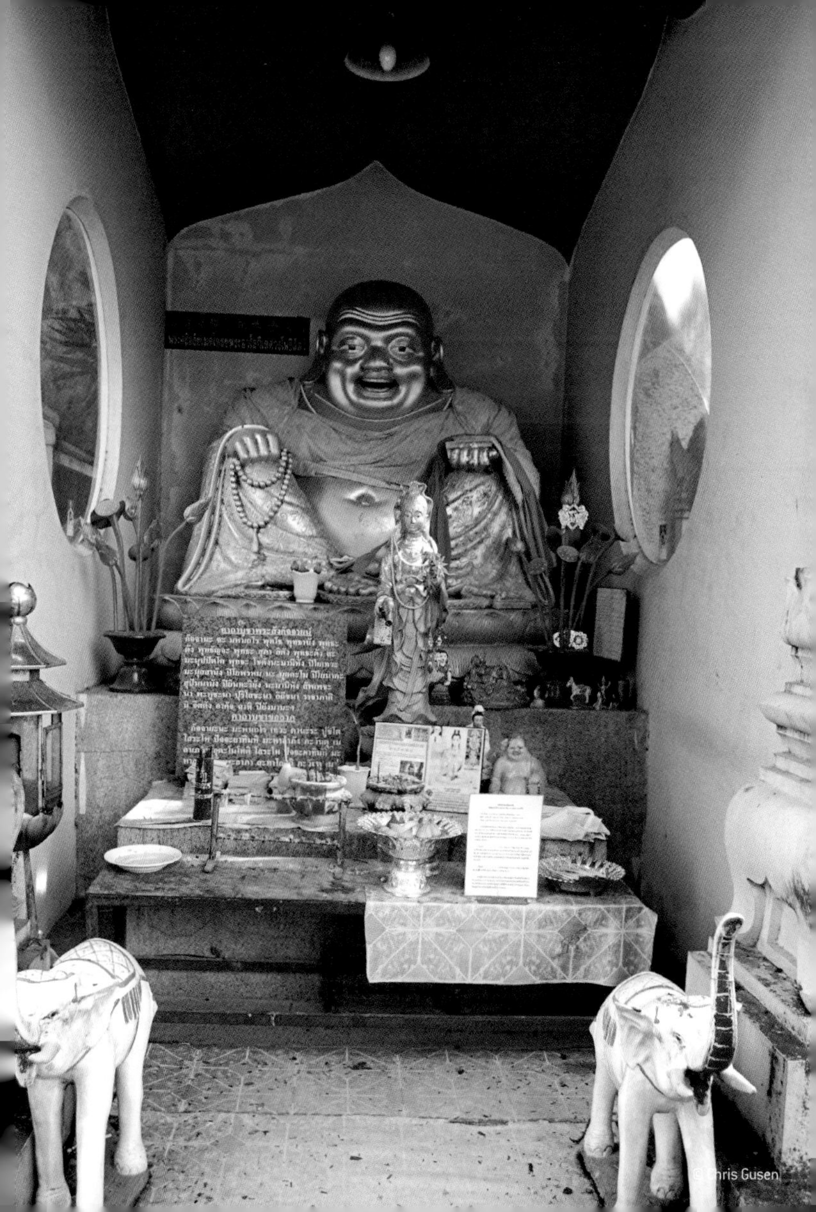

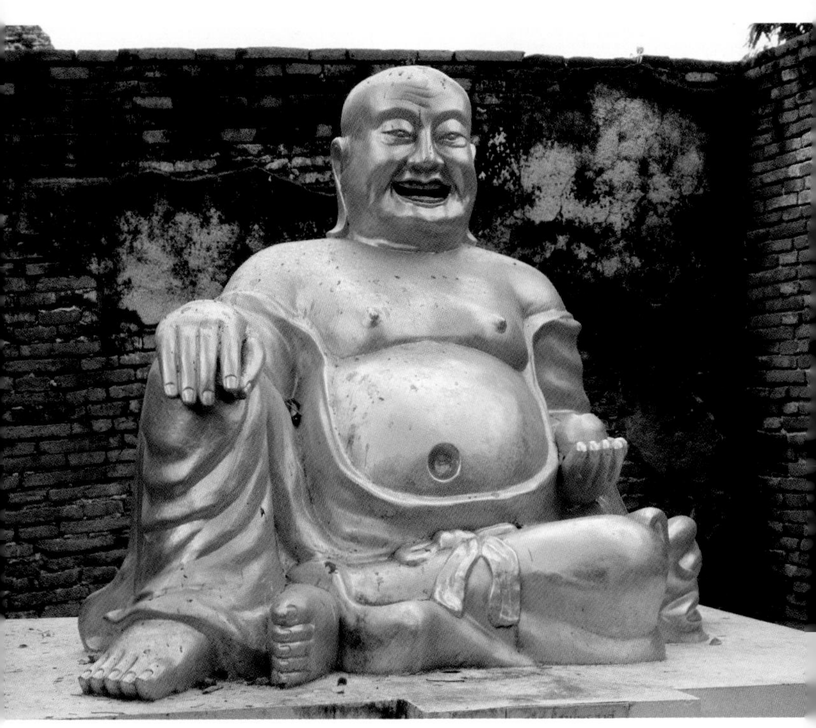

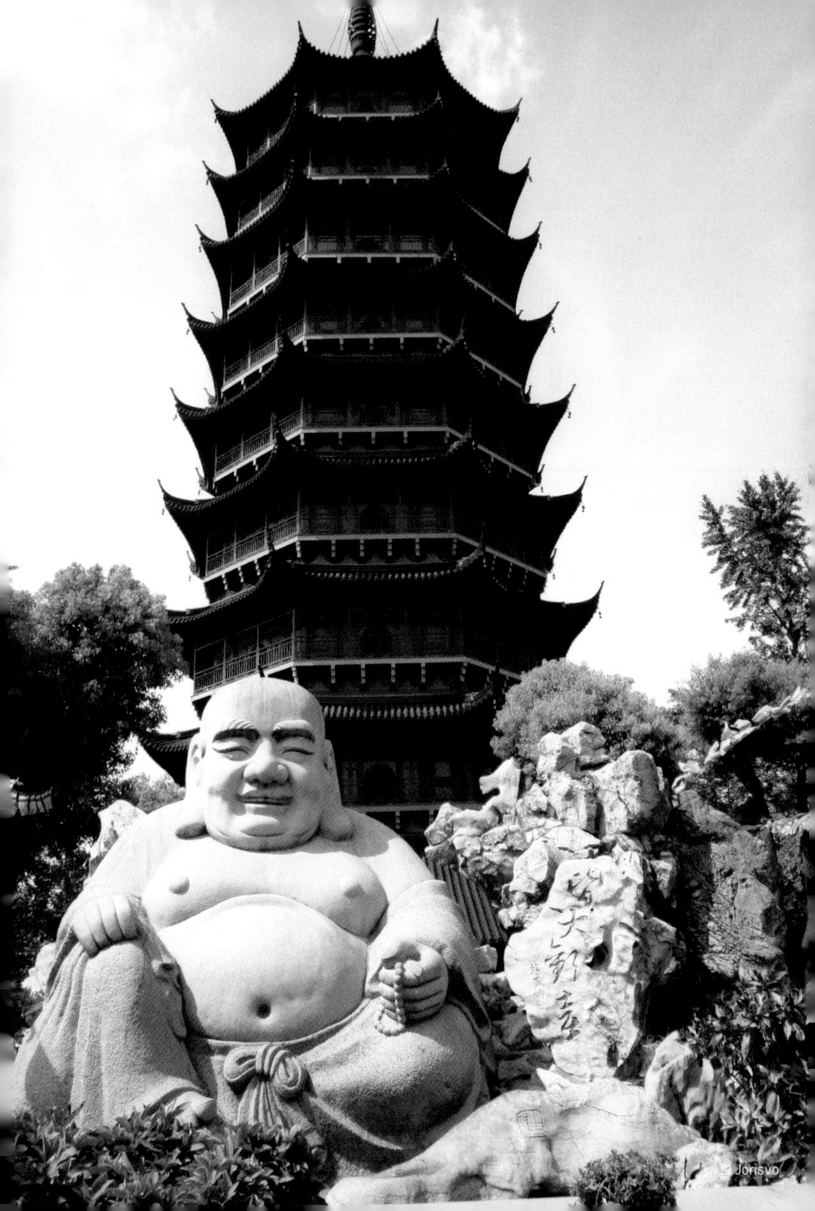
© Jorisvo

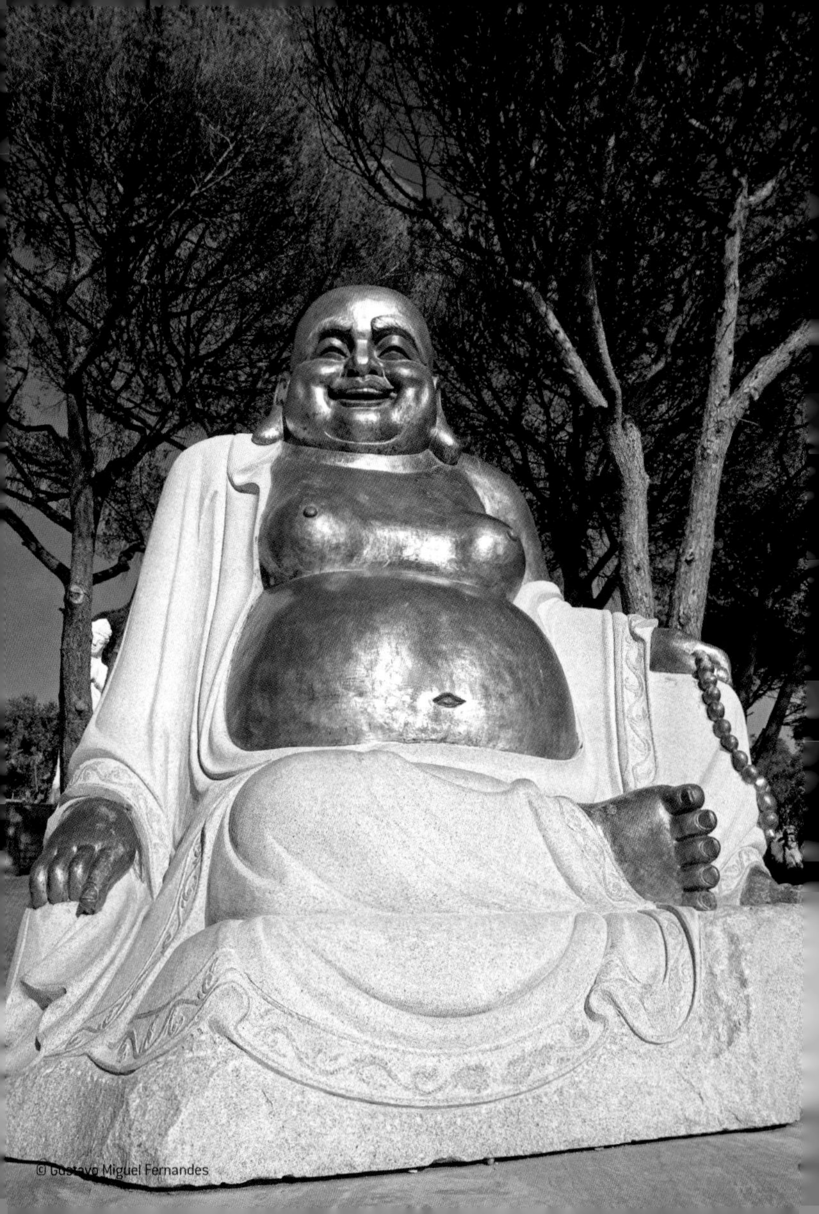

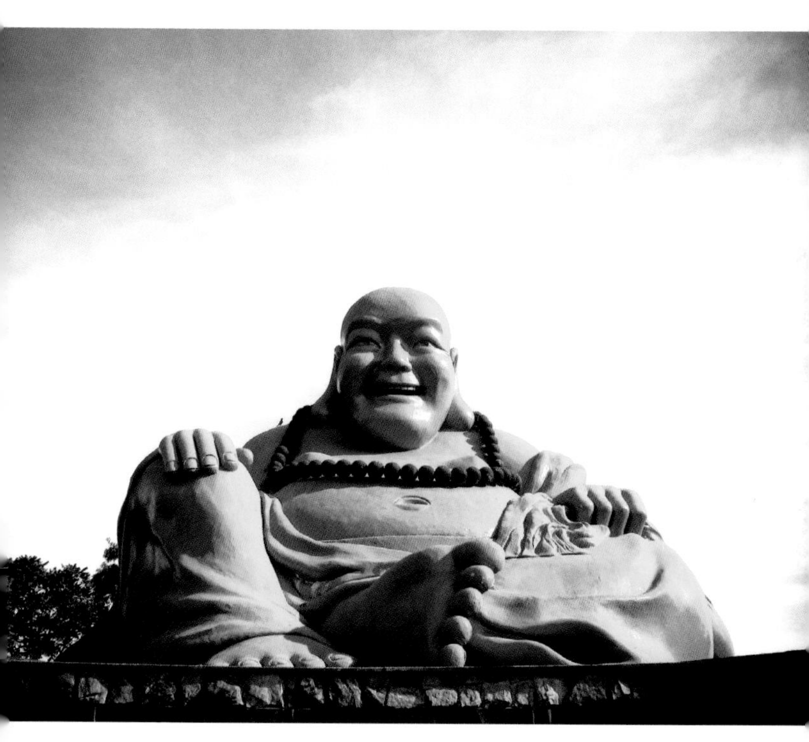

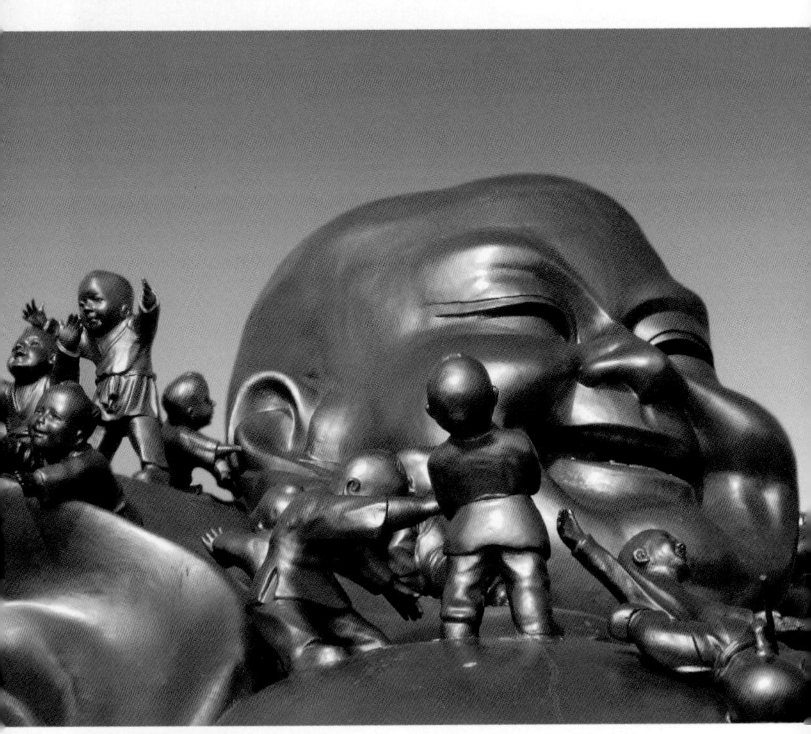

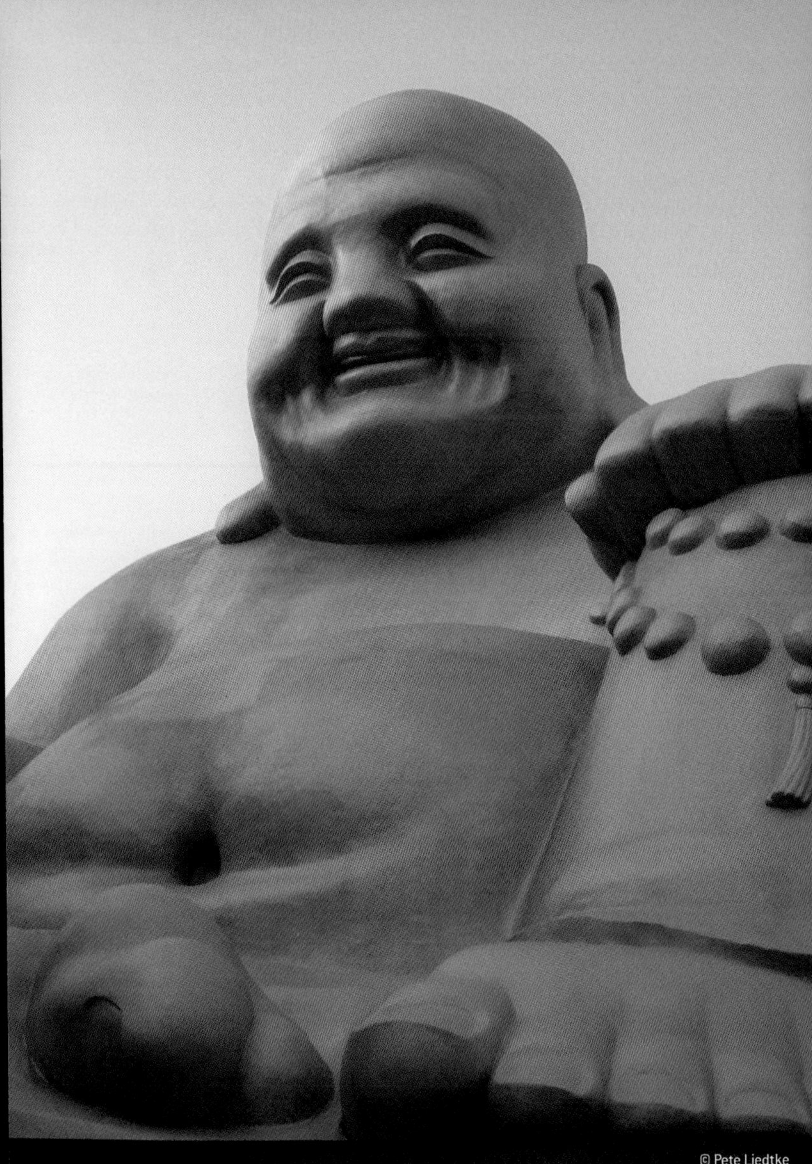

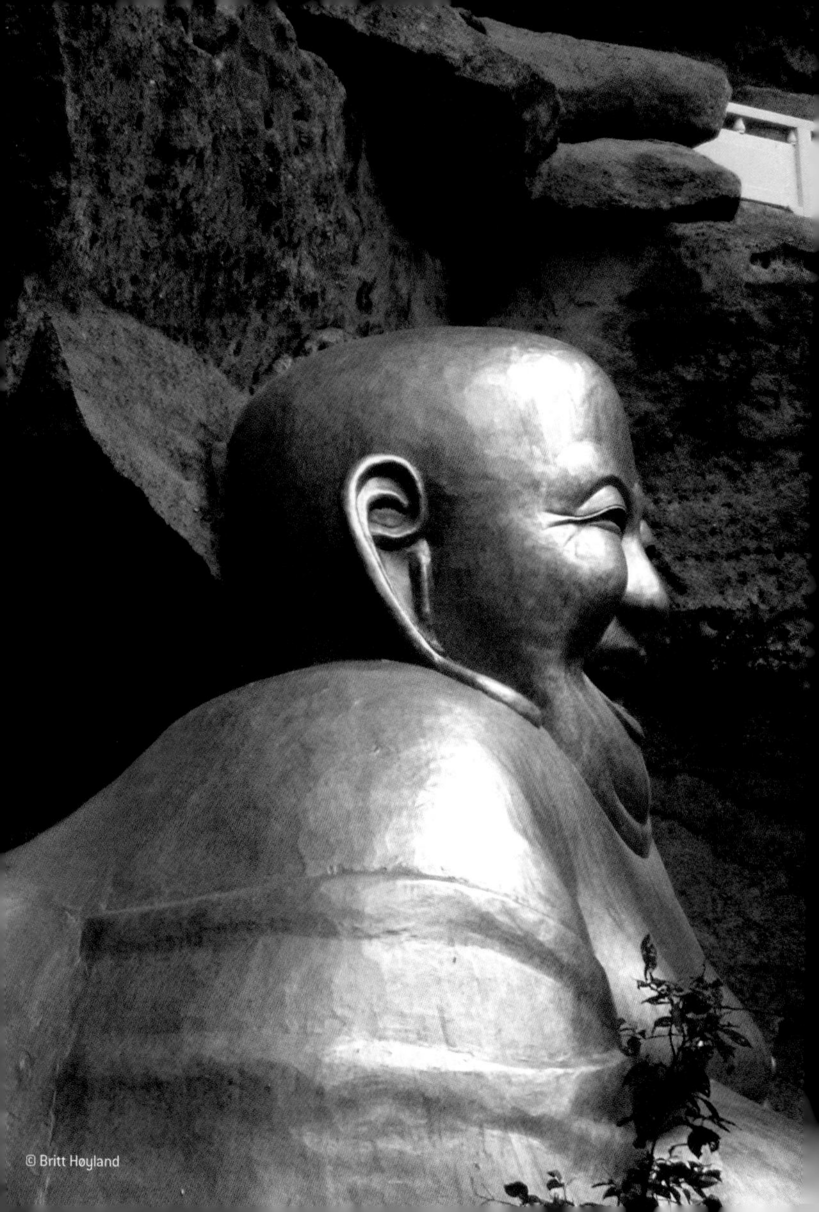

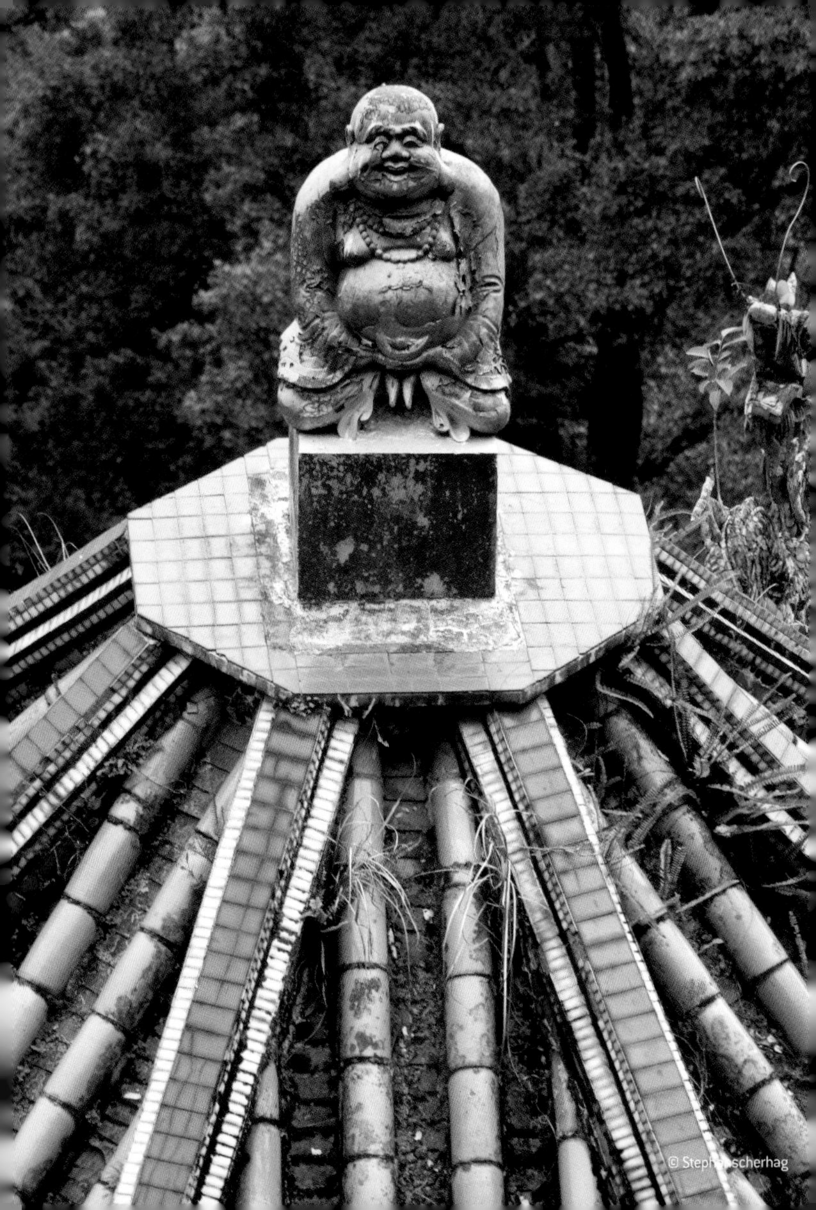

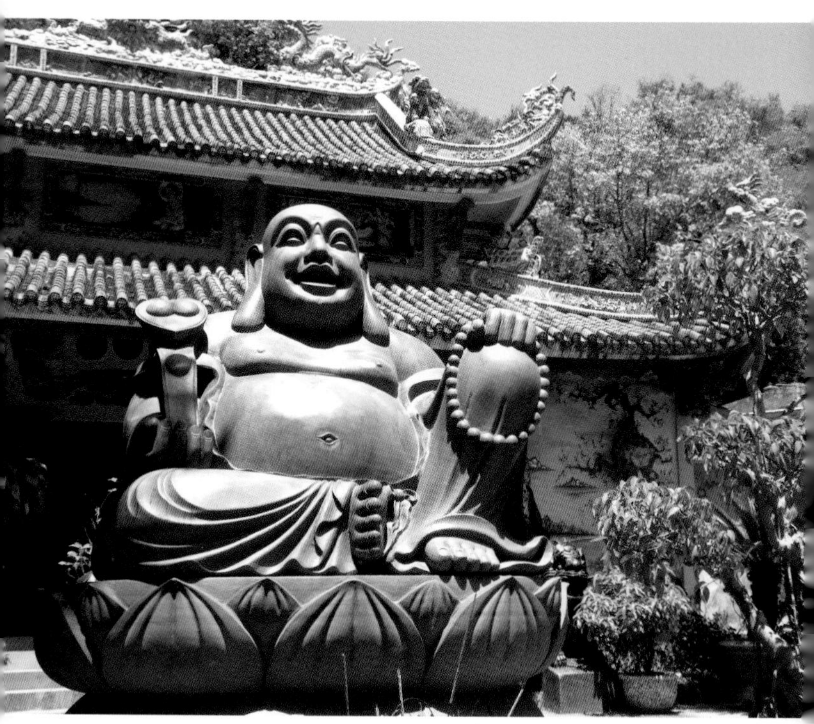

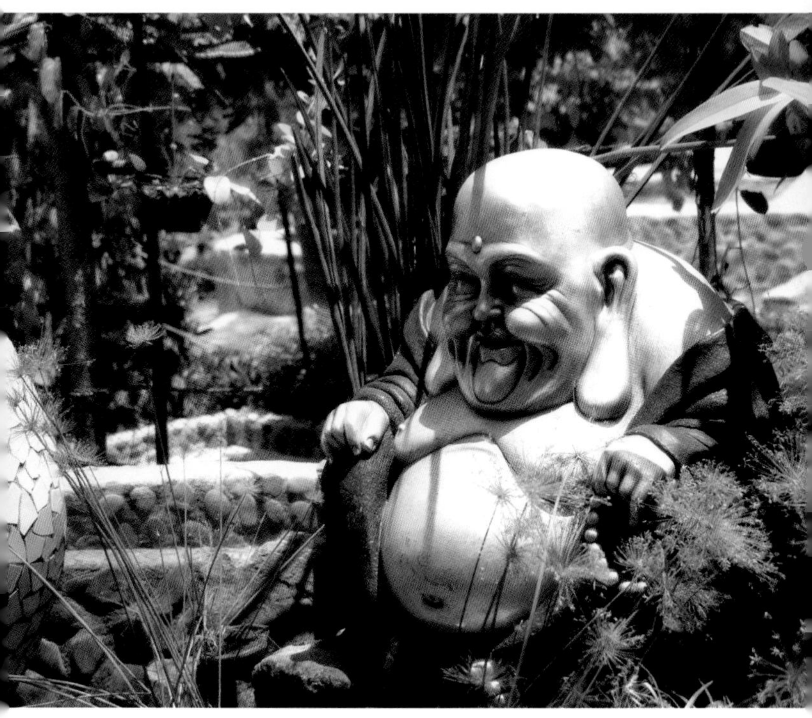

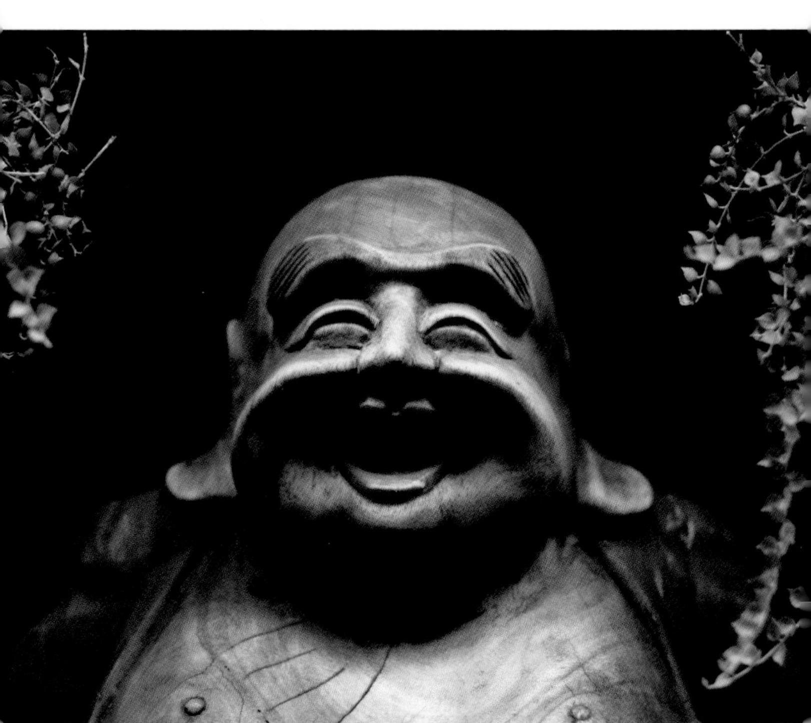

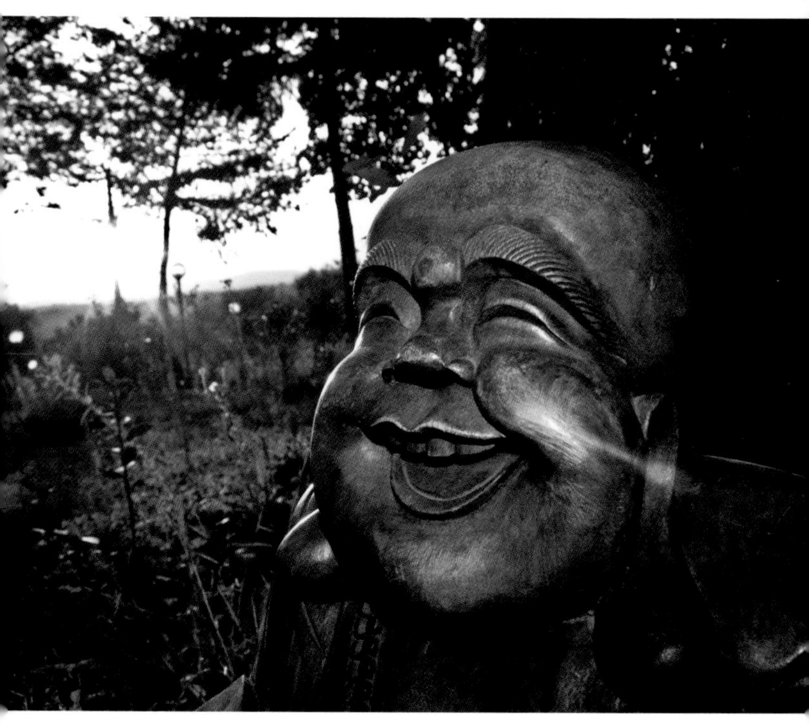

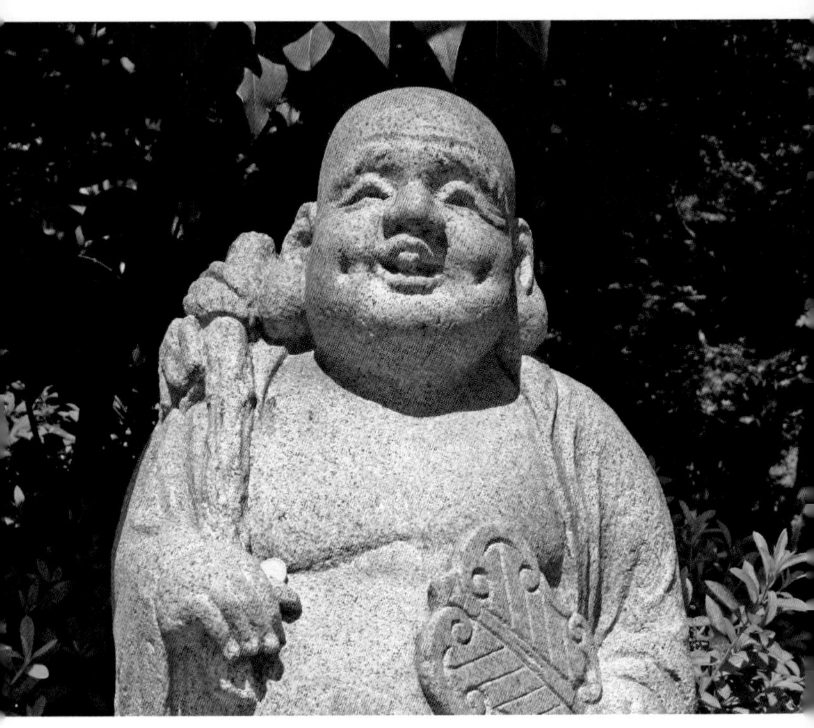

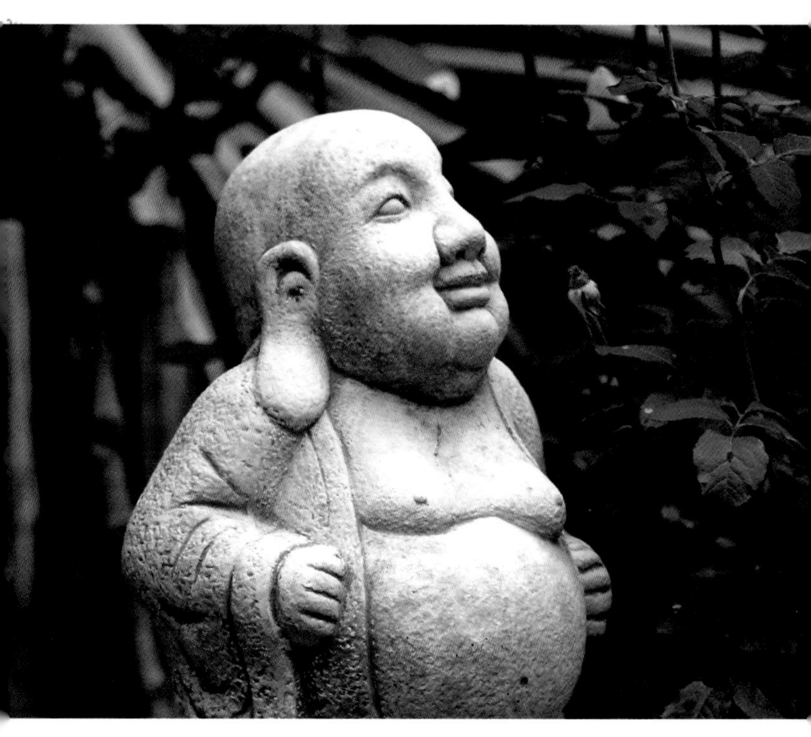

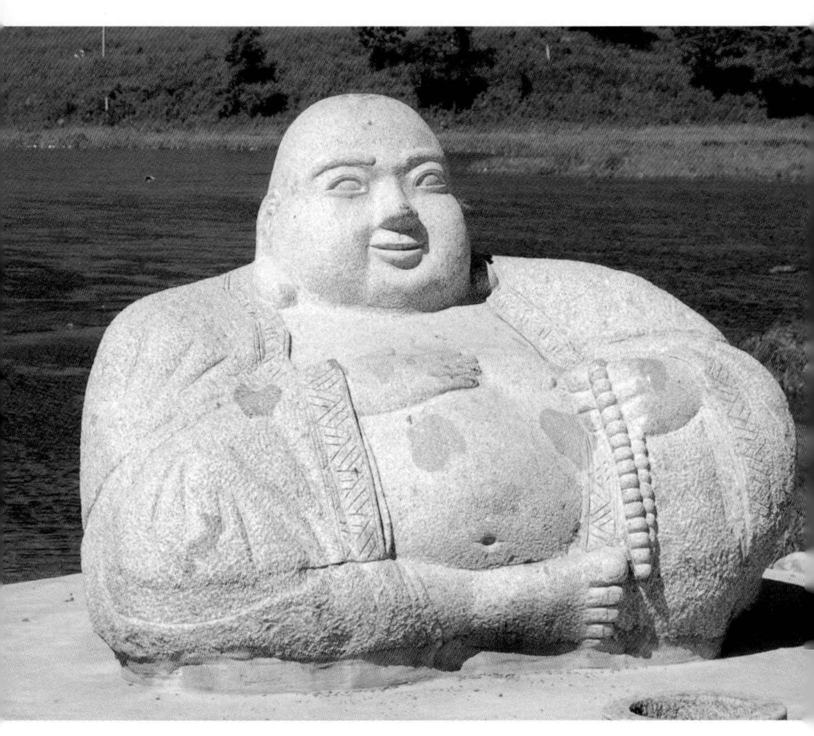

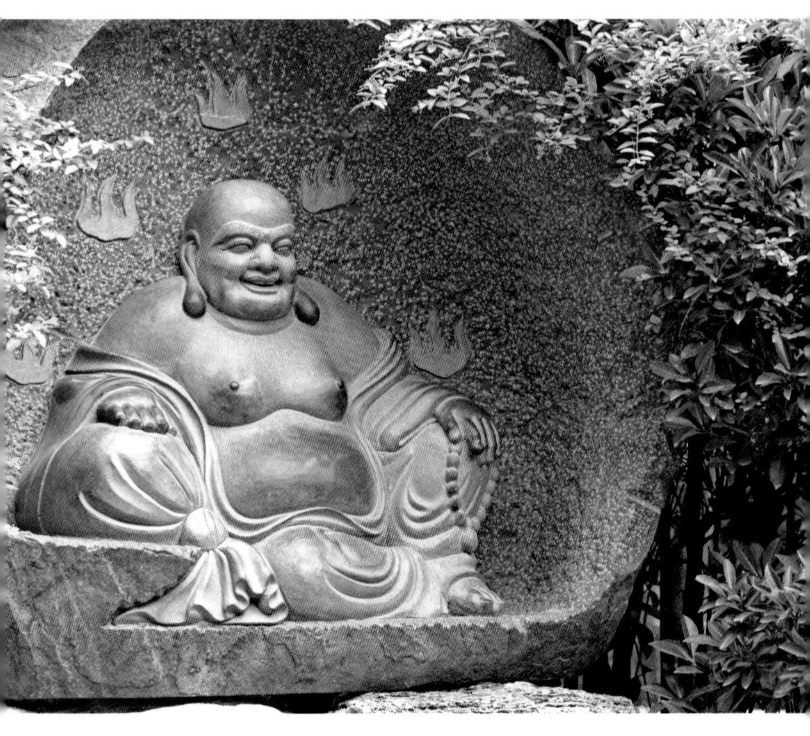

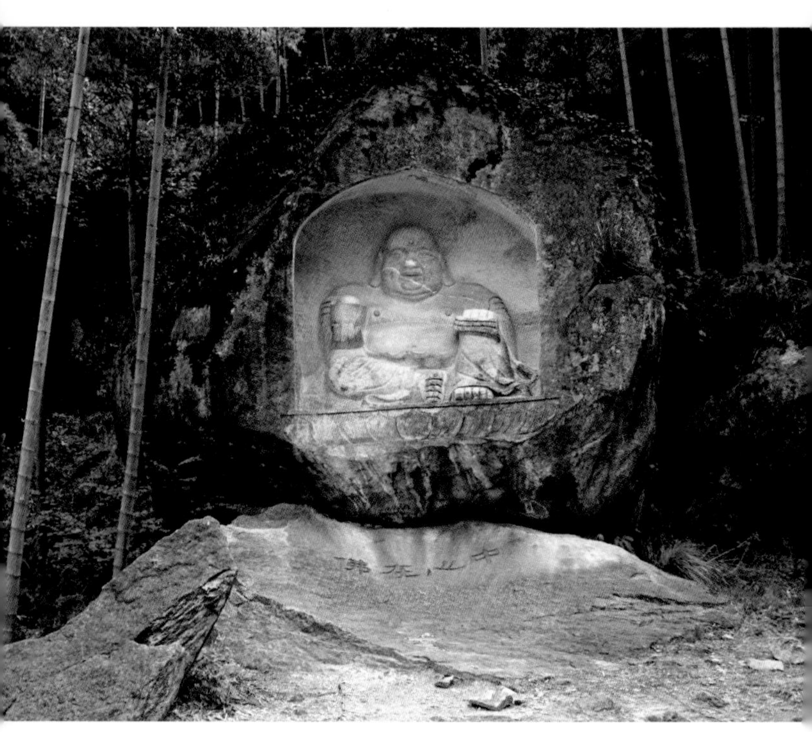

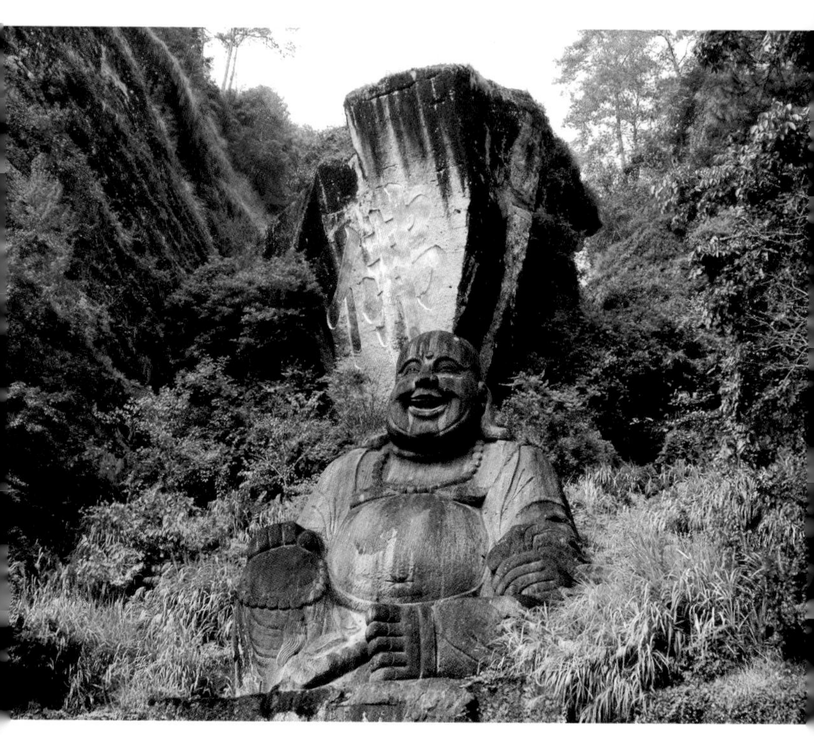

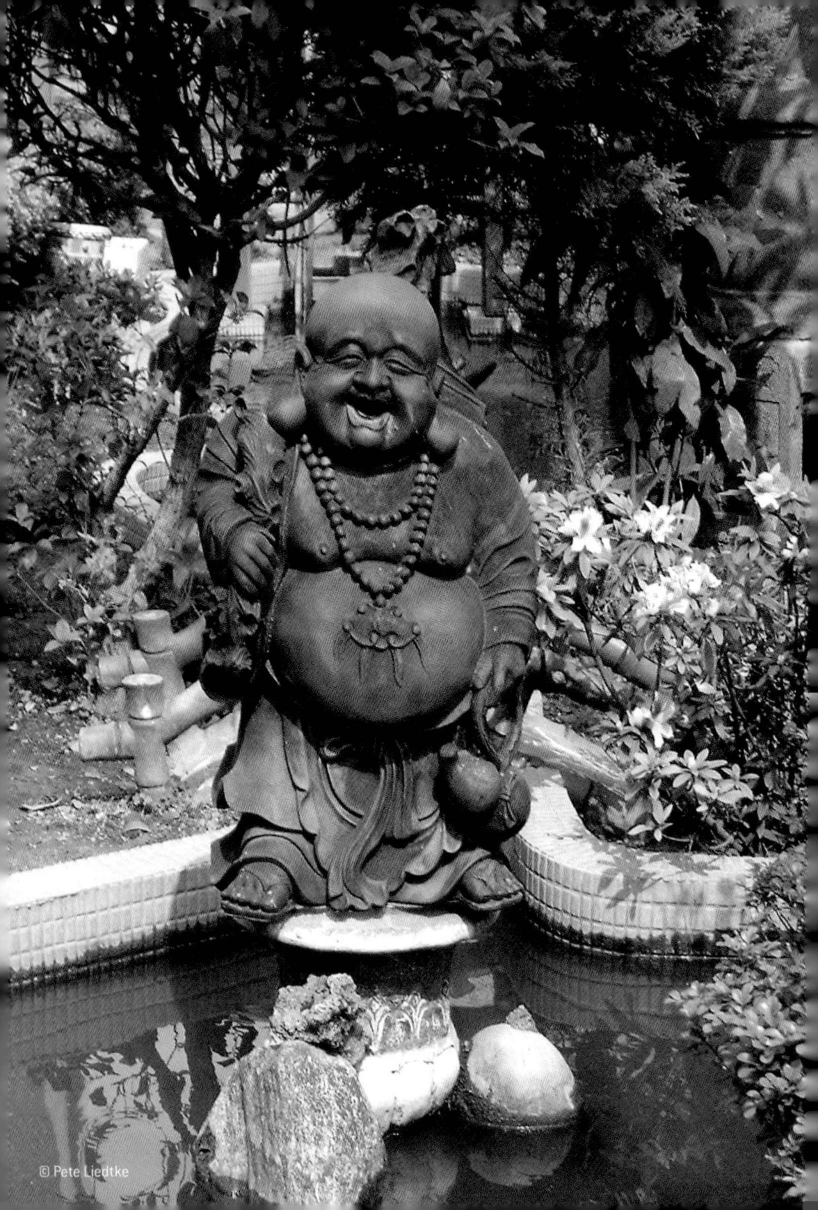

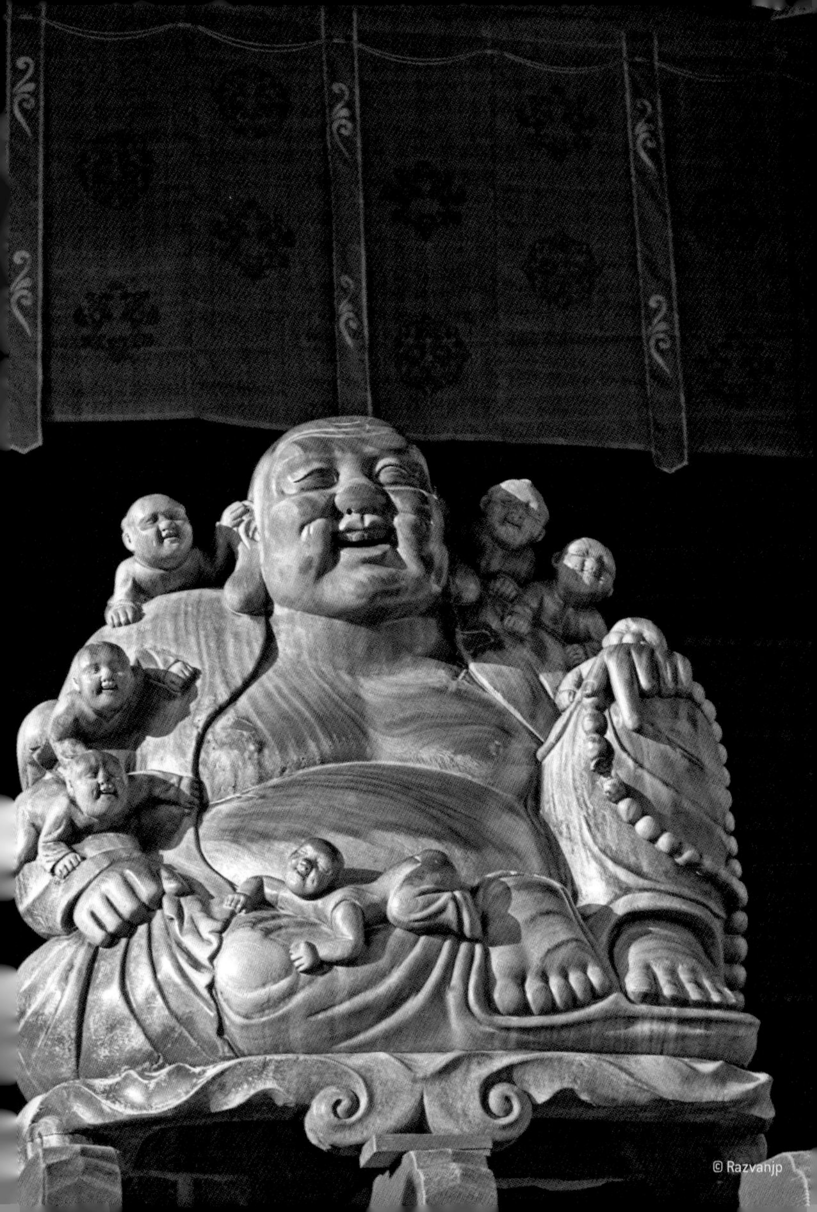

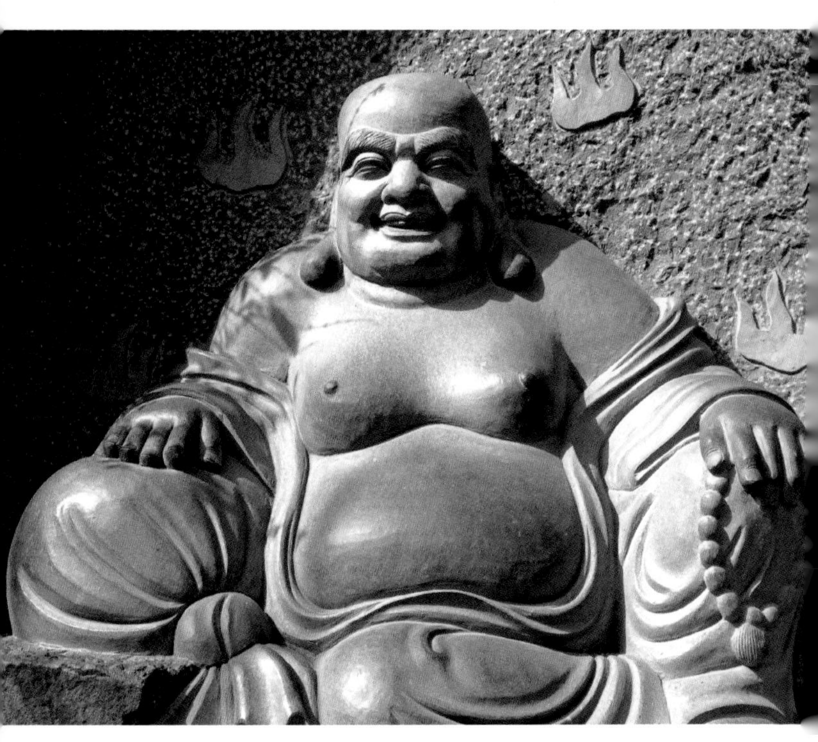

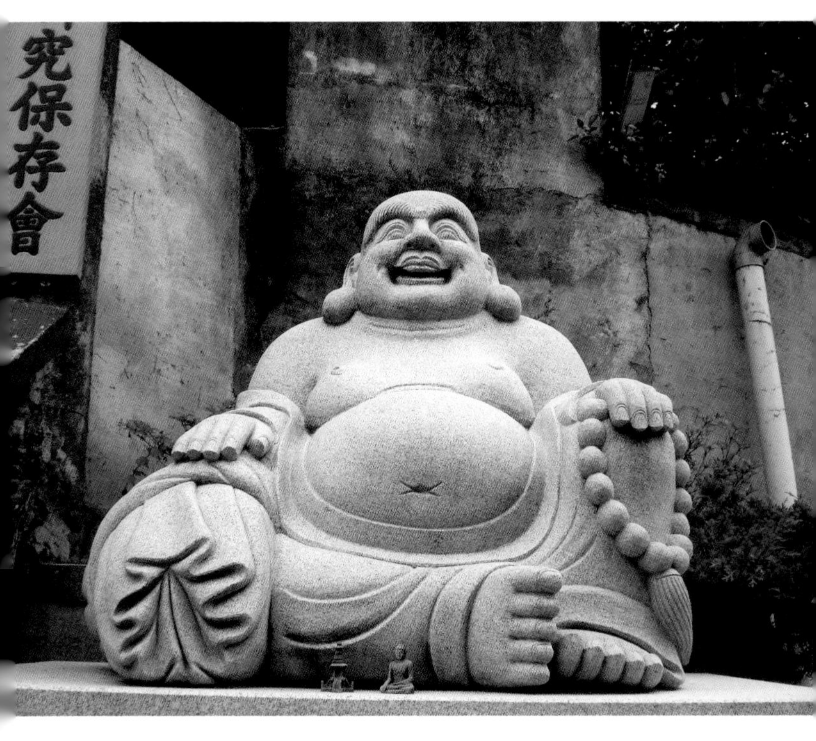
究保存會

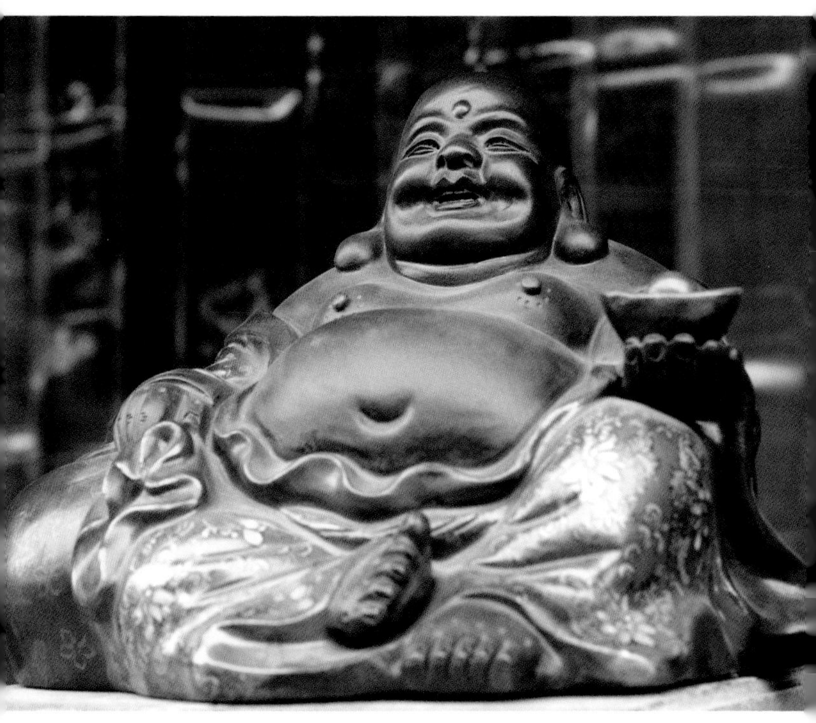

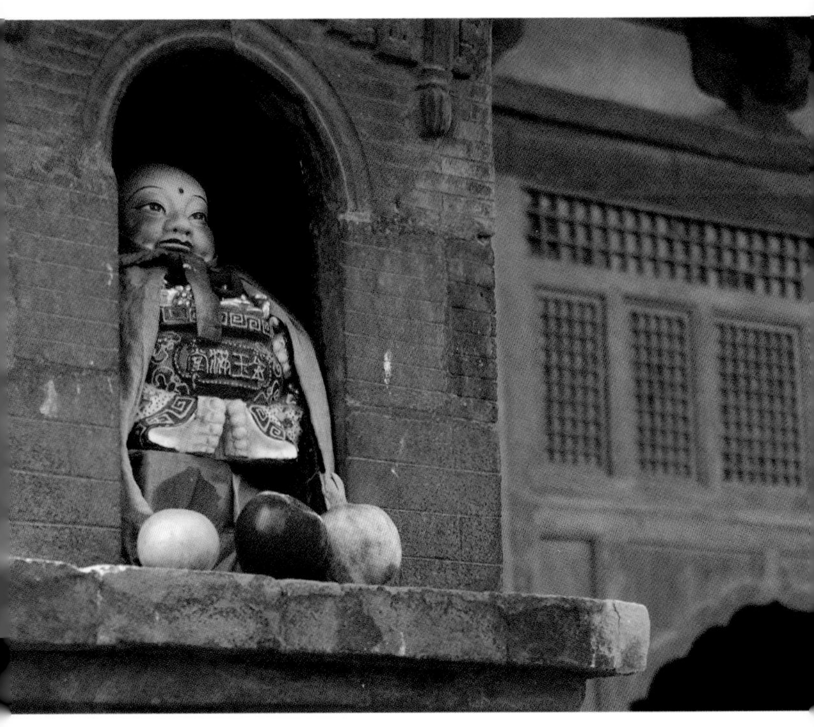

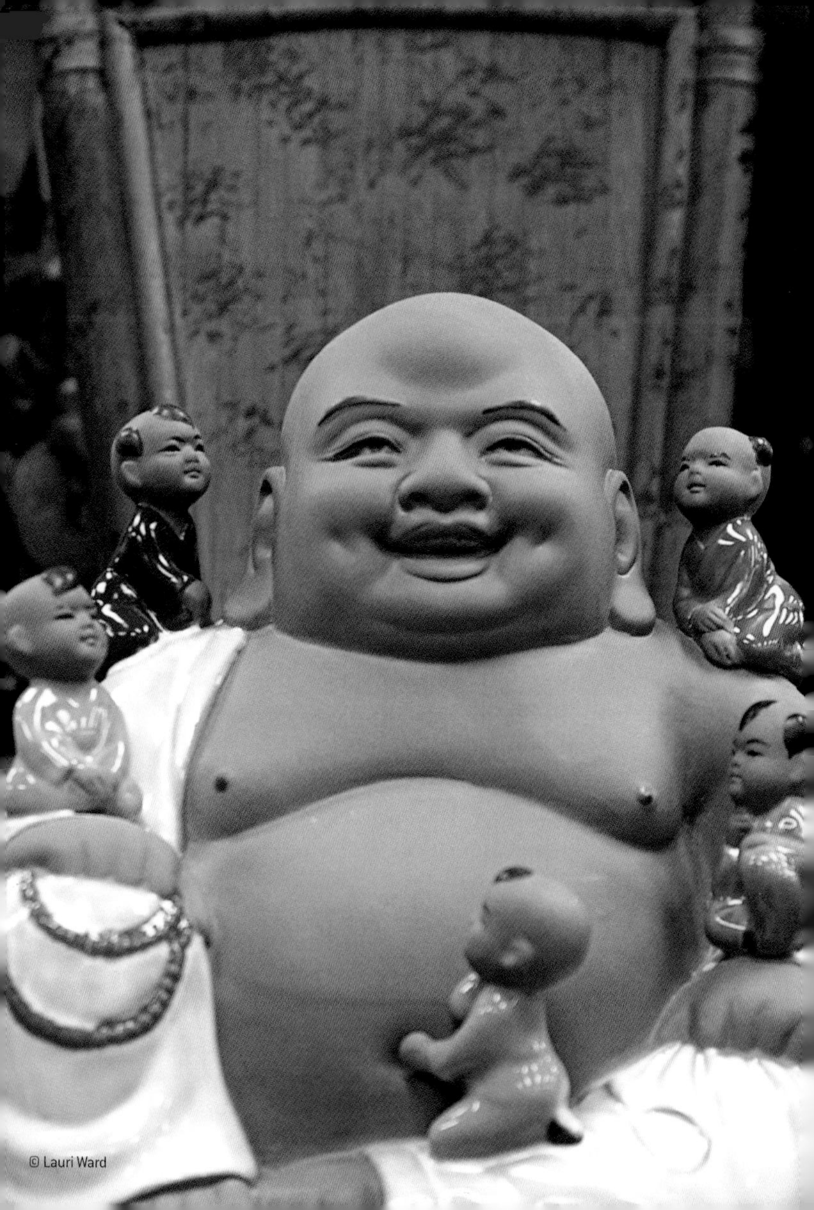

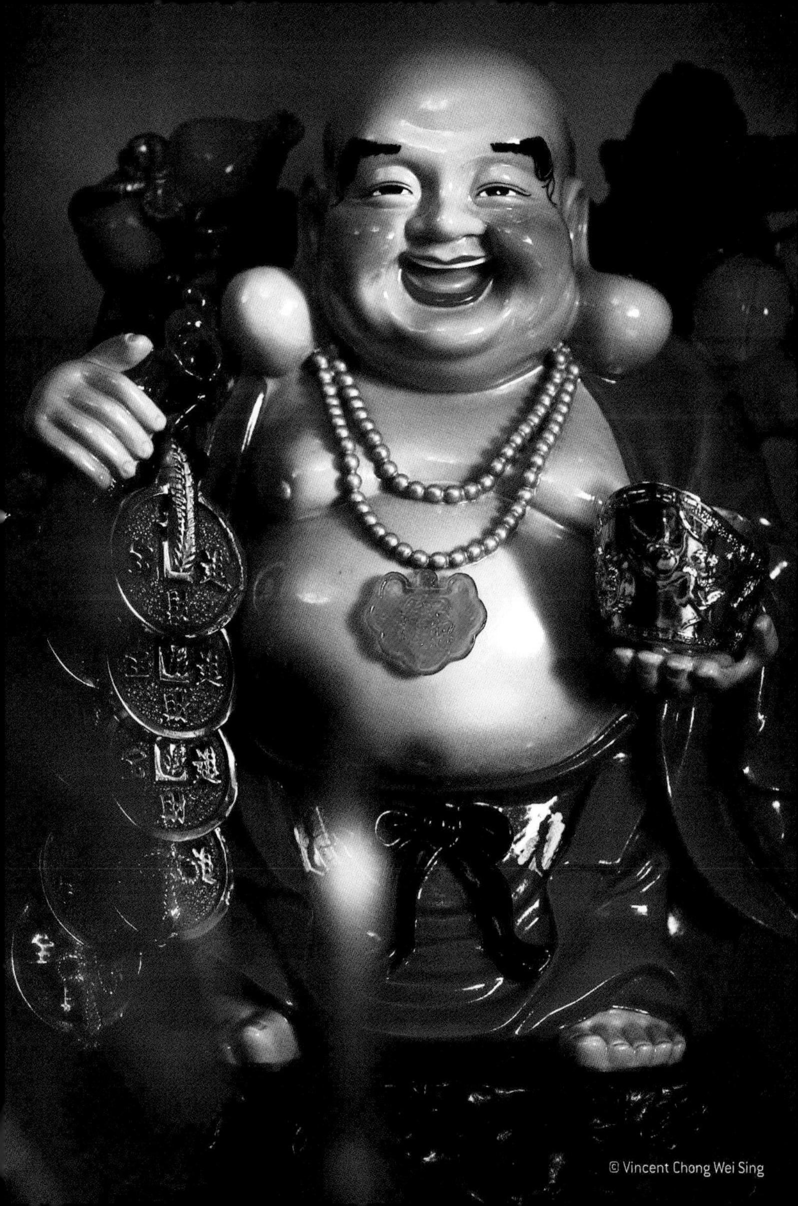

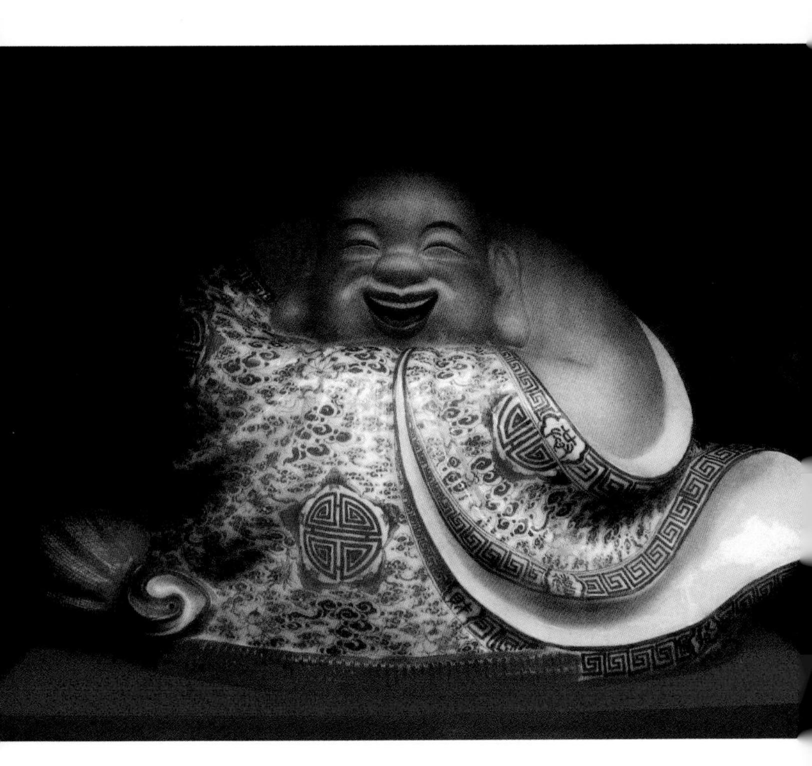

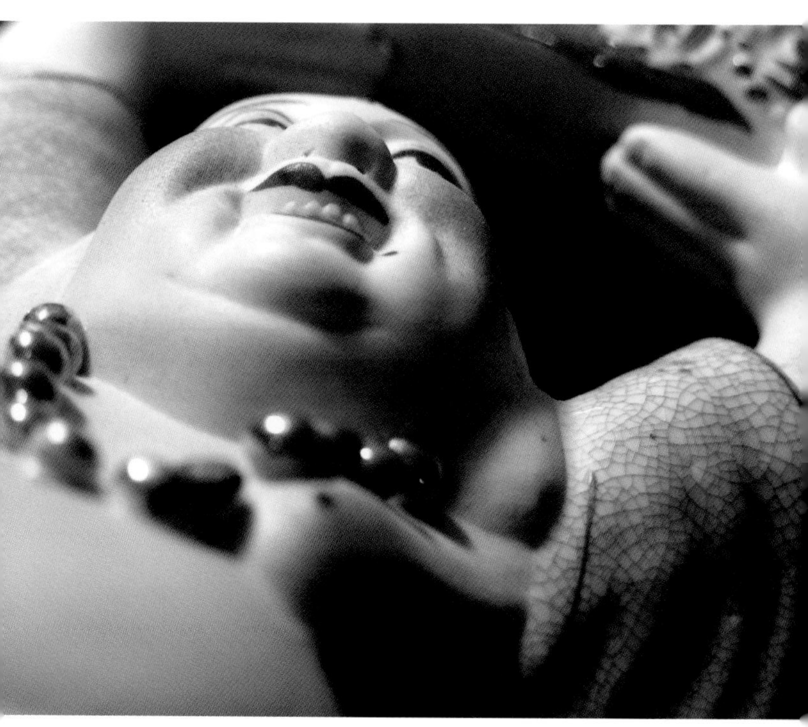

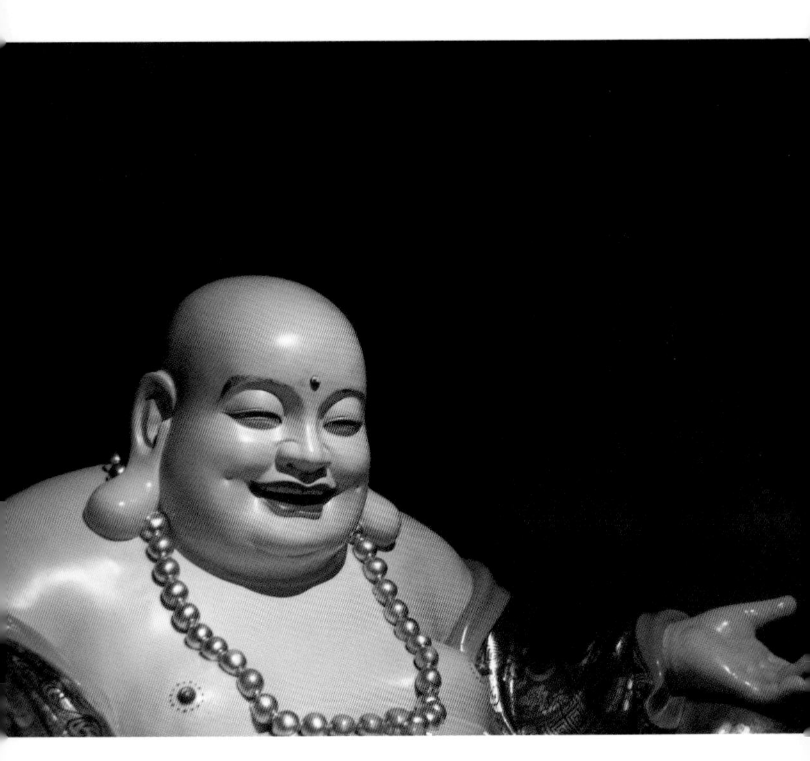

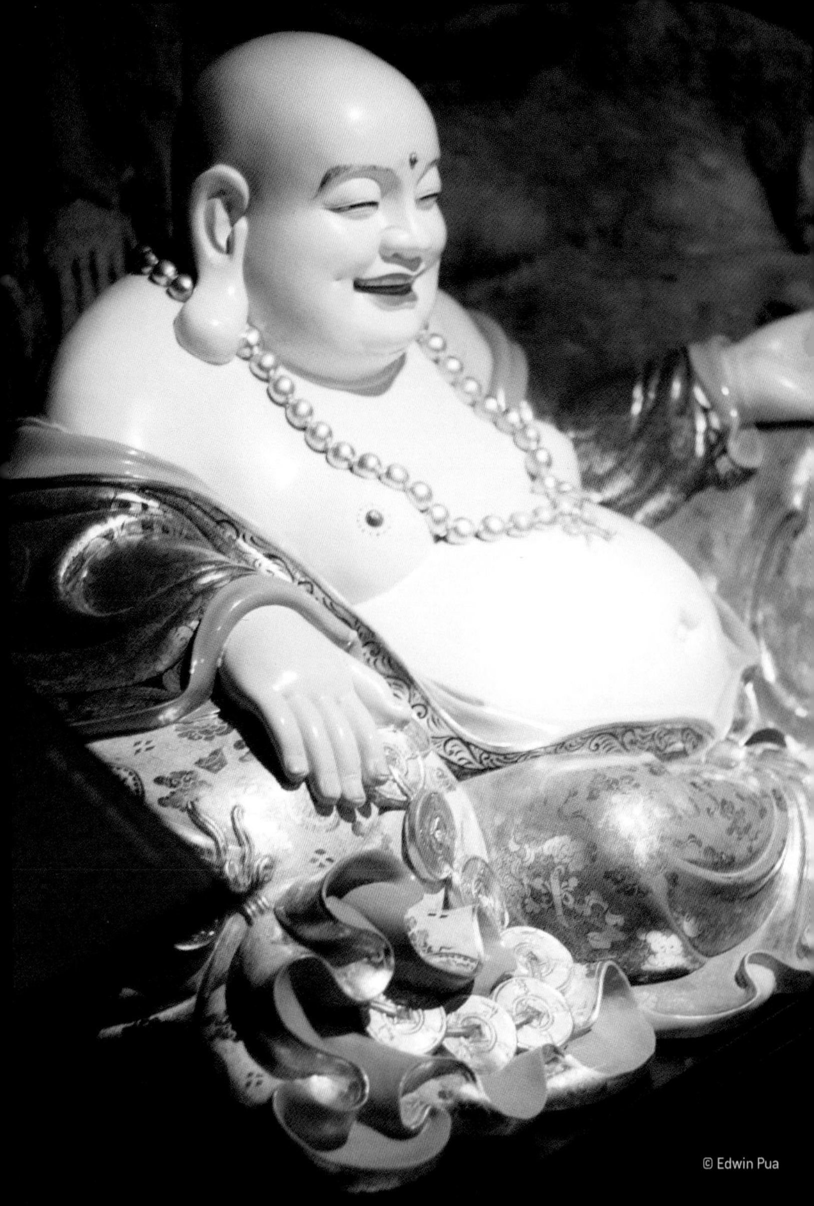

© Edwin Pua

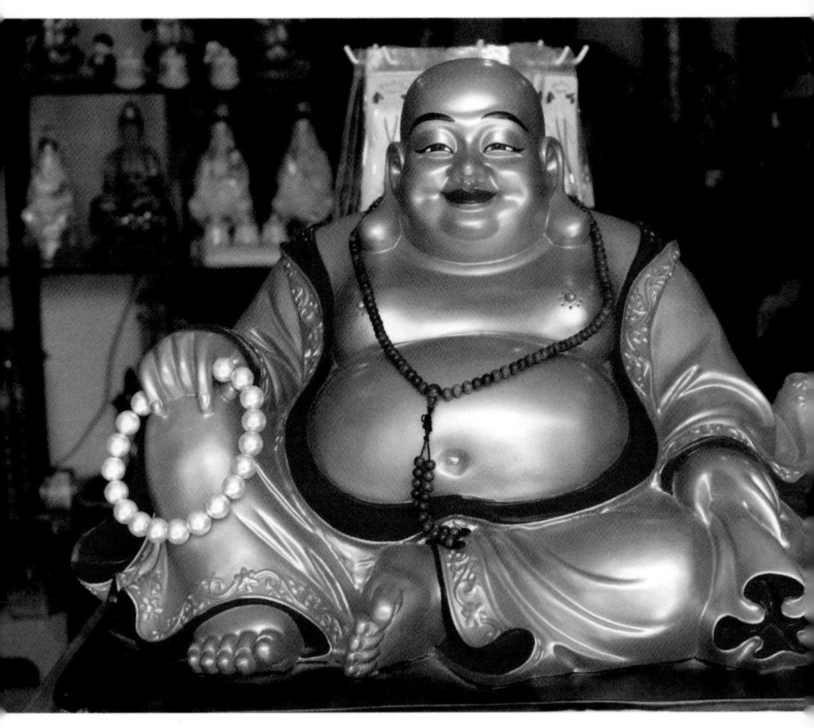

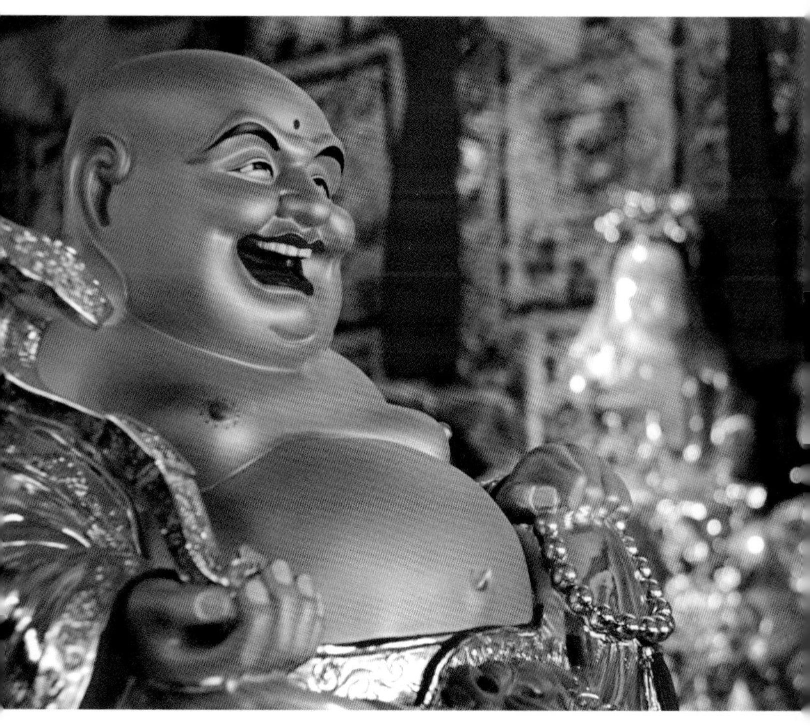

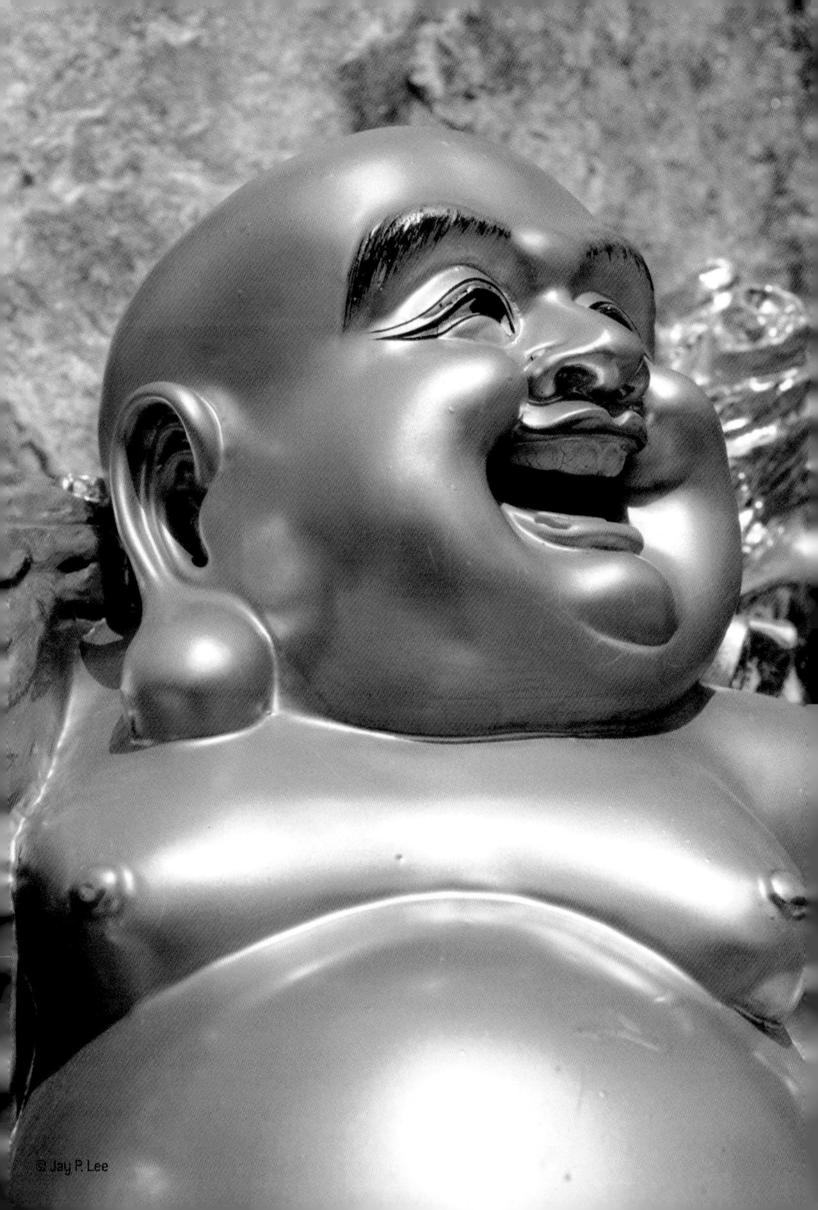

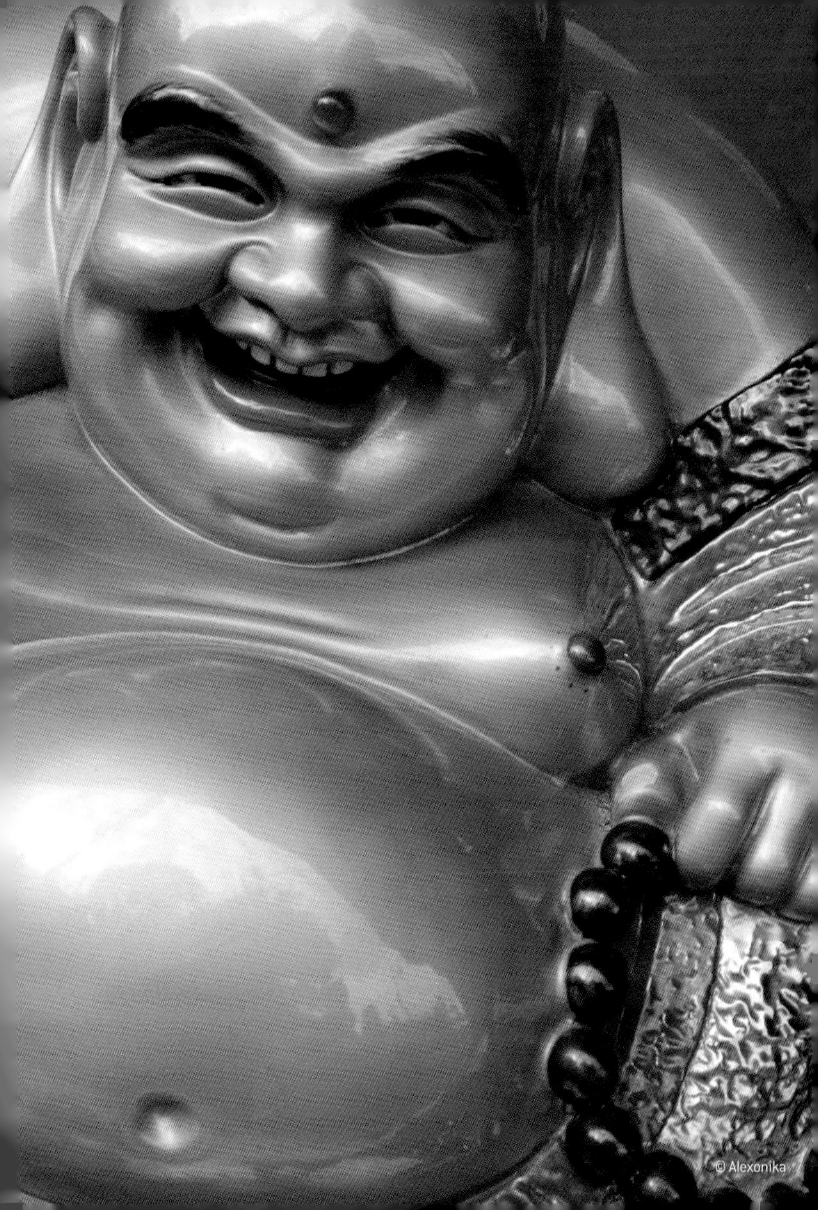

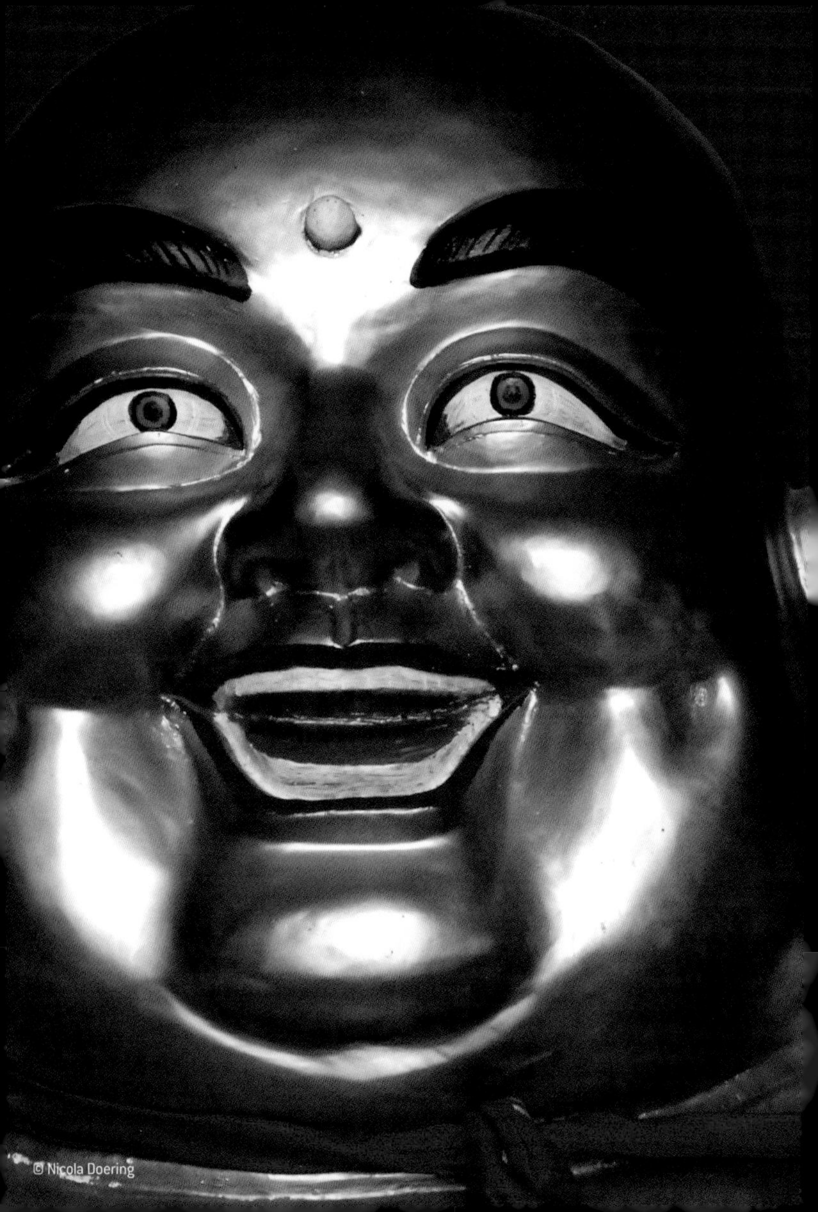

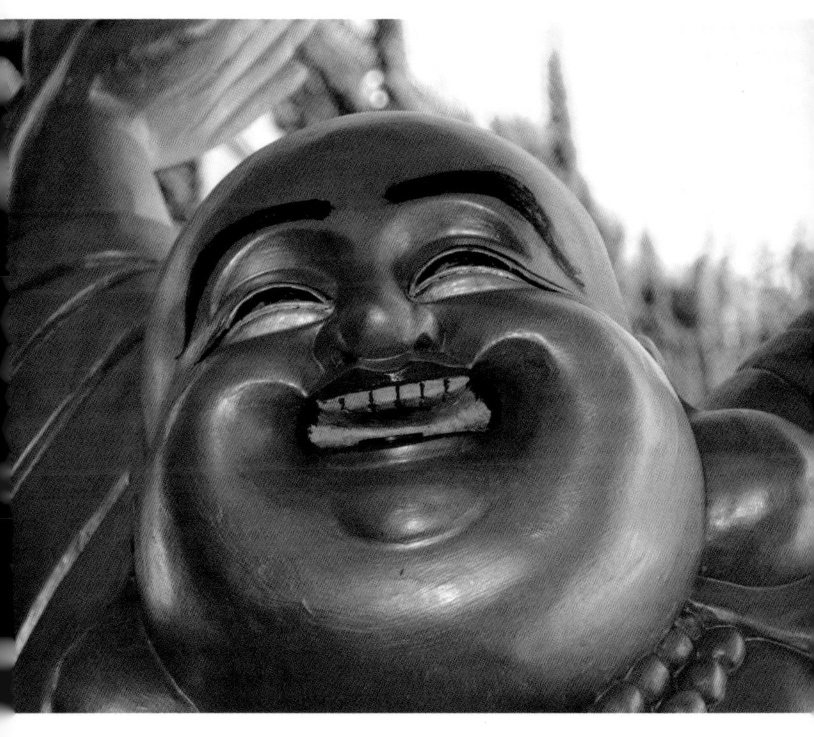

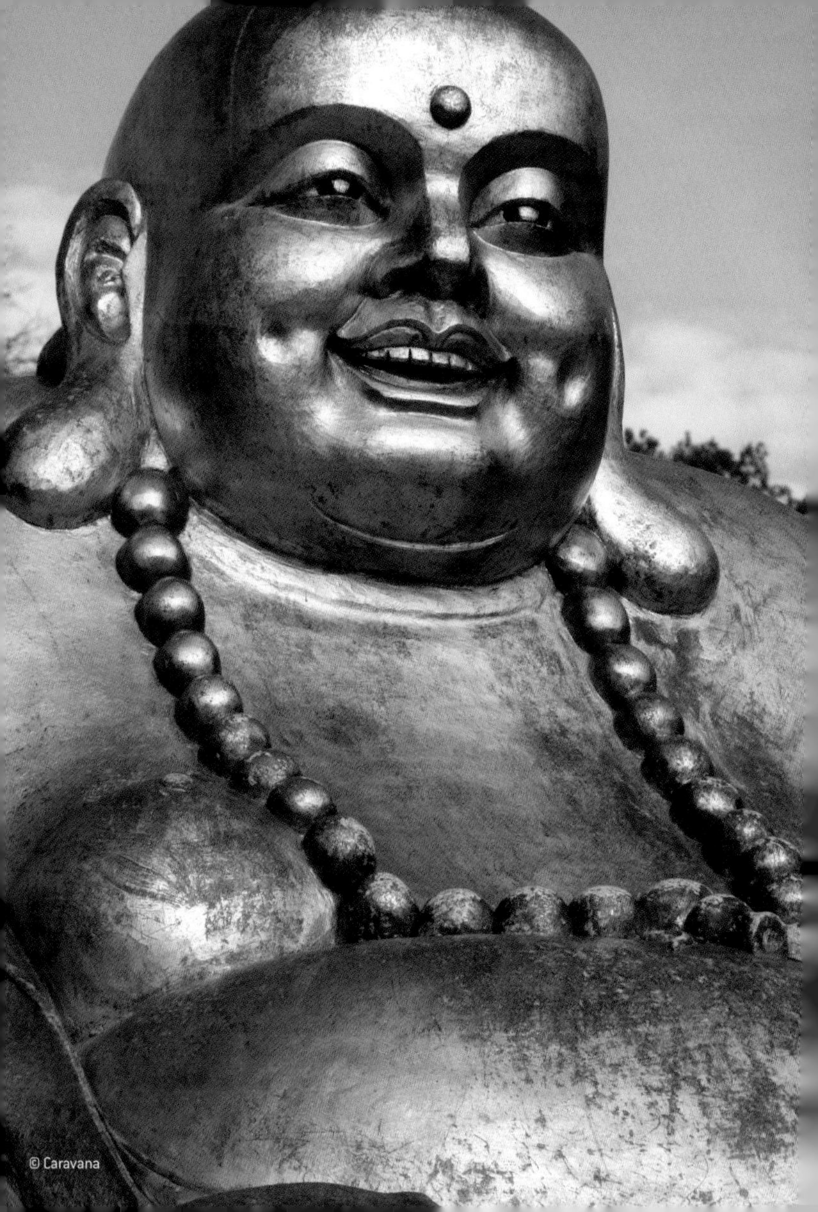

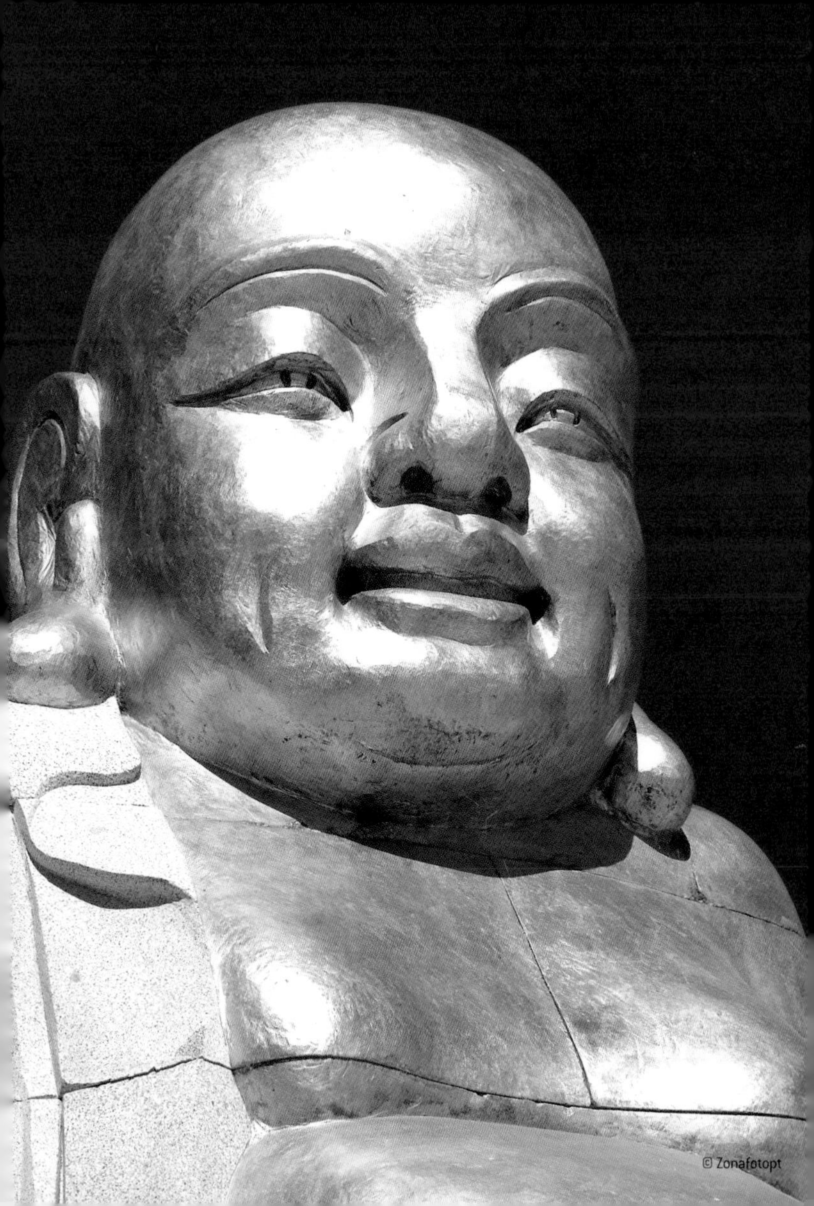

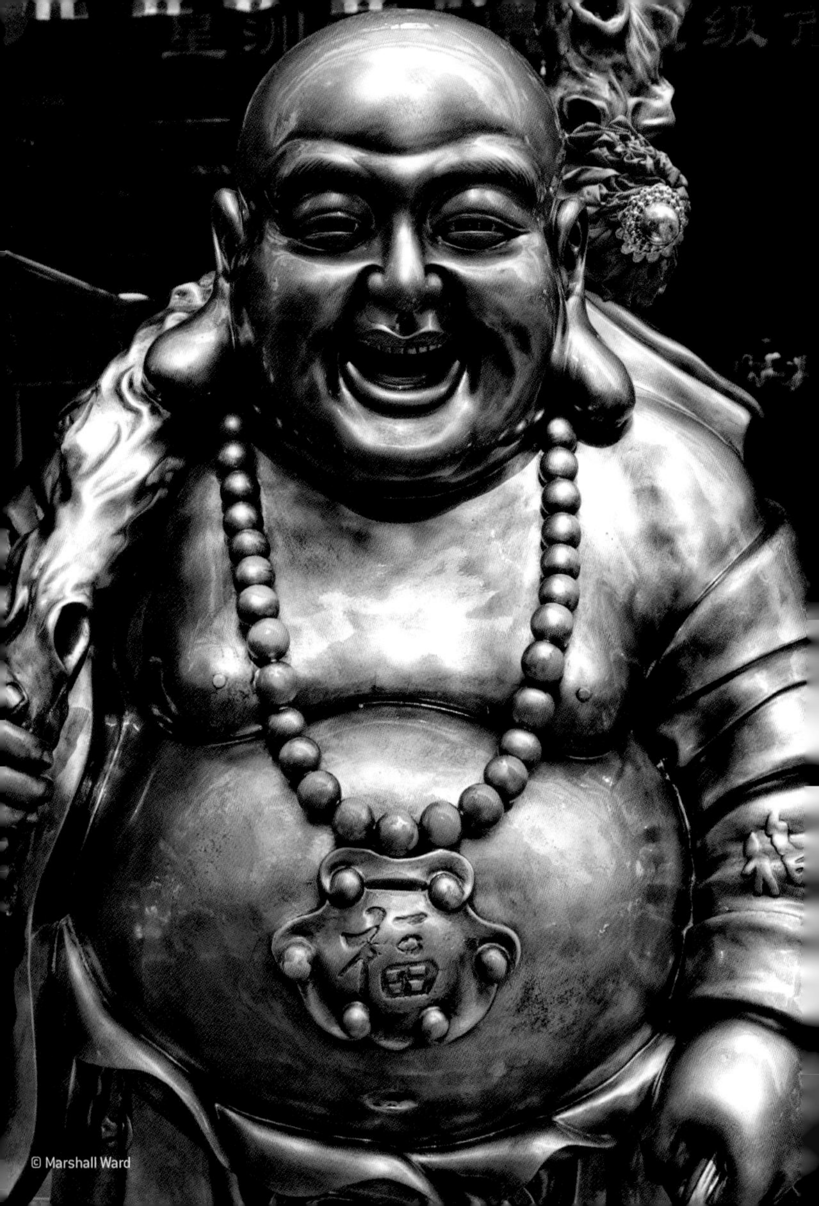

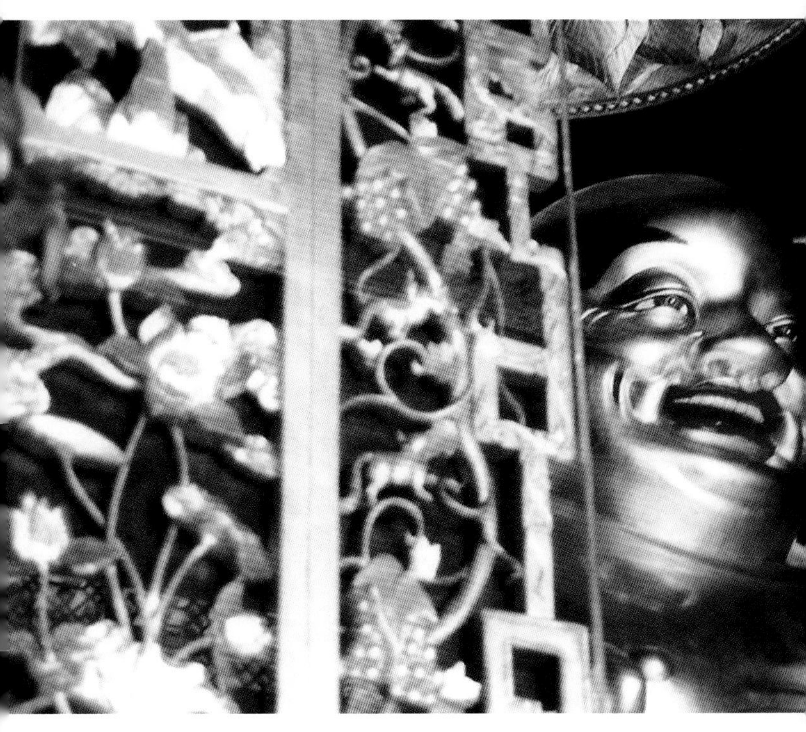

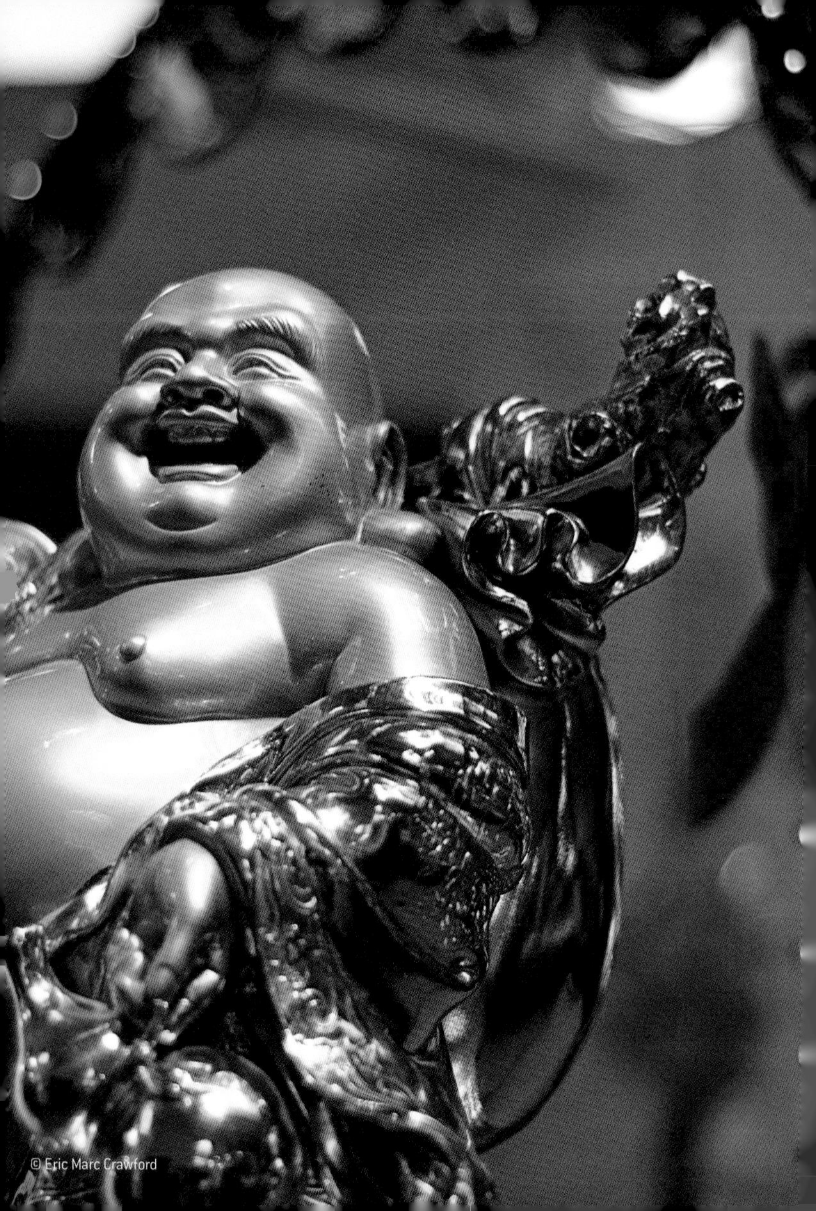

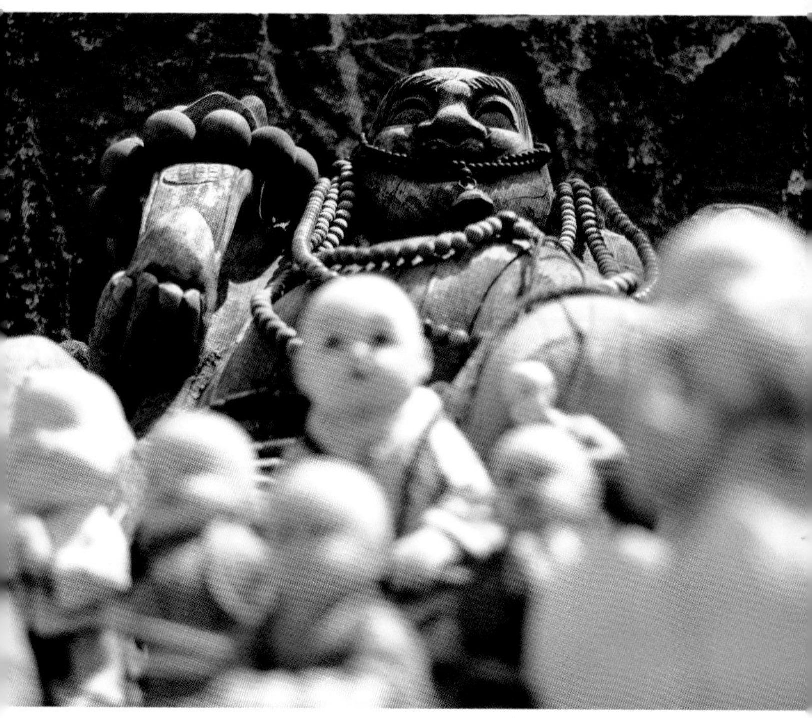

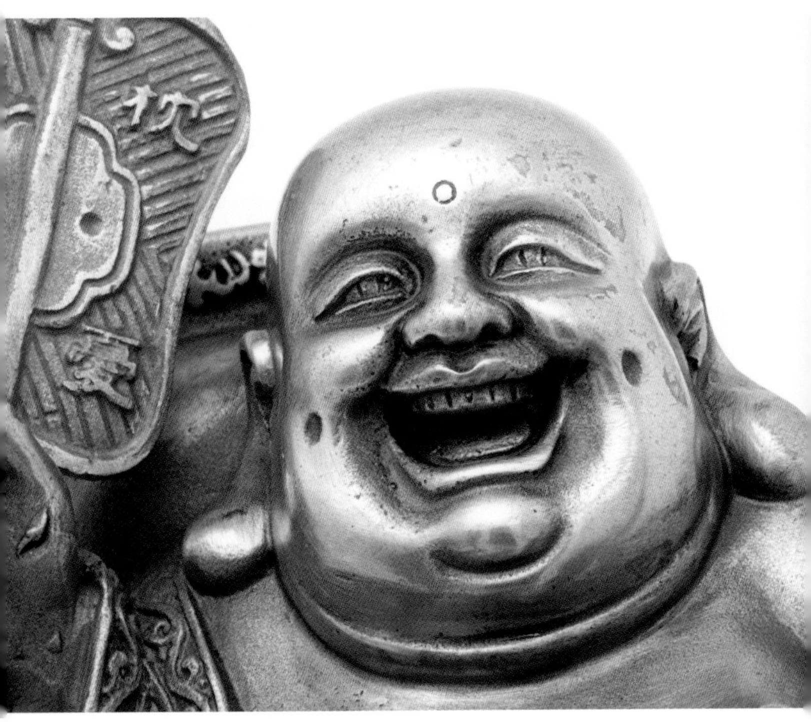

© Andrey Lavrenov

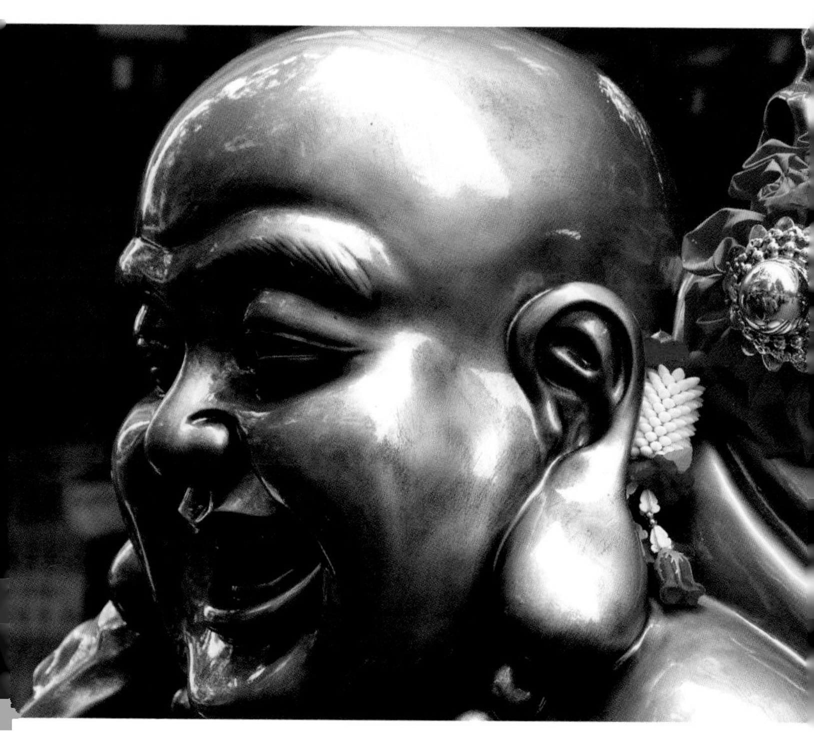

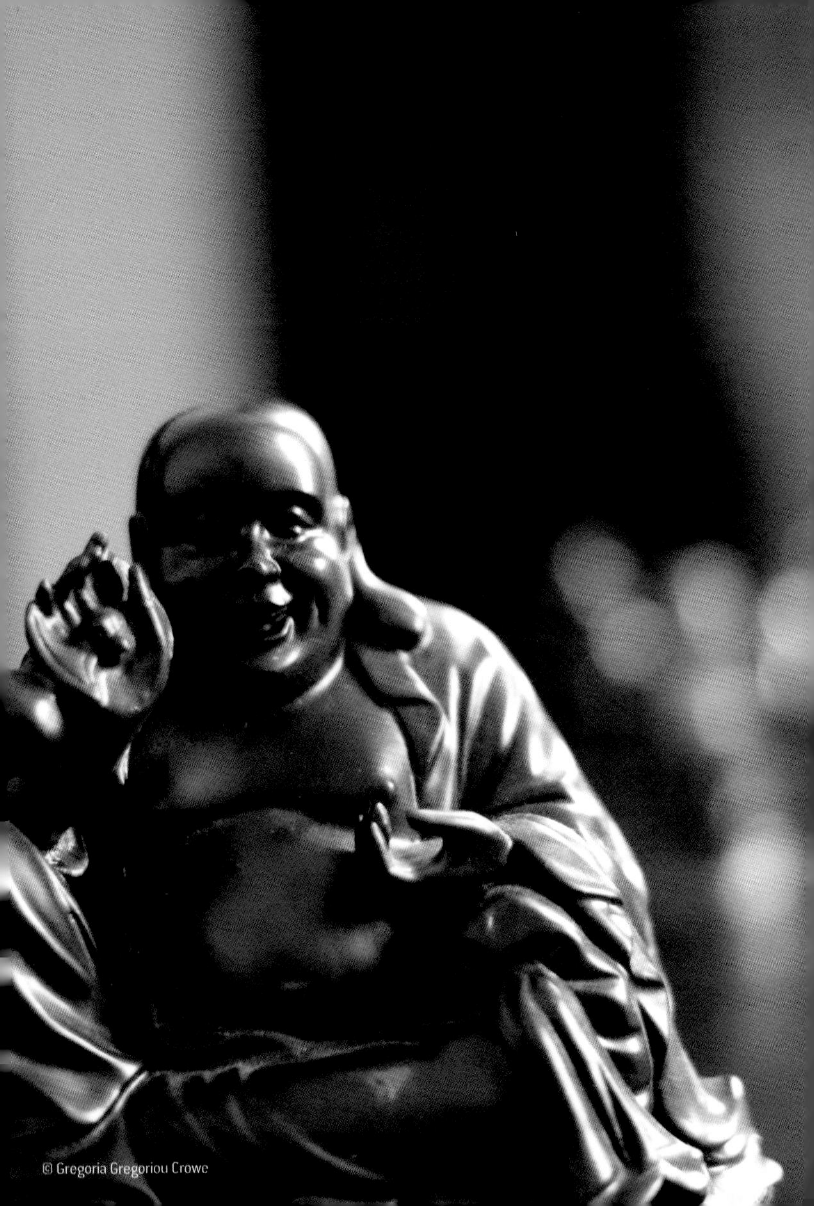

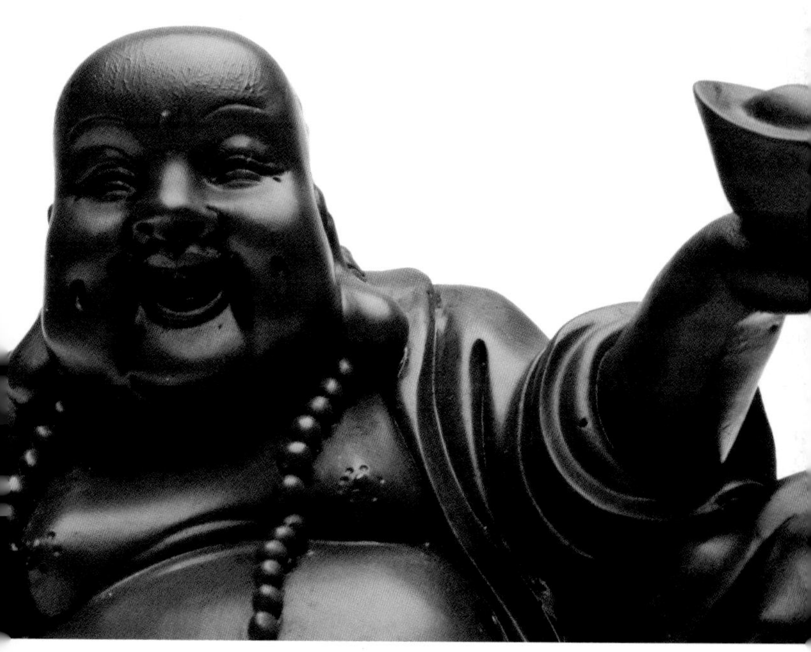

Sitting Buddha
Bouddha assis
Sitzender Buddha
Zittende Boeddha

The sitting Buddha is perhaps the most famous of all of the representations. In this position we can see that he has very long arms, since, sitting and with a straight back, Buddha can touch his seat. In this position, we can also see his rounded and meaty chest in retribution for the food and sustenance that he has offered to others.
In this chapter we can quickly see Buddha's body, which draws our attention to the detail of the veins and ribs, something which cannot be seen in any of the other representations. Even so, his chest is held upright, symbolising the everlasting consideration that he shows towards all other beings on Earth, despite his original social position, as well as the care he takes to never humiliate or mistreat others.

Le bouddha assis est probablement la représentation la plus connue de toutes. Dans cette position, on peut voir que ses bras sont très longs, car étant assis et avec le dos droit, il arrive à toucher son siège. Cette position fait également ressortir sa poitrine arrondie et charnue, tel un signe de gratitude pour les aliments et les substances qu'il a offerts aux autres.
Dans ce chapitre, on peut apprécier la représentation du Bouddha jeûnant, dont le détail des veines et des côtes attire l'attention, et que l'on n'observe dans aucune autre représentation. Malgré cela, son torse reste dressé, symbolisant la considération qu'il a toujours eue envers les habitants de la Terre, en dépit de sa position sociale originelle, et le soin qu'il a pris de ne jamais les humilier ni les maltraiter.

Der sitzende Buddha ist vielleicht die populärste Darstellung von allen. In dieser Position können wir sehen, dass seine Arme sehr lang sind, da er in sehr aufrechter Haltung sitzend Buddha seinen Sitz berühren kann. Bei dieser Position fällt auch die Tatsache auf, dass seine Brust rund und fleischig ist, als Vergütung für die Lebensmittel und Nährstoffe, die er anderen geboten hat. In diesem Kapitel kann man auch die Figur des fastenden Buddhas würdigen, die wegen der detaillierten Hervorhebung seiner Venen und Rippen auffällt, etwas, was man bei keiner anderen Darstellung sehen kann. Dennoch bleibt seine Brust aufgerichtet und symbolisiert so die Achtung vor allen Lebewesen, die die Erde bewohnen, trotz seiner ursprünglichen gesellschaftlichen Stellung, ebenso wie die Sorgfalt, die er aufbrachte, um diese niemals zu demütigen oder zu misshandeln.

De zittende boeddha is misschien wel de populairste voorstelling van allemaal. In deze positie kunnen we zien dat zijn armen erg lang zijn, aangezien Boeddha zittend en met rechte rug zijn zetel kan aanraken. Eveneens valt in deze houding zijn ronde en vlezige borst op ter compensatie van de etenswaren en voedingsmiddelen die hij anderen heeft aangeboden.
In dit hoofdstuk kan men ook de figuur van de vastende Boeddha zien. De aandacht wordt hier gevestigd op het detail waarmee zijn aders en ribben worden benadrukt, iets wat in geen andere voorstelling kan worden waargenomen. Desalniettemin houdt hij zijn borst recht. Dit symboliseert het respect dat hij, ondanks zijn oorspronkelijke sociale positie, altijd heeft gehad voor alle andere wezens die de aarde bewonen, alsmede de zorg waarmee hij heeft geprobeerd hen nooit te vernederen of te mishandelen.

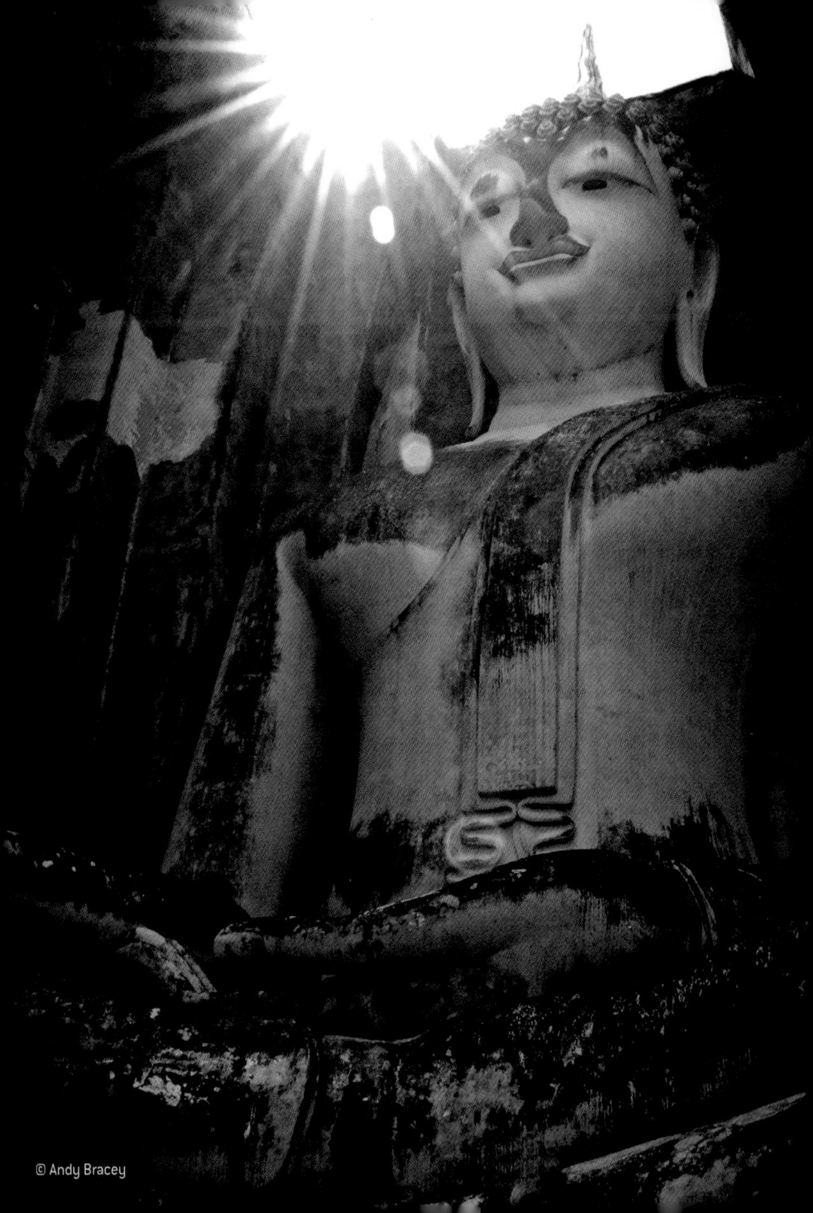

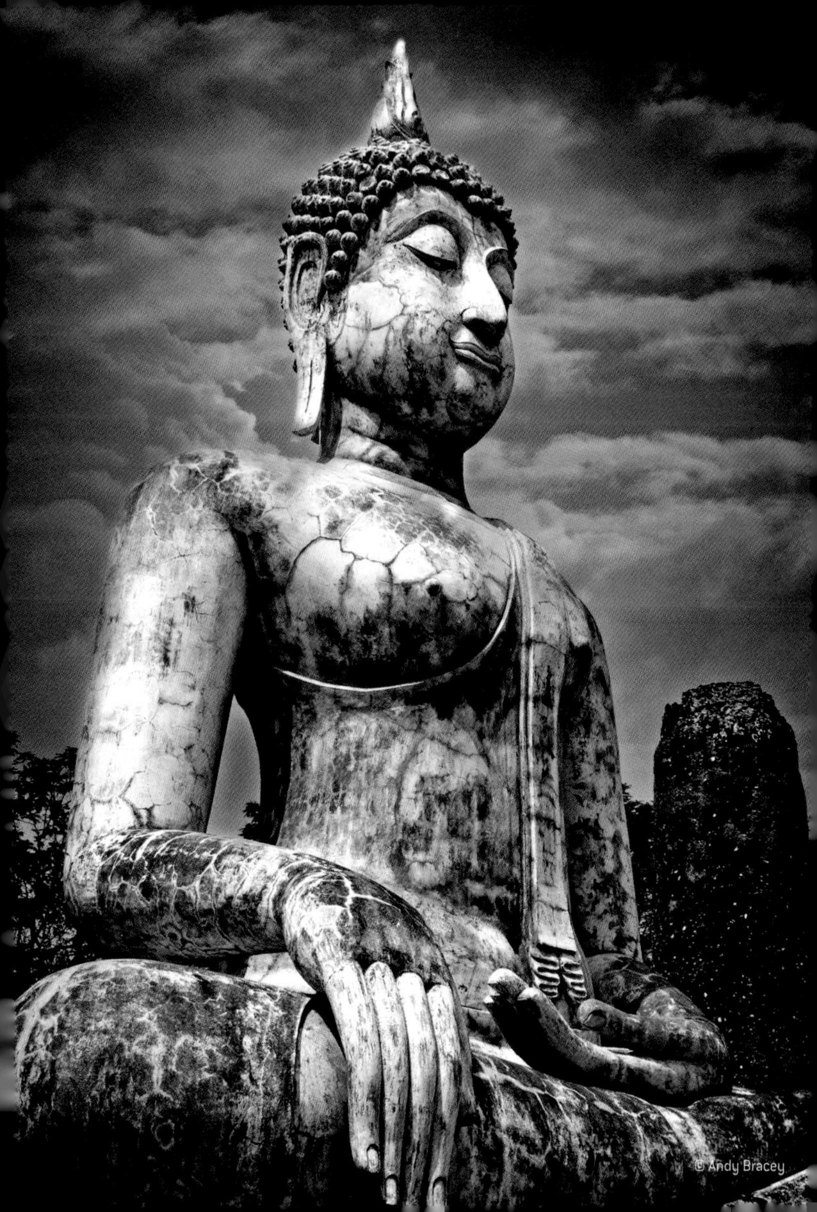

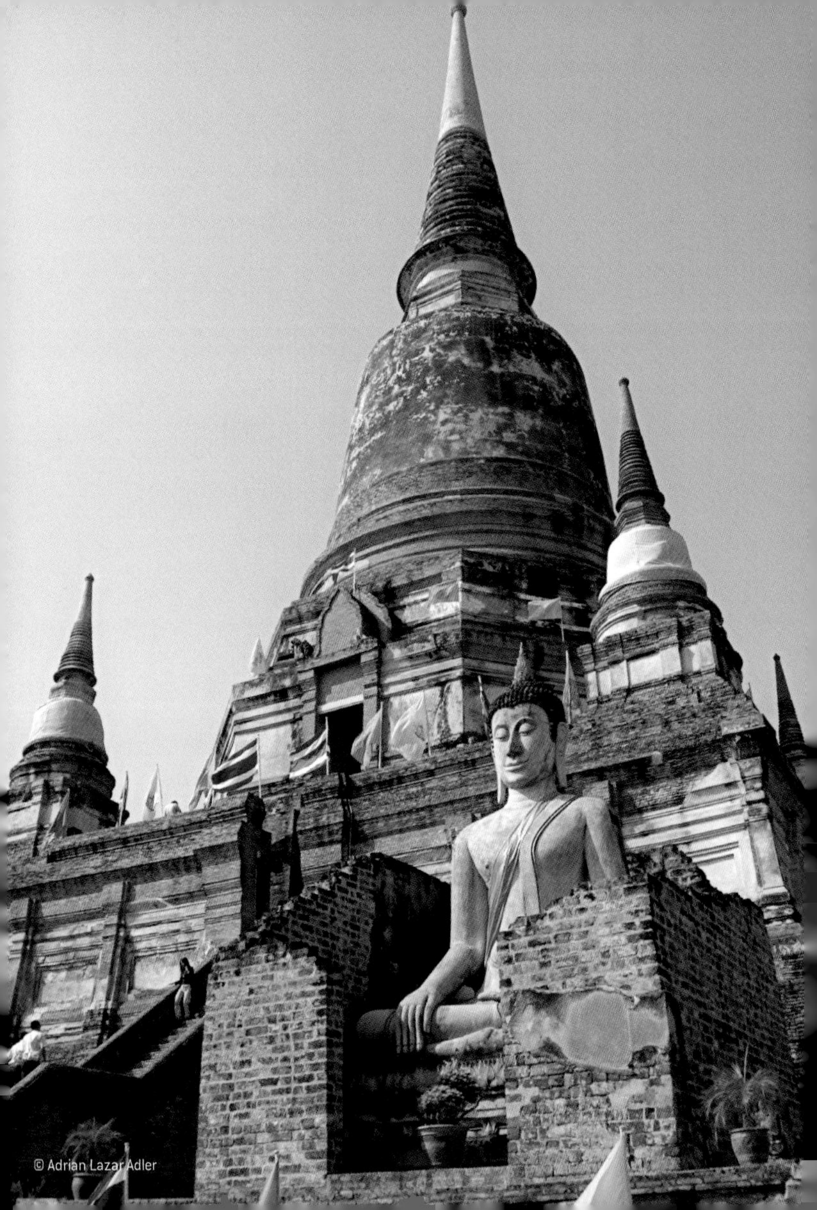

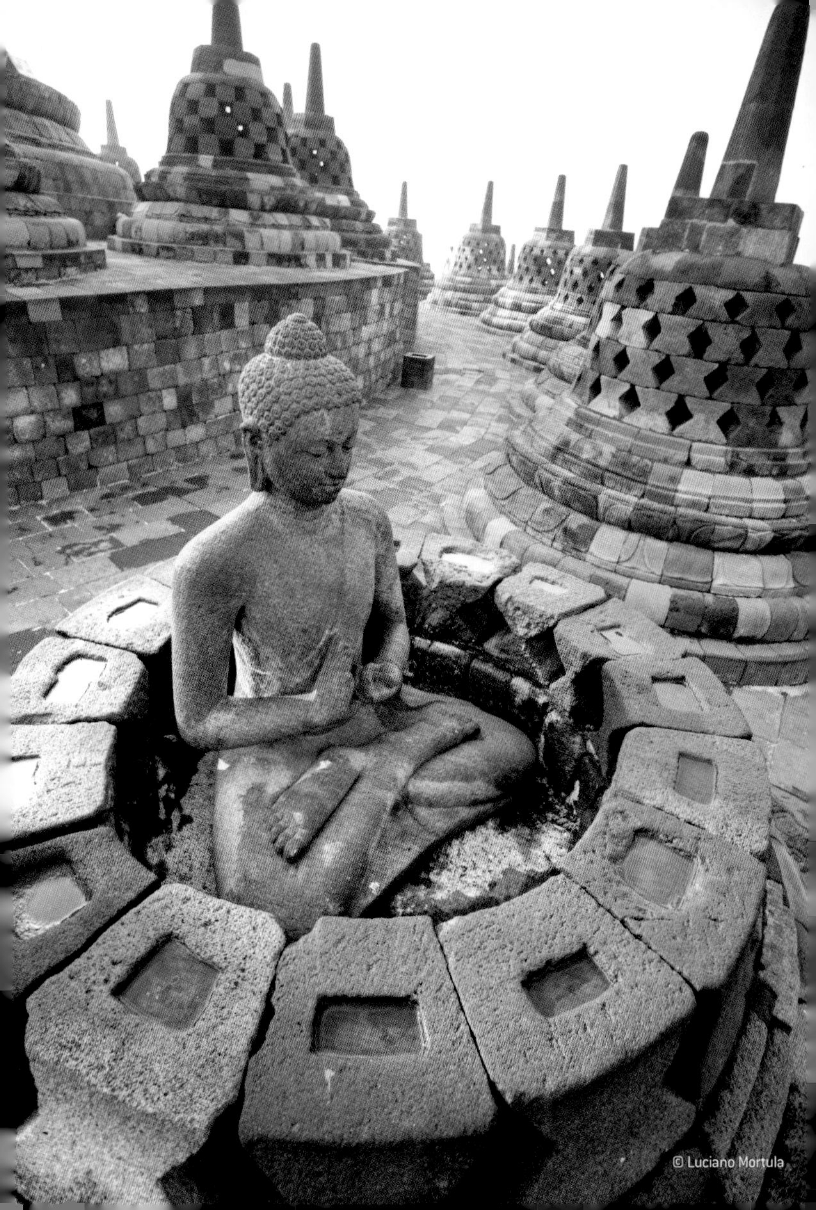

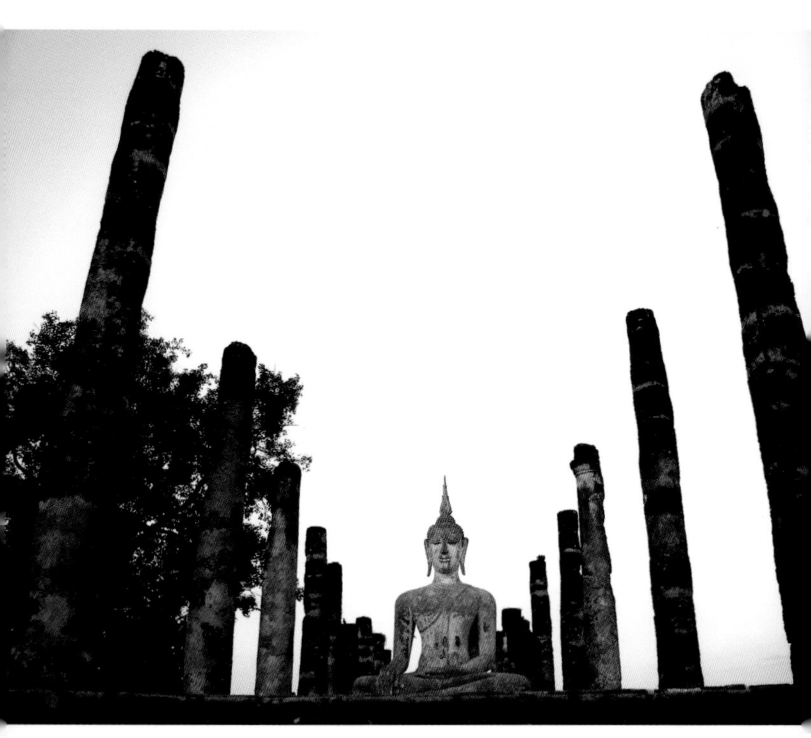

© Jutamas Klib-Ngern

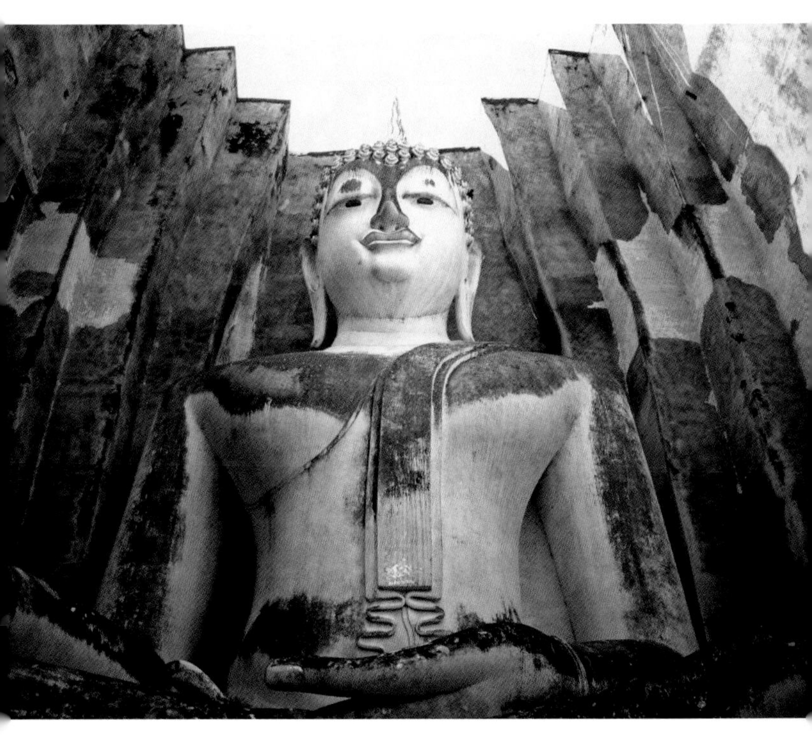

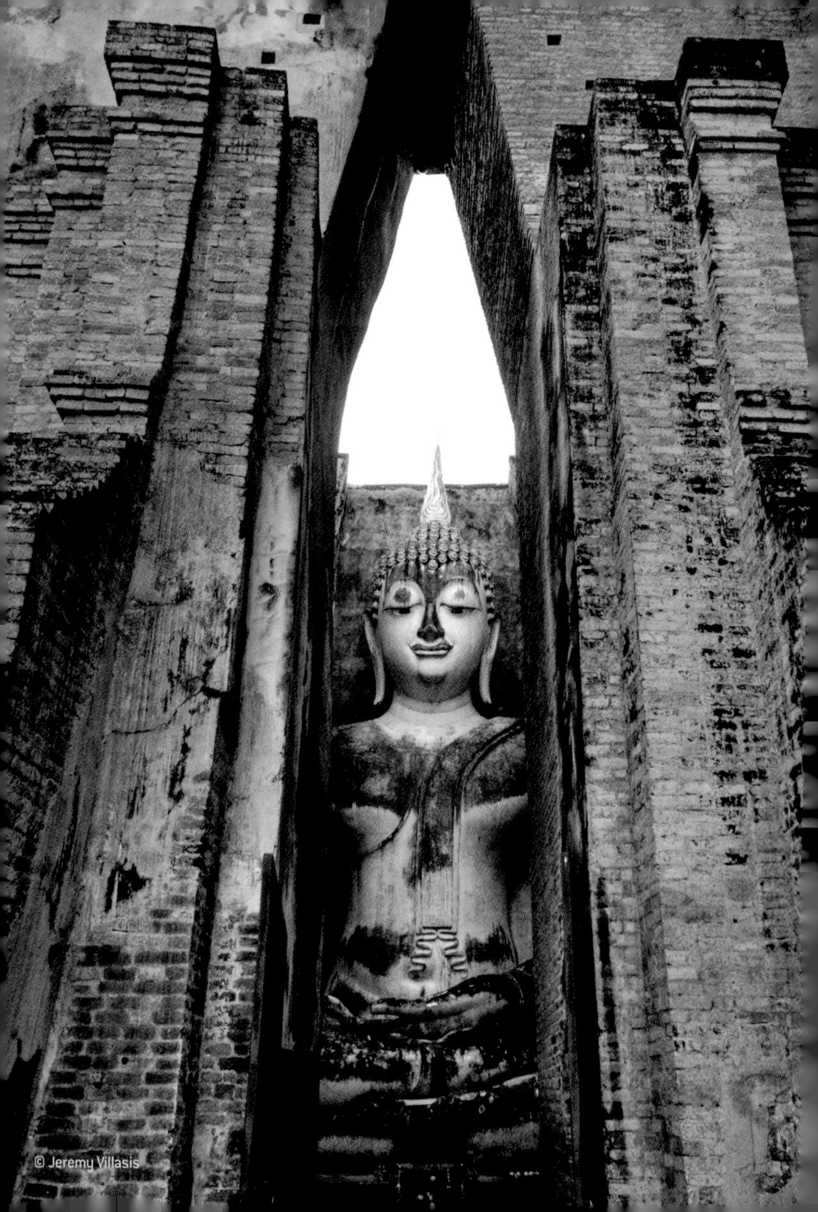
© Jeremy Villasis

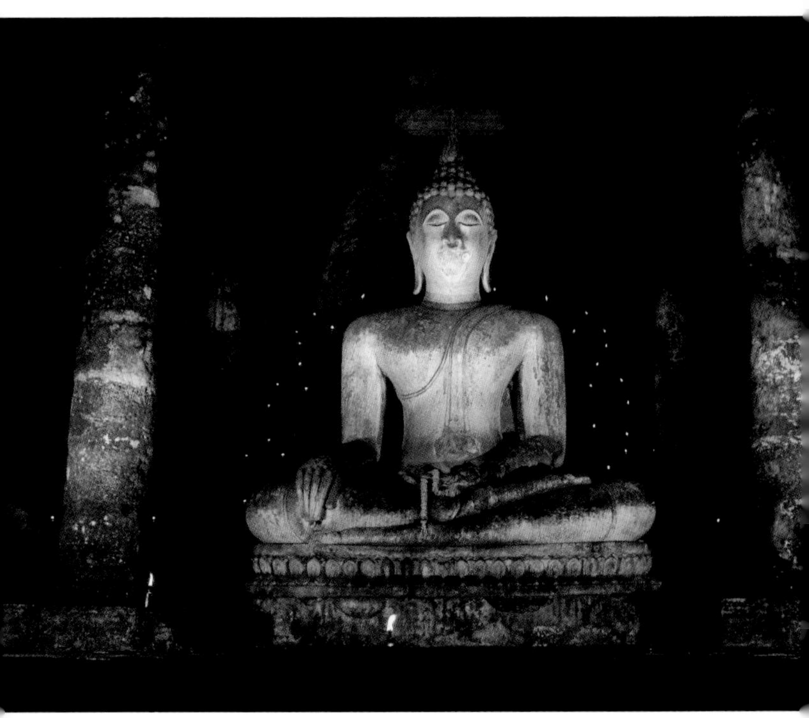

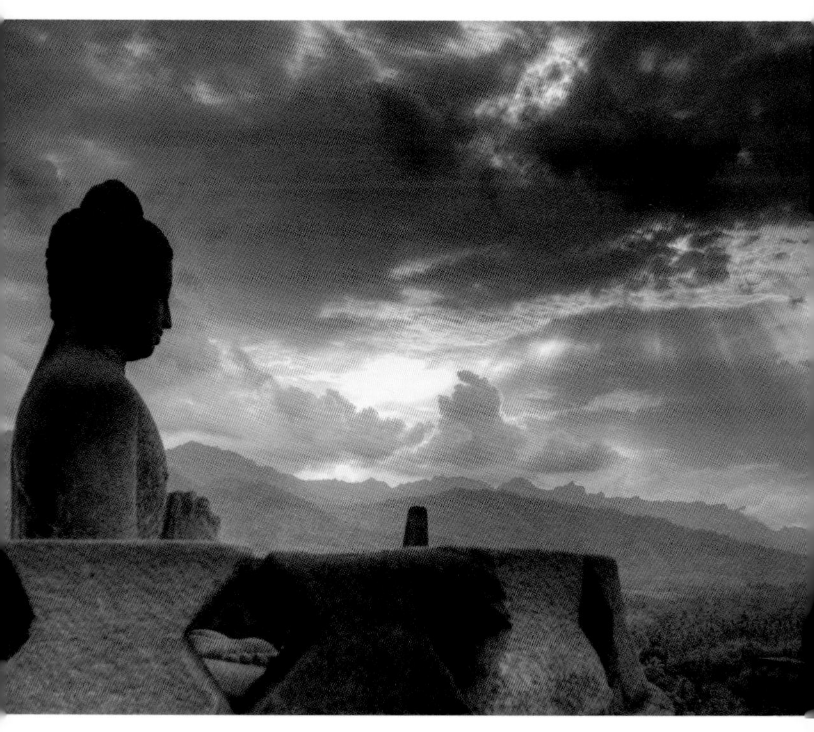

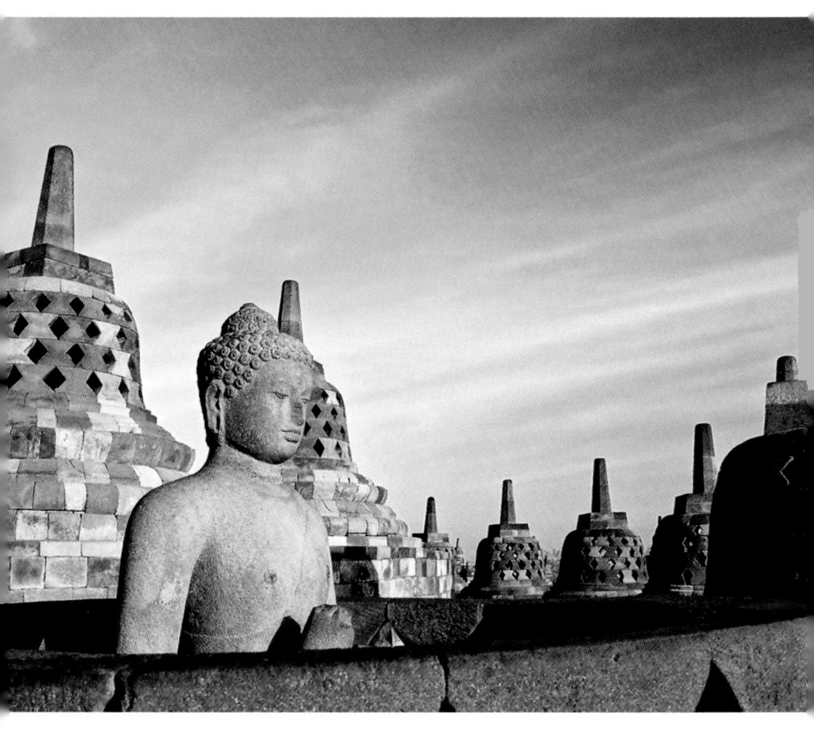

© Igor Prahin

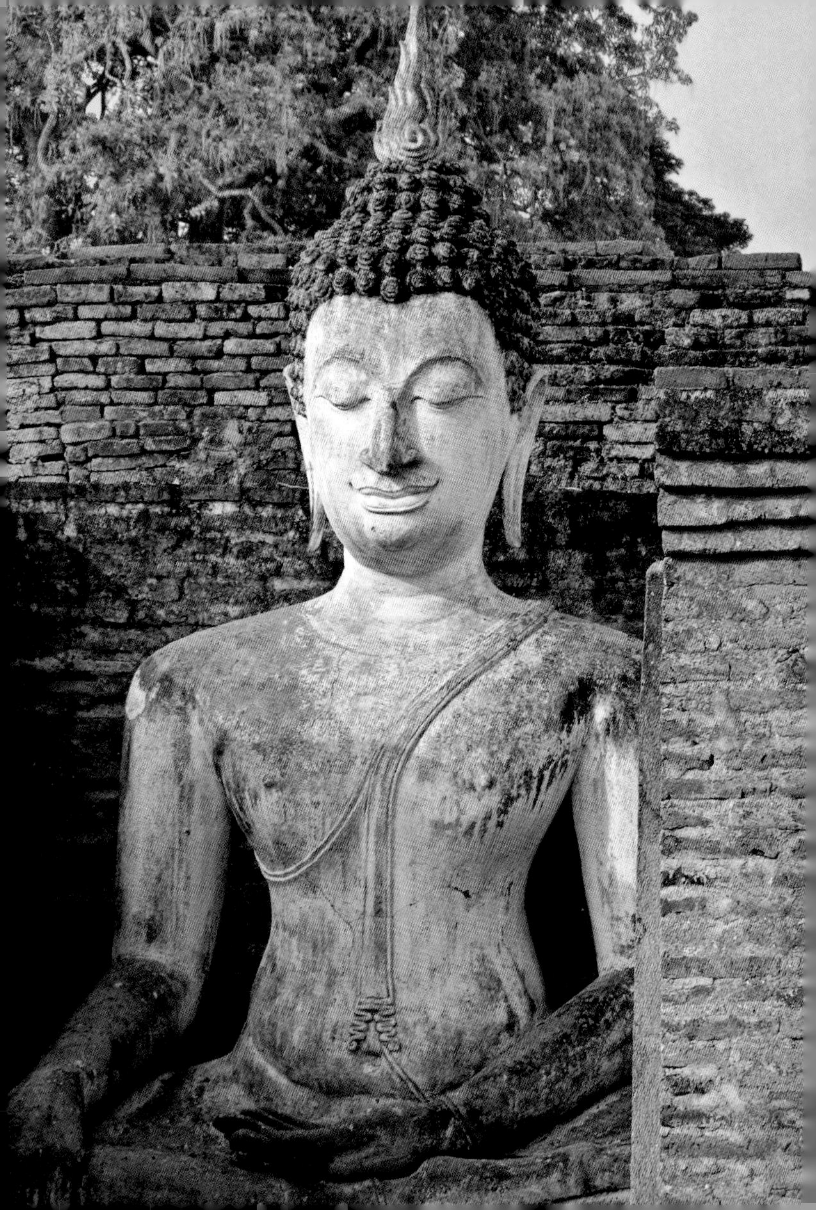

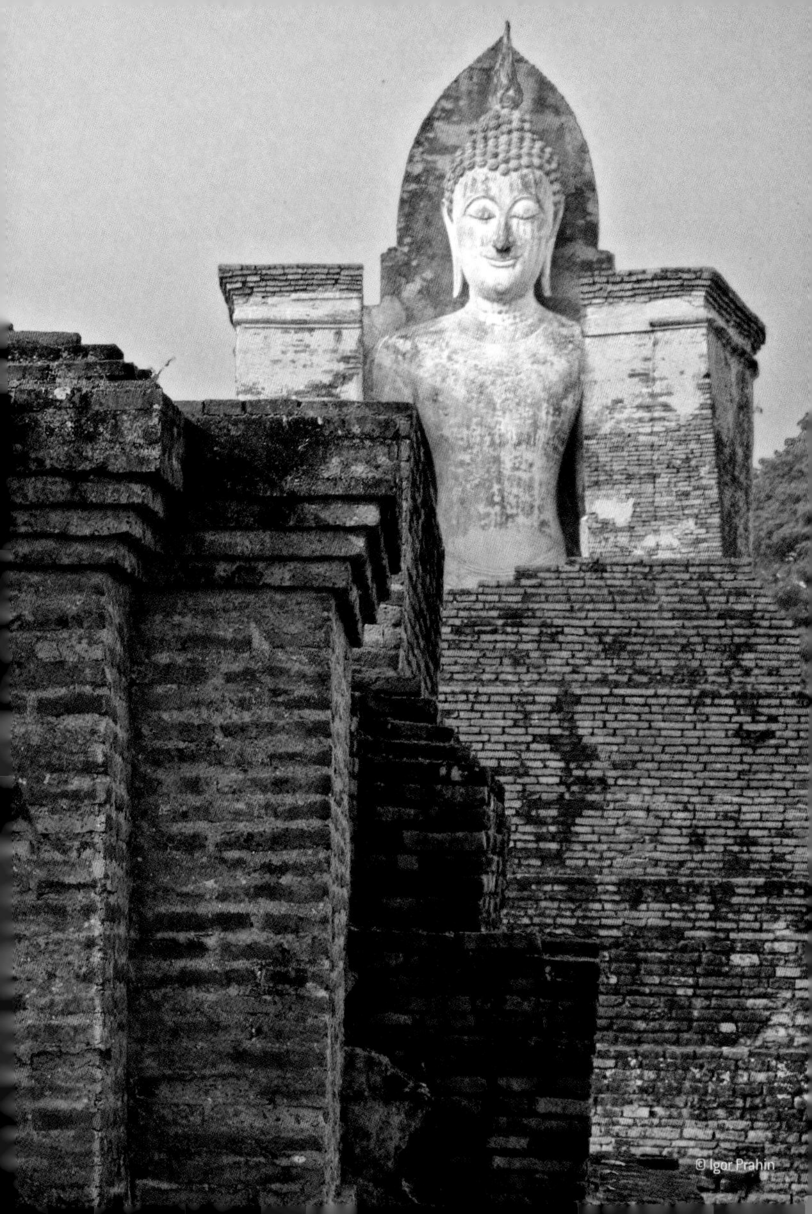
© Igor Prahin

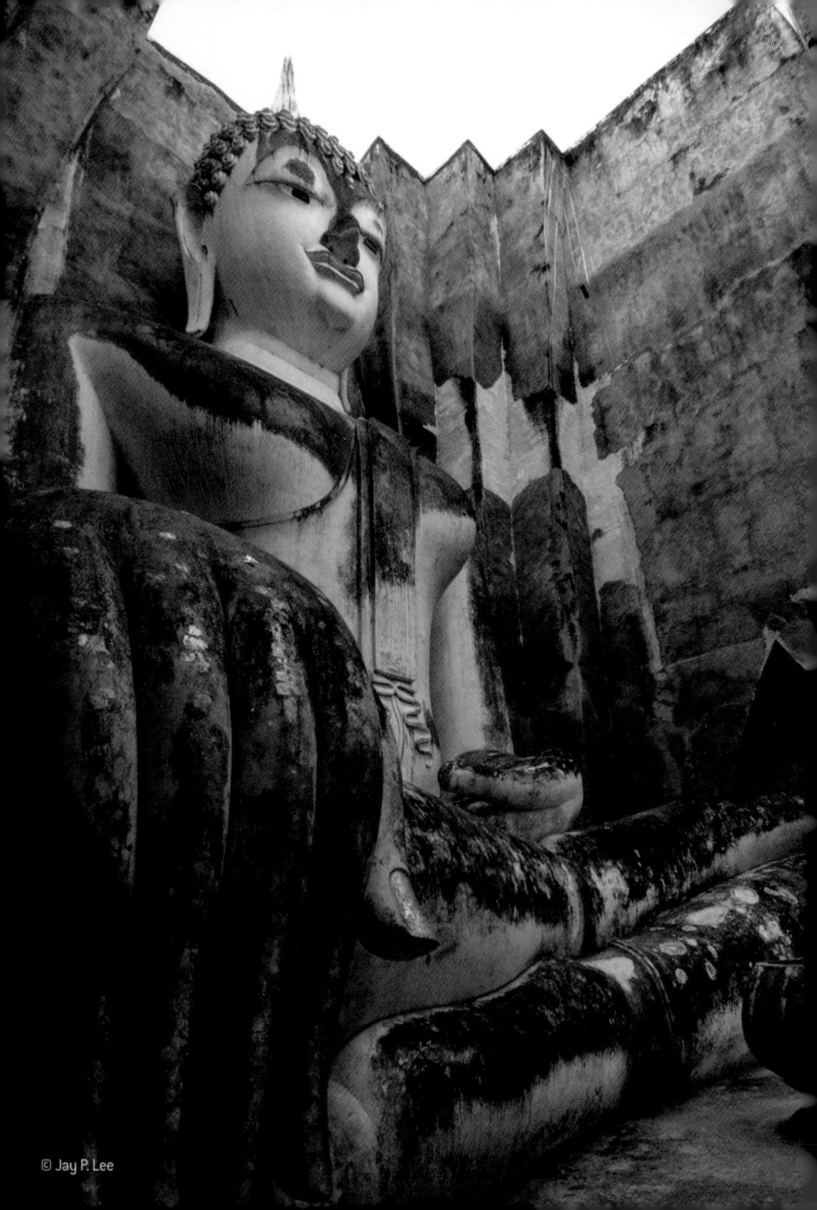

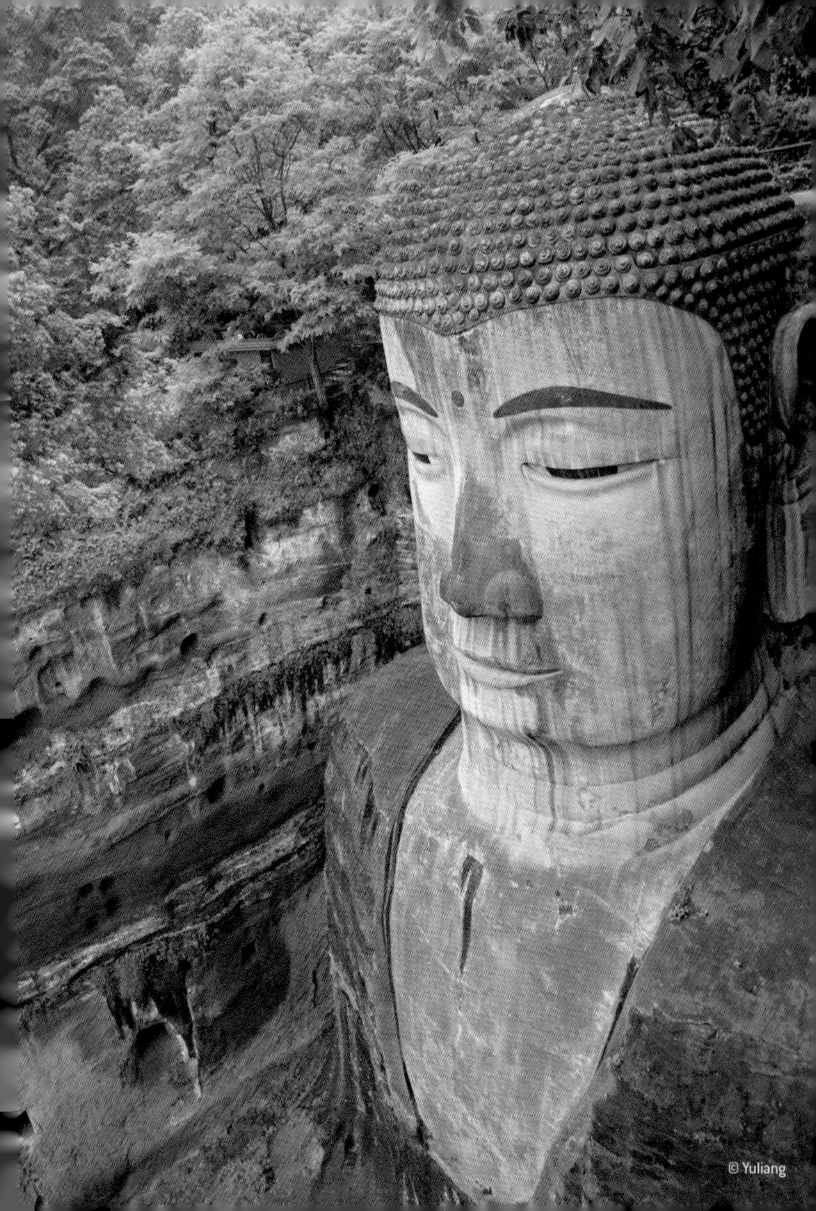

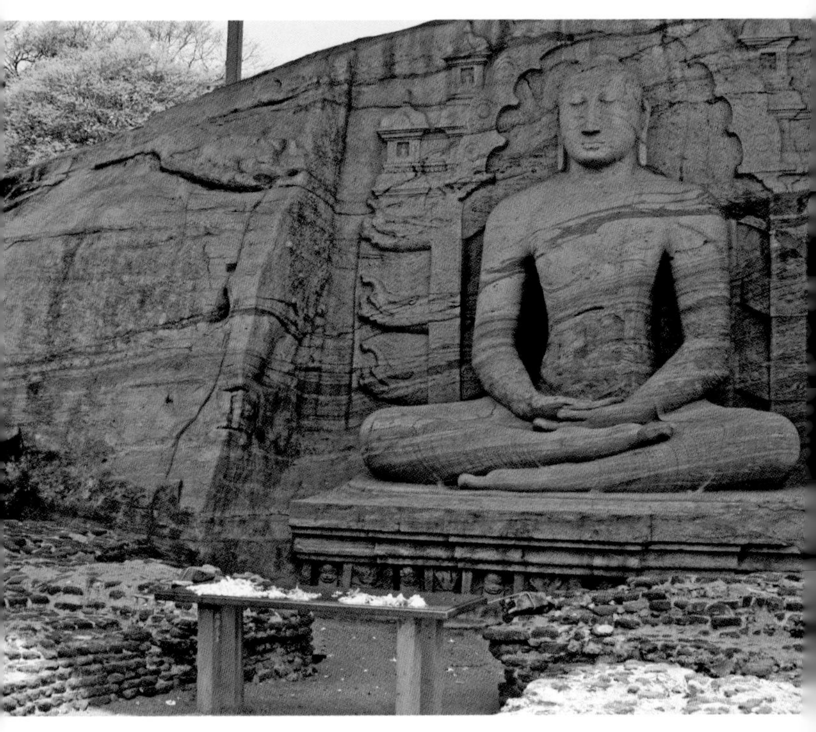

©Dhaneesha Senaratne

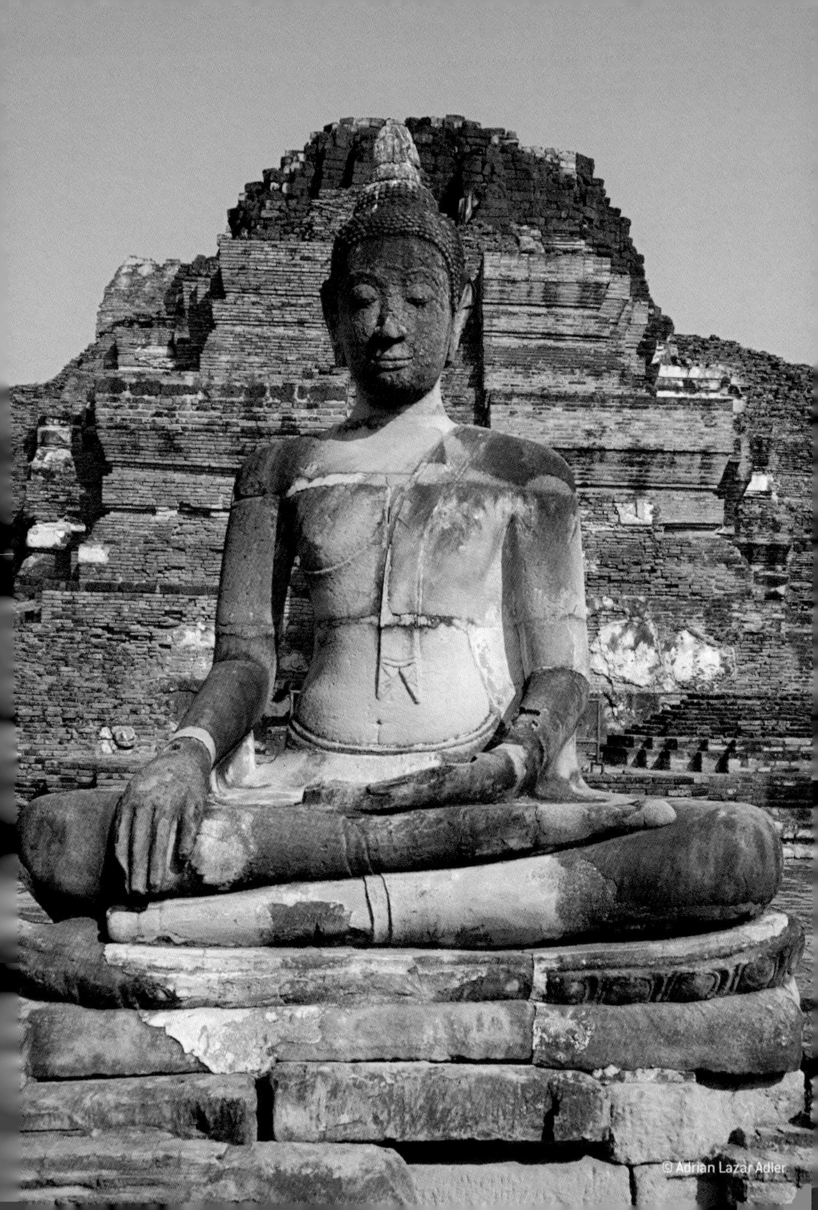

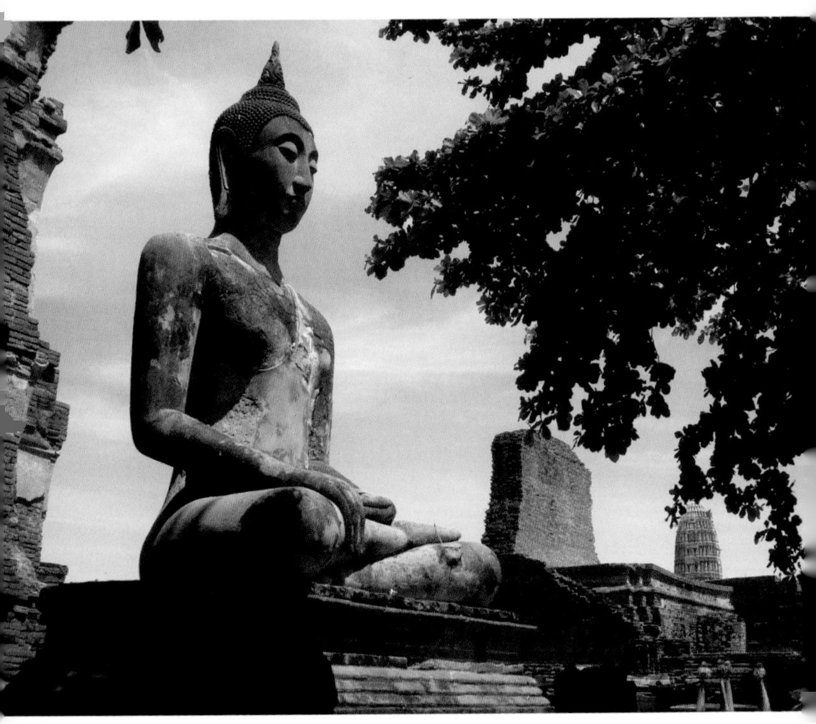

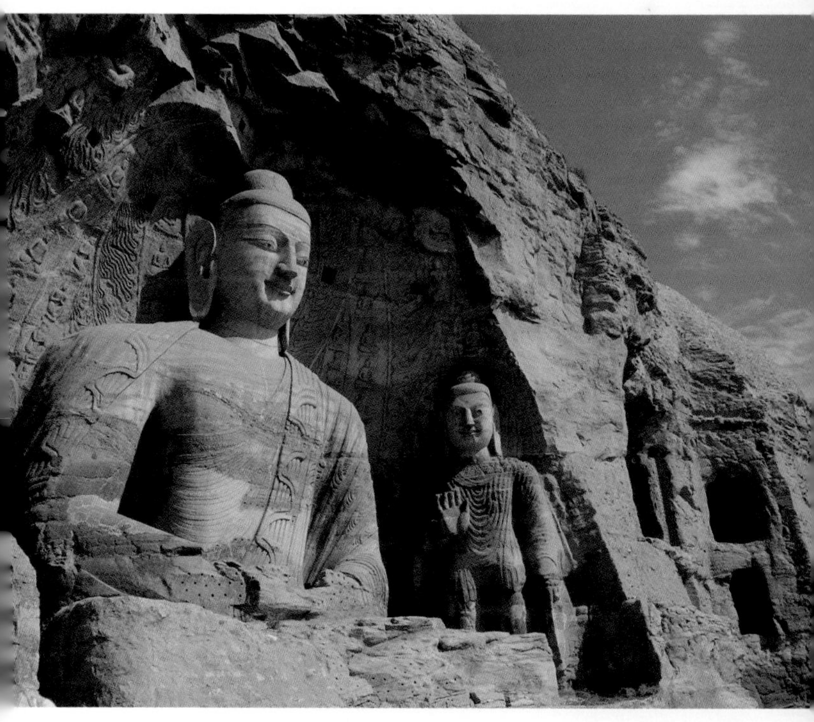

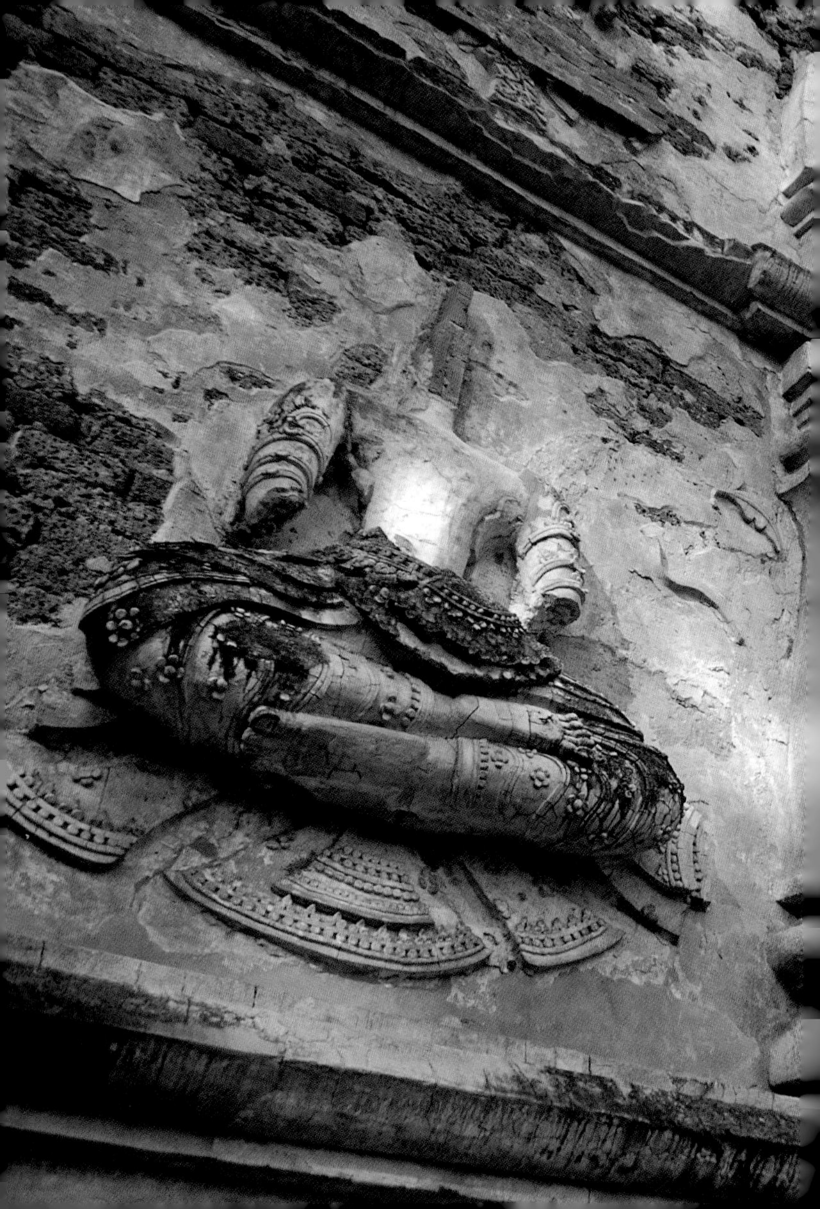

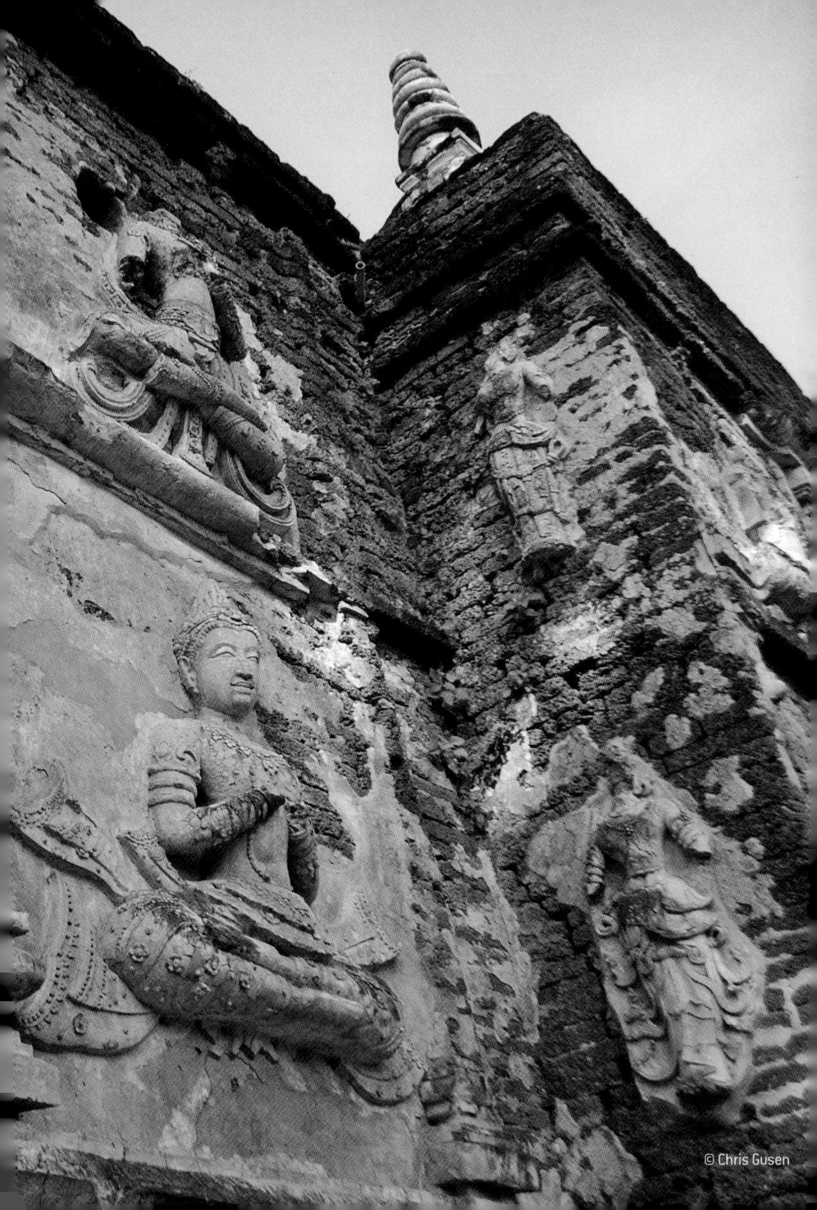

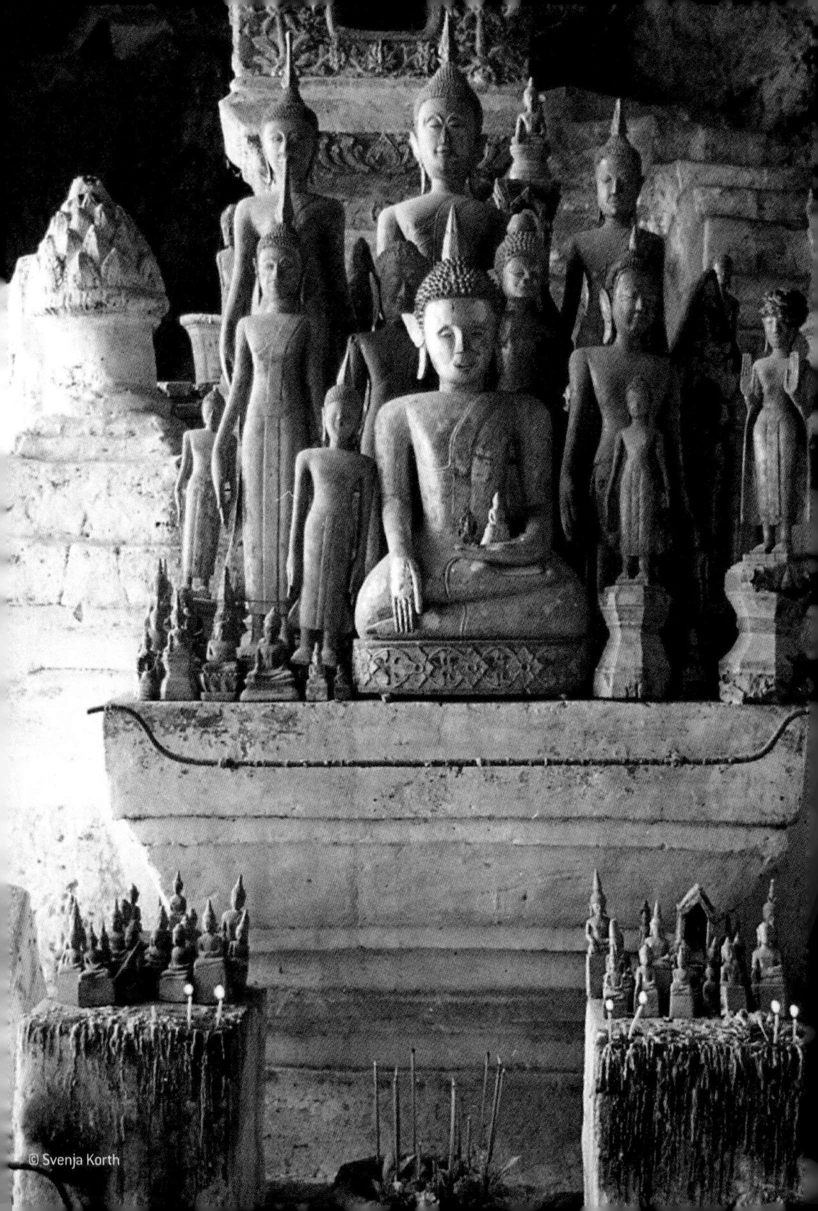

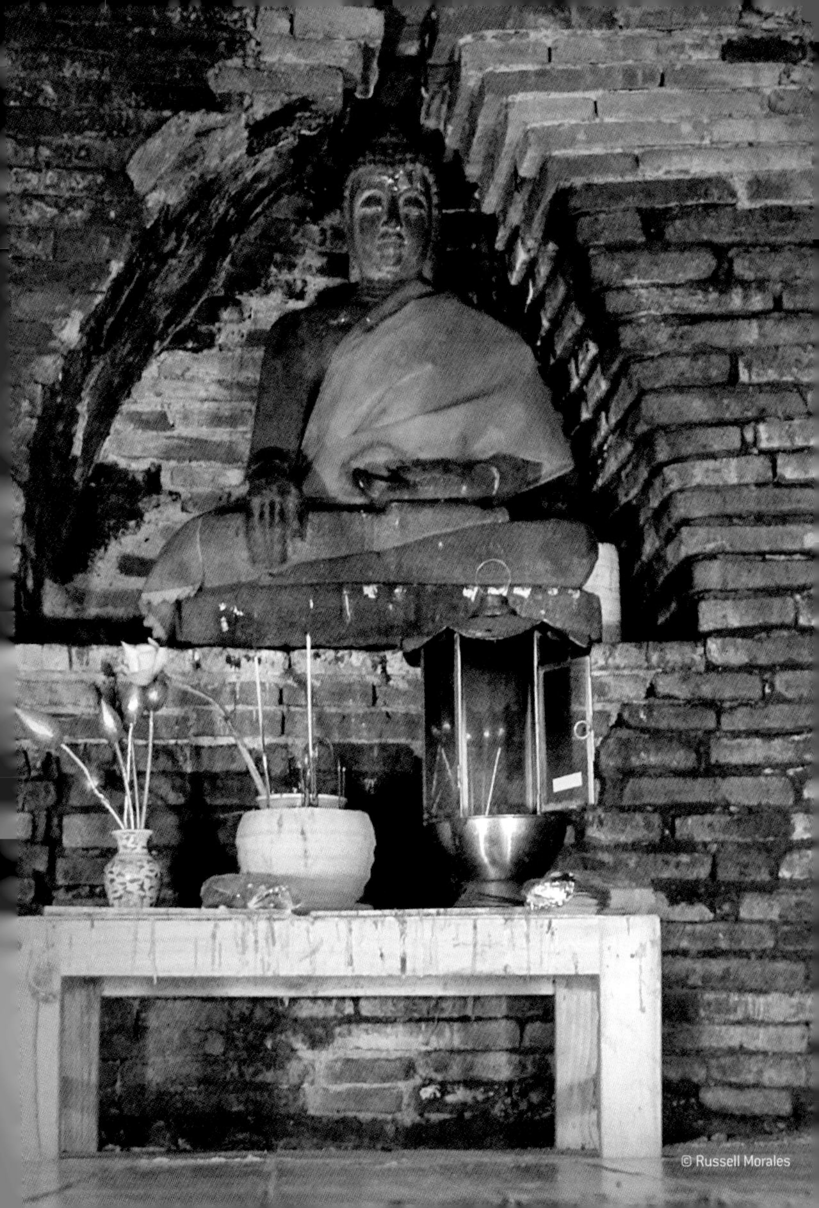

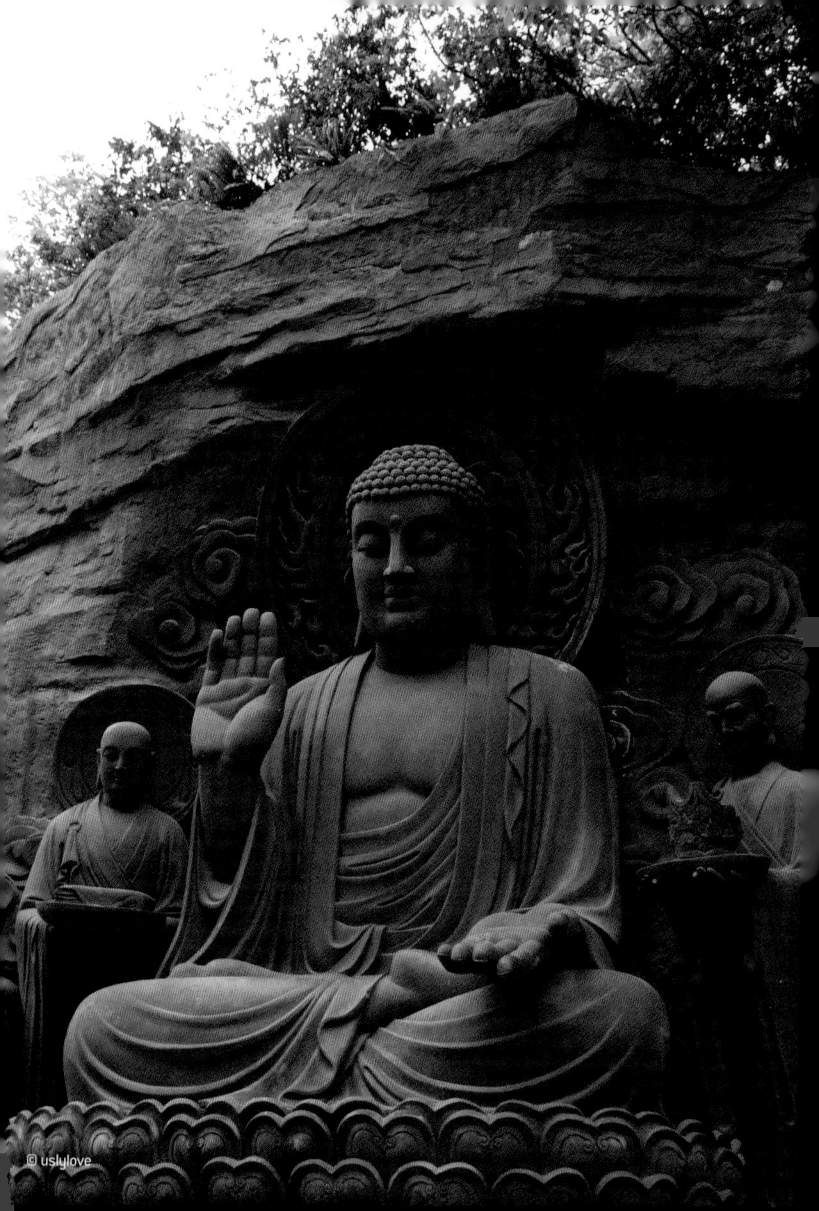
© uslylove

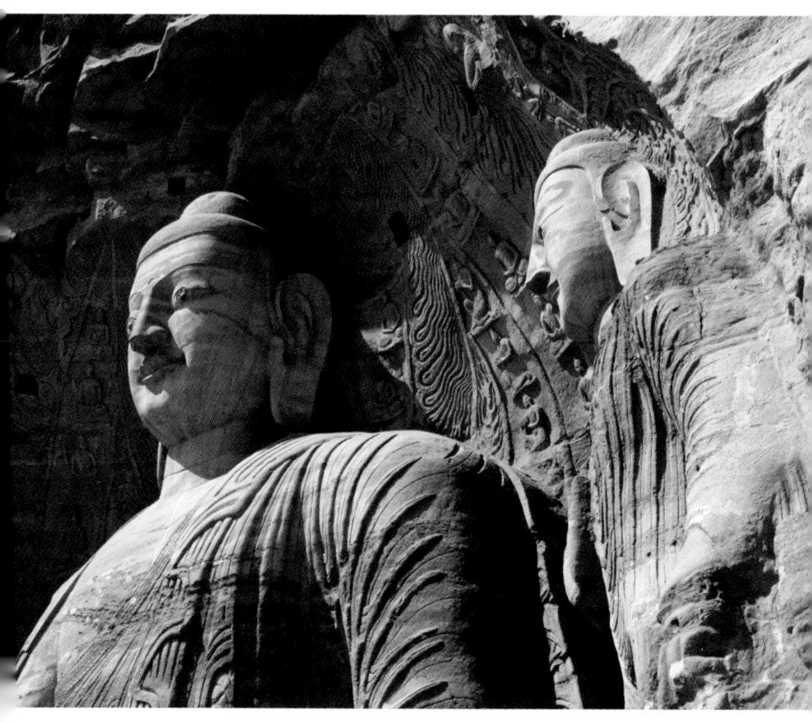

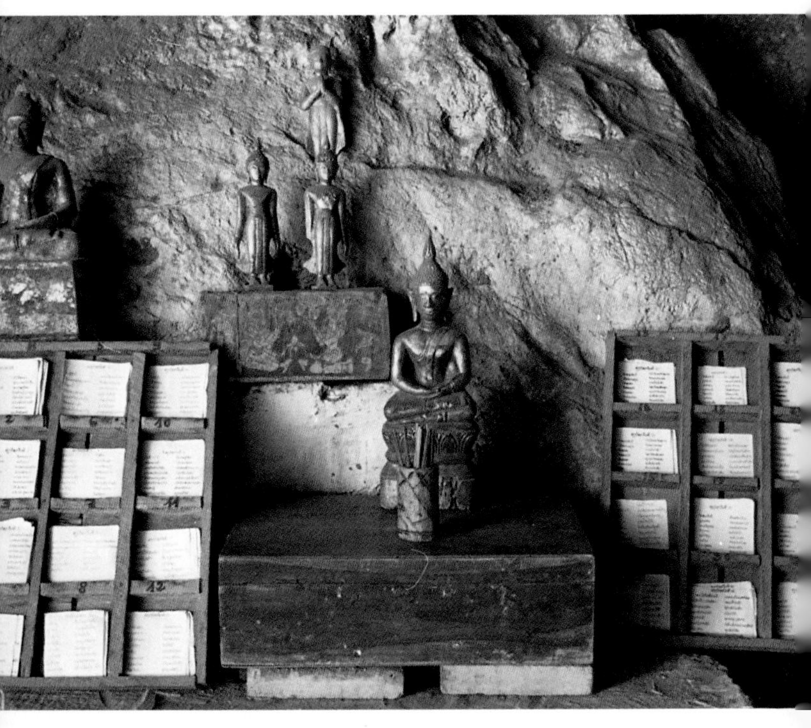

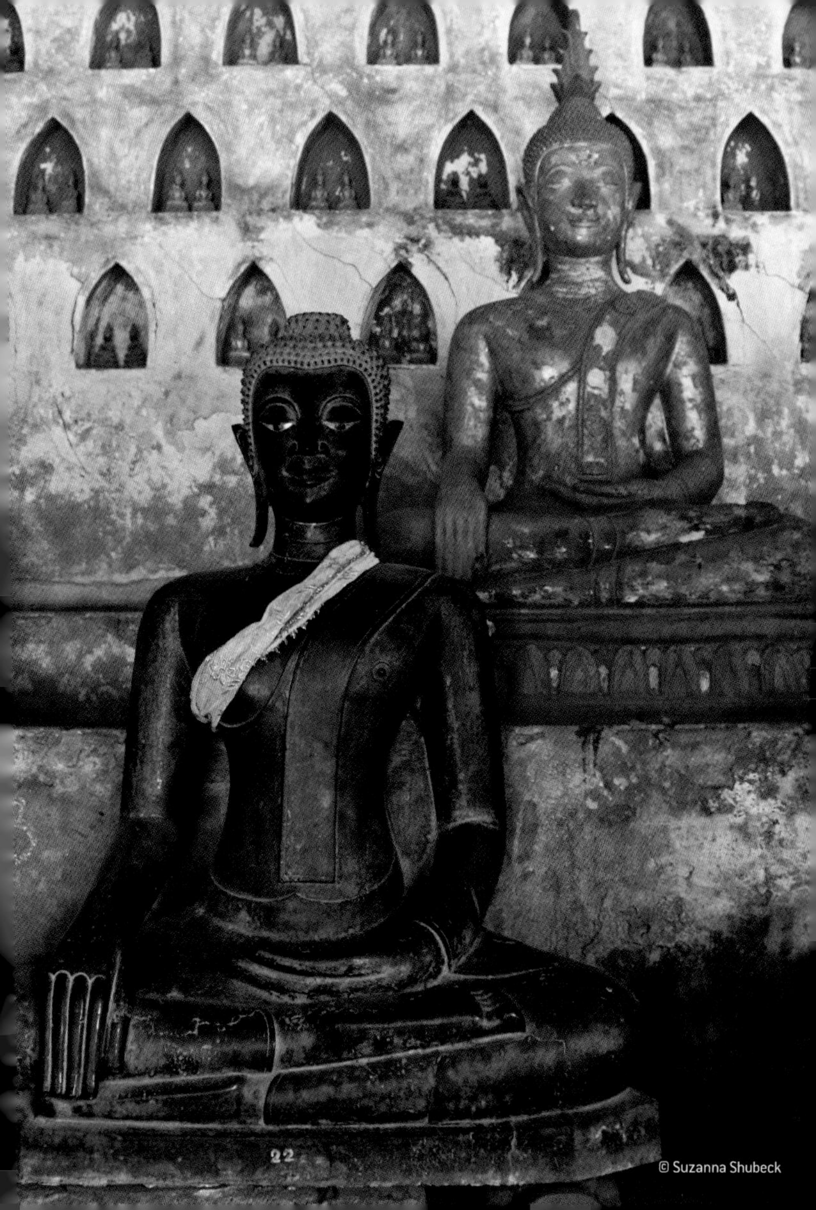
22

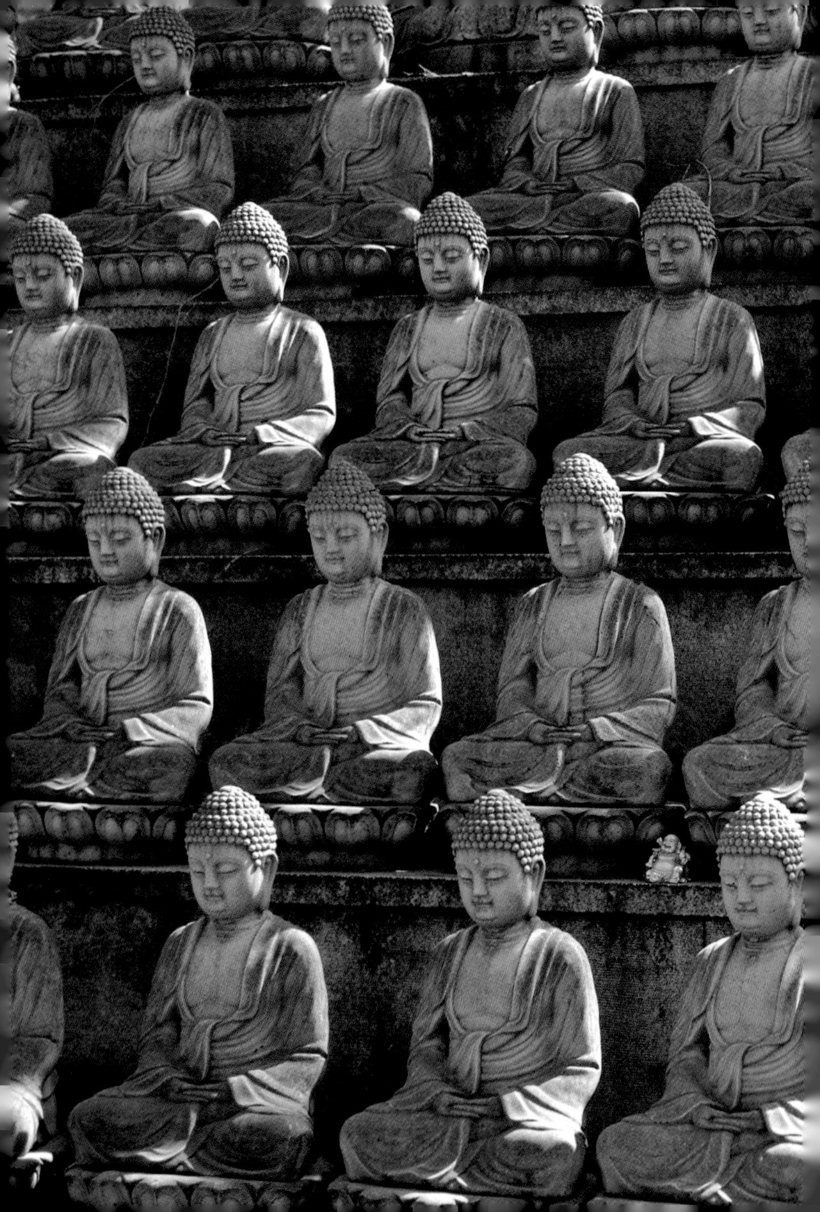

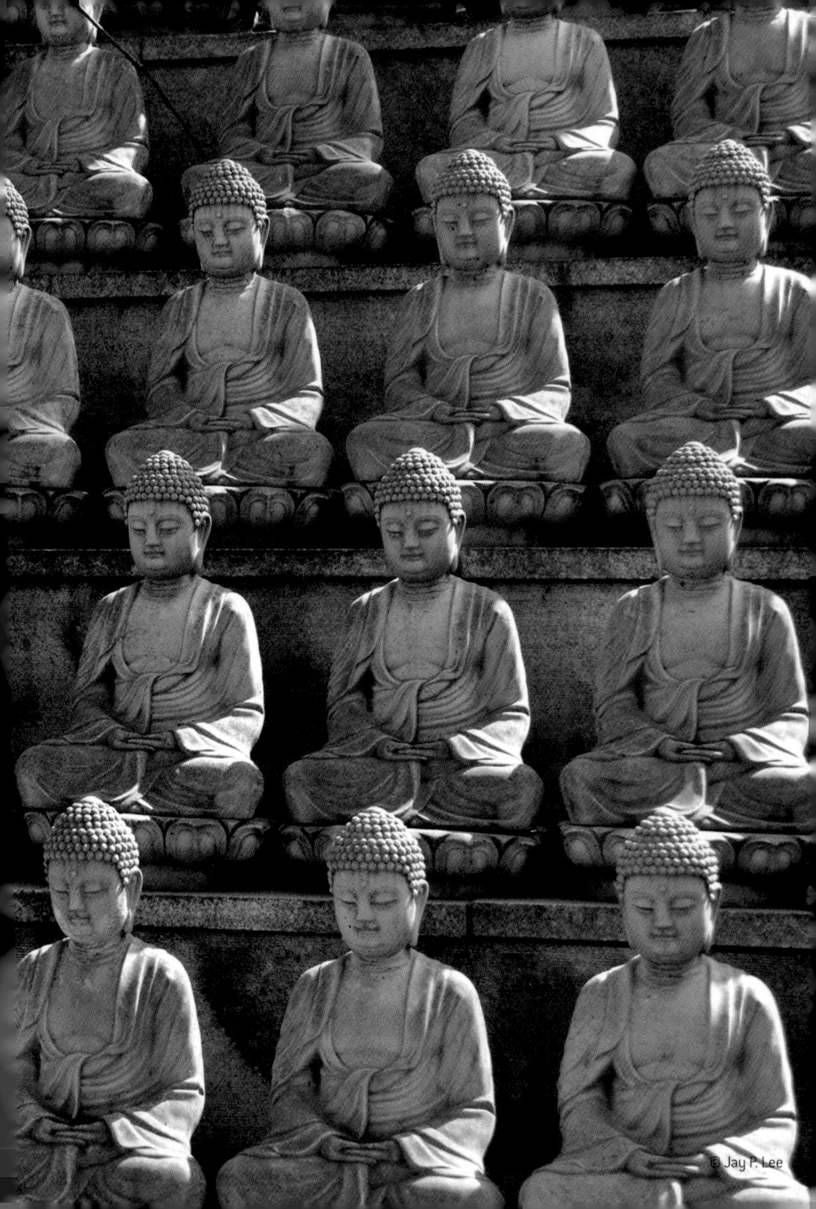
© Jay P. Lee

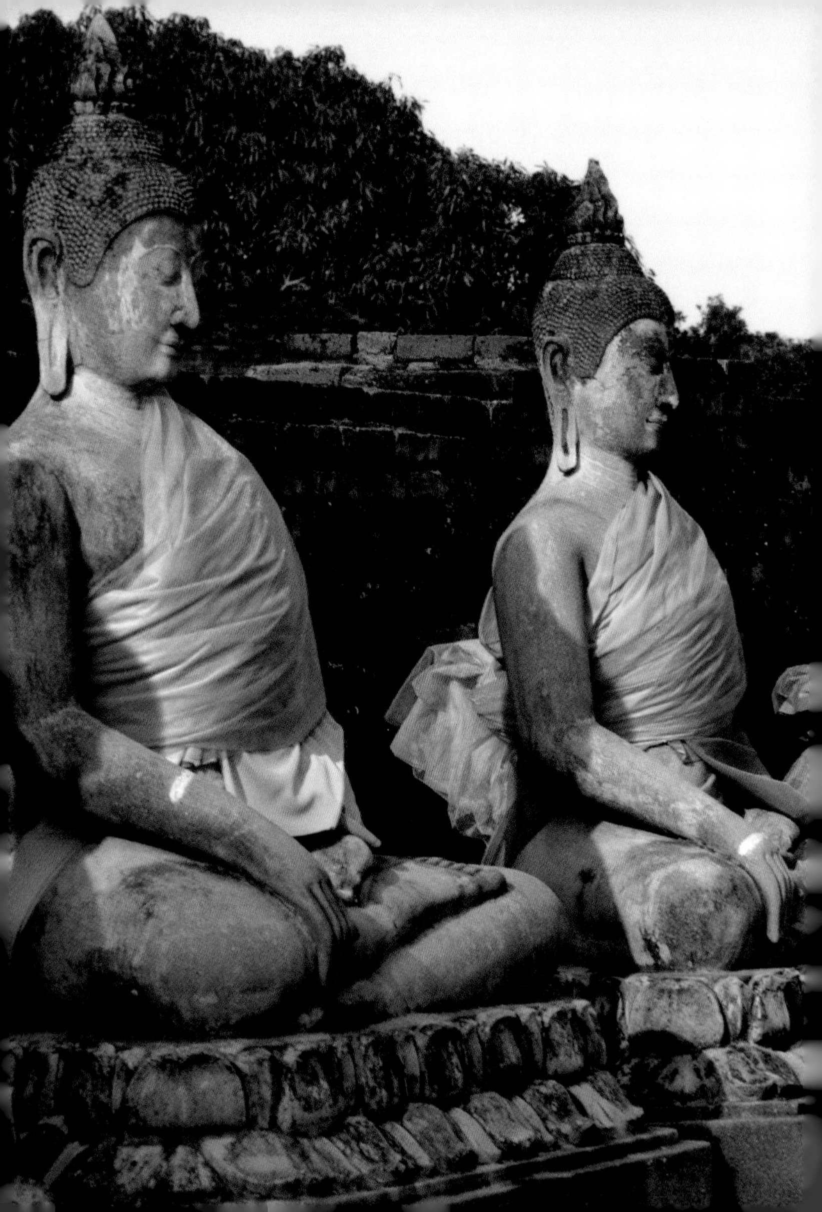

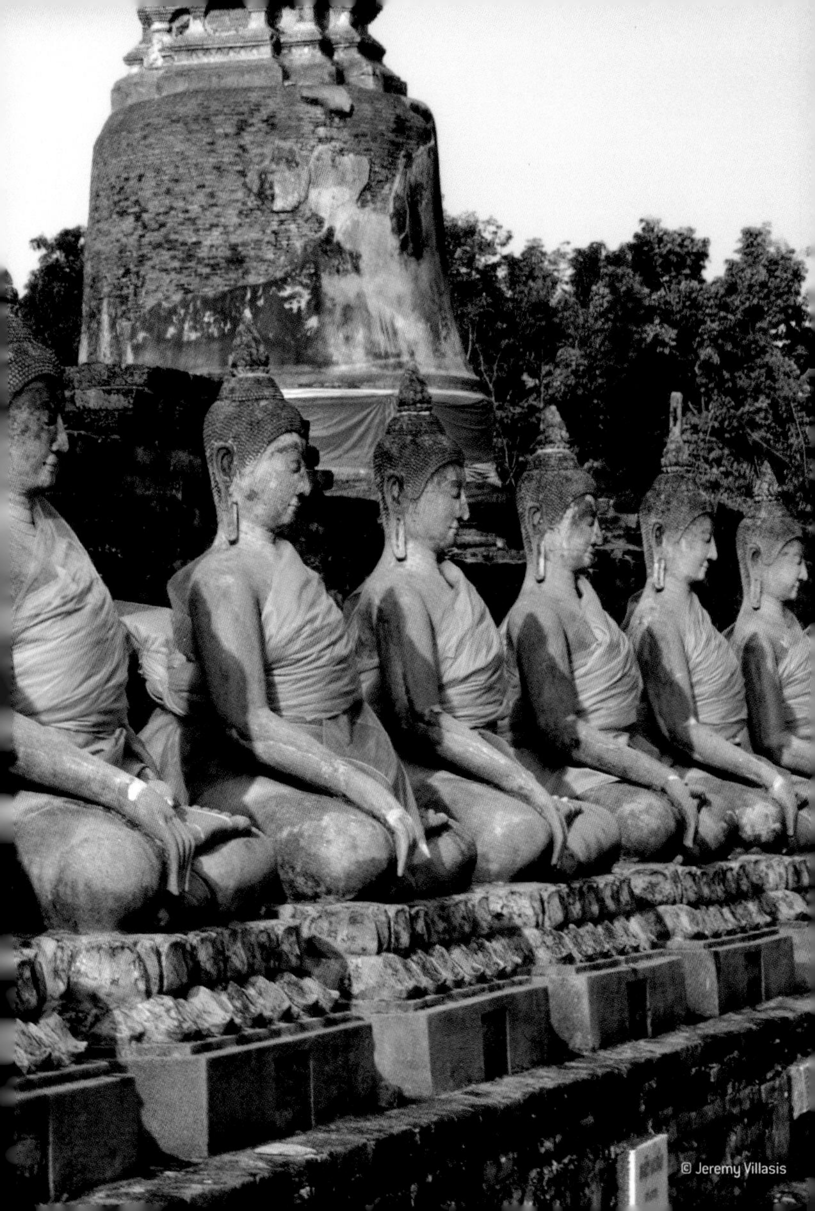

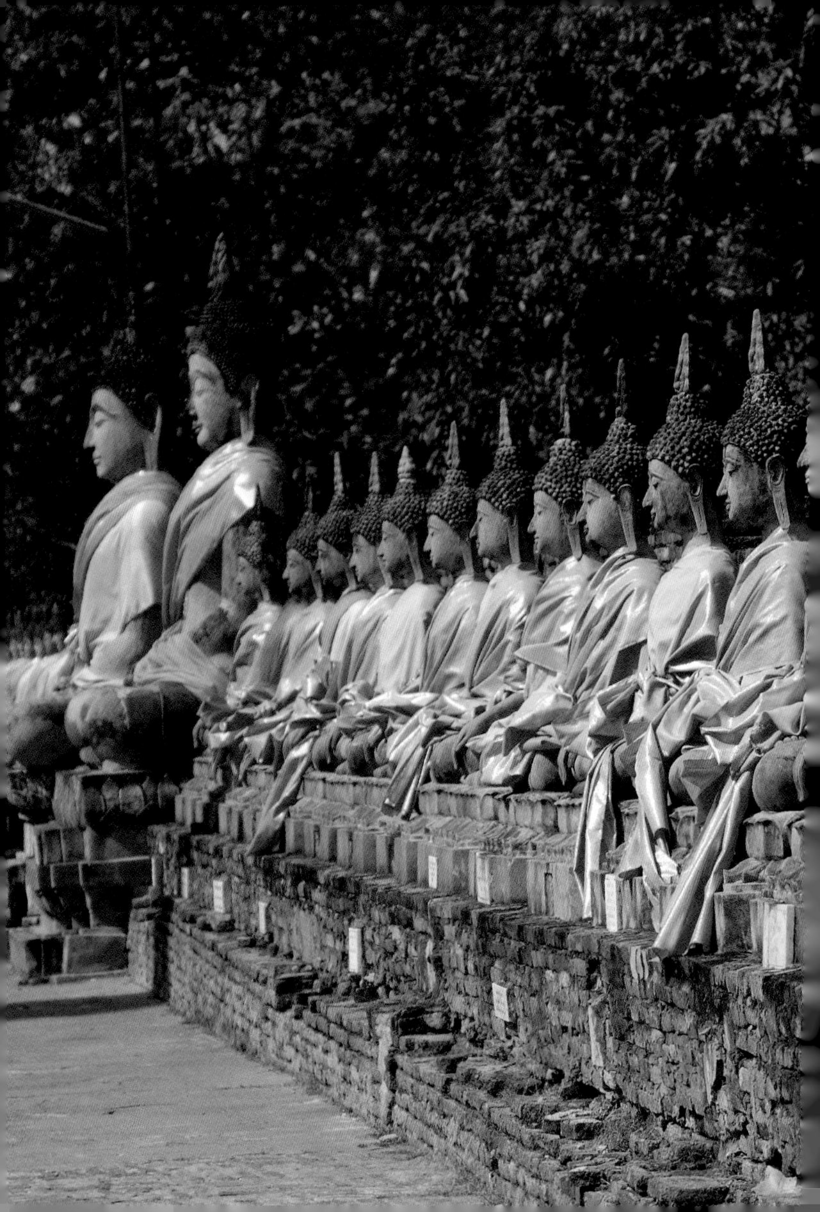

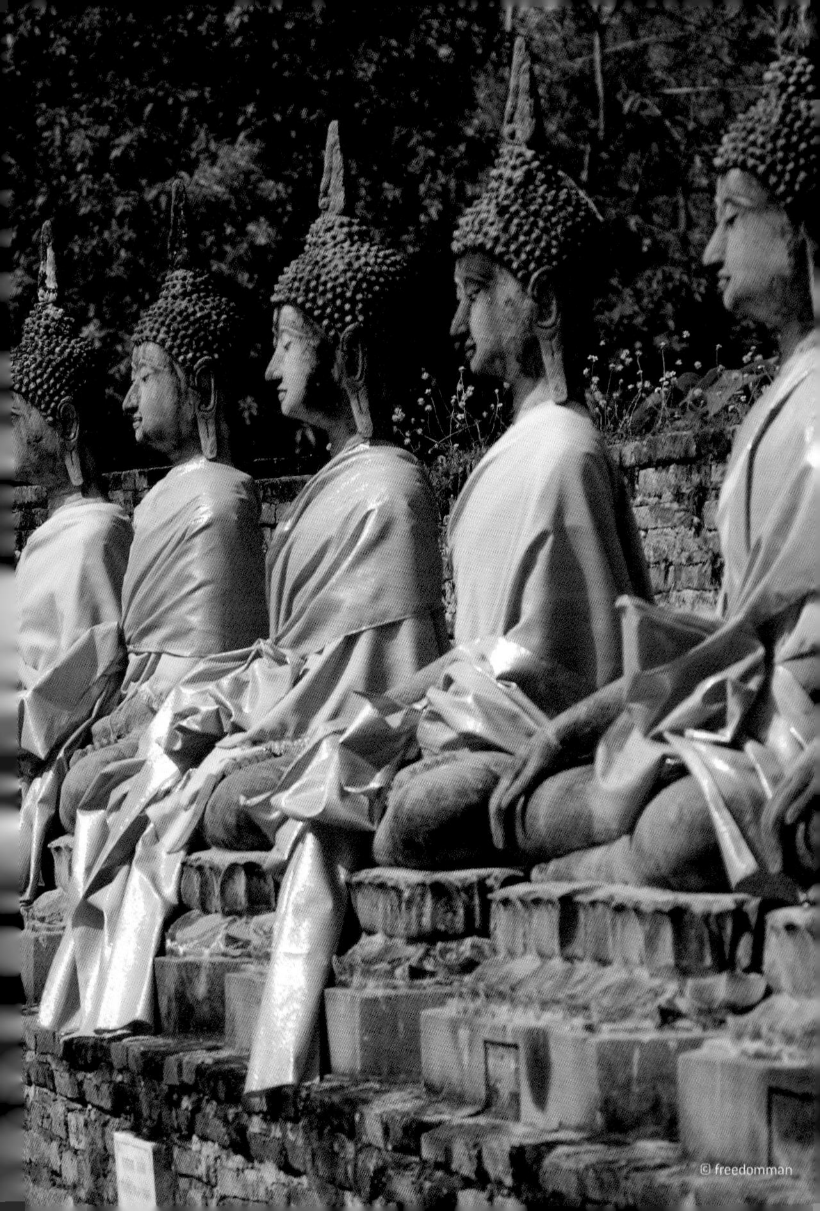

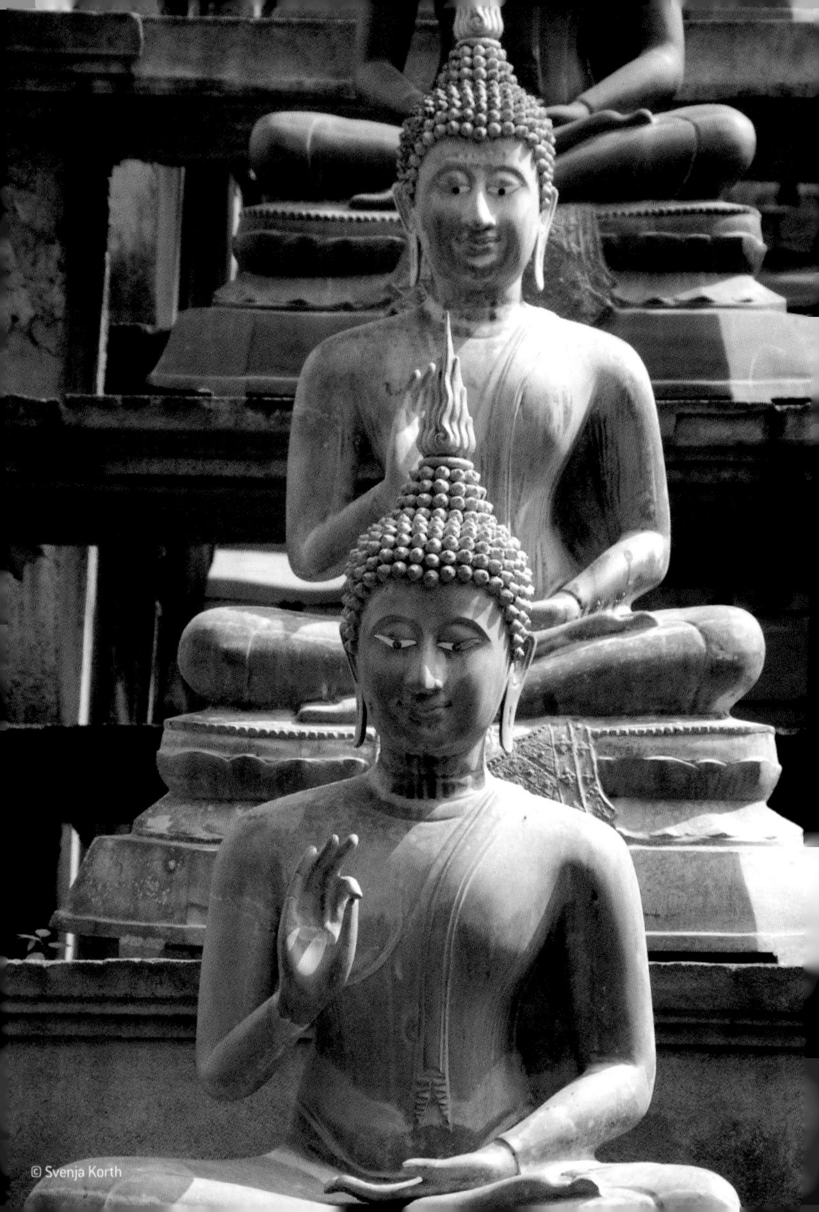

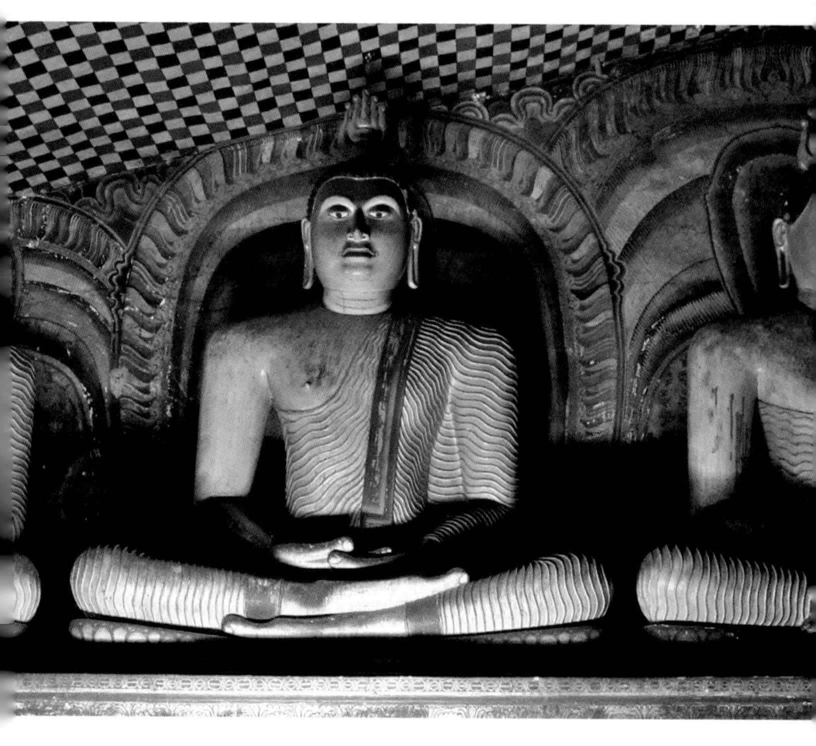

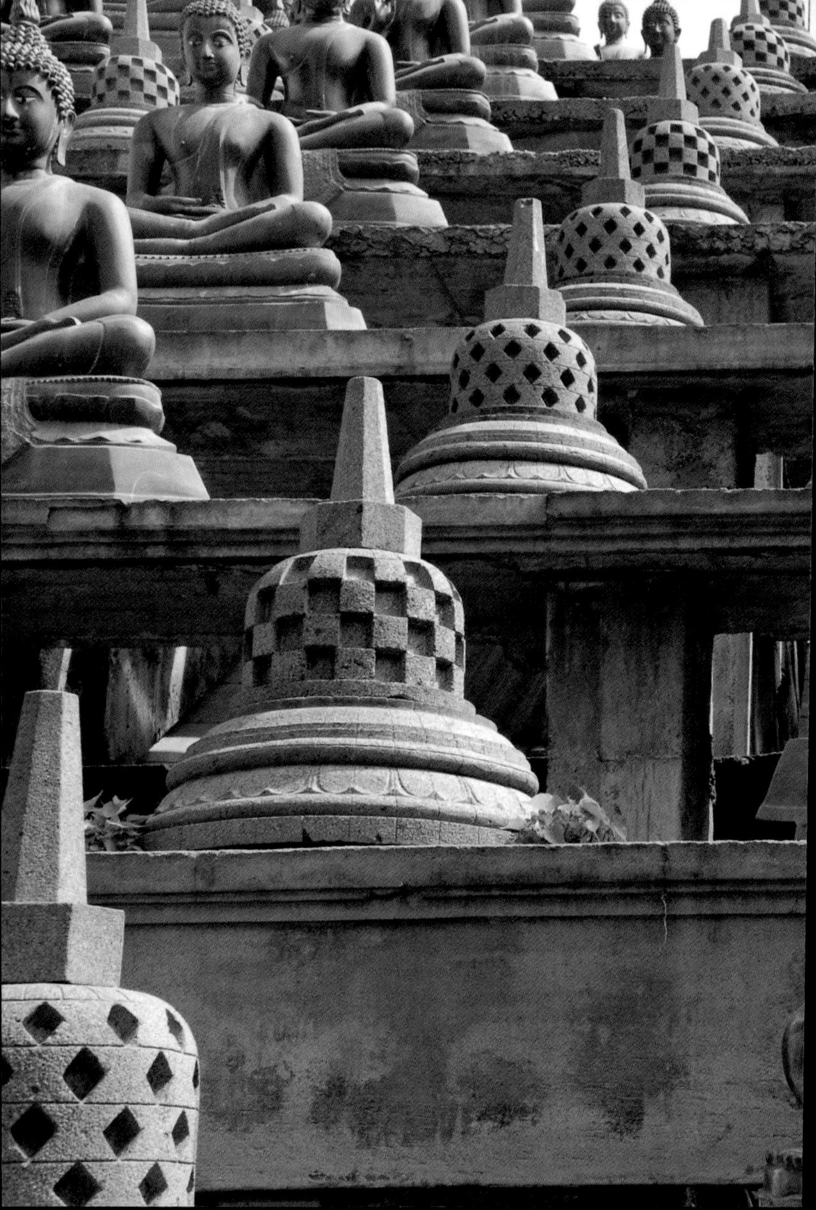

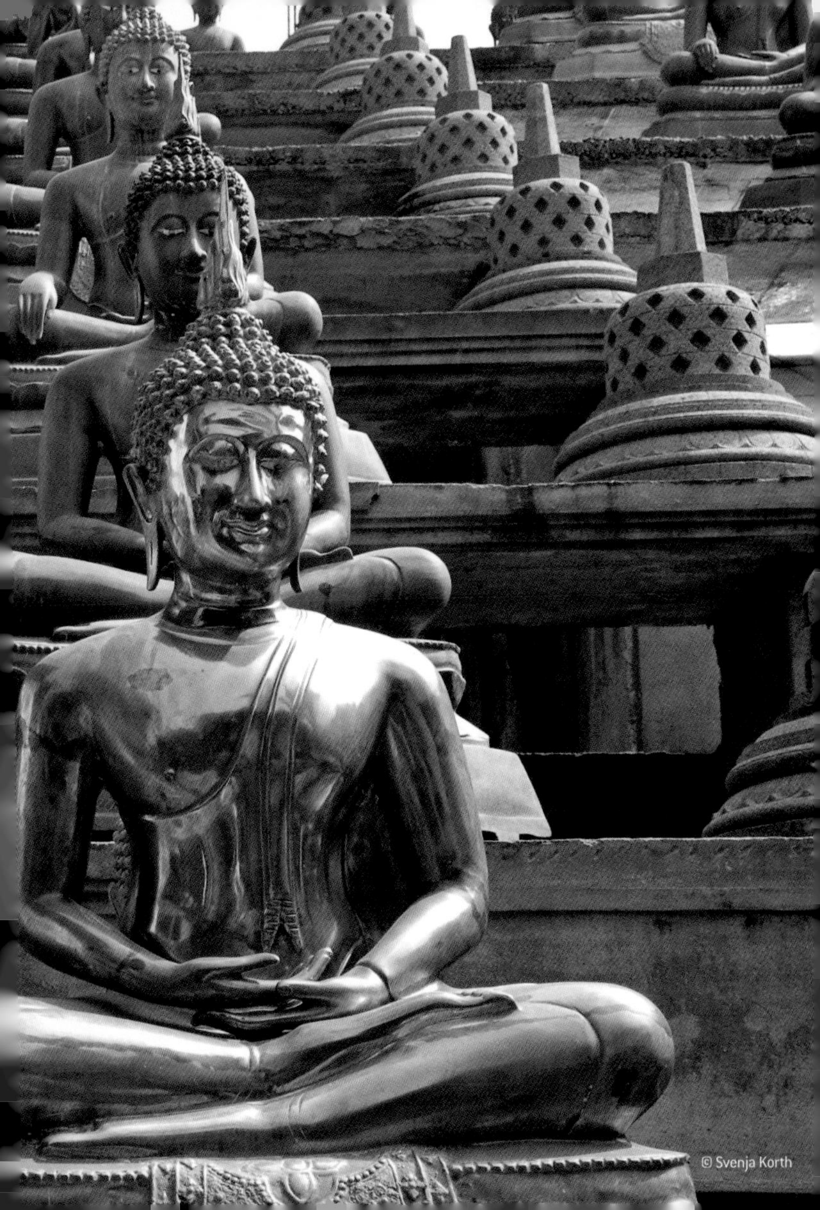

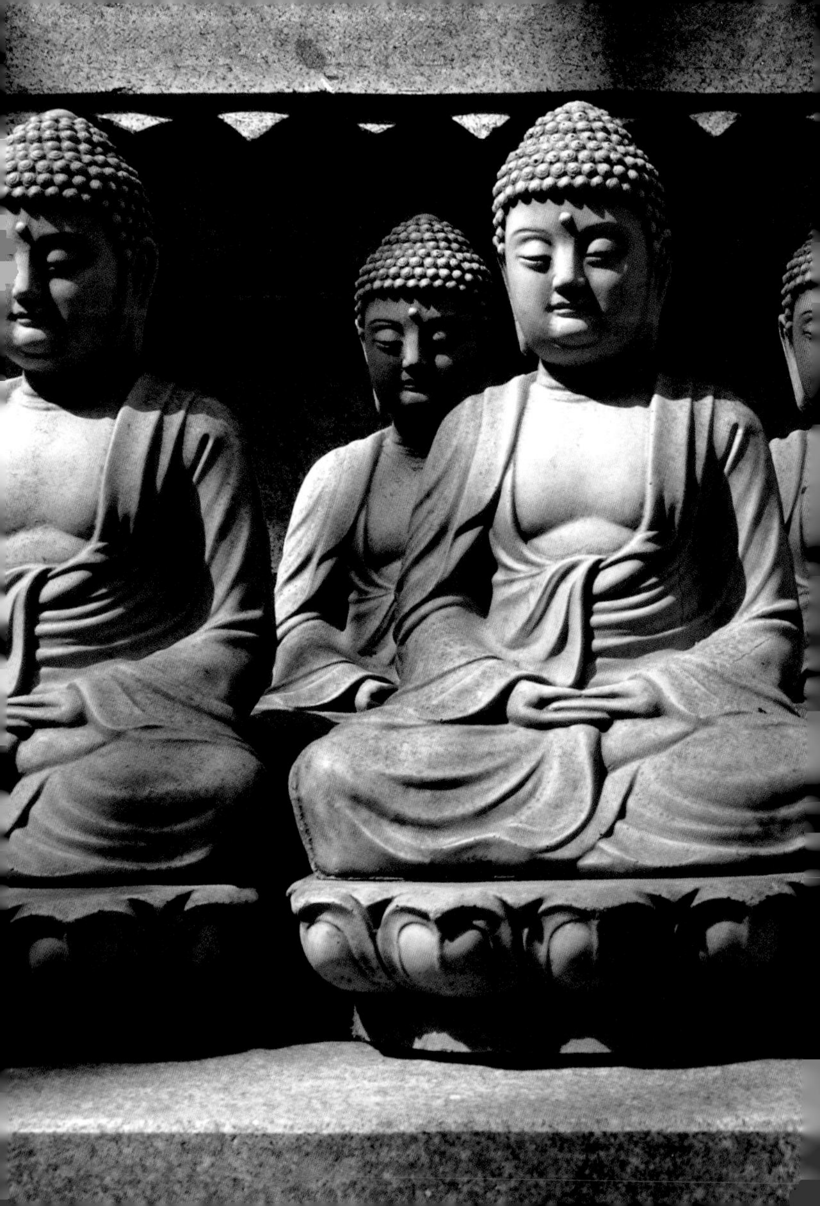

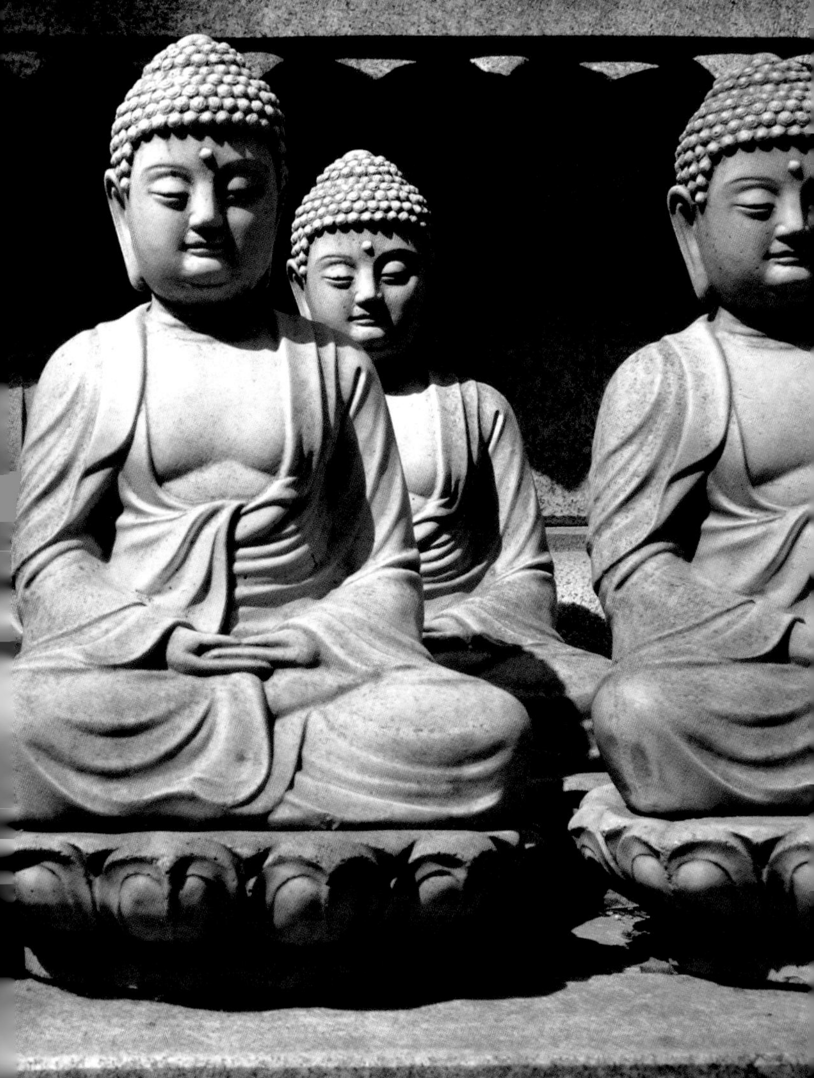
© Jay P. Lee

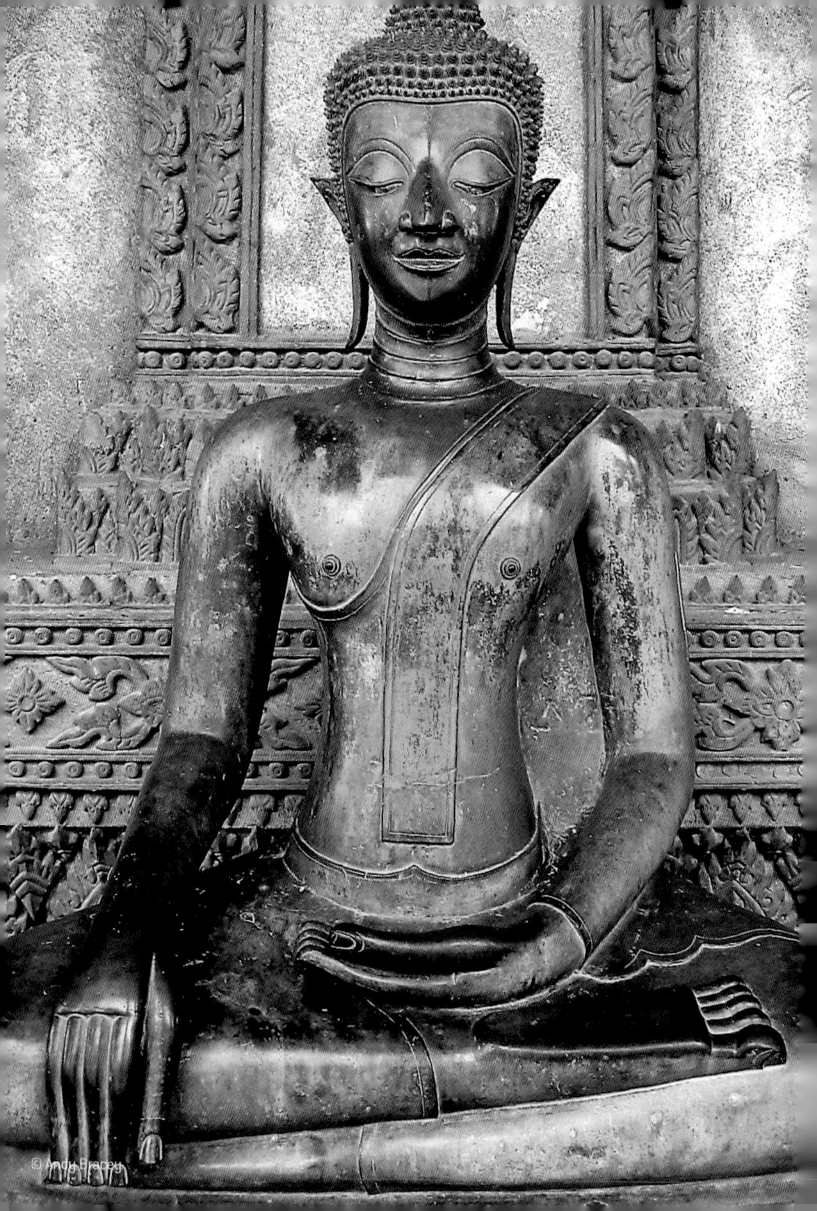

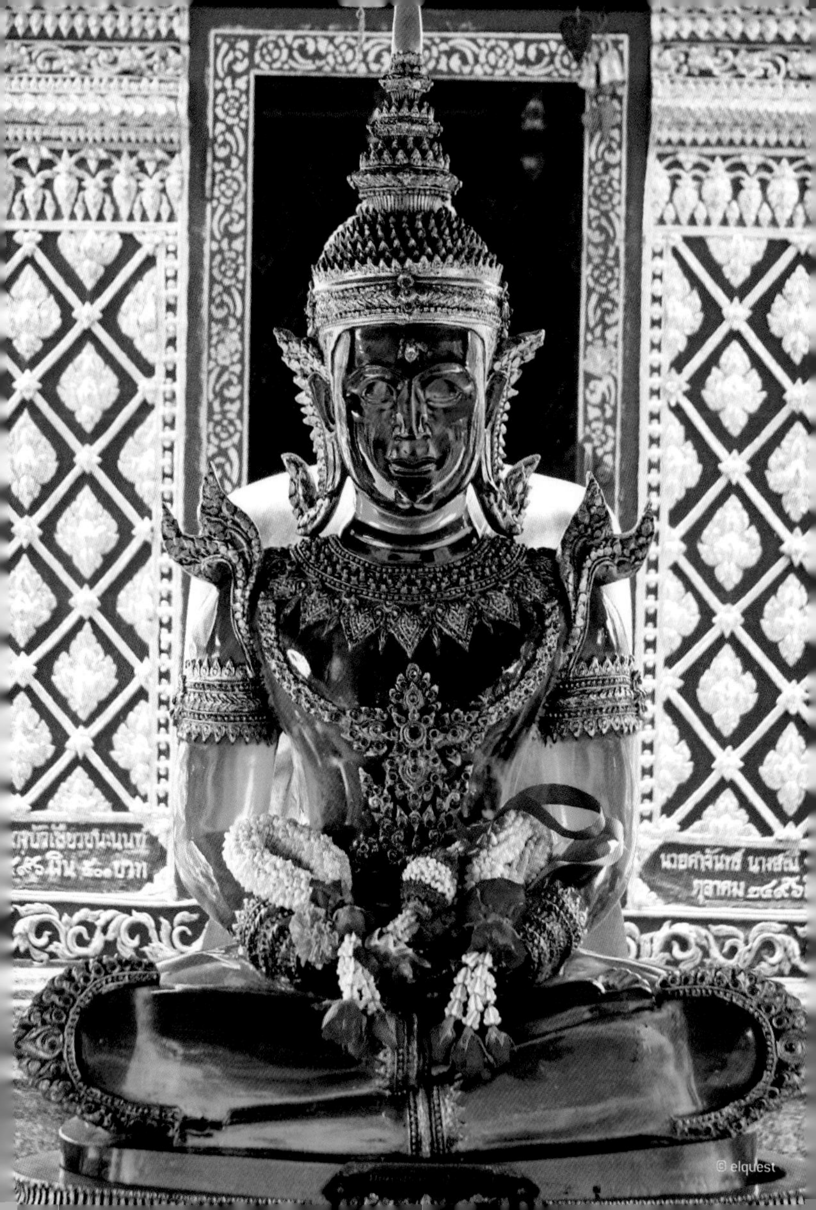

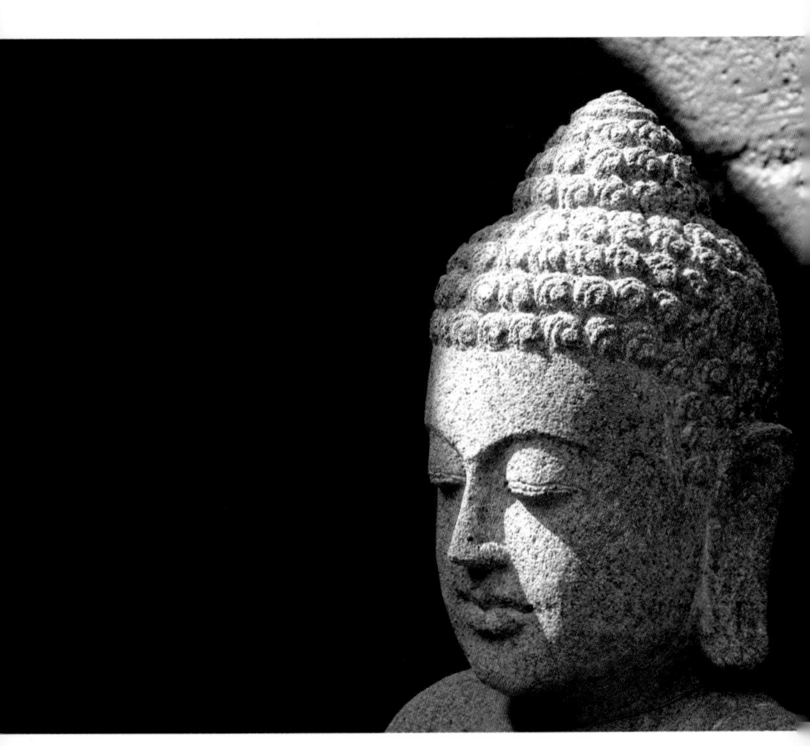

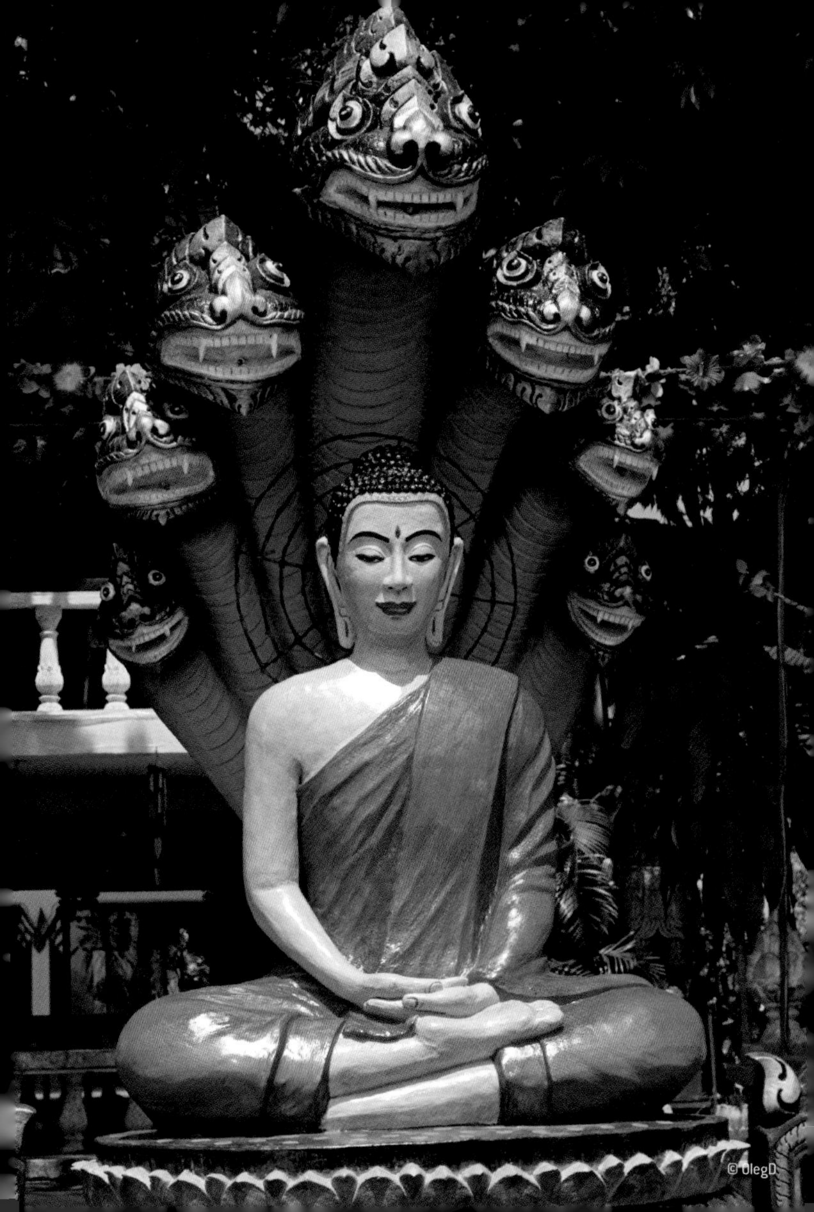
© OlegD

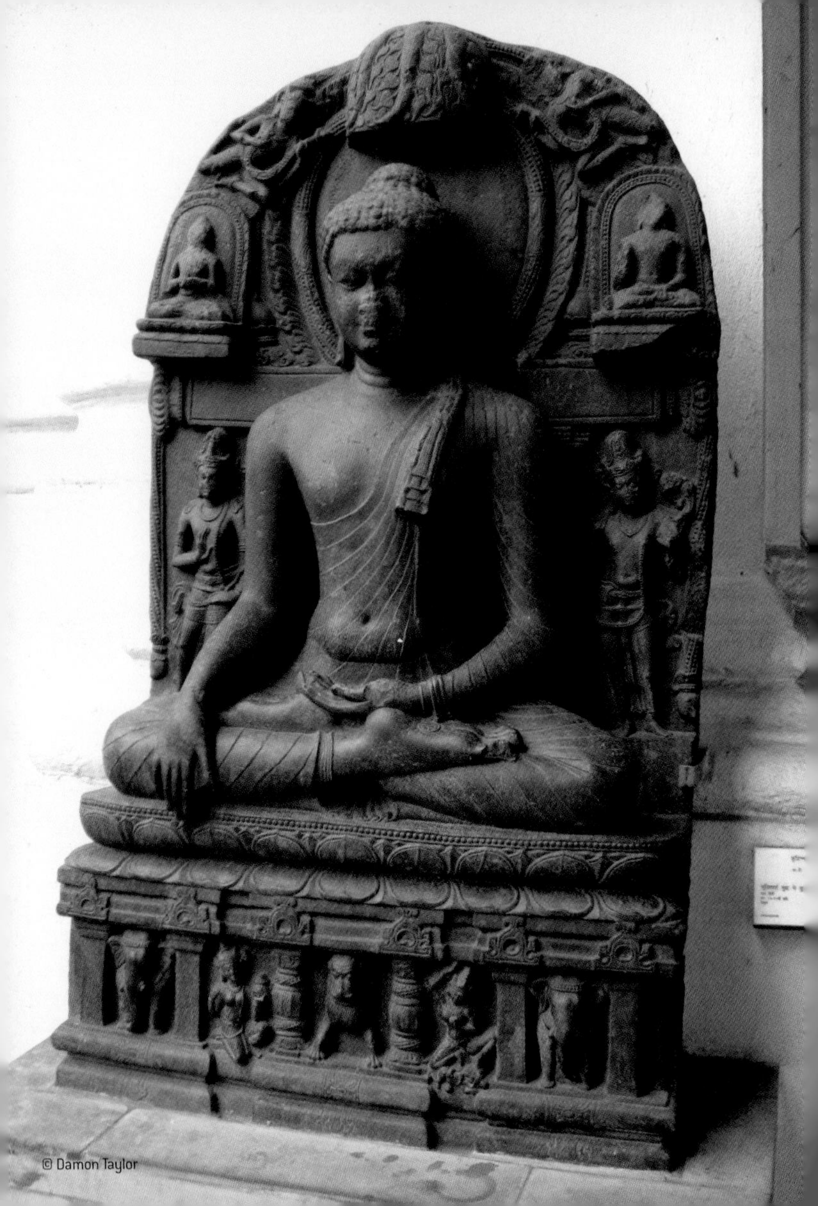
© Damon Taylor

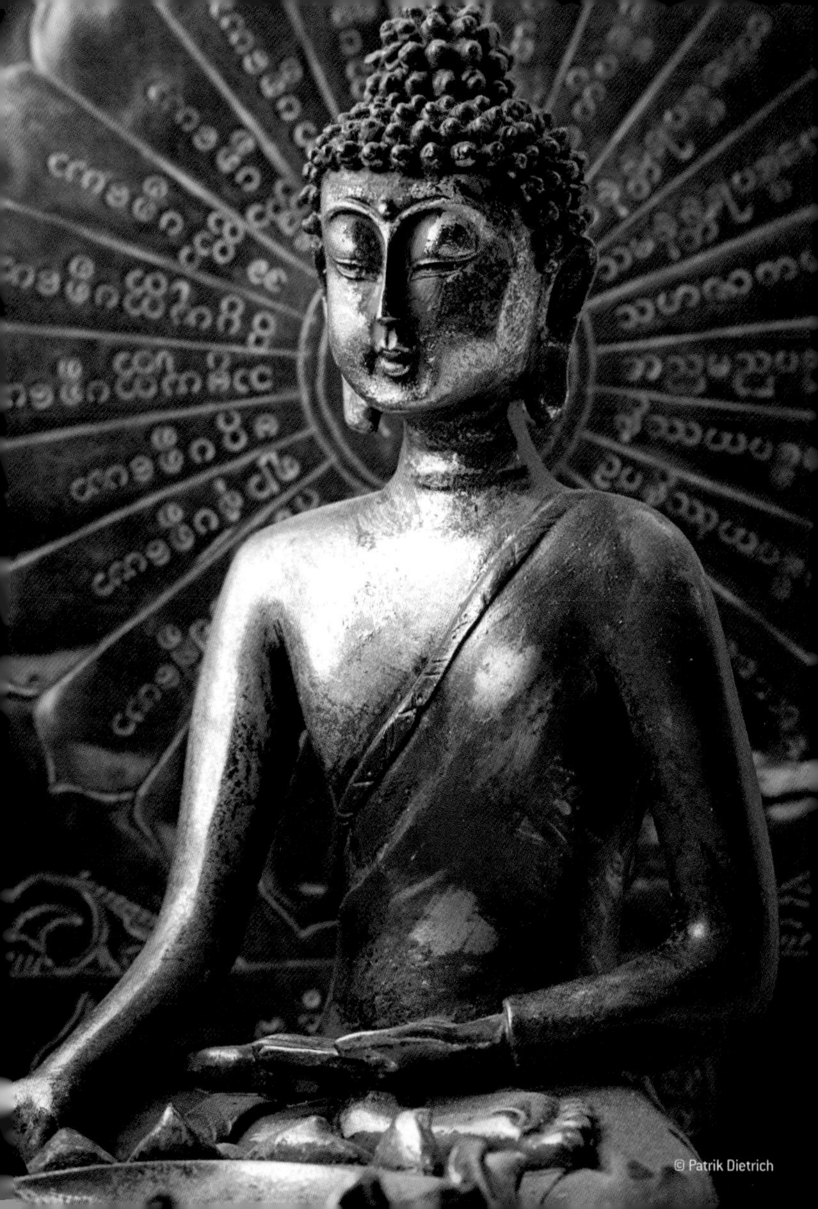

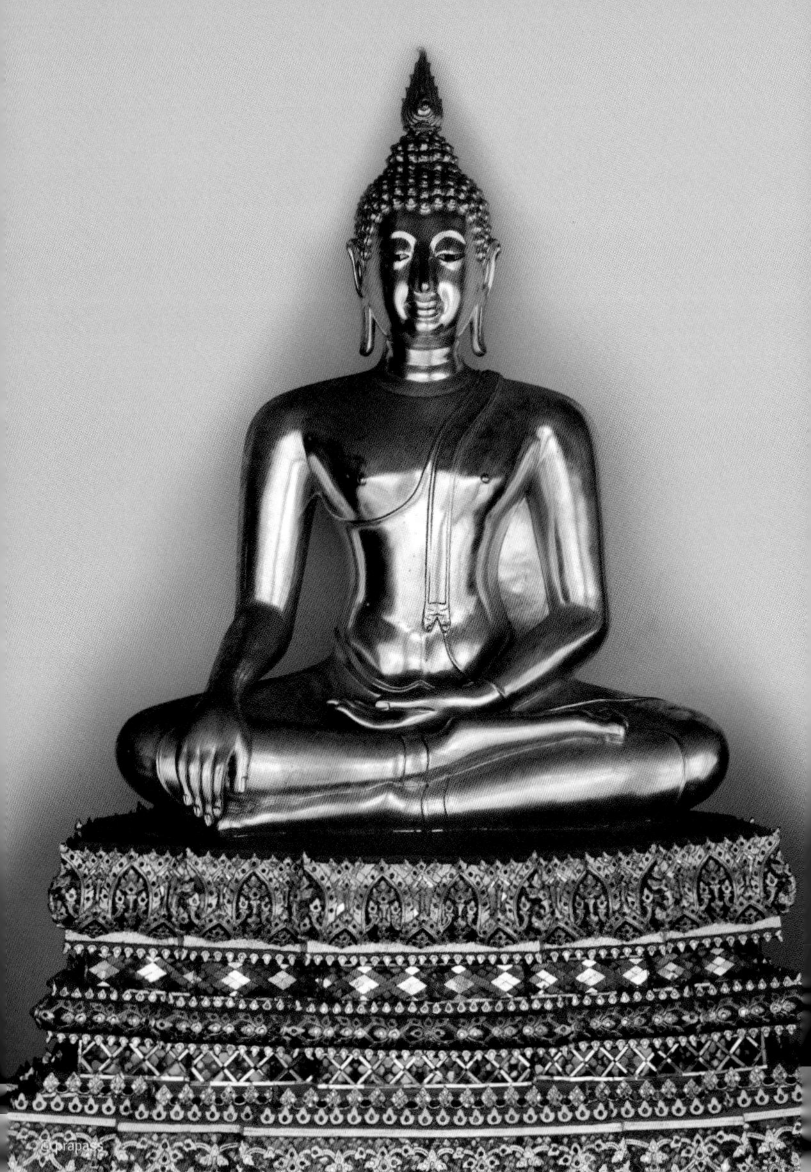
© prapass

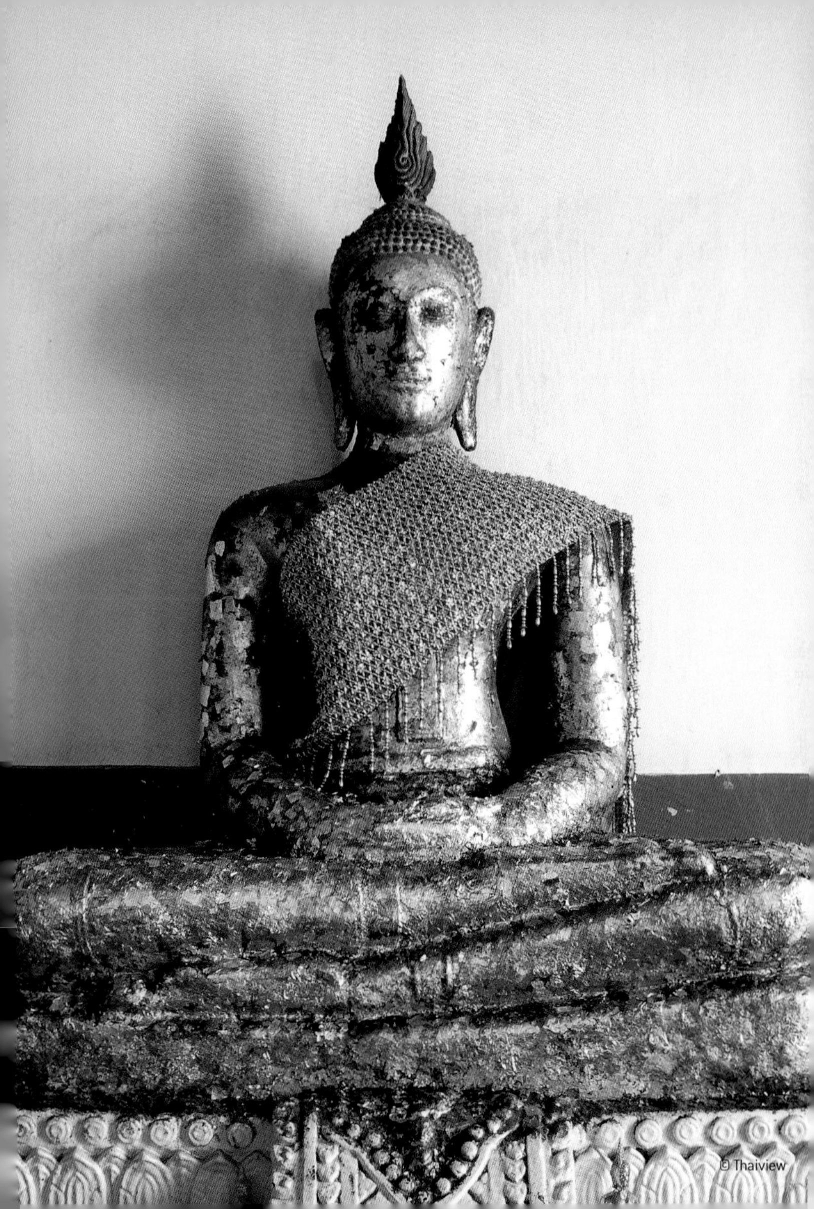

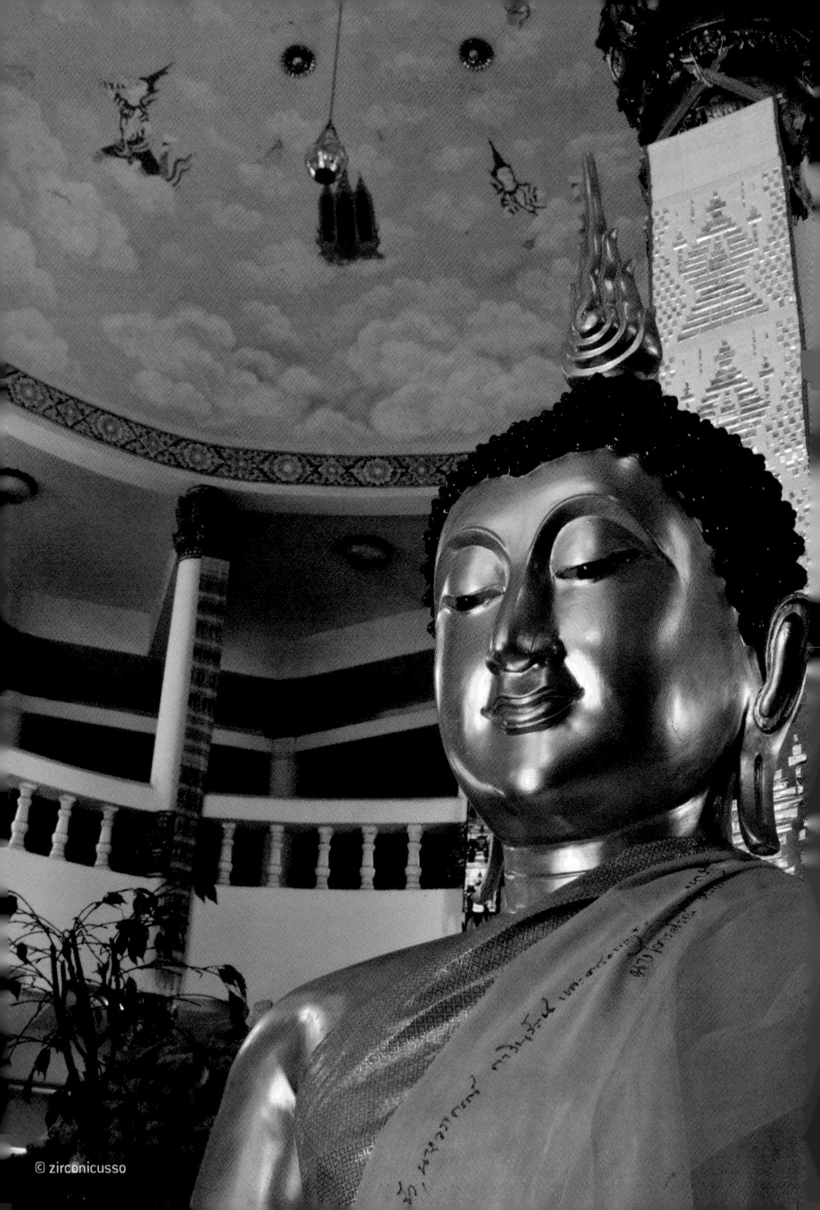

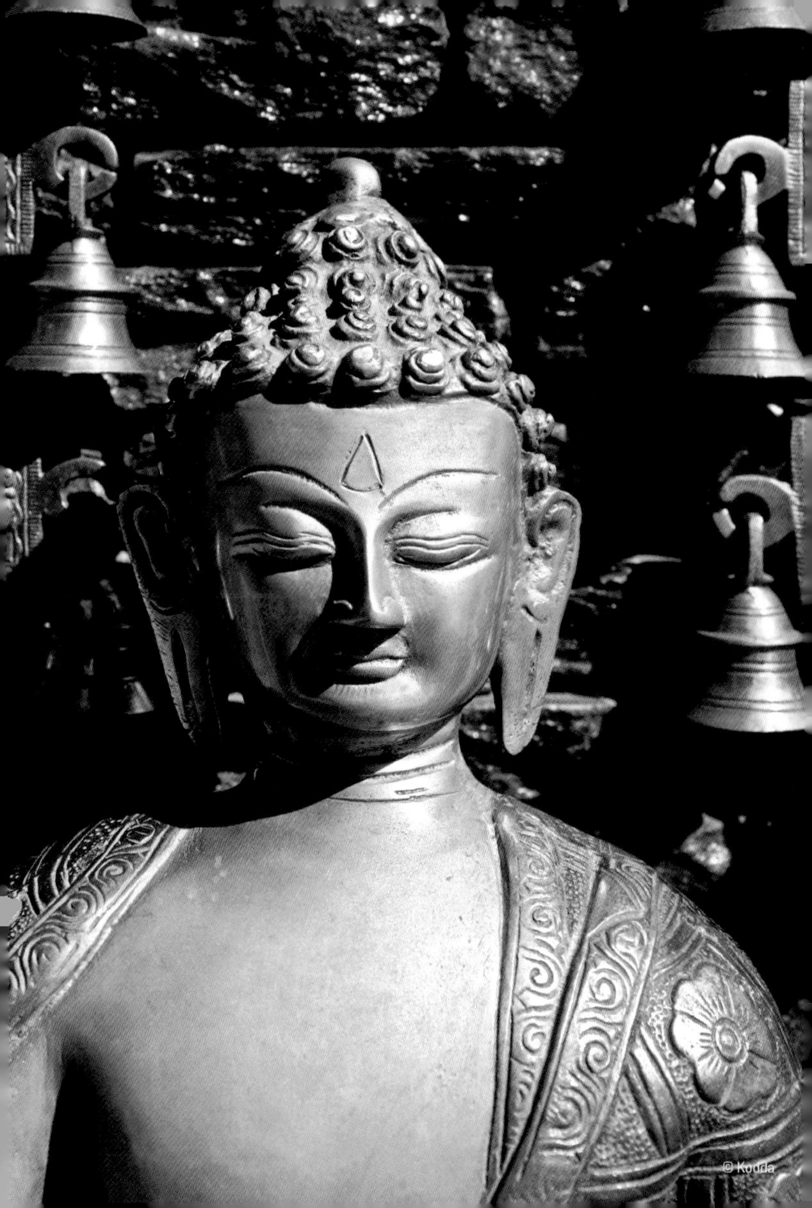

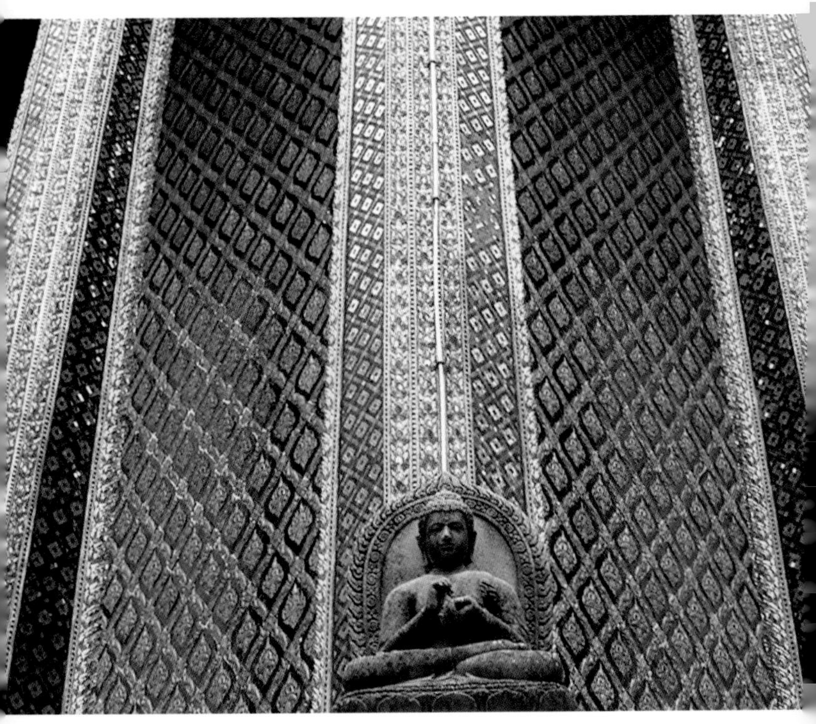

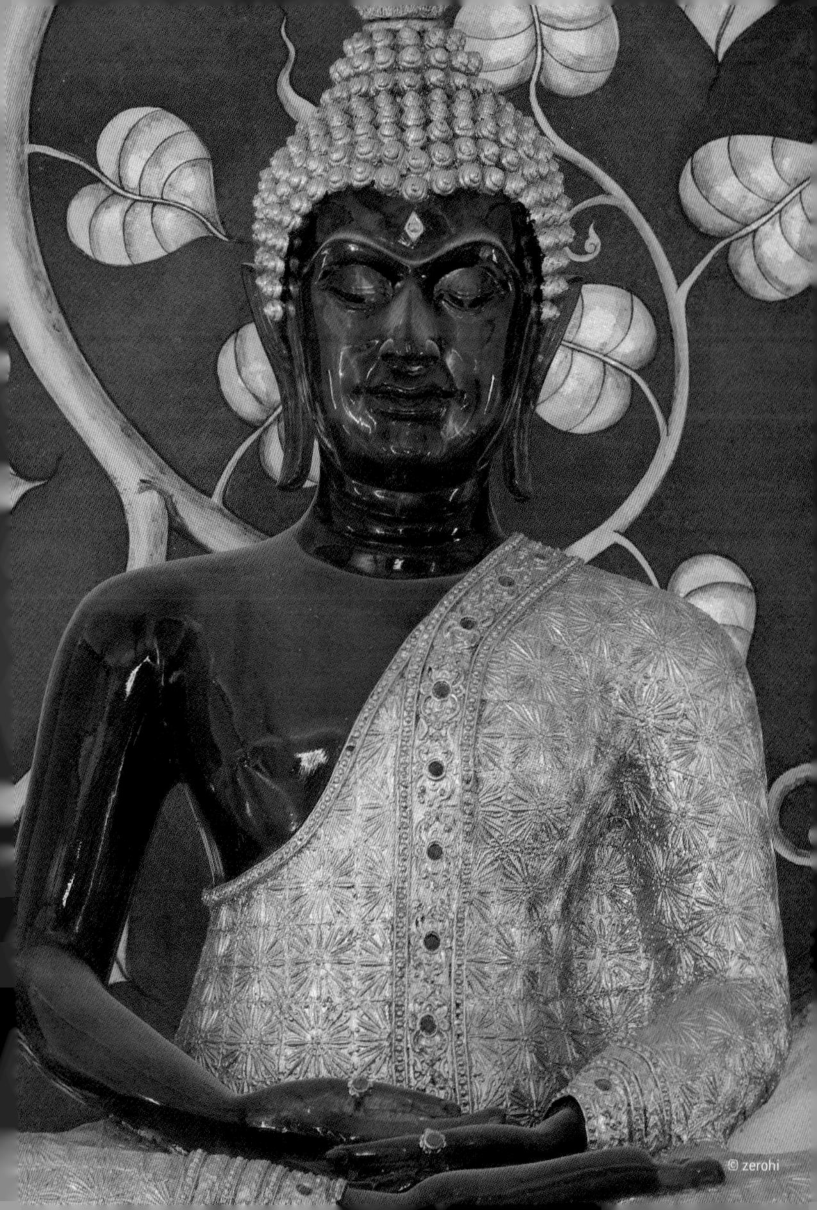

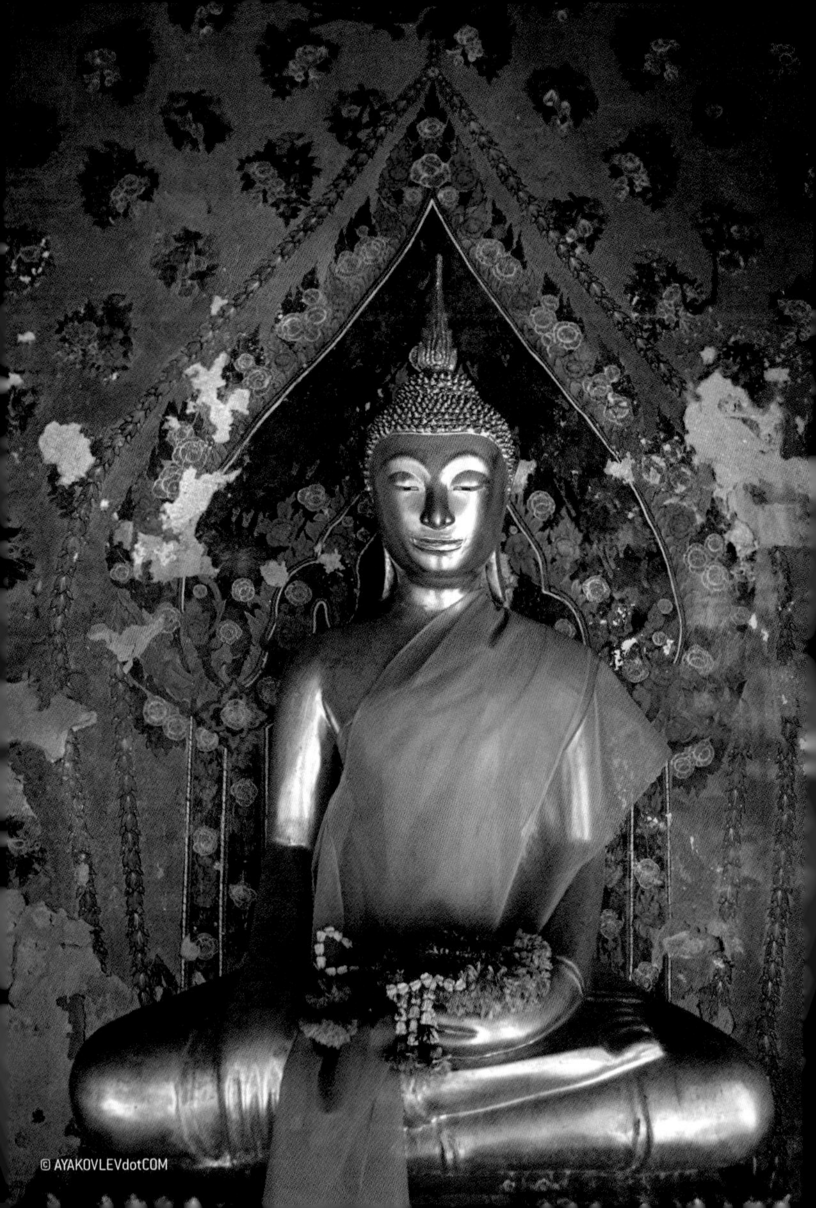

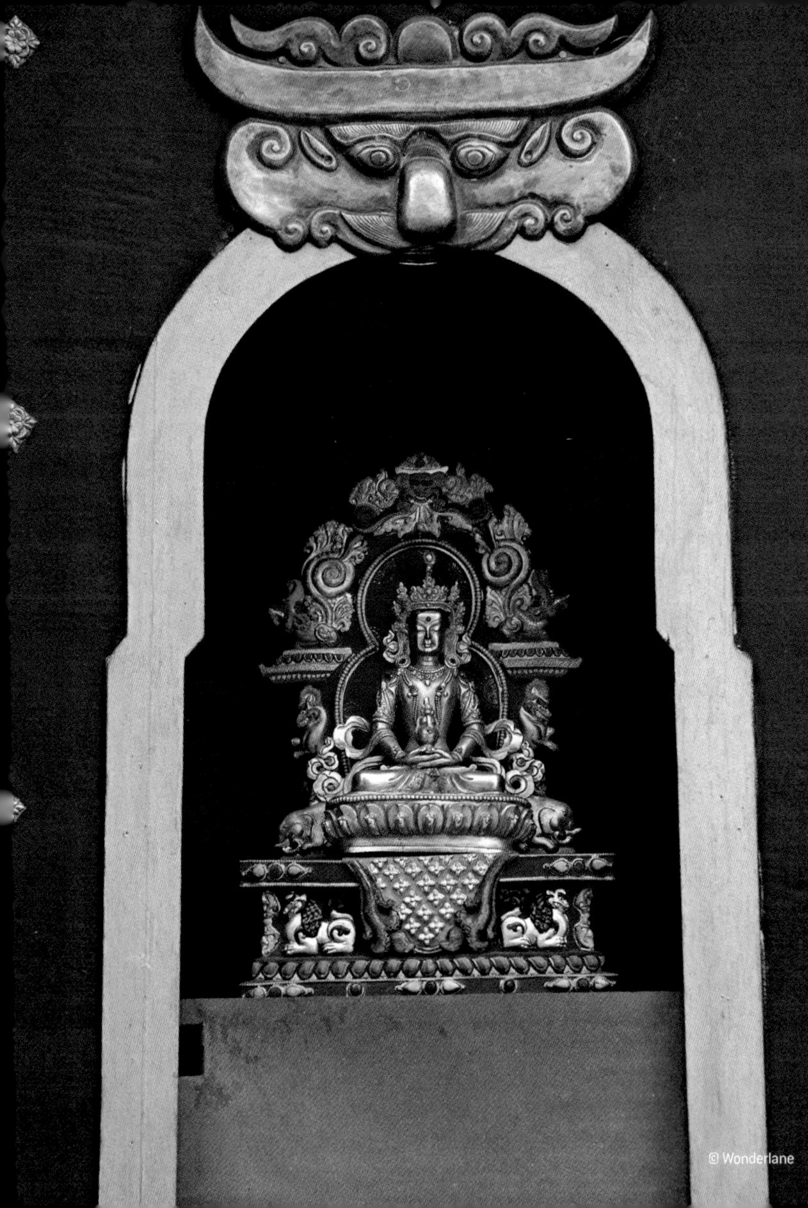

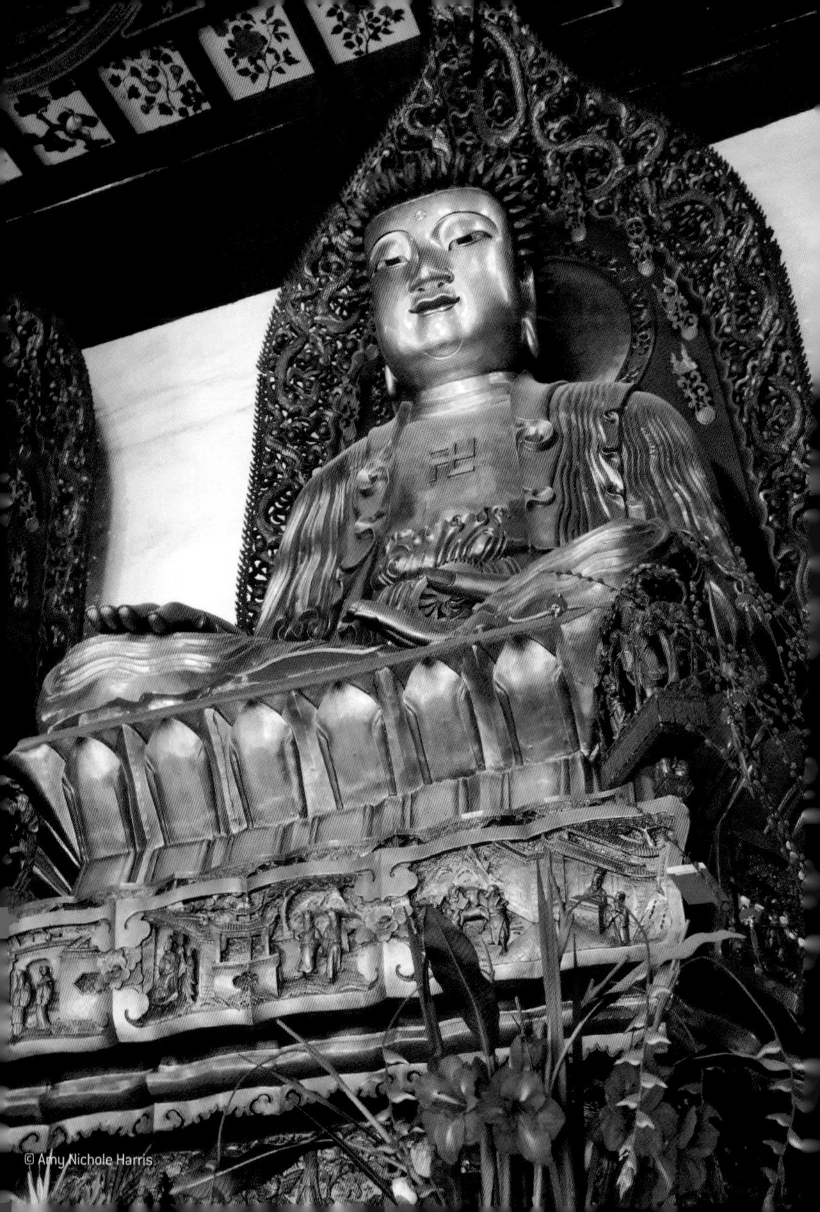

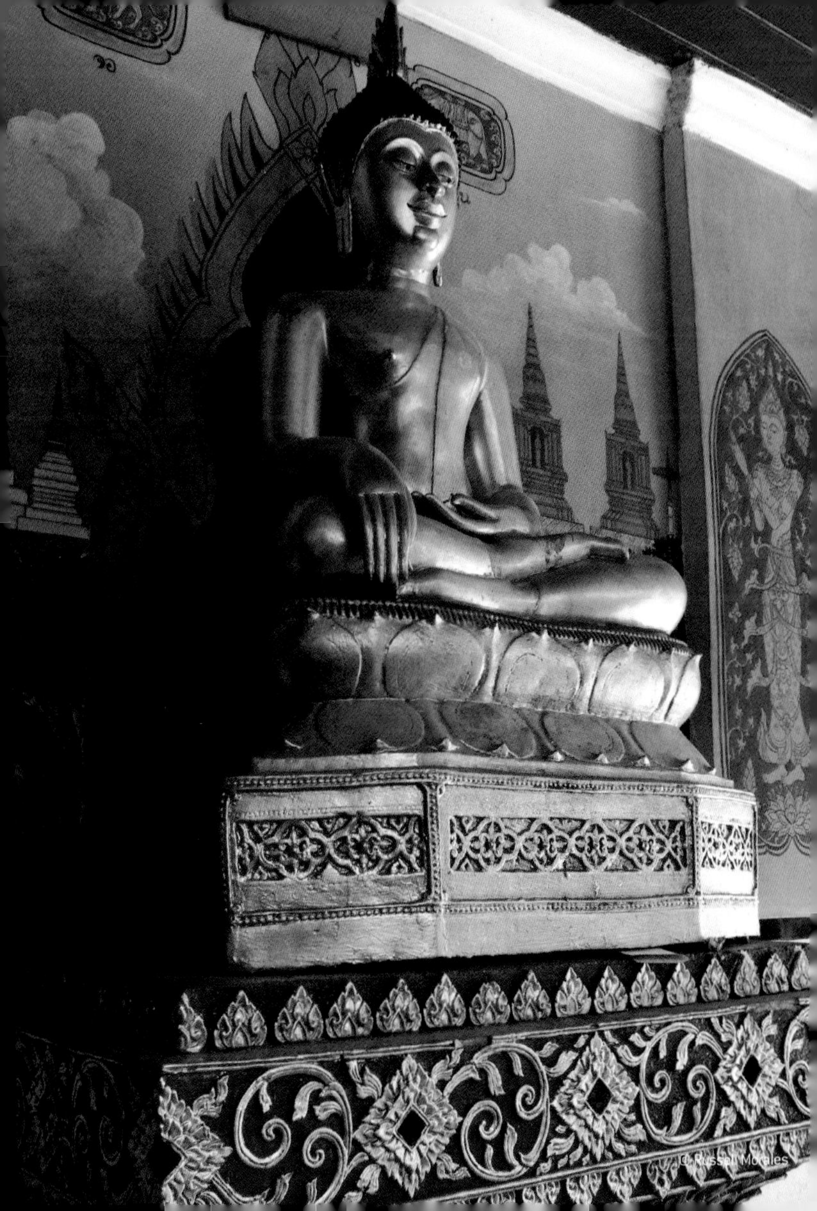
© Russell Morales

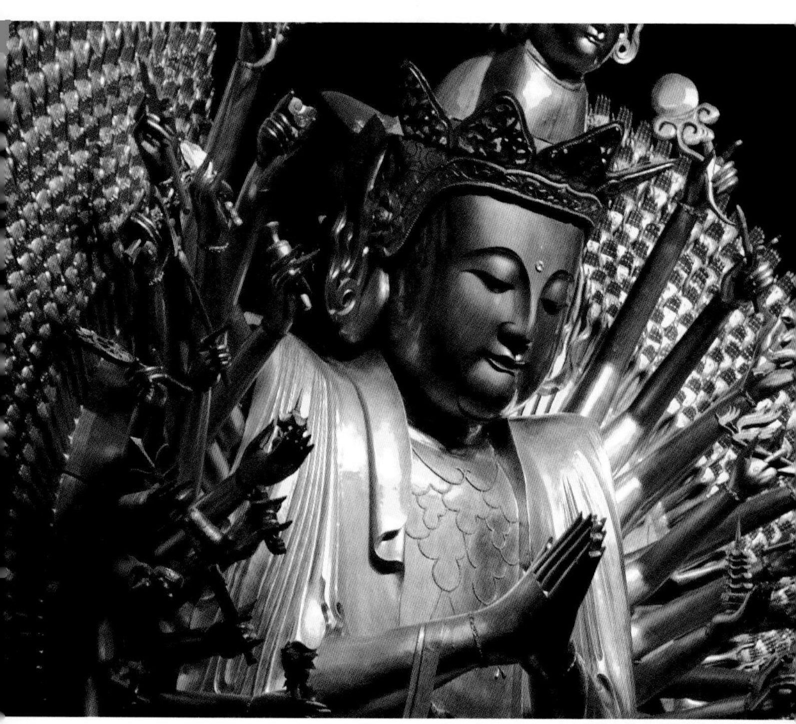

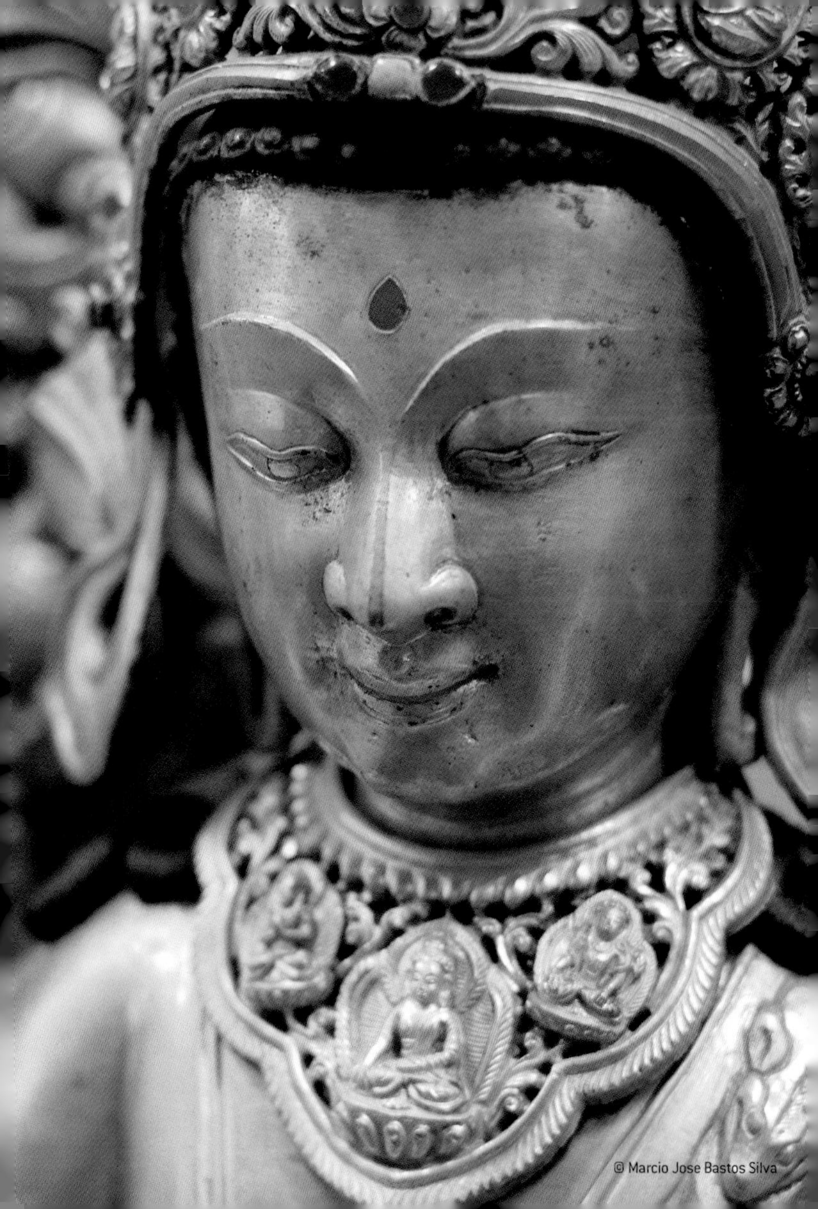

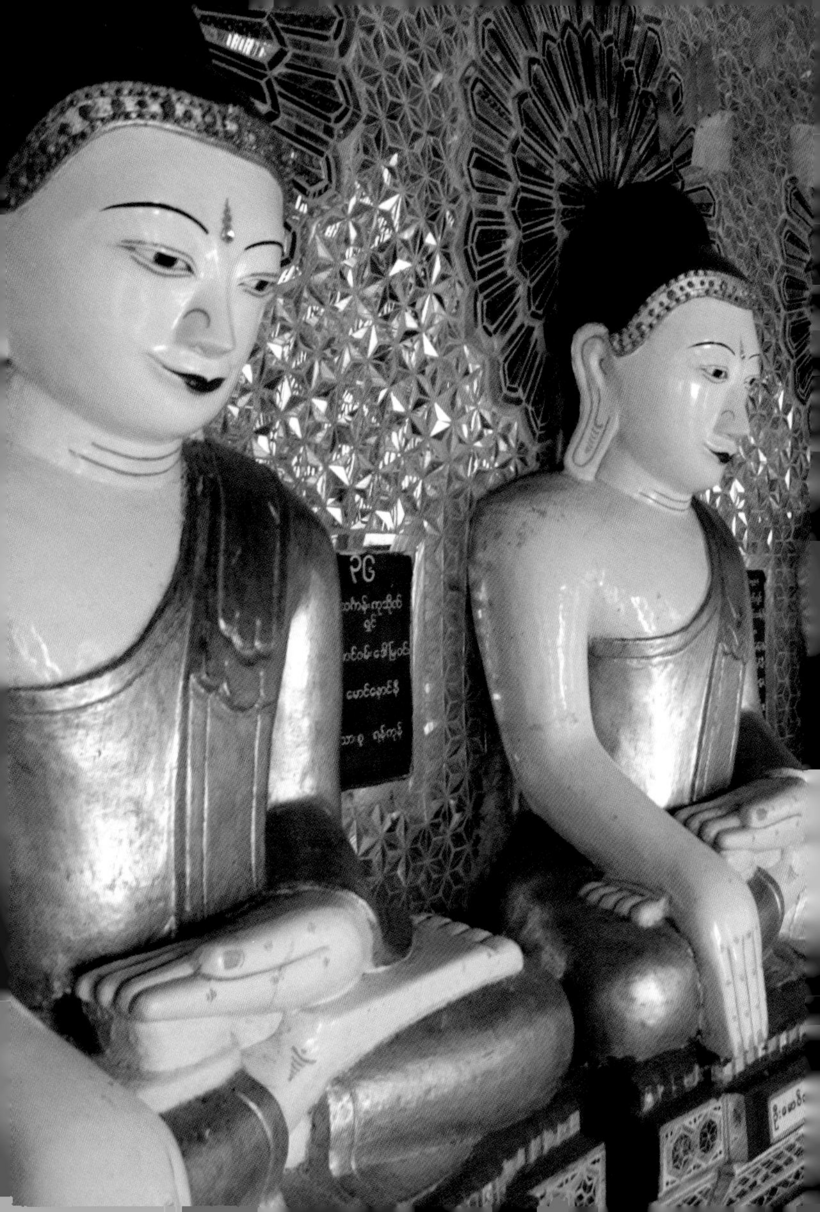

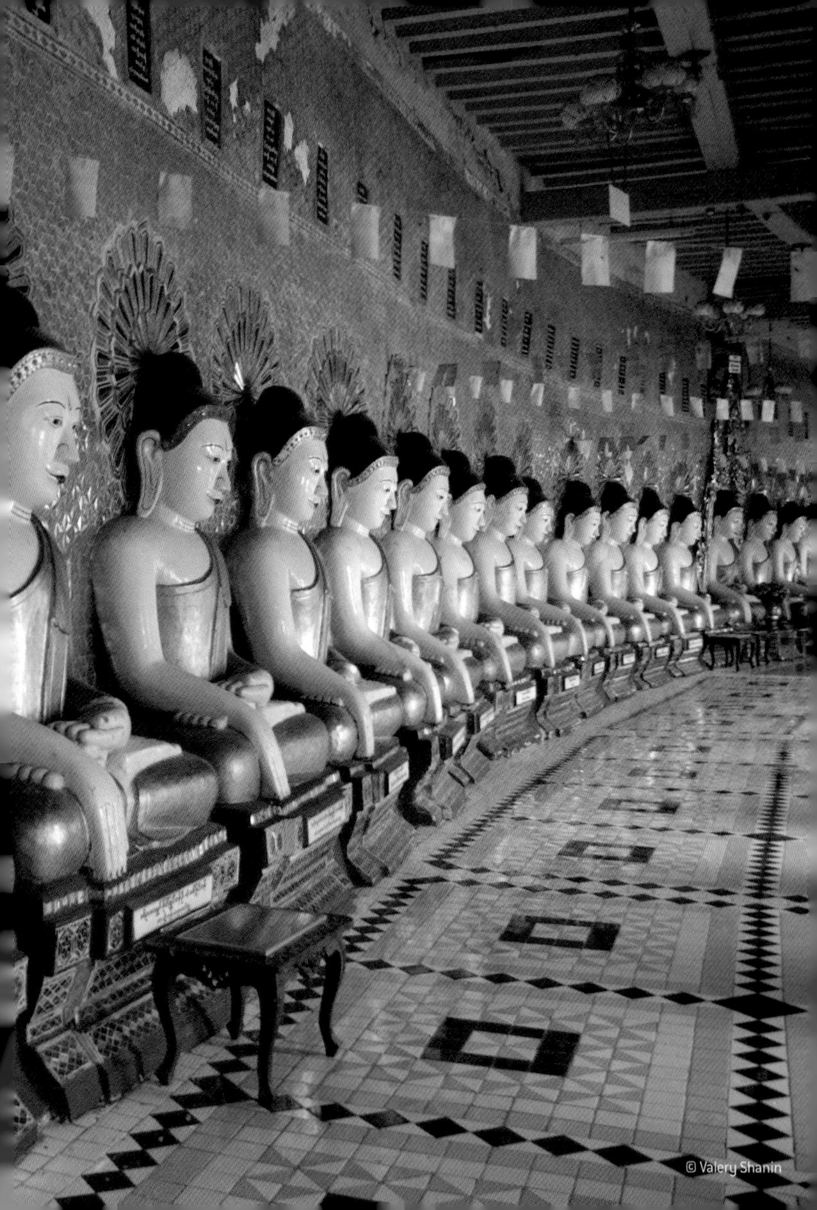
© Valery Shanin

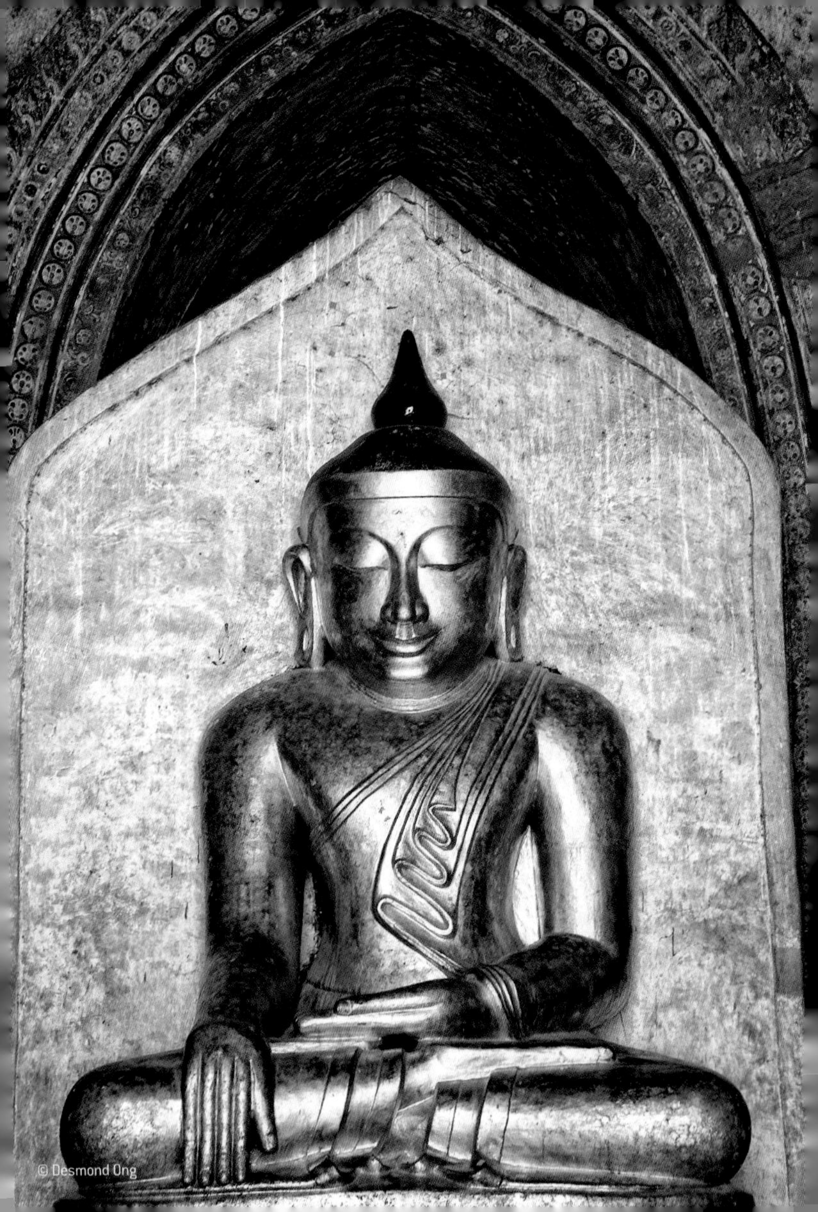

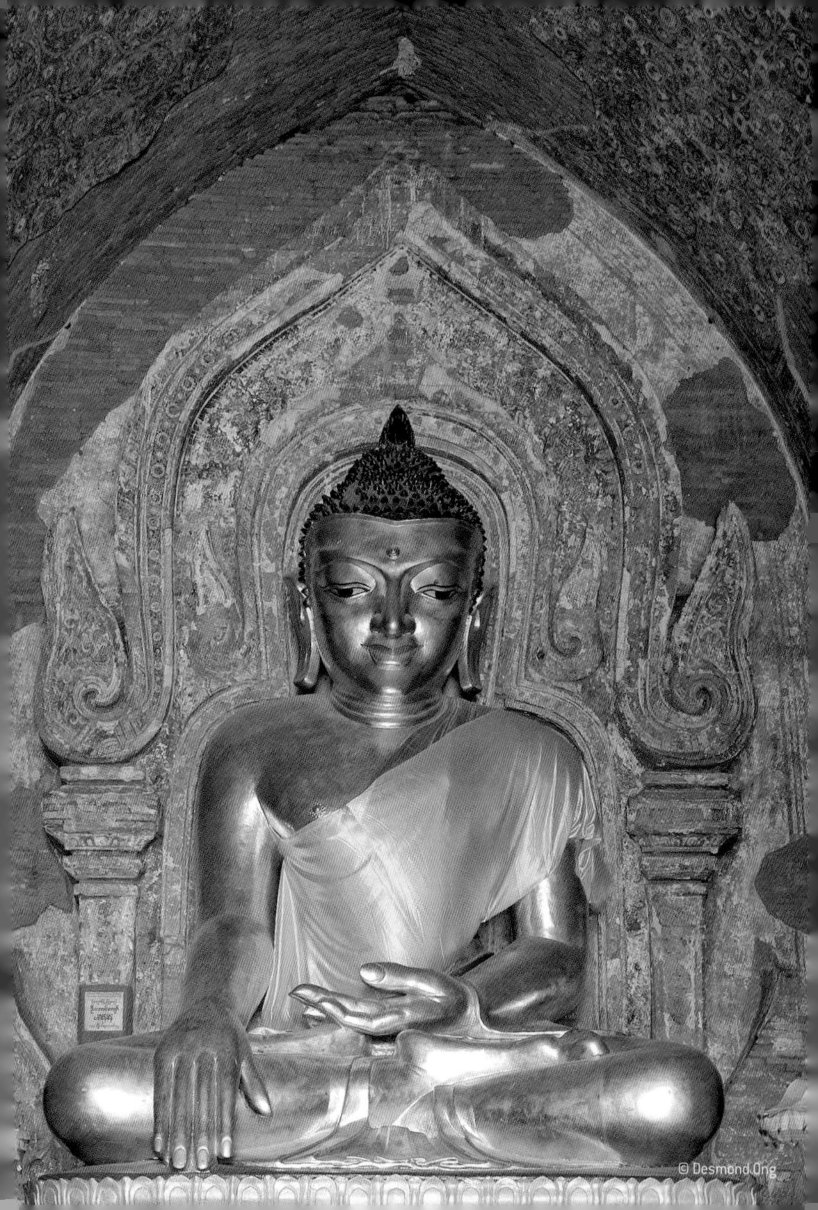

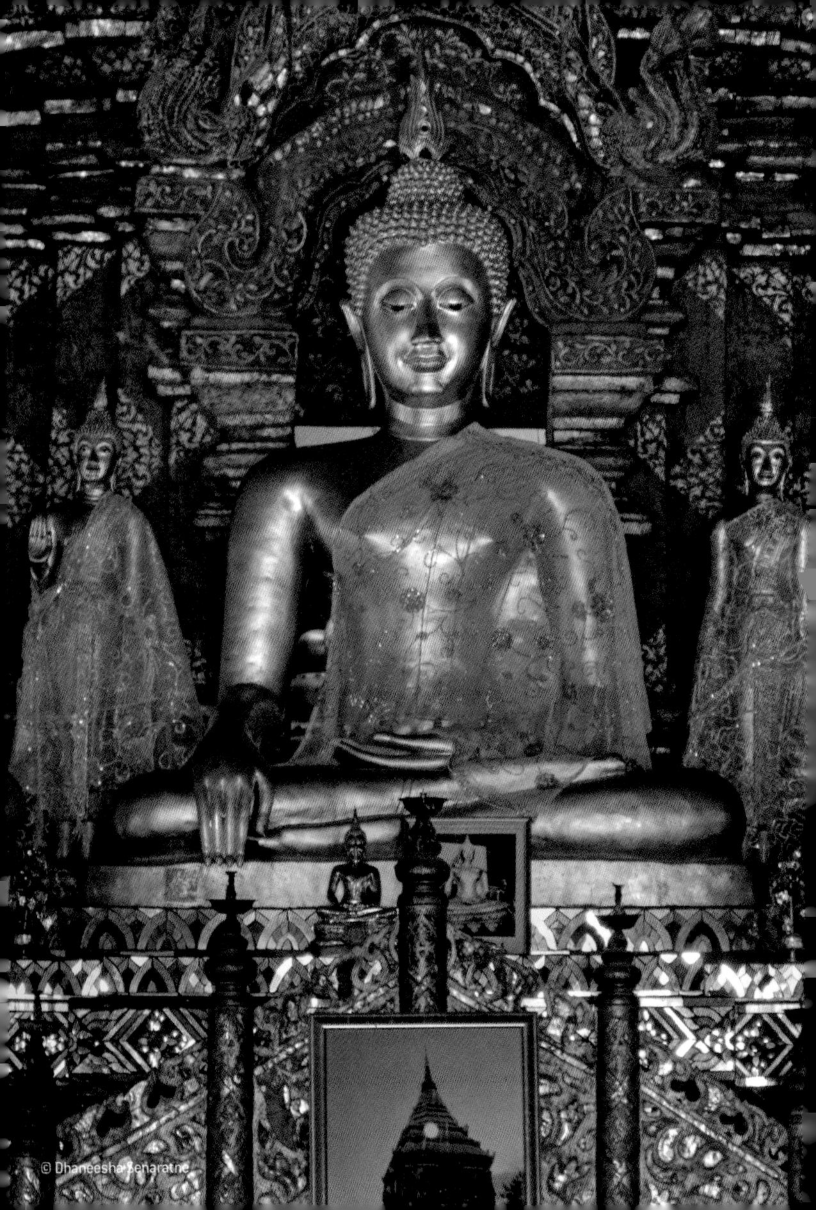

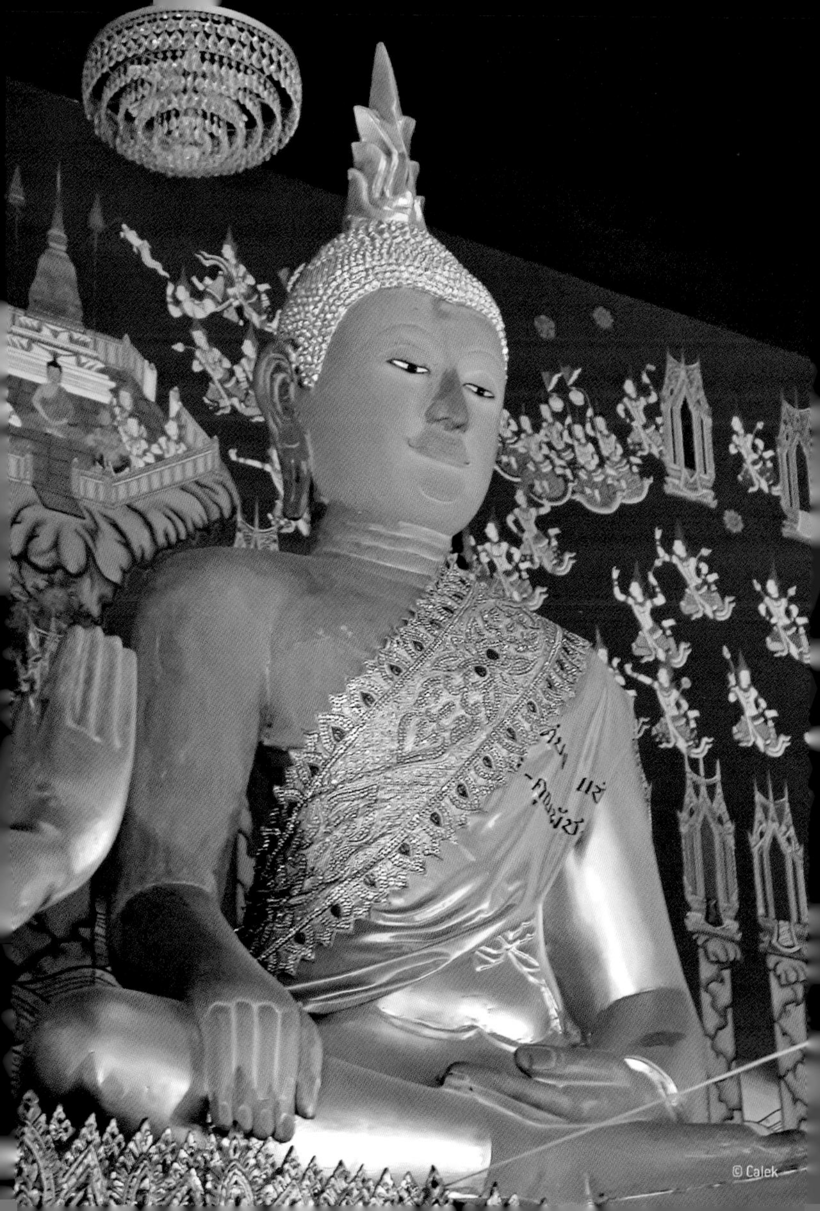

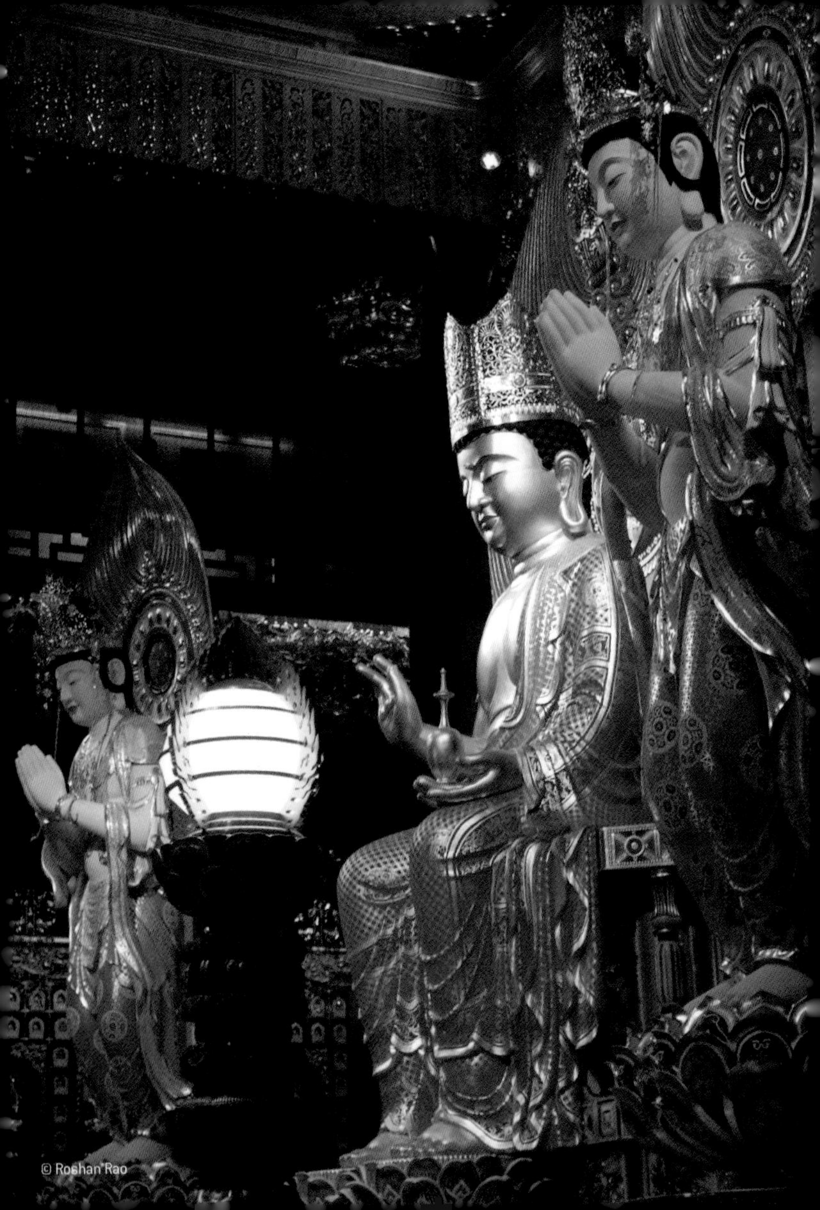

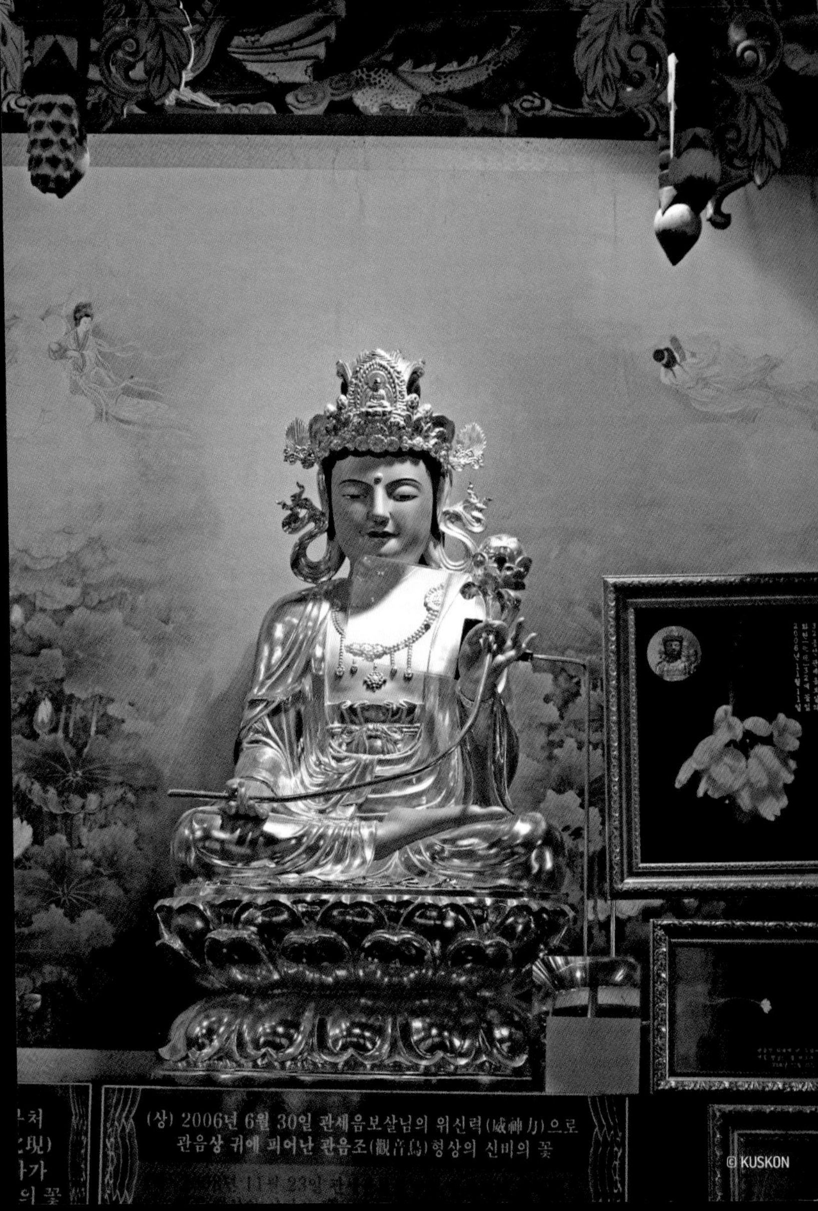
(상) 2006년 6월 30일 관세음보살님의 위신력(威神力)으로
관음상 귀에 피어난 관음조(觀音鳥)형상의 신비의 꽃

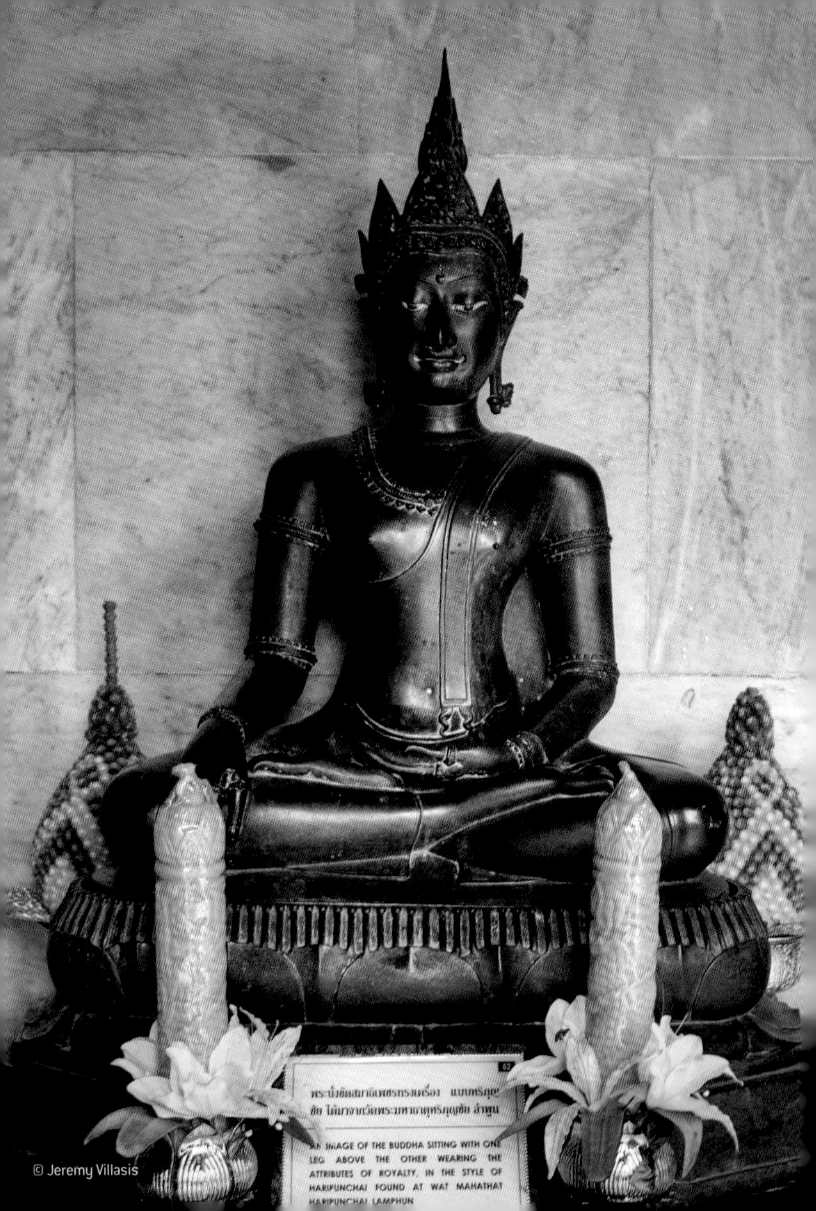
IMAGE OF THE BUDDHA SITTING WITH ONE
LEG ABOVE THE OTHER WEARING THE
ATTRIBUTES OF ROYALTY, IN THE STYLE OF
HARIPUNCHAI FOUND AT WAT MAHATHAT
HARIPUNCHAI LAMPHUN

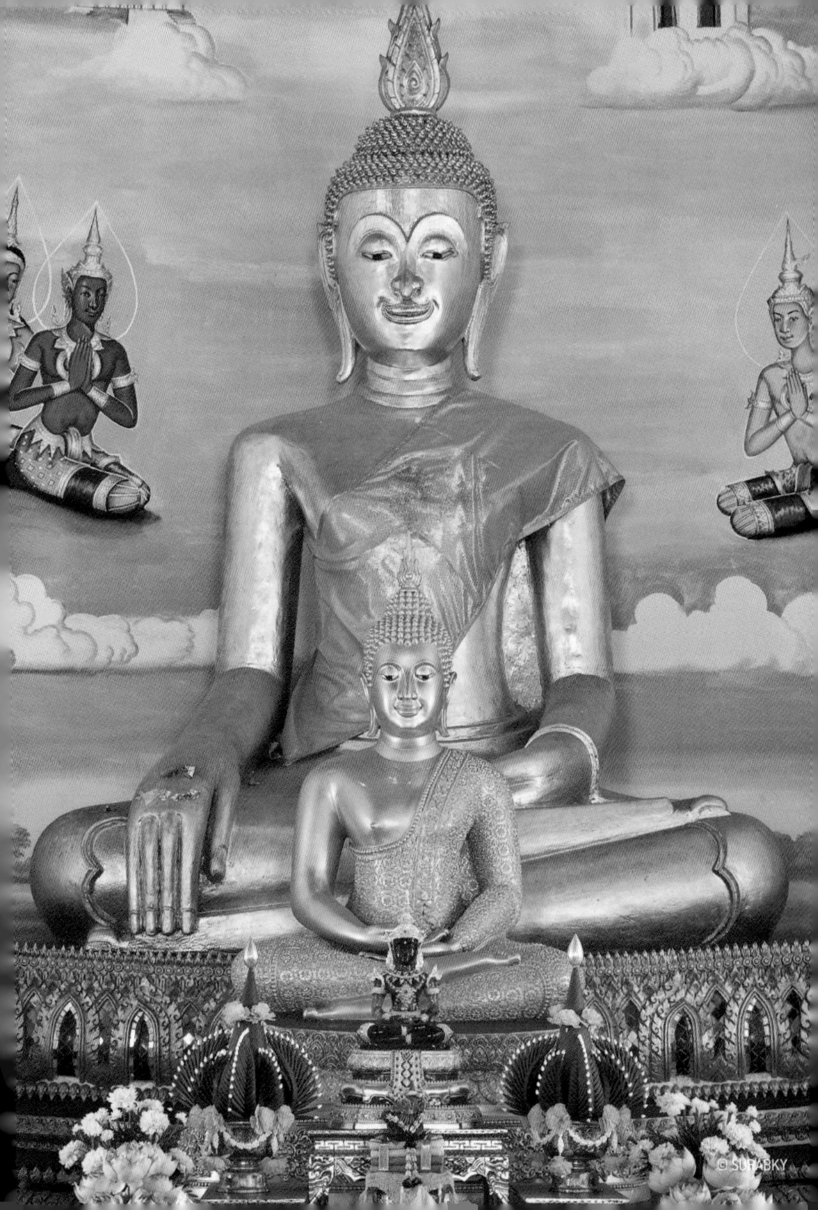

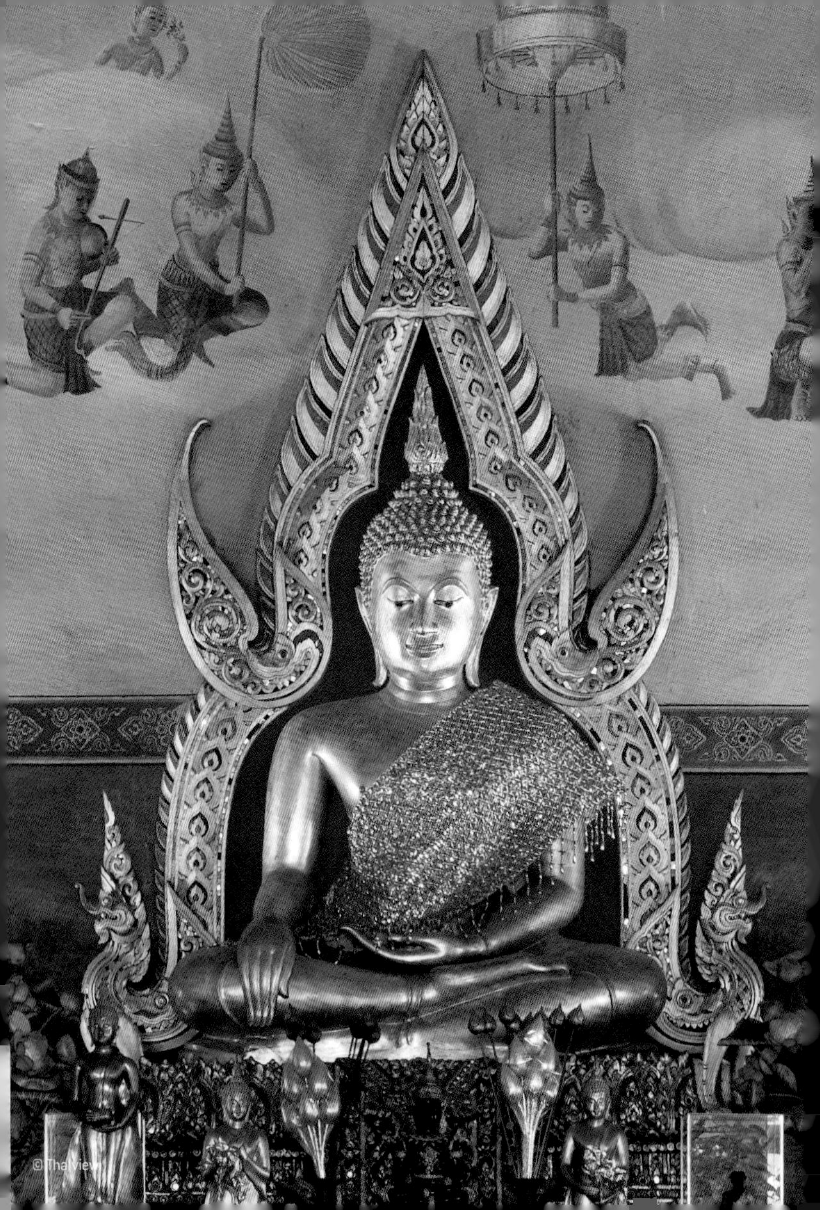

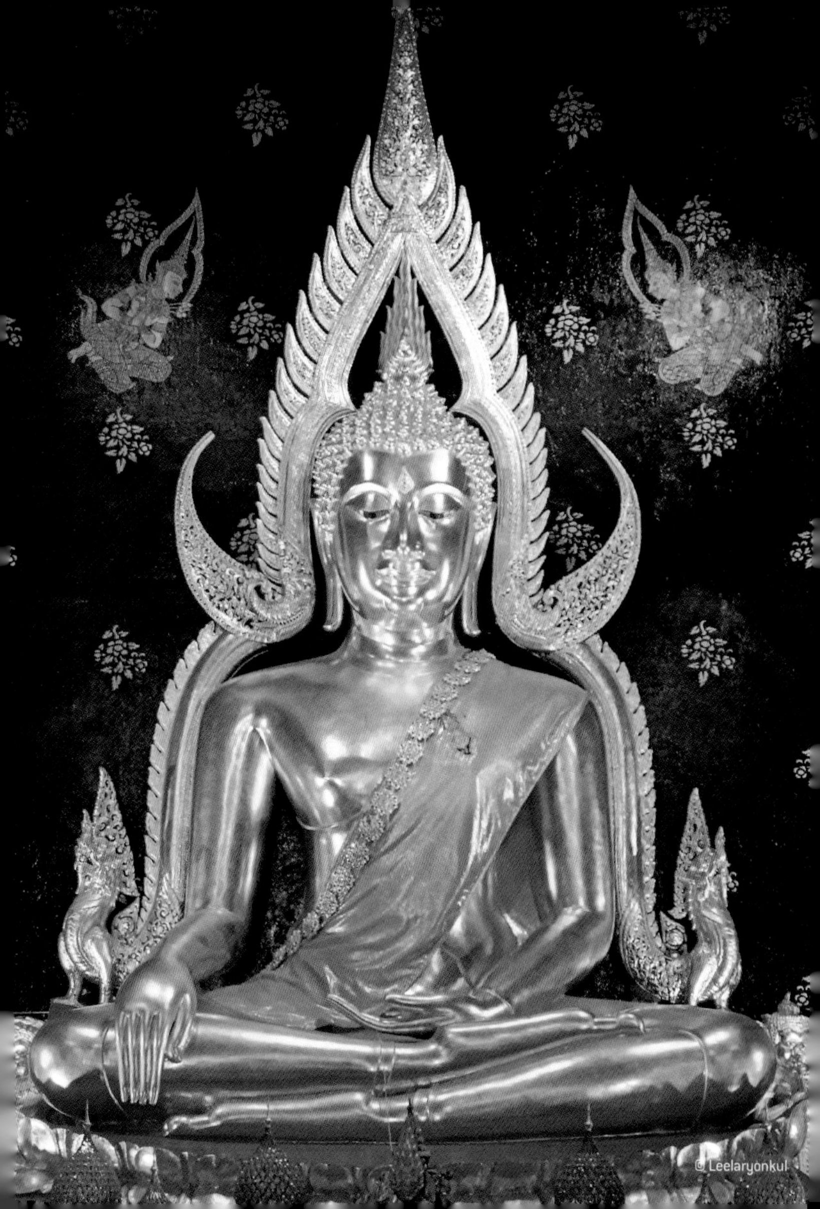
© Leelaryonkul

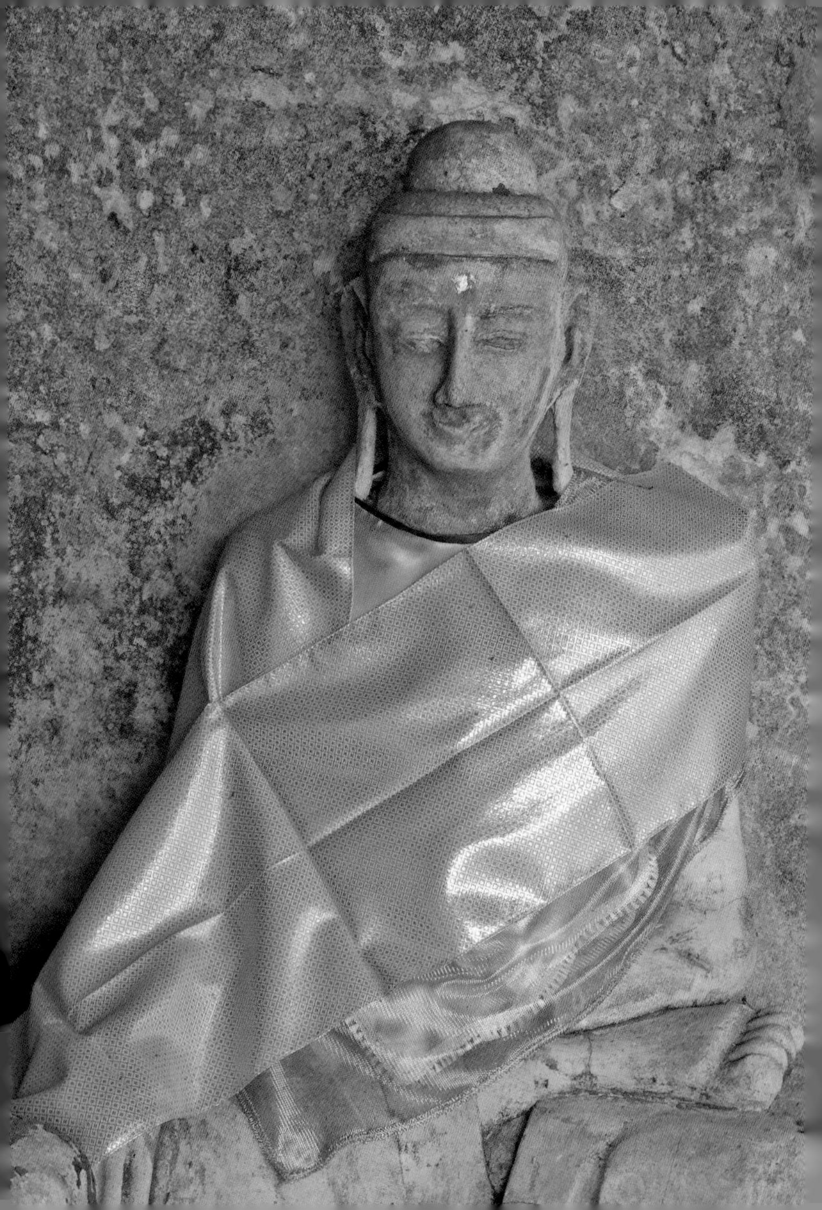

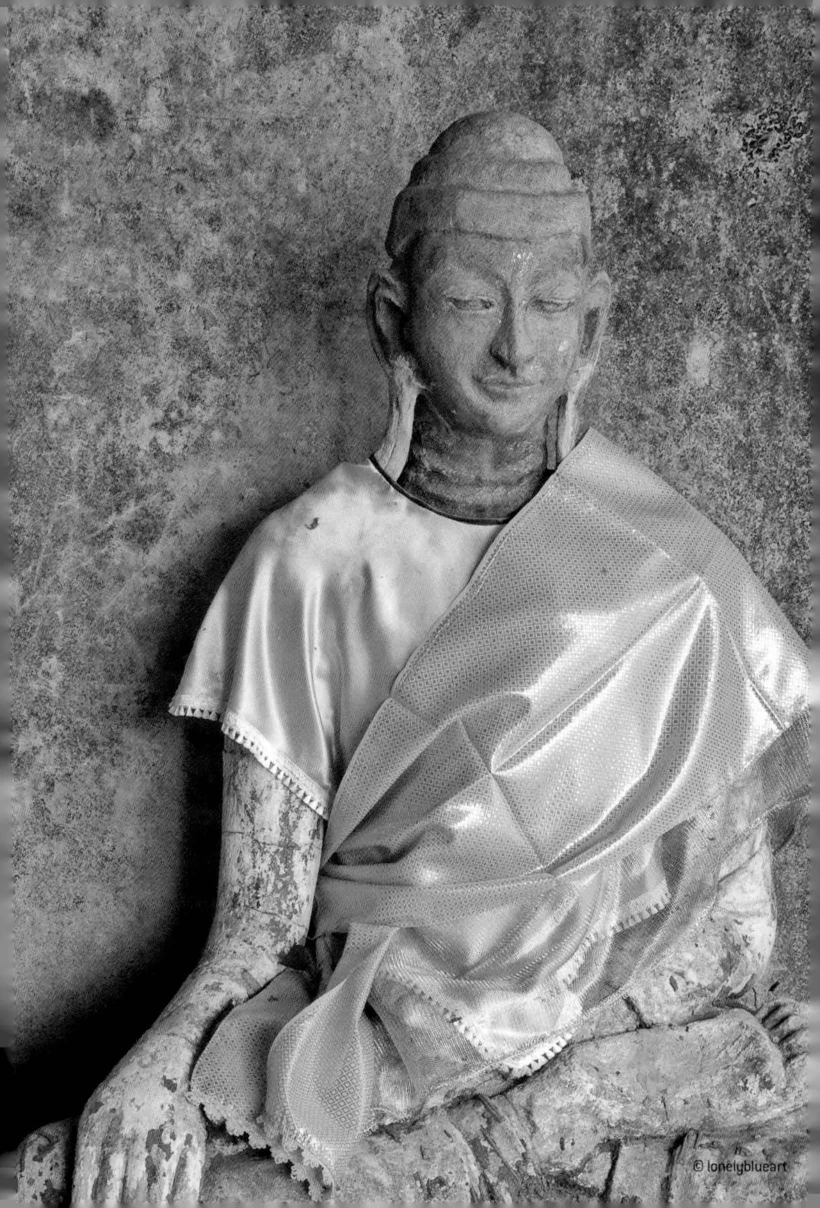
© lonelyblueart

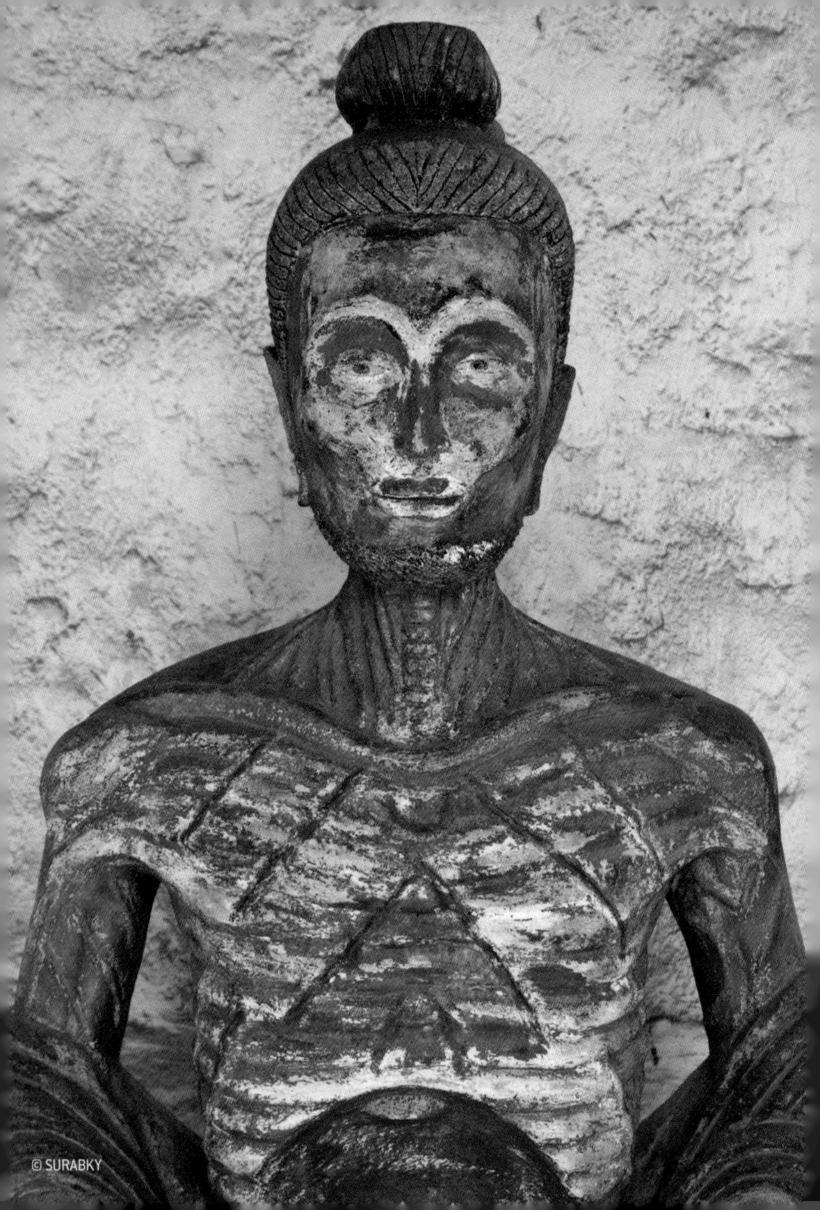

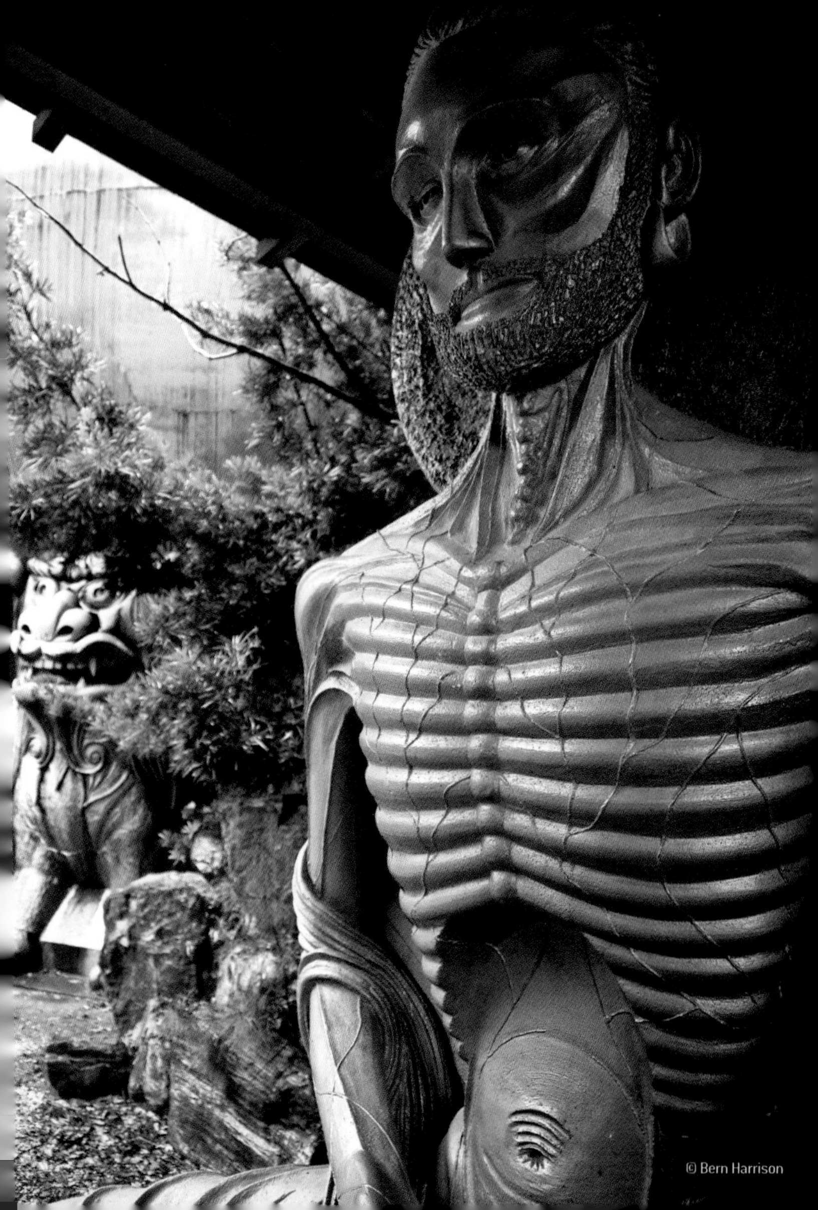
© Bern Harrison

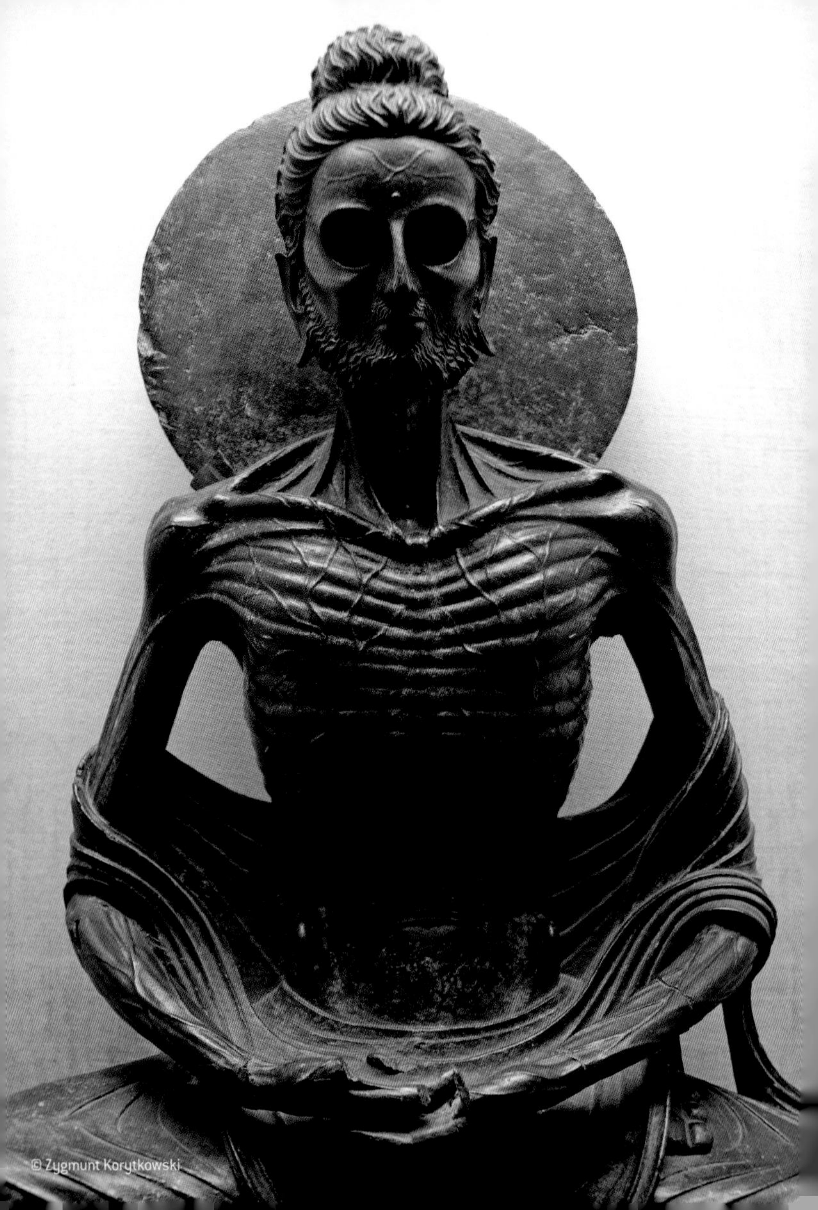

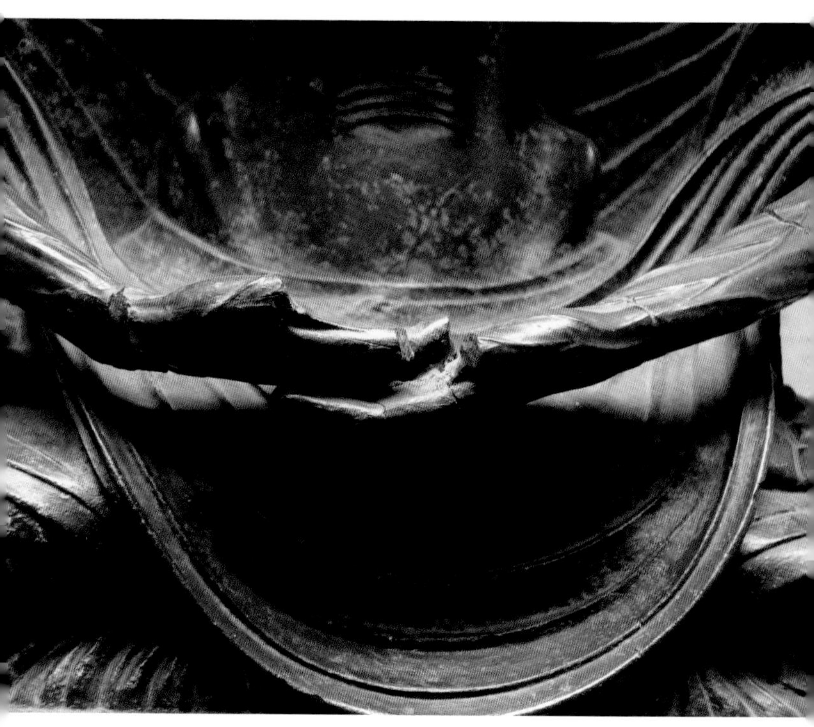

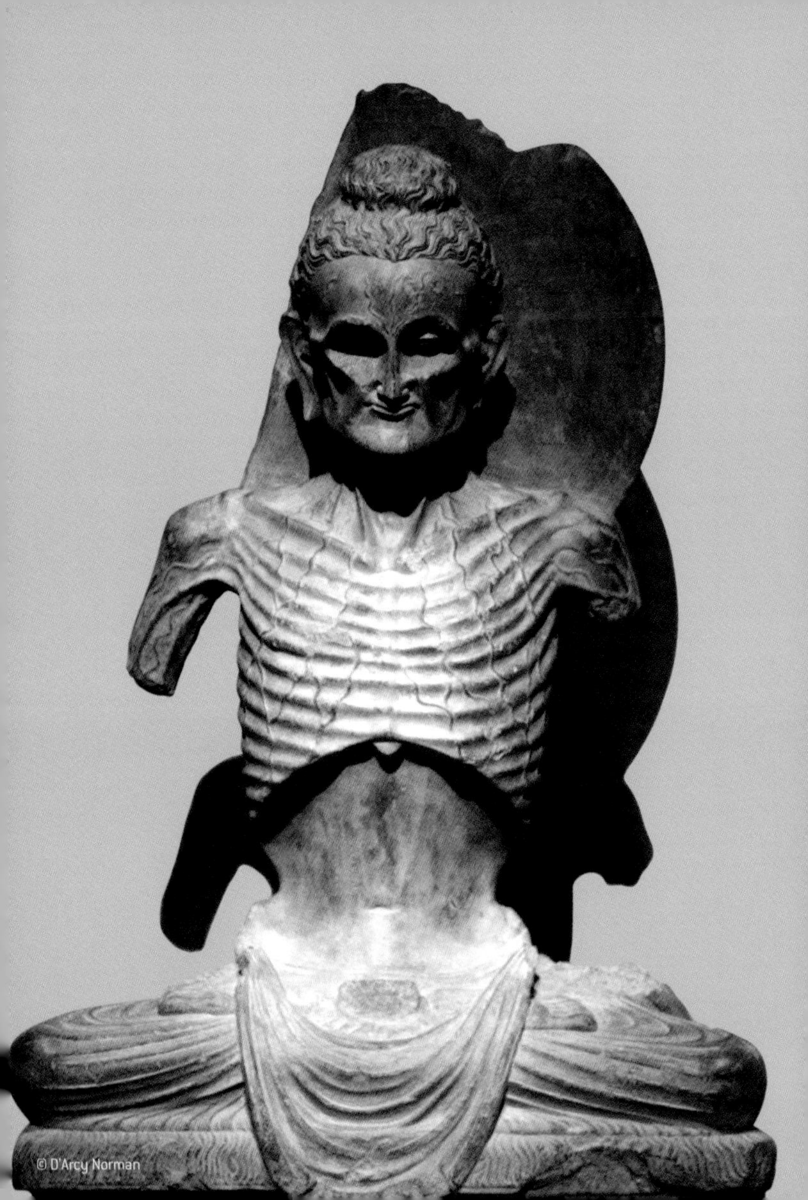

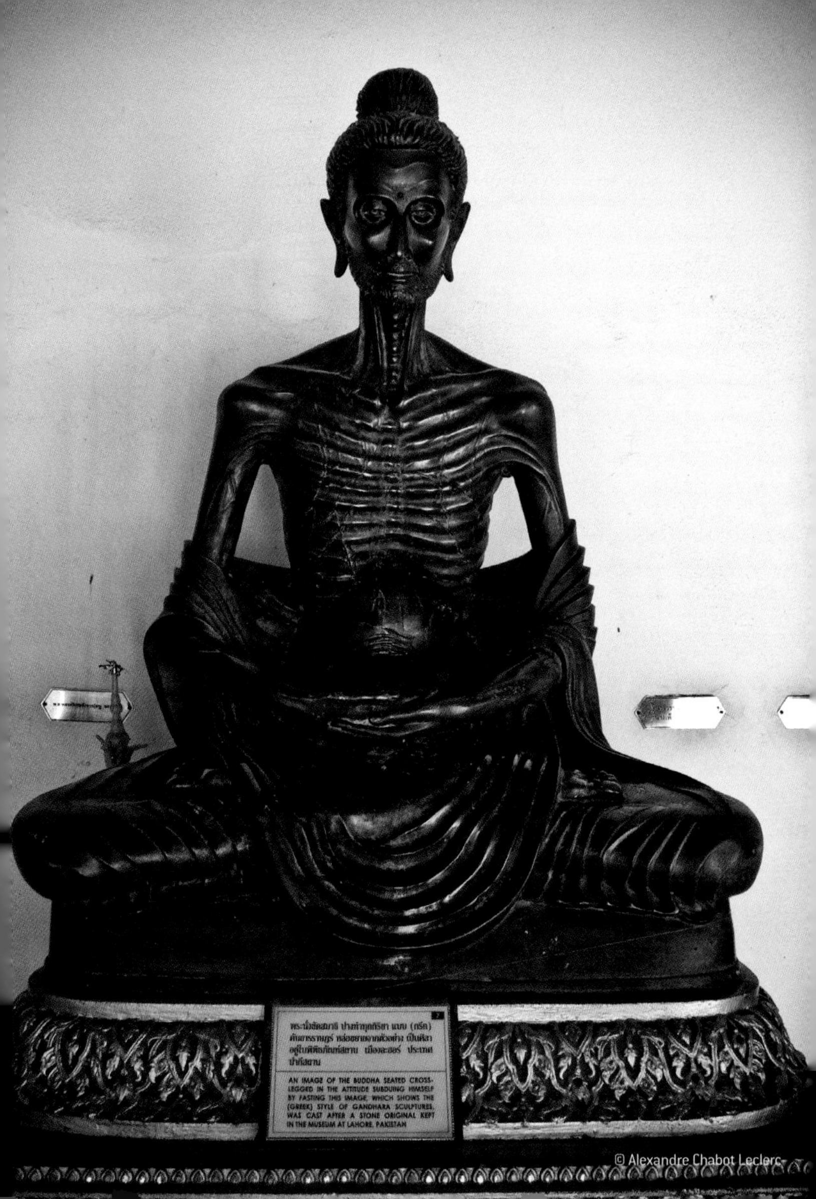
AN IMAGE OF THE BUDDHA SEATED CROSS-
LEGGED IN THE ATTITUDE SUBDUING HIMSELF
BY FASTING THIS IMAGE, WHICH SHOWS THE
(GREEK) STYLE OF GANDHARA SCULPTURES,
WAS CAST AFTER A STONE ORIGINAL KEPT
IN THE MUSEUM AT LAHORE, PAKISTAN

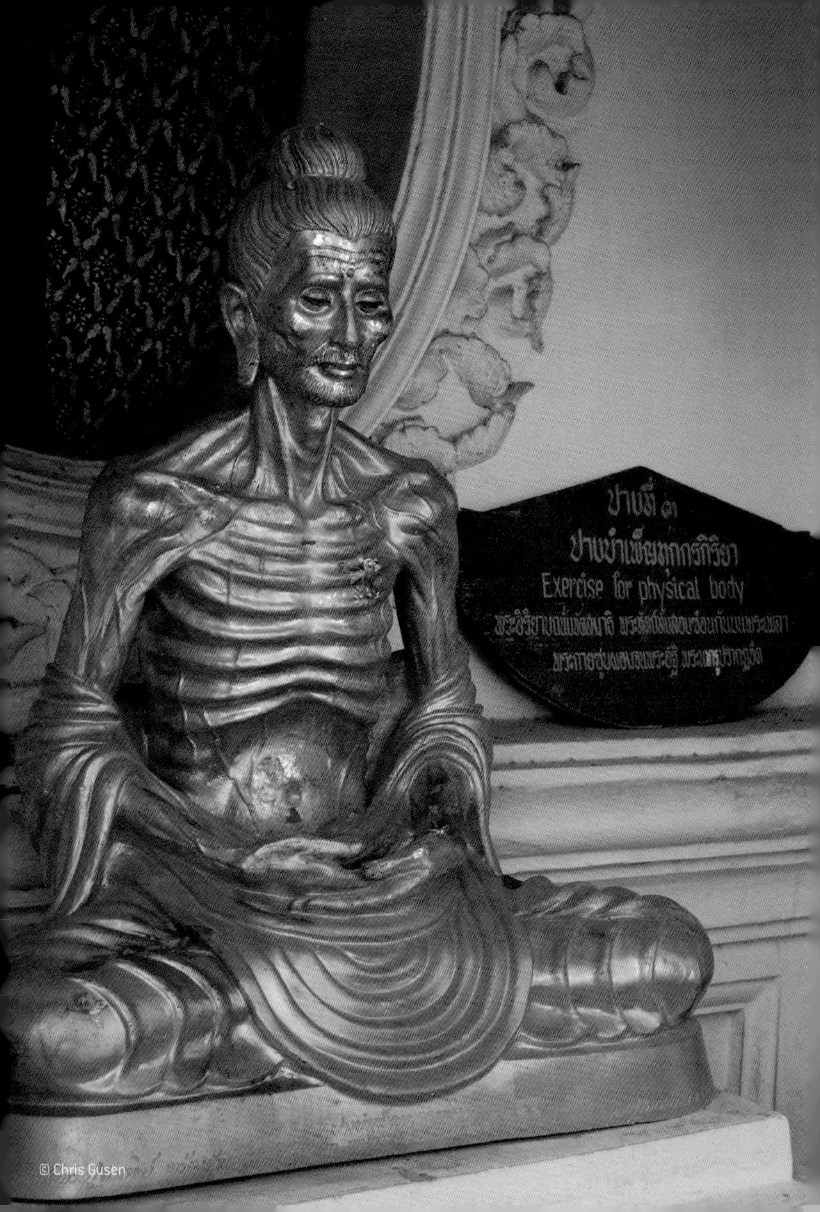
ปางที่ ๓
ปางบำเพ็ญทุกรกิริยา
Exercise for physical body

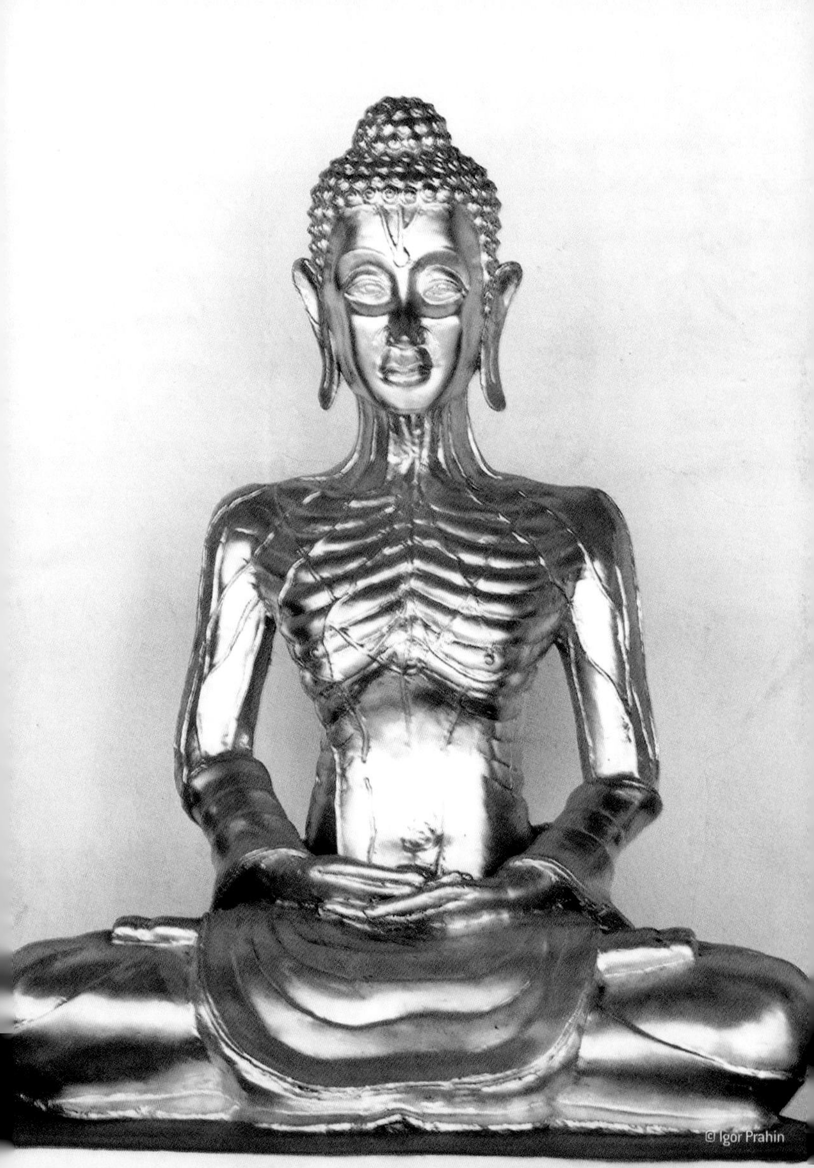
© Igor Prahin

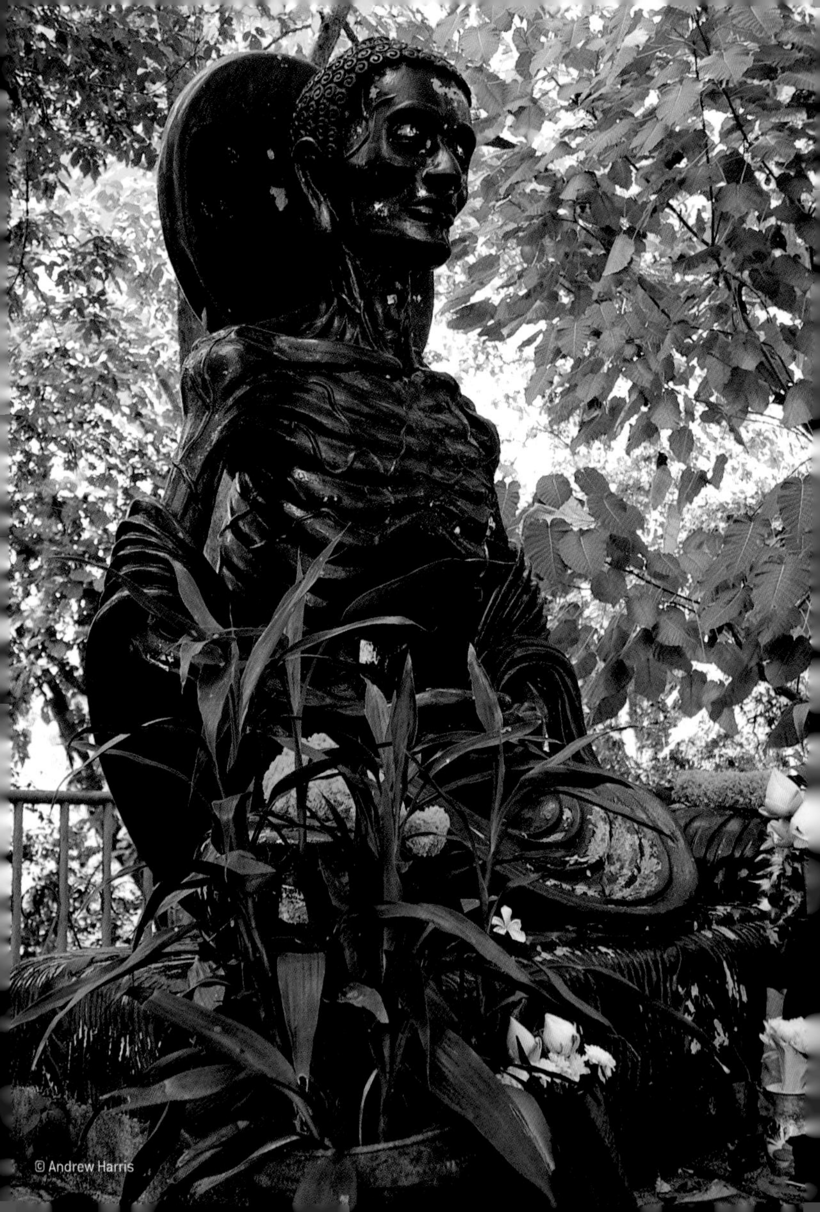
© Andrew Harris

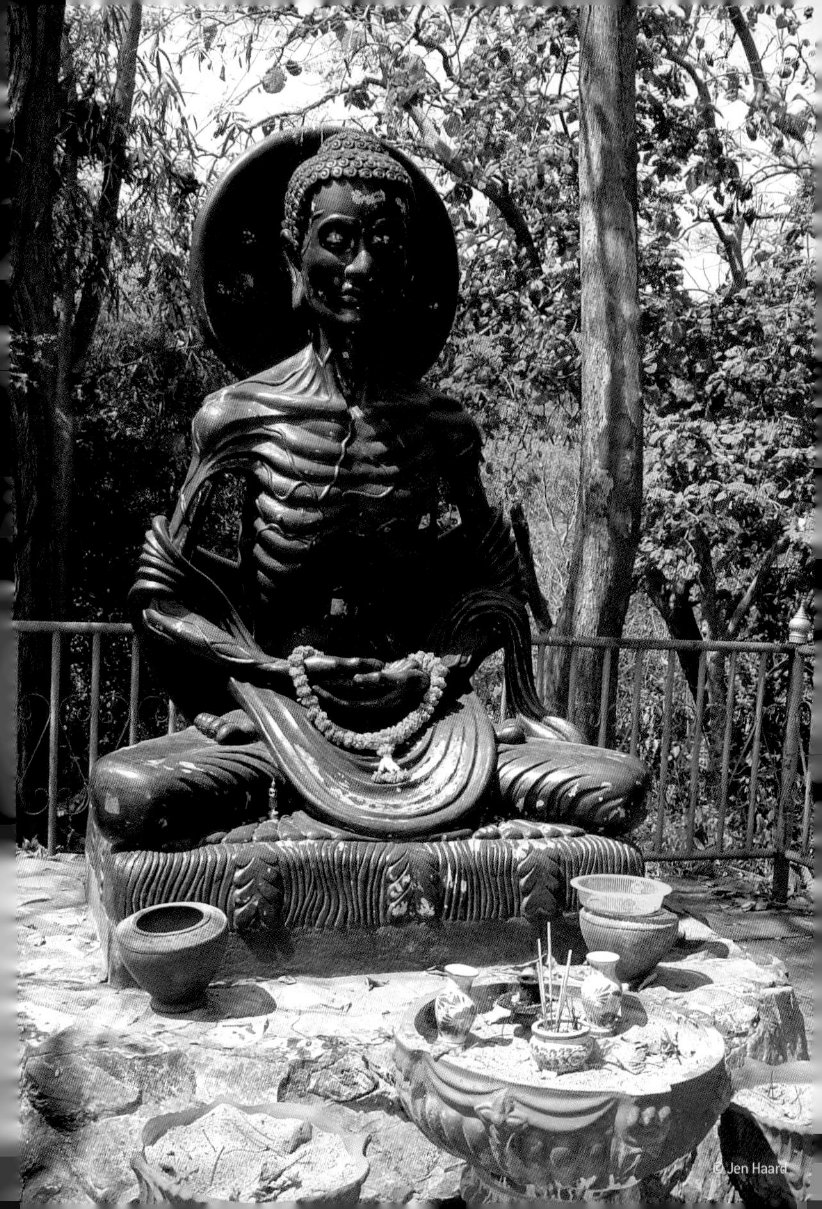
© Jen Haard

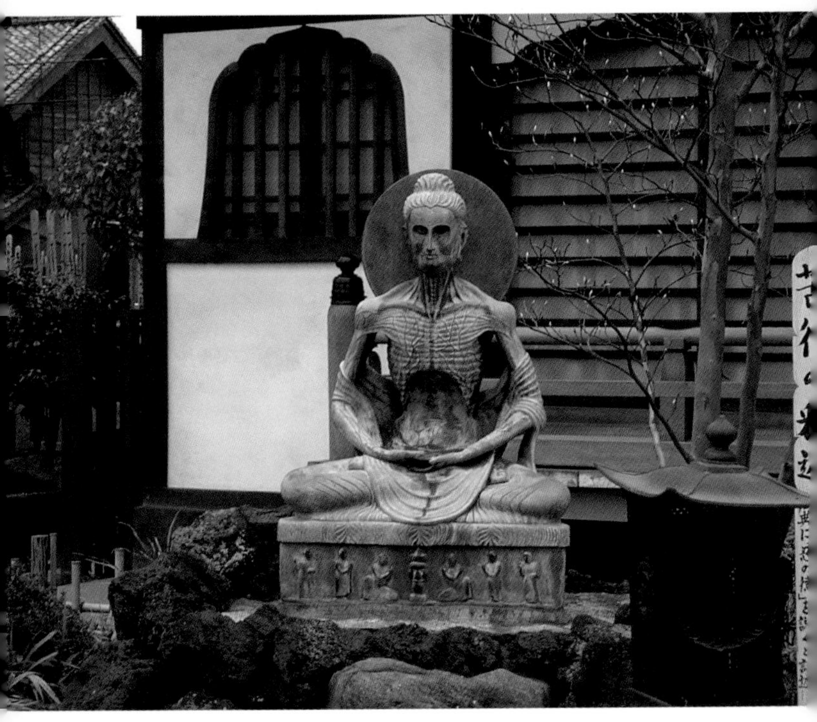

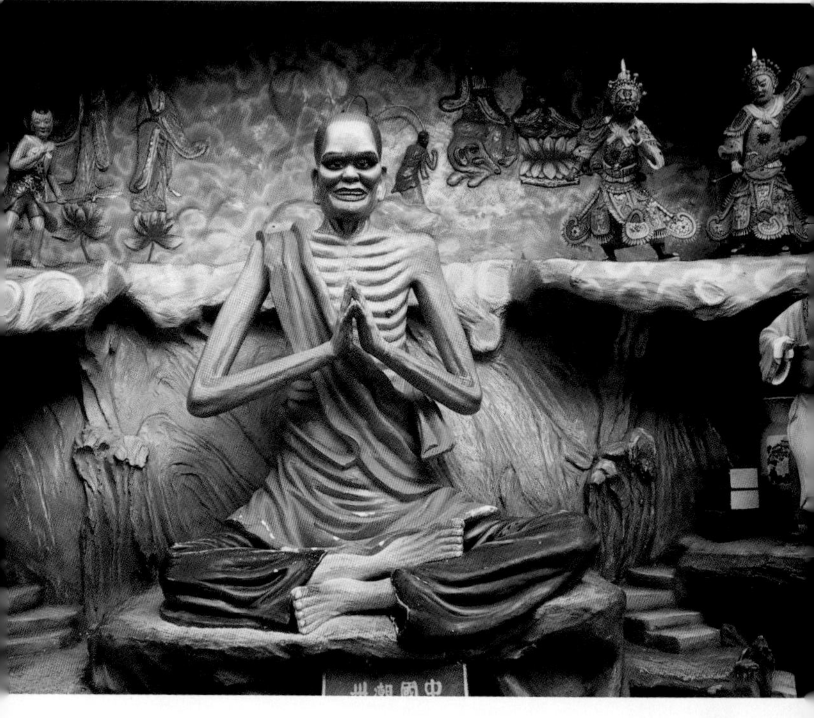

© Seet

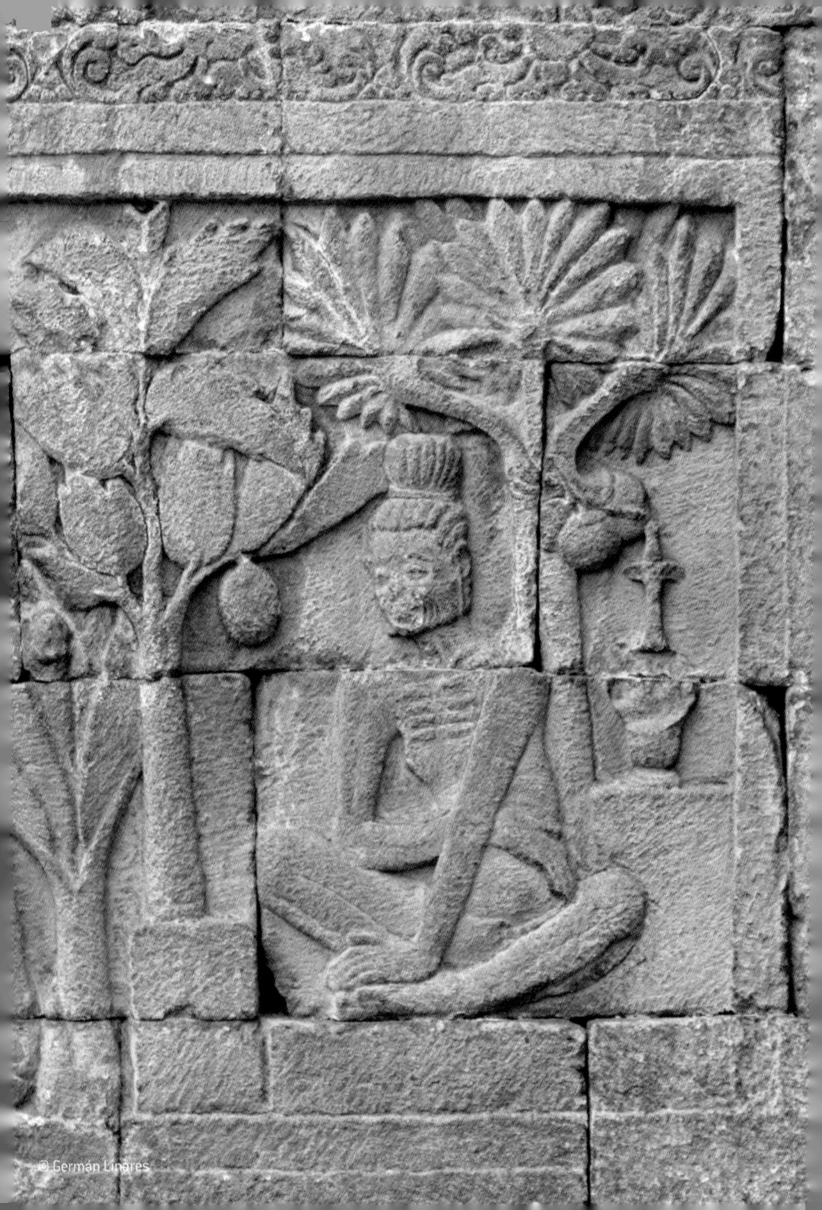
© Germán Linares

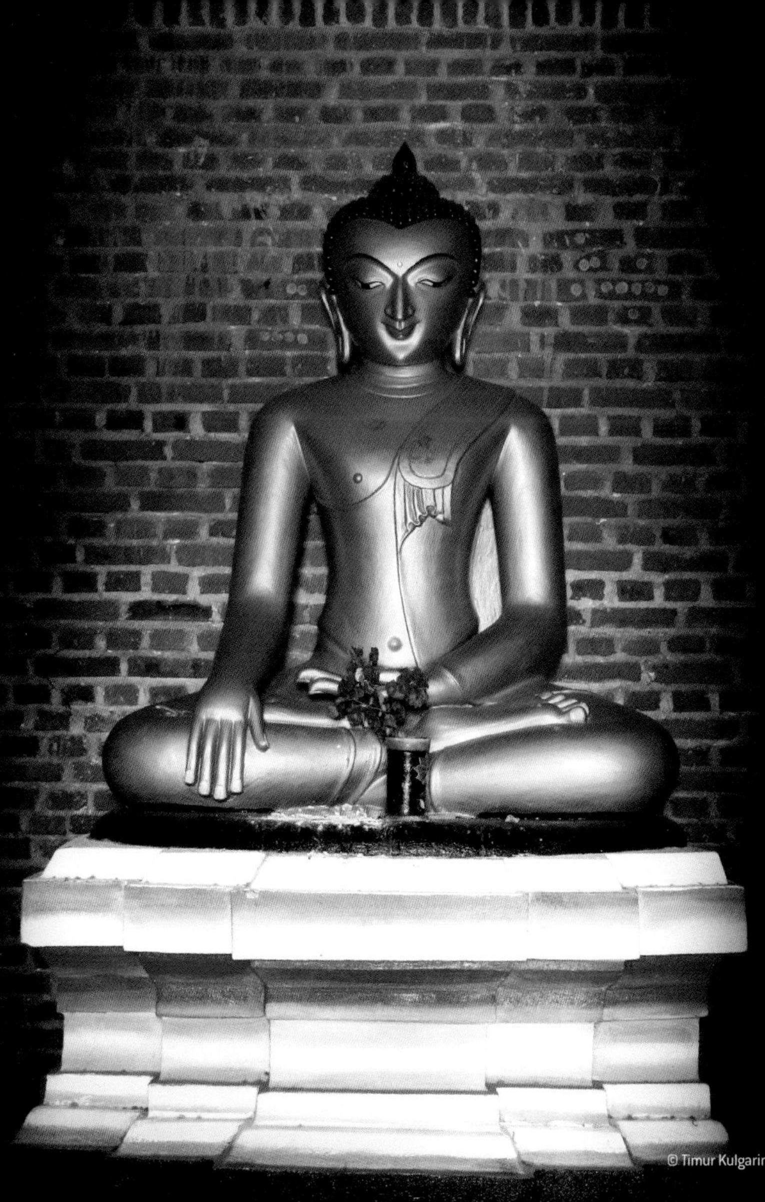

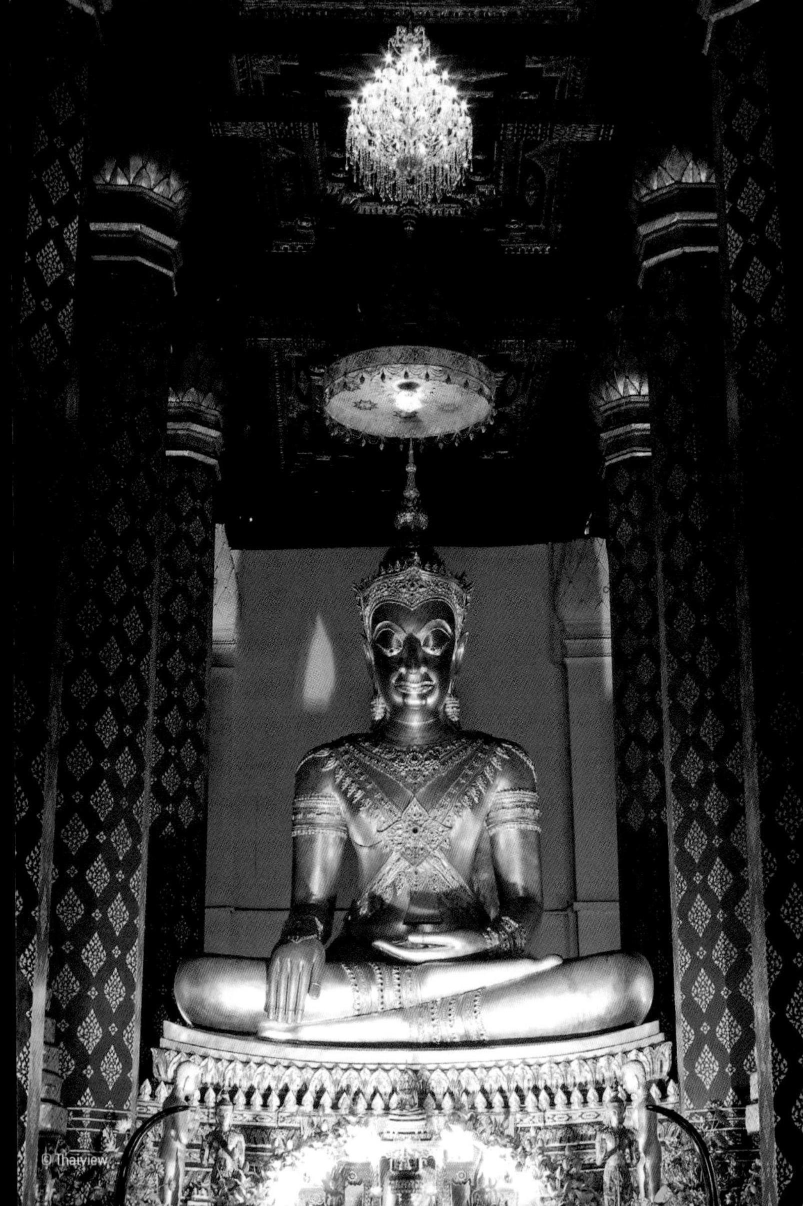

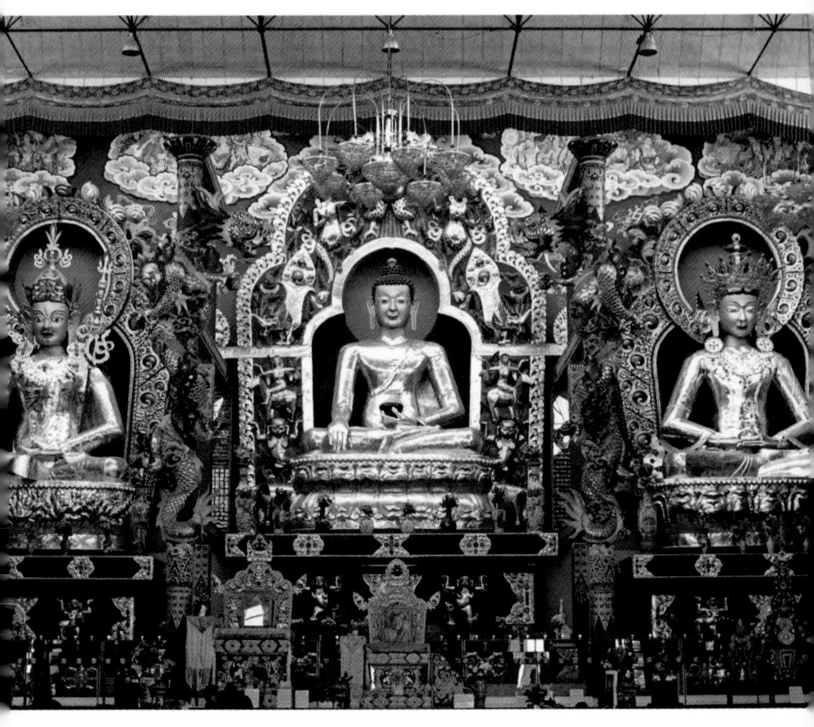

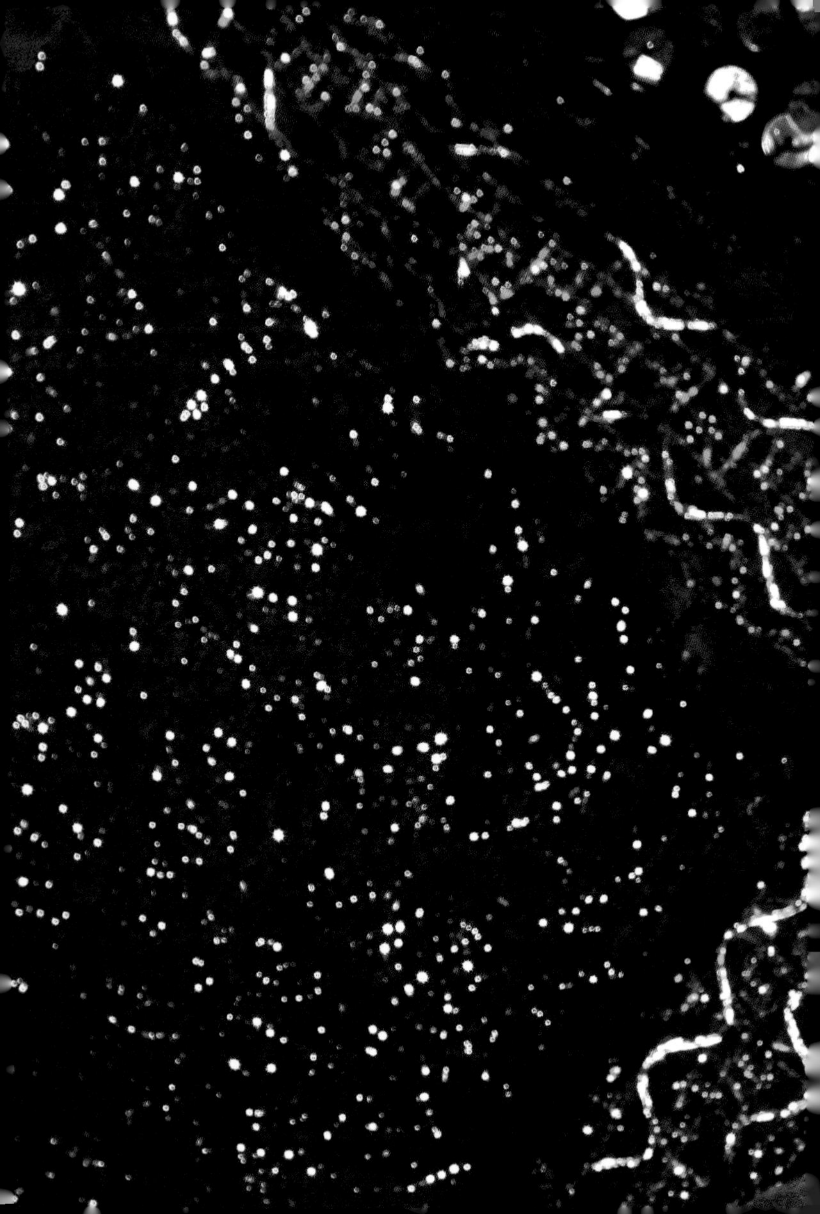

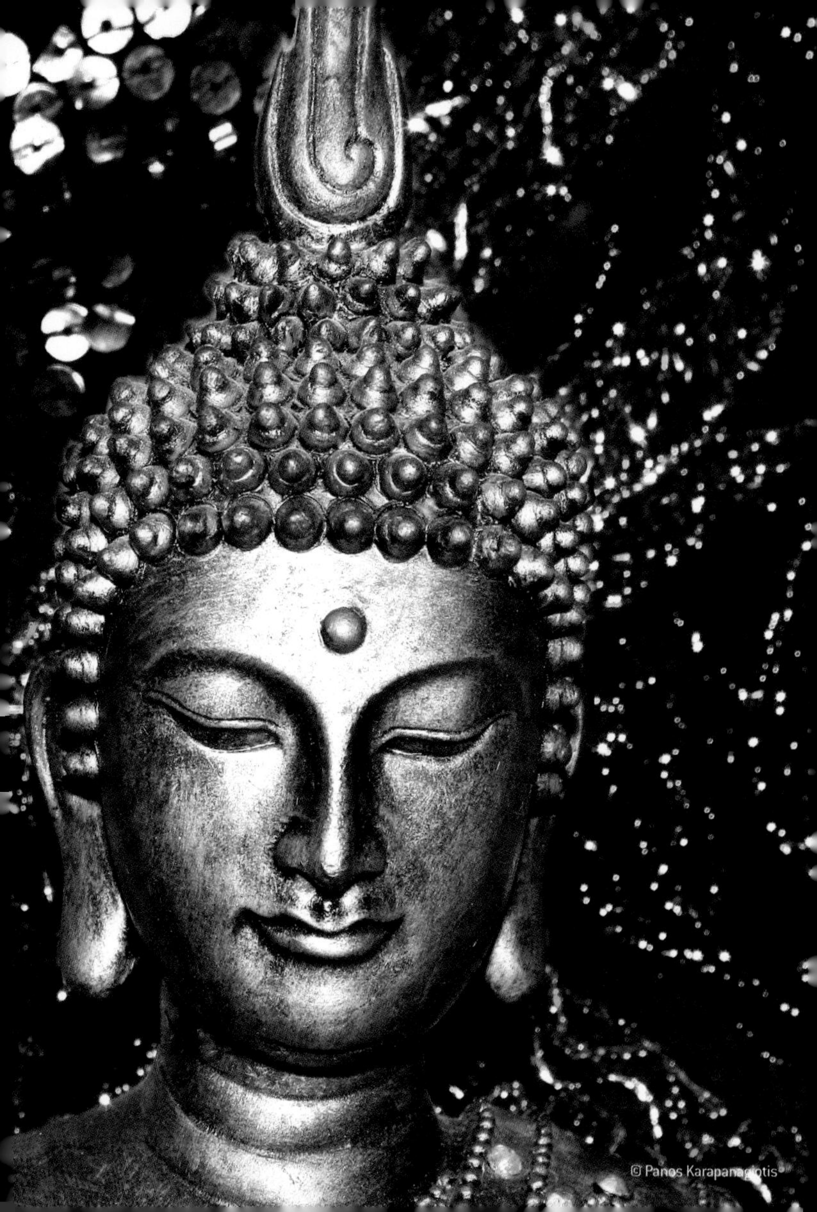
© Panos Karapanagiotis

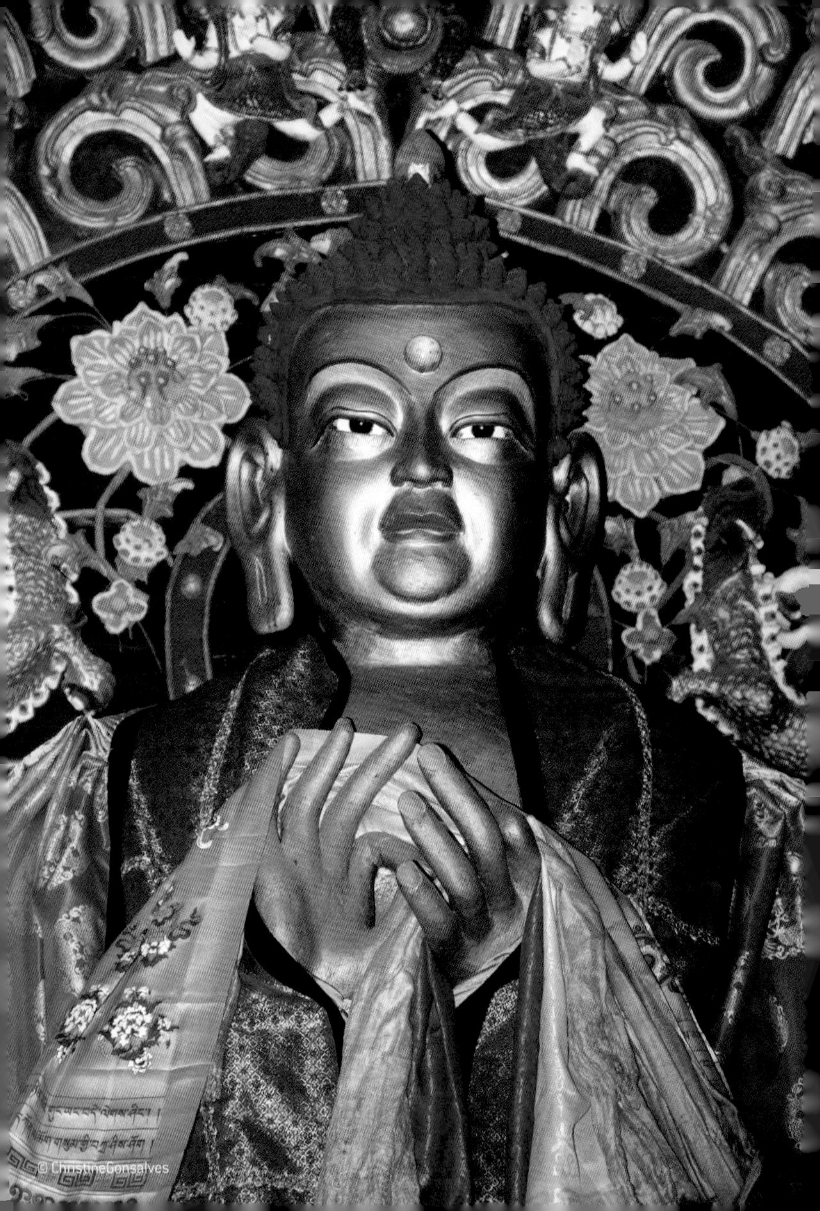

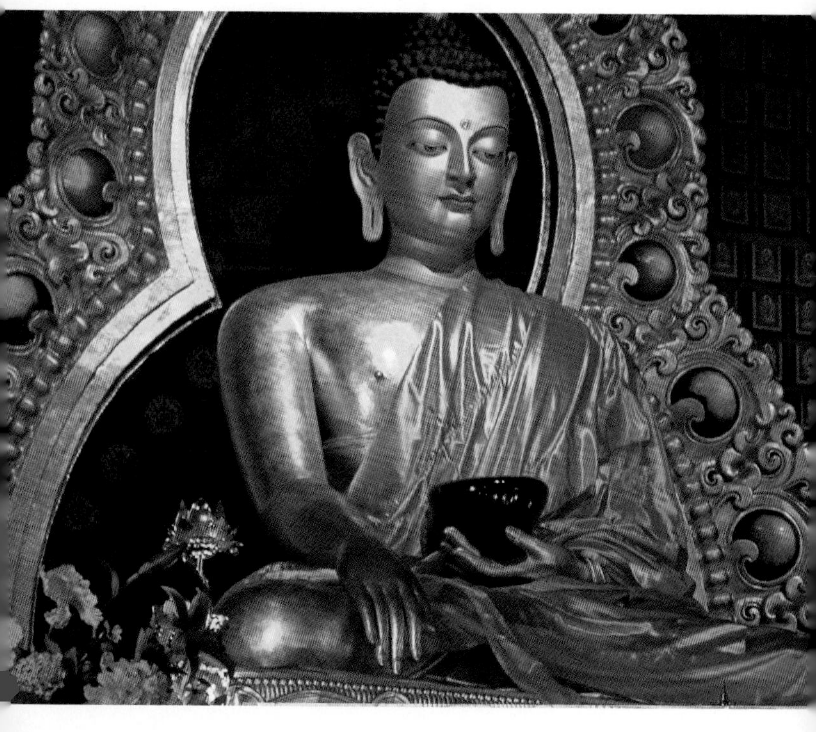

© Wonderlane

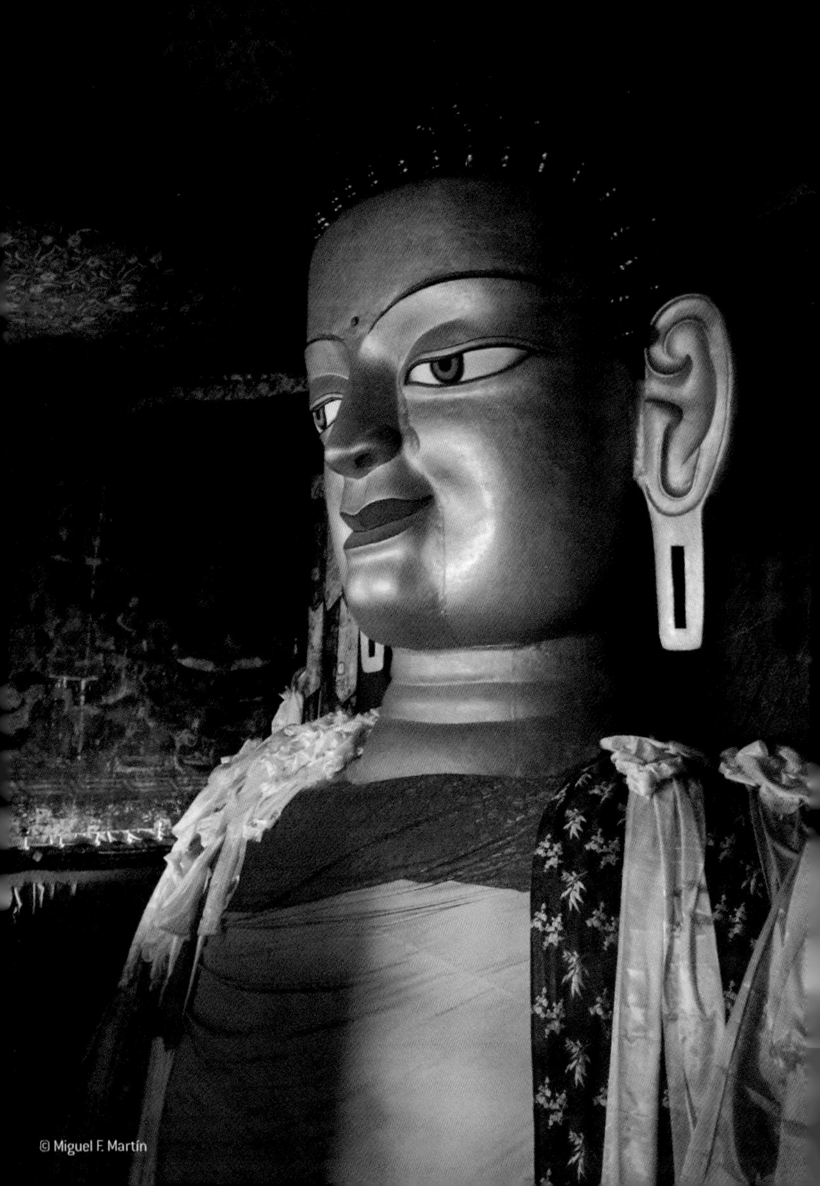

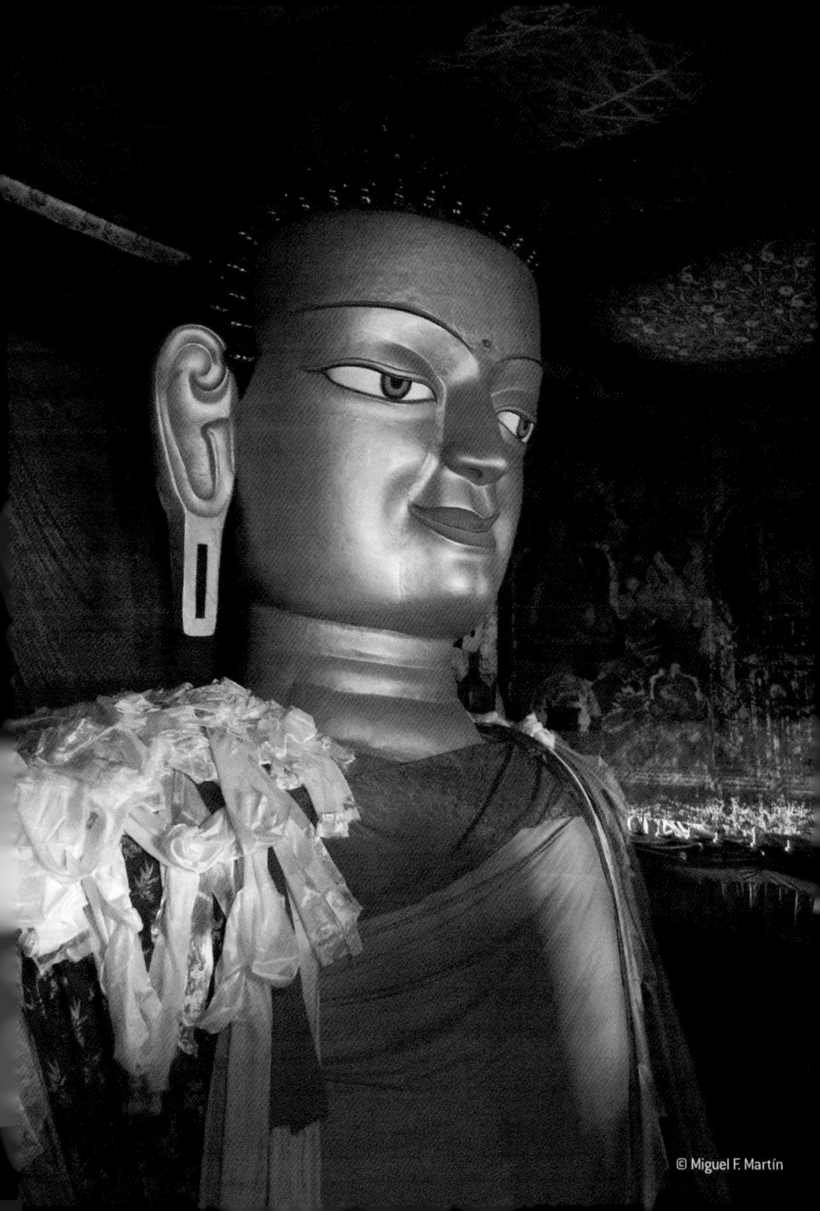

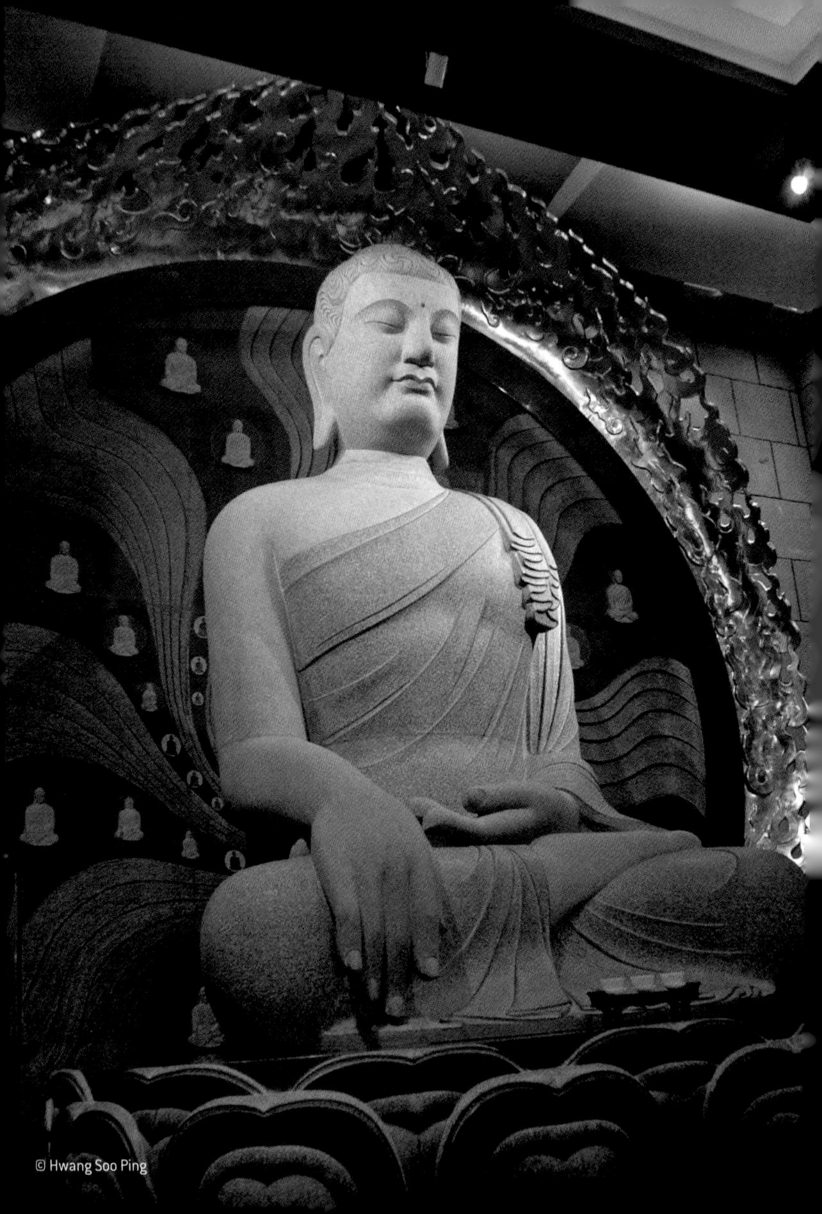

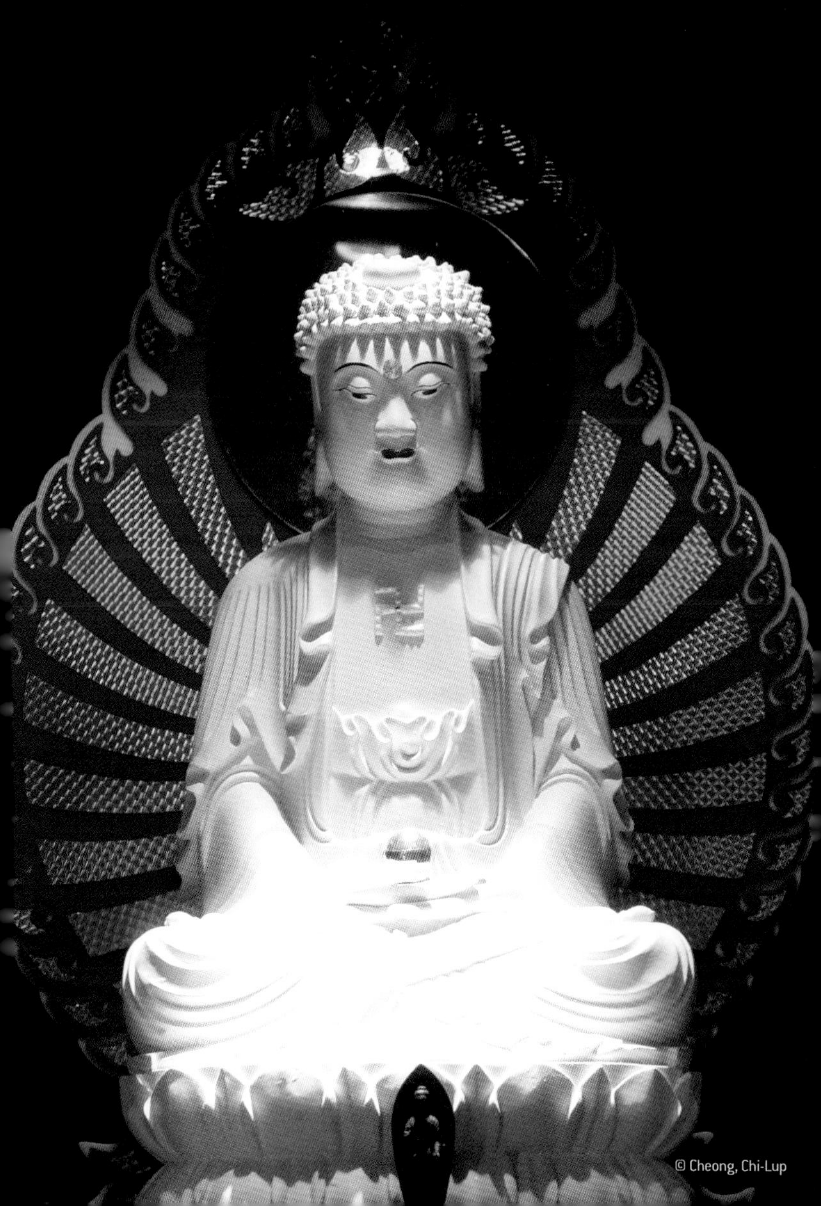

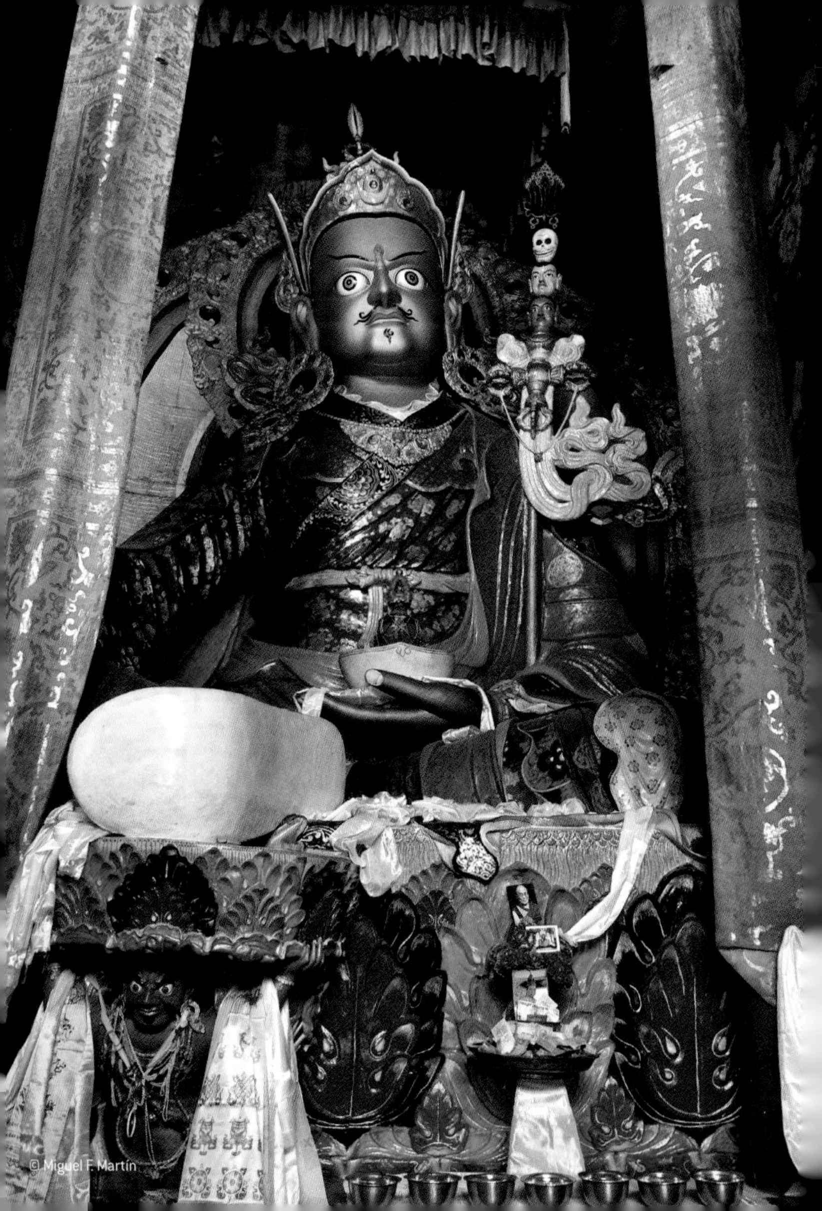

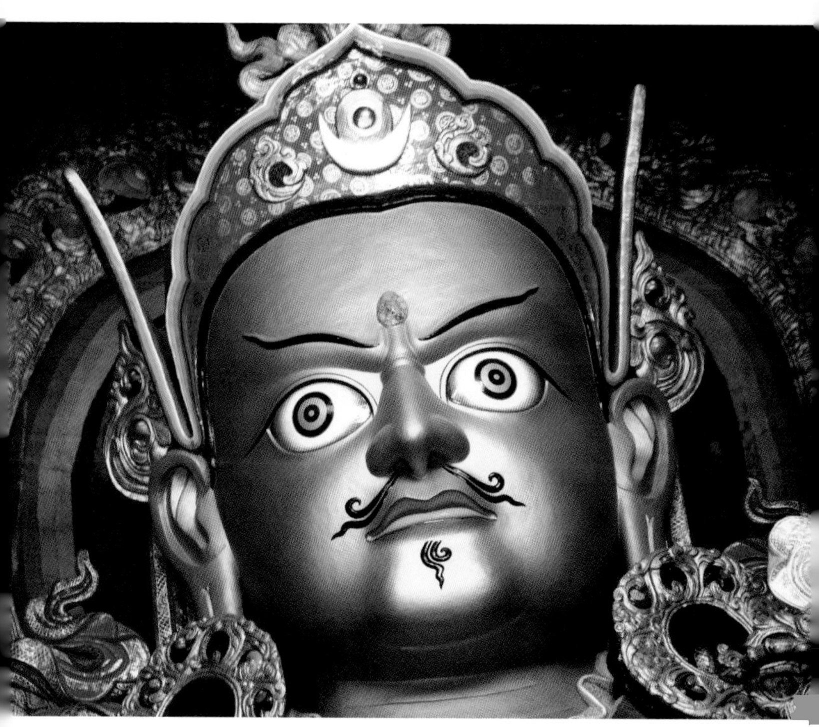

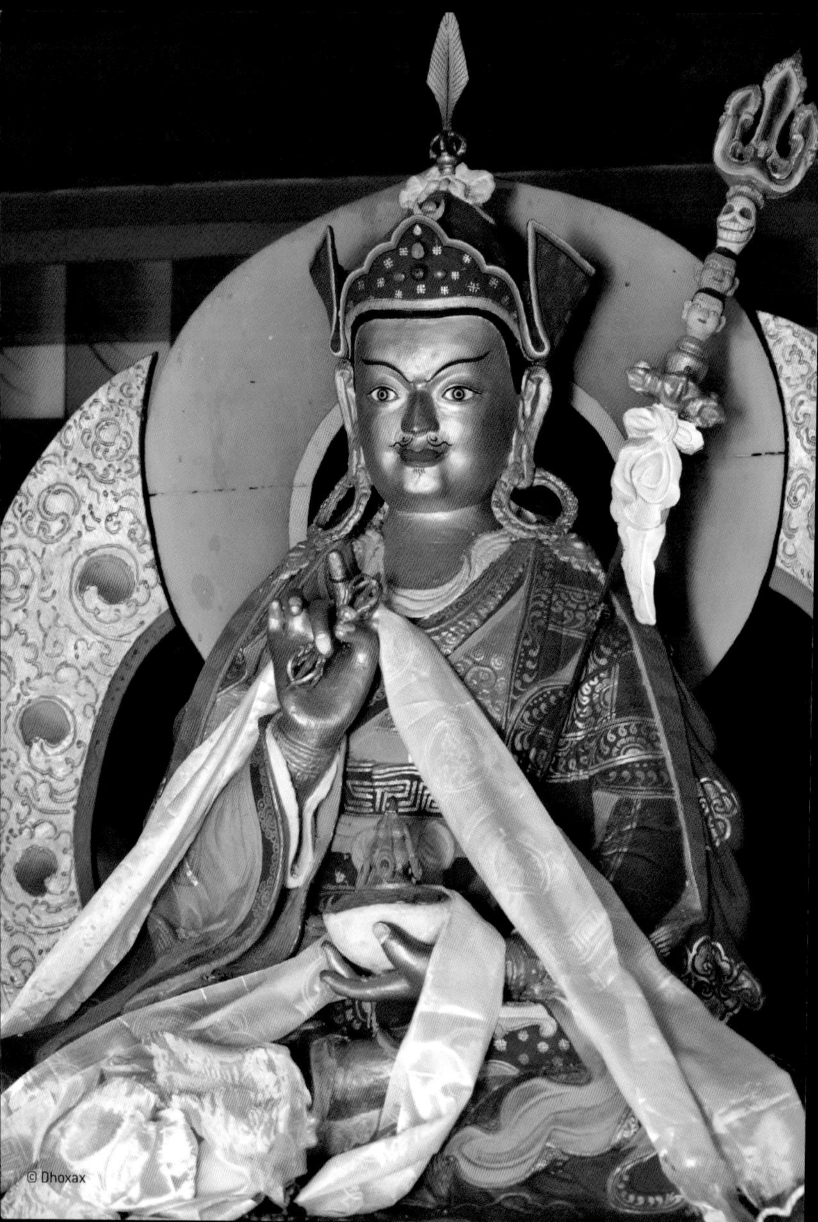

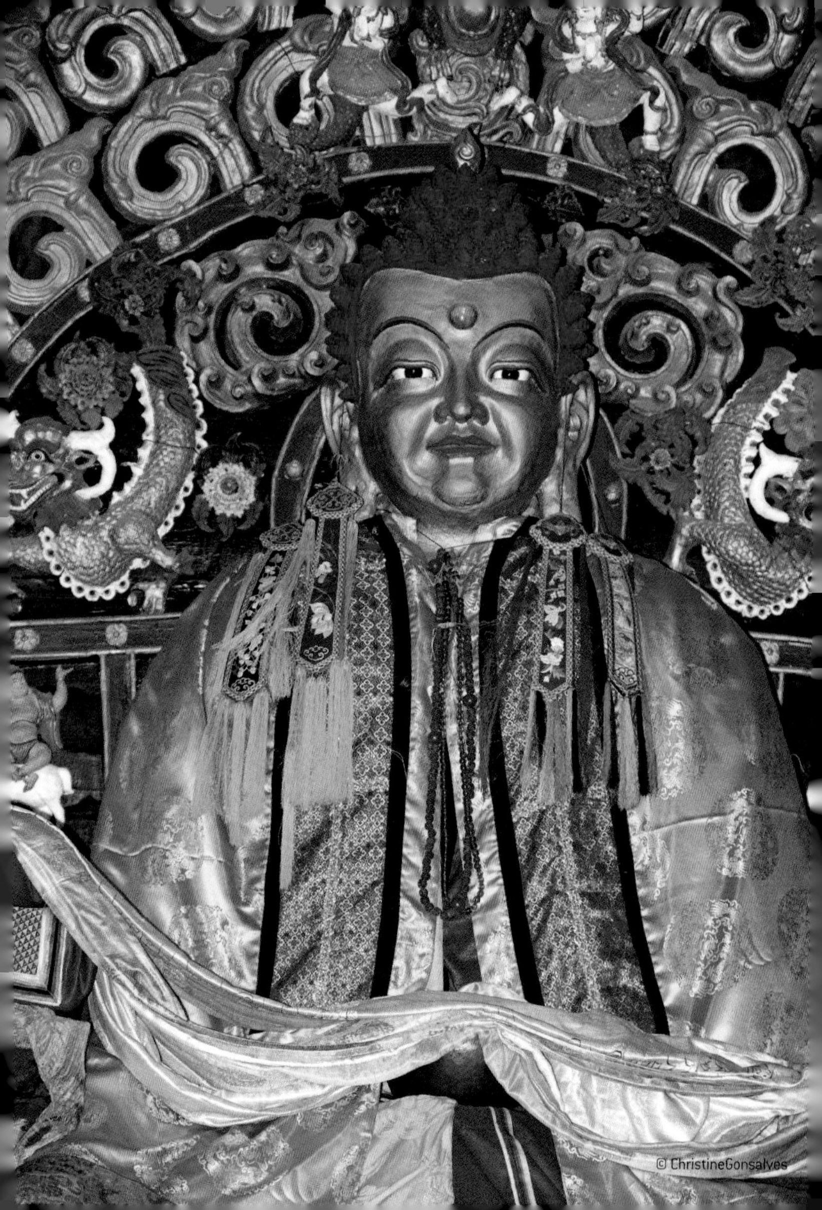

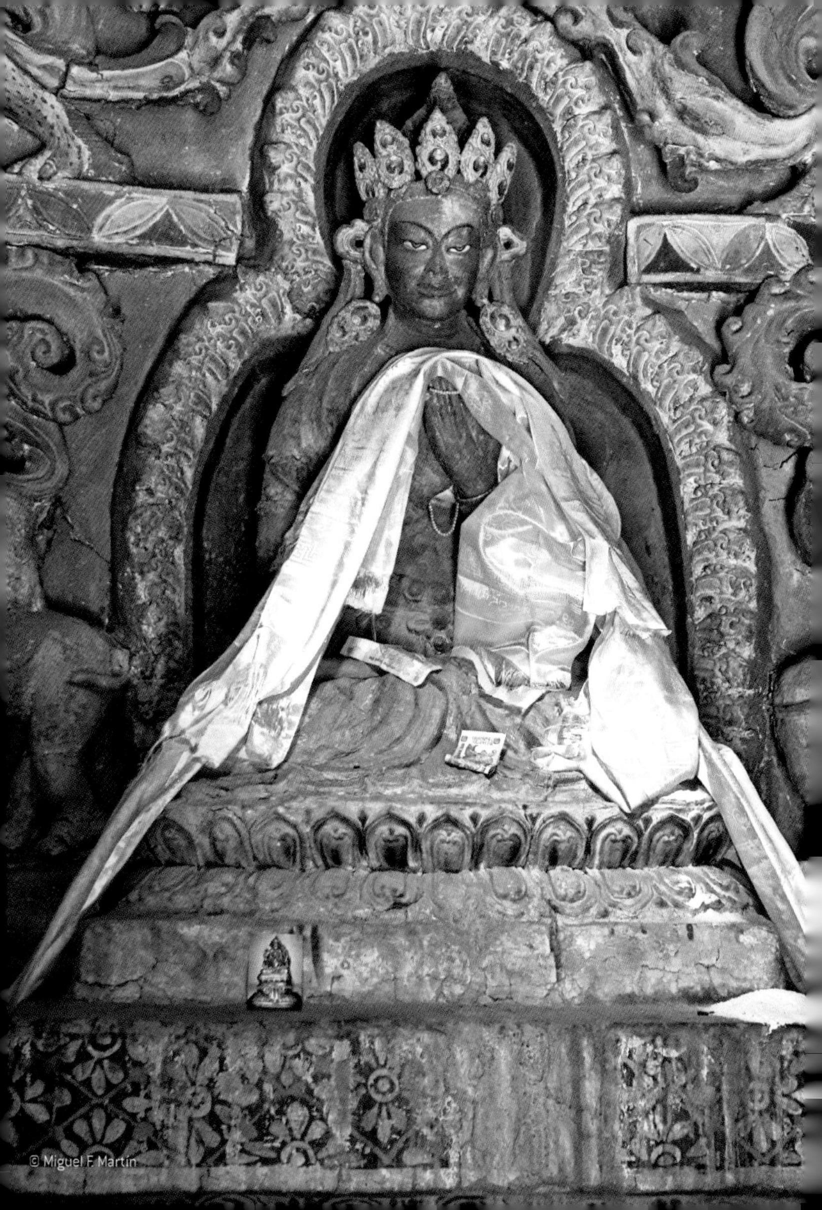

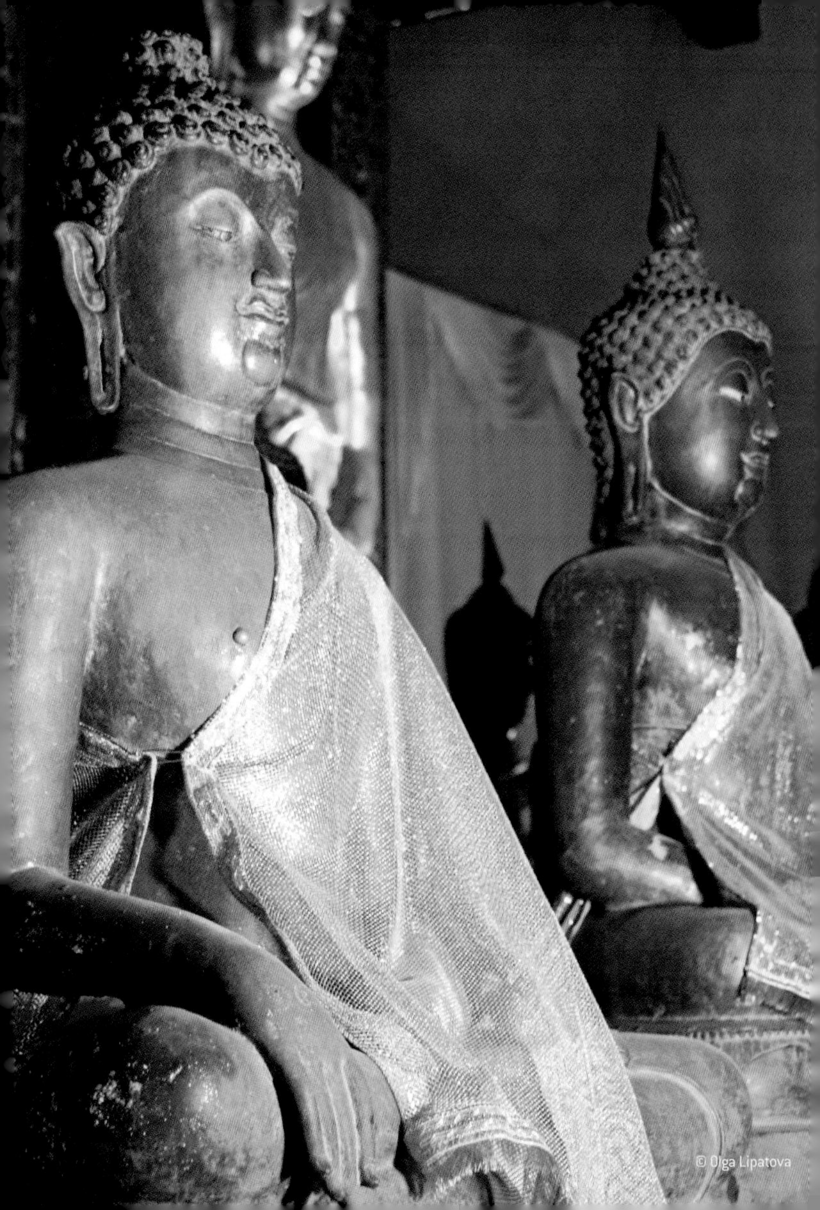

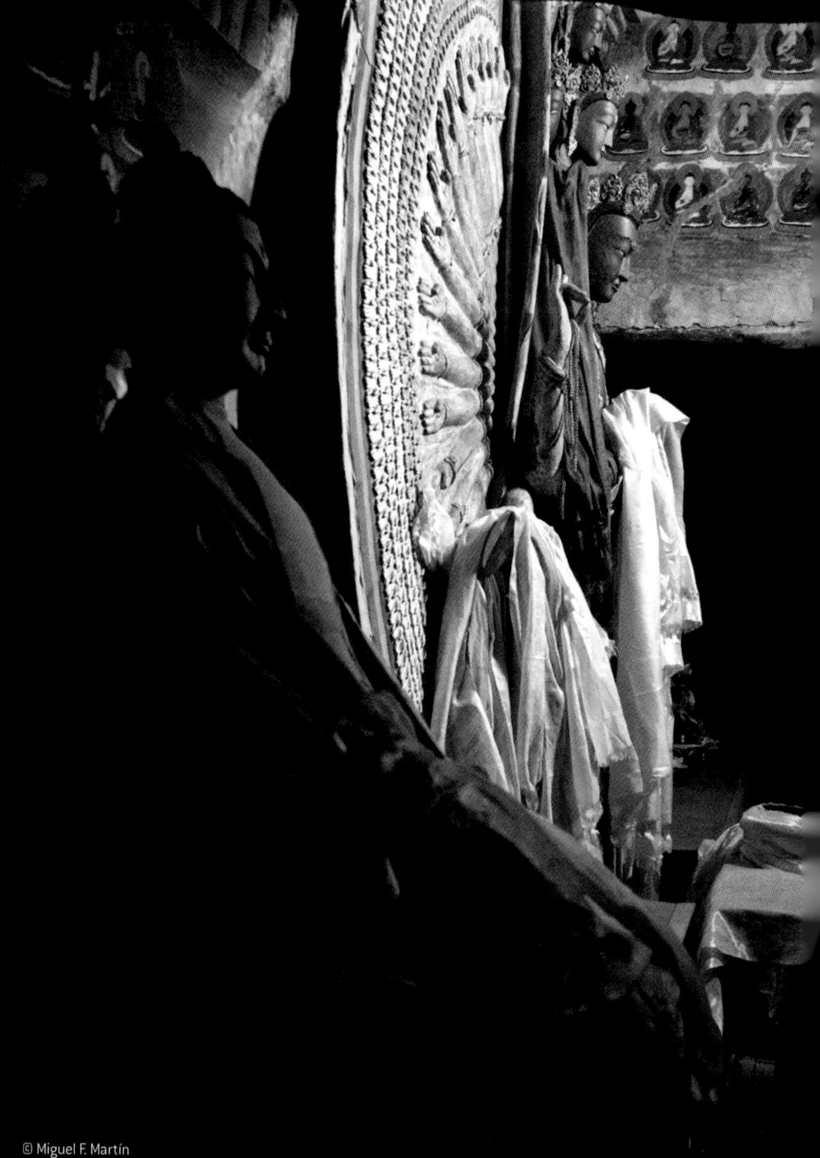

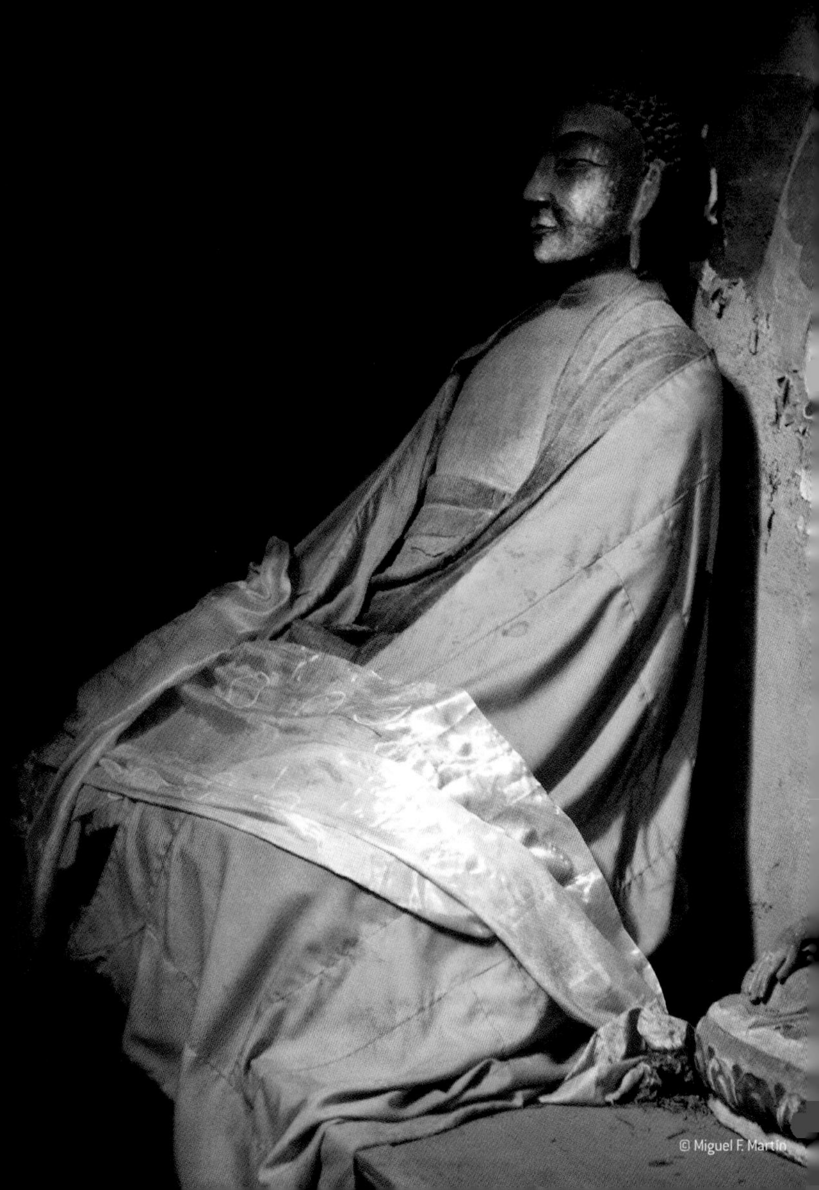

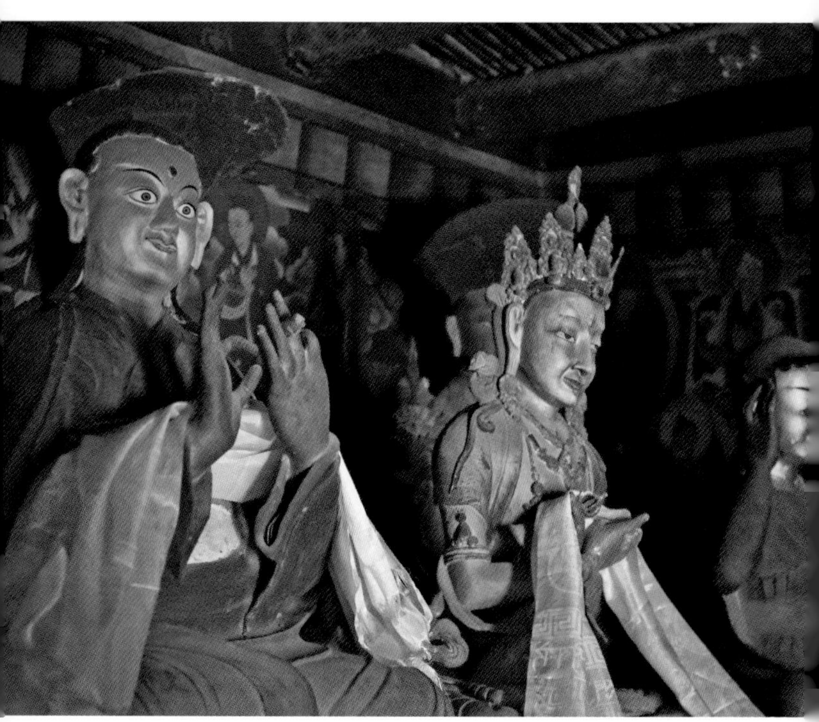

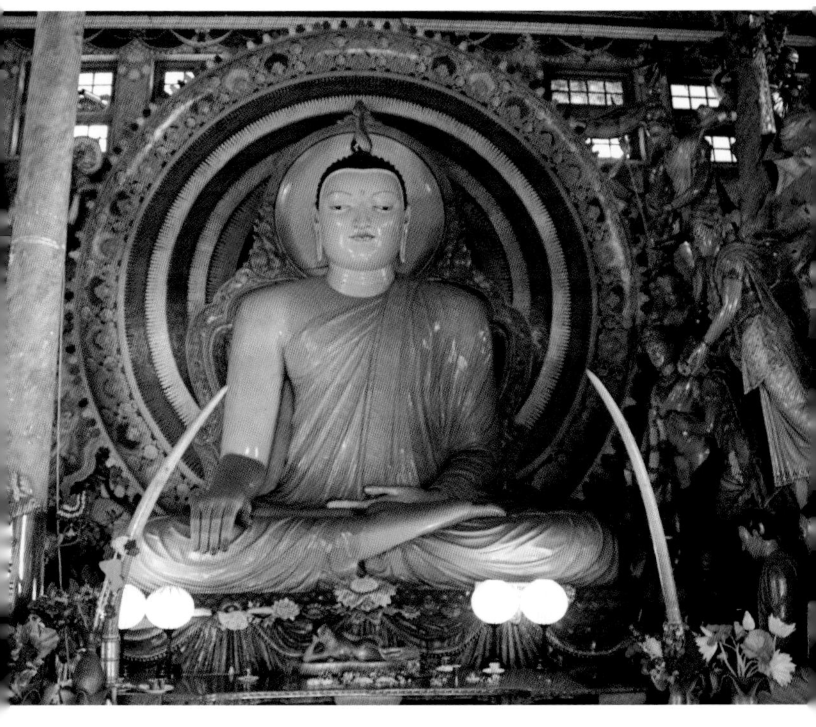

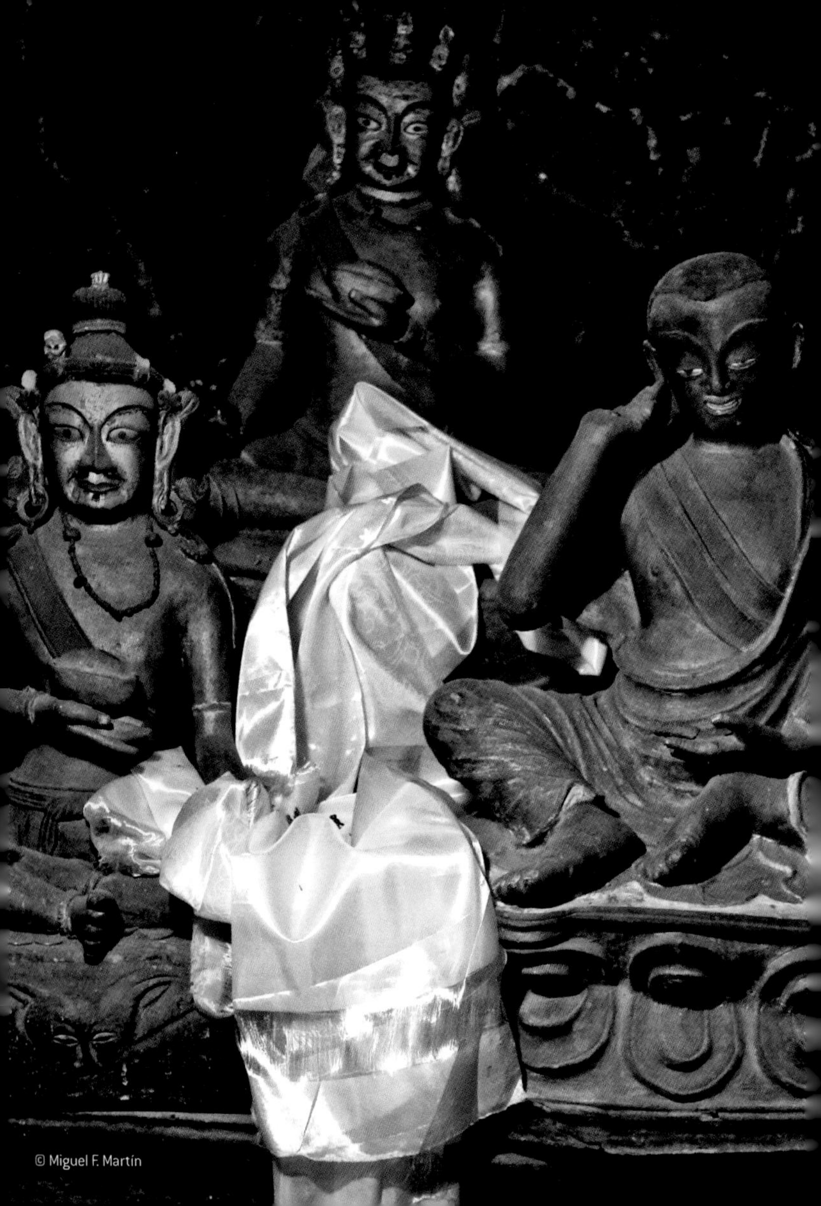

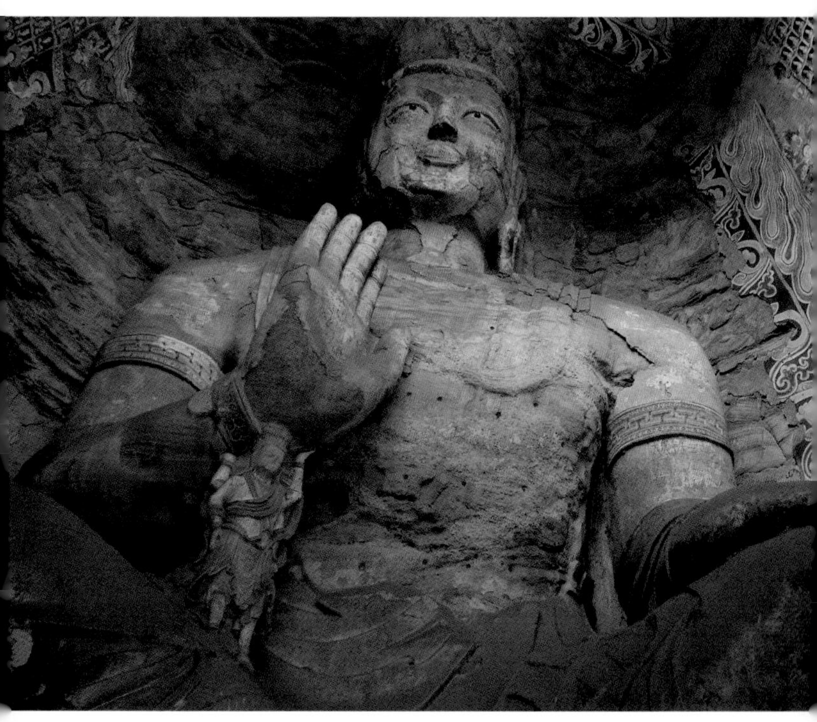

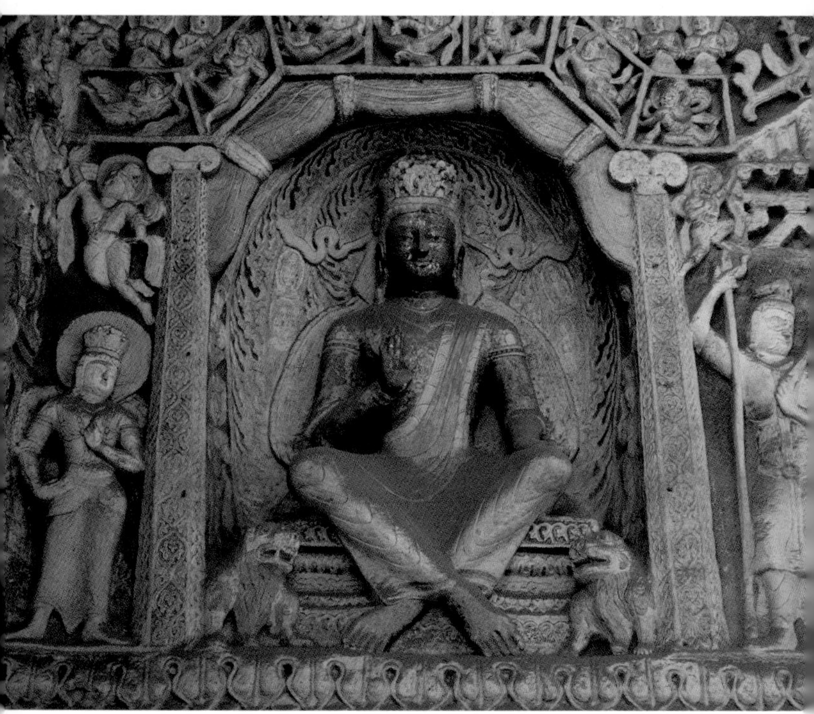

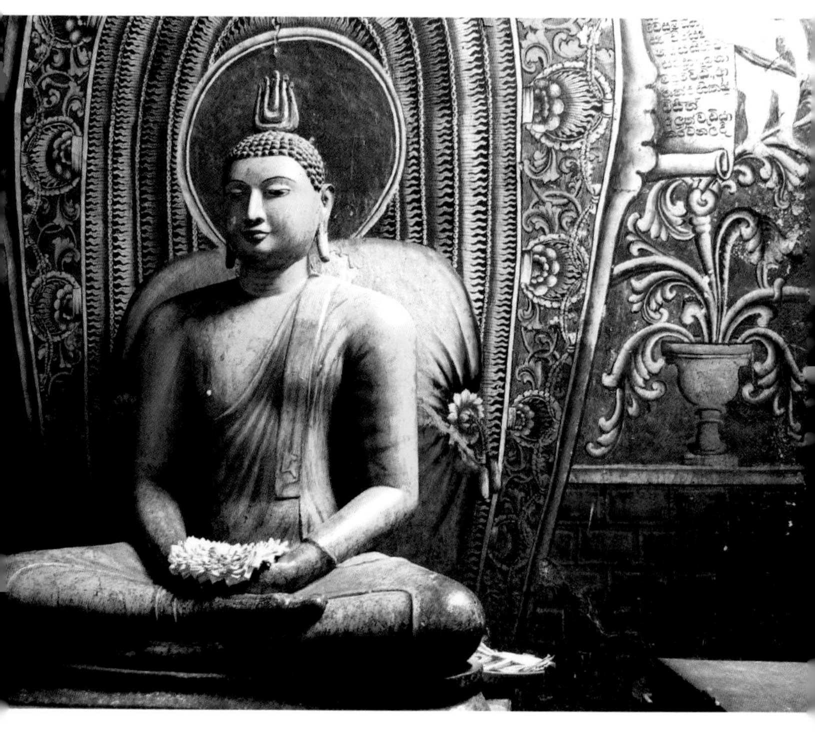

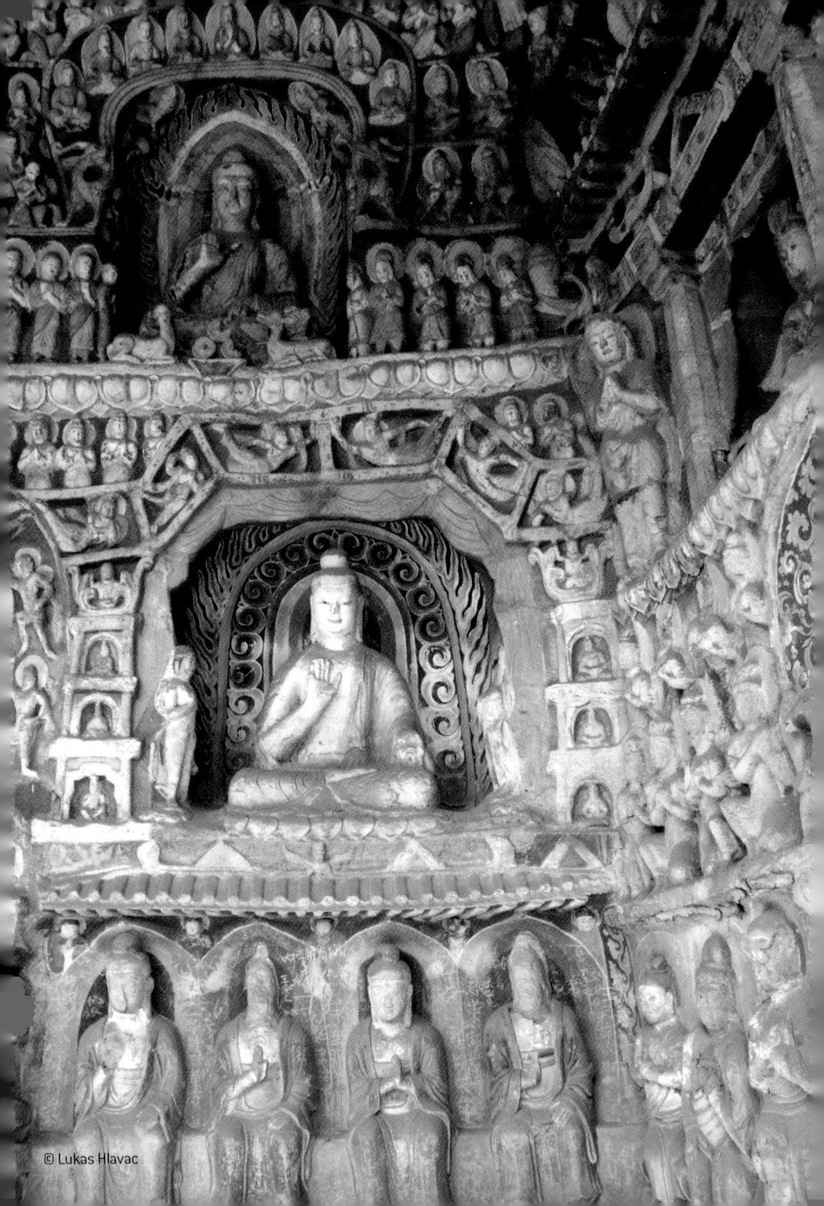

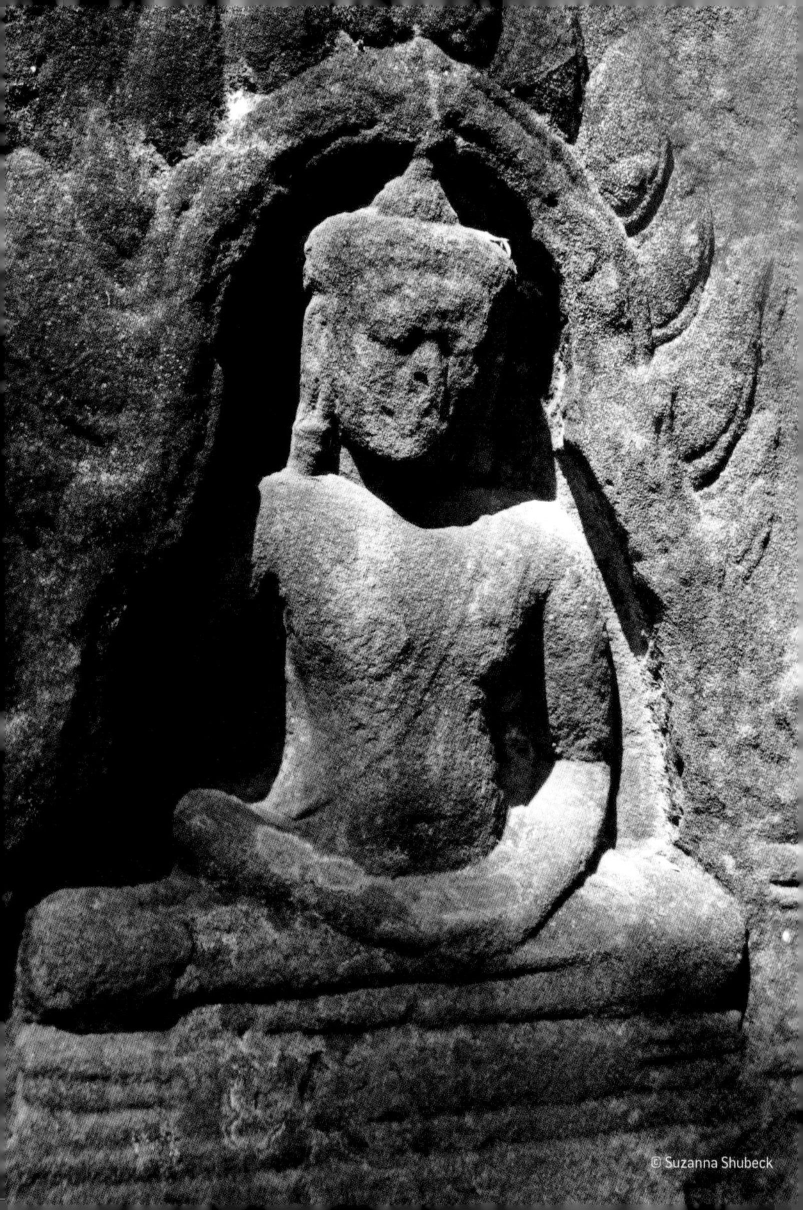

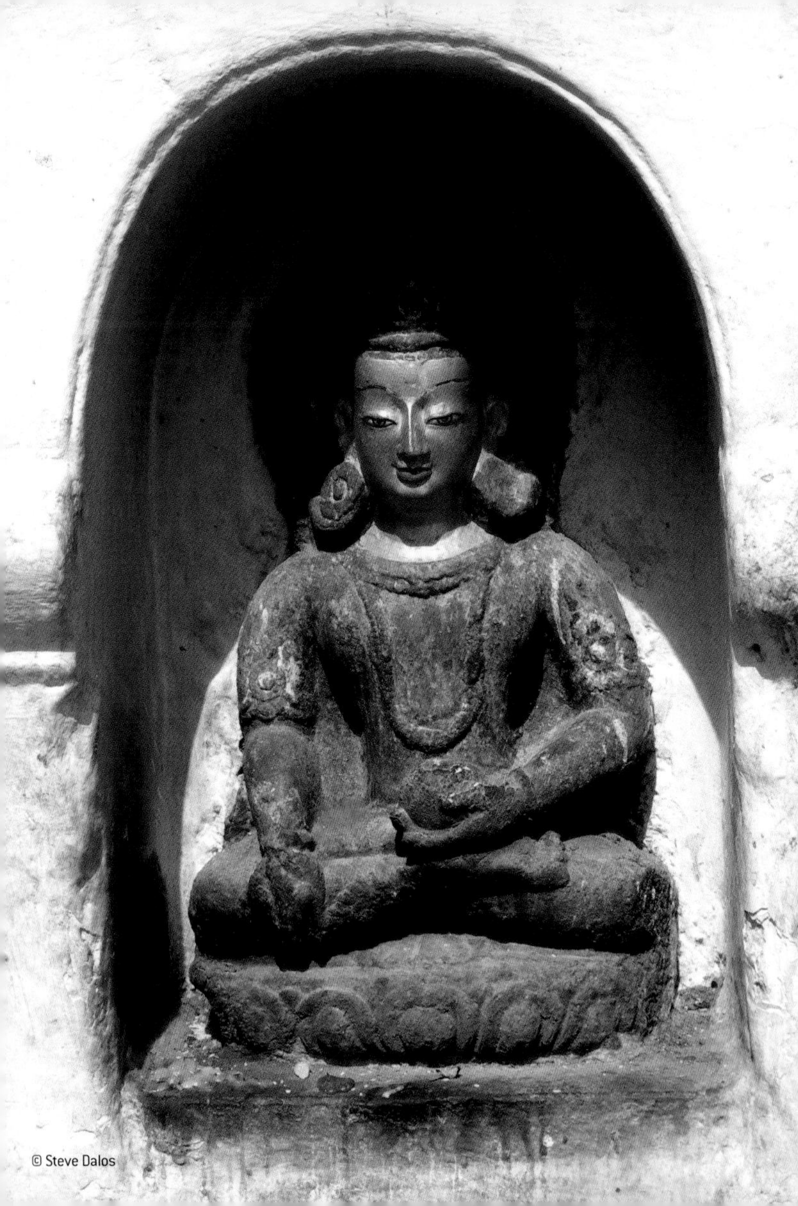

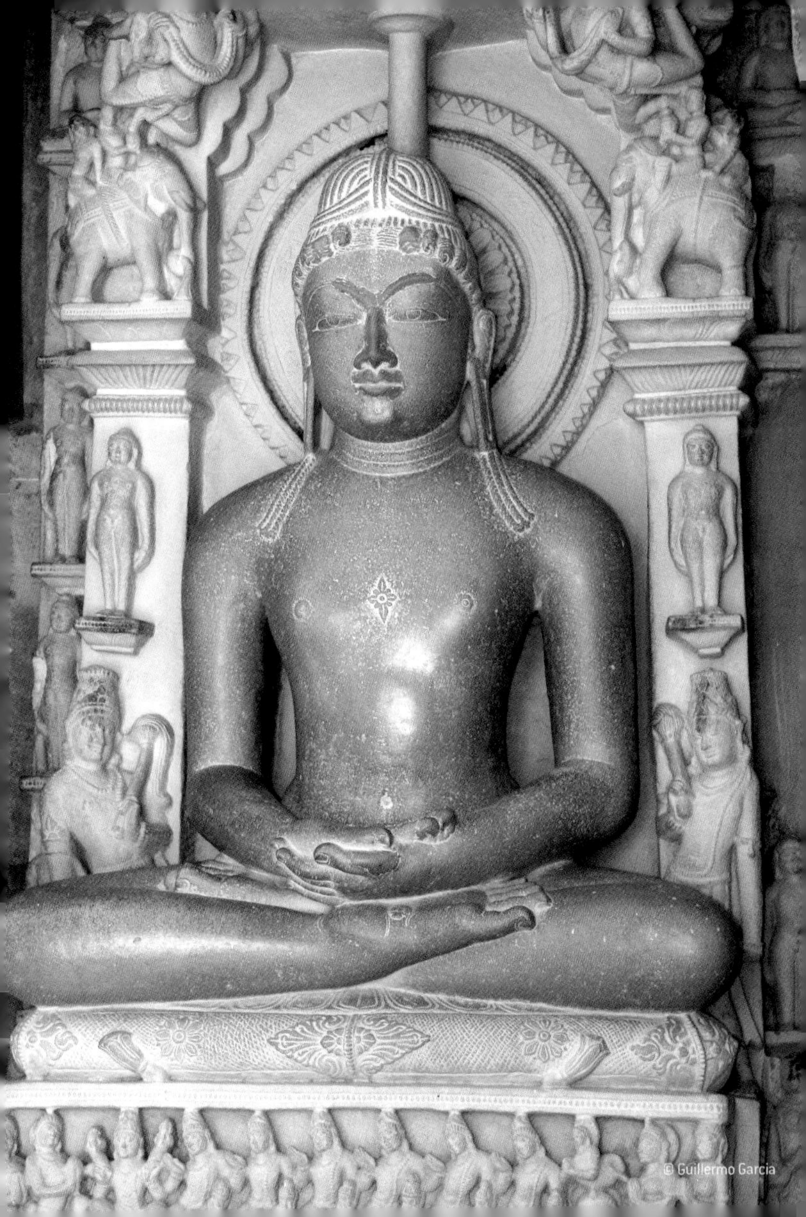

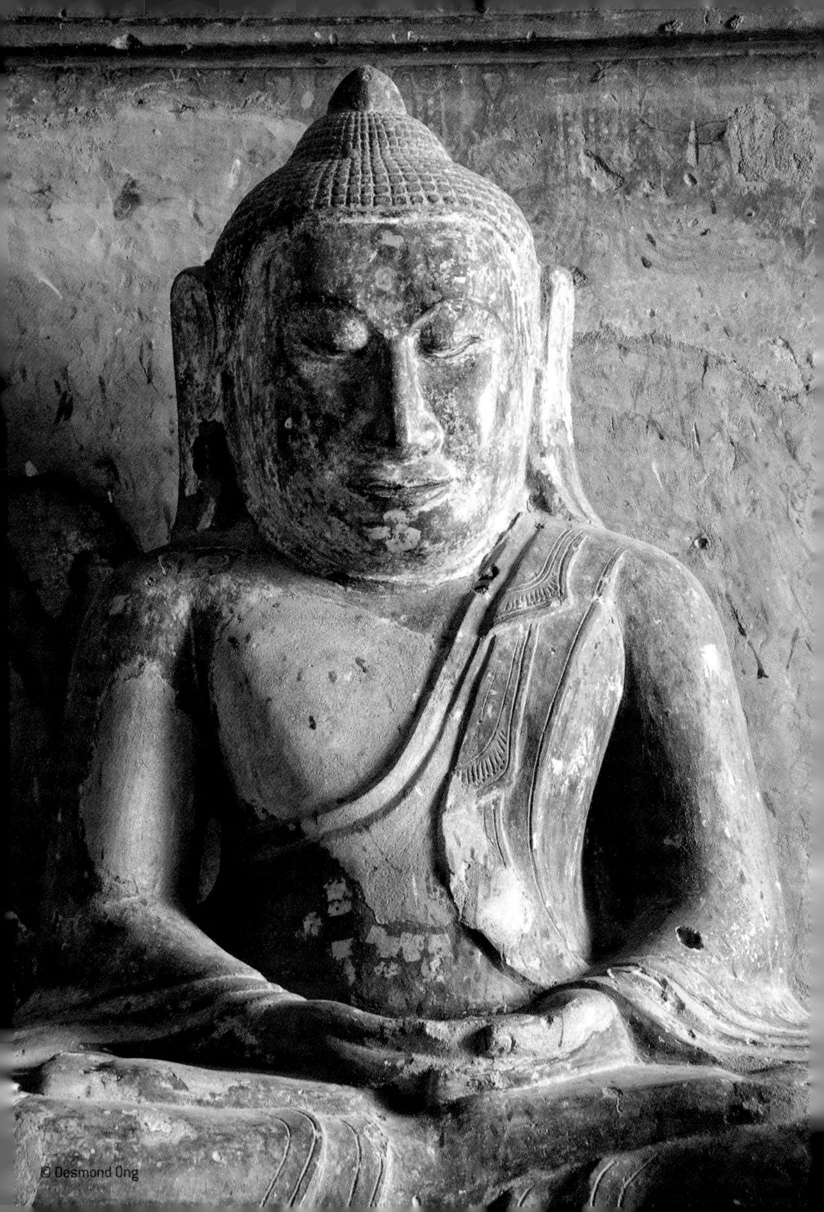

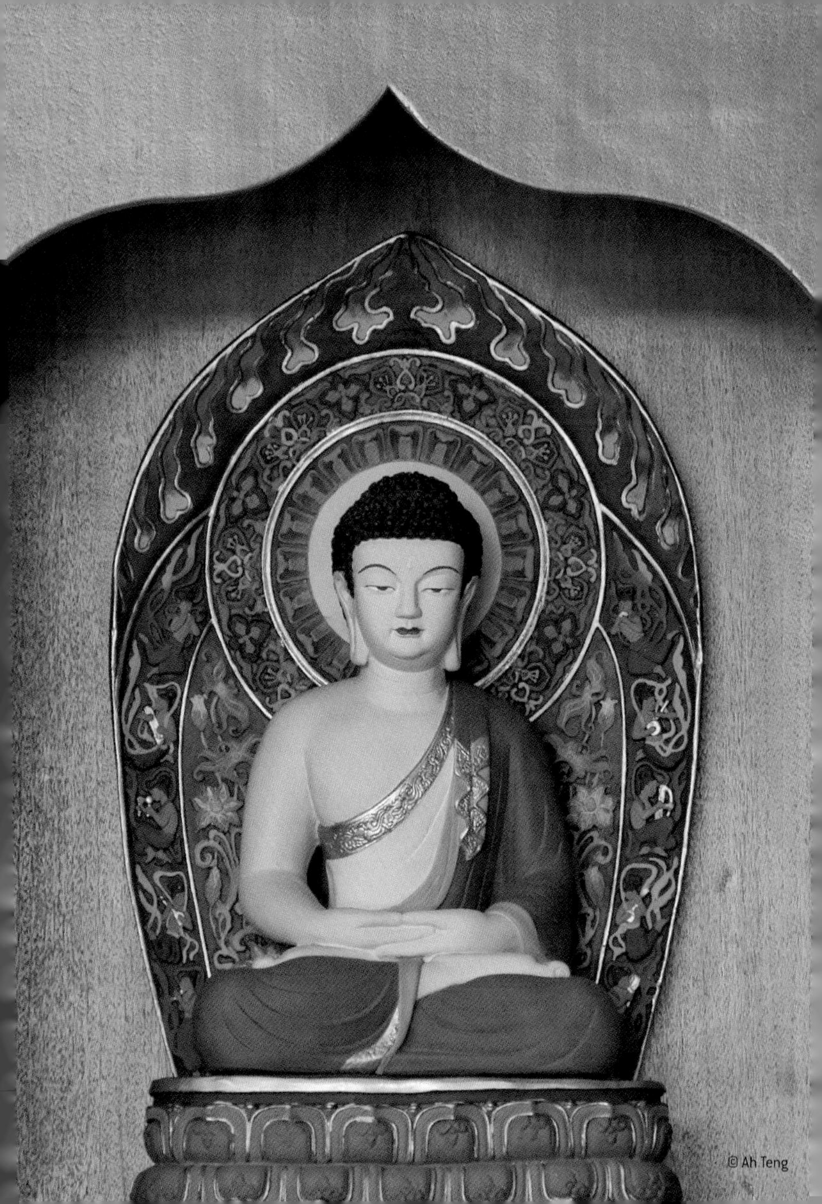

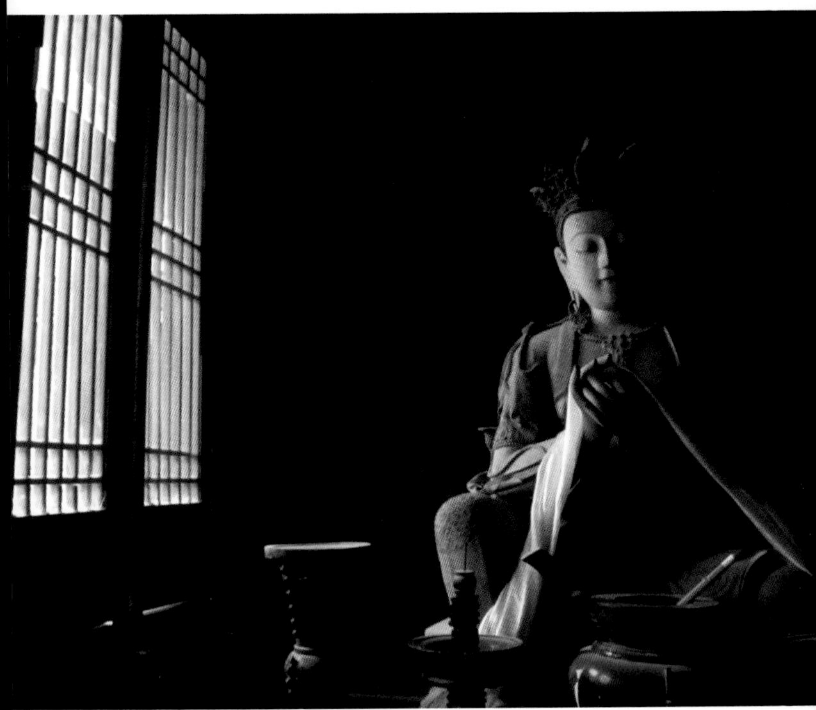

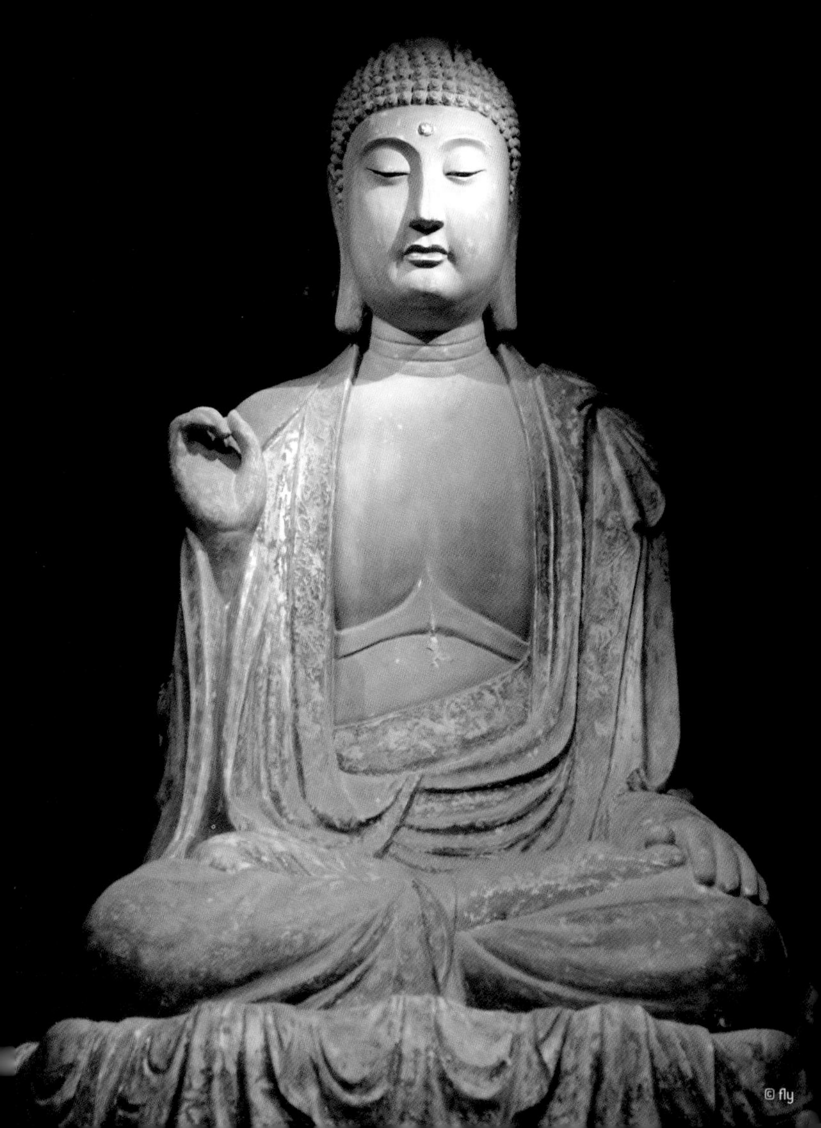
© fly

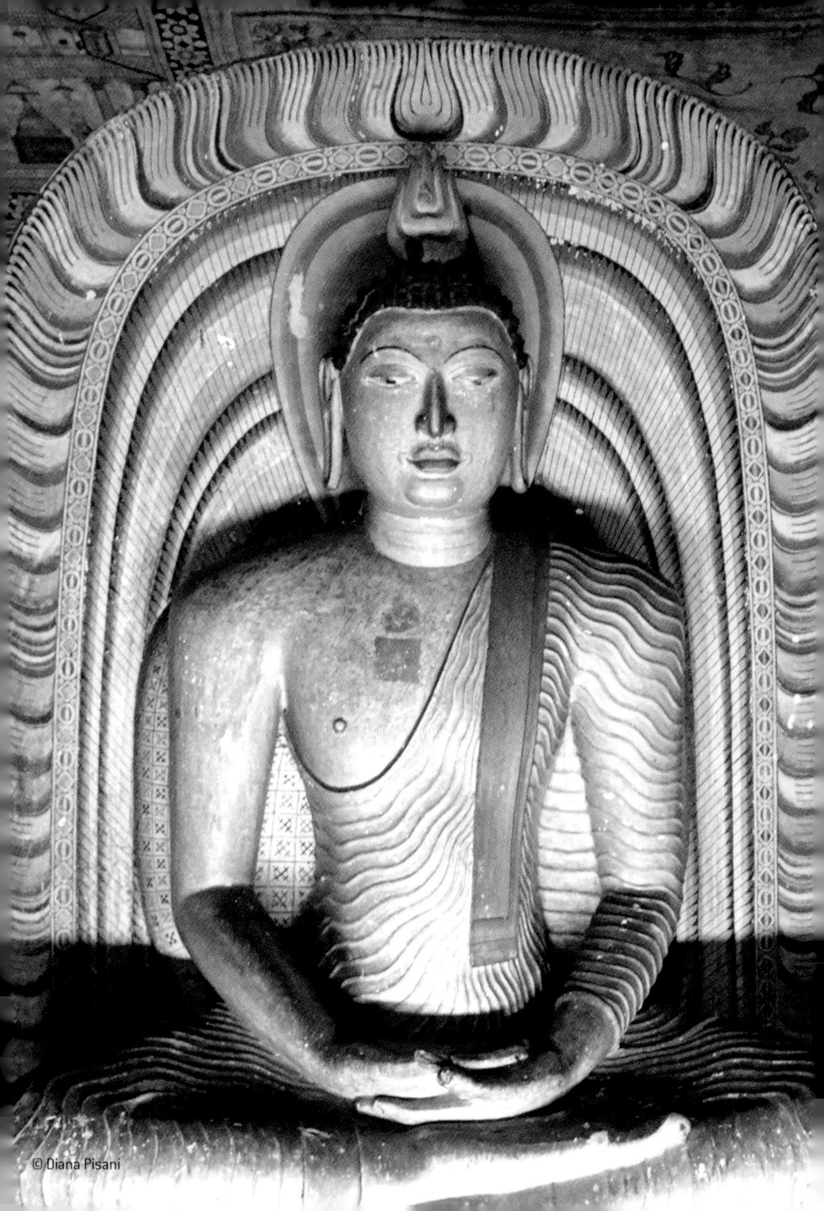

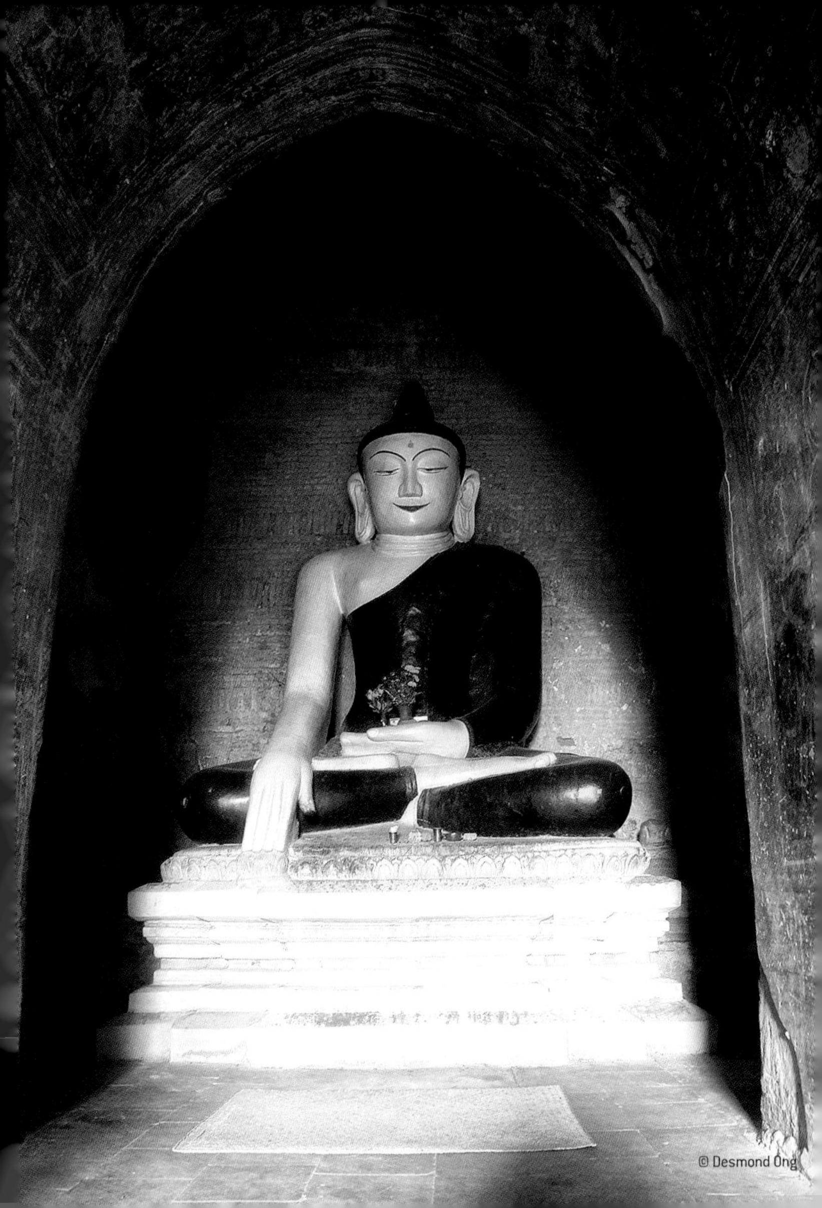

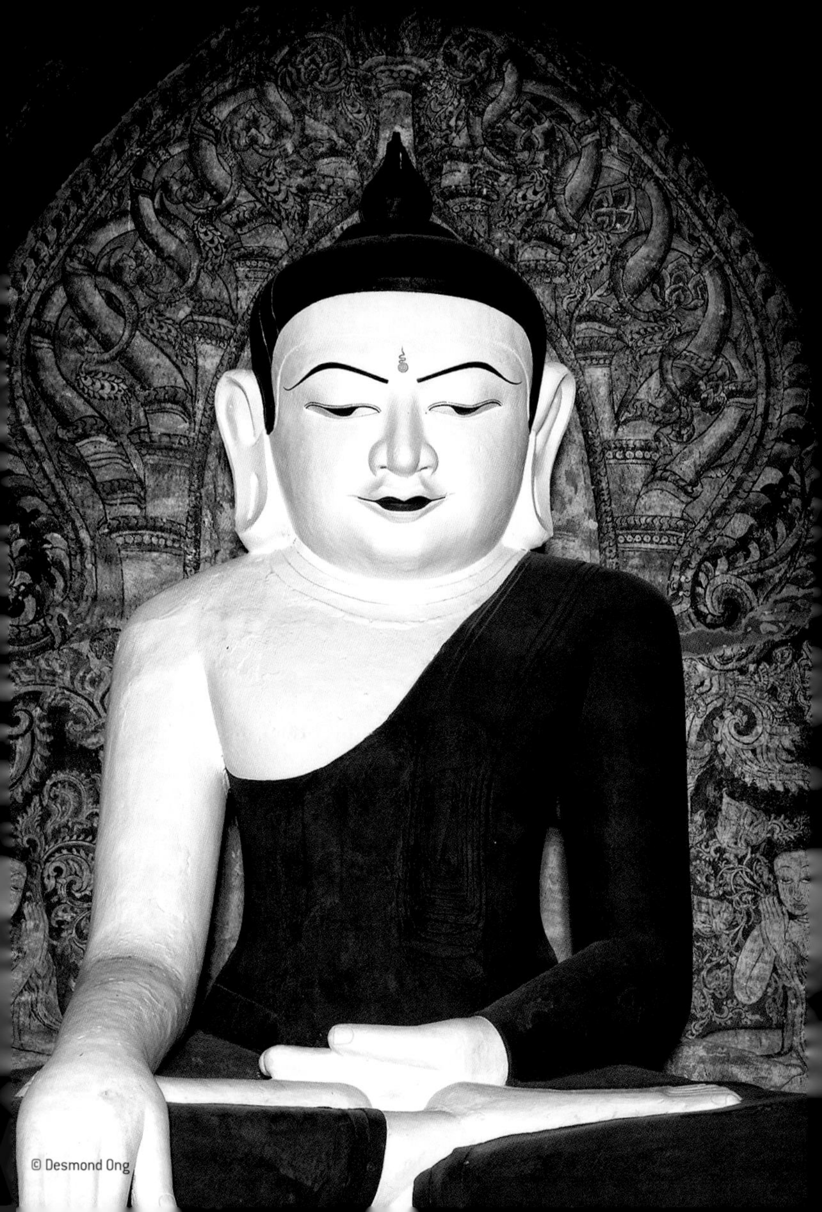

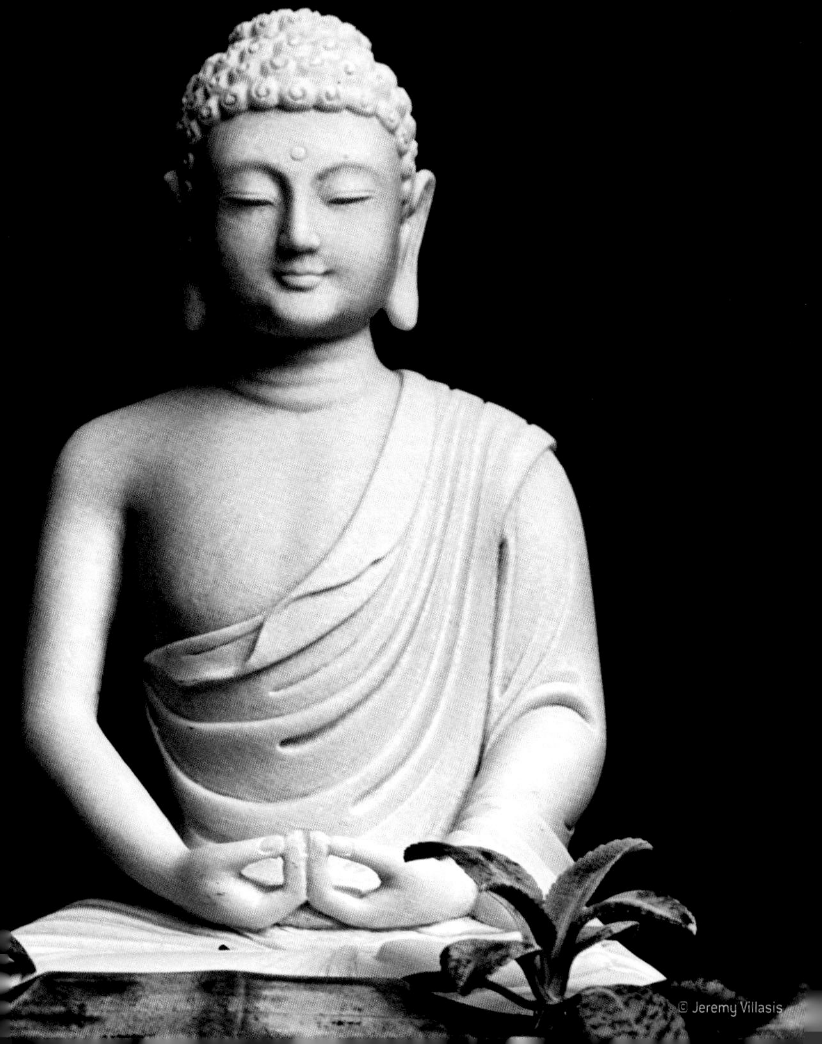

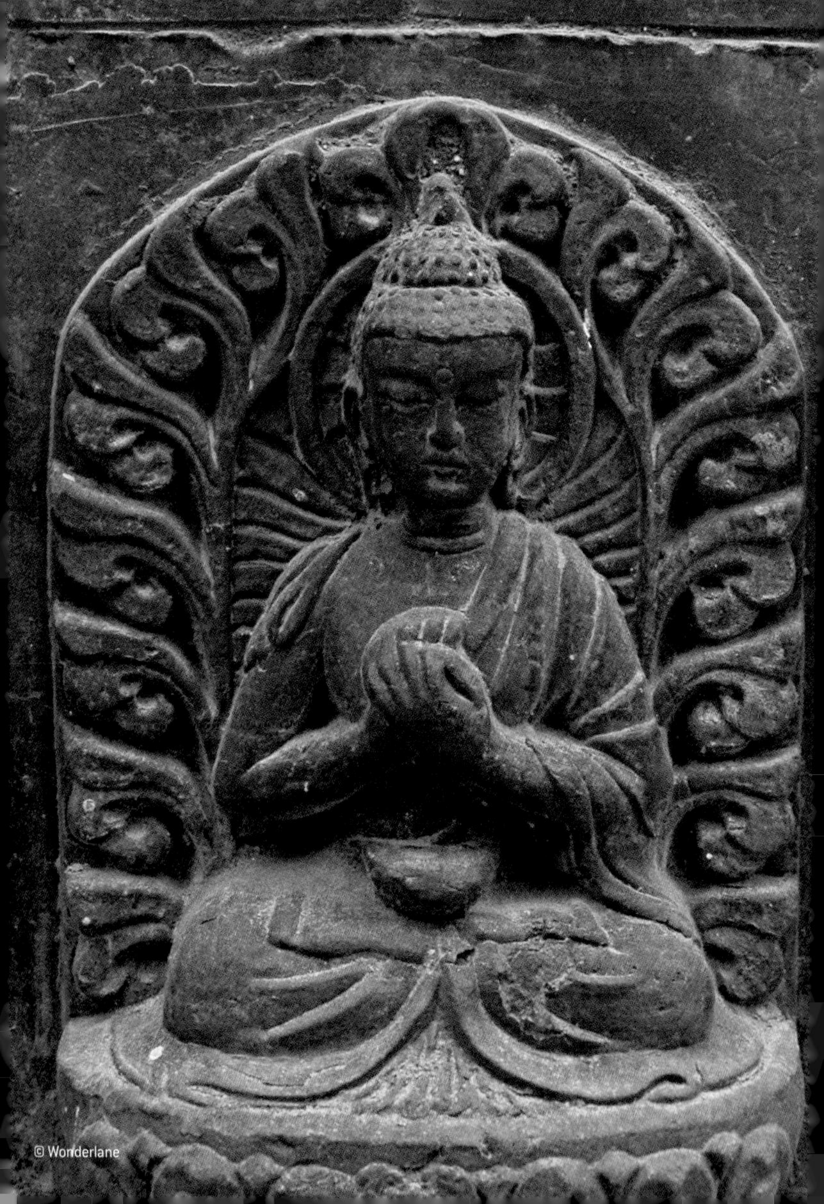

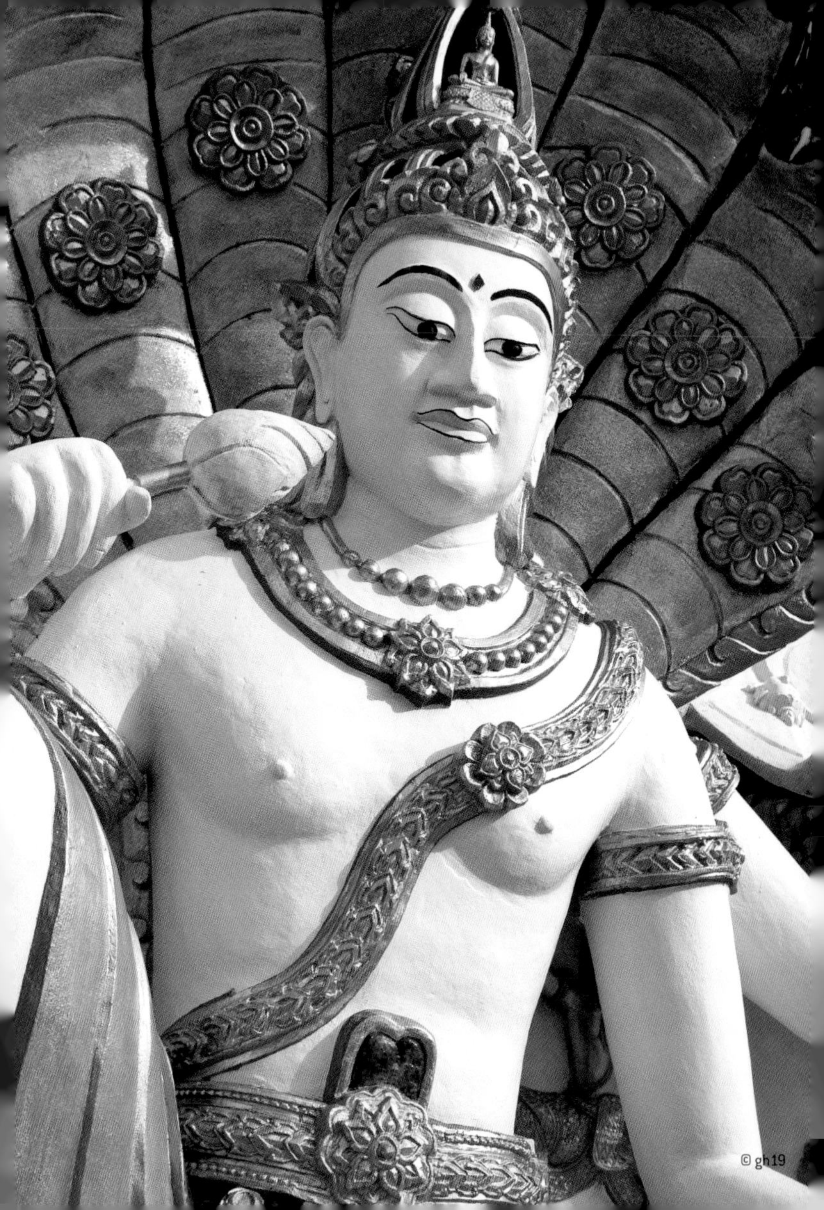
© gh19

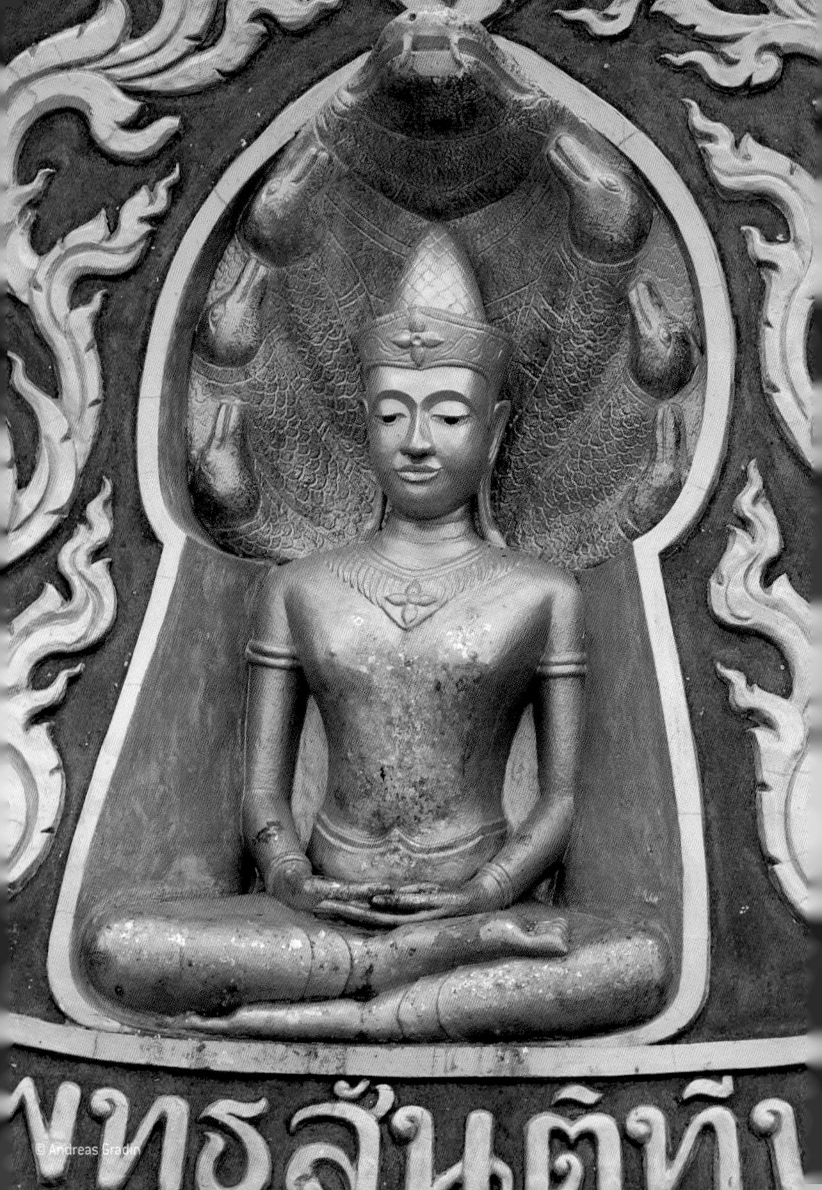

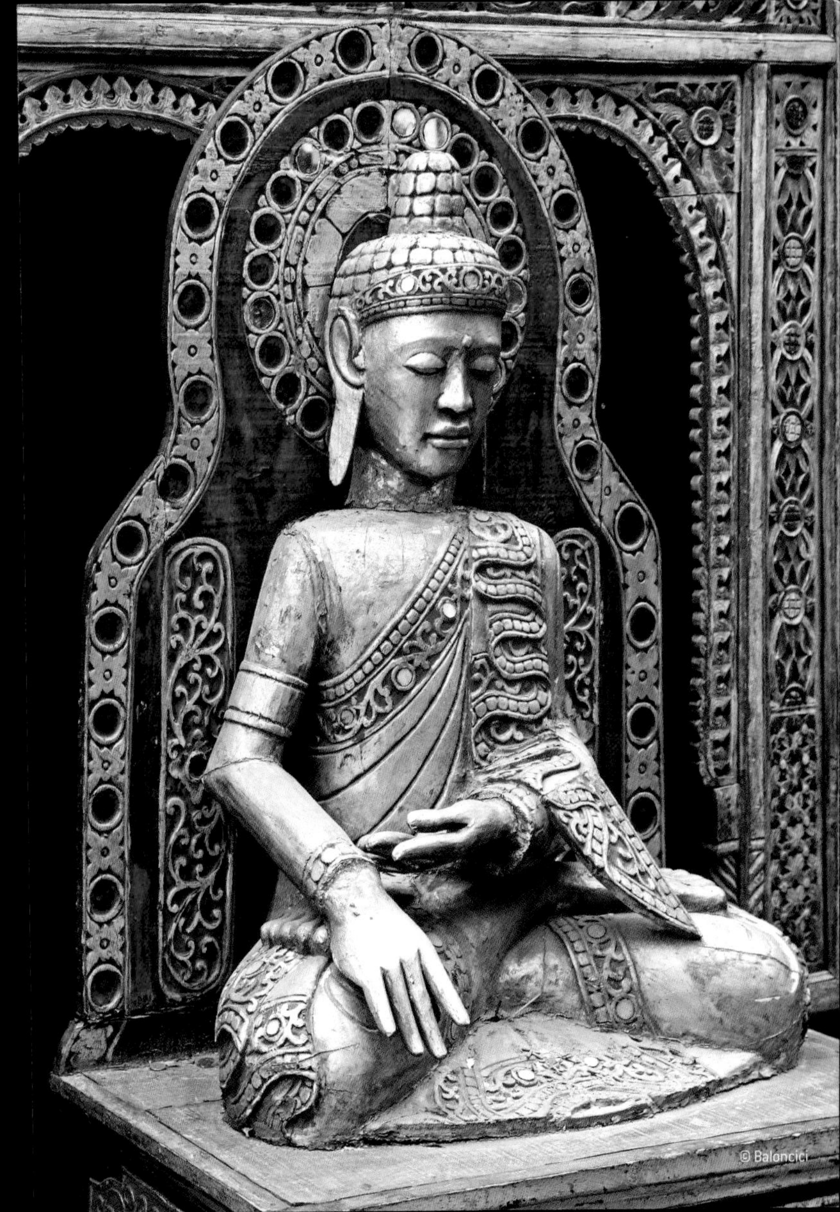
© Baloncici

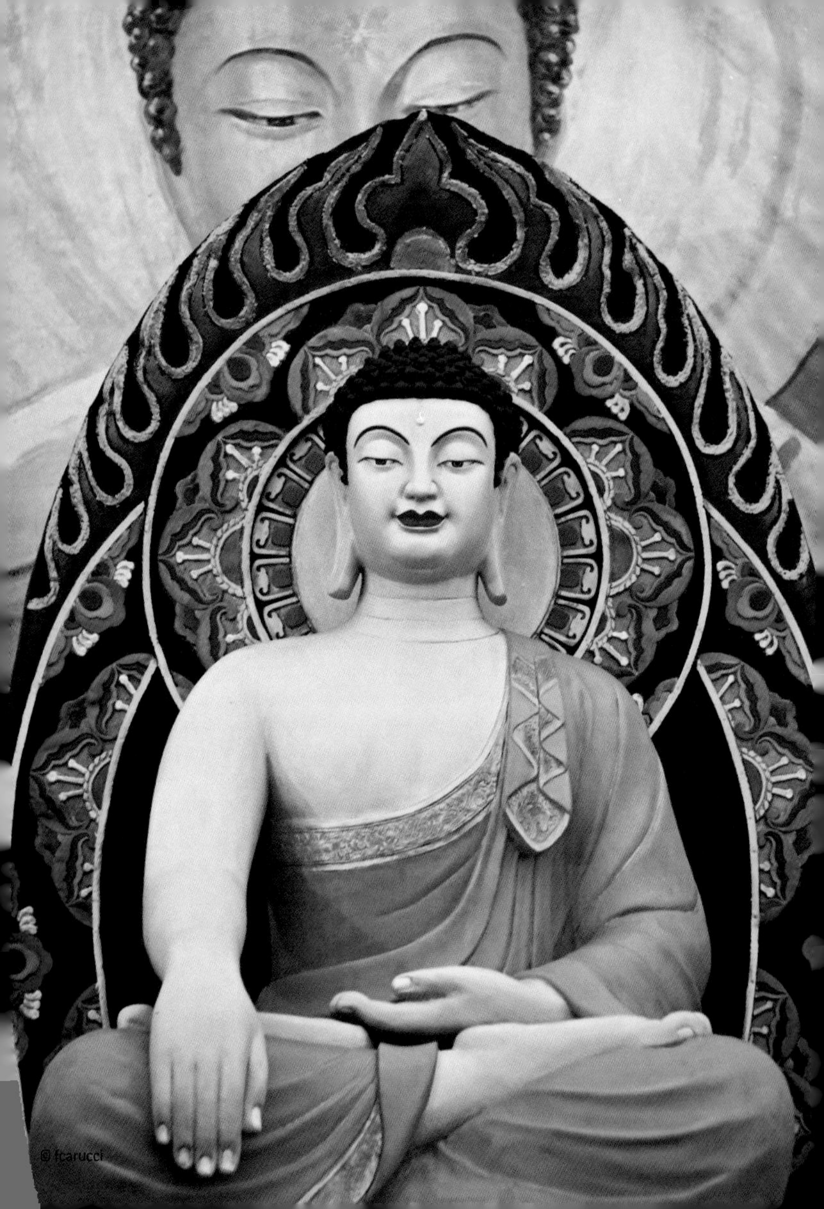
© fcarucci

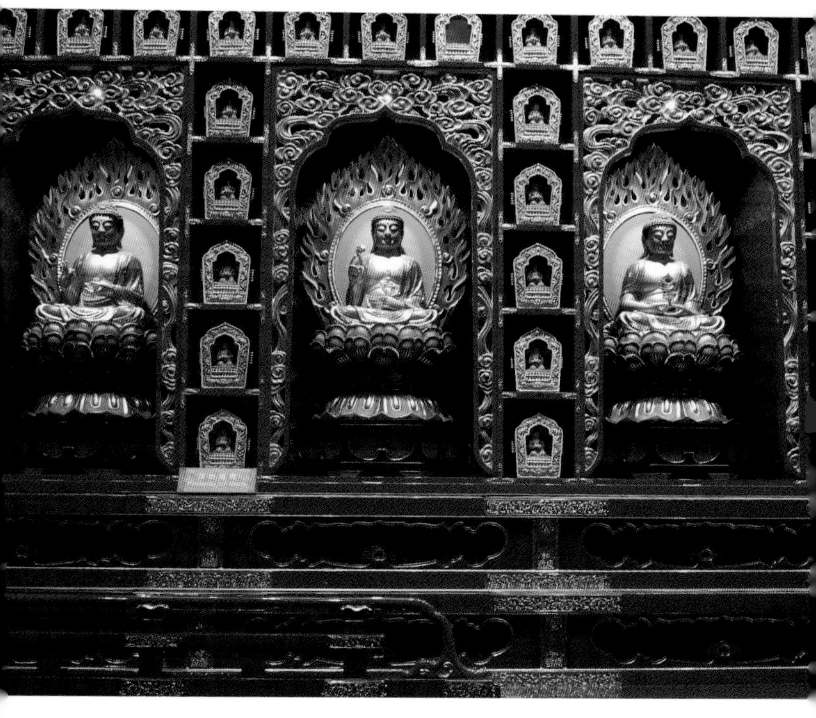

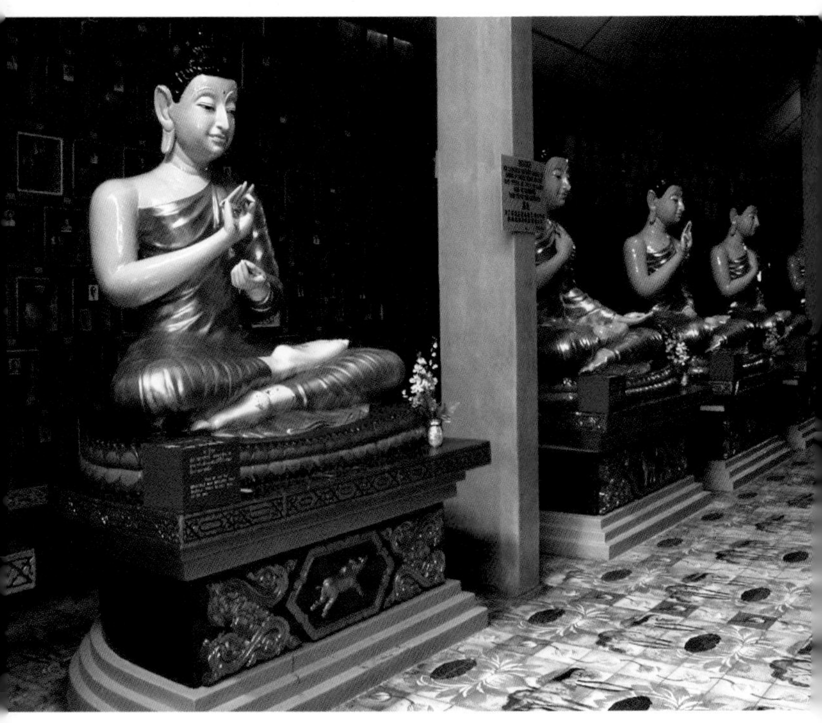

© Tan Yoke Liang

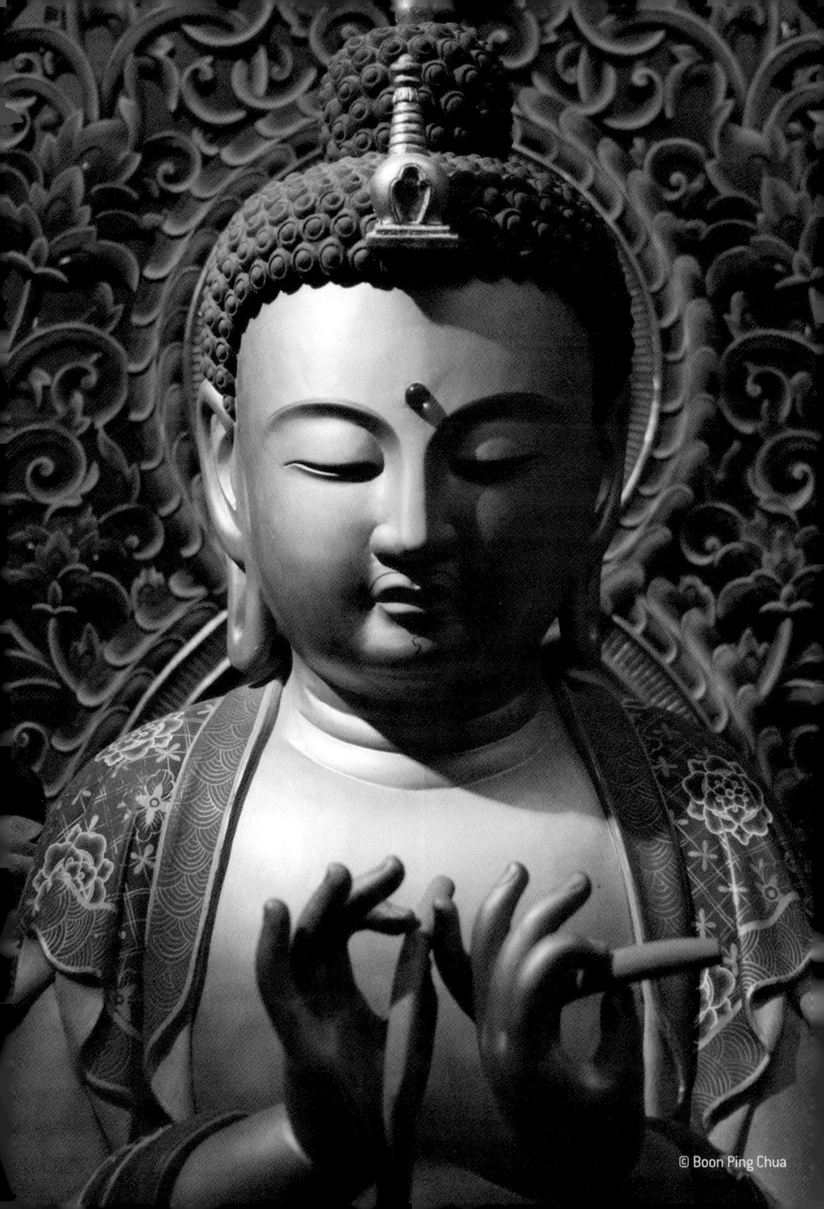

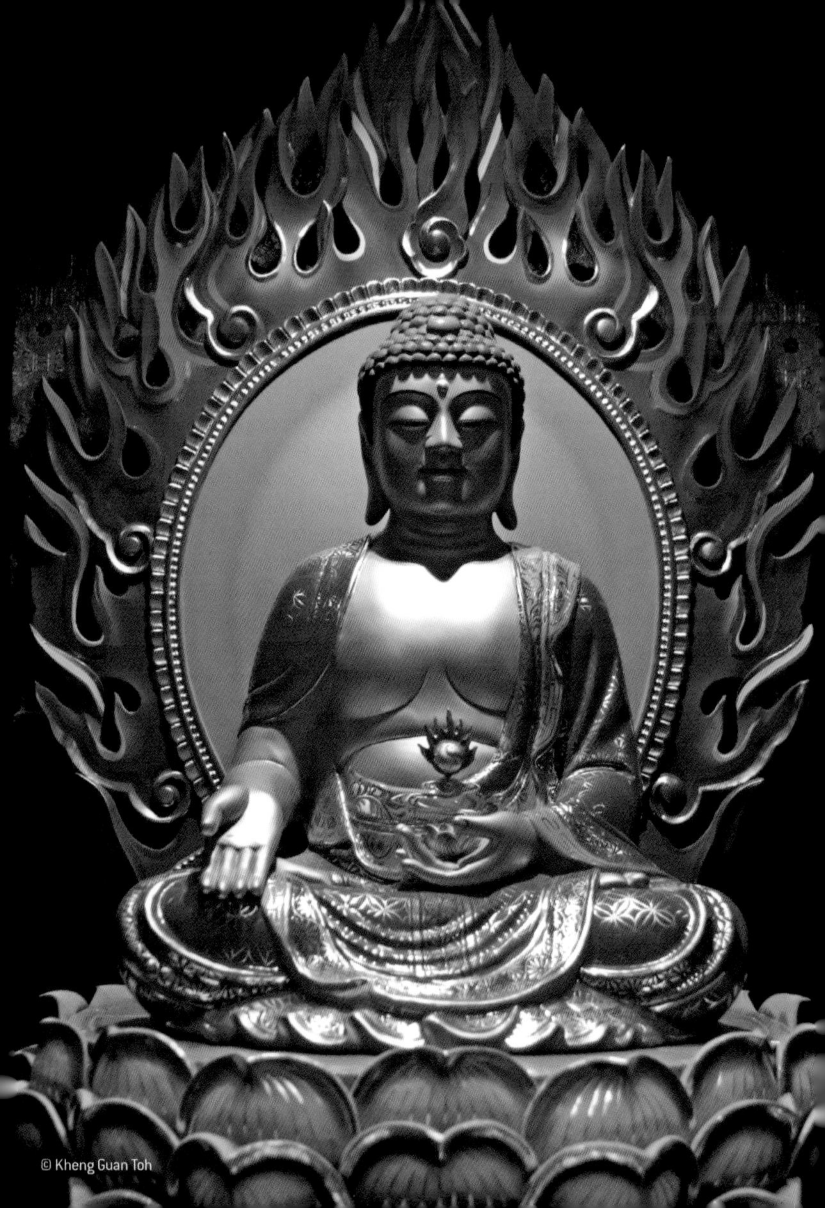

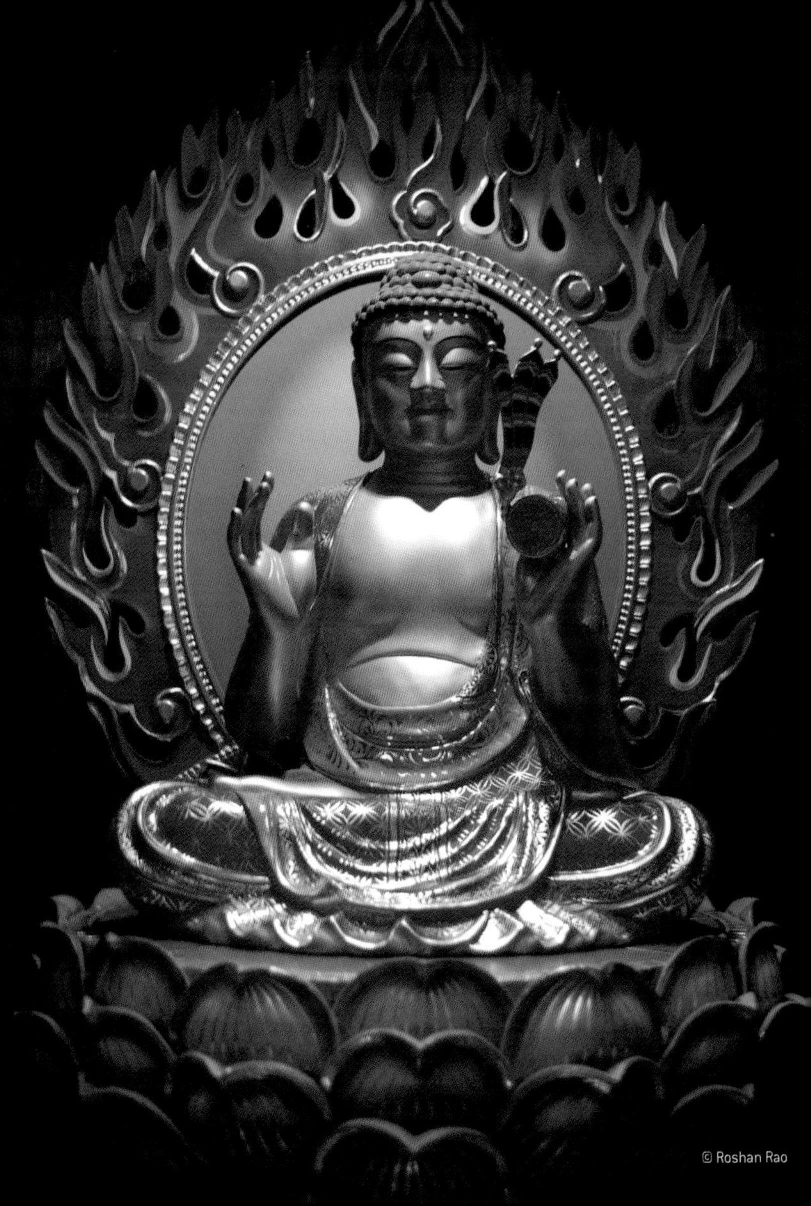

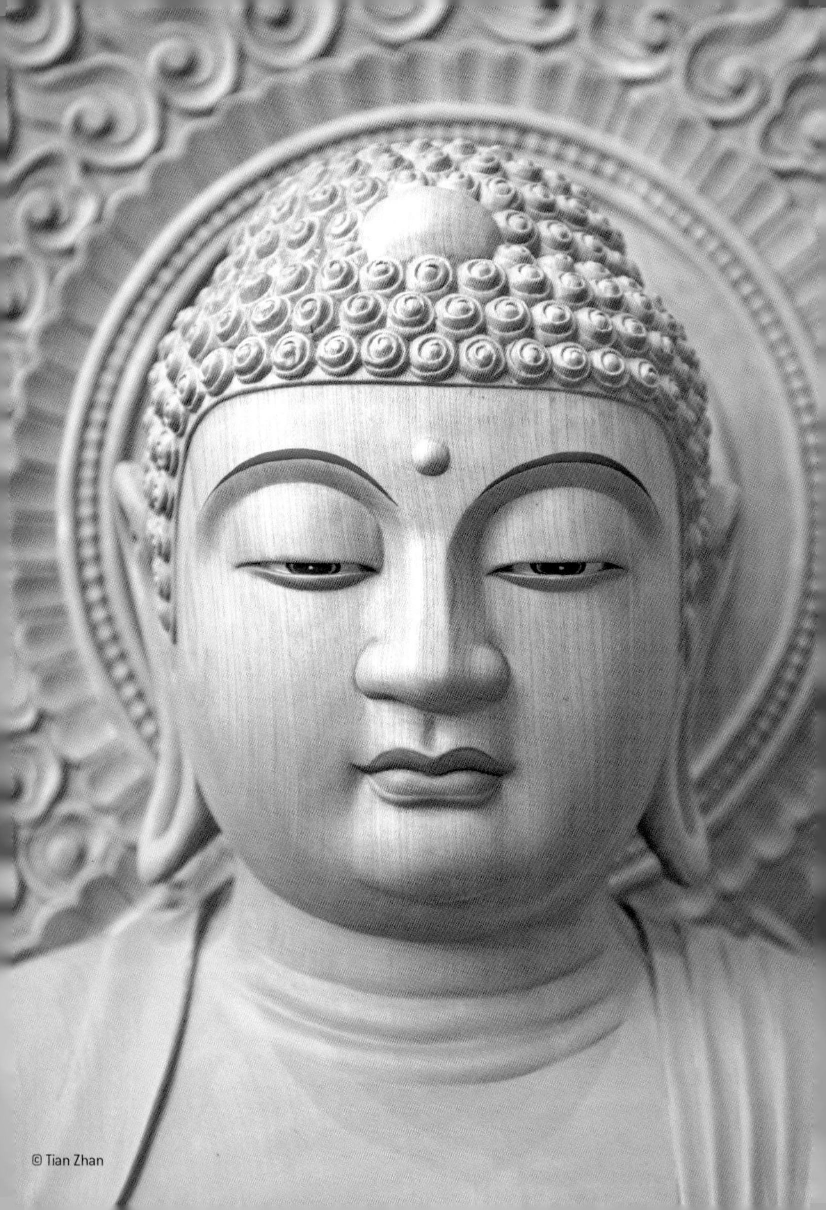

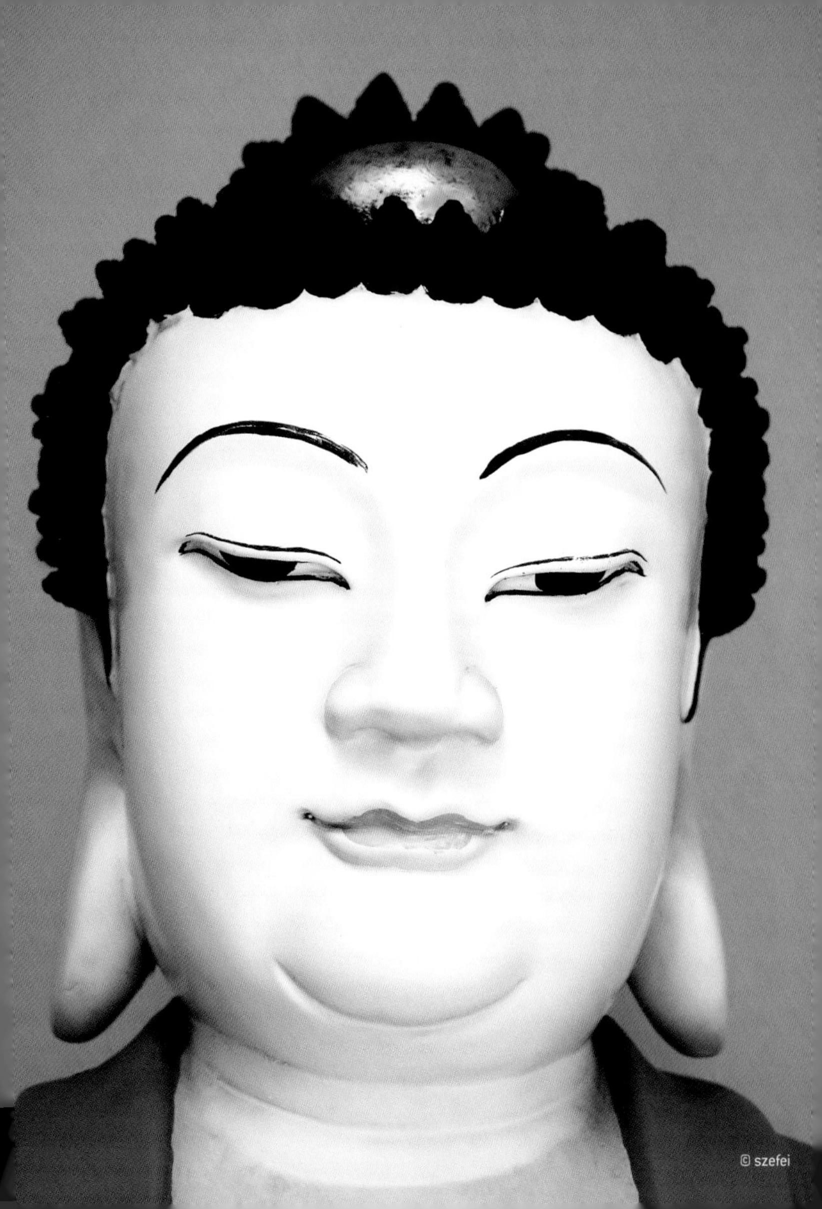

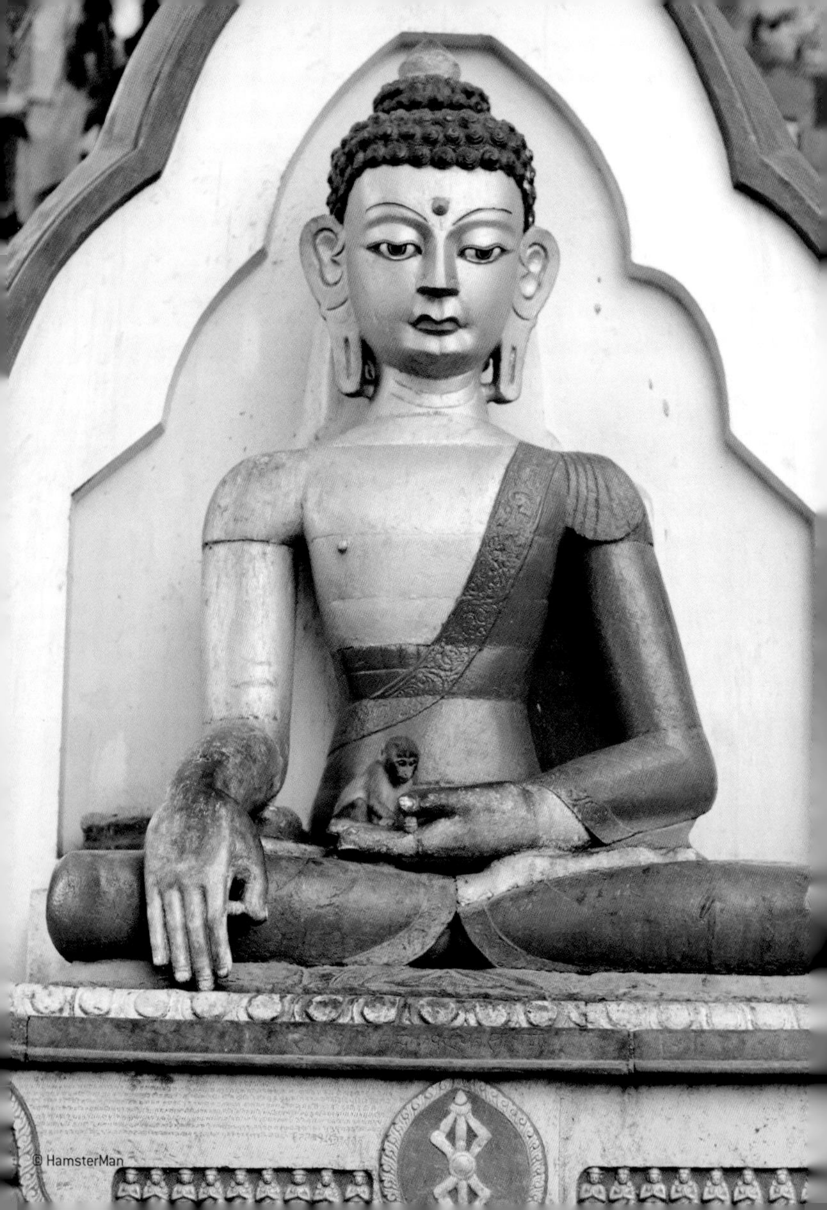

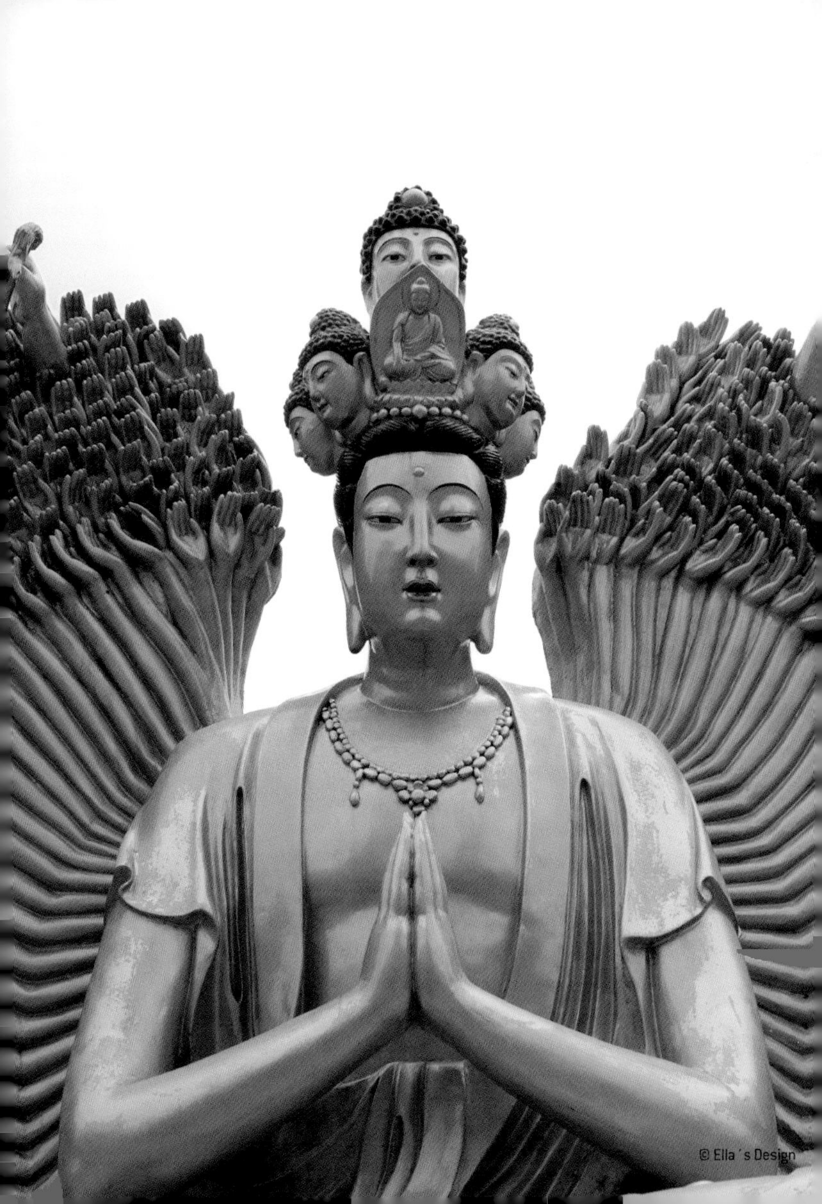
© Ella´s Design

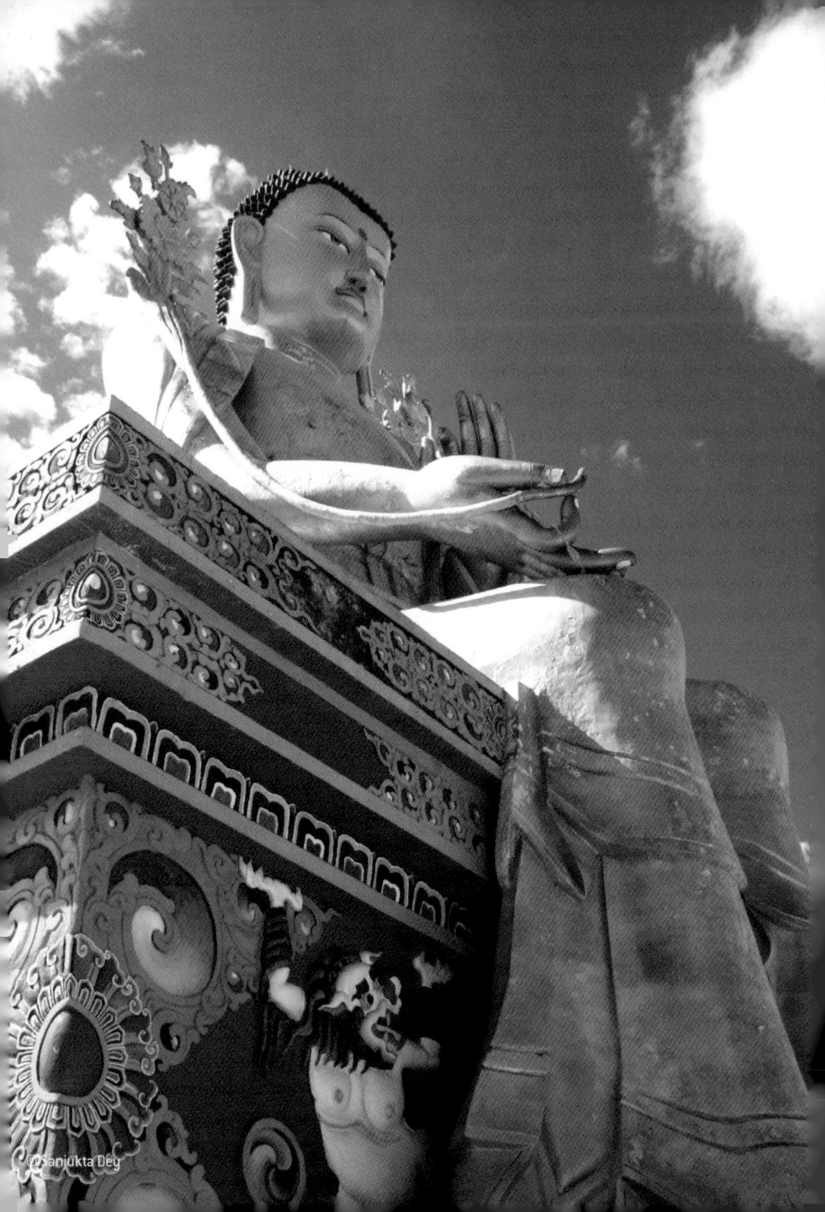
©Sanjukta Dey

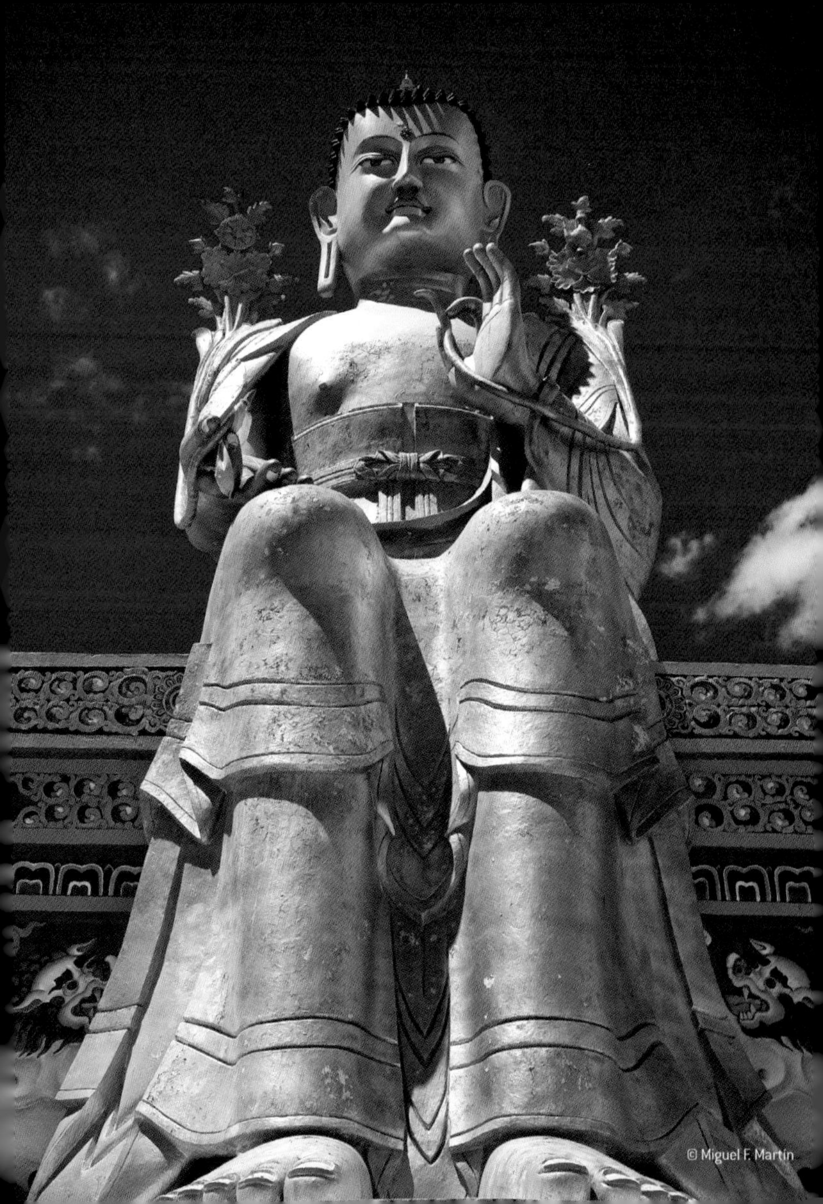

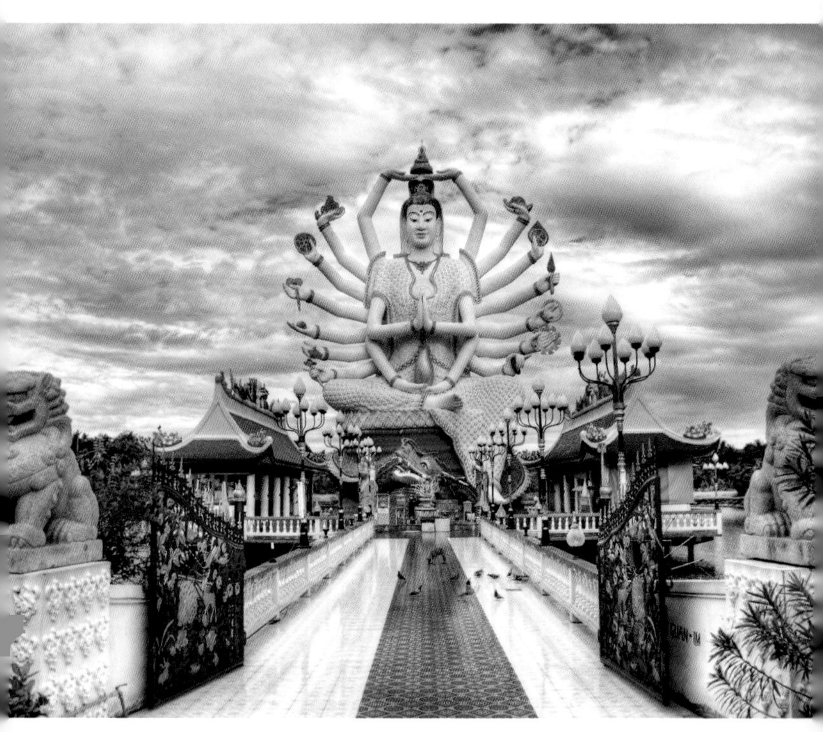

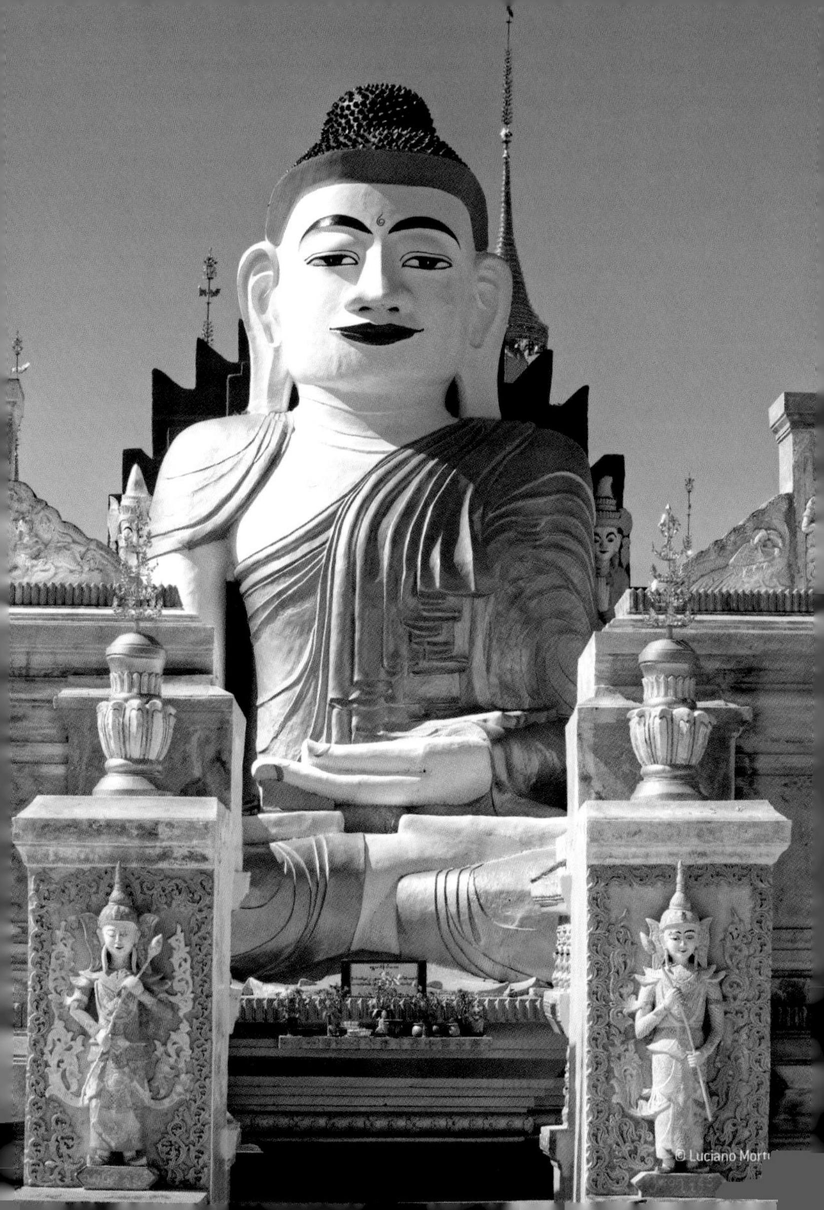
© Luciano Mort

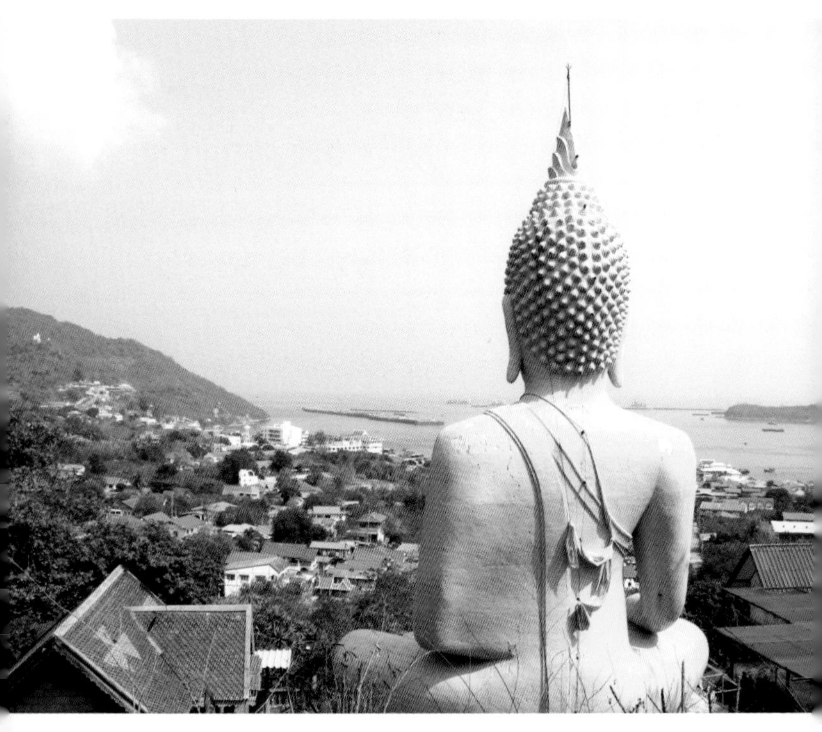

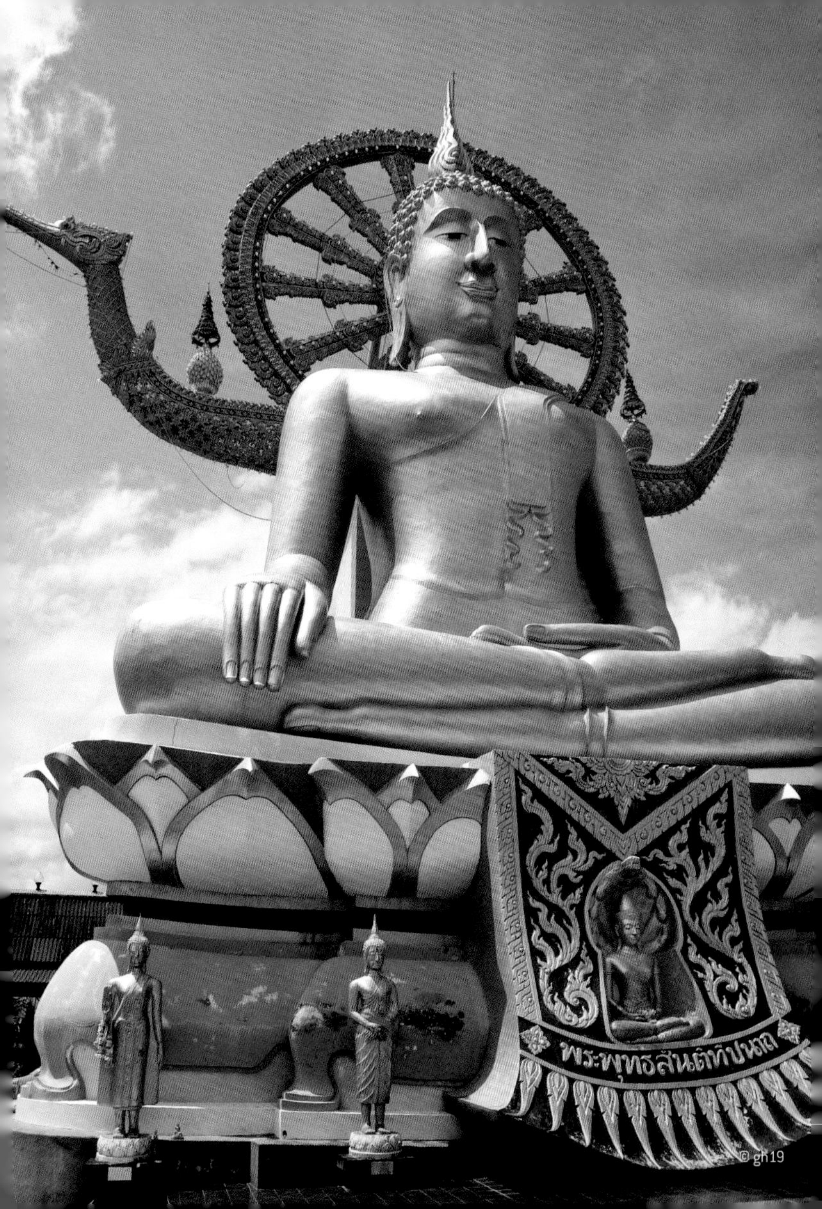
พระพุทธสันติทิปนฤ
© gh19

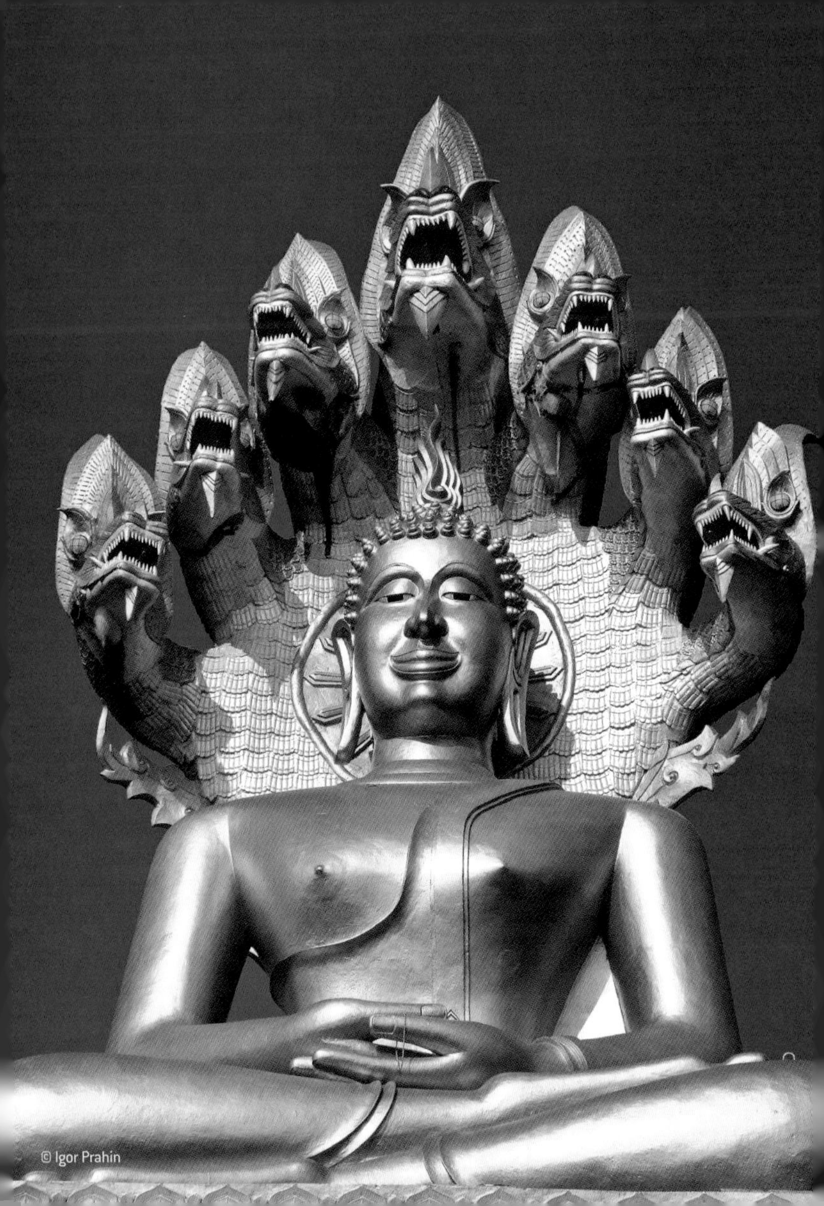

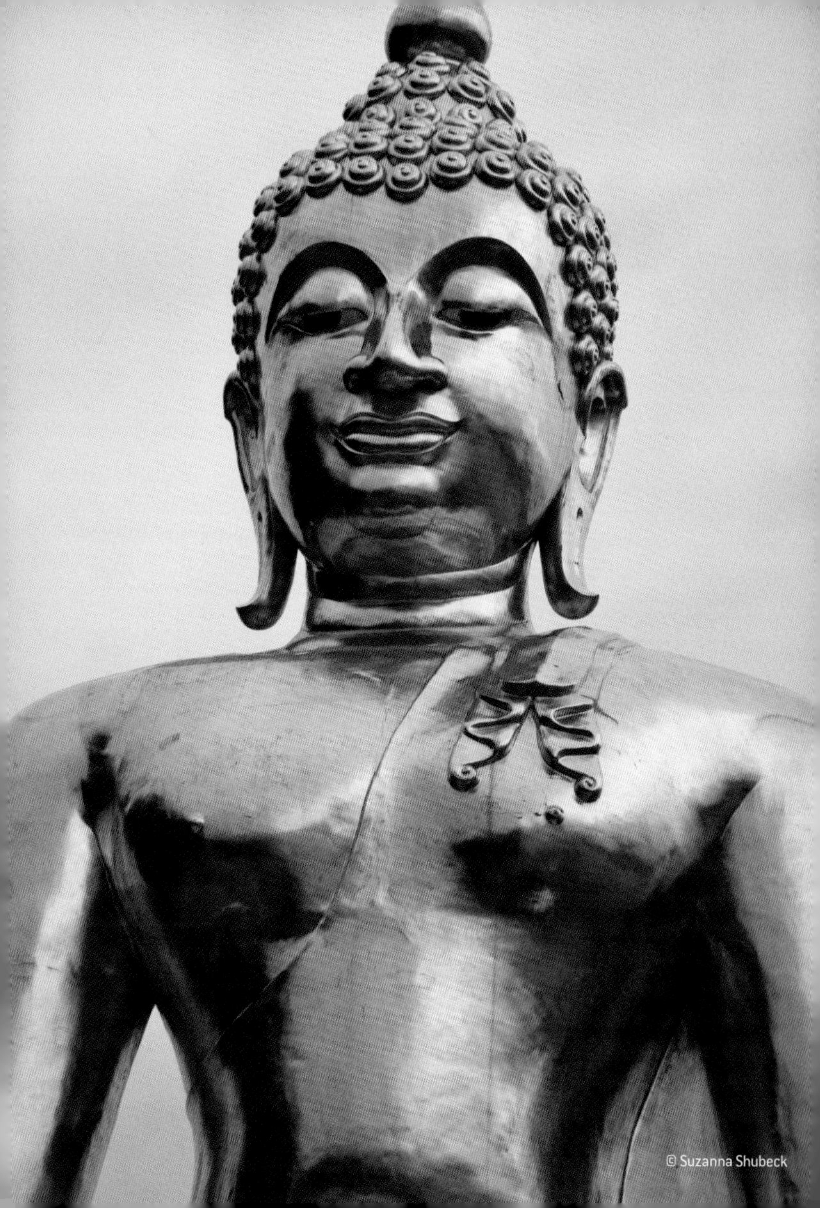

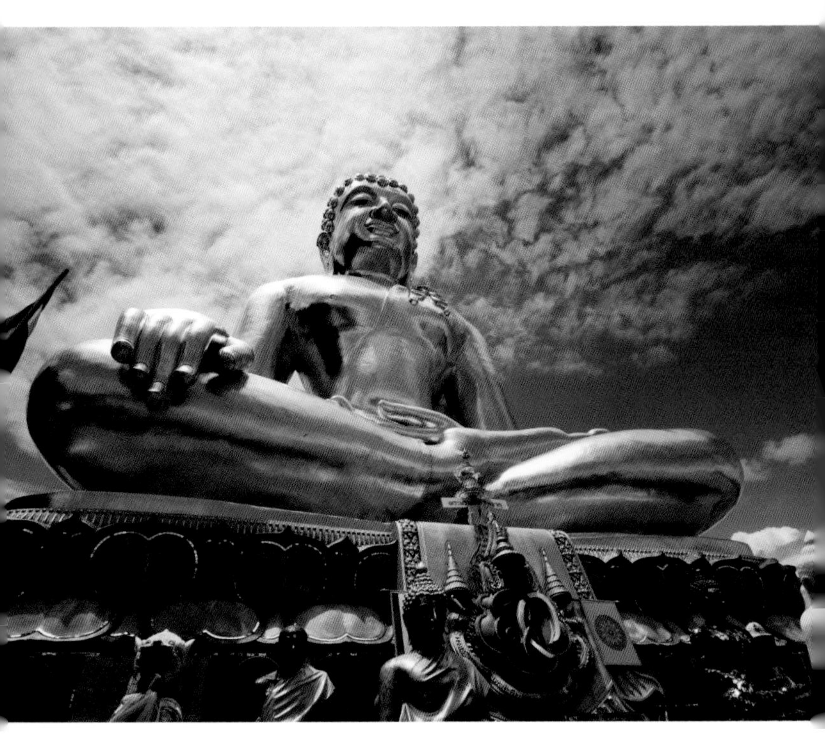

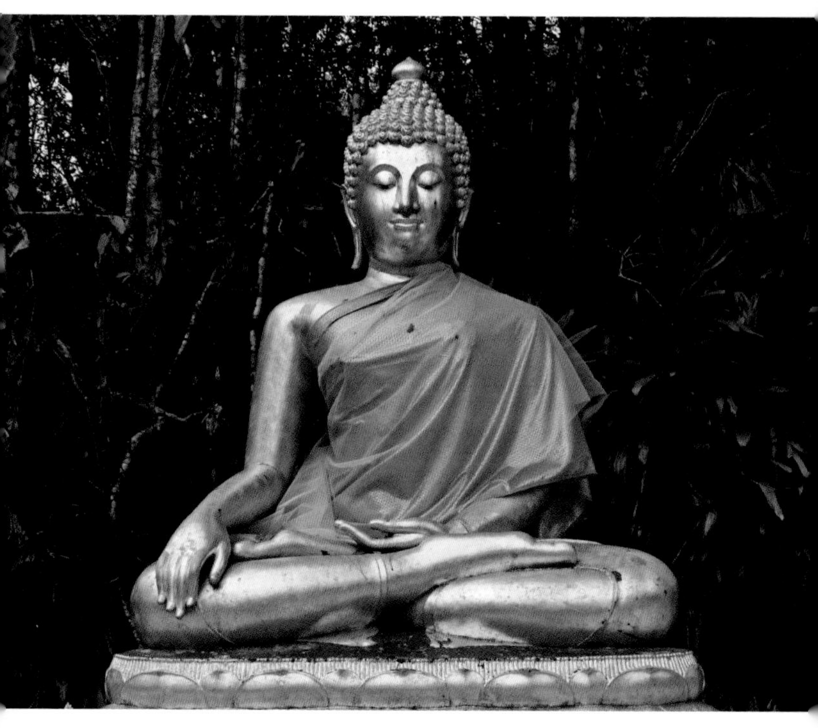

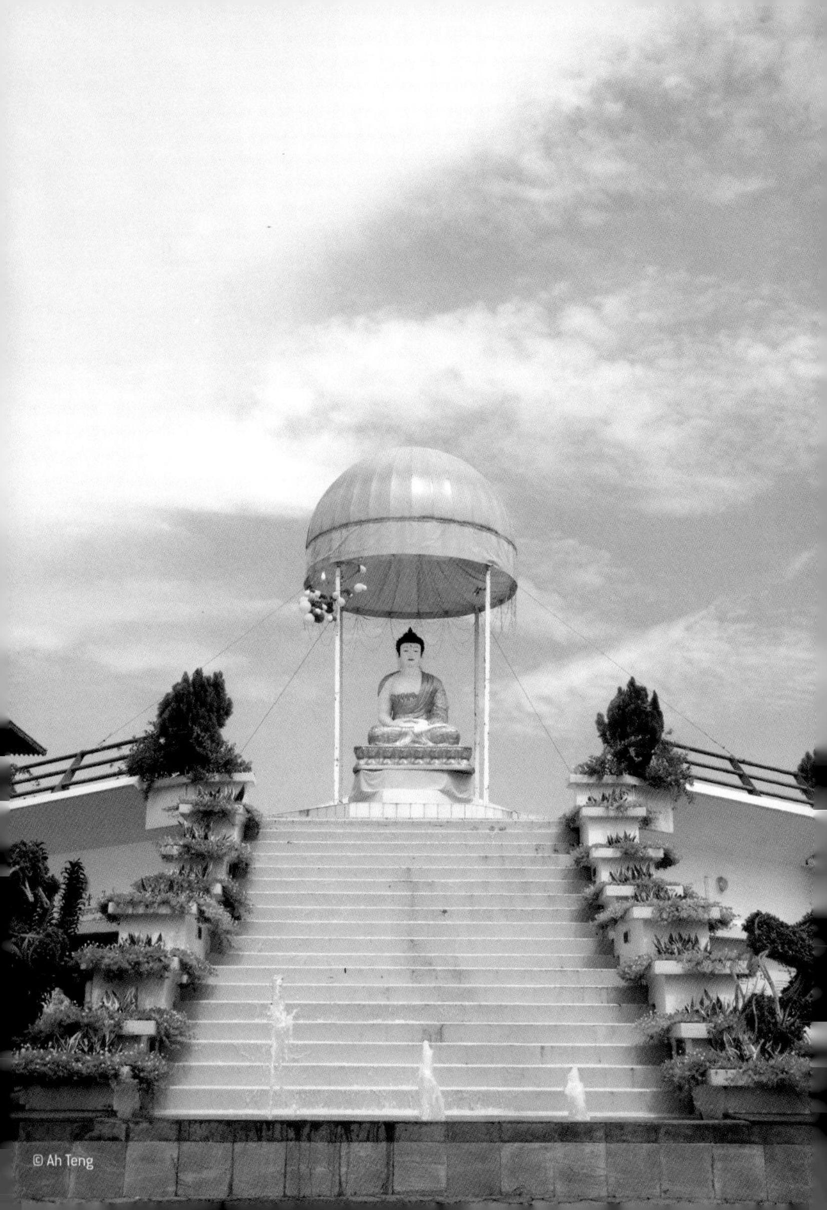

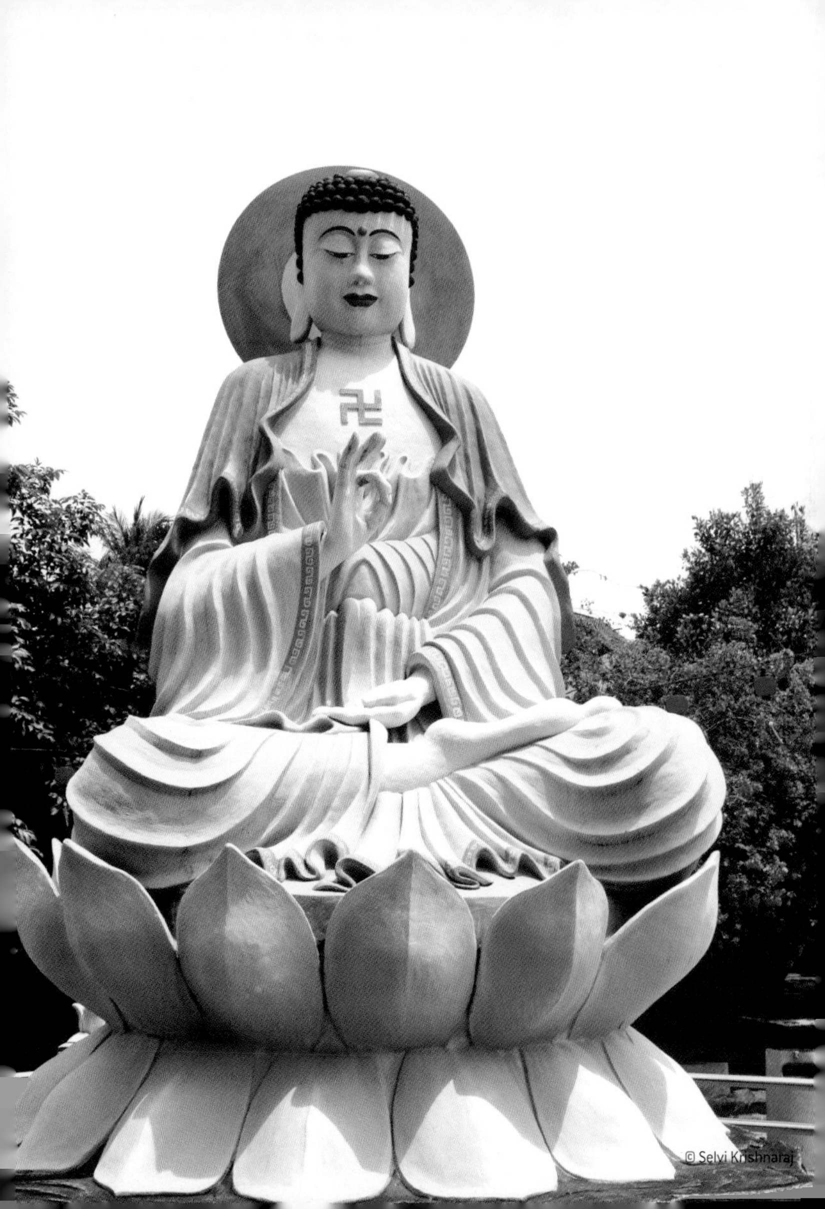
© Selvi Krishnaraj

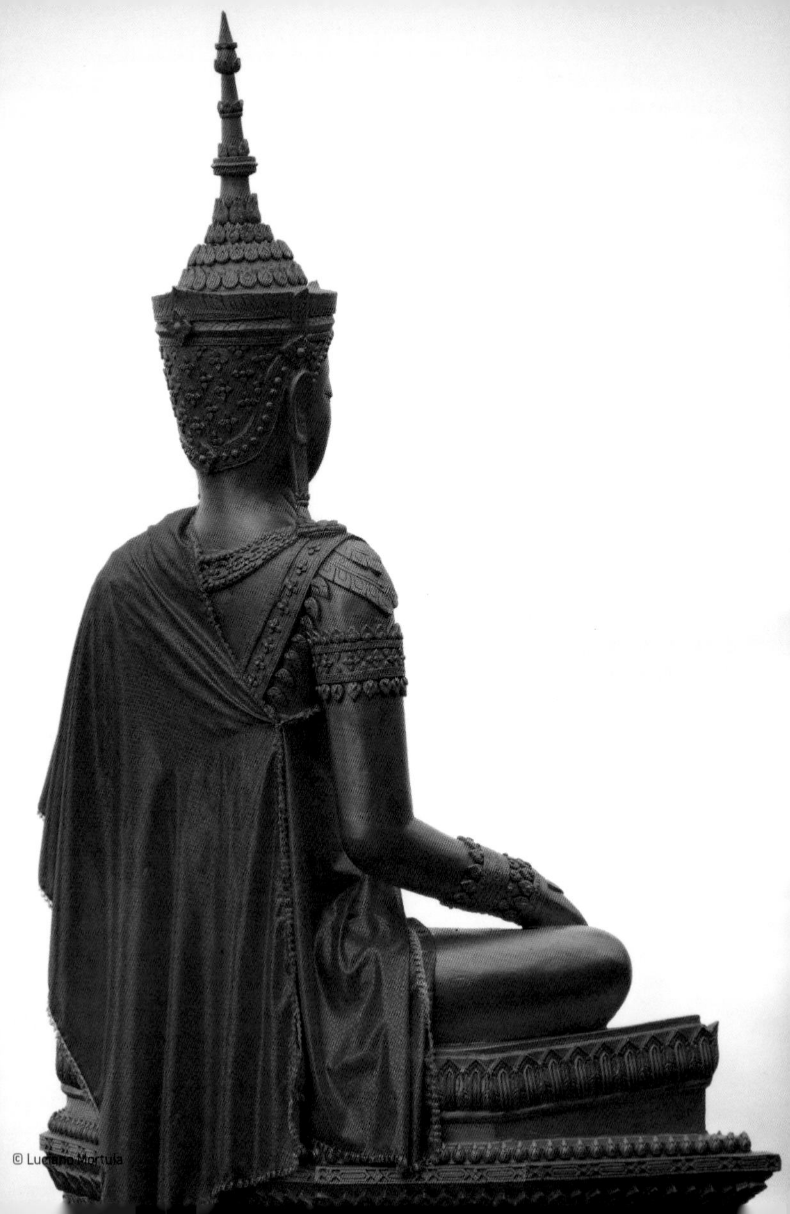

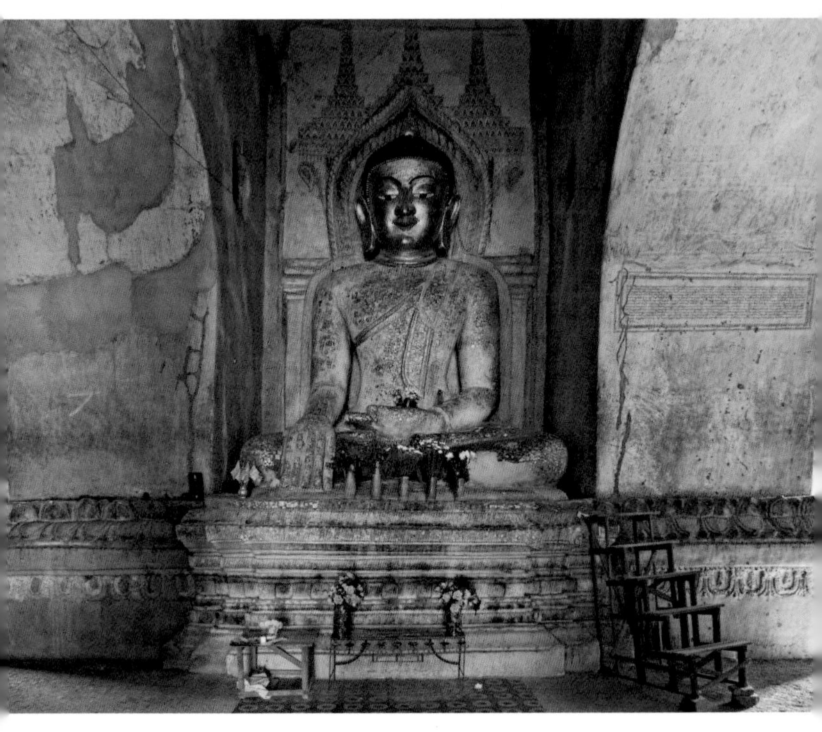

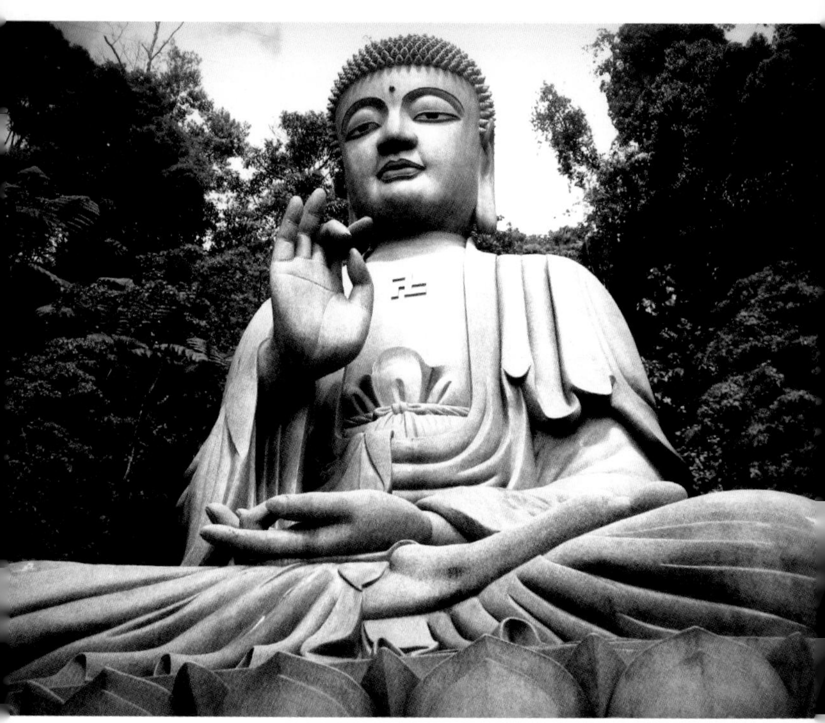

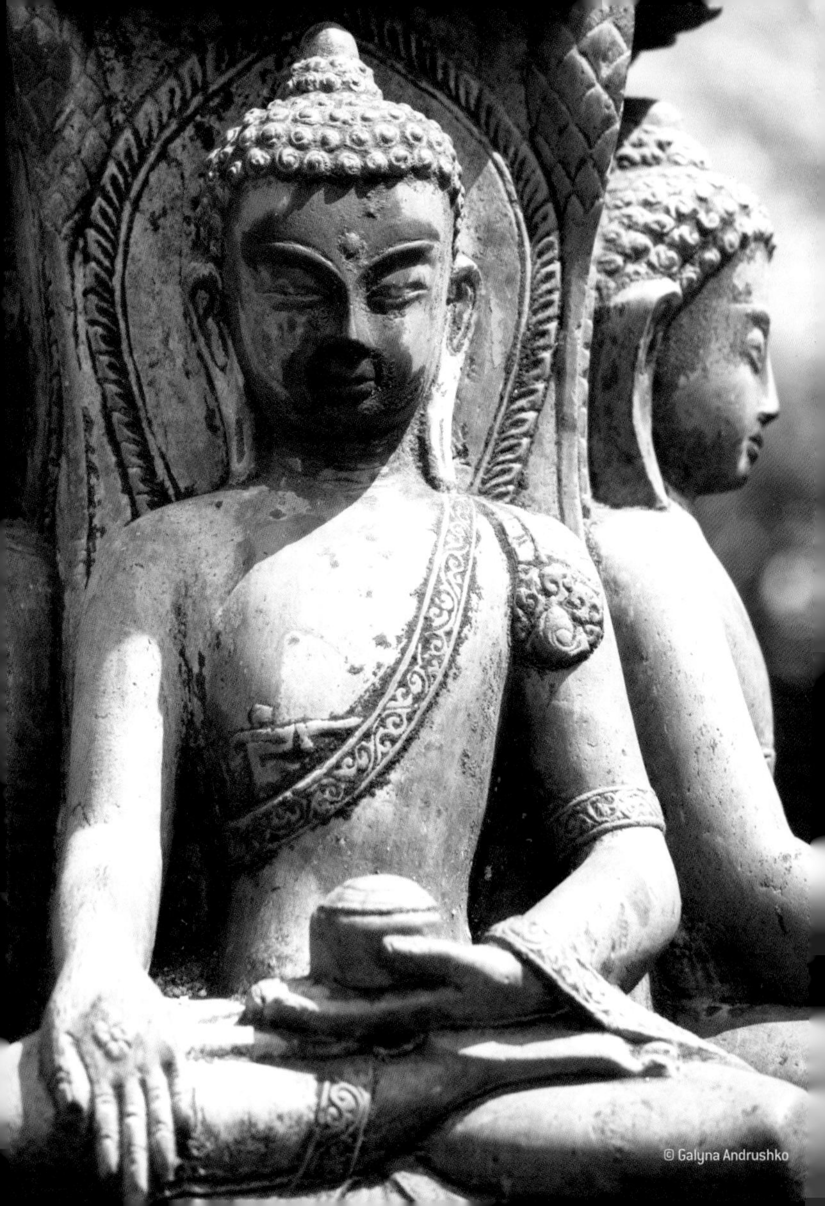

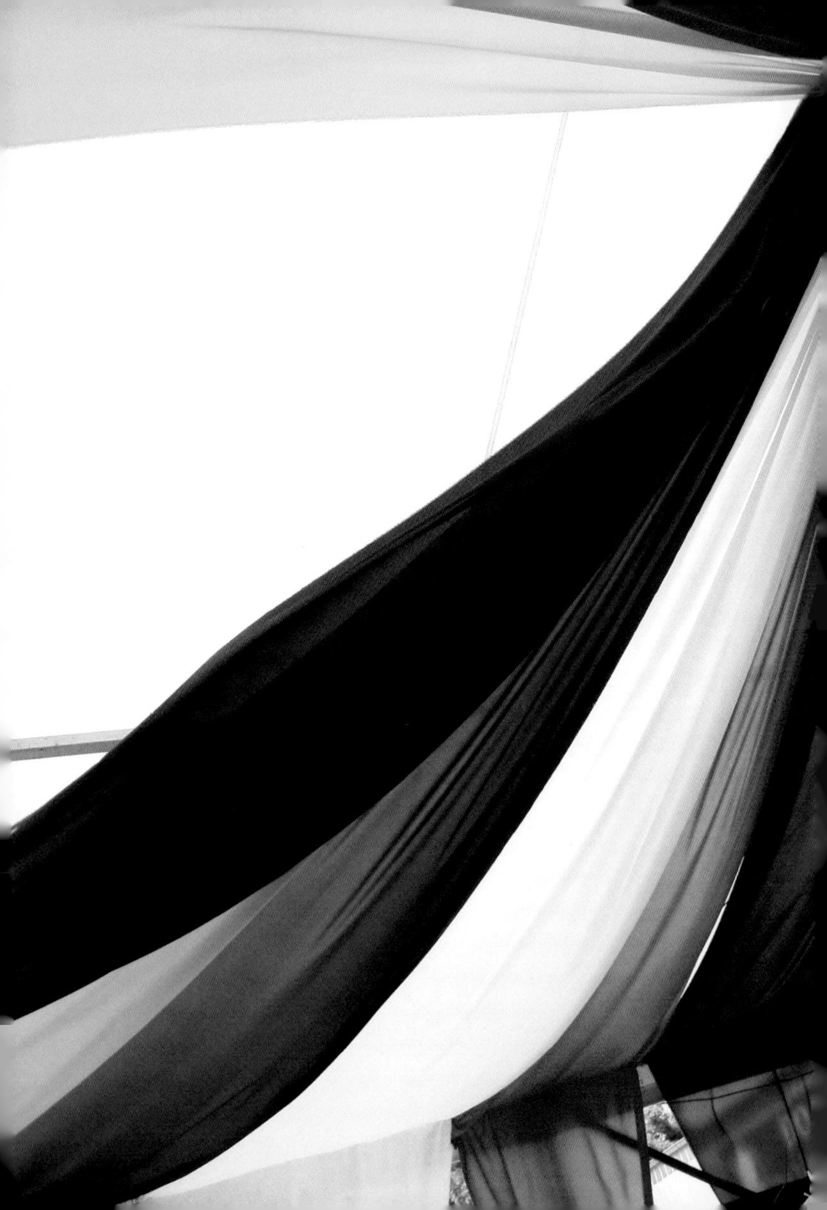

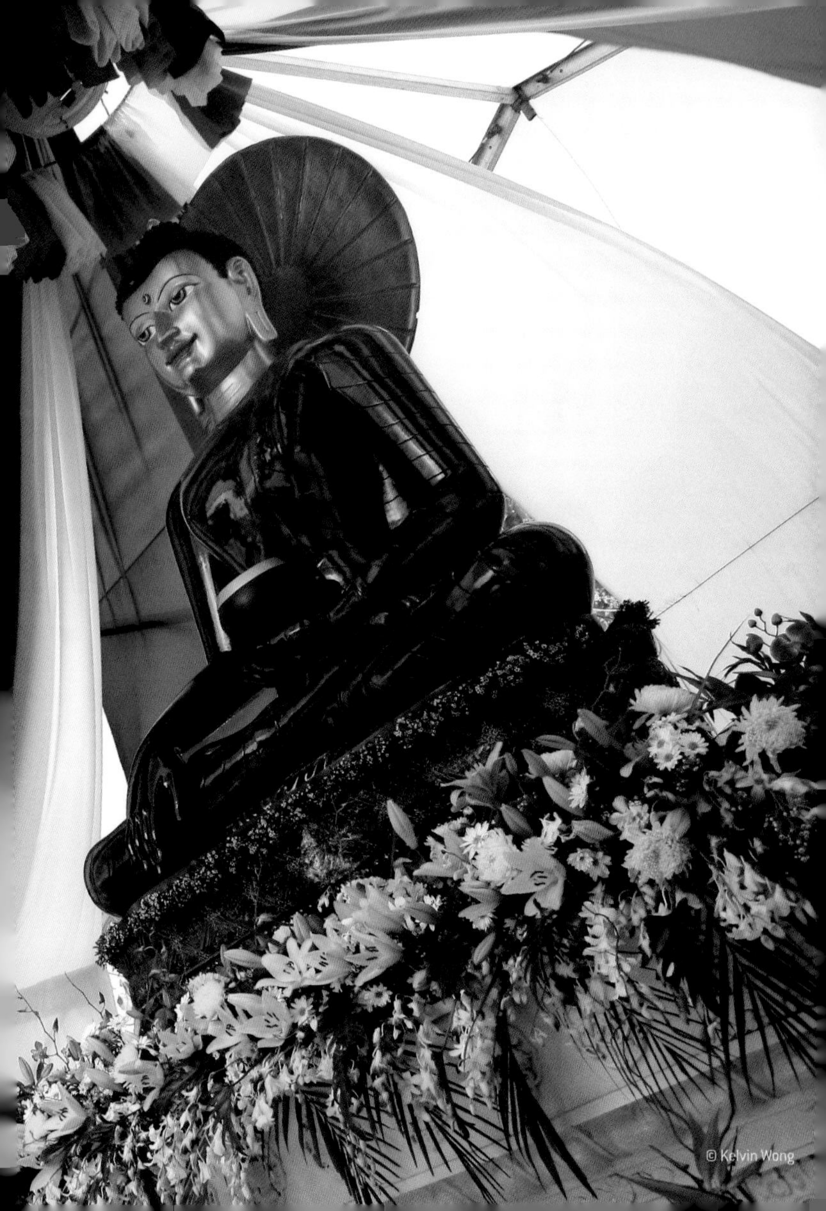

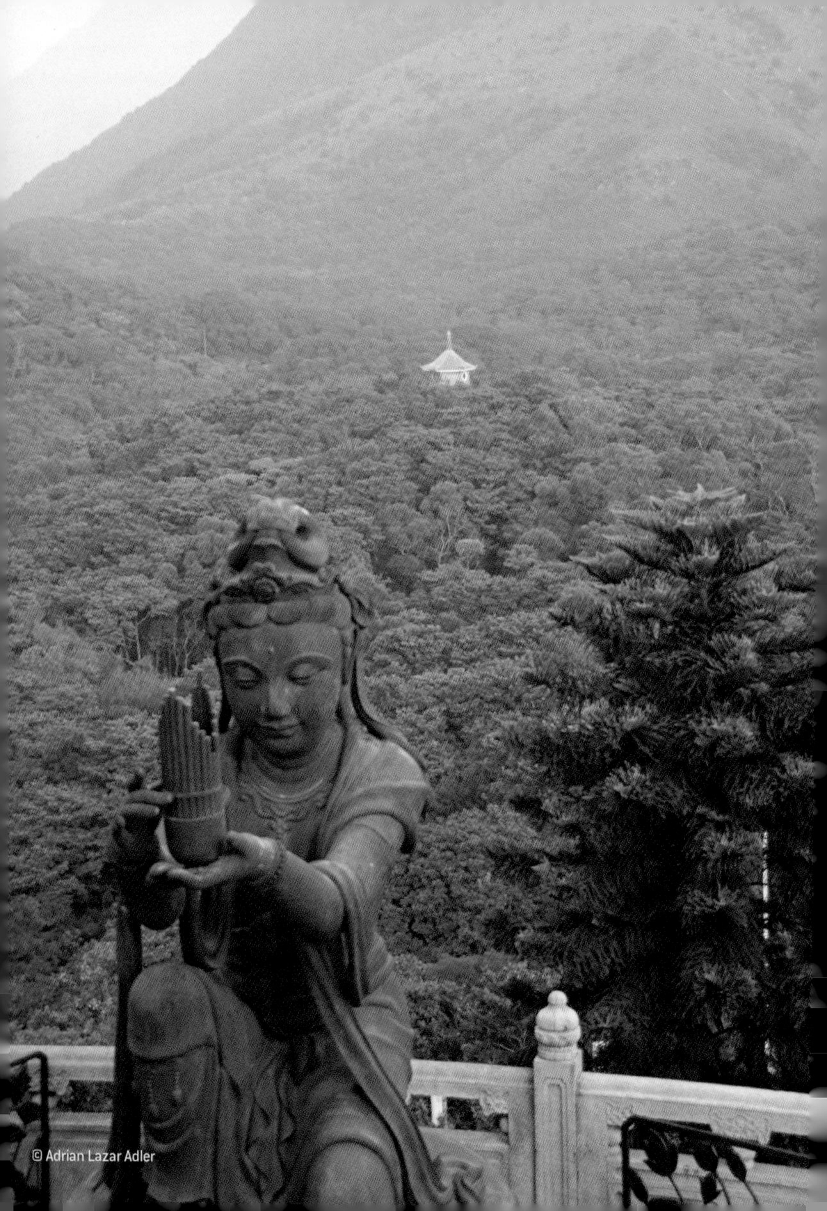

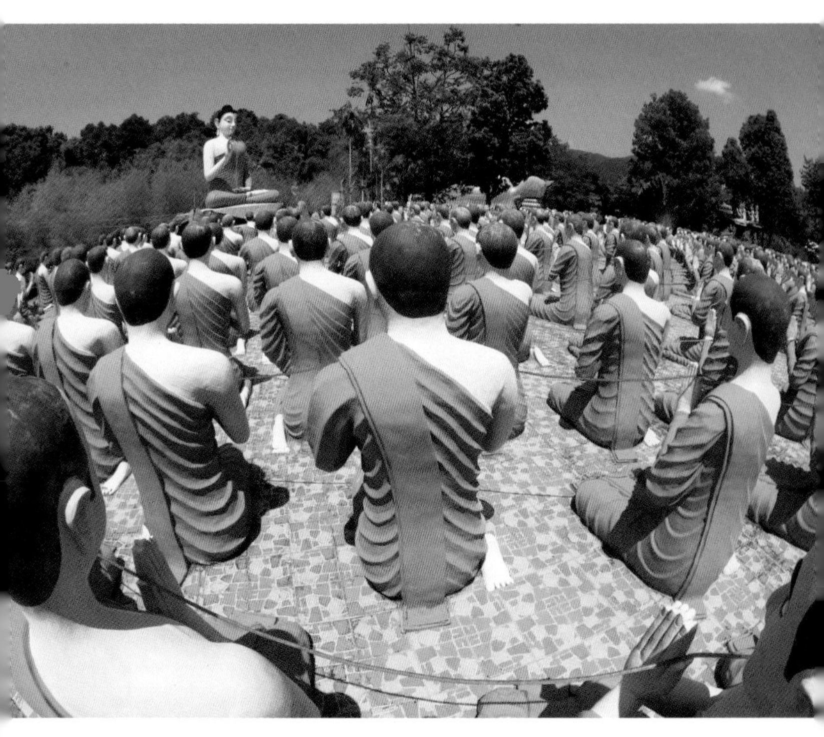

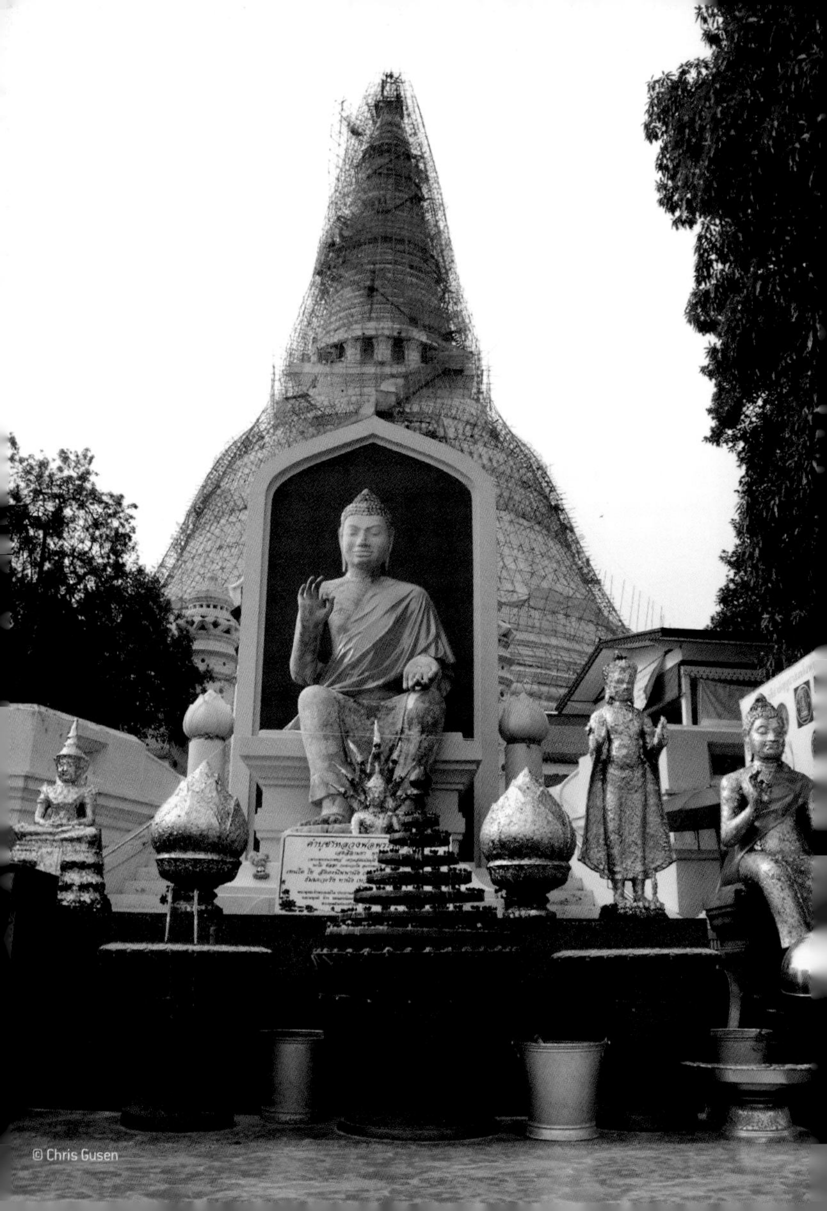

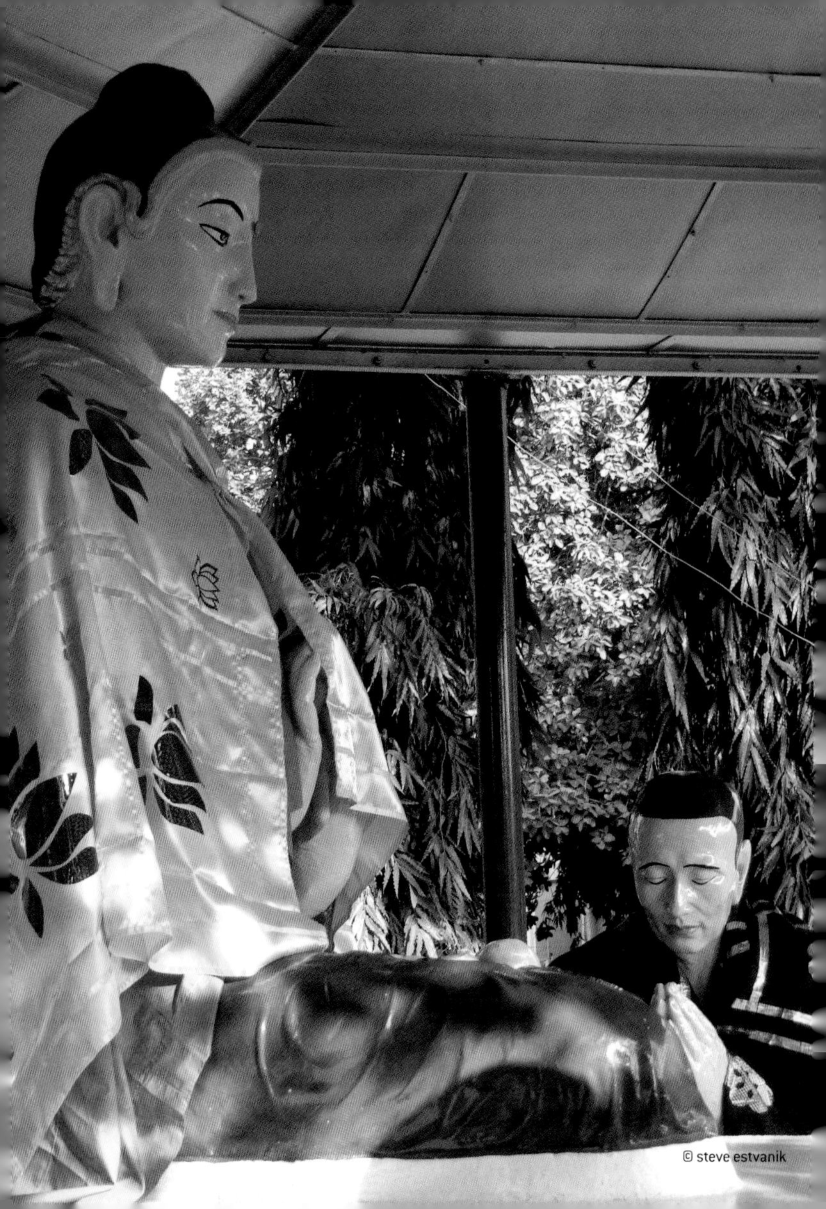

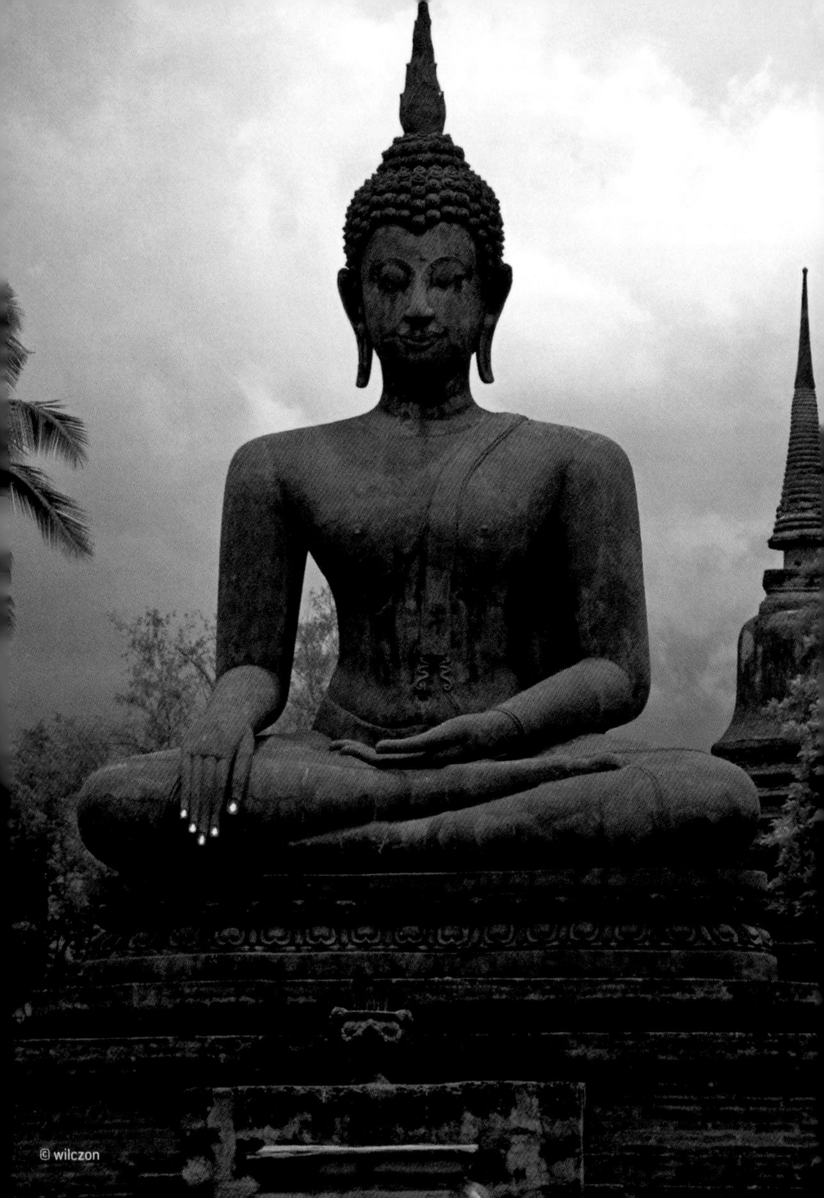

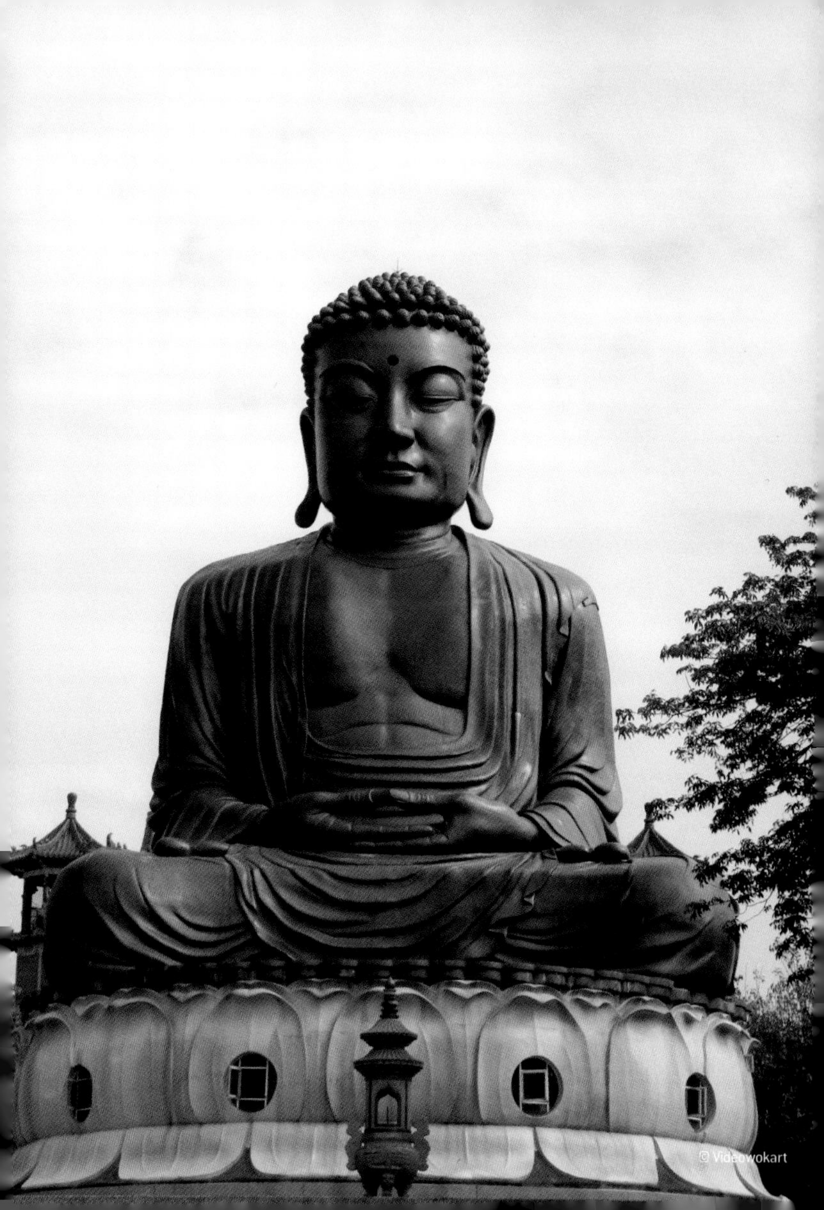

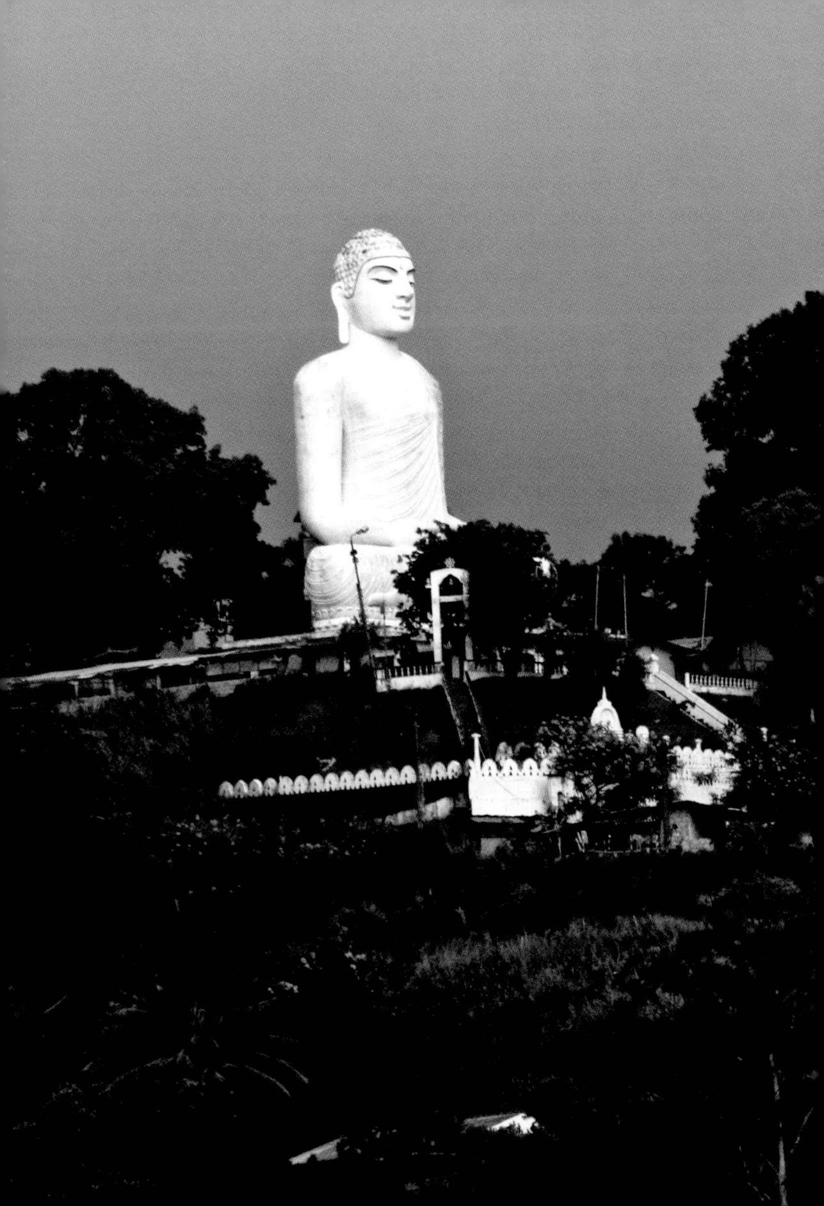

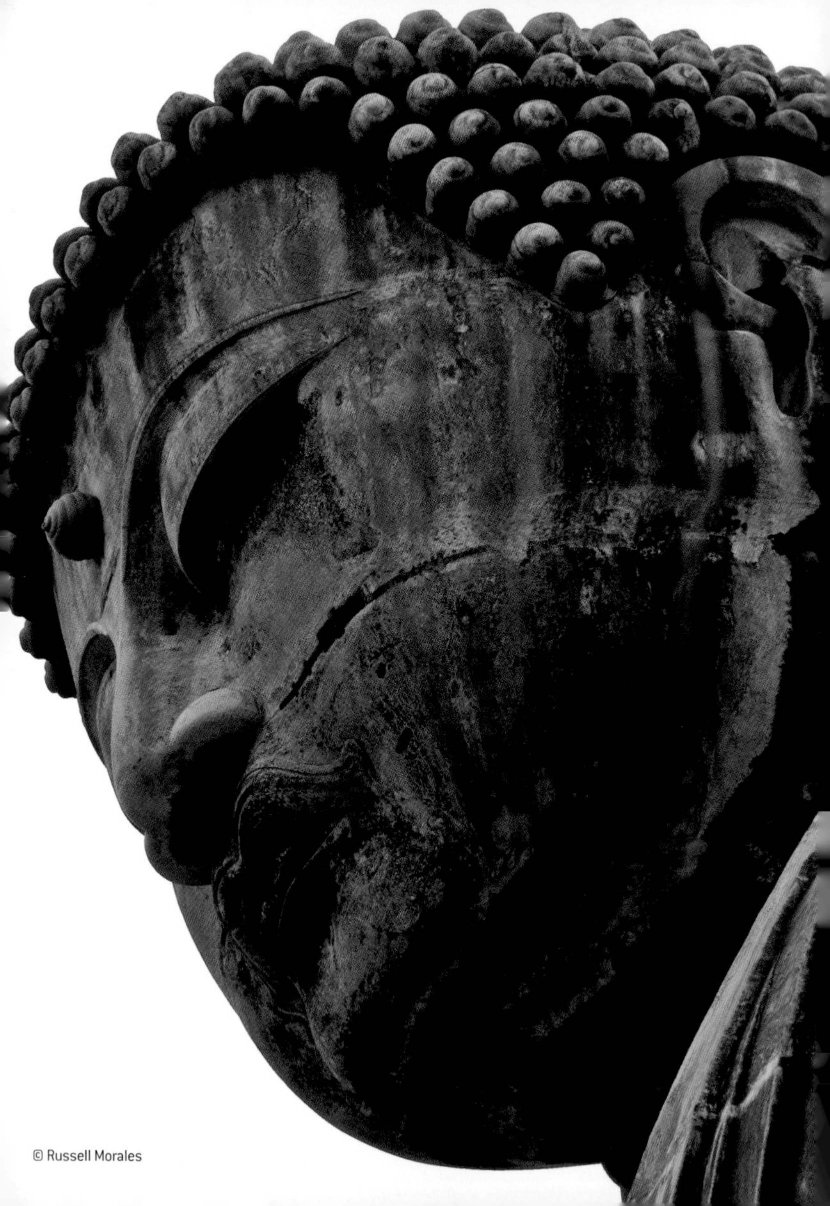

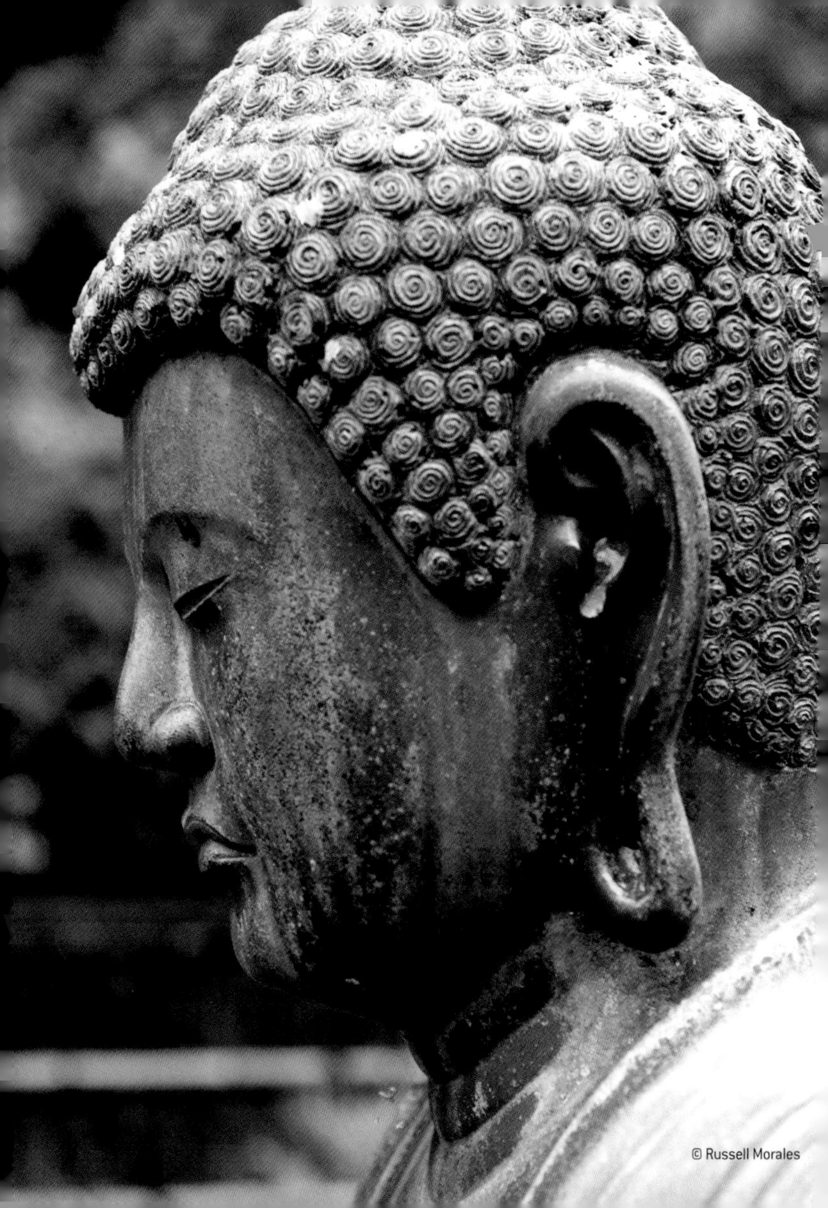

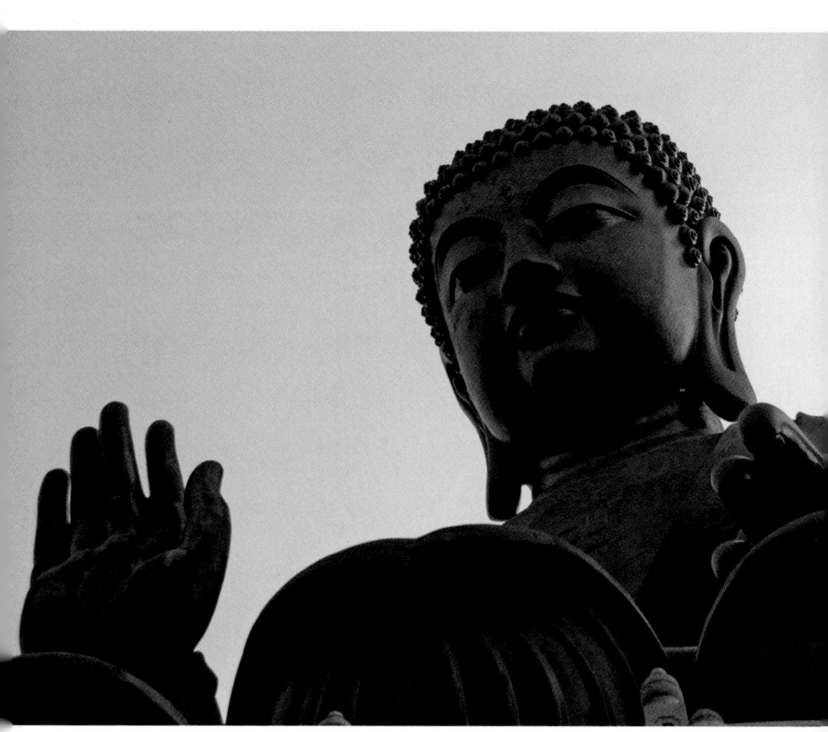

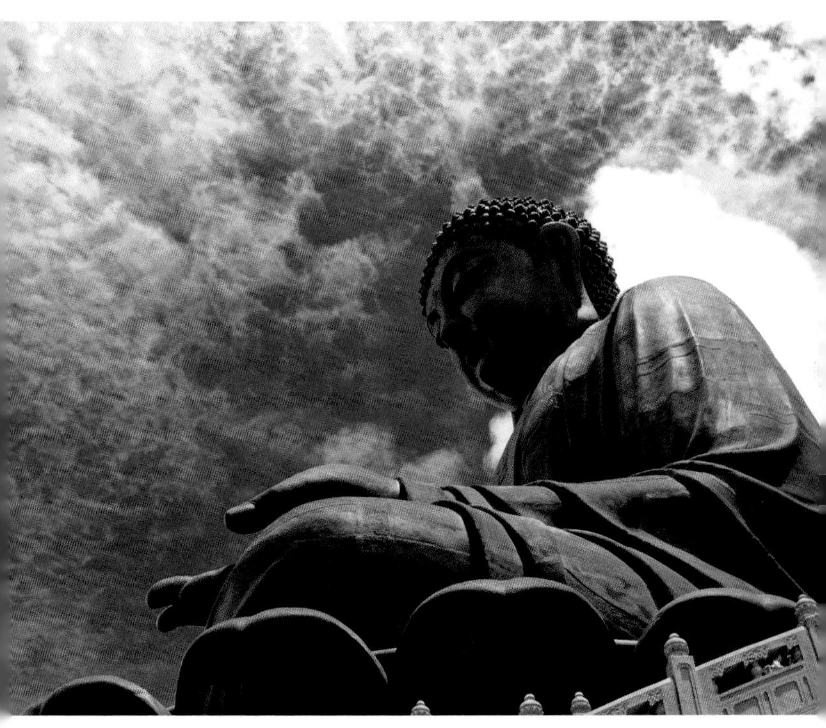

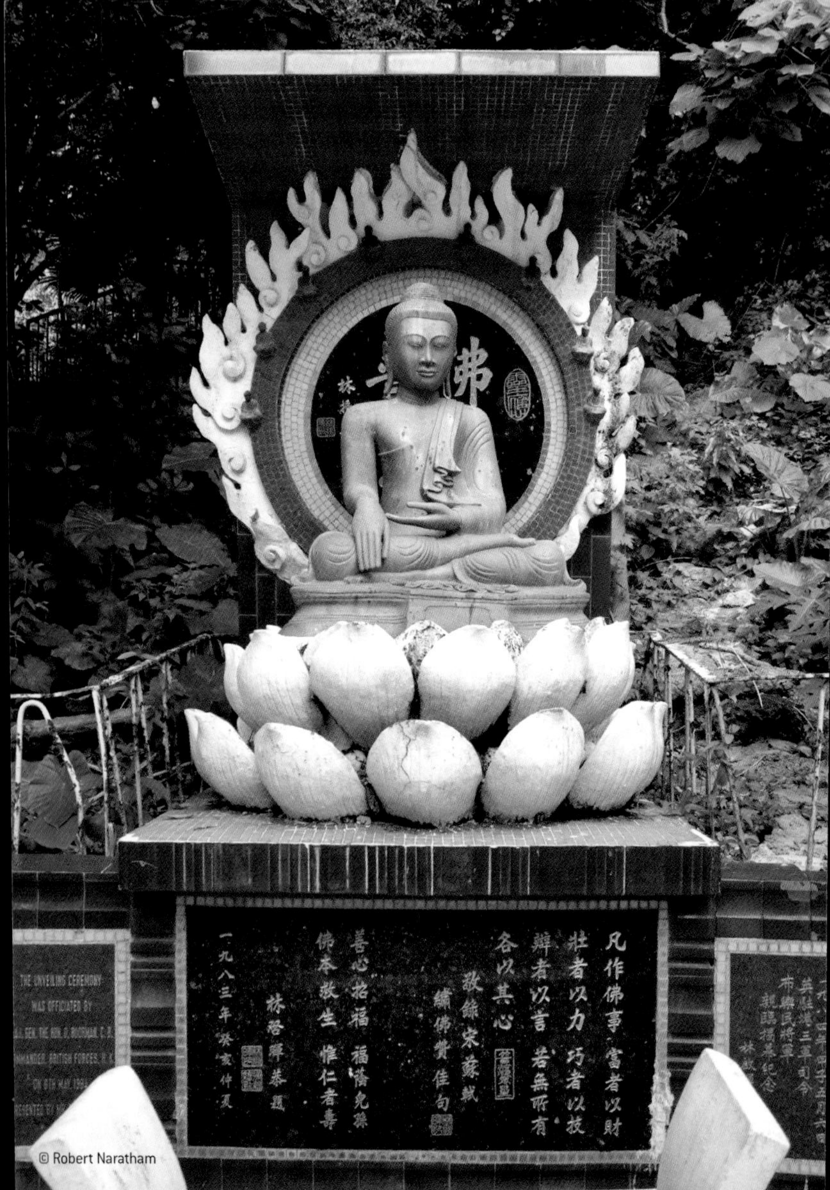
凡作佛事 富者以財
壯者以力 巧者以技
辯者以言 若無所有
各以其心
敬錄宋蘇軾
繡佛贊佳句
善心招福 福蔭兒孫
佛本救生 惟仁者壽
一九八三年癸亥仲夏
THE UNVEILING CEREMONY
WAS OFFICIATED BY

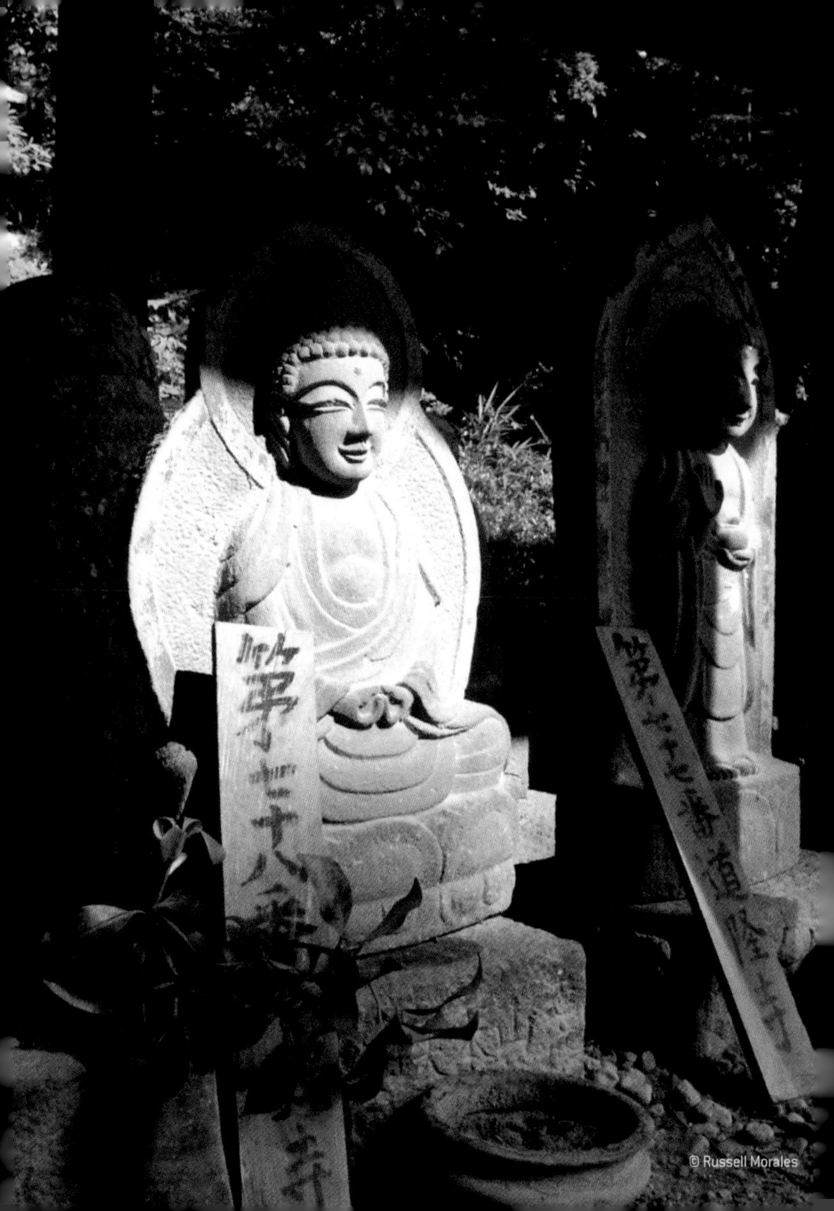
© Russell Morales

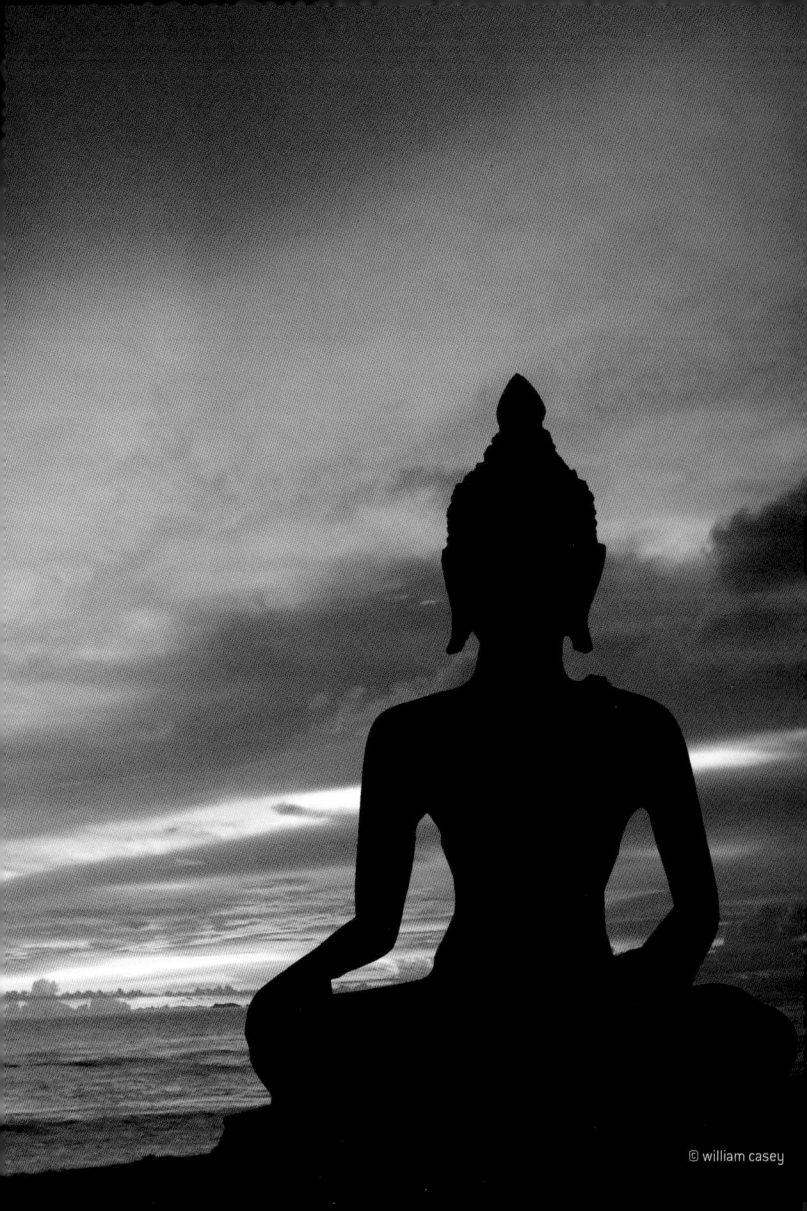

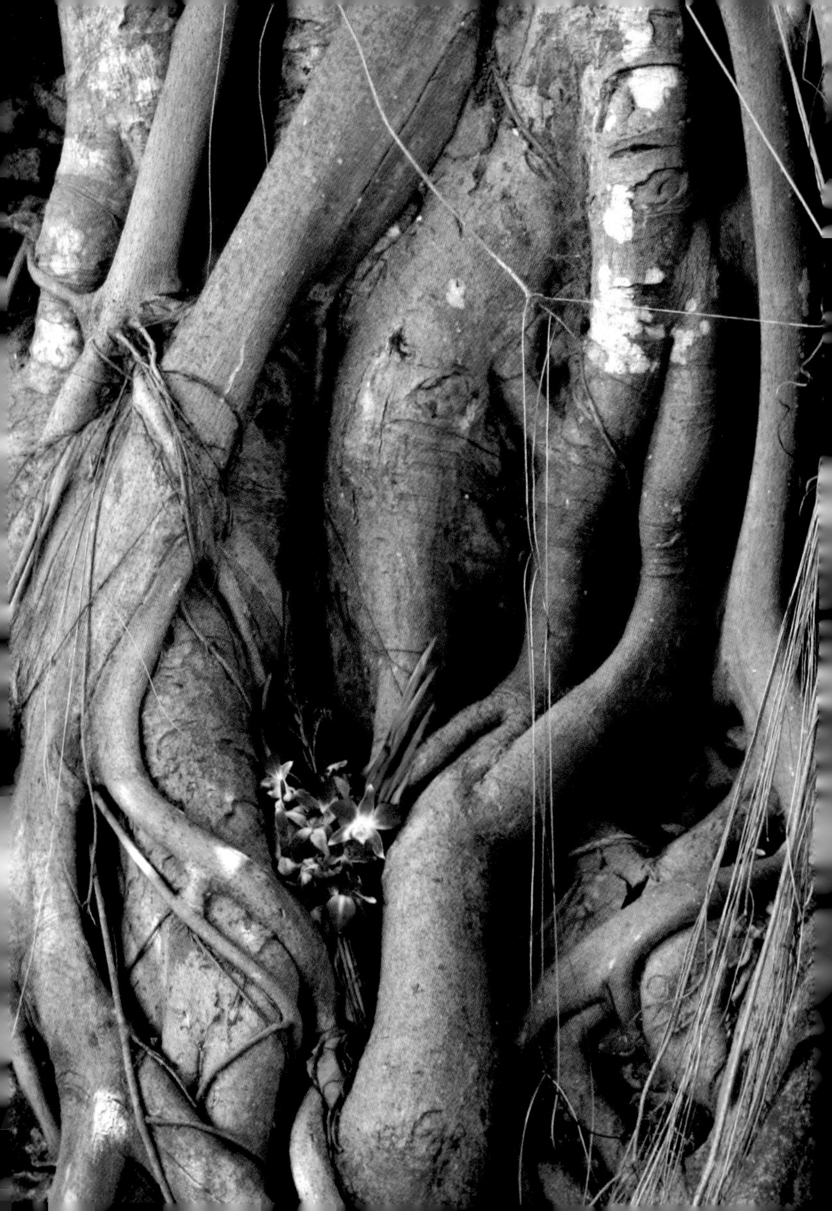

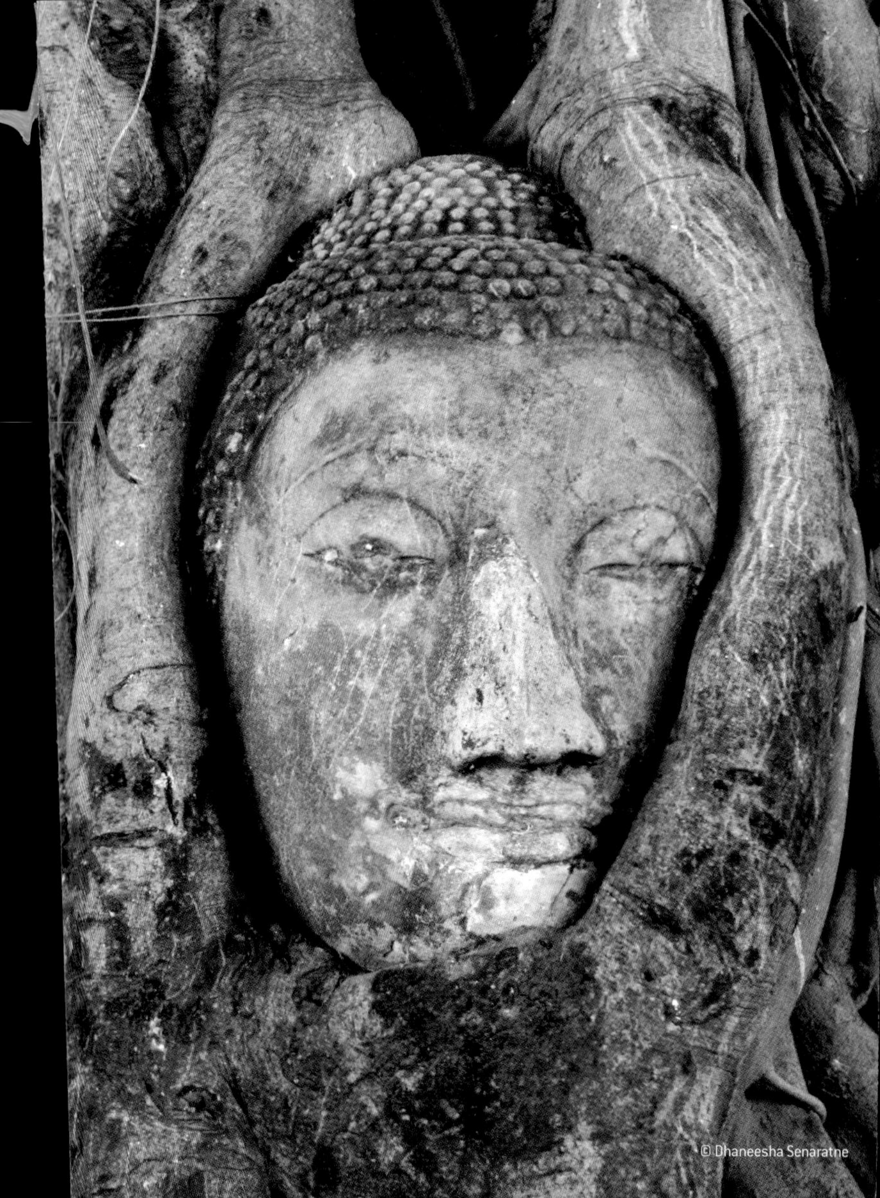